STRUCTURED
Cobol

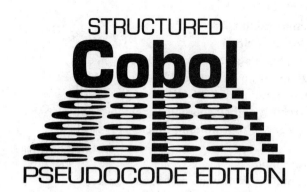

PSEUDOCODE EDITION

SHELLY and CASHMAN PUBLICATIONS

Computer Fundamentals for an Information Age
Workbook and Study Guide to accompany Computer Fundamentals for an Information Age
Computer Lab Software Projects Diskette (IBM PC, Apple II, TRS-80 Model 3 and Model 4)
Introduction to Computers and Data Processing
Student Workbook and Study Guide
    to accompany Introduction to Computers and Data Processing

Structured COBOL — Flowchart Edition
Structured COBOL — Pseudocode Edition
Introduction to Computer Programming Structured COBOL
Advanced Structured COBOL Program Design and File Processing
Introduction to Computer Programming ANSI COBOL
ANSI COBOL Workbook — Testing and Debugging Techniques and Exercises
Advanced ANSI COBOL Disk/Tape Programming Efficiencies

Introduction to BASIC Programming
Introduction to BASIC Programming Workbook and Study Guide
Introduction to BASIC Programming Apple Computer Supplement

Computer Programming RPG II
Introduction to Computer Programming RPG

Introduction to Flowcharting and Computer Programming Logic
Business Systems Analysis and Design

Introduction to Computer Programming IBM Systems/360 Assembler Language
IBM System/360 Assembler Language Workbook Core Dump Analysis and
    Debugging Techniques
IBM System/360 Assembler Language Disk/Tape Advanced Concepts

DOS Utilities Sort/Merge Multiprogramming
OS Job Control Language
DOS Job Control for Assembler Language Programmers
DOS Job Control for COBOL Programmers

STRUCTURED
Cobol

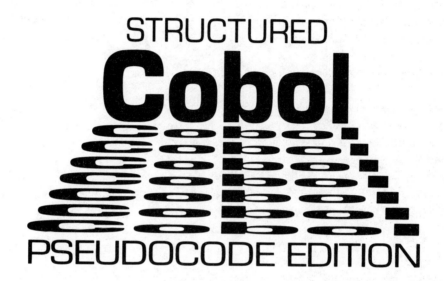

PSEUDOCODE EDITION

Gary B. Shelly
Educational Consultant
Brea, California

Thomas J. Cashman, CDP, B.A., M.A.
Long Beach City College
Long Beach, California

Steven G. Forsythe, B.S., M.A.
Educational Consultant
Brea, California

ANAHEIM PUBLISHING COMPANY, INC.
2632 Saturn St., P. O. Box 9600
Brea, CA 92622-9600
(714) 993-3700

Library of Congress Catalog Card Number 85-071235

ISBN 0-88236-127-9

Printed in the United States of America

TABLE OF CONTENTS

INTRODUCTION TO COMPUTER PROGRAMMING

1

INTRODUCTION TO STRUCTURED DESIGN

2

INPUT / OUTPUT OPERATIONS

3

ARITHMETIC OPERATIONS; REPORT EDITING

4

COMPARING; FINAL TOTALS

5

DATA EDITING AND NESTED IF STATEMENTS

6

CONTROL BREAKS; TABLE PROCESSING

7

MULTIPLE LEVEL CONTROL BREAKS; TABLE PROCESSING

8

TABLE SEARCHING; MULTIPLE LEVEL TABLES

9

SORTING; EXTERNAL TABLES

10

ADDITIONAL COBOL STATEMENTS

11

PREFACE

One of the most significant developments in the history of computer programming has been the acceptance and use of structured programming as a methodology for the improvement of the quality of software. Of equal importance has been the practical implementation of the theory of structured design, in conjunction with structured programming, to assist in the improvement of the quality of computer programs. It is now generally recognized that structured design is the basis for writing "good" structured programs.

The most important issue faced by computer programming educators today is how to teach students to design computer programs that will be error free, reliable, and easy to modify and maintain. Toward this end, the objective of this textbook is to teach students, from the very beginning, the proper methods of structured design and structured COBOL programming. Unlike other beginning COBOL textbooks, where the methods for developing the structure of a program are never explained and the student is left to wonder how a program structure is developed, this text explains, in simple, straightforward terms, the methods used to derive a program hierarchy chart.

Based upon the structured design methodology developed by Larry Constantine and Ed Yourdon, this text uses IPO Charts to decompose programs into small, cohesive, functional modules. Logic for programs can be designed using either pseudocode or flowcharts. In this text, the logic for each module is designed using pseudocode as the primary design tool. Those instructors who wish to also expose their students to flowcharts will find the flowcharts for all of the programs in Appendix D. An instructor who wishes to use flowcharting as the primary design tool should use the text, *Structured COBOL, Flowchart Edition,* by Shelly/Cashman/Forsythe, published by Anaheim Publishing Company, Copyright 1985.

The first program illustrated for analysis in the text has been carefully designed and could serve as a model program in industry. The style and programming standards serve as a guideline for all subsequent programs the student will write, both in class and as a COBOL programmer in industry. Indeed, an entire appendix (Appendix C) is dedicated to specifying coding standards and style which should be used by COBOL programmers.

The student is immediately introduced to a sample program so that the programming process can begin almost immediately in the course. In the chapters that follow, the programs become more complex, building upon the knowledge and skills already attained from previous chapters and programs, and introduce additional techniques of structured design and structured COBOL coding.

In every case, the COBOL coding is carefully explained. All coding throughout the textbook is shown using COBOL coding forms, so the student can see exactly how the coding should be written. Thus, beginning with the very first chapters, the student studies structured design and structured programming as well as the COBOL language itself. Perhaps even more importantly, when students write their first programs, they will be producing properly designed and coded COBOL programs. Students will not have to discard techniques learned in early chapters when they come to chapters on structured programming, as is the case in so many introductory COBOL texts. Instead, they learn the correct way to design and write programs beginning with their very first program.

The textbook is designed to be used in a one quarter or one semester course to teach the beginning student of computer programming how to DESIGN and WRITE structured programs using COBOL. No prior knowledge of computer programming is required. A problem-oriented approach is used throughout the book, wherein the student is introduced to structured design and structured programming through a series of programs illustrating typical applications. Those statements and segments of the language necessary in the solution of the problem are explained.

The student, therefore, learns programming in relation to the total problem and is not burdened with the task of remembering a series of isolated facts concerning the individual segments of the language. Upon completion of the text, the student will have gained experience in designing and writing a variety of business-oriented programs using COBOL.

The programs explained in each of the chapters include the following subjects: Basic Input/Output, Addition, Subtraction, Multiplication, Division, Compute Statement, Report Editing, Comparing Operations, Nested If Statement, Single and Multiple Level Control Breaks, Table Processing, Table Searching, Multiple Level Tables, External Tables, and Sorting.

The reviewer of this text is encouraged to examine the Table of Contents. The instructions covered, design techniques illustrated, and programming methods taught in this book are specified in more detail than can be covered in this preface.

Several important features found in these chapters should be noted. First, tables are extensively covered in four chapters of the text. Included are single level tables, multiple level tables, tables in which data is loaded through use of the COBOL Value clause, and tables where the data is loaded dynamically during program execution. This coverage of tables is the most extensive found in an introductory COBOL textbook. It is the authors' experience that tables are an extremely important aspect of COBOL programming. A knowledge of tables is vital if the student is to obtain a complete and meaningful education in the use of the COBOL language.

A second important feature of this textbook is that the important subject of data editing and data validation is explained. An entire program and chapter are devoted to explaining the need for data validation and the techniques which can be implemented to edit input data and ensure valid processing.

A third important feature is that sequential disk files are illustrated throughout the textbook. Recognizing that disk input/output is the most important type of I/O used in COBOL programs, the authors have included sequential disk input files in the first program students see. In this manner, students learn the most important input/output methods immediately. The use of obsolete punched cards and the fixed 80-character input record will not be found in this textbook.

A fourth important feature of this textbook is that it satisfies all of the requirements of the DPMA curriculum course CIS-2, Application Program Development I. As such, it has been recommended for use in that curriculum.

At the conclusion of each chapter, there are four types of activities which should be performed by the student. The first activity is a set of Review Questions which requires the student to apply the knowledge learned within the chapter to a set of questions. The second activity, COBOL Coding Exercises, requires the student to correctly code sections of a COBOL program. The third activity, Structured Walkthrough Exercises, requires the student to find errors in program logic, the use of the COBOL language itself, or in the programming standards which should be used. Each structured walkthrough exercise is designed to simulate the actual structured walkthrough activities encountered by a computer programmer in business.

The fourth activity involves actually writing COBOL programs. Four programming assignments are included in each chapter. The first assignment is relatively close to the program illustrated in the text and requires a basic understanding of the problem and the concepts presented in the chapter. The second programming assignment presents a slight variation of the sample program developed in the text and requires more creative thinking to arrive at the solution of the problem. The third and fourth assignments are increasingly complex and are designed to challenge the student with more difficult programming assignments. At the conclusion of the text, three case studies are presented. These case studies are designed to encompass many of the concepts discussed in previous chapters and to provide the student with the opportunity to write a program that closely approximates the types of situations one would encounter in industry.

The Appendices also provide valuable information. Appendix A contains the six sets of test data which can be used for the programming assignments in the text. Each of the programming assignments presented within the text will use one of the six sets of test data in the appendix. There is, therefore, no need to prepare extensive test data for each programming assignment. Appendix B contains a list of the COBOL reserved words. Appendix C contains the Coding Standards which are applied to every program in the text. It is strongly suggested that instructors introduce these standards at the beginning of the course and insist upon strict adherence to them throughout the course. By doing this, the programmer leaving the course will be of a better quality than one trained in a less exacting manner.

Appendix D, as mentioned, contains the flowcharts for each of the sample programs explained in the text. These flowcharts are presented in this appendix for those instructors who wish to expose their students to the use of flowcharts for developing program logic, and to compare flowcharts to the primary logic design tool in this textbook, pseudocode. Appendix E contains the COBOL format notations for the COBOL statements explained in the text.

After the study of the material contained in the text has been completed, the student should have a firm foundation in the concepts and techniques of structured program design and structured COBOL programming, and should be capable of solving a wide variety of business-application problems using COBOL. With the widespread use of structured COBOL in industry and the implementation of the language by a variety of computer manufacturers, the student will have taken a significant step in gaining the knowledge required to enter the computer programming profession.

Instructors' materials developed for this textbook include an Instructor's Guide and Answer Manual as well as Transparency Masters. The Instructor's Guide and Answer Manual contains answers to all Review Questions, COBOL Coding Exercises, and Structured Walkthrough Exercises. In addition, the IPO Charts, Pseudocode, and Source Listings for all programs found in the Student Programming Assignments are included. The Transparency Masters contain an enlarged drawing of every figure in the entire textbook, which has in excess of 400 illustrations.

The authors would like to thank Ken Russo for the cover design, and Ellana Russo, Ken Russo, and Mike Broussard for the text illustrations, page design, and preparing the finished copy. They would also like to thank Marilyn Martin for typesetting the manuscript, and Joan Parsons for her help in the final push over the top. The publication of any book is time-consuming, and at times, exhaustive work. The finished product would be of far less quality were it not for the devotion and creative contributions of the individuals mentioned here.

Steven Forsythe would also like to acknowledge two groups of individuals who have either directly or indirectly influenced the writing of this textbook. The first is the Board of Trustees, administration, and instructional staff at St. Clair County Community College in Port Huron, Michigan. Throughout the many years of our association, these individuals have put the desire for quality education and the welfare of the students above all else. As such, they have been a model for myself and a model for colleges everywhere.

Secondly, Steve Forsythe would like to acknowledge the support and encouragement received from his wife Jill, son Matthew, and daughter Jennefer, who willingly embarked on a 2,500 mile journey away from family and friends to be part of this newest adventure, and dedicate this book to Kimberly, our newest addition.

Gary Shelly says thank you to wife Kathleen, sons Philipp, Konrad and Hans, and daughters Tammra, Kristin, and Leigh, for their patience and understanding. The time in this book was time away from them.

Tom Cashman again says thank you to his wife, Merilyn, and family for their continued support during the writing of this book.

Gary B. Shelly
Thomas J. Cashman
Steven F. Forsythe

ACKNOWLEDGMENT

The following information is reprinted from COBOL Edition 1965, published by the Conference on Data Systems Languages (CODASYL).

"Any organization interested in reproducing the COBOL report and specifications in whole or in part, using ideas taken from this report as the basis for an instruction manual or for any other purpose is free to do so. However, all such organizations are requested to reproduce this section as part of the introduction to the document. Those using a short passage, as in a book review, are requested to mention "COBOL" in acknowledgment of the source, but need not quote this entire section.

"COBOL is an industry language and is not the property of any company or group of companies, or of any organization or group of organizations.

"No warranty, expressed or implied, is made by any contributor or by the COBOL Committee as to the accuracy and functioning of the programming system and language. Moreover, no responsibility is assumed by any contributor, or by the committee, in connection therewith.

"Procedures have been established for the maintenance of COBOL. Inquiries concerning the procedures for proposing changes should be directed to the Executive Committee of the Conference on Data Systems Languages.

"The authors and copyright holders of the copyrighted material used herein

FLOW-MATIC (Trademark of Sperry Rand Corporation), Programming for the Univac (R) I and II, Data Automation Systems copyrighted 1958, 1959, by Sperry Rand Corporation; IBM Commercial Translator Form No. F28-8013, copyrighted 1959 by IBM; FACT, DSI 27A5260-2760, copyrighted 1960 by Minneapolis-Honeywell

have specifically authorized the use of this material in whole or in part, in the COBOL specifications. Such authorization extends to the reproduction and use of COBOL specifications in programming manuals of similar publications."

CHAPTER ONE

INTRODUCTION TO COMPUTER PROGRAMMING

INTRODUCTION
COMPUTER OPERATIONS
COMPONENTS OF A COMPUTER
COMPUTER PROGRAMS
PROGRAM CATEGORIES
DATA ORGANIZATION
THE BASICS OF A COMPUTER PROGRAM
STRUCTURED PROGRAMMING
SEQUENCE CONTROL STRUCTURE
IF-THEN-ELSE CONTROL STRUCTURE
LOOPING CONTROL STRUCTURE
SINGLE ENTRY POINT/SINGLE EXIT POINT RULE
PROGRAM DESIGN
PROGRAMMING LANGUAGES
THE HISTORY OF COBOL
ADVANTAGES AND DISADVANTAGES OF COBOL
CODING COMPUTER PROGRAMS
STRUCTURED WALKTHROUGHS
CONDUCTING A STRUCTURED WALKTHROUGH
PROGRAM EXECUTION
CHAPTER SUMMARY
REVIEW QUESTIONS

INTRODUCTION TO COMPUTER PROGRAMMING

1

INTRODUCTION

In 1975, Dr. Harlan Mills, a leading authority in the information processing industry, wrote, "Computer programming as a practical activity is some 25 years old, a short time for intellectual development. Yet computer programming has already posed the greatest intellectual challenge that mankind has faced in pure logic and complexity."

As noted by Dr. Mills, the task of computer programming has posed some difficult challenges for programmers. Many programs contain hundreds, and even thousands, of individual statements. Each of these statements must be placed in exactly the right sequence for the correct output to be produced.

This textbook is concerned with teaching the COBOL programming language, which is a widely used language for writing business application programs. Prior to beginning a detailed study of COBOL, however, it is useful to review some principles of computers and computer programming.

Computer Operations

A computer is an electronic device, operating under the control of instructions stored in its own memory unit, which can accept and store data, perform arithmetic and logical operations on that data without human intervention, and produce output from the processing. To accomplish this, all computers, regardless of their size, perform basically the same operations. These operations include:

1. Input operations, which allow data to be entered into the computer for processing.
2. Arithmetic operations, which involve performing addition, subtraction, multiplication, and division calculations.
3. Logical operations, which allow the computer to compare data and determine if one value is less than, equal to, or greater than another value.
4. Output operations, which make information generated from processing on the computer available for use.
5. Storage operations, which include electronically storing data on an external device for future reference.

All operations that are carried out by a computer require access to data. Data is numbers, words, and phrases which are suitable for processing in some manner on a computer to produce information. Information produced by processing data can be used for whatever functions are required by the user of the computer. The production of information by processing data on a computer is called information processing, or sometimes electronic data processing.

COMPONENTS OF A COMPUTER

Processing data on a computer is performed by specific units (Figure 1–1). These units, called the computer hardware, are:

1. Input units
2. Processor unit
3. Output units
4. Auxiliary storage units

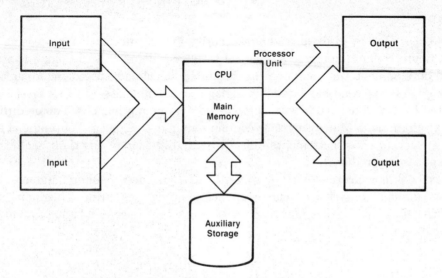

Figure 1 - 1 Components of a Computer

Input units are used to enter data into a computer. Commonly used input units include the keyboard (Figure 1–2), magnetic tape, and magnetic disk. As data enters the computer, it is stored in main computer memory.

Figure 1 - 2 Example of a Keyboard

The processor unit of a computer is composed of two distinct parts: main computer memory and the central processing unit. Main computer memory consists of components which electronically store data, including letters of the alphabet, numbers, and special characters such as decimal points or dollar signs. When data is entered into a computer from an input unit, it is stored in main computer memory. When a computer processes this data, instructions directing the processing are required. These instructions are also stored in main memory.

The central processing unit (CPU) contains the electronic circuits which actually cause processing to occur by interpreting and executing the instructions to the computer and controlling the input, output, and storage operations of the computer.

Figure 1-3 Printer

Figure 1-4 CRT Terminal

Figure 1-5 Magnetic Tape Drives

Figure 1-6 Magnetic Disk Drives

Output from a computer can be presented in many forms. The two most commonly found output units when the computer is used for business applications are the printer (Figure 1–3) and the television-like screen called a cathode ray tube, or CRT (Figure 1–4).

Main computer memory is used to store instructions and data while the instructions are being executed and the data is being processed. In most applications, however, these instructions and data must be stored elsewhere when they are not being used because main computer memory is not large enough to store the instructions and data for all applications at one time. Auxiliary storage units are used to store instructions and data when they are not being used in main computer memory. Two common forms of auxiliary storage are magnetic tape (Figure 1–5) and magnetic disk (Figure 1–6).

COMPUTER PROGRAMS

A computer is directed to perform the input, arithmetic, logical, output, and storage operations by a series of instructions called a **computer program**. A computer program specifies what operations are to be performed and the sequence in which they are to be performed. Computer programs are commonly referred to as computer software.

When a computer program is executed on a computer, the instructions in the program must be stored in main computer memory. The actual instructions which are executed must be in the form of machine language, which is a set of instructions the electronics of the computer can interpret and execute.

The basic task of a computer programmer is to design, write, test, and implement a computer program which directs the computer to process data in the manner required to solve a given problem. Although the instructions which are actually executed by the computer must be in a form called machine language, the programmer who writes the program does not normally write in machine language. Instead, the programmer uses a source language. A source language allows the programmer to write instructions in a manner which is easy for people to read and understand. COBOL is an example of a source programming language. After the program is written using a source language, the instructions written in the source language must be translated into machine language for actual execution on the computer.

The COBOL programming language has instructions which fall into seven major categories. These categories are: 1) Statements that define the data bases, files, records, and fields to be processed by the program; 2) Statements to define other data within the program, such as headings which will appear on a report; 3) Statements which cause data to be read into main computer memory from input or auxiliary storage devices and statements which cause data to be written from main computer memory to output devices or auxiliary storage devices; 4) Statements which move data from one location in main computer memory to another; 5) Statements which cause arithmetic operations to occur; 6) Statements which cause data to be compared and perform alternative operations based upon the results of the comparison; 7) Statements which document, or explain, the program.

Program Categories

Programming performed in companies today falls into two broad categories: 1) Systems programming; 2) Applications programming. Systems programming involves maintaining the set of programs, called an operating system, which interface between the computer user or computer programs and the computer hardware itself to control and manage the operations of the computer. A systems programmer makes updates to the operating system and generally ensures the computer is operational from a software point of view. Individuals trained to be systems programmers usually require an extensive technical background in programming for the specific computer which is being used.

Applications programming involves writing programs that are needed to solve problems related to business, science, and government. There are two general areas in applications programming: 1) Scientific programming; 2) Business application programming. Scientific programming refers to programming computers for scientific or engineering activities. This might include such diverse activities as writing a program to control a nuclear reactor or a space vehicle, or to perform long range weather forecasting. Individuals who are scientific programmers normally have a bachelor's or master's degree in the area of mathematics or computer science.

Business application programming involves writing programs which process business applications, such as payroll, accounts receivable, accounts payable, and inventory control. An individual interested in business application programming must be thoroughly trained in one or more programming languages and be capable of designing the logic to solve specific problems. A knowledge of accounting and business procedures is also valuable. Many large companies require business application programmers to have a four-year college degree or a two-year technical degree in computer programming. COBOL is widely used by business application programmers.

DATA ORGANIZATION

Data is used in each operation on a computer, including input operations, arithmetic operations, logical operations, output operations, and storage operations. It is important, therefore, to understand something about the data which is processed by a computer program.

Each unit of data is referred to as a data item, or field. For example, the payroll register illustrated in Figure 1–7 contains the social security number field, employee name field, and the paycheck amount field. Although each field can be processed in some manner on a computer, most of the time a single field is not useful or meaningful. A field is often useful only when it is combined with other fields or when a relationship to other fields is established. To illustrate, the social security number, by itself, is not useful. When, however, it is related to the other fields (employee name and paycheck amount), it becomes meaningful.

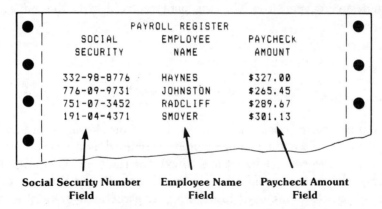

Figure 1 - 7 The Payroll Register

In order to be processed on a computer, data is normally organized based upon the application and data item relationships. Data fields are often combined to form records for processing on a computer. A record is a collection of related data items, or fields. Each record normally corresponds to a specific unit of information. For example, a record that could be used to produce the payroll register is illustrated in Figure 1–8.

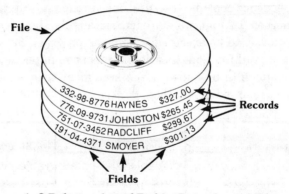

Figure 1 - 8 Relationship of Fields, Records, and Files

The fields in the record are the social security number field, the employee name field, and the paycheck amount field. This is the data used to prepare the payroll register. The first record in Figure 1–8 contains all of the data concerning the first employee, Haynes. The second record contains all of the data concerning the second employee, Johnston. Each subsequent record contains all of the data for a given employee. It can be seen how the related fields have been grouped together to form a record.

The collection of records seen in Figure 1–8 is called a file. A file contains all of the related records for an application. Therefore, the payroll file shown in Figure 1–8 contains all the records required to produce the payroll register. Files are stored on auxiliary storage devices, such as magnetic tape or magnetic disk.

THE BASICS OF A COMPUTER PROGRAM

As noted, a computer program must process data in the proper sequence under the proper conditions in order to produce the desired output. Therefore, a key element of a computer program is the logic which is implemented by the computer program. Program logic specifies the sequence in which instructions will be executed by the program in order to process data and produce the desired output. The following paragraphs identify the manner in which program logic is expressed.

Structured Programming

In well-written computer programs, program logic is developed according to the rules of structured programming. Structured programming is defined as a method of developing program logic that uses three control structures to express the logic of a program. These three control structures, called the sequence control structure, the if-then-else control structure, and the looping control structure, are used to form highly structured units of computer instructions that are easily read and understood. The following paragraphs contain an explanation of these three control structures.

Sequence Control Structure

When using the sequence control structure, one statement, or program instruction, occurs immediately after another. In Figure 1–9, each rectangular box represents a statement, or program instruction, that is to be executed within the program. For example, the instruction could cause data to be moved from one location in main computer memory to another location or could cause two numbers to be added. Each statement takes place in the exact sequence specified, one statement followed by another.

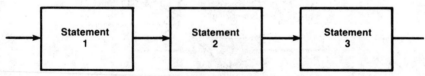

Figure 1-9 Sequence Control Structure

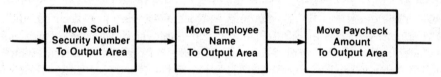

Figure 1-10 Example of the Use of the Sequence Control Structure

In the example in Figure 1-10, the three statements shown consist of moving the social security number, the employee name, and the paycheck amount to an output area in main computer memory prior to printing the fields on the report.

If-Then-Else Control Structure

The second control structure used in structured programming is called the if-then-else control structure (Figure 1-11). This structure is used for conditional statements where a condition within a program is tested, and alternative operations are performed depending upon the results of the test. In Figure 1-11, if the condition tested is true, statement 1 would be executed; if the condition tested is false, statement 2 would be executed.

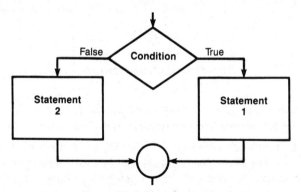

Figure 1-11 If-Then-Else Control Structure

In the example in Figure 1-12, the "if" portion of the structure (represented by the diamond-shaped symbol) tests if an employee worked overtime. The true portion of the if-then-else control structure (represented by the answer "yes" to the question, "Did the employee work overtime?") is executed if the condition tested is true. Thus in Figure 1-12, if the employee worked overtime, the regular pay and the overtime pay are calculated.

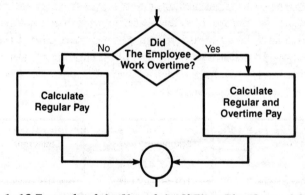

Figure 1-12 Example of the Use of the If-Then-Else Control Structure

The false portion of the if-then-else control structure (represented in Figure 1-12 by the answer "no" to the question, "Did the employee work overtime?") is executed when the condition tested is not true. Thus in Figure 1-12, if the employee did not work overtime, only the regular pay is calculated. The term if-then-else is derived from the manner in which the statement is read: IF the condition is true, THEN perform the true processing, ELSE perform the false processing.

Looping Control Structure

The third control structure, the looping control structure, is used to allow program looping. Looping means that one or more statements are executed so long as a given condition remains true. In Figure 1-13, the condition is tested. If the condition is true, statement 1 and statement 2 will be executed. The same condition is then tested again. If it is still true, then statement 1 and statement 2 will be executed again. This looping will continue until the condition being tested is not true. At that time, control will exit from the loop and subsequent processing will occur.

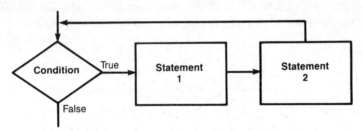

Figure 1-13 Looping Control Structure

The statements which are executed within the loop must at some point change the condition which is tested at the beginning of the loop. Otherwise, the loop will never end (called an infinite loop).

The example in Figure 1-14 illustrates a loop wherein the interest for a given amount of money is calculated and printed for each year for a period of ten years. The decision at the start of the loop determines if interest for ten years has been calculated. If so, the loop is exited. If not, the interest is calculated and printed, and then the value 1 is added to the year count. As a result of this addition, when ten years have been calculated the year count will show that ten years have been calculated and the loop can then be exited.

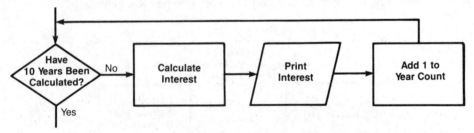

Figure 1-14 Example of the Use of the Looping Control Structure

The terms, true and false, and yes and no, should not be confused when reading the loop control structure or any of the three control structures. For example, in Figure 1-13 the word "true" specifies that the condition tested is true, and therefore, the loop is entered. In Figure

1–14, the word "no" is used to indicate that if ten years have not been calculated, the loop should be entered. The word "true" in Figure 1–13 and the word "no" in Figure 1–14 are equivalent because both answers indicate that the loop should be entered. For each question asked in a decision symbol (the diamond), the programmer must analyze the question and the resulting answer to determine if a loop should be entered.

These three control structures, the sequence control structure, the if-then-else control structure, and the looping control structure, should be used to solve any programming logic problem. They form the basis for a scientific approach to computer programming.

Single Entry Point/Single Exit Point Rule

When utilizing the three control structures of structured programming, a most important rule that must be followed is the single entry point/single exit point rule. An entry point in a control structure is the point at which the control structure is entered. An exit point is the point at which the control structure is exited. In Figure 1–15, the entry point to the if-then-else control structure is at the point where the condition is tested. The exit point from the if-then-else control structure is represented by the circle. When the control structure is executed, it is entered and the condition is tested. If the condition is true, then statement 1 is executed; if the condition is false, statement 2 is executed. Regardless of whether the condition is true or the condition is false, control is then passed to the exit point of the control structure.

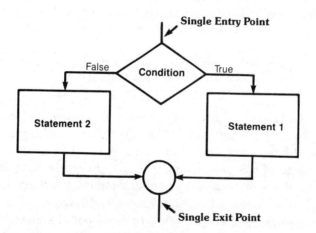

Figure 1-15 Illustration of the Single Entry/Single Exit Point Rule

The single entry point/single exit point rule states that there must be only one entry point and only one exit point for each control structure. In the example in Figure 1–15, the single entry point is where the condition is tested and the single exit point is represented by the circle. Regardless of the processing that takes place in statement 1 and statement 2, control must always be passed to the single exit point within the control structure.

Following the single entry point/single exit point rule substantially improves the ability of a programmer to read and understand a program because the programmer can be assured that whatever happens within a structure, control will always exit at the single exit point. Prior to the use of structured programming, many programmers would pass control to other parts of a program without following the single entry point/single exit point rule. This practice led to programs which were extremely difficult to read and understand.

Program Design

Program design is the process of developing the structure and logic of a program. The logic utilized in a computer program dictates the exact sequence and under what conditions instructions will be executed. The development of the logic used in a program is part of the process of designing a program.

Another major part of the program design process is to identify all of the tasks which are required for a program to process data and produce the required output. Each computer program has a number of tasks which must be accomplished in order to produce the desired output. For example, to produce the payroll register report in Figure 1–7, two of the tasks to be completed are to read the records which contain the data for the report and to print the report on the printer. The process of identifying these tasks, sometimes called structured design, is an important ingredient in the program design process, for if all the tasks are not identified, the logic for accomplishing the tasks will not be developed.

Therefore, the program design process consists of two major steps: 1) Identify the tasks which must be accomplished by the program in order to process data and produce the desired output; 2) Develop the logic to implement each of the required tasks. The programmer will normally spend a significant amount of time designing a program to ensure that the program which is designed will produce the correct output.

At the end of the design phase of a computer program, the structure and logic of the program should be detailed in such a fashion that the resulting program code from the design will be efficient, will always produce correct output (reliable), will work under all conditions (robust), and will be easily modified (maintainable).

PROGRAMMING LANGUAGES

Once a program is designed, it must be coded in a programming language in order to be implemented on a computer. Although more than 400 different programming languages have been developed during the past forty years, most have achieved limited use in industry, science, and education. Some of the programming languages which have played an important part in the development of the information processing industry include Assembler Language, FORTRAN, COBOL, PL/I, BASIC, RPG, Ada, Pascal, and Logo.

Assembler languages use symbolic notation to represent the instruction which is to be executed. These languages are closely related to the internal architecture of the machine on which they are used. They are called low-level programming languages because they are so closely related to the computer's internal design.

A programming language in which the program statements are not closely related to the internal characteristics of the computer on which the program will be executed is called a high-level programming language. As a general rule, one statement in a high-level programming language will develop a number of machine language instructions which are then executed by the computer hardware.

The History of COBOL

As has been noted, one of the most widely used high-level programming languages for business applications is COBOL (COmmon Business Oriented Language). COBOL was developed by a group of computer users and manufacturers and was released in 1960 as a high-level, business-oriented programming language.

One of the stated objectives when COBOL was developed was that the language should be machine independent, meaning that a program written in COBOL should be able to be run on a variety of computers from a variety of manufacturers with little or no change. COBOL was also designed to be written in English-like form and to be self-documenting. Nearly every manufacturer of medium and large-scale computers has undertaken the implementation of COBOL. It has also been implemented on a number of personal computers.

The success of COBOL can be credited to two major factors. First, since programming in a low-level language was difficult and error-prone, there was a definite need in 1960 for a high-level business-oriented programming language. Secondly, there was strong pressure from the federal government to establish a common language for business applications. Recognizing the need for such a language, the federal government in the early 1960's specified that if a company wanted to sell or lease computers to the federal government, it had to have COBOL software available unless it could be demonstrated that COBOL was not needed for the particular class of problems to be solved. Since the federal government was the single largest user of computers, manufacturers quickly recognized the value of developing this software.

After going through a number of revisions, COBOL was officially approved as a United States Standard in 1968. Subsequent revisions of the language led to the 1974 ANSI (American National Standards Institute) Standard COBOL, which is in use on many computers. A revision of the Standard COBOL was approved in 1985. The programs in this textbook are all compatible with the current versions of ANSI Standard COBOL.

Advantages and Disadvantages of COBOL

COBOL has several important advantages. One of the most important is that COBOL is designed to be machine independent. A program written in COBOL can be run on any computer that supports the COBOL language, regardless of manufacturer, with very minor changes.

In addition, COBOL has strong file handling capabilities, meaning that it can both write and read files stored on most media, including tape and disk; and can write and read files stored in a variety of formats, including sequential, indexed, and relative or direct files. Access to data base systems and data communications software is also available through COBOL. COBOL, as well, is relatively easy to write and, if properly written, can be easily understood by other programmers.

Some observers consider the "wordiness" of COBOL a disadvantage, for more coding must be written to produce a given result than is required when using some other high-level programming languages, such as BASIC.

It is important to recognize that, notwithstanding the disadvantages, many hundreds of thousands of programs have been written in COBOL during the past twenty-five years. It is apparent, therefore, that because of its widespread use, COBOL will remain an important programming language for many years to come.

Coding Computer Programs

Once a computer program has been designed, it is coded using a programming language.

In this text, after a program has been designed, it will be coded using the COBOL programming language. Coding a program is an activity that must be performed with care and precision. In general, errors made when coding a program can be traced to two reasons: Either the programmer was careless or the programmer did not know how to use the programming language. Neither reason is valid when coding a program. Computer programs should be coded in such a manner that errors are very rarely committed.

Structured Walkthroughs

Since designing and coding a computer program requires a considerable amount of care and attention to detail, it is possible that a programmer may inadvertently make an error. Therefore, to aid in the detection of errors in both program design and program coding, program reviews of both the program design and the program coding are normally conducted. These reviews are often called structured walkthroughs.

A structured walkthrough is an organized review of program design and program code by programmers other than the programmer who developed the material being reviewed. The intent of the walkthrough is to find any errors which have been made in the program, including either errors in the use of a programming language, called syntax errors, or errors in the design of the program.

In order for a walkthrough to be successful, it is mandatory that the programmer whose work is being reviewed adopt the attitude that a discovery of errors is welcome, since the program will be a valued asset to the company for which the programmer works only when it contains no errors. The discovery of an error in a walkthrough is not an indictment of the individual programmer. The review of the program design and program code is an important step in the development of a program, and should be part of each programming project.

Conducting a Structured Walkthrough

A structured walkthrough is normally conducted in the following manner. The programmer whose work is to be reviewed will select from 3 to 7 programmers within the department to act as reviewers. The programmer will then make copies of the work to be reviewed, whether it be program design material or program code. These copies will be distributed to the reviewers several days before the review is to take place so that those who are reviewing the work will have an opportunity to look at the copies and formulate their questions concerning the program design or the program code. In addition, prior to the meeting the reviewers will normally search for any syntax errors, such as misspelled words or missing punctuation, so that time is not spent on relatively minor errors such as these.

At the review meeting, the programmer whose work is being reviewed will walk each reviewer through the design or the code, explaining why and how things were done. Then, the reviewers will ask questions which they have formulated as a result of their examination of the work. These questions will normally focus on the completeness, accuracy, and general quality of the work produced. In particular, questionable areas in program logic and the organization of the program will be discussed.

During this process, the reviewers will not tell the programmer how to correct errors in the program. Instead, they only point out errors, and/or they raise issues which they feel may cause the program to function incorrectly or inefficiently or which may cause the program to be unintelligible to others. After the meeting, the programmer will go over the questions and suggestions made by the reviewers with the view of correcting the program.

The process of program review has been found to be a significant factor in producing quality, error-free programs. Structured walkthroughs should be conducted on all programs, whether they are designed and written for personal use, for use in industry, or for use in the classroom.

Program Execution

After the program has been designed, coded, and reviewed in a structured walkthrough, the instructions are entered into the computer and the program is executed. At this time, the design and code in the program are tested to ensure that they produce the correct results.

Chapter Summary

The input operations, arithmetic operations, logical operations, output operations, and storage operations performed by computer hardware are carried out under the direction of instructions found in a computer program. A computer program must be designed and coded by a computer programmer. The program operates on data which can be organized into fields, records, and files.

When developing the logic within a computer program, a programmer should adhere to the rules of structured programming. Three control structures are used with structured programming — sequence, if-then-else, and looping. Each of these control structures must have a single entry point and a single exit point.

In addition to designing the logic for a program, the programmer must determine the tasks to be completed by the program. After the design is complete, the programmer writes the program using a programming language. Both the program design and the program code should be formally reviewed through the use of structured walkthroughs.

The remainder of this textbook will be concerned with teaching both the techniques of program design using structured programming and structured design, and the rules and use of the COBOL programming language.

REVIEW QUESTIONS

1. Explain the input, arithmetic, logical, output, and storage operations performed by a computer.

2. Explain the function of the input units, processor unit, output units, and auxiliary storage units.

3. What is a computer program? Explain the difference between machine language and a source language.

4. List the seven major categories in which COBOL program instructions fall.

5. Describe the differences between systems programming, scientific programming, and business application programming.

6. Explain the relationship of data items, records, and files.

7. Define program logic. Define structured programming.

8. Draw and identify the three basic control structures used in structured programming.

9. What is an entry point into a control structure? What is an exit point from a control structure? Explain the single entry point/single exit point rule of structured programming.

10. What is meant by structured design?

11. Explain the difference between a low-level programming language and a high-level programming language.

12. Describe the history of the COBOL programming language.

13. List the advantages and disadvantages of the COBOL programming language.

14. What is a structured walkthrough? Describe the manner in which a structured walkthrough is conducted.

CHAPTER TWO

INTRODUCTION TO STRUCTURED DESIGN

INTRODUCTION TO STRUCTURED DESIGN

2

INTRODUCTION

As mentioned in Chapter 1, when programmers first began programming computers, the process was very much an individual effort. This approach to programming created programs that were unreliable and that were difficult to modify and maintain. Today, more is known about the methods and techniques which can and should be used to design and write computer programs.

Although computer programs written for business applications can be small, the majority of programs written are large and complex. As a result of the complexity of programs written for business, it is important that computer programmers write programs in a systematic, disciplined manner. The purpose of this chapter is to identify and explain the proper methodology for developing a computer program.

SAMPLE APPLICATION

Prior to analyzing the methodology for developing a computer program, it is essential to have an overall understanding of how the processing of data occurs within a computer. To illustrate the processing of data, a sample application is developed in this chapter in which a list of people who have purchased insurance policies is to be prepared. This Policy Report is to contain the Policy Number, Customer Name, Agent Name, and Insurance Type. An example of the printed report that is to be prepared is illustrated in Figure 2-1.

(Policy Number)	(Customer Name)	(Agent Name)	(Insurance Type)
HM-9083-6762	FRANKEN, PETER	JEAN, BARBARA	HOME
AN-3453-9834	GARCIA, WILLIAM	BENSON, GLORIA	ANNUITY
AM-9878-5647	GARFIELD, JOEY	ANDERSON, JAMES	AUTOMOBILE
TL-6763-0093	PARNELLI, FRANK	BENSON, GLORIA	TERM LIFE
HM-8767-8788	SOLENFELD, NANCY	JACOBSON, PETER	HOME
WL-7682-0903	WINDER, ROBERT	ANDERSON, JAMES	WHOLE LIFE

Figure 2-1 Sample Output of Policy Report

The data to prepare the Policy Report is stored in a file on magnetic disk and is named the Policy Disk File. Each record within the file contains the Customer Name, Agent Name, Insurance Type, and Policy Number. Together the four data items, or fields, will be used to produce one line of output on the Policy Report. The format of a Policy Disk Record is illustrated in Figure 2-2.

Policy Disk Record			
FIELD DESCRIPTION	POSITION	LENGTH	ATTRIBUTE
Customer Name	1 – 20	20	Alphanumeric
Agent Name	21 – 40	20	Alphanumeric
Insurance Type	41 – 50	10	Alphanumeric
Policy Number	51 – 62	12	Alphanumeric
Record Length		62	

Figure 2-2 Format of Policy Disk Records

The actual records to be processed by the program to produce the Policy Report are shown in Figure 2–3.

Records to be Processed			
Customer Name (Positions 1 – 20)	Agent Name (Positions 21 – 40)	Insurance Type (Positions 41 – 50)	Policy Number (Positions 51 – 62)
Franken, Peter	Jean, Barbara	Home	HM-9083-6762
Garcia, William	Benson, Gloria	Annuity	AN-3453-9834
Garfield, Joey	Anderson, James	Automobile	AM-9878-5647
Parnelli, Frank	Benson, Gloria	Term Life	TL-6763-0093
Solenfeld, Nancy	Jacobson, Peter	Home	HM-8767-8788
Winder, Robert	Anderson, James	Whole Life	WL-7682-0903

Figure 2-3 Data to be Processed by the Policy Report Program

Thus, the actual Policy Disk File stored on magnetic disk contains six records to be processed by the Policy Report program. Each of the six records in the Policy Disk File contains four fields: customer name (positions 1 - 20), agent name (positions 21 - 40), insurance type (positions 41 - 50), and policy number (positions 51-62). The data in each disk record will be processed to produce one line of output on the Policy Report.

A computer program in main memory controls the processing of the data needed to produce the Policy Report. The processing to prepare the Policy Report consists of reading an input disk record into an input area in main memory, moving each of the fields from the input area of main memory to an output area of main memory, and writing a line on the printer. This processing is repeated as long as there are input records to be processed. These steps are illustrated in the diagrams in Figure 2-4.

In step 1, the data contained in the disk input record is read into an input area in main memory. In step 2, each field in the input area is moved to the output area reserved for the data to be printed on the report. The report is then written (step 3). This sequence of events will continue as long as there are input records to be processed.

The fields on the printed report are not in the same sequence as the fields in the input record. For example, the policy number is the last field in the input record but is the first field to appear on the printed report. The arrangement of the fields on the report is controlled by the programmer when the program is written. It is important for the programmer to understand this basic processing in order to be able to properly design a program.

Step 1: A disk record containing the Customer Name, Agent Name, Insurance Type, and Policy Number is read into an input area.

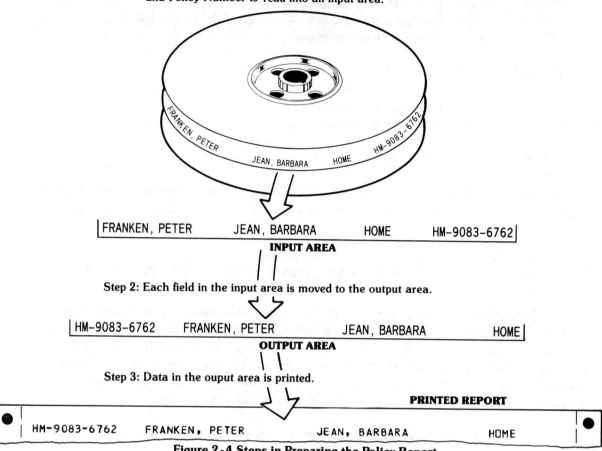

| FRANKEN, PETER | JEAN, BARBARA | HOME | HM-9083-6762 |

INPUT AREA

Step 2: Each field in the input area is moved to the output area.

| HM-9083-6762 | FRANKEN, PETER | JEAN, BARBARA | HOME |

OUTPUT AREA

Step 3: Data in the ouput area is printed.

PRINTED REPORT

| HM-9083-6762 | FRANKEN, PETER | JEAN, BARBARA | HOME |

Figure 2-4 Steps in Preparing the Policy Report

THE PROGRAM DEVELOPMENT CYCLE

Because of the complexity of writing large business programs, it is imperative that the programmer approaches writing a program in a systematic, disciplined manner. Toward this end, a program development cycle consisting of five phases has been established. These five phases, together with some intermediate steps, are listed below.

PHASE 1: REVIEW SYSTEM AND PROGRAMMING SPECIFICATIONS

PHASE 2: DESIGN THE PROGRAM
    Step 1: Analyze the program requirements in terms of the output, input, and processing.
    Step 2: Analyze the processing specified on the IPO Chart and decompose the module if required.
    Step 3: Design the logic necessary to perform the processing specified in step 1 and step 2.
    Step 4: Conduct a structured walkthrough of the program logic.
    Step 5: Specify the data bases, files, records, and fields required for the program.

PHASE 3: CODE THE PROGRAM
          Step 1: Write the source code.
          Step 2: Conduct a structured walkthrough of the source code.
          Step 3: Compile the source code.

PHASE 4: TEST THE PROGRAM
          Step 1: Create the test data.
          Step 2: Develop a testing sequence.
          Step 3: Execute the program.

PHASE 5: DOCUMENT THE PROGRAM

A detailed explanation of each of the steps in the program development cycle together with an explanation of each of the intermediate steps is contained on the following pages.

PHASE 1: REVIEW SYSTEM AND PROGRAMMING SPECIFICATIONS

A systems analyst in an information systems department reviews current operations and designs new systems for use within an organization. Upon completion of the design of a new system, the systems analyst will give the system and programming specifications to the programmer. These specifications illustrate the format of the output to be produced from the program, the format of the input to be used in the program, and the processing that is to occur within the program. System and programming specifications can consist of:

1. A printer spacing chart defining the format of any printed report that is to be prepared.

2. A disk record description defining the fields that appear in the input record.

3. A program narrative explaining the processing which is to occur to produce the output information from the input data.

Printer Spacing Chart

A printer spacing chart is used to define the format of a report. It specifies where the fields are to be printed on the report and whether the report is to be single or double spaced. Figure 2-5 contains the printer spacing chart for the Policy Report.

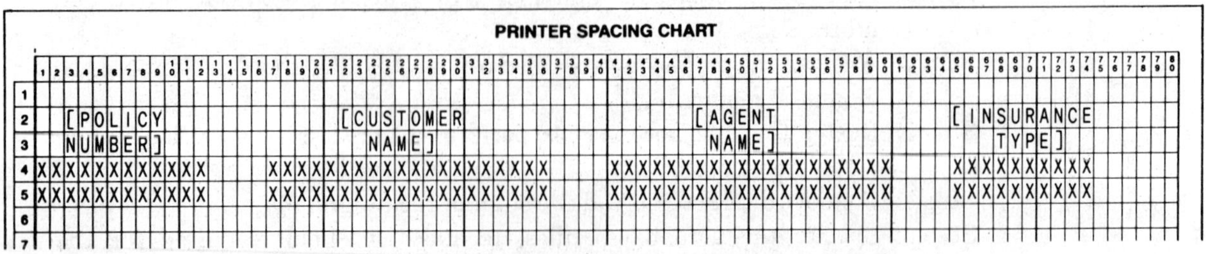

Figure 2-5 Printer Spacing Chart for the Policy Report

The small numbers at the top of the printer spacing chart represent the actual printing positions on the computer's printer. To lay out a report on a printer spacing chart, the analyst selects the print positions which are to be used to print the fields from the input record and makes an "X" notation in each print position. From the printer spacing chart in Figure 2-5 it can be seen that the Policy Number will be printed in positions 1-12 on the report, the Customer Name will be printed in positions 17-36, the Agent Name will appear in positions 41-60, and the Insurance Type is printed in positions 65-74.

At least two lines of X's are recorded in order to indicate whether the report is to be single, double, or triple spaced. For example, if the report is to be double spaced, a blank line would appear between each row of X's. Note from the printer spacing chart that the Policy Report is to be single spaced.

The titles that appear on the printer spacing chart surrounded by square brackets do not appear on the printed report but are simply to identify the contents of each field on the report.

When the input data is stored on disk, the format of the disk records must be defined. The format of the Policy Disk Records is again shown in Figure 2-6.

Policy Disk Record			
FIELD DESCRIPTION	**POSITION**	**LENGTH**	**ATTRIBUTE**
Customer Name	1 – 20	20	Alphanumeric
Agent Name	21 – 40	20	Alphanumeric
Insurance Type	41 – 50	10	Alphanumeric
Policy Number	51 – 62	12	Alphanumeric
Record Length		62	

Figure 2-6 Format of Policy Disk Records

In the Policy Disk Record, the Customer Name field is recorded in positions 1-20 and has a length of 20 characters. The Customer Name field is specified as an alphanumeric field, meaning that it can contain letters of the alphabet, numbers, and any special characters which are available on the computer. The Agent Name is stored in positions 21-40 of the Policy Disk Record. It contains 20 characters and is alphanumeric. The alphanumeric field Insurance Type is 10 characters in length and is stored in positions 41-50 of the Policy Disk Record. The last field in the record, the Policy Number, is an alphanumeric field stored in positions 51-62 with a length of 12 characters. The total length of every record in the Policy Disk File, which is determined by adding the length of each individual field, is 62 positions.

Processing

The processing which the program is to accomplish is normally specified by the systems analyst on a program narrative form. At the top of the program narrative form, space is provided for general information about the narrative, such as the subject of the narrative, the date the narrative was written, the individual who is to receive the narrative, the individual who is writing the narrative, and page numbering. The body of the program narrative form contains a description of the processing which is to occur in the program. The program narrative form used for the Policy Report program is illustrated in Figure 2-7.

PROGRAM NARRATIVE

SUBJECT		DATE		PAGE 1 OF 1
	Policy Report		October 3	
TO	Programmer	FROM	Systems Analyst	

A program is to be written to prepare a Policy Report. The format of the input record and the printer spacing chart are included with this narrative. The program should be written to include the following processing:

1. The program should read the input records and create the Policy Report as per the format illustrated on the printer spacing chart. The report shall contain Policy Number, Customer Name, Agent Name, and Insurance Type.

2. One line is to be printed on the report for each record that is read.

3. The report is to be single spaced.

4. The program should be written in COBOL.

Figure 2-7 Program Narrative

The printer spacing chart, disk record description, and program narrative — commonly referred to as the programming specifications — are used by the analyst to provide the programmer with the information required to design the program and produce the required output.

When the programming specifications have been received from the system analyst, the programmer must carefully review the specifications so that every aspect of the program which is to be written is fully understood. Too much emphasis cannot be placed on the requirement that the programmer fully understands the processing which is to take place within a program. It is quite obvious that if the programmer does not understand what is required in a program, the program cannot possibly contain the proper coding to process the data. In addition, a programmer can often find errors or omissions within the programming specifications which must be corrected prior to the programming effort. An extremely detailed check of the programming specifications must always be undertaken before beginning the task of programming.

PHASE 2: DESIGN THE PROGRAM

After the system and programming specifications have been carefully reviewed, the programmer begins the next phase of the program development cycle - designing the structure and logic of the program. Program design is one of the most important phases in the program development cycle, for if a program is properly designed, it will be easy to write in the selected programming language.

Recognizing the importance of program design and the need for a design methodology that would allow the overall structure of a program to be designed, Wayne Stevens, Glenford Myers, and Larry Constantine published an article entitled "Structured Design" in the *IBM Systems Journal* in 1974. This article described a design methodology called structured design which, when used, resulted in a program consisting of many small groups of computer instructions called modules. Each module performs a given function within the program.

The structured design methodology presents a technique to decompose a large program into small modules. The major benefit of this technique is that each of the modules is logically fairly simple, particularly when compared to the logic required for a very large program. By combining the processing of each of these small modules into a complete program, the program accomplishes the desired result.

To design a program using the structured design methodology, a series of well-defined steps must be followed. These steps are outlined below.

1. Analyze the programming specifications in terms of output, input, and functions to be performed by the program and determine the major processing tasks necessary to convert the input to output. Record this information on an IPO Chart (Input/Processing/Output Chart).

2. Further analyze the major processing tasks of the program and decompose any complex processing into simpler, more easily understood levels of processing.

3. Design the logic necessary to perform the processing specified in step 1 and step 2 by recording the detailed steps using English-like statements called Pseudocode.

4. Conduct a structured walkthrough of the program structure and program logic as shown by the pseudocode.

5. Analyze the pseudocode and identify all data bases, files, records, and fields required by the program.

Program design is an iterative process in which the design is continuously reviewed at each step and revised, if necessary, so that the optimal solution to the program will result. In particular, Steps 1 and 2 will be continually repeated, since each time the processing is decomposed into more detailed levels of processing, a new IPO Chart will be prepared for the new level of processing.

In addition, it is not at all uncommon to reach Step 3 or Step 4 only to find that the design of the program is not entirely correct. In this case, it would be required to begin a redesign of the program with Step 1 and Step 2. Although it is preferable that this type of redesigning be kept to a minimum, in actual practice it occurs quite frequently, especially with more complex programming.

Thus, a programmer should not feel that a poor job of design has been done if steps within the design process must be repeated. It should be kept in mind that the end result of the design phase is to have a program which will be efficient, will always produce correct output, will work under all conditions, and will be easily modified. Therefore, any corrections which are necessary in the design phase of the program serve only to enhance the probabilities of a correct program. A programmer should continue the repetitive process of design until the program is correct.

A detailed explanation of the design steps used for the program which creates the Policy Report follows.

Step 1: Analyze the Programming Specifications in
Terms of the Output, Input, and Processing

As the first step in program design, the programmer must specify: 1) The output to be produced from the program; 2) The input to be used to produce the output; 3) The major processing tasks which must occur to transform the input to the desired output. This information is recorded on an IPO Chart.

The output to be produced from the sample program consists of the printed Policy Report. An appropriate entry reflecting this is recorded in the OUTPUT section of the IPO Chart as shown in Figure 2-8.

IPO CHART				
PROGRAM: Policy Report		PROGRAMMER: Forsythe		DATE: Oct. 4
MODULE NAME: Create Policy Report	REF: A000	MODULE FUNCTION: Create the Policy Report		
INPUT	PROCESSING		REF:	OUTPUT
				1. Policy Report

Figure 2-8 Example of IPO Chart with the Output Entry

The entry POLICY REPORT is recorded in the column labeled Output on the IPO Chart to specify the output produced by the program. The heading sections on the IPO Chart are used to identify the program (POLICY REPORT), the programmer (FORSYTHE), the date (OCT. 4), the module name (CREATE POLICY REPORT), the reference number (A000), and the module function (CREATE THE POLICY REPORT). The Reference Number (REF) is a number given to each module within a program for identification purposes. In the sample program, the processing is not complex, so only one module is required to create the Policy Report. When the program consists of only one module, the reference number A000 is used.

The REF entry in the heading line with the Input, Processing, and Output headings is used to specify those processing tasks which will be performed by separate modules within the program. As discussed above, in the sample program in this chapter only one module is required, so an entry in this column is not made.

The input to the program is the Policy Disk File. This information should be recorded on the IPO Chart in the section marked INPUT, as illustrated in Figure 2-9.

IPO CHART				
PROGRAM: Policy Report		PROGRAMMER: Forsythe		DATE: Oct. 4
MODULE NAME: Create Policy Report	REF: A000	MODULE FUNCTION: Create the Policy Report		
INPUT	PROCESSING		REF:	OUTPUT
1. Policy Disk File				1. Policy Report

Figure 2-9 Example of IPO Chart with the Input Entry Added

At this point in the design process, the input to the program is recorded in the INPUT portion of the IPO Chart, and the output is recorded in the OUTPUT portion of the IPO Chart. The programmer must next determine the major processing tasks which are necessary to accomplish the function of the module defined on the IPO Chart. In the example, the function of the module is to Create the Policy Report. The major processing tasks to accomplish this are specified in the PROCESSING section as illustrated in Figure 2-10.

IPO CHART

PROGRAM: Policy Report		PROGRAMMER: Forsythe		DATE: Oct. 4
MODULE NAME: Create Policy Report	REF: A000	MODULE FUNCTION: Create the Policy Report		

INPUT	PROCESSING	REF:	OUTPUT
1. Policy Disk File	1. Initialize		1. Policy Report
	2. Obtain the input data		
	3. Format the print line		
	4. Write the report		
	5. Terminate		

Figure 2-10 Example of IPO Chart with the Processing Entry Added

The first entry on the IPO Chart under PROCESSING is "Initialize." Most computer programs require some type of initialization processing which prepares data bases, files, records, and fields for processing. In the sample program, initialization is required. Therefore, one of the tasks which must be specified is Initialize.

Another major processing task which must normally be performed within a business program is obtaining the input data because most business programs process some type of input data and create some type of output information. Since the program in this chapter is to process records from the Policy Disk File, input records must be read from the Policy Disk File. Therefore, "Obtain the input data" is one of the processing tasks which must be accomplished within the program.

Another task which must be accomplished within the program is to "Format the print line," which means prepare the line to be printed as specified on the printer spacing chart. Any detailed steps which may be involved in formatting the print line, such as moving individual fields from the input area to the output area, are not specified on the IPO Chart. At this step in the design process, only the major processing tasks are specified. At a later time the information on the IPO Chart will be further analyzed to define specific steps which must be taken.

In order to produce output from the program, the report must be printed. Therefore, another task to be accomplished within the program is to "Write the report." In addition, most business programs require some type of termination processing. Thus, "Terminate" is one of the processing tasks which must be specified on the IPO Chart.

The entries in the PROCESSING section of the IPO Chart do not specify the manner in which any of the processing is to be accomplished nor are they necessarily listed in the sequence in which the processing is to take place within the program. Instead, the IPO Chart is used merely to specify the major processing tasks which must occur within the program. Thus, the IPO Chart is used to specify WHAT is to take place within the program, not WHEN and HOW.

Step 2: Analyze the Processing Specified on the IPO Chart and Decompose the Module (if Required)

The program module defined on the IPO Chart in Figure 2-10 performs a given function (Create the Policy Report). It is composed of the major processing tasks (Initialize, Obtain the input data, Format the print line, Write the report, and Terminate) which must be performed in order to create the Policy Report. After the tasks have been defined on the IPO Chart, the programmer should analyze the processing to determine if the module requires further "decomposition." A module should be decomposed when the module becomes too complex to read and understand easily. A general rule used in structured programming is that a module becomes too complex when more than 20-30 statements are required in a programming language to write the module. The ability to recognize when a module becomes too complex and must be decomposed improves with the experience of the programmer.

If it appears that the processing for a module, as specified on the IPO Chart, will be too complex, then those tasks which perform a unique function within the module should themselves be made modules of the program. Each of these new modules will accomplish a given function within the program. Whenever this occurs, an IPO Chart for these new modules must be developed by the programmer. This process of decomposing a program will continue until all modules are easy to understand. The primary concept is to decompose large complex modules of a program into simpler, more easily understood modules. The general rule which limits modules to 20-30 program language statements is only a guideline to assist in the decomposition of modules and to lead to an effective program design.

In the sample program in this chapter, an analysis of the processing to be accomplished in the module whose function is to Create the Policy Report reveals that none of the major processing tasks is of such a size as to cause the entire module to be greater than 20-30 program language statements in length. Therefore, further decomposition of the module specified on the IPO Chart in Figure 2-10 is not required.

After the IPO Charts have been completed, the programmer would normally consult with the system analyst to ensure that the programmer has properly understood the problem to be solved and has provided a viable solution to the problem. The discussion should include such questions as: 1) Has the proper input been identified? 2) Has the proper output been identified? 3) Does the processing identified constitute all of the processing which should occur within the program?

In large programming projects, the processing to be performed may be extremely complex, with many different functions to be performed. Therefore, at this time it may be desirable to conduct a structured walkthrough with other programmers to review the IPO Charts created. If the basic design appears satisfactory, the programmer then begins the next step in the structured design process by defining the logic necessary in the solution of the problem.

Step 3: Design the Logic Necessary to Perform the Processing Specified in Step 1 and Step 2

After the input, processing, and output have been specified for a module, it is necessary to design the program logic, which specifies the sequence in which instructions will be executed by the program in order to process the data. A design tool called pseudocode has been developed to facilitate this process.

Pseudocode enables the programmer to express the logical flow of program processing in a straightforward, easy to understand manner using the English language. Pseudocode has few rules. Each phrase written by the programmer represents a programming statement or process which must be performed. Pseudocode is written at a level of completeness and detail which allows the programmer to code the program directly from the pseudocode statements.

Pseudocode statements are developed from the processing which is specified in the PROCESSING portion of the IPO Chart. The object of pseudocode is to specify the logic and methods of implementing the major processing tasks which are required to accomplish the function of the module. It will be recalled that the processing specified on the IPO Chart indicates WHAT is to occur; the processing specified in pseudocode indicates WHEN and HOW this processing will be performed. The pseudocode for the production of the Policy Report is illustrated in Figure 2-11.

PSEUDOCODE SPECIFICATIONS

PROGRAM: Policy Report		PROGRAMMER: Forsythe		DATE: Oct. 4
MODULE NAME: Create Policy Report	REF: A000	MODULE FUNCTION: Create the Policy Report		

PSEUDOCODE	REF:	DATA BASES, FILES, RECORDS, FIELDS REQUIRED

Open the files
Read an input record
PERFORM UNTIL no more input records
    Clear the output area
    Move the policy number, customer name,
      agent name, insurance type to output
      area
    Write the line on the report
    Read an input record
ENDPERFORM
Close the files
Stop run		

Figure 2-11 Pseudocode for the Policy Report Program

Pseudocode statements are recorded on a form entitled "Pseudocode Specifications." This form is used to specify the logic which is to be employed in the program as well as the Data Bases, Files, Records, and Fields which are required in the program. The heading sections on the Pseudocode Specifications are the same as those on the IPO Chart. The REF (Reference) column in the center of the form is used to specify the Reference Number of other modules which are referenced within the pseudocode. In the sample program in this chapter, there is only one module, so an entry in this portion of the form is not required.

As illustrated in Figure 2-11, pseudocode is a series of statements which indicate the sequence in which operations are to be executed and also under what conditions they are to be executed. The first operation to occur is to "Open the files." This is the initialization processing which was noted previously. It readies the files to be processed. Whenever a file is to be used for either input or output in a COBOL program, it must be opened.

The next statement is "Read an input record." Thus, the first record in the Policy Disk File will be read into main memory. Note that the statements in the pseudocode are NOT COBOL statements; rather, they are English statements of what operations are to take place.

After the first input record is read, a "PERFORM UNTIL" statement is specified. This statement says, "Perform the following statements until there are no more input records." All of the statements between the words PERFORM UNTIL and the word ENDPERFORM will be executed in a "loop," which means they will be continually executed until there is no more data to be processed.

The first job of the PERFORM UNTIL statement is to determine if there are any more input records. Assuming there is at least one input record which was read by the previous read statement, the statements within the "Perform Loop" would be executed.

The first statement within the loop specifies "Clear the output area." This consists of placing blanks in the output area so that improper data will not appear in the print line. After the output area has been cleared, the data in the input area is moved to the output area. This is specified in pseudocode by the "Move" statement. Thus, the Policy Number, Customer Name, Agent Name, and Insurance Type will be moved from the input area, where it was stored when read from the disk file, to the output area, from which it will be printed.

After the data is moved from the input area to the output area, the data is ready to be printed. Therefore, the next step is to "Write the line on the report." This will cause the data in the output area to be printed on the report.

After the line has been printed on the report, the first record read has been completely processed. The next step, therefore, is to read another input record, as is specified in the pseudocode in Figure 2-11. After the next input record is read, control passes back to the Perform Until statement, which will determine if there is another input record to process. If there is, then the statements within the "Perform Loop" will again be executed. If there is no more data, then the statement following the word "ENDPERFORM" will be executed. As can be seen, it is the Perform statement which determines when the looping process should be terminated.

After all records have been read and printed on the report, the loop will be terminated. At that time, the "Close the files" statement will be executed. Closing the files is the termination processing which is required whenever files are processed using COBOL. All files which have been opened must be closed. After the files are closed, the program is stopped.

To further illustrate the processing which will occur as a result of the pseudocode statements in Figure 2-11, assume there are three records in the input file. The following steps would take place within the program:

1. The files are opened.
2. The first input record is read.
3. Since there is a record to be processed, the following occur:
   a. The output area is cleared.
   b. The data from the first record is moved from the input area to the output area.
   c. The data in the output area is printed.
   d. The second record is read from the input file.
4. Since there is another record to be processed, the following occur:
   a. The output area is cleared.
   b. The data from the second record is moved from the input area to the output area.
   c. The data in the output area is printed.
   d. The third record is read from the input file.
5. Since there is another record to be processed, the following occur:
   a. The output area is cleared.
   b. The data from the third record is moved from the input area to the output area.
   c. The data in the output area is printed.
   d. An attempt is made to read the next record; however, there are no more records to be processed.
6. Since there are no more records to be processed, the loop is terminated and the files are closed.
7. The program is stopped.

This concept of performing statements within a loop as long as there are more records to process is very important since most COBOL programs employ this identical logic to process sequential input records. Therefore, it is imperative that the programmer understands this concept and is able to use it in programs.

As a result of the processing specified in the pseudocode, the tasks identified on the IPO Chart in Figure 2–10 are accomplished. This relationship is illustrated in Figure 2–12.

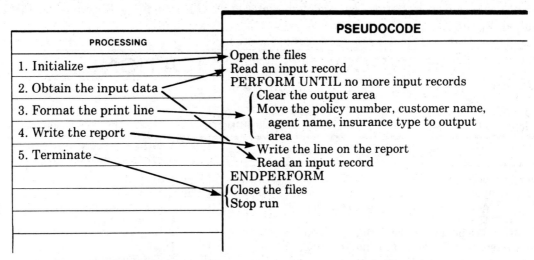

Figure 2 - 12 Relationship of Processing Entries on the IPO Chart to Pseudocode

All of the major processing tasks which had to be accomplished, as identified in the PROCESSING portion of the IPO Chart, are accomplished by the sequence of statements that appear in the PSEUDOCODE portion of the Pseudocode Specifications form. It must be noted again that the processing specified on the IPO Chart consists of the major processing tasks which must be performed; it does not specify the sequence in which events are to take place nor how they are to be accomplished. It is only when these tasks are translated into pseudocode that the methods to be used in the program are specified.

In the pseudocode in Figure 2–12, the PERFORM UNTIL and ENDPERFORM words are in capital letters. This is because these words have special meaning within pseudocode — they indicate the entry point into a loop and the exit point from a loop. In addition, the statements which are to be executed within the loop are indented so that they are more easily seen. This convention of capitalizing the PERFORM UNTIL and ENDPERFORM words and indenting the statements to be executed within the loop should always be followed.

Step 4: Conduct a Structured Walkthrough of the Program Logic

---

After the pseudocode is completed, it can be reviewed by three to seven programmers on the programming staff to find any logic errors which occurred when the pseudocode was written. The programmers will review the pseudocode to determine if the programmer has made any logical mistakes which would prevent the proper output from being produced. If any questionable logic and techniques are found, the original programmer should again review the pseudocode and justify what is taking place within the program. After all reviewing programmers and the original programmer are satisfied that the logic of the program is correct as specified in the pseudocode, then the programmer should determine the Data Bases, Files, Records, and Fields required for the program.

Step 5: Specify the Data Bases, Files, Records, and Fields Required for the Program

---

Each statement within the pseudocode is examined to determine what data bases, files, records, or fields must be available for that particular statement. This information is recorded on the pseudocode specifications in the column labeled Data Bases, Files, Records, and Fields Required (Figure 2–13).

PSEUDOCODE SPECIFICATIONS				
PROGRAM: Policy Report		**PROGRAMMER:** Forsythe		**DATE:** Oct. 4
MODULE NAME: Create Policy Report		**REF:** A000	**MODULE FUNCTION:** Create the Policy Report	

PSEUDOCODE	REF:	DATA BASES, FILES, RECORDS, FIELDS REQUIRED

Open the files
Read an input record
PERFORM UNTIL no more input records
    Clear the output area
    Move the policy number, customer name,
       agent name, insurance type to output
       area
    Write the line on the report
    Read an input record
ENDPERFORM
Close the files
Stop run
		Policy disk file
		Policy report file
		Input area for input record
		    Customer name
		    Agent name
		    Insurance type
		    Policy number
		Indicator for no more records
		Printer output area
		    Policy number
		    Customer name
		    Agent name
		    Insurance type

Figure 2-13 Determination of Data Bases, Files, Records, and Fields Required

In order to "Open the files," the Policy Disk File and the Policy Report File must be defined. When an input record is read, there must be an input area in which to store the input record. Therefore, the input area for the input record must be defined. Within that input area will be areas for the Customer Name, Agent Name, Insurance Type, and Policy Number because these fields are referenced within the program (see Figure 2-6 for the input record description).

The loop to format the print line, write the line on the report, and read the next record will be performed until there are no more input records. Therefore, it is mandatory that some means be used to indicate there are no more input records so that the loop can be terminated. The method used is an "indicator" which can be tested to determine if there are no more data records. The definition of the indicator and the method in which it can be set to indicate no more data records will be discussed in detail in Chapter 3.

In order to clear the output area, the printer output area must be defined within the program. Therefore, the printer output area is specified together with the fields which are found within the printer output area (see Figure 2-5 for the output record format). The remainder of the statements in the pseudocode reference files, records, or fields which have already been specified, so there is no need for further entries on the form.

Once the pseudocode has been defined and approved in a walkthrough, and the data bases, files, records, and fields have been specified, the design phase is complete. Therefore, the programmer must move to the third phase — that of coding the program.

PHASE 3: CODE THE PROGRAM

The third phase of the program development cycle consists of coding the program in the programming language chosen. This phase is made up of three steps:

1. Write the source code.
2. Conduct a structured walkthrough of the source code.
3. Compile the source code.

A detailed explanation of each of these steps is contained in the following paragraphs.

Step 1: Write the Source Code

High-level programming languages are designed so the programmer can write source code, which consists of the instructions and statements in the program, clearly and with ease, leading to a program which is easily understood by others. In addition, a high-level language is independent of the internal characteristics of a particular computer, which allows programs written in high-level source languages to be used on many different computers.

Although the instructions which are actually executed by the computer must be in a form called machine language, a COBOL programmer codes a program using the COBOL source language. After the program is written in COBOL, the source instructions must be translated to machine language for actual execution on the computer. A portion of the COBOL source program to solve the sample problem in this chapter is illustrated in Figures 2-14 and 2-15.

The COBOL statements in Figures 2-14 and 2-15 are somewhat readable without having a proficiency in the language. They resemble the pseudocode which was developed for the solution of the problem (see Figure 2-11). The program code should be written directly from

Figure 2-14 Example of a COBOL Program (Part 1 of 2)

COBOL Coding Form

SYSTEM							PUNCHING INSTRUCTIONS							PAGE 2 OF 2	
PROGRAM	POLICY REPORT						GRAPHIC	O	O	2	Z				
PROGRAMMER	FORSYTHE		DATE OCT. 10				PUNCH	O$_H$	ZER$_O$	TW$_O$	ZE$_E$				

```
SEQUENCE                          COBOL STATEMENT                                    IDENTIFICATION
005010              POLICY-REPORT-FILE.                                              POLRPT
005020      STOP RUN.                                                                POLRPT
005030                                                                              POLRPT
005040                                                                              POLRPT
005050                                                                              POLRPT
005060  A001-FORMAT-PRINT-LINE.                                                     POLRPT
005070                                                                              POLRPT
005080      MOVE SPACES TO POLICY-REPORT-LINE.                                      POLRPT
005090      MOVE POLICY-NUMBER-INPUT TO POLICY-NUMBER-REPORT.                       POLRPT
005100      MOVE CUSTOMER-NAME-INPUT TO CUSTOMER-NAME-REPORT.                       POLRPT
005110      MOVE AGENT-NAME-INPUT TO AGENT-NAME-REPORT.                             POLRPT
005120      MOVE INSURANCE-TYPE-INPUT TO INSURANCE-TYPE-REPORT.                     POLRPT
005130      WRITE POLICY-REPORT-LINE                                                POLRPT
005140          AFTER ADVANCING 1 LINES.                                            POLRPT
005150      READ POLICY-INPUT-FILE                                                  POLRPT
005160          AT END                                                              POLRPT
005170              MOVE 'NO ' TO ARE-THERE-MORE-RECORDS.                           POLRPT
```

Figure 2-15 Example of a COBOL Program (Part 2 of 2)

the pseudocode specifications form. A detailed explanation of the use of the COBOL code in Figures 2-14 and 2-15 is contained in Chapter 3.

Step 2: Conduct a Structured Walkthrough of the Source Code

After the coding has been written on the coding forms, a structured walkthrough should be conducted to review the coding and detect any errors which have been incorporated into the source code. In particular, the reviewer should check the code to be sure that no syntax errors have occurred and that the coding corresponds to the pseudocode which was developed for the program. Syntax errors are errors which occur when the rules of the programming language are violated. For example, if required punctuation is omitted or punctuation is included where it cannot be, a syntax error has occurred. It is the function of this walkthrough to detect these errors so they will not occur when the program is compiled.

When the structured walkthrough is completed, the programmer and the reviewers should be completely confident that the coding is correct, that no errors will occur as a result of misuse of the programming language, and that the logic as implemented in the programming language is correct. The program should not be placed on the computer until all possible care has been taken to ensure that it is correct.

Step 3: Compile the Source Code

For processing on the computer, the COBOL program can be entered into main memory using a CRT (Cathode Ray Tube) terminal. The diagram in Figure 2-16 illustrates a segment of the COBOL program as it appears on the screen of the terminal. For each line of coding in the program, a single line is entered on the terminal.

Figure 2-16 A Segment of a COBOL Program as Seen on a CRT Screen

A computer can only execute instructions stored in memory in a machine language format. Therefore, COBOL statements written by the programmer must be translated into machine language instructions in order to be executed by the computer. For example, the COBOL word "MOVE" must be converted to a code which can be interpreted by the computer electronics in order for the move operation to be executed.

A special program, called a compiler or translator, has been developed to translate computer programs written by programmers in a source language into machine language instructions. The drawing in Figure 2-17 on page 2.18 illustrates the processing performed by the COBOL compiler to compile a COBOL program, that is, convert the COBOL source program statements written by the programmer into machine language instructions.

The processing performed by the compiler, as shown in Figure 2-17, includes the following: 1) The COBOL compiler, stored on auxiliary storage, is read into main memory; 2) The COBOL program written by the programmer on coding sheets is entered into the main memory; 3) The compiler analyzes each COBOL source statement and produces the following output: a) The object program, which contains the machine language instructions; b) A source listing of the COBOL source statements; c) A diagnostic listing identifying any syntax errors detected within the source program.

With careful coding and a thorough structured walkthrough, there should never be any compilation errors to correct. Only if there are errors that go undetected during the process of entering the source program into the computer should compilation errors be found. Once a "clean compilation" has been obtained, that is, once the compilation has been made without any diagnostics, then the programmer is ready for the fourth phase of the program development cycle, that of program testing.

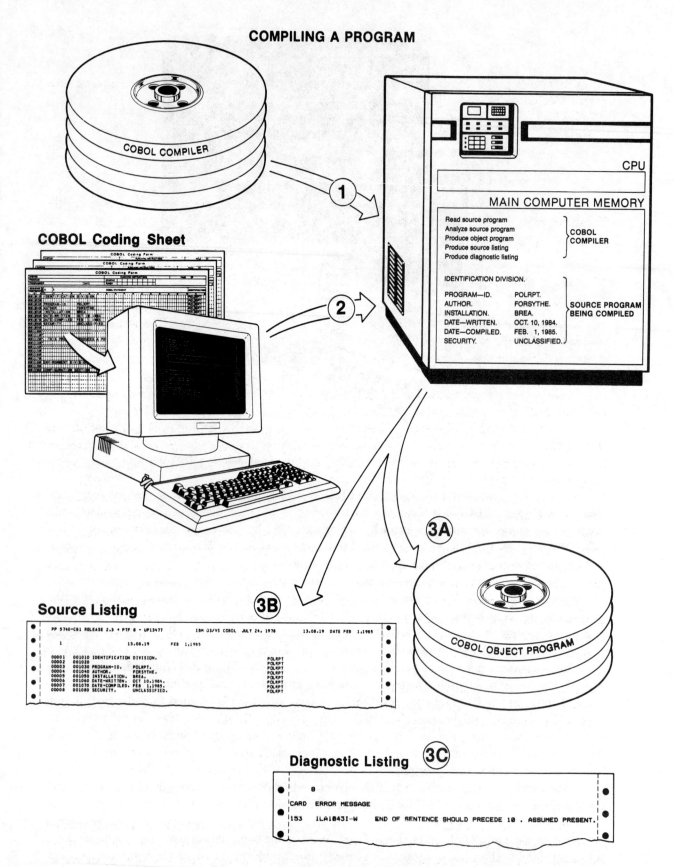

Figure 2-17 Steps in Compiling a COBOL Program

PHASE 4: TEST THE PROGRAM

The fourth phase of the program development cycle consists of testing the source program. This phase is made up of three steps:

1. Create the test data.
2. Develop a testing sequence.
3. Execute the program.

A detailed explanation of each of the steps in this phase of the program development cycle is contained in the following paragraphs.

Step 1: Create the Test Data

Creating the test data with which to test a computer program is an important responsibility of a computer programmer. The development of adequate test data, together with good program design and coding, are the most important tasks accomplished by a computer programmer.

There are several elements to developing test data. These are: 1) What type of data should be developed? 2) Who should develop the test data? 3) Who will check the test data?

Test data should be designed to find errors in the program. Although it has been shown that testing — no matter how extensive — cannot be used to prove a program is entirely error-free, it has been found that properly designed test data can be used to show a high probability that errors do not exist.

Therefore, the task of developing test data should be approached with the same seriousness as designing and coding the program. Test data should be developed which requires the program to execute all the instructions within the program at least one time. To do this, test data will normally fall into two major areas: 1) Data which is in the correct format and which will cause the instructions that process correct data to be executed; 2) Data which contains predefined errors, causing the error routines within the program to be executed.

To test a program, data must be produced which will allow the instructions within a program to be executed in order to determine if the program is operating correctly. Although many times the programmer will be required to make up test data, it has been found that when a programmer makes test data to test a program, the data is many times biased to test what the programmer knows the program should do, as opposed to testing what the program was designed to do. Therefore, in recent years, the trend is to have the test data prepared by someone other than the programmer who wrote the program. In this manner, unbiased test data is produced, leading to a program that will be adequately tested.

Step 2: Develop a Testing Sequence

A program will not normally be tested by being executed just one time. The programmer should develop a test plan which, among other things, specifies the number of test runs to be executed, the portions of the program that are to be tested on each run, and the objectives of each test run.

Step 3: Execute the Program

In the past there has been great emphasis on the testing phase of the program development cycle because it was felt that this was the proper place to ensure a program did not contain errors. Although this thinking has been largely discounted with the increased emphasis on program design, it still remains that the program must be executed and tested prior to implementation in a production environment.

The errors found in programs can be in many forms. Typical errors include logic errors which produce results other than those intended for the program, errors in design which will cause the program to be unable to process the required types of input data, and inadvertent omission of program statements which causes invalid output to be produced by the program. An example of the latter type of error is found in the listing in Figure 2-18.

```
HM-9083-6762JEAN, BARBARA          FRANKEN, PETER          HOME
AN-3453-9834BENSON, GLORIA         GARCIA, WILLIAM         ANNUITY
AM-9878-5647ANDERSON, JAMES        GARFIELD, JOEY          AUTOMOBILE
TL-6763-0093BENSON, GLORIA         PARNELLI, FRANK         TERM LIFE
HM-8767-8788JACOBSON, PETER        SOLENFELD, NANCY        HOME
WL-7682-0903ANDERSON, JAMES        WINDER, ROBERT          WHOLE LIFE
```

Figure 2-18 Example of Output Produced From a Program Error

In the sample report illustrated in Figure 2-18, the spaces between the Policy Number field and the next field on the printed report have been omitted. When an error such as this occurs, the programmer must closely examine the source program to determine why the error occurred and then carefully make corrections to the program. In making a correction, the programmer must be sure that the correction which is made does not cause an error elsewhere in the program. This is not an infrequent occurrence and, therefore, must be considered.

After any test run, the programmer must carefully examine the output to find all errors which occurred in the test. For example, in the output in Figure 2-18, it is obvious that the print line is spaced incorrectly. It is less obvious, however, that the Agent Name and the Customer Name have been reversed. Thus, the test run which produced the output in Figure 2-18 revealed two distinct errors in the program. It is the responsibility of the programmer to find ALL of the errors which are produced from the test run and make the proper corrections. After corrections are made, the report will be printed correctly, as illustrated in Figure 2-19.

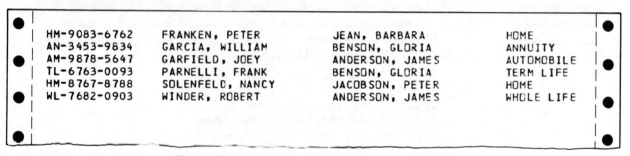

```
HM-9083-6762    FRANKEN, PETER      JEAN, BARBARA       HOME
AN-3453-9834    GARCIA, WILLIAM     BENSON, GLORIA      ANNUITY
AM-9878-5647    GARFIELD, JOEY      ANDERSON, JAMES     AUTOMOBILE
TL-6763-0093    PARNELLI, FRANK     BENSON, GLORIA      TERM LIFE
HM-8767-8788    SOLENFELD, NANCY    JACOBSON, PETER     HOME
WL-7682-0903    WINDER, ROBERT      ANDERSON, JAMES     WHOLE LIFE
```

Figure 2-19 Example of Correct Program Output

In Figure 2-19, both of the errors have been corrected. Again, although program testing is an important phase in the program development cycle, it must be emphasized that proper program design will keep the number of errors to a minimum; in fact, there should be NO errors when a program is compiled and tested. The programmer must constantly work toward this goal when designing and writing the program.

PHASE 5: DOCUMENT THE PROGRAM

Program documentation is an important but often neglected part of the programming process. In an organization with many hundreds or even thousands of programs, the lack of documentation available with programs can determine the success or failure of using the program. The documentation of each program should include the following:

1. An abstract and general description of the program.
2. Record layouts for report output, terminal output, files on auxiliary storage, user views of data bases used, and any other data which is necessary in the execution of the program.
3. A system flowchart or data flow diagram illustrating where the particular program fits within the system.
4. A detailed description of the processing which occurs within the program.
5. A hierarchy chart of the modules within the program illustrating the structure of the program.
6. The logic utilized within each module of the program.
7. A listing of the source program.
8. A listing of the test data used to test the program and the results of the testing.
9. A console run form which includes the job control statements and any other information necessary to specify how the program is to be run on the computer.
10. A user guide specifying how to use the program.

SUMMARY

The programmer who follows a disciplined approach when writing a program and closely adheres to the steps in the program development cycle with care and diligence will generate programs that are efficient, that will always produce correct output, that will work under all conditions, and that will be easily modified. A summary of the phases in the program development cycle follows:

PHASE 1: REVIEW SYSTEM AND PROGRAMMING SPECIFICATIONS

PHASE 2: DESIGN THE PROGRAM
          Step 1: Analyze the program requirements in terms of the output, input, and processing.
          Step 2: Analyze the processing specified on the IPO Chart and decompose the module (if required).
          Step 3: Design the logic necessary to perform the processing specified in step 1 and step 2.
          Step 4: Conduct a structured walkthrough of the program logic.

Step 5: Specify the data bases, files, records, and fields required for the program.

PHASE 3: CODE THE PROGRAM
Step 1: Write the source code.
Step 2: Conduct a structured walkthrough of the source code.
Step 3: Compile the source code.

PHASE 4: TEST THE PROGRAM
Step 1: Create the test data.
Step 2: Develop a testing sequence.
Step 3: Execute the program.

PHASE 5: DOCUMENT THE PROGRAM

The key to developing good programs is to perform good program design. The design of a program is, without question, the most important aspect of programming. By using the three control structures found in structured programming, as described in Chapter 1, together with a well-designed modular program, the programmer will develop a program which can subsequently be easily coded and implemented.

Coding a program, thoroughly testing it, and documenting it properly are all very important in obtaining understandable, maintainable programs. A failure in any of these areas will result in a poor program, notwithstanding the good design. Without good design, however, success in coding, testing, and placing the program into production is unlikely.

REVIEW QUESTIONS

1. Summarize the steps required to produce a printed report from a disk input record.

2. List the five phases in the program development cycle.

3. What are the steps in Phase 2 of the program development cycle?

4. What are the steps in Phase 3 of the program development cycle?

5. What are the steps in Phase 4 of the program development cycle?

6. What types of information should be recorded on an IPO Chart?

7. In the sample program designed in this chapter, is it necessary to move the Customer Name, Agent Name, Insurance Type, and Policy Number from the input area to the output area? Why is this information not recorded under PROCESSING on the IPO Chart?

8. What is the purpose of pseudocode?

9. What is a compiler? What are the steps in compiling a COBOL program?

10. What is a source listing? What is a diagnostic listing?

11. What documentation should be prepared for each program?

PROGRAM DESIGN ASSIGNMENT 1

INSTRUCTIONS

An Inventory Report is to be prepared. Design the program to create the Inventory Report by preparing the IPO Chart and writing the required pseudocode. Retain the IPO Chart and pseudocode for use in Chapter 3.

INPUT

Input consists of Inventory Records that contain a Part Number, Part Description, Quantity on Hand, and Quantity Sold. The format of the Inventory Disk Record is illustrated below. The portions of the record designated UNUSED are not used in this programming assignment.

Inventory Disk Record			
FIELD DESCRIPTION	POSITION	LENGTH	ATTRIBUTE
UNUSED	1 – 5	5	Alphanumeric
Part Number	6 – 9	4	Alphanumeric
UNUSED	10 – 29	20	Alphanumeric
Part Description	30 – 49	20	Alphanumeric
UNUSED	50 – 55	6	Alphanumeric
Quantity on Hand	56 – 58	3	Alphanumeric
Quantity Sold	59 – 61	3	Alphanumeric
Record Length		61	

OUTPUT

Output consists of an Inventory Report listing the Part Number, Quantity Sold, Part Description, and Quantity on Hand. The printer spacing chart for the report is illustrated below.

PRINTER SPACING CHART

```
       1         2         3         4         5         6         7         8
123456789012345678901234567890123456789012345678901234567890123456789012345678901234567890
1
2 [PART      [QUANTITY                                   [QUANTITY
3 NUMBER]     SOLD]           [DESCRIPTION]               ON HAND]
4
5 XXXX        XXX       XXXXXXXXXXXXXXXXXXXX              XXX
6 XXXX        XXX       XXXXXXXXXXXXXXXXXXXX              XXX
7
8
9
10
```

PROGRAM DESIGN ASSIGNMENT 2

INSTRUCTIONS

A Sales Report is to be prepared. Design the program to create the Sales Report by preparing the IPO Chart and writing the required pseudocode. Retain the IPO Chart and pseudocode for use in Chapter 3.

INPUT

Input consists of Sales Disk Records that contain a Store Number, Department Number, Salesperson Number, Salesperson Name, and Sales Amount. The format of the Sales Disk Record is illustrated below. Those portions of the record designated UNUSED are not used in this programming assignment.

Sales Disk Record			
FIELD DESCRIPTION	**POSITION**	**LENGTH**	**ATTRIBUTE**
UNUSED	1 – 6	6	Alphanumeric
Store Number	7 – 8	2	Alphanumeric
Department Number	9 – 10	2	Alphanumeric
Salesperson Number	11 – 12	2	Alphanumeric
Salesperson Name	13 – 32	20	Alphanumeric
UNUSED	33 – 53	21	Alphanumeric
Sales Amount	54 – 59	6	Alphanumeric
UNUSED	60 – 67	8	Alphanumeric
Record Length		67	

OUTPUT

Output consists of a Sales Report listing the Salesperson Number, Salesperson Name, Store Number, Department Number, and Sales Amount. The printer spacing chart for the report is illustrated below. Note that the report is double spaced.

PRINTER SPACING CHART

PROGRAM DESIGN ASSIGNMENT 3

INSTRUCTIONS

Two listings of a Food Store's inventory are to be prepared. Since two listings are required, it has been decided to print each of the fields twice on the same print line. Design the program to create the listing by preparing the IPO Chart and writing the required pseudocode. Retain the IPO Chart and pseudocode for use in Chapter 3.

INPUT

Input consists of Food Disk Records that contain the Food Number and Food Description. The format of the Food Disk Record is illustrated below. The portions of the record designated UNUSED are not used in this programming assignment.

Food Disk Record			
FIELD DESCRIPTION	**POSITION**	**LENGTH**	**ATTRIBUTE**
UNUSED	1 – 6	6	Alphanumeric
Food Number	7 – 10	4	Alphanumeric
UNUSED	11 – 16	6	Alphanumeric
Food Description	17 – 36	20	Alphanumeric
UNUSED	37 – 64	28	Alphanumeric
Record Length		64	

OUTPUT

Output consists of a Food Report listing the same Food Number and Food Description twice. The printer spacing chart for the report is illustrated below.

PRINTER SPACING CHART

[NUMBER]   [DESCRIPTION]   [NUMBER]   [DESCRIPTION]

XXXX   XXXXXXXXXXXXXXXXXXXX   XXXX   XXXXXXXXXXXXXXXXXXXX
XXXX   XXXXXXXXXXXXXXXXXXXX   XXXX   XXXXXXXXXXXXXXXXXXXX

(NOTE: EACH RECORD IS PRINTED TWICE)

PROGRAM DESIGN ASSIGNMENT 4

INSTRUCTIONS

A Computer User Report is to be prepared listing new computer users. Design the program to create the Computer User Report by preparing the IPO Chart and writing the required pseudocode. Retain the IPO Chart and pseudocode for use in Chapter 3.

INPUT

Input consists of User Disk Records that contain the CRT Number, Connect Date, and User Name. The format of the User Disk Record is illustrated below. The portions of the record designated UNUSED are not used in this programming assignment.

User Disk Record			
FIELD DESCRIPTION	POSITION	LENGTH	ATTRIBUTE
CRT Number	1 – 2	2	Alphanumeric
UNUSED	3 – 33	31	Alphanumeric
Connect Date	34 – 39	6	Alphanumeric
User Name	40 – 59	20	Alphanumeric
UNUSED	60 – 73	14	Alphanumeric
Record Length		73	

OUTPUT

Output consists of a Computer User Report listing the User ID, User Name, Connect Date, and CRT Number. User ID is generated as follows: The first four characters of the User ID are the first four characters of the User Name. This is followed by the last four characters of the Connect Date, followed by the CRT Number. Thus, the User ID for ABCD COMPUTER CORP. whose Connect Date is 010386 and who uses CRT Number 01 would be ABCD038601. The printer spacing chart for the report is illustrated below.

PRINTER SPACING CHART

CHAPTER THREE

INPUT / OUTPUT OPERATIONS

INTRODUCTION
OUTPUT
INPUT
IPO CHART
PSEUDOCODE — REQUIRED DATA
    BASES, FILES, RECORDS,
    AND FIELDS
COBOL CODING FORM
IDENTIFICATION DIVISION
FORMAT NOTATION
SUMMARY — IDENTIFICATION
    DIVISION
ENVIRONMENT DIVISION
CONFIGURATION SECTION
INPUT-OUTPUT SECTION
SELECT CLAUSE
DATA DIVISION
FILE SECTION
RECORD CONTAINS CLAUSE
LABEL RECORDS CLAUSE
DATA RECORD CLAUSE
RECORD DESCRIPTION
LEVEL NUMBERS
PICTURE CLAUSE
DEFINITION OF THE REPORT FILE
WORKING-STORAGE SECTION
VALUE CLAUSE
DATA DESIGN
PROCEDURE DIVISION

COMMENTS
OPEN STATEMENT
READ STATEMENT
PERFORM STATEMENT
CLOSE STATEMENT
STOP RUN STATEMENT
PERFORMED PARAGRAPH
MOVE STATEMENTS
MULTIPLE RECEIVING FIELDS
DIFFERENT LENGTH FIELDS
RECEIVING FIELD LONGER THAN
    SENDING FIELD
RECEIVING FIELD SHORTER THAN
    SENDING FIELD
LITERALS
WRITE STATEMENT
PROGRAMMING TIPS
SAMPLE PROGRAM
OUTPUT
INPUT
SOURCE LISTING
PRINTED OUTPUT
REVIEW QUESTIONS
COBOL CODING EXERCISES
STRUCTURED WALKTHROUGH
    EXERCISES
PROGRAMMING ASSIGNMENTS

INPUT/OUTPUT OPERATIONS

3

INTRODUCTION

As explained in Chapter 2, the program development cycle consists of reviewing the specifications of the problem to be solved, designing the program to solve the problem, coding the program, testing the program, and documenting the program. One of the steps in coding the program is to write the source code. This chapter is devoted to explaining the entries required to write the COBOL source code to produce the Policy Report from the Policy Disk File.

OUTPUT

In review, the Policy Report contains the Policy Number, Customer Name, Agent Name, and Insurance Type. The printer spacing chart for the report is illustrated in Figure 3-1.

PRINTER SPACING CHART

```
      [POLICY              [CUSTOMER              [AGENT            [INSURANCE
      NUMBER]               NAME]                  NAME]             TYPE]
     XXXXXXXXXXXX    XXXXXXXXXXXXXXXXXXXX    XXXXXXXXXXXXXXXXXXXX    XXXXXXXXXX
     XXXXXXXXXXXX    XXXXXXXXXXXXXXXXXXXX    XXXXXXXXXXXXXXXXXXXX    XXXXXXXXXX
```

Figure 3-1 Printer Spacing Chart for Policy Report

INPUT

Each record in the Policy Disk File contains a Customer Name, Agent Name, Insurance Type, and Policy Number. The format of the input record is illustrated in Figure 3-2.

Policy Disk Record			
FIELD DESCRIPTION	POSITION	LENGTH	ATTRIBUTE
Customer Name	1 – 20	20	Alphanumeric
Agent Name	21 – 40	20	Alphanumeric
Insurance Type	41 – 50	10	Alphanumeric
Policy Number	51 – 62	12	Alphanumeric
Record Length		62	

Figure 3-2 Policy Disk Record Format

IPO CHART

The IPO Chart for the program which produces the Policy Report is illustrated in Figure 3–3. The IPO Chart contains the input, output, and major processing tasks that are to be performed to transform the input to the output.

IPO CHART

PROGRAM: Policy Report	PROGRAMMER: Forsythe	DATE: Oct. 4

MODULE NAME: Create Policy Report	REF: A000	MODULE FUNCTION: Create the Policy Report

INPUT	PROCESSING	REF:	OUTPUT
1. Policy Disk File	1. Initialize		1. Policy Report
	2. Obtain the input data		
	3. Format the print line		
	4. Write the report		
	5. Terminate		

Figure 3-3 IPO Chart

PSEUDOCODE - REQUIRED DATA BASES, FILES, RECORDS, AND FIELDS

The pseudocode, which specifies the detailed steps required in the solution of the problem, together with a listing of the required data bases, files, records, and fields to be referenced in the program, are contained on the Pseudocode Specifications in Figure 3–4.

PSEUDOCODE SPECIFICATIONS

PROGRAM: Policy Report	PROGRAMMER: Forsythe	DATE: Oct. 4

MODULE NAME: Create Policy Report	REF: A000	MODULE FUNCTION: Create the Policy Report

PSEUDOCODE	REF:	DATA BASES, FILES, RECORDS, FIELDS REQUIRED

Open the files
Read an input record
PERFORM UNTIL no more input records
    Clear the output area
    Move the policy number, customer name,
      agent name, insurance type to output
      area
    Write the line on the report
    Read an input record
ENDPERFORM
Close the files
Stop run
		Policy disk file
		Policy report file
		Input area for input record
		    Customer name
		    Agent name
		    Insurance type
		    Policy number
		Indicator for no more records
		Printer output area
		    Policy number
		    Customer name
		    Agent name
		    Insurance type

Figure 3-4 Pseudocode Specifications

After the pseudocode has been written and the required data bases, files, records, and fields have been specified, the programmer is ready to write the COBOL source code. The COBOL source code written to process the Policy Disk File and create the Policy Report is illustrated in Figure 3-5 and Figure 3-6.

COBOL Coding Form

SYSTEM
PROGRAM POLICY REPORT
PROGRAMMER FORSYTHE DATE OCT. 10
PUNCHING INSTRUCTIONS
GRAPHIC O 0 2 Z
PUNCH O_H Zero Two Zee
PAGE 1 OF 6

```
001010  IDENTIFICATION DIVISION.                                    POLRPT
001020                                                              POLRPT
001030  PROGRAM-ID.      POLRPT.                                    POLRPT
001040  AUTHOR.          FORSYTHE.                                  POLRPT
001050  INSTALLATION.    BREA.                                      POLRPT
001060  DATE-WRITTEN.    OCT 10,1984.                               POLRPT
001070  DATE-COMPILED.   FEB  1,1985.                               POLRPT
001080  SECURITY.        UNCLASSIFIED.                              POLRPT
001090                                                              POLRPT
001100 ******************************************************       POLRPT
001110 *                                                      *     POLRPT
001120 *  THIS PROGRAM PRODUCES A POLICY REPORT.              *     POLRPT
001130 *                                                      *     POLRPT
001140 ******************************************************       POLRPT
001150                                                              POLRPT
001160                                                              POLRPT
001170                                                              POLRPT
001180  ENVIRONMENT DIVISION.                                       POLRPT
001190                                                              POLRPT
001200  CONFIGURATION SECTION.                                      POLRPT
```

```
002010                                                              POLRPT
002020  SOURCE-COMPUTER.   IBM-4381.                                POLRPT
002030  OBJECT-COMPUTER.   IBM-4381.                                POLRPT
002040                                                              POLRPT
002050  INPUT-OUTPUT SECTION.                                       POLRPT
002060                                                              POLRPT
002070  FILE-CONTROL.                                               POLRPT
002080      SELECT POLICY-INPUT-FILE                                POLRPT
002090          ASSIGN TO UT-S-POLINPUT.                            POLRPT
002100      SELECT POLICY-REPORT-FILE                               POLRPT
002110          ASSIGN TO UT-S-POLPRINT.                            POLRPT
002120 /                                                            POLRPT
002130  DATA DIVISION.                                              POLRPT
002140                                                              POLRPT
002150  FILE SECTION.                                               POLRPT
002160                                                              POLRPT
002170  FD  POLICY-INPUT-FILE                                       POLRPT
002180      RECORD CONTAINS 62 CHARACTERS                           POLRPT
002190      LABEL RECORDS ARE STANDARD                              POLRPT
002200      DATA RECORD IS POLICY-INPUT-RECORD.                     POLRPT
```

```
003010  01  POLICY-INPUT-RECORD.                                    POLRPT
003020      05  CUSTOMER-NAME-INPUT      PICTURE X(20).             POLRPT
003030      05  AGENT-NAME-INPUT         PICTURE X(20).             POLRPT
003040      05  INSURANCE-TYPE-INPUT     PICTURE X(10).             POLRPT
003050      05  POLICY-NUMBER-INPUT      PICTURE X(12).             POLRPT
003060                                                              POLRPT
003070  FD  POLICY-REPORT-FILE                                      POLRPT
003080      RECORD CONTAINS 133 CHARACTERS                          POLRPT
003090      LABEL RECORDS ARE OMITTED                               POLRPT
003100      DATA RECORD IS POLICY-REPORT-LINE.                      POLRPT
003110  01  POLICY-REPORT-LINE.                                     POLRPT
```

Figure 3-5 COBOL Source Code — Part 1 of 2

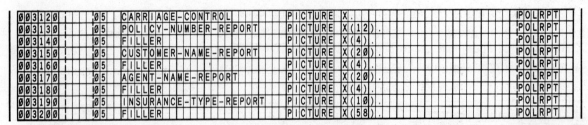

```
003120    05  CARRIAGE-CONTROL           PICTURE  X.                  POLRPT
003130    05  POLICY-NUMBER-REPORT       PICTURE  X(12).              POLRPT
003140    05  FILLER                     PICTURE  X(4).               POLRPT
003150    05  CUSTOMER-NAME-REPORT       PICTURE  X(20).              POLRPT
003160    05  FILLER                     PICTURE  X(4).               POLRPT
003170    05  AGENT-NAME-REPORT          PICTURE  X(20).              POLRPT
003180    05  FILLER                     PICTURE  X(4).               POLRPT
003190    05  INSURANCE-TYPE-REPORT      PICTURE  X(10).              POLRPT
003200    05  FILLER                     PICTURE  X(58).              POLRPT
```

```
004210                                                                POLRPT
004020  WORKING-STORAGE SECTION.                                      POLRPT
004030                                                                POLRPT
004040  01  PROGRAM-INDICATORS.                                       POLRPT
004050      05  ARE-THERE-MORE-RECORDS   PICTURE X(3) VALUE 'YES'.    POLRPT
004060 /                                                              POLRPT
004070  PROCEDURE DIVISION.                                           POLRPT
004080                                                                POLRPT
004090  ***************************************************************  POLRPT
004100  *                                                          *  POLRPT
004110  *  THIS PROGRAM READS THE POLICY INPUT RECORDS AND CREATES THE  *  POLRPT
004120  *  POLICY REPORT.  IT IS ENTERED FROM THE OPERATING SYSTEM AND  *  POLRPT
004130  *  EXITS TO THE OPERATING SYSTEM.                           *  POLRPT
004140  *                                                          *  POLRPT
004150  ***************************************************************  POLRPT
004160                                                                POLRPT
004170  A000-CREATE-POLICY-REPORT.                                    POLRPT
004180                                                                POLRPT
004190      OPEN INPUT  POLICY-INPUT-FILE                             POLRPT
004200           OUTPUT POLICY-REPORT-FILE.                           POLRPT
```

```
005010      READ POLICY-INPUT-FILE                                   POLRPT
005020          AT END                                               POLRPT
005030              MOVE 'NO ' TO ARE-THERE-MORE-RECORDS.            POLRPT
005040      PERFORM A001-FORMAT-PRINT-LINE                           POLRPT
005050          UNTIL ARE-THERE-MORE-RECORDS = 'NO '.                POLRPT
005060      CLOSE POLICY-INPUT-FILE                                  POLRPT
005070            POLICY-REPORT-FILE.                                POLRPT
005080      STOP RUN.                                                POLRPT
005090                                                               POLRPT
005110                                                               POLRPT
005120  A001-FORMAT-PRINT-LINE.                                      POLRPT
005130                                                               POLRPT
005140      MOVE SPACES TO POLICY-REPORT-LINE.                       POLRPT
005150      MOVE POLICY-NUMBER-INPUT TO POLICY-NUMBER-REPORT.        POLRPT
005160      MOVE CUSTOMER-NAME-INPUT TO CUSTOMER-NAME-REPORT.        POLRPT
005170      MOVE AGENT-NAME-INPUT TO AGENT-NAME-REPORT.              POLRPT
005180      MOVE INSURANCE-TYPE-INPUT TO INSURANCE-TYPE-REPORT.      POLRPT
005190      WRITE POLICY-REPORT-LINE                                 POLRPT
005200          AFTER ADVANCING 1 LINES.                             POLRPT
```

```
006010      READ POLICY-INPUT-FILE                                   POLRPT
006020          AT END                                               POLRPT
006030              MOVE 'NO ' TO ARE-THERE-MORE-RECORDS.            POLRPT
```

Figure 3-6 COBOL Source Code — Part 2 of 2

An explanation of the entries on each line of the COBOL coding forms is contained on the following pages.

COBOL CODING FORM

The COBOL program is normally written on a special COBOL coding form. A segment of the coding form is illustrated in Figure 3-7.

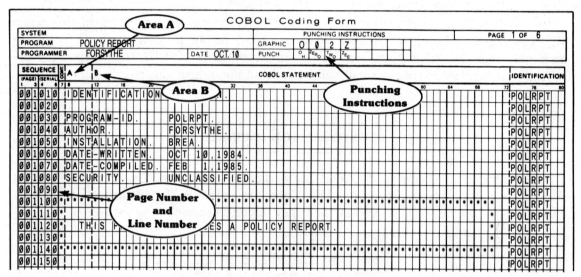

Figure 3-7 COBOL Coding Form

At the top of the form, space is provided for general information about the program, including the system name, program name, programmer, and date. Instructions for data entry can be given in the section labeled "Punching instructions." To prevent confusion when entering a character written on a coding form into the computer, an explanation of the character may be given in this section. For example, on the coding form in Figure 3-7, the letter "O" is explained using the word "OH," and the number "0" is explained using the word "ZERO." In the upper right corner of the form, space is provided to record the Page Number and the total number of pages of coding for the program.

In columns 73-80, space is reserved for the "Identification." This area on the form is used to give an identification to each of the coded lines. Any numbers, letters of the alphabet, or special characters, including blanks, may be used. The "Identification" has no effect on the object program or the compiler even though this information is entered into columns 73-80 of the lines comprising the COBOL source program. It is used merely for identification purposes. In the sample program, the value "POLRPT," representing Policy Report, has been chosen by the programmer as the identification.

Columns 1-6, labeled "Sequence," are used to number the lines of coding on the form. Columns 1, 2, and 3 are used for page number identification, and columns 4, 5, and 6 are used to identify each line number (serial number). Each succeeding line is given a higher number. Columns 4 and 5 are sometimes prenumbered on the coding form. Use of the columns 1-6 for sequence numbering program lines is optional and is not required for most COBOL compilers. As a good programming practice, however, they should be included. All programs in this textbook include the page and line numbers.

If columns 1-6 are used, Page Number (1-3) and Serial Number (4-6) should contain only numeric digits. Letters of the alphabet or special characters are not allowed by most COBOL compilers. In Figure 3-7, the method of numbering allows additional instructions to be inserted at a later date, if required, without disturbing the ascending sequence of instructions. For example, if an additional line of coding is to be inserted between line 010 and line 020, the line could be identified as line 015 and be inserted into the main program without disturbing the sequence of lines comprising the COBOL program.

The continuation indicator area (column 7) must be blank on all lines except when a special type of COBOL word called a non-numeric literal must be continued on a second line, or when comments are to be placed in the source program. This use of the continuation column is explained in detail later in the text.

Columns 8-72 are used for program entries. The columns are grouped into two areas, AREA A (columns 8-11) and AREA B (columns 12-72). Certain portions of the COBOL program must begin in AREA A and certain portions must begin in AREA B. The specific rules for recording the various entries are discussed in detail throughout this chapter.

IDENTIFICATION DIVISION

The Identification Division of a COBOL program is written first. This Division specifies information which serves to identify and document the program. The Identification Division of the COBOL program used to prepare the Policy Report is shown in Figure 3-8.

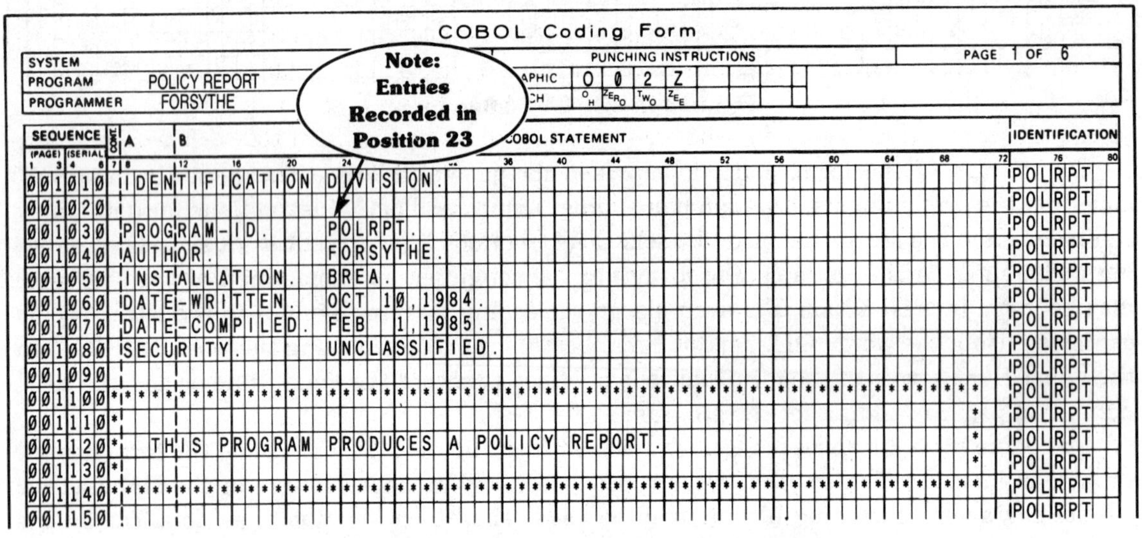

Figure 3-8 Example of Identification Division

When writing a COBOL program, the method of recording the Division Names and related entries, the spacing, and the presence or absence of the period is extremely important. The following statements summarize the rules for recording entries in the Identification Division.

1. The beginning of the Identification Division is marked by the "Division Header Entry" which consists of the name IDENTIFICATION DIVISION. A Division Header entry always begins on a line by itself, must begin in Area A, and must be followed by a period.
2. The Identification Division is made up of "Paragraph Headers." These Paragraph Headers consist of a series of fixed names (PROGRAM-ID, AUTHOR, INSTALLATION, DATE-WRITTEN, DATE-COMPILED, and SECURITY). Paragraph Headers must begin in Area A and be followed by a period and a space.
3. The words or sentences following the Paragraph Headers must be contained within Area B.

4. The Program Name following PROGRAM-ID must consist of alphabetic and numeric characters, one of which must be alphabetic. The first eight characters of the Program Name identify the object program.

5. The words following the Paragraph Header entries AUTHOR, INSTALLATION, DATE-WRITTEN, DATE-COMPILED, and SECURITY may be originated at the discretion of the programmer and may contain any characters available on the computer. Coding may not be extended into columns 73-80. The programmer may break off the coding anywhere before column 73 and record the following entries on the next line beginning in Area B.

6. Each of the entries in the Identification Division must be terminated by a period.

The entries recorded for the sample program in Figure 3-8 are used to identify the program and the programmer. The program name is POLRPT and it was written by Forsythe. The program was written at the Brea installation on Oct. 10, 1984, and compiled on Feb. 1, 1985. The date on which a program is to be compiled is often not known to the programmer when the program is written. In addition, it may be compiled a number of times in order to correct mistakes, make changes to the program, or for other reasons. Therefore, most COBOL compilers will insert the date on which the compilation takes place automatically if the DATE-COMPILED Paragraph Header is included in the Identification Division.

In the coding in Figure 3-8, line number 001020 is blank, and each of the entries following the Paragraph Header entries begins in column 23. Although not required, these entries are recorded in this manner so that the listing will be clear and easy to read. It is extremely important that the source listing be easy to read. One way in which this can be done is to utilize uniform ways of recording information on the coding form. The coding conventions illustrated in Figure 3-8 for the Identification Division will be used throughout this text.

An asterisk (*) is included in column 7 for lines 001100 through 001140. Whenever an asterisk is included in column 7, the statement is treated as a comment statement. A comment statement will appear on the source listing but will not become a part of the machine language instructions generated by the compiler. The comments in the Identification Division appear on the source listing as illustrated in Figure 3-9.

```
PP 5740-CB1 RELEASE 2.3 + PTF 8 - UP13477          IBM OS/VS COBOL  JULY 24, 1978          13.08.19  DATE FEB  1,1985

       1                          13.08.19          FEB 11,1985

00001    001010 IDENTIFICATION DIVISION.                                                    POLRPT
00002    001020                                                                             POLRPT
00003    001030 PROGRAM-ID.      POLRPT.                                                     POLRPT
00004    001040 AUTHOR.          FORSYTHE.                                                   POLRPT
00005    001050 INSTALLATION.    BREA.                                                       POLRPT
00006    001060 DATE-WRITTEN.    OCT 10,1984.                                                POLRPT
00007    001070 DATE-COMPILED.   FEB 11,1985.                                                POLRPT
00008    001080 SECURITY.        UNCLASSIFIED.                                               POLRPT
00009    001090                                                                             POLRPT
00010    001100********************************************************************         POLRPT
00011    001110*                                                                  *         POLRPT
00012    001120*   THIS PROGRAM PRODUCES A POLICY REPORT.                         *         POLRPT
00013    001130*                                                                  *         POLRPT
00014    001140********************************************************************         POLRPT
00015    001150                                                                             POLRPT
00016    001160                                                                             POLRPT
00017    001170                                                                             POLRPT
00018    001180 ENVIRONMENT DIVISION.                                                        POLRPT
00019    001190                                                                             POLRPT
00020    001200 CONFIGURATION SECTION.                                                      POLRPT
00021    002010                                                                             POLRPT
00022    002020 SOURCE-COMPUTER. IBM-4381.                                                   POLRPT
00023    002030 OBJECT-COMPUTER. IBM-4381.                                                   POLRPT
00024    002040                                                                             POLRPT
```

Figure 3-9 Example of Comment Statements

Comments are normally used to specify or help clarify the processing which takes place within the program. Any characters available on the computer can appear in the comment statements. When used in the Identification Division, comments usually specify the processing which is to take place within the program. In the sample program, the comments specify that the program produces the Policy Report.

When coding the Identification Division, the Paragraph Headers (PROGRAM-ID, AUTHOR, etc.) must begin in Area A of the coding form. The words or sentences following the Paragraph Headers must be contained within Area B. They do not, however, have to be on the same line. The example in Figure 3-10 illustrates an alternative method of recording the entries for the Identification Division on the COBOL coding form.

SEQUENCE		A	B	COBOL STATEMENT
(PAGE)	(SERIAL)			

```
001010  IDENTIFICATION DIVISION.
001020
001030  PROGRAM-ID.
001040      POLRPT.
001050  AUTHOR.
001060      FORSYTHE.
001070  INSTALLATION.
001080      BREA.
001090  DATE-WRITTEN.
001100      OCT 04,1984.
001110  DATE-COMPILED.
001120      FEB 01,1985.
001130  SECURITY.
001140      UNCLASSIFIED.
001150
001160  *****************************************************************
001170  *                                                               *
001180  *  THIS PROGRAM PRODUCES THE POLICY REPORT.                     *
001190  *                                                               *
001200  *****************************************************************
```

Figure 3-10 Identification Division with Entries on Separate Lines

Format Notation

Technical reference manuals developed for the COBOL programming language provide a standard format notation for the various elements of COBOL. These generalized descriptions are intended to guide the programmer when writing COBOL programs. The format notation for the Identification Division is illustrated in Figure 3-11.

```
IDENTIFICATION DIVISION.

PROGRAM-ID.  program-name.

[AUTHOR.  [comment-entry ]  ... ]

[INSTALLATION.  [comment-entry]  ...]

[DATE-WRITTEN.  [comment-entry]  ...]

[DATE-COMPILED.  [comment-entry]  ...]

[SECURITY.  [comment-entry]  ...]
```

Figure 3-11 Format Notation for Identification Division

It is imperative that the COBOL programmer thoroughly understands this system of notation. The basic rules as related to the Identification Division are summarized in the following paragraphs.

1. All words printed entirely in capital letters are reserved words. These words have preassigned meanings in the COBOL language and are not to be used for any other purpose. In all formats, words written in capital letters and selected for use in a COBOL program must be duplicated exactly as they appear in the format notation. A complete list of reserved words is given in Appendix B.

2. All underlined reserved words are required unless the portion of the format containing them is itself optional. These are key words. If any such word is missing or is incorrectly spelled, it is considered an error in the program. Reserved words which are not underlined may be used or omitted at the programmer's option, but if they are included, they must be spelled properly.

3. Lower case words represent information that must be supplied by the programmer.

4. Punctuation, except for commas and semicolons, is required where it is shown. Commas and semicolons are always optional.

5. Square brackets ([...]) are used to indicate that the enclosed item may be used or omitted, depending on the requirements of the particular program.

6. When braces ({...}) enclose a portion of a general format, one of the options within the braces must be explicitly specified or a default value will be used.

7. Options are indicated in a general format by vertically stacking alternative possibilities, by a series of brackets or braces, or by a combination of both. An option is selected by specifying one of the possibilities from a stack of alternative possibilities or by specifying a unique combination of possibilities from a series of brackets or braces.

8. Except where noted, clauses must be written in the sequence given in the general formats.

By applying the above rules of format notation to the Identification Division, it can be seen that AUTHOR, INSTALLATION, DATE-WRITTEN, DATE-COMPILED, and SECURITY are enclosed in brackets and are optional. These paragraphs are not required entries in the Identification Division. The only required entries in the Identification Division are the Division Header, IDENTIFICATION DIVISION, and the PROGRAM-ID. In well-written programs, however, all the entries in the Identification Division are used in order to properly document the program.

Summary — Identification Division

The Identification Division is recorded on a COBOL coding form. There are two areas on the COBOL coding form, Area A (columns 8-11) and Area B (columns 12-72). The Division Header, IDENTIFICATION DIVISION, must begin in Area A and be followed by a period. This entry must appear on a line by itself.

The Paragraph Headers, PROGRAM-ID, AUTHOR, INSTALLATION, DATE-WRITTEN, DATE-COMPILED, and SECURITY must also begin in Area A and must be followed immediately by a period and then a space. Sentences within a paragraph may start on the same line as the Paragraph Header or on a separate line. Succeeding lines of the paragraph must begin within Area B.

ENVIRONMENT DIVISION

The next division of the COBOL program to be coded is the Environment Division. The Environment Division contains two Sections, the Configuration Section and the Input-Output Section. The Configuration Section identifies the computer on which the program is to be compiled and executed. The Input-Output Section assigns files to input and output devices and may also specify special input/output techniques.

Configuration Section

The COBOL coding form in Figure 3–12 illustrates the suggested entries for the Configuration Section of the Environment Division.

```
001170
001180  ENVIRONMENT DIVISION.
001190
001200  CONFIGURATION SECTION.
002010
002020  SOURCE-COMPUTER.  IBM-4381.
002030  OBJECT-COMPUTER.  IBM-4381.
002040
```

Figure 3-12 Environment Division — Configuration Section

The Division Header, ENVIRONMENT DIVISION, the Section Header, CONFIGURATION SECTION, and the Paragraph Headers, SOURCE-COMPUTER and OBJECT-COMPUTER, must begin in Area A and be followed by a period. There must always be at least one blank space following a period. The entries following SOURCE-COMPUTER and OBJECT-COMPUTER must be contained within Area B.

The SOURCE-COMPUTER paragraph identifies the computer on which the COBOL program is to be compiled. The OBJECT-COMPUTER paragraph identifies the computer on which the program is to be executed. In the sample program, the computer on which the program is compiled and on which it is executed is an IBM 4381 computer. Therefore, the term IBM-4381 is specified for both the SOURCE-COMPUTER and OBJECT-COMPUTER. These entries are treated strictly as comments and, therefore, have no value except for documentation purposes. Each manufacturer has specific entries which may be placed in these paragraphs, depending upon the model of the computer being used and other manufacturer-dependent specifications.

The COBOL format notation for the Configuration Section is illustrated in Figure 3–13.

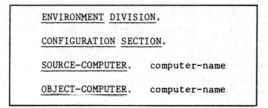

```
ENVIRONMENT DIVISION.

CONFIGURATION SECTION.

SOURCE-COMPUTER.   computer-name

OBJECT-COMPUTER.   computer-name
```

Figure 3-13 Format Notation for Configuration Section

In the format notation illustrated in Figure 3–13, the terms CONFIGURATION

SECTION, SOURCE-COMPUTER, and OBJECT-COMPUTER must be included as shown. The computer-name describes the source and object computers.

Input-Output Section

The Input-Output Section of the Environment Division contains the File-Control paragraph. The File-Control paragraph is used to name the files to be processed and associate those files with the input/output devices being used. In the sample program, the Policy Disk File and the Policy Report File must be defined.

The entries used in the sample program for the Input-Output Section of the Environment Division are shown in Figure 3–14.

```
002050 INPUT-OUTPUT SECTION.
002060
002070 FILE-CONTROL.
002080     SELECT POLICY-INPUT-FILE
002090          ASSIGN TO UT-S-POLINPUT.
002100     SELECT POLICY-REPORT-FILE
002110          ASSIGN TO UT-S-POLPRINT.
```

Figure 3-14 Input-Output Section

Select Clause

The general format of the Select statement within the File-Control paragraph is illustrated in Figure 3–15.

```
SELECT  file-name

ASSIGN TO implementor-name-1 [, implementor-name-2] ...
```

Figure 3-15 Format Notation for Select and Assign Clauses

In the Select clause, the word Select is used to name each file within the program. The Assign clause is used to assign a file to a device on the computer. The Select and Assign clauses used for the disk input file in the sample program are illustrated in Figure 3–16.

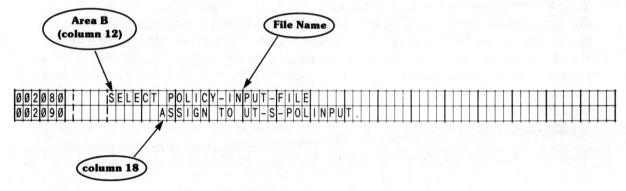

Figure 3-16 Select Clause and Assign Clause

The Select clause must begin with the word SELECT and be followed by a file-name. The file-name, chosen by the programmer, is the name by which the file is referenced throughout the program. A file-name should be chosen that is descriptive of the file being processed. It may be composed of a combination of not more than 30 characters chosen from the following set of 37 characters:

> 0 through 9 (numeric digits)
> A through Z (alphabetic letters)
> - (hyphen)

A file-name must contain at least one alphabetic character. The name must not begin or end with a hyphen but a hyphen may be contained within the name. The end of a file-name is detected by the COBOL compiler by the space at the end of the name. Therefore, no blanks are permitted within the name. The name of each file must be unique within the program and should be descriptive of the file to be processed.

The file-name chosen for the Policy Disk File is POLICY-INPUT-FILE. This name was chosen because it is descriptive.

The Assign clause is used to relate the file to a particular input/output device. In the example in Figure 3-16 the words ASSIGN TO begin the Assign Clause. The word ASSIGN is required in the clause and the word TO may be used at the option of the programmer. It is not required (see Figure 3-15).

Although the COBOL language is designed to be used on any computer hardware regardless of the manufacturer, there are several areas within the program where the entries depend upon the COBOL compiler being used. One of these areas is the Assign clause used within the program. In the general format in Figure 3-15, the entry used with the Assign clause is "implementor-name-1." This means the value to be placed in the Assign clause is defined by the implementor of the COBOL compiler, and can change based upon the computer and the COBOL compiler being used.

The sample program is implemented using an IBM-4381 COBOL compiler executed under the OS/MVS operating system. The implementor-name UT-S-POLINPUT is used in the sample program because this name has meaning to the particular computer and software being used. The UT stands for Utility, meaning the file can be stored on any device which will support sequential files. The entry, S, indicates that the file will be a sequential file. The name POLINPUT stands for Policy Input and identifies the name of the file as stored on disk. These entries may vary from one computer to another. The reference manual for the particular computer and compiler being used should be consulted to determine proper entries for the Assign clause.

In Figure 3-16, the Select clause (line 080) for the POLICY-INPUT-FILE is continued on line 090. This continued line must begin within Area B. For readability, the "ASSIGN TO..." line was indented six spaces to begin in column 18. In all sample programs within this text, any continuing lines will be indented six spaces. It should be noted, however, that the continued line could begin in column 12 or any column within Area B. In addition, it is not required that the Assign Clause be placed on a separate line. It could have been placed on the same line as the Select Clause, with one blank between the last letter of the file-name and the word ASSIGN.

The Select and Assign clauses for the POLICY-REPORT-FILE are illustrated in Figure 3-17.

```
002100 │    SELECT POLICY-REPORT-FILE
002110 │        ASSIGN TO UT-S-POLPRINT.
```

Figure 3-17 Select Clause for Policy Report File

The same format is used for the printer output file as is used for the disk input file. The sentence must always start with the word SELECT. The file-name used for the printer output file is POLICY-REPORT-FILE which, again, is a name chosen because it is descriptive of the file to be processed.

The Assign clause must use an implementor-name. In the sample program, the entry used is UT-S-POLPRINT. This entry is the same as that used for the disk input file except that the last term used is POLPRINT, not POLINPUT. The entry POLPRINT will associate the file with the printer on the computer. The entries for other compilers and computers may differ from the entries described because they are defined by the implementor.

The Select and Assign clauses are used to give a name to a file and to indicate the type of hardware to be used for the file. It remains, however, to indicate the other attributes of the file, such as the length and format of the records in the file. These definitions are made in the Data Division of the COBOL program.

DATA DIVISION

The Data Division of a COBOL source program describes the files and data to be processed by the program. The Data Division is subdivided into Sections. In the sample program in this chapter which creates the Policy Report, the File Section and Working-Storage Section of the Data Division are used.

File Section

The File Section describes the content and organization of the files to be processed. In addition to describing the files to be processed, Record Description entries which describe the individual fields contained in the records of a file are required.

The first segment of the File Section of the Data Division used in the sample program consists of the entries illustrated in Figure 3–18.

```
002130  DATA DIVISION.
002140
002150  FILE SECTION.
002160
002170  FD  POLICY-INPUT-FILE
002180      RECORD CONTAINS 62 CHARACTERS
002190      LABEL RECORDS ARE STANDARD
002200      DATA RECORD IS POLICY-INPUT-RECORD.
```

Figure 3 - 18 Data Division — File Section

The entries in Figure 3–18 are used to provide a general description of the content and organization of the records contained in the file. The format notation for the entries used in the sample program in the File Section of the Data Division are illustrated in Figure 3–19 which appears on page 3.14.

The Division Header, DATA DIVISION, is a required statement and must be spelled as shown. It must appear on a line by itself and be followed by a period and a space. The entire File Section is optional because it is enclosed within brackets. The File Section is optional only if there are no files to be processed by the program. In the programs within this text, the File

```
      DATA DIVISION.

     [FILE SECTION.

     [FD  file-name

         [; RECORD CONTAINS [integer-3 TO]  integer-4 CHARACTERS]

          ; LABEL  {RECORD IS  }  {STANDARD}
                   {RECORDS ARE}  {OMITTED }

         [; DATA  {RECORD IS  }  data-name-3  [, data-name-4] ...]
                  {RECORDS ARE}

         [record-description-entry] ... ] ...
```

Figure 3-19 Format Notation for File Section

Section will be required because files are to be processed.

The words FILE SECTION are required if a File Section is to be used and must appear on a separate line with the correct spelling. Both the words DATA DIVISION and the words FILE SECTION begin in column 8 of the coding form. The requirement is that they begin in Area A. In all programs in this text, they will begin in column 8. The DATA DIVISION and FILE SECTION entries are separated by a blank line. Although this is not required, it is suggested that it be done to increase the readability of the source listing.

The FD level indicator (File Description) in Figure 3–20 describes each file to be processed by the program. The name following the FD must be the same file-name used in the Select clause of the File-Control paragraph. The letters FD must begin in Area A and the file-name must begin in Area B.

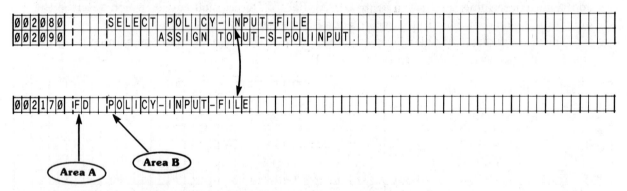

Figure 3-20 Select Clause and FD Entry for Policy Input File

Although any columns within Area A may be used for the FD level indicator, all programs in this textbook will use column 8. In the same manner, the file-name may begin in any column within Area B. In the programs in this book, the file-name always begins in column 12.

Record Contains Clause

Following the FD level indicator is the Record Contains clause. The Record Contains clause is used to specify the number of characters in a record. The entry from the sample program is illustrated in Figure 3-21.

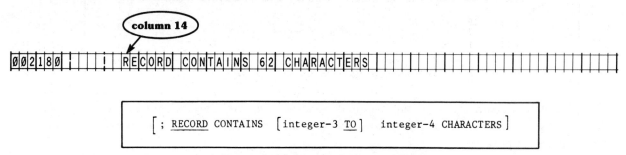

Figure 3-21 Record Contains Clause

The Record Contains clause must begin in Area B. In Figure 3-21 it begins in column 14 to increase readability. Integer-4 in the format notation specifies the number of positions in the record found in the file. In the program for this chapter, the entry RECORD CONTAINS 62 CHARACTERS is used because each input record in the POLICY-INPUT-FILE contains 62 characters.

The Record Contains clause is not required (note the brackets in the format notation). It is suggested, however, that the entry be included for documentation purposes. Record lengths are determined by the compiler regardless of whether or not the clause is specified.

Label Records Clause

The Label Records clause specifies the presence or absence of standard or non-standard labels on a file. Labels are used to identify files stored on magnetic tape or disk. The entry used in the sample program is illustrated in Figure 3-22.

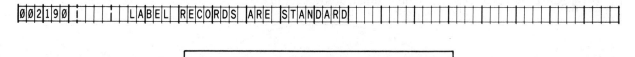

Figure 3-22 Label Records Clause

The format notation in Figure 3-22 specifies that the Label Records clause is required in the FD statement (no brackets). Therefore, whenever a file is being defined with the FD statement in the File Section of the Data Division, the Label Records clause must be included. In the example, the word STANDARD is used because the file named POLICY-INPUT-FILE, which is stored on disk, uses standard labels for identification purposes.

Data Record Clause

The Data Record clause specifies the name of the records within a file. The Data Record clause used in the sample program is illustrated in Figure 3-23 on page 3.16.

```
002200 |       |   DATA RECORD IS POLICY-INPUT-RECORD.
```

```
[ ; DATA { RECORD IS  } data-name-3 [ , data-name-4 ] ... ]
           { RECORDS ARE }
```

Figure 3-23 Data Record Clause

The Data Record clause is not required because it is contained within brackets in the format. Again, however, it is suggested that the clause be included in the source code for documentation purposes.

The entry for "data-name-3..." in the Data Record clause is for the purpose of assigning a symbolic name to the individual records of a file. In the sample problem, the entry DATA RECORD IS POLICY-INPUT-RECORD is specified. Thus, the name POLICY-INPUT-RECORD may be used in subsequent sections of the program to reference the individual records from the POLICY-INPUT-FILE. More than one type of record may be contained within a single file. The ellipsis (...) following the entry data-name-4 indicates that additional record names can be specified in order to give names to all the types of records found in the file.

The formation of a data-name follows the rules of data-name formation. These rules state the name must contain at least one alphabetic character and be composed of not more than 30 characters. The characters may be numbers, letters of the alphabet, or the hyphen. The hyphen must not be the first or last character of the name.

In the code in Figure 3-23 a period follows the data-name because the data-name is the last entry in the FD statement. As mentioned previously, the use of the period is critical when writing COBOL programs. Strict attention must be paid to the format notation and the examples given in the text so that punctuation errors are not made.

At this point in the COBOL program, the programmer has assigned a symbolic name to the entire file (POLICY-INPUT-FILE) and a symbolic name to each record within the file (POLICY-INPUT-RECORD). This is illustrated in Figure 3-24.

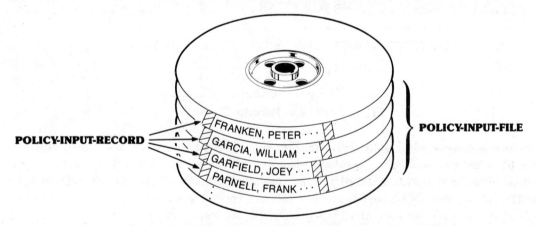

Figure 3-24 Illustration of File and Records within a File

Record Description

After the file has been described by the Record Contains, Label Records, and Data Record clauses, the individual records within the file are described. Figure 3-25 contains the entries in the COBOL program in this chapter that describe the record stored in the POLICY-INPUT-FILE.

```
002130 DATA DIVISION.
002140
002150 FILE SECTION.
002160
002170 FD  POLICY-INPUT-FILE
002180         RECORD CONTAINS 62 CHARACTERS
002190         LABEL RECORDS ARE STANDARD
002200         DATA RECORD IS POLICY-INPUT-RECORD.
003010 01  POLICY-INPUT-RECORD.
003020     05  CUSTOMER-NAME-INPUT        PICTURE X(20).
003030     05  AGENT-NAME-INPUT           PICTURE X(20).
003040     05  INSURANCE-TYPE-INPUT       PICTURE X(10).
003050     05  POLICY-NUMBER-INPUT        PICTURE X(12).
```

Figure 3-25 Record Description Entries

A Record Description entry in the File Section of the Data Division specifies the characteristics of each field in a record. Every item in the record must be described as a separate entry in the same order in which the item appears in the record. Each Record Description entry in the sample program in this chapter consists of a Level-Number, a Data-Name, and a Picture clause.

The general format of the Record Description entry used in the sample program is illustrated in Figure 3-26.

```
level-number  {data-name-1}
              {FILLER     }

[ ; {PICTURE}  IS character-string ]
    {PIC    }
```

Figure 3-26 Format Notation for Record Description Entries

Level Numbers

Level numbers are used to show how data items (fields) are related to each other. The level number 01 is used to specify an individual record within a file. In the sample program, the individual record of the POLICY-INPUT-FILE is identified by the entry 01 POLICY-INPUT-RECORD, as illustrated in Figure 3-27.

```
002200          DATA RECORD IS POLICY-INPUT-RECORD.
003010 01  POLICY-INPUT-RECORD.
```

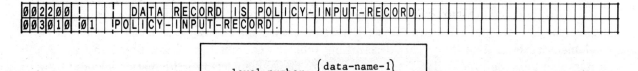

```
level-number  {data-name-1}
              {FILLER     }
```

Figure 3-27 Record Description Entry

In Figure 3-27 level number 01 is specified in Area A and the data-name POLICY-INPUT-RECORD is specified in Area B. All 01 level numbers must be specified in Area A.

Subordinate data items that constitute a record are grouped in a hierarchy, and are identified with level numbers 02 through 49. In the sample program, level number 05 is used to identify the fields within a record. Any number higher than 01 could have been selected. Identifying the fields within a record with a level number of 05 allows further subdivisions of the record if required at some future time.

Figure 3-28 illustrates the entries to describe the fields within the record named POLICY-INPUT-RECORD.

```
003010 01  POLICY-INPUT-RECORD.
003020     05  CUSTOMER-NAME-INPUT        PICTURE X(20).
003030     05  AGENT-NAME-INPUT           PICTURE X(20).
003040     05  INSURANCE-TYPE-INPUT       PICTURE X(10).
003050     05  POLICY-NUMBER-INPUT        PICTURE X(12).
```

Figure 3-28 Entries to Describe Fields Within a Record

The entries on lines 020, 030, 040, and 050 in Figure 3-28 are used to describe the fields within the record. When describing the fields within a record, a data-name or the COBOL word FILLER must be specified following the level number. The data-name selected may contain up to 30 characters. The construction of the name follows the same rules as those for the formation of file-names. In the coding in Figure 3-28, the data-names CUSTOMER-NAME-INPUT, AGENT-NAME-INPUT, INSURANCE-TYPE-INPUT, and POLICY-NUMBER-INPUT have been selected to reference the corresponding fields in the input record. These names have been chosen because they represent the content of each field within the record. Whenever data-names are used, they should always indicate the contents of the field — this is mandatory in order to make the program as readable as possible.

The suffix "INPUT" is used on all data-names to indicate that the names refer to fields in the input record. Whenever data-names are used to describe fields within an input or output record, a suffix should be used to indicate the use of field.

When the data-names are written on the coding form, they are indented two spaces following the level 05 entry. This indentation is designed to improve the readability of the source code.

The subdivisions of a record that are not themselves subdivided are called elementary items. In Figure 3-28, the fields with the data-names CUSTOMER-NAME-INPUT, AGENT-NAME-INPUT, INSURANCE-TYPE-INPUT, and POLICY-NUMBER-INPUT are elementary items. Data items which are subdivided are called group items. Thus, the record name POLICY-INPUT-RECORD is a group item.

Picture Clause

With each elementary item (identified by level-number 05 in the sample program), there must be an associated Picture clause. A Picture clause specifies a detailed description of an elementary level data item. This description indicates the number of characters in the data item and also the type of data, such as letters of the alphabet only (alphabetic); letters of the alphabet, numbers, and/or special symbols (alphanumeric); or numbers only (numeric). The Picture clauses used for the fields in the input record in the sample program are illustrated in Figure 3-29.

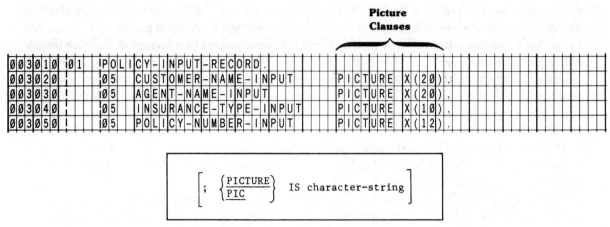

Figure 3-29 Example of Picture Clause

The word PICTURE is followed by a character string. This character string is used to specify the type of data which is contained within the field and also the number of characters which are in the field. In the sample program, the data is alphanumeric, meaning that the fields being described may contain any of the characters which are available on the computer. In order to define an alphanumeric field, the notation "X" is used following the word PICTURE.

The value within the parentheses specifies the number of characters in the field. The CUSTOMER-NAME-INPUT field contains 20 alphanumeric characters as a result of the entry X(20) following the word PICTURE. Similarly, the AGENT-NAME-INPUT field contains 20 alphanumeric characters, the INSURANCE-TYPE-INPUT field contains 10 alphanumeric characters, and the POLICY-NUMBER-INPUT field contains 12 alphanumeric characters.

These field sizes correspond to the disk record format, as illustrated in Figure 3-30.

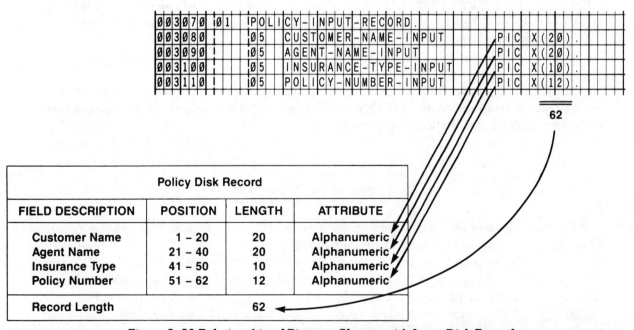

Figure 3-30 Relationship of Pictures Clauses with Input Disk Record

The field lengths specified in the disk record format in Figure 3-30 correspond to the field sizes as specified in the Picture clauses. The attribute of the fields (ALPHANUMERIC)

corresponds to the use of the "X" in the Picture clauses. In addition, the fields are specified on the coding form in the same sequence in which they are found in the input record. Thus, the Customer Name field is first, followed by the Agent Name, Insurance Type, and Policy Number fields.

Instead of specifying the value 20 within the parentheses to indicate the number of characters in the CUSTOMER-NAME-INPUT and AGENT-NAME-INPUT fields, 20 separate X's could be written. The use of the parentheses provides a convenient method for representing the number of occurrences of the X and greatly reduces the amount of writing required. When, however, the number of positions in a field is small, then an X can be written for each position in the field. For example, a field that contains two characters could have a Picture clause written as PICTURE X(2) or as PICTURE XX.

After the POLICY-INPUT-RECORD has been defined, a check should be performed to ensure that the number of characters in the POLICY-INPUT-RECORD (the sum of the X's from the coding form) agrees with the record length as specified in the disk record format and also with the number of characters in the record as described by the Record Contains clause (see Figure 3-21). As can be seen, all agree there are 62 characters.

In the sample program, the word PICTURE begins in column 40 of the coding form. Although the word could have begun after one blank space following the data-name, it is recorded in column 40 so that all Picture clauses for the program will begin in the same column. This coding convention contributes to the readability of the source program listing.

As shown in the format notation in Figure 3-29, the word PICTURE need not be spelled out completely. It is valid to use the abbreviation PIC instead of the entire word. If this were done, the record description for the disk input record would appear as illustrated in Figure 3-31.

```
003070 01  POLICY-INPUT-RECORD.
003080     05  CUSTOMER-NAME-INPUT             PIC X(20).
003090     05  AGENT-NAME-INPUT                PIC X(20).
003100     05  INSURANCE-TYPE-INPUT            PIC X(10).
003110     05  POLICY-NUMBER-INPUT             PIC X(12).
```

Figure 3-31 Example of PIC Entry

The only change in Figure 3-31 from the coding in Figure 3-30 is that the value "PIC" is used instead of the entire word "PICTURE." The use of this abbreviation is intended to save coding and writing time for the programmer.

Definition of the Report File

The next entry in the sample program is used to define the Report File and the Report Line that is to be used in the program (Figure 3-32).

As with the input file, the printer output file is defined through the use of the FD statement. The name following the FD level indicator must be the same as the name specified in the Select clause of the File-Control paragraph (see Figure 3-17). Thus, the name used is POLICY-REPORT-FILE. The remaining entries for the printer file are quite similar to the entries for the input file.

The Record Contains clause indicates that the record is to contain 133 characters. The maximum number of print positions available on most printers is 132. The extra position is specified to allow for a special carriage control character which is specified as the first

```
003070 FD  POLICY-REPORT-FILE
003080 I       RECORD CONTAINS 133 CHARACTERS
003090 I       LABEL RECORDS ARE OMITTED
003100 I       DATA RECORD IS POLICY-REPORT-LINE.
003110 01  POLICY-REPORT-LINE.
003120 I       05  CARRIAGE-CONTROL           PICTURE X.
003130 I       05  POLICY-NUMBER-REPORT       PICTURE X(12).
003140 I       05  FILLER                     PICTURE X(4).
003150 I       05  CUSTOMER-NAME-REPORT       PICTURE X(20).
003160 I       05  FILLER                     PICTURE X(4).
003170 I       05  AGENT-NAME-REPORT          PICTURE X(20).
003180 I       05  FILLER                     PICTURE X(4).
003190 I       05  INSURANCE-TYPE-REPORT      PICTURE X(10).
003200 I       05  FILLER                     PICTURE X(58).
```

Figure 3 - 32 File and Record Definition for Print File

character in the definition of the print line. This carriage control character is used to control single spacing, double spacing, etc. It is not printed when the line is printed on the report. The 132 actual print positions plus the additional print position required for the carriage control character equals the "133" specified in the Record Contains clause.

Some printers do not require a carriage control character. The programmer should check the COBOL compiler and operating system manuals for the machine being used to determine if a carriage control character must be defined.

The Label Records clause is included next. Whenever a printer is used for a file, there are no labels. Therefore, LABEL RECORDS ARE OMITTED must be included in the FD statement.

The Data Record clause is the last clause of the FD statement. This clause is used to specify the name of the print line which is to be printed. Here, the name of the print line is POLICY-REPORT-LINE. Note the period following the Data Record clause to indicate the end of the FD statement.

The print line as specified on the printer spacing chart must then be defined. Like the input file, the 01 level number is used for the name of the entire record. Here, the name POLICY-REPORT-LINE is specified. It must be the same name as is specified in the Data Record clause.

The 05 level numbers below the entry for the POLICY-REPORT-LINE are used to describe the format of the output line. The first entry is a one position field (PICTURE X) called CARRIAGE-CONTROL. The first position of the output line will contain a special code that controls the functions of spacing and skipping when printing a line. Although this character is not referenced in the program, it is given the name CARRIAGE-CONTROL for clarity purposes. This single character, which is not printed, must be present in the definition of a print line on many computers.

The next entry is the 05 level number with the related data-name POLICY-NUMBER-REPORT. This entry describes where the Policy Number is to be printed on the report line. The Policy Number will be printed in the first 12 positions of the report line. The suffix REPORT is appended to the name POLICY-NUMBER to identify the field as part of the report line.

The entry following POLICY-NUMBER-REPORT consists of the level number 05, the word FILLER, and the Picture clause PICTURE X(4). This entry indicates there are four unused positions following the POLICY-NUMBER-REPORT field. When the POLICY-REPORT-LINE is written on the printer, these four unused positions described using the word FILLER will cause four blank spaces to appear following the Policy Number. The word

FILLER may be used to describe unused positions in either input or output records.

The remaining entries describe where the Customer Name, Agent Name, and Insurance Type fields are to be printed on the output report. The diagram in Figure 3–33 illustrates the entries for the POLICY-REPORT-LINE and the relationship of the Picture clauses with the printed report.

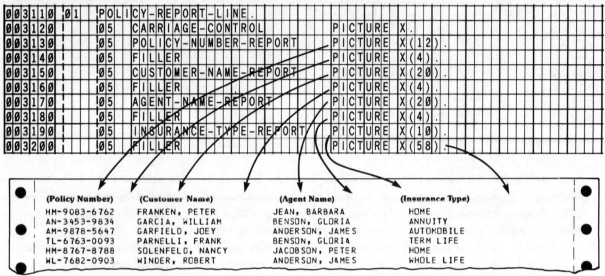

Figure 3 - 33 Record Description Entries for POLICY-REPORT-LINE and Related Output

When the POLICY-REPORT-LINE has been defined, a check should be made to ensure that the number of characters in the POLICY-REPORT-LINE (the sum of the X's) agrees with the number of characters in the record as described by the Record Contains clause and as shown on the printer spacing chart (including the carriage control character). In this instance, all three agree there are 133 characters.

Working-Storage Section

The File Section of the Data Division is used to describe the content and organization of the files to be processed within the program. However, the only data which can be described within the File Section is the data which is found in the records to be processed, namely the disk input record and the printer output record.

In many programs, such as the sample program in this chapter, data other than that found in the input and output records must be defined for use. This data is defined in the Working-Storage Section of the Data Division. The Working-Storage Section used in the sample program is illustrated in Figure 3–34.

The entry WORKING-STORAGE SECTION must be written on a line by itself, as shown in Figure 3–34. It must begin in Area A of the coding form. Following the Working-Storage Section entry may be one or more record description entries. These entries follow the same rules as discussed for record description entries in the File Section. They consist of a level number plus a data name for group items; and a level number, a data-name, and a Picture clause for elementary items.

In Figure 3–34, the first entry in the Working-Storage Section is 01 PROGRAM-INDICATORS. The 01 level number is used to indicate that a group item is being defined. The data-name, which is chosen by the programmer, reflects the fact that the elementary items

```
004020 WORKING-STORAGE SECTION.
004030
004040 01  PROGRAM-INDICATORS.
004050     05  ARE-THERE-MORE-RECORDS  PICTURE X(3) VALUE 'YES'.
```

```
 ┌ WORKING-STORAGE SECTION.                      ┐
 │ ┌ 77-level-description-entry ┐                │
 │ │ record-description-entry   │  ...           │
 └ └                            ┘                ┘
```

Figure 3-34 Working-Storage Section

within the group are to be used as indicators. An indicator is a field within a program which can have one value to indicate one condition and another value to indicate another condition. For example, if the indicator field contains the value YES, it could mean there are more input records to process; if the indicator field contains the value NO , it could indicate there are no more input records to process. The value in the indicator field will be checked by instructions within the program.

The elementary item within the group item is defined using the level number 05. The elementary item will act as the indicator. The data-name chosen by the programmer is ARE-THERE-MORE-RECORDS. This data-name is chosen to reflect the question which will be answered by the indicator. In this instance, the question which the indicator will answer by the value stored in the indicator is, "Are there more records?"

The field will be three characters in length, as designated by the entry PICTURE X(3). Whenever a field is used as an indicator, it is usually necessary to give the field an initial value. An initial value is the value which will be stored in the indicator field when the execution of the program begins. The initial value will have meaning within the program and will be tested by instructions within the program. In the sample program, the value YES in the indicator field ARE-THERE-MORE-RECORDS is used to indicate there are more input records left to process. Therefore, prior to beginning the execution of the program, the indicator field should contain the value YES to indicate there are input records to process.

Value Clause

In order to give a field an initial value, the Value clause is used. The format of the Value clause is illustrated in Figure 3-35.

```
 ┌ ; VALUE IS literal ┐
 └                    ┘
```

Figure 3-35 Format of Value Clause

The word VALUE is required and the word IS is an optional word. Following the words VALUE IS, a literal is specified. A literal is the actual value which will be contained in the field at the beginning of the program.

When the Picture Clause describes an alphanumeric field, that is, when Picture X is used, then the literal specified must be enclosed within quotes as illustrated in Figure 3-36.

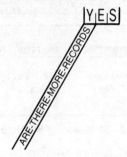

Figure 3-36 Example of Value Clause

The literal specified must be the same length or a lesser length than the field length as defined by the Picture clause. As a result of the Value clause in Figure 3–36, the ARE-THERE-MORE-RECORDS field will contain the value YES when program execution begins. The value will be in the field at the beginning of the execution of the program and will remain there until it is changed by an instruction within the program.

Data Design

It will be recalled that prior to beginning the coding of the program, the data bases, files, records, and fields required for the program were specified on the Pseudocode Specifications form (see Figure 3–4). As the coding of the Data Division progressed, the programmer would be referencing these specifications and coding the program from them. At the conclusion of the coding of the Data Division, the programmer should review the data bases, files, records, and fields required for the program to ensure that they are contained in the program. The data bases, files, records, and fields required for the sample program and the resulting Data Division are illustrated in Figure 3–37.

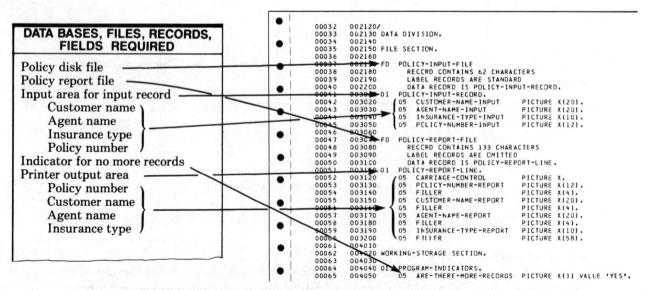

Figure 3-37 Data Design and Data Division

The data bases, files, records, and fields which are required for the program, as determined when the program was designed, are defined in the Data Division of the sample program. Thus, the program design is quite an important phase in the programming of the problem because it is from the design that the source program will be coded. Since all of the data bases, files, records, and fields required for the program are defined, the coding of the Data Division is completed and the coding of the Procedure Division can begin.

PROCEDURE DIVISION

The Procedure Division of a COBOL program specifies those procedures necessary to solve a given problem. These steps (computations, logical decisions, input/output, etc.) are expressed in meaningful statements, similar to English, which employ the concept of verbs to denote actions, and statements and sentences to describe procedures. The Procedure Division is coded directly from the pseudocode which was developed in the program design phase of the program development cycle. The pseudocode and Procedure Division for the sample program are illustrated in Figure 3-38.

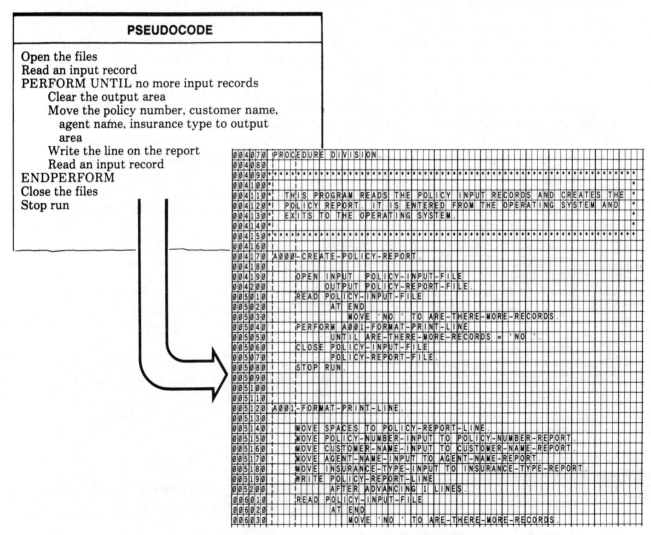

PSEUDOCODE

Open the files
Read an input record
PERFORM UNTIL no more input records
    Clear the output area
    Move the policy number, customer name, agent name, insurance type to output area
    Write the line on the report
    Read an input record
ENDPERFORM
Close the files
Stop run

```
004070 PROCEDURE DIVISION.
004080
004090 *..............................................................*
004100 *                                                              *
004110 *   THIS PROGRAM READS THE POLICY INPUT RECORDS AND CREATES THE*
004120 *   POLICY REPORT.  IT IS ENTERED FROM THE OPERATING SYSTEM AND*
004130 *   EXITS TO THE OPERATING SYSTEM.                             *
004140 *                                                              *
004150 *..............................................................*
004160
004170 A000-CREATE-POLICY-REPORT.
004180
004190     OPEN INPUT  POLICY-INPUT-FILE
004200          OUTPUT POLICY-REPORT-FILE.
005010     READ POLICY-INPUT-FILE
005020         AT END
005030             MOVE 'NO ' TO ARE-THERE-MORE-RECORDS.
005040     PERFORM A001-FORMAT-PRINT-LINE
005050         UNTIL ARE-THERE-MORE-RECORDS = 'NO '.
005060     CLOSE POLICY-INPUT-FILE
005070           POLICY-REPORT-FILE.
005080     STOP RUN.
005090
005100
005110
005120 A001-FORMAT-PRINT-LINE.
005130
005140     MOVE SPACES TO POLICY-REPORT-LINE.
005150     MOVE POLICY-NUMBER-INPUT TO POLICY-NUMBER-REPORT.
005160     MOVE CUSTOMER-NAME-INPUT TO CUSTOMER-NAME-REPORT.
005170     MOVE AGENT-NAME-INPUT TO AGENT-NAME-REPORT.
005180     MOVE INSURANCE-TYPE-INPUT TO INSURANCE-TYPE-REPORT.
005190     WRITE POLICY-REPORT-LINE
005200         AFTER ADVANCING 1 LINES.
006010     READ POLICY-INPUT-FILE
006020         AT END
006030             MOVE 'NO ' TO ARE-THERE-MORE-RECORDS.
```

Figure 3-38 Pseudocode and Procedure Division

The Division Header, PROCEDURE DIVISION, begins in Area A (column 8) and is on a line by itself, followed by a period. The basic structure of the Procedure Division consists of paragraphs, containing a series of sentences.

Paragraphs are logical entities consisting of one or more sentences. Each paragraph must start with a paragraph name, which is written beginning in Area A. The sample program has two paragraphs — the A000-CREATE-POLICY-REPORT paragraph and the A001-FORMAT-PRINT-LINE paragraph. A paragraph ends at the next paragraph name or at the end of the Procedure Division.

The paragraph name, also called a procedure name, may be composed of not more than 30 characters and may consist of the digits 0 — 9, the letters of the alphabet A through Z, and the hyphen (-). The paragraph name cannot begin or end with a hyphen. Paragraph names may be composed solely of numeric characters. No blanks are permitted within the name.

Paragraph names selected should be meaningful. They should indicate the type of processing which is to take place within the paragraph. In addition, it is recommended that a prefix number be placed on each paragraph name. This number should correspond to the Reference Number which is defined on the IPO Chart and the Pseudocode Specifications. The numbers will appear in an ascending sequence within the source program listing, allowing easier reference to a particular paragraph name within the Procedure Division.

A sentence is a single statement or series of statements terminated by a period and followed by a space. A single comma or semicolon or the word THEN may be used as a separator between statements. Commas, semicolons, and the word THEN have no effect on the program and are used merely to improve readability. The period, on the other hand, is a required punctuation symbol which indicates the end of a sentence.

Each statement consists of a syntactically valid combination of words and symbols beginning with a COBOL verb. A COBOL verb indicates the processing which is to occur. The basic classification of the COBOL verbs is presented in the following list.

Arithmetic

ADD
COMPUTE
DIVIDE
MULTIPLY
SUBTRACT

Compiler-Directing

COPY
REPLACE
ENTER
USE

Conditional

EVALUATE
IF

Ending

STOP

Inter-Program Communicating

CALL
CANCEL

Data Movement

INITIALIZE
INSPECT
MOVE
STRING
UNSTRING

Procedure Branching

ALTER
EXIT
GO TO
PERFORM

Input-Output

ACCEPT
CLOSE
DELETE
DISPLAY
OPEN
REWRITE
START
WRITE

Table Handling

SEARCH
SET

Ordering

MERGE
RELEASE
RETURN
SORT

Comments

Following the Division Header, PROCEDURE DIVISION, in Figure 3–38 is a series of comment statements (asterisks in column 7). These comments are used to explain the function of the program. The comments do not say how the function is to be performed, merely what is to take place. In general, comments should be included at the start of a program or program module to explain the function of the module.

In addition, the comments state that the program is entered from and exits to the operating system. The operating system is a series of programs which allow for interaction of the program with the actual computer hardware. Application programs are always given control from the operating system, and when they are complete, they return control back to the operating system. Comments which explain the function of a program or of a module within a program should normally identify where control is received from and where control is returned at the conclusion of the processing.

Open Statement

The first statement in the A000-CREATE-POLICY-REPORT paragraph is the Open statement, as illustrated in Figure 3–39.

```
004170  A000-CREATE-POLICY-REPORT.
004180
004190      OPEN INPUT   POLICY-INPUT-FILE
004200           OUTPUT  POLICY-REPORT-FILE.
```

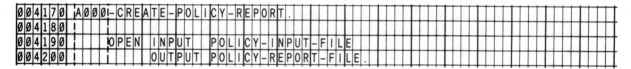

Figure 3-39 Example of Open Statement

The Open statement initiates the processing of files and must be executed prior to any other input/output statement for a file. The Open statement, by itself, does not make an input record available for processing; a Read statement must be executed in order to obtain the first record. For an output file, an Open statement makes available an area for development of the first output record.

In the general format of the Open statement illustrated in Figure 3–39, it can be seen that the word INPUT must precede the file-name of the input file to be opened. Similarly, the word OUTPUT must precede the file-name of the output file to be opened. Thus, in the coded portion of the sample program in Figure 3–39, the OPEN verb is followed by the word INPUT and then the file-name of the input file, POLICY-INPUT-FILE. Since there is only one input file, the word OUTPUT is specified next, followed by the name of the printer output file, POLICY-REPORT-FILE. The OPEN verb need be specified only one time in order to open both the disk input file and the printer output file.

In the coding illustrated, the input file and the output file are specified on different lines of the coding form and are vertically aligned. This is to aid in the readability of the program and has no consequence concerning the Open statement itself. The termination of the Open statement is indicated by the period and blank space following the name of the output file.

Read Statement

The next statement in the sample program is the Read statement (Figure 3–40).

```
004170 A000-CREATE-POLICY-REPORT.
004180
004190      OPEN INPUT   POLICY-INPUT-FILE
004200           OUTPUT  POLICY-REPORT-FILE.
005010      READ POLICY-INPUT-FILE
005020           AT END
005030           MOVE 'NO ' TO ARE-THERE-MORE-RECORDS.
```

```
READ file-name RECORD [INTO identifier] [; AT END imperative-statement]
```

Figure 3-40 Example of Read Statement

The function of the Read statement is to make available a record from an input file and to allow the performance of specified operations when end-of-file is detected. For sequential input files that are stored on disk, end-of-file is detected by the presence of an end-of-file marker placed at the end of all records in the disk file when the file was created.

When a Read statement is executed, the next record in the file named in the Read statement becomes available for processing in the input area defined by the associated Record Description entry in the Data Division. The file-name which is specified must be defined by a File Description (FD) entry in the Data Division. In the coded portion of the sample program in Figure 3–40, the file-name POLICY-INPUT-FILE is specified, since this is the name of the input file as defined in the Data Division.

After a record is read into the input area defined in the Data Division, it remains available for processing in the input area until the next Read statement (or until a Close statement) is executed for that file.

The At End option is required for files which are accessed sequentially, such as the POLICY-INPUT-FILE. The At End portion of the Read statement is executed when an end-of-file condition is detected by the end-of-file marker being read.

In Figure 3–40, when end-of-file is detected, the value NO will be moved to the field ARE-THERE-MORE-RECORDS. It will be recalled that the field ARE-THERE-MORE-RECORDS is used as an indicator to specify whether more records are available for processing. It was given the initial value of YES through the use of the Value clause in the Data Division (see Figure 3–36). So long as the ARE-THERE-MORE-RECORDS field contains the value YES, it indicates there are more input records to process. When, however, the value NO is moved to the field as a result of the At End portion of the Read statement, the indicator specifies that there are no more records in the input file to be processed.

Once the At End portion of the Read statement has been executed for a file, any subsequent attempts to read from that file or to refer to records in that file might cause the program to be abnormally terminated.

In Figure 3–40 the words AT END are on a separate coding line from the Read verb and file-name, and the words are indented six spaces. Although this is not required, the convention within the programs in this text, and one that is recommended, is that any statement which must be continued onto the next coding line be indented six spaces from the previous line. In this manner, it is easy to see that the statement has been continued onto the next line.

In addition, the processing specified following the AT END words will not take place each time an input record is read. It takes place only when the end-of-file marker has been read. Therefore, the At End clause is called a conditional clause since it will be executed only under a given condition. Within all programs in this text, instructions which are to be executed based upon a given condition will be on a separate line from the statement of the condition and will be indented three spaces. In the example in Figure 3-40, the condition is "AT END." Therefore, the statement which is to be executed on that condition (the Move Statement) is placed on the next coding line and is indented three spaces.

These conventions for writing the statements within the program are again illustrated in Figure 3-41.

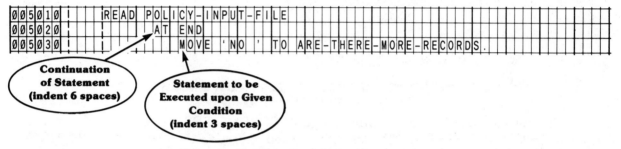

Figure 3-41 Example of Coding Conventions

In Figure 3-41 the continuation of the Read statement is indented six spaces and the statement to be executed when the condition is satisfied is indented three spaces. This spacing convention will be used throughout the text in order to make the program listing more readable. It is the suggested convention when writing COBOL programs.

Perform Statement

The next statement in the sample program is the Perform statement, which is illustrated in Figure 3-42.

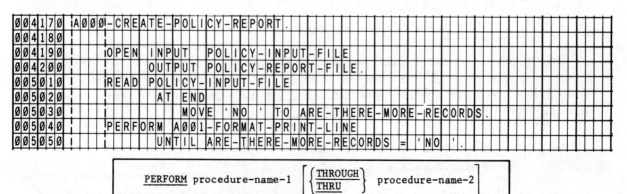

Figure 3-42 Example of Perform Statement

The Perform statement is used to transfer control to the paragraph specified as procedure-name-1 in the format notation. The statements within the paragraph specified as procedure-name-1 will be executed until "condition-1" is true, at which time control will be returned to the statement following the Perform statement in the program.

In the sample program, the Perform statement works in the following manner:

Step 1: The condition ARE-THERE-MORE-RECORDS = 'NO ' is checked first by comparing the value in the field ARE-THERE-MORE-RECORDS to the value NO (Figure 3–43).

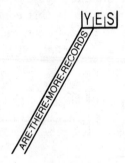

Figure 3-43 Condition in Indicator Field is Checked

The value in the field ARE-THERE-MORE-RECORDS is YES, which indicates there are more input records to process. Therefore, it is desired to execute the A001-FORMAT-PRINT-LINE paragraph, which will format and print the output record.

Step 2: Since the condition tested is not true, the statements in the A001-FORMAT-PRINT-LINE paragraph will be executed (Figure 3–44).

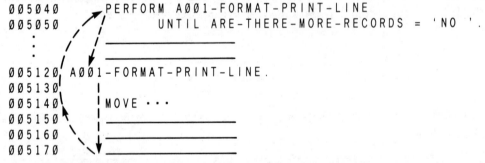

Figure 3-44 Example of Perform Statement Execution

The Perform statement causes control to be transferred to the A001-FORMAT-PRINT-LINE paragraph, where all of the statements within that paragraph will be executed.

After the A001-FORMAT-PRINT-LINE paragraph has been executed one time, the condition specified in the Perform statement will again be checked.

Step 3: The condition in the Perform Statement is again checked to determine if the field ARE-THERE-MORE-RECORDS contains the value NO (Figure 3–45).

In Step 3, after the instructions within the A001-FORMAT-PRINT-LINE paragraph have been executed one time, the condition specified in the Perform statement is again checked. In Figure 3–45, the value in the ARE-THERE-MORE-RECORDS field has not changed because

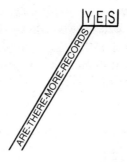

Figure 3-45 Condition in Indicator Field is Checked Again

the end-of-file marker was not found. Therefore, the A001-FORMAT-PRINT-LINE paragraph will be executed again.

This processing will continue until the value NO is found in the ARE-THERE-MORE-RECORDS field. At that time, the statement following the Perform statement will be executed.

There must be instructions within the A001-FORMAT-PRINT-LINE paragraph which will change the value in the ARE-THERE-MORE-RECORDS field from YES to NO . If there are not, then this "looping" will never terminate because the value NO will never be found. Therefore, whenever a paragraph is performed until a certain condition occurs, that condition must occur within the performed paragraph so that the loop can be terminated. The instructions within the A001-FORMAT-PRINT-LINE paragraph will be examined following the completion of the discussion of the A000-CREATE-POLICY-REPORT paragraph.

Close Statement

After the operation of the Perform statement has been completed, which includes the execution of the A001-FORMAT-PRINT-LINE paragraph that prints the report, the processing of the input data is completed. Therefore, the termination processing must be accomplished. In the sample program, the termination consists of closing the files and stopping the program.

In order to close the files, the Close statement illustrated in Figure 3-46 is used.

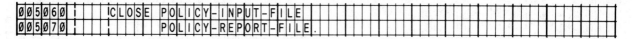

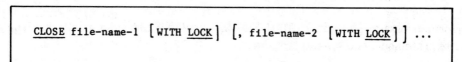

Figure 3-46 Example of Close Statement

The Close statement begins with the Close verb. It is followed by the file-names of those files to be closed. Prior to terminating the program, it is necessary to close any files which have been previously opened. Therefore, the file-names POLICY-INPUT-FILE and POLICY-REPORT-FILE are specified because they are the files which were previously opened (see

Figure 3–39). After a file has been closed, it cannot be referenced in a Read or Write statement unless the file is reopened through the use of the Open statement.

Stop Run Statement

In order to terminate the program, the Stop Run statement is used (Figure 3–47).

```
005080        STOP RUN.
```

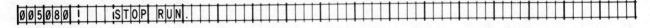

Figure 3-47 Example of Stop Statement

The Stop Run statement terminates the execution of the program and returns control to the operating system. It is the last statement executed in a program.

Performed Paragraph

It will be recalled that the processing required to format and print the report is performed (see Figure 3–42). The paragraph which is performed is illustrated in Figure 3–48.

```
005120   A001-FORMAT-PRINT-LINE.
005130
005140       MOVE SPACES TO POLICY-REPORT-LINE.
005150       MOVE POLICY-NUMBER-INPUT TO POLICY-NUMBER-REPORT.
005160       MOVE CUSTOMER-NAME-INPUT TO CUSTOMER-NAME-REPORT.
005170       MOVE AGENT-NAME-INPUT TO AGENT-NAME-REPORT.
005180       MOVE INSURANCE-TYPE-INPUT TO INSURANCE-TYPE-REPORT.
005190       WRITE POLICY-REPORT-LINE
005200           AFTER ADVANCING 1 LINES.
006010       READ POLICY-INPUT-FILE
006020           AT END
006030           MOVE 'NO ' TO ARE-THERE-MORE-RECORDS.
```

Figure 3-48 Performed Paragraph

The performed paragraph, named A001-FORMAT-PRINT-LINE, consists of Move statements, a Write statement, and a Read statement.

Move Statements

The Move statement is used to move data from one location in main memory to another. The format of the Move statement is illustrated in Figure 3–49.

```
MOVE  {identifier-1}  TO identifier-2  [, identifier-3] ...
      {literal     }
```

Figure 3-49 Format Notation for Move Statement

In the format notation for the Move statement, "identifier-1" refers to the data-name of the field containing the data to be moved. "Identifier-2," "identifier-3," etc. refers to the data-names of the fields to which the data from "identifier-1" will be moved. There must be at least one field to which the data is to be moved (called the receiving field), but there can be more than one field if required. There can be only one field from which the data is moved (called the sending field). The sending field can be either a data-name (identifier-1) or a literal. The concept of a literal will be explained in detail later in this chapter.

The first Move statement in Figure 3-48 is used to move spaces (blanks) to the printer output area so that the printer output area will not contain any extraneous data when the contents of the printer output area are printed on the report. The operation of this Move statement is illustrated in Figure 3-50.

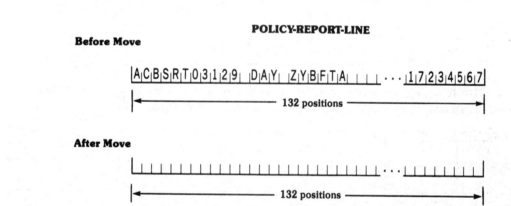

POLICY-REPORT-LINE

Figure 3-50 Example of Move Spaces Statement

Prior to the execution of the Move statement, the printer output area (POLICY-REPORT-LINE) contains meaningless data. The meaningless data in this area may originate from the data previously stored in the printer output area or from other sources. This data must not be present when the data to be printed is moved to the printer output area. Thus, the Move statement to move blanks to the printer output area is required to eliminate any meaningless data in the printer output area. After the execution of the Move statement, the POLICY-REPORT-LINE area contains blanks, which is the desired result.

The word SPACES in Figure 3-50 illustrates the use of a figurative constant. A figurative constant is a standard COBOL data-name to which a value has been assigned. The figurative constant SPACE or SPACES represents one or more "blanks" or "spaces" when specified in a COBOL statement. Therefore, the effect of the Move statement in Figure 3-50 is to move blanks to the printer output area.

Once the printer output area has been cleared, the contents of the input area can be moved to the output area. The Move statements used to move the data from the input area to the printer output area are illustrated in Figure 3-51.

0 0 5 1 5 0	MOVE POLICY-NUMBER-INPUT TO POLICY-NUMBER-REPORT.
0 0 5 1 6 0	MOVE CUSTOMER-NAME-INPUT TO CUSTOMER-NAME-REPORT.
0 0 5 1 7 0	MOVE AGENT-NAME-INPUT TO AGENT-NAME-REPORT.
0 0 5 1 8 0	MOVE INSURANCE-TYPE-INPUT TO INSURANCE-TYPE-REPORT.

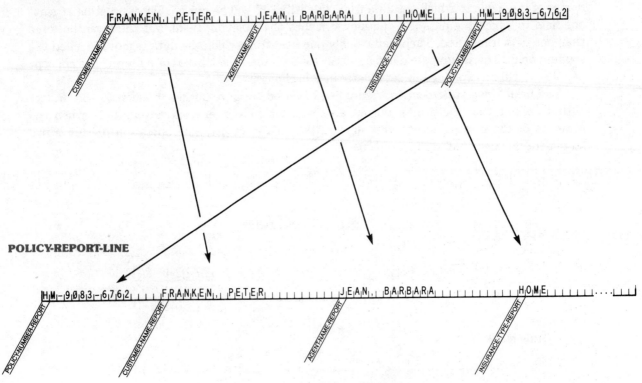

Figure 3-51 Example of Move Statements

The Move statements in Figure 3–51 are used to move data from fields in the input area (POLICY-INPUT-RECORD) to fields in the printer output area (POLICY-REPORT-LINE). Each Move statement identifies both the field from which the data is moved and the field to which the data is moved. For example, the Move statement on line 005150 will move the data in the POLICY-NUMBER-INPUT field to the POLICY-NUMBER-REPORT field. All of the fields used in Move statements must have been previously defined in the Data Division.

When the COBOL Move statement is executed, the data is not actually moved; rather, it is duplicated in the receiving field. Therefore, after the execution of the Move statement, the data is stored in both the sending field and the receiving field.

Multiple Receiving Fields

In the previous examples, the data in one sending field has been moved to one receiving field. It is also possible to move the data in one sending field to more than one receiving field using only one Move statement. This is illustrated in Figure 3–52.

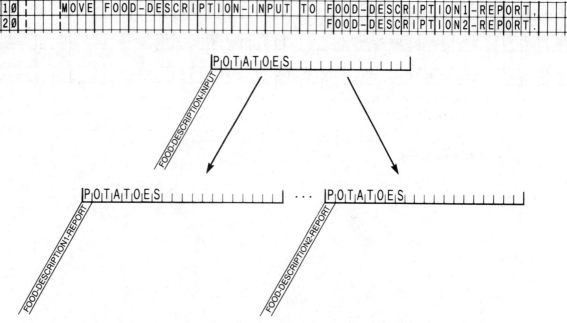

Figure 3-52 Example of Multiple Receiving Fields in Move Statement

In Figure 3–52 the Move statement contains one sending field, FOOD-DESCRIPTION-INPUT. Two receiving fields are specified — FOOD-DESCRIPTION1-REPORT and FOOD-DESCRIPTION2-REPORT. When the Move statement is executed, the data in FOOD-DESCRIPTION-INPUT is moved to both FOOD-DESCRIPTION1-REPORT and FOOD-DESCRIPTION2-REPORT. This format of the Move statement is useful when the data in a single field must be moved to multiple fields within main memory. In Figure 3–52, the names of the two receiving fields are on separate lines and are separated by a comma. This is done to make the Move statement more readable and is not required.

Different Length Fields

In all previous examples, the sending field and the receiving field each contain the same number of characters in their Picture clauses in the Data Division. For example, in the program in this chapter the CUSTOMER-NAME-INPUT field and the CUSTOMER-NAME-REPORT field are the same length — both contain 20 characters. To make the object program as efficient as possible, both the sending and receiving fields in a Move statement should be the same length. If, for some reason however, the sending and receiving fields in a Move statement are different lengths, COBOL will process the fields based upon specific rules.

Receiving Field Longer Than Sending Field

If the receiving field is longer than the sending field when moving alphanumeric (Picture X) data, the data from the sending field will be moved to the receiving field starting with the leftmost positions. Those positions of the receiving field which are not filled with data from the sending field will be filled with blanks (Figure 3–53).

Before Execution

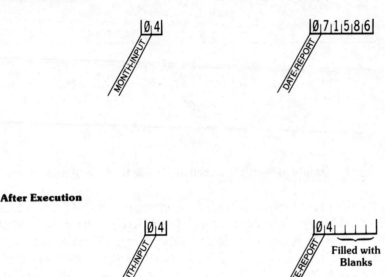

After Execution

Figure 3-53 Example of Receiving Field Longer Than Sending Field

In Figure 3-53, the sending field, MONTH-INPUT, contains two characters and the receiving field, DATE-REPORT, contains six characters. Before the execution of the Move statement, the MONTH-INPUT field contains the value 04, and the DATE-REPORT field contains the value 071586. When the data in MONTH-INPUT is moved to the DATE-REPORT field, the two characters in the MONTH-INPUT field (04) are moved to the two leftmost positions of the DATE-REPORT field. The remaining positions in the DATE-REPORT field are filled with blanks. Thus, after the execution, the contents of the MONTH-INPUT field remain unchanged while the DATE-REPORT field contains the value 04 followed by four blank spaces.

Receiving Field Shorter Than Sending Field

If the receiving field is shorter than the sending field when moving alphanumeric (Picture X) data, the data from the sending field will be placed in the receiving field, starting at the leftmost position, until all the positions in the receiving field are filled. The remaining characters from the sending field are truncated, meaning they are not moved to the receiving field (Figure 3-54).

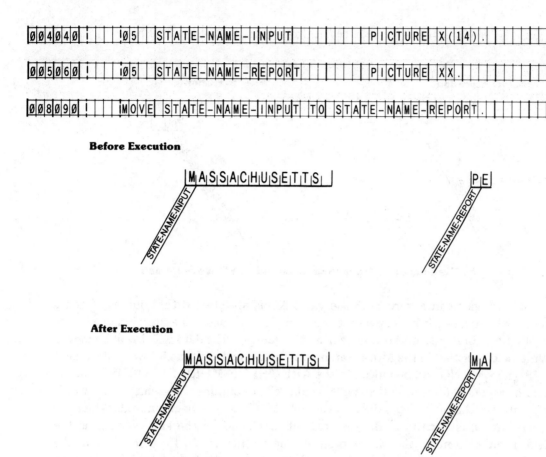

```
004040       05   STATE-NAME-INPUT            PICTURE X(14).
005060       05   STATE-NAME-REPORT           PICTURE XX.
008090       MOVE STATE-NAME-INPUT TO STATE-NAME-REPORT.
```

Before Execution

MASSACHUSETTS   STATE-NAME-INPUT

PE   STATE-NAME-REPORT

After Execution

MASSACHUSETTS   STATE-NAME-INPUT

MA   STATE-NAME-REPORT

Figure 3-54 Example of Receiving Field Shorter Than Sending Field

The Move statement in Figure 3-54 moves data from a sending field (STATE-NAME-INPUT) to a receiving field (STATE-NAME-REPORT) that is shorter than the sending field. Before the execution of the Move statement, the STATE-NAME-INPUT field contains the name MASSACHUSETTS and the STATE-NAME-REPORT field contains the two characters PE. The leftmost characters in the STATE-NAME-INPUT field are moved until the two positions in the STATE-NAME-REPORT field are filled. At that time, the execution of the Move statement ceases, and the STATE-NAME-REPORT field contains the two characters MA.

In most cases, the lengths of the two fields involved in a Move statement will be the same. The programmer should be careful, however, to note those times when they are not the same in order to ensure that the Move statement will produce the desired results.

Literals

In the previous examples, the sending field in the Move statement has been defined in the Data Division. It is also possible to define data to be moved in the Move statement itself through the use of a literal. A literal is a set of characters which act as the data to be processed, rather than as an identifier referencing a main memory area which contains the data to be processed. The data contained within a literal is data that will not change during the execution of the program. The use of an alphanumeric literal in a Move statement is illustrated in Figure 3-55.

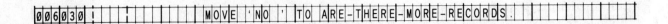

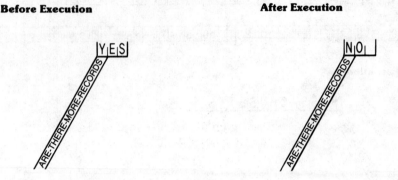

Figure 3-55 Example of an Alphanumeric Literal in a Move Statement

In the Move statement in Figure 3-55 the value NO is specified within quotes. When a value is placed within quotes, it indicates that the value is to be used as a literal instead of as an identifier of a field. In addition, the value within the quotes is the data which will be moved to the receiving field specified in the Move statement. Thus, as a result of the Move statement in Figure 3-55, the value NO will be moved to the ARE-THERE-MORE-RECORDS field.

The literal in Figure 3-55 is specified as "N-O-blank." It contains three characters, which is the same number of characters contained in the field to which it is being moved. Whenever an alphanumeric literal is used in a Move statement, it should be the same length as the receiving field in order to make the object program more efficient. If, for some reason, the literal is not the same length as the receiving field, the rules for different length fields discussed previously are applied.

Write Statement

After the fields have been moved to the printer output area, the Write statement is used to cause a line to be printed on the printer. The Write statement used in the sample program is illustrated in Figure 3-56.

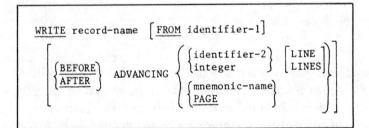

Figure 3-56 Example of Write Statement

The Write statement in Figure 3-56 will cause the data stored in the record POLICY-

REPORT-LINE to be printed on the printer. The record-name entry in the general format refers to the record which is defined for the print file in the File Section of the Data Division (see Figure 3–32). In the sample program, this record-name is POLICY-REPORT-LINE. The "FROM" clause shown in the general format is not used in the sample program — it is an optional entry.

The Advancing option is used to control the spacing on the report. It specifies whether the line is to be printed before spacing the printer (BEFORE) or after spacing the printer (AFTER). In Figure 3–56, the After Advancing option is used, which means that the printer will be spaced and then the line will be printed.

The value specified as "integer" in the general format is used to indicate the number of lines to be spaced. Any value from 0 through 99 can be specified. In Figure 3–56, the value 1 is specified (ie. — AFTER ADVANCING 1 LINES). Therefore the printer will be spaced one line each time a line is to be printed on the report. The value 2 would be used if double spacing were desired, the value 3 for triple spacing, etc. When the Advancing option is used for a file, every Write statement for records in the same file must contain an Advancing option.

An Open statement must be executed for the file prior to executing the first Write statement. After the Write statement is executed, the record named by "record-name" is no longer available for processing.

After the Write statement has been executed and the line has been written on the printer, the processing for the record is complete. Therefore, the next statement in the performed paragraph is a Read statement which will read the next record to be processed (see Figure 3–48). After the last record has been processed, control will be returned to the statement following the Perform statement. The files will then be closed and program execution will be terminated.

PROGRAMMING TIPS

A program should compile and execute the first time it is placed on the computer. In order for this to occur, each phase within the program development cycle must be followed exactly. One of the phases within the cycle is coding the program. Within this phase, one of the steps which must take place is a structured walkthrough of the code in the program. Common mistakes which are made in coding the COBOL program, and which should be looked for in the structured walkthrough, include the following:

1. All required punctuation, required COBOL words, and the COBOL formatting must be correct. Frequent errors include periods placed at the wrong point, or periods which are omitted when they should be included; misspelled COBOL reserved or required words; statements beginning in the wrong columns on the coding form; and omission of required COBOL words.

2. The definitions of the fields in the Data Division must correspond exactly to the program specifications for that data.

3. Data-names should reflect the fields which they are defining.

4. The data-names used must be spelled the same in the Procedure Division as they are in the Data Division.

5. The coding in the Procedure Division must correspond exactly to the logic expressed in the pseudocode.

6. Comments should be used where necessary to explain what is to occur within a program module.

7. Indentation and the physical structure of the program should be according to established standards. The source program should be easily read. The indentation rules used in this text will be discussed in the appropriate chapters. In all programs in this book, the Data Division and the Procedure Division will begin on new source listing pages. This page skipping can be caused by placing the character slash (/) in column 7. If words are contained on the same line as the slash, the words are treated as comments by the COBOL compiler. A summary of all coding rules and standards used in this book is contained in Appendix C.

Remember, A PROGRAM SHOULD WORK THE FIRST TIME. If the steps in the program development cycle are followed closely, and if the program is designed and written with care and concentration, then there is every chance that it will. If any of the steps within the program development cycle are omitted, however, there is every likelihood that it will not.

SAMPLE PROGRAM

The following pages illustrate the Output, Input, IPO Chart, Pseudocode Specifications, Source Listing, and Printed Output of the sample program to create the Policy Report.

Output

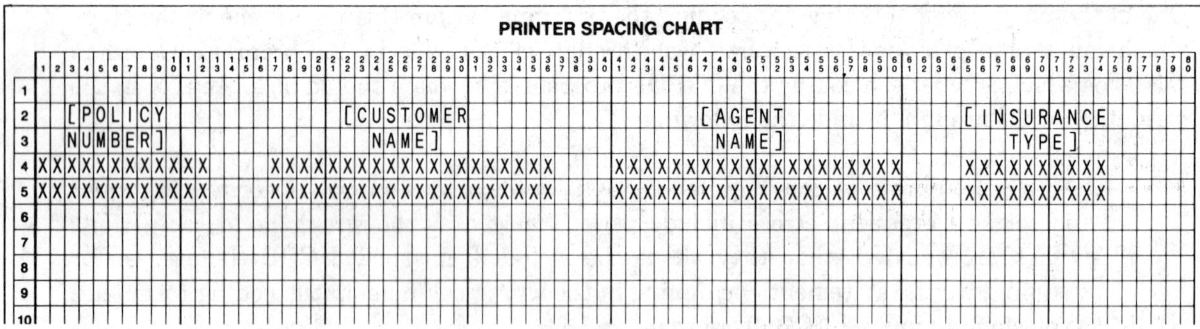

PRINTER SPACING CHART

	[POLICY	[CUSTOMER	[AGENT	[INSURANCE
	NUMBER]	NAME]	NAME]	TYPE]
	XXXXXXXXXXX	XXXXXXXXXXXXXXXXXXXX	XXXXXXXXXXXXXXXXXXXXX	XXXXXXXXXX
	XXXXXXXXXXX	XXXXXXXXXXXXXXXXXXXX	XXXXXXXXXXXXXXXXXXXXX	XXXXXXXXXX

Figure 3-57 Printer Spacing Chart

Input

Policy Disk Record			
FIELD DESCRIPTION	POSITION	LENGTH	ATTRIBUTE
Customer Name	1 – 20	20	Alphanumeric
Agent Name	21 – 40	20	Alphanumeric
Insurance Type	41 – 50	10	Alphanumeric
Policy Number	51 – 62	12	Alphanumeric
Record Length		62	

Figure 3-58 Policy Disk Record Format

IPO CHART

PROGRAM: Policy Report		PROGRAMMER: Forsythe		DATE: Oct. 4
MODULE NAME: Create Policy Report	REF: A000	MODULE FUNCTION: Create the Policy Report		

INPUT	PROCESSING	REF:	OUTPUT
1. Policy Disk File	1. Initialize		1. Policy Report
	2. Obtain the input data		
	3. Format the print line		
	4. Write the report		
	5. Terminate		

Figure 3-59 IPO Chart

PSEUDOCODE SPECIFICATIONS

PROGRAM: Policy Report		PROGRAMMER: Forsythe		DATE: Oct. 4
MODULE NAME: Create Policy Report	REF: A000	MODULE FUNCTION: Create the Policy Report		

PSEUDOCODE	REF:	DATA BASES, FILES, RECORDS, FIELDS REQUIRED

Open the files
Read an input record
PERFORM UNTIL no more input records
    Clear the output area
    Move the policy number, customer name,
      agent name, insurance type to output
      area
    Write the line on the report
    Read an input record
ENDPERFORM
Close the files
Stop run
		Policy disk file
		Policy report file
		Input area for input record
		    Customer name
		    Agent name
		    Insurance type
		    Policy number
		Indicator for no more records
		Printer output area
		    Policy number
		    Customer name
		    Agent name
		    Insurance type

Figure 3-60 Pseudocode Specifications

Source Listing

```
PP 5740-CB1 RELEASE 2.3 + PTF 8 - UP13477          IBM OS/VS COBOL  JULY 24, 1978        13.08.19  DATE FEB  1,1985

      1                        13.08.19      FEB  1,1985

   00001    001010 IDENTIFICATION DIVISION.                                          POLRPT
   00002    001020                                                                   POLRPT
   00003    001030 PROGRAM-ID.      POLRPT.                                          POLRPT
   00004    001040 AUTHOR.          FORSYTHE.                                        POLRPT
   00005    001050 INSTALLATION.    BREA.                                            POLRPT
   00006    001060 DATE-WRITTEN.    OCT 10,1984.                                     POLRPT
   00007    001070 DATE-COMPILED.   FEB 11,1985.                                     POLRPT
   00008    001080 SECURITY.        UNCLASSIFIED.                                    POLRPT
   00009    001090                                                                  POLRPT
   00010    001100****************************************************************  POLRPT
   00011    001110*                                                              *  POLRPT
   00012    001120*   THIS PROGRAM PRODUCES A POLICY REPORT.                     *  POLRPT
   00013    001130*                                                              *  POLRPT
   00014    001140****************************************************************  POLRPT
   00015    001150                                                                  POLRPT
   00016    001160                                                                  POLRPT
   00017    001170                                                                  POLRPT
   00018    001180 ENVIRONMENT DIVISION.                                            POLRPT
   00019    001190                                                                  POLRPT
   00020    001200 CONFIGURATION SECTION.                                           POLRPT
   00021    002010                                                                  POLRPT
   00022    002020 SOURCE-COMPUTER. IBM-4381.                                       POLRPT
   00023    002030 OBJECT-COMPUTER. IBM-4381.                                       POLRPT
   00024    002040                                                                  POLRPT
   00025    002050 INPUT-OUTPUT SECTION.                                            POLRPT
   00026    002060                                                                  POLRPT
   00027    002070 FILE-CONTROL.                                                    POLRPT
   00028    002080     SELECT POLICY-INPUT-FILE                                     POLRPT
   00029    002090         ASSIGN TO UT-S-POLINPUT.                                 POLRPT
   00030    002100     SELECT POLICY-REPORT-FILE                                    POLRPT
   00031    002110         ASSIGN TO UT-S-POLPRINT.                                 POLRPT
```

```
      2                        13.08.19      FEB  1,1985

   00032    002120/                                                                 POLRPT
   00033    002130 DATA DIVISION.                                                   POLRPT
   00034    002140                                                                  POLRPT
   00035    002150 FILE SECTION.                                                    POLRPT
   00036    002160                                                                  POLRPT
   00037    002170 FD  POLICY-INPUT-FILE                                            POLRPT
   00038    002180     RECORD CONTAINS 62 CHARACTERS                                POLRPT
   00039    002190     LABEL RECORDS ARE STANDARD                                   POLRPT
   00040    002200     DATA RECORD IS POLICY-INPUT-RECORD.                          POLRPT
   00041    003010 01  POLICY-INPUT-RECORD.                                         POLRPT
   00042    003020     05  CUSTOMER-NAME-INPUT    PICTURE X(20).                    POLRPT
   00043    003030     05  AGENT-NAME-INPUT       PICTURE X(20).                    POLRPT
   00044    003040     05  INSURANCE-TYPE-INPUT   PICTURE X(10).                    POLRPT
   00045    003050     05  POLICY-NUMBER-INPUT    PICTURE X(12).                    POLRPT
   00046    003060                                                                  POLRPT
   00047    003070 FD  POLICY-REPORT-FILE                                           POLRPT
   00048    003080     RECORD CONTAINS 133 CHARACTERS                               POLRPT
   00049    003090     LABEL RECORDS ARE OMITTED                                    POLRPT
   00050    003100     DATA RECORD IS POLICY-REPORT-LINE.                           POLRPT
   00051    003110 01  POLICY-REPORT-LINE.                                          POLRPT
   00052    003120     05  CARRIAGE-CONTROL       PICTURE X.                        POLRPT
   00053    003130     05  PCLICY-NUMBER-REPORT   PICTURE X(12).                    POLRPT
   00054    003140     05  FILLER                 PICTURE X(4).                     POLRPT
   00055    003150     05  CUSTOMER-NAME-REPORT   PICTURE X(20).                    POLRPT
   00056    003160     05  FILLER                 PICTURE X(4).                     POLRPT
   00057    003170     05  AGENT-NAME-REPORT      PICTURE X(20).                    POLRPT
   00058    003180     05  FILLER                 PICTURE X(4).                     POLRPT
   00059    003190     05  INSURANCE-TYPE-REPORT  PICTURE X(10).                    POLRPT
   00060    003200     05  FILLER                 PICTURE X(58).                    POLRPT
   00061    004010                                                                  POLRPT
   00062    004020 WORKING-STORAGE SECTION.                                         POLRPT
   00063    004030                                                                  POLRPT
   00064    004040 01  PROGRAM-INDICATORS.                                          POLRPT
   00065    004050     05  ARE-THERE-MORE-RECORDS PICTURE X(3) VALUE 'YES'.         POLRPT
```

Figure 3-61 Sample Program — Part 1 of 2

```
      3               13.08.19      FEB 1,1985

00066  004060/                                                       POLRPT
00067  004070 PROCEDURE DIVISION.                                    POLRPT
00068  004080                                                        POLRPT
00069  004090*******************************************************  POLRPT
00070  004100*                                                    *  POLRPT
00071  004110*   THIS PROGRAM READS THE POLICY INPUT RECORDS AND CREATES THE * POLRPT
00072  004120*   POLICY REPORT. IT IS ENTERED FROM THE OPERATING SYSTEM AND  * POLRPT
00073  004130*   EXITS TO THE OPERATING SYSTEM.                     *  POLRPT
00074  004140*                                                    *  POLRPT
00075  004150*******************************************************  POLRPT
00076  004160                                                        POLRPT
00077  004170 A000-CREATE-POLICY-REPORT.                             POLRPT
00078  004180                                                        POLRPT
00079  004190     OPEN INPUT  POLICY-INPUT-FILE                      POLRPT
00080  004200          OUTPUT POLICY-REPORT-FILE.                    POLRPT
00081  005010     READ POLICY-INPUT-FILE                             POLRPT
00082  005020         AT END                                        POLRPT
00083  005030             MOVE 'NO ' TO ARE-THERE-MORE-RECORDS.      POLRPT
00084  005040     PERFORM A001-FORMAT-PRINT-LINE                     POLRPT
00085  005050         UNTIL ARE-THERE-MORE-RECORDS = 'NO '.          POLRPT
00086  005060     CLOSE POLICY-INPUT-FILE                            POLRPT
00087  005070           POLICY-REPORT-FILE.                          POLRPT
00088  005080     STOP RUN.                                          POLRPT
00089  005090                                                        POLRPT
00090  005100                                                        POLRPT
00091  005110                                                        POLRPT
00092  005120 A001-FORMAT-PRINT-LINE.                                POLRPT
00093  005130                                                        POLRPT
00094  005140     MOVE SPACES TO POLICY-REPORT-LINE.                 POLRPT
00095  005150     MOVE POLICY-NUMBER-INPUT TO POLICY-NUMBER-REPORT.  POLRPT
00096  005160     MOVE CUSTOMER-NAME-INPUT TO CUSTOMER-NAME-REPORT.  POLRPT
00097  005170     MOVE AGENT-NAME-INPUT TO AGENT-NAME-REPORT.        POLRPT
00098  005180     MOVE INSURANCE-TYPE-INPUT TO INSURANCE-TYPE-REPORT. POLRPT
00099  005190     WRITE POLICY-REPORT-LINE                           POLRPT
00100  005200         AFTER ADVANCING 1 LINES.                       POLRPT
00101  006010     READ POLICY-INPUT-FILE                             POLRPT
00102  006020         AT END                                        POLRPT
00103  006030             MOVE 'NO ' TO ARE-THERE-MORE-RECORDS.      POLRPT
```

Figure 3-62 Sample Program — Part 2 of 2

Printed Output

```
HM-9083-6762   FRANKEN, PETER     JEAN, BARBARA      HOME
AN-3453-9834   GARCIA, WILLIAM    BENSON, GLORIA     ANNUITY
AM-9878-5647   GARFIELD, JOEY     ANDERSON, JAMES    AUTOMOBILE
TL-6763-0093   PARNELLI, FRANK    BENSON, GLORIA     TERM LIFE
HM-8767-8788   SOLENFELD, NANCY   JACOBSON, PETER    HOME
WL-7682-0903   WINDER, ROBERT     ANDERSON, JAMES    WHOLE LIFE
```

Figure 3-63 Printed Output

REVIEW QUESTIONS

1. What information should be recorded in the area called Punching Instructions on the COBOL coding form?

2. What is the purpose of the Identification Division?

3. List the Paragraph Headers that make up the Identification Division. What is the only Paragraph Header required in the Identification Division?

4. What occurs when an asterisk (*) is recorded in column 7 of the COBOL coding form?

5. What do square brackets indicate in COBOL format notation?

6. What do underlined words in capital letters signify in COBOL format notation?

7. What do lower-case words represent in COBOL format notation?

8. What is specified in the File-Control paragraph of the Input-Output Section in the Environment Division?

9. What are the rules for construction of a file-name?

10. What is the purpose of the Data Division? What are two of the sections within the Data Division?

11. How are fields in an input record defined within the Data Division?

12. What is the purpose of Level Numbers in the Data Division? Why is level number 05 used to identify the fields in a record?

13. When a field is defined with a Picture X, what characters may be contained within that field?

14. What is the purpose of the Procedure Division?

15. What are the rules for the construction of a paragraph name used within the Procedure Division?

16. Explain the operation of the statement PERFORM A001-FORMAT-PRINT-LINE UNTIL ARE-THERE-MORE-RECORDS = 'NO '.

17. What occurs when a Read statement is executed?

18. Explain the processing that occurs when a Move statement moves data from a sending field that is shorter than a receiving field. What happens when the sending field is longer than the receiving field?

19. Explain the operation of the After Advancing option when used with a Write statement.

COBOL CODING EXERCISES

1. Write the COBOL code for the Identification Division of a program. The Program-ID is Farmlist. You are the programmer, the program is written on the current date, and is written in your installation. The program produces a listing of all the farm owners in Harris County.

2. Write the COBOL code required in the Environment Division to define the disk input file and the printer output file for the program identified in problem #1 above. The names of the files are chosen by the programmer. The files are to be used on devices in your installation.

3. The format for the input records in the disk file for the problem specified in problems #1 and #2 is as follows: Farmer Name, positions 1-20; Tract Number, positions 31-38; City Name, positions 41-60. All fields are alphanumeric. Write the COBOL code required in the Data Division to define the input file and the records in the input file.

4. The format for the report line to be printed on the printer for the problem specified in problem #1 and #2 is as follows: Tract Number, positions 6 - 13; Farmer Name, positions 21 - 40; City Name, positions 48 - 67. Write the COBOL code required in the Data Division to define the printer output file and the line to be printed.

5. Write the COBOL Read statement required to read a record from the disk file defined in problem #2 and problem #3.

6. Write the COBOL Move statements required to move the input fields defined in problem #3 to the output fields defined in problem #4.

7. Write the COBOL Write statement required to write a line on the printer using the file defined in problem #4.

STRUCTURED WALKTHROUGH EXERCISES

The following portions of COBOL code contain one or more errors in program logic, in the use of the COBOL language itself, or in the programming standards which should be followed. Review the code in each exercise in the same manner used for structured walkthroughs. Identify the errors and make the appropriate corrections.

1.

```
001010 IDENTIFICATION DIVISION
001020 PROGRAM-ID. FARMRPT.
001030 AUTHOR. HILLIARD.
001040 INSTALLATION. LONG BEACH
001050 DATE. FEB 24,1986.
001060
001070
001080
001090 ENVIRONMENT DIVISION
```

2.

```
003010 DATA DIVISION.
003020
003030 FILE-SECTION
003040 FD SALES-INPUT-FILE
003050    RECORD CONTAINS 72 CHARACTERS
003060    LABEL RECORDS ARE STANDARD.
003070 01 SALES-INPUT-RECORD.
003080    05 SALES-NUMBER-INPUT        PICTURE X(6).
003090    05 FILLER                    PICTURE X(31.
003100    05 SALES-TERRITORY-INPUT     PICTURE X(4).
003110    05 FILLER                    PICTURE X(28)
003120    05 SALES-TYPE-INPUT          PICTURE X(4).
```

3.

```
005010 WORKING-STORAGE-SECTION.
005020
005030 01 PROGRAM-INDICATORS
005040    05 ARE-THERE-MORE-RECORDS  PICTURE X(3) VALUE YES.
```

4.

```
007070 A000-CREATE-SALES-REPORT.
007080
007090    OPEN SALES-INPUT-FILE,
007100         SALES-REPORT-FILE.
007110    READ SALES-REPORT-FILE
007120    AT END MOVE 'NO' TO ARE-THERE-MORE-RECORDS.
```

5.

```
008150 A001-FORMAT-PRINT-LINE.
008160     MOVE BLANKS TO SALES-REPORT-LINE.
008170     MOVE SALES-TYPE-INPUT TO SALESTYPEREPORT.
```

6.

```
008010     WRITE SALES-REPORT-FILE
008020         AFTER ADVANCING 1 LINE.
008030     READ SALES-INPUT-RECORD
008040         AT EOF
008050             MOVE 'YES' TO ARE-THERE-MORE-RECORDS.
```

PROGRAMMING ASSIGNMENT 1

INSTRUCTIONS

An Inventory Report is to be prepared. Write the COBOL program to create the Inventory Report. The IPO Chart and Pseudocode Specifications prepared in Chapter 2 should be used when coding the program. Use Test Data Set 1 in Appendix A.

INPUT

Input consists of Inventory Records that contain a Part Number, Part Description, Quantity on Hand, and Quantity Sold. The format of the Inventory Disk Record is illustrated below. The portions of the record designated UNUSED are not used in this programming assignment.

Inventory Disk Record			
FIELD DESCRIPTION	POSITION	LENGTH	ATTRIBUTE
UNUSED	1 – 5	5	Alphanumeric
Part Number	6 – 9	4	Alphanumeric
UNUSED	10 – 29	20	Alphanumeric
Part Description	30 – 49	20	Alphanumeric
UNUSED	50 – 55	6	Alphanumeric
Quantity on Hand	56 – 58	3	Alphanumeric
Quantity Sold	59 – 61	3	Alphanumeric
Record Length		61	

OUTPUT

Output consists of an Inventory Report listing the Part Number, Quantity Sold, Part Description, and Quantity on Hand. The printer spacing chart for the report is illustrated below.

PRINTER SPACING CHART

PROGRAMMING ASSIGNMENT 2

INSTRUCTIONS

A Sales Report is to be prepared. Write the COBOL program to create the Sales Report. Use the IPO Chart and Pseudocode Specifications prepared in Chapter 2 when coding the program. Use Test Data Set 2 in Appendix A.

INPUT

Input consists of Sales Disk Records that contain a Store Number, Department Number, Salesperson Number, Salesperson Name, and Sales Amount. The format of the Sales Disk Record is illustrated below. Those portions of the record designated UNUSED are not used in this programming assignment.

Sales Disk Record			
FIELD DESCRIPTION	**POSITION**	**LENGTH**	**ATTRIBUTE**
UNUSED	1 – 6	6	Alphanumeric
Store Number	7 – 8	2	Alphanumeric
Department Number	9 – 10	2	Alphanumeric
Salesperson Number	11 – 12	2	Alphanumeric
Salesperson Name	13 – 32	20	Alphanumeric
UNUSED	33 – 53	21	Alphanumeric
Sales Amount	54 – 59	6	Alphanumeric
UNUSED	60 – 67	8	Alphanumeric
Record Length		67	

OUTPUT

Output consists of a Sales Report listing the Salesperson Number, Salesperson Name, Store Number, Department Number, and Sales Amount. The printer spacing chart for the report is illustrated below. Note that the report is double spaced.

PROGRAMMING ASSIGNMENT 3

INSTRUCTIONS

Two listings of a Food Store's inventory are to be prepared. Since two listings are required, it has been decided to print each of the fields twice on the same print line. Write the COBOL program to prepare the listing. The IPO Chart and Pseudocode Specifications prepared in Chapter 2 should be used when coding the program. Use Test Data Set 3 in Appendix A.

INPUT

Input consists of Food Disk Records that contain the Food Number and Food Description. The format of the Food Disk Record is illustrated below. The portions of the record designated UNUSED are not used in this programming assignment.

Food Disk Record			
FIELD DESCRIPTION	**POSITION**	**LENGTH**	**ATTRIBUTE**
UNUSED	1 – 6	6	Alphanumeric
Food Number	7 – 10	4	Alphanumeric
UNUSED	11 – 16	6	Alphanumeric
Food Description	17 – 36	20	Alphanumeric
UNUSED	37 – 64	28	Alphanumeric
Record Length		64	

OUTPUT

Output consists of a Food Report listing the same Food Number and Food Description twice. The printer spacing chart for the report is illustrated below.

PROGRAMMING ASSIGNMENT 4

INSTRUCTIONS

A Computer User Report is to be prepared listing new computer users. Write the COBOL program to create the Computer User Report. The IPO Chart and Pseudocode Specifications prepared in Chapter 2 should be used when coding the program. Use Test Data Set 4 in Appendix A.

INPUT

Input consists of User Disk Records that contain the CRT Number, Connect Date, and User Name. The format of the User Disk Record is illustrated below. The portions of the record designated UNUSED are not used in this programming assignment.

User Disk Record			
FIELD DESCRIPTION	POSITION	LENGTH	ATTRIBUTE
CRT Number	1 – 2	2	Alphanumeric
UNUSED	3 – 33	31	Alphanumeric
Connect Date	34 – 39	6	Alphanumeric
User Name	40 – 59	20	Alphanumeric
UNUSED	60 – 73	14	Alphanumeric
Record Length		73	

OUTPUT

Output consists of a Computer User Report listing the User ID, User Name, Connect Date, and CRT Number. User ID is generated as follows: The first four characters of the User ID are the first four characters of the User Name. This is followed by the last four characters of the Connect Date, followed by the CRT Number. Thus, the User ID for ABCD COMPUTER CORP. whose Connect Date is 010386 and who uses CRT Number 01 would be ABCD038601. The printer spacing chart for the report is illustrated below.

PRINTER SPACING CHART

CHAPTER FOUR

ARITHMETIC OPERATIONS; REPORT EDITING

ARITHMETIC OPERATIONS; REPORT EDITING

4

INTRODUCTION

The addition, subtraction, multiplication, and division arithmetic operations are essential for many business applications. Most business reports also require editing numeric data on a printed report. Report editing refers to the process of printing numeric fields with special characters, such as the dollar sign, comma, and decimal point; and zero suppression, which is suppressing the printing of leading non-significant zeros. The sample program developed in this chapter illustrates arithmetic operations and editing of numeric data.

THE PROBLEM

In the sample problem, a Telephone Billing Report is created. The Telephone Billing Report is a summary of the long distance telephone charges incurred by companies subscribing to a long distance telephone service. The printer spacing chart and program output is illustrated in Figure 4-1.

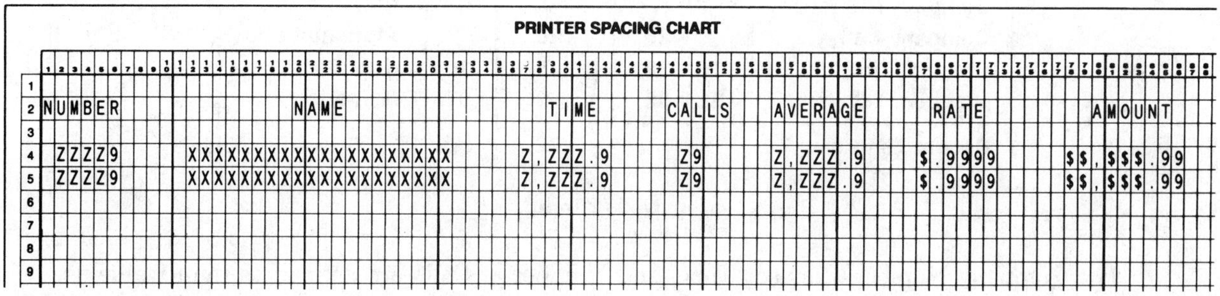


```
NUMBER          NAME                      TIME     CALLS   AVERAGE      RATE          AMOUNT

  2045     JACKSON PRINTING CO.          291.3       4        72.8     $.2175          $63.36
  9348     AJAX PETROLEUM CORP.        2,307.4       8       288.4     $.2175         $501.86
 11756     ANDERSON ACCOUNTING         9,632.9       4     2,408.2     $.2175       $2,095.16
 29644     PATHWAY BICYCLE SHOP          175.5       2        87.8     $.2175          $38.17
```

Figure 4-1 Printer Spacing Chart and Program Output

The Telephone Billing Report contains the company number of the company being billed (NUMBER), the company name (NAME), the total minutes of telephone connect time (TIME), the total number of telephone calls made (CALLS), the average time of each telephone call

(AVERAGE), the billing rate (RATE), and the billing amount (AMOUNT). The average length of each telephone call (AVERAGE) is obtained by dividing the total minutes of telephone connect time (TIME) by the total number of telephone calls made (CALLS). The billing amount (AMOUNT) is obtained by multiplying the total minutes of telephone connect time (TIME) by the billing rate (RATE). Headings are printed to identify the values contained in each of the columns on the report.

Report editing is used to cause zero suppression and to include punctuation, such as commas, periods, and dollar signs, for the numeric fields on the report. In Figure 4-1, the Company Number, Time, Calls, and Average fields have the letter Z within their specifications on the printer spacing chart. The letter Z indicates that the numeric fields are to be zero suppressed. The value 9, representing a numeric digit, indicates where zero suppression is to stop. In the Time field, for example, the rightmost digit will always be printed even if the digit is a zero.

The Rate field and the Billing Amount field contain dollar signs. A single dollar sign is specified for the Rate field. This indicates that the dollar sign is a fixed dollar sign, meaning it will be printed in the column specified regardless of the value in the Rate field. A series of dollar signs is specified for the Billing Amount field in the same manner as a series of Z's are specified for the fields to be zero suppressed. The series of dollar signs indicates that the dollar sign is to be printed as a floating dollar sign, which is a dollar sign printed to the left of and adjacent to the first significant digit in the number being edited.

The input consists of a Billing Disk File with records containing the Company Number, Company Name, Connect Time, and Number of Calls. The format of the input record is illustrated in Figure 4-2.

Billing Disk Record				
FIELD DESCRIPTION	POSITION	LENGTH	DEC	ATTRIBUTE
Company Number	1 – 5	5	0	Numeric
Company Name	6 – 25	20		Alphanumeric
Connect Time	26 – 30	5	1	Numeric
Number of Calls	31 – 32	2	0	Numeric
Record Length		32		

Figure 4-2 Input

The Company Number, Connect Time, and Number of Calls are defined as numeric fields. Numeric fields can contain digits to the right of the decimal point. For example, a dollars and cents field contains two digits to the right of the decimal point. In Figure 4-2, the length of the field (Length) and the number of digits to the right of the decimal point (Dec) are listed in the input format. Company Number is a numeric field that can contain five numeric digits with no decimal positions. Connect time is a numeric field 5 digits in length with one digit to the right of the decimal point. Number of Calls is a 2-digit numeric field with no decimal positions.

The decimal point in these numeric fields is not actually part of the input record and does not take up space in the record. Each record in the Billing Disk File contains 32 positions.

PROCESSING

The requirements for the program processing are specified in the Program Narrative. The

Program Narrative for the sample program is illustrated in Figure 4–3.

PROGRAM NARRATIVE			
SUBJECT Telephone Billing Report	**DATE** October 18		**PAGE** 1 **OF** 1
TO Programmer	**FROM** Systems Analyst		

A program is to be written to prepare a Telephone Billing Report. The format of the input record and the printer spacing chart are included with this narrative. The program should be written to include the following processing:

1. The program should read the input records and create the Telephone Billing Report as per the format illustrated on the printer spacing chart. The report shall contain Company Number, Company Name, Connect Time (in minutes), Number of Calls, Average Time, Billing Rate, and Billing Amount.

2. The Billing Rate for all calls is $.2175 per minute.

3. The Average Time is calculated by dividing the Connect Time by the Number of Calls.

4. Billing Amount is calculated by multiplying the Connect Time by the Billing Rate.

5. One line is to be printed on the report for each record that is read.

6. The report is to be single spaced.

7. The program should be written in COBOL.

Figure 4 - 3 Program Narrative

PHASE 1: REVIEW SYSTEM AND PROGRAMMING SPECIFICATIONS

After receiving the program narrative and prior to designing the program, the programmer must analyze the program narrative together with the format of the input records and printer spacing chart to understand the processing which will occur on each input record. The diagrams on the following pages illustrate the steps which must occur in order to process an input record.

The first processing step reads the input record into the input area and moves the fields from the input area to the output area (Figure 4–4).

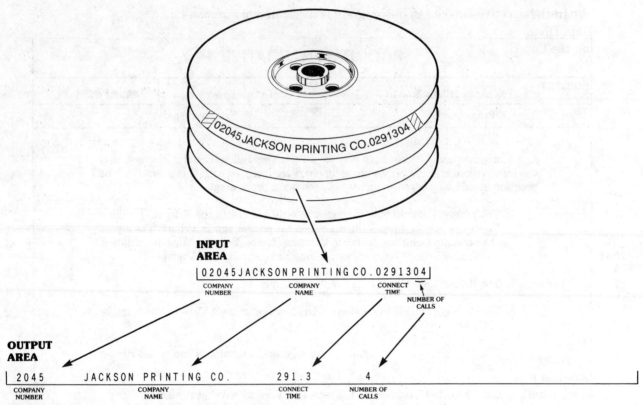

Figure 4 - 4 Data is Read and Moved to the Output Area

After the input record is read into the input area, the Company Number, Company Name, Connect Time, and Number of Calls are moved from the input area to the output area. In the process of being moved from the input area to the output area, all numeric fields are edited.

After the data is moved to the output area, the next step is to calculate the Average Time by dividing the Connect Time by the Number of Calls. As part of the process of calculating the Average Time, the result is moved to the output area. In the process of being moved to the output area, the Average Time is edited (Figure 4–5).

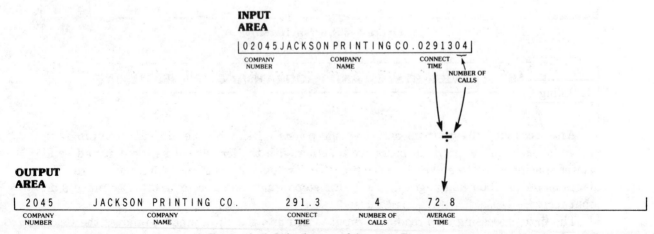

Figure 4 - 5 Calculation of Average Time

In the next step, the Billing Rate, which is defined in the Working-Storage Section of the Data Division, is moved to the output area, and the Billing Amount is calculated by multiplying the Connect Time by the Billing Rate.

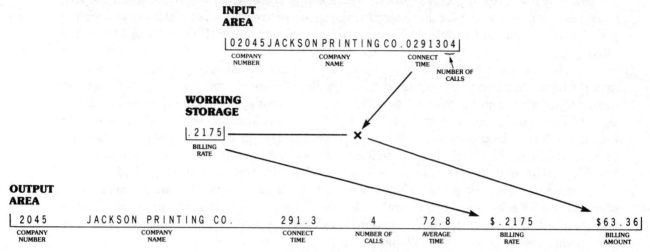

Figure 4-6 Calculation of Billing Amount

After the calculations are completed, the line is printed on the report and another input record is read. This processing will continue until there are no more records to process, at which time processing will be terminated.

Once the programmer is satisfied that the processing is understood, then the second phase of the program development cycle, program design, can begin.

PHASE 2: DESIGN THE PROGRAM

The first step in the program design is to prepare the IPO Chart. The first entry recorded on the IPO Chart is the output to be produced. The output from the sample program is the Billing Report. This entry is recorded in the Output portion of the IPO Chart as shown in Figure 4-7 (Step 1).

IPO CHART				
PROGRAM: Billing Report		**PROGRAMMER:** Forsythe		**DATE:** Oct. 18
MODULE NAME: Create Billing Report	**REF:** A000	**MODULE FUNCTION:** Create Billing Report		
INPUT	**PROCESSING**		**REF:**	**OUTPUT**
1. Billing Disk File	1. Initialize			1. Billing Report
	2. Obtain the input data			
Step 2	3. Perform the calculations			Step 1
	4. Format the print line			
Step 3	5. Write the report			
	6. Terminate			

Figure 4-7 IPO Chart with Input, Processing, and Output Entries

The second entry recorded on the IPO Chart is the input to the program. The input to the sample program is the Billing Disk File. This entry is recorded in the Input portion of the IPO Chart (Figure 4-7, Step 2).

Once the input to the program and the output from the program are specified on the IPO Chart, the programmer must then determine the major processing tasks which are required to transform the input to the output. These steps are recorded on the IPO Chart in Figure 4-7 (Step 3).

As with most programs, the sample program requires initialization processing. In addition, the input records must be obtained for processing. As noted previously, calculations must be performed within this program. Therefore, one of the processing tasks is "Perform calculations." The details concerning the calculations are not specified on the IPO Chart shown in Figure 4-7. These details are left until the development of the pseudocode. The print line must be formatted and the report must be written, so these processing tasks are specified on the IPO Chart. The final step is the termination processing which must be accomplished.

These major processing steps specified on the IPO Chart in Figure 4-7 are not necessarily specified in the same sequence in which they will take place within the program. This is because the major processing tasks on the IPO Chart are used to specify WHAT is to take place within the program, not HOW and WHEN.

After the major processing tasks have been specified, the programmer should review each task to determine if any of them would make the module too complex or difficult to understand. If any task would cause the module to be too complex or difficult to understand, it should be decomposed into simpler, more easily understood tasks. In the sample program, none of the major processing tasks is large enough or complex enough to require further decomposition; so the IPO Chart for the program is complete.

After the IPO Chart is completed, the programmer would normally review the entries with the systems analyst, and perhaps the user of the system, to ensure that a viable solution has been developed for the problem.

Pseudocode

After the processing on the IPO Chart has been approved, the programmer must design the logic to implement the processing. As noted previously, the tool used is pseudocode. The pseudocode for the sample program is illustrated in Figure 4-8.

The pseudocode developed for this application is similar to the pseudocode developed for the application in Chapter 2 and Chapter 3. First, the files are opened to make them available for processing.

After the files are opened, the heading is printed on the report. The heading is always printed prior to printing any of the detail lines. After the heading is printed, the spacing for the report must be set to double spacing. Double spacing is used because there will be one blank line following the heading line (see Figure 4-1). The technique to accomplish this will be explained later in this chapter.

After the heading has been printed and the spacing set, the first input record is read. The routine to format and print the report is then performed until there are no more input records, at which time the files are closed and the program is terminated.

Within the routine which formats and prints the report, the printer output area is cleared with blanks and then data from the input record (Company Number, Company Name, Connect Time, and Number of Calls) is moved from the input area to the printer output area. The Average Time is then calculated by dividing the Connect Time by the Number of Calls. This

PSEUDOCODE SPECIFICATIONS		
PROGRAM: Billing Report	**PROGRAMMER:** Forsythe	**DATE:** Oct. 18
MODULE NAME: Create Billing Report	**REF:** A000 **MODULE FUNCTION:**	Create Billing Report

PSEUDOCODE	REF:	DATA BASES, FILES, RECORDS, FIELDS REQUIRED

Open the files
Write the heading line
Set space control for double spacing
Read an input record
PERFORM UNTIL no more input records
    Clear the output area
    Move the company number, company name,
        connect time, and number of calls to the
        output area
    Calculate average time = connect time / number
        of calls
    Move the billing rate to the output area
    Calculate billing amount = connect time x
        billing rate
    Write the line on the report
    Set space control for single spacing
    Read an input record
ENDPERFORM
Close the files
Stop run		

Figure 4-8 Pseudocode for Sample Program

Average Time is placed in the output area. The Billing Rate is moved from Working-Storage to the output area. Then the Billing Amount is calculated by multiplying the Connect Time by the Billing Rate, and the result is placed in the output area.

After the report line is formatted, it is written on the report. The spacing is then set for single spacing so the remainder of the report will be single spaced, as specified on the printer spacing chart (see Figure 4-1). The next record to be processed is then read.

After the programmer has completed the pseudocode, a structured walkthrough would normally be conducted. The pseudocode should be reviewed by all other programmers on the programming team to find any logic errors which occurred when the pseudocode was written. The programmers will review the pseudocode to determine if any logical mistakes have been made which would prevent the proper output from being produced. If any questionable logic and techniques are found, the programmer should review the pseudocode and justify what is taking place within the program. After all programmers on the team are satisfied that the logic of the program is correct as specified in the pseudocode, the programmer continues with the design of the program.

Definition of Data Bases, Files, Records, and Fields

The data bases, files, records, and fields required for the program must be specified next. The entries on the pseudocode specifications form for the program in this chapter are illustrated in Figure 4-9.

PSEUDOCODE SPECIFICATIONS

PROGRAM: Billing Report		PROGRAMMER: Forsythe		DATE: Oct. 18
MODULE NAME: Create Billing Report	REF: A000	MODULE FUNCTION:	Create Billing Report	

PSEUDOCODE	REF:	DATA BASES, FILES, RECORDS, FIELDS REQUIRED

Open the files
Write the heading line
Set space control for double spacing
Read an input record
PERFORM UNTIL no more input records
    Clear the output area
    Move the company number, company name, connect time, and number of calls to the output area
    Calculate average time = connect time / number of calls
    Move the billing rate to the output area
    Calculate billing amount = connect time x billing rate
    Write the line on the report
    Set space control for single spacing
    Read an input record
ENDPERFORM
Close the files
Stop run
		Billing disk file
		Billing report file
		Heading line
		Printer spacing field
		Double space control character
		Input area for input record
		    Company number
		    Company name
		    Connect time
		    Number of calls
		No more records indicator
		Printer output area
		    Company number
		    Company name
		    Connect time
		    Number of calls
		    Average time
		    Billing rate
		    Billing amount
		Billing rate constant
		Single space control character

Figure 4-9 Data Bases, Files, Records, and Fields Required for the Program

The data bases, files, records, and fields required for the program are determined from the processing specified by the pseudocode. The Billing Disk File is the input file for the program, and the Billing Report File is the printed report file. Since a heading line is to be printed on the report, a heading line containing the values to be printed in the heading must be defined.

As shown by the printer spacing chart in Figure 4–1, the report is double spaced after the heading is printed, but the remainder of the report is single spaced. Therefore, a printer spacing field which contains the control character to designate either single or double spacing must be defined. In addition, the control character to cause the double spacing must be defined within the program.

In order to read an input record, an input area must be defined. Within the input area are fields for the Company Number, Company Name, Connect Time, and Number of Calls. A no more records indicator to indicate that all of the data in the input file has been read is defined next. To clear the printer line, the printer output area must be defined. Within the printer output area are the fields for the Company Number, Company Name, Connect Time, Number of Calls, Average Time, Billing Rate, and Billing Amount.

Since the Billing Rate appears on the output report and is used in the calculation of the Billing Amount, the Billing Rate constant must be defined. In addition, the report is to be single spaced, so the control character to cause single spacing must be defined.

Once the pseudocode and the data bases, files, records, and fields for the program have been defined, the third phase of the development cycle, program coding, can begin.

PHASE 3: CODE THE PROGRAM

Much of the coding required for the sample program will be similar to that used in the previous program and will not be discussed in detail in this chapter. The following pages discuss the concepts and coding of arithmetic operations and report editing.

Definition of Numeric Data

The definition of the Billing Input File and the record format is illustrated in Figure 4-10. The length of each record is 32 characters. The data record to be processed is named the BILLING-INPUT-RECORD in the program.

Billing Disk Record				
FIELD DESCRIPTION	POSITION	LENGTH	DEC	ATTRIBUTE
Company Number	1 – 5	5	0	Numeric
Company Name	6 – 25	20		Alphanumeric
Connect Time	26 – 30	5	1	Numeric
Number of Calls	31 – 32	2	0	Numeric
Record Length		32		

```
002200 FILE SECTION.
003010
003020 FD  BILLING-INPUT-FILE
003030     RECORD CONTAINS 32 CHARACTERS
003040     LABEL RECORDS ARE STANDARD
003050     DATA RECORD IS BILLING-INPUT-RECORD.
003060 01  BILLING-INPUT-RECORD.
003070     05  COMPANY-NUMBER-INPUT      PIC 9(5).
003080     05  COMPANY-NAME-INPUT        PIC X(20).
003090     05  CONNECT-TIME-INPUT        PIC 9(4)V9.
003100     05  NUMBER-OF-CALLS-INPUT     PIC 99.
```

Figure 4-10 Definition of Numeric Fields

In Chapter 3, the data in the input record was alphanumeric data. The Picture X clause was used to define each field. The COMPANY-NAME-INPUT field is an alphanumeric field in the Billing Input Record. Therefore, PIC X(20) is used to define the field.

When data is used in arithmetic operations such as addition, subtraction, multiplication, or division, or is to be edited on a report, the data must be defined as numeric data. Numeric data is defined using the Picture 9 clause, where the "9" indicates that the data stored in the field is numeric.

In the definition of the BILLING-INPUT-RECORD in Figure 4-10, the COMPANY-NUMBER-INPUT field is a numeric field. It must be defined as a numeric field because it will be zero suppressed on the report. The Picture clause PIC 9(5) states there are five numeric digits in the field. The five in parentheses indicates the number of digits in the field; the nine outside the parentheses indicates the characters in the field are numeric.

As with Picture X fields, the numeric Picture clause can be written without parentheses. Thus, PIC 99999 could be written instead of PIC 9(5). The programming standards used for programs in this text state that if more than three characters or digits are found in the field, parentheses should be used in the Picture clause. Therefore, parentheses are used for the Company Number Picture clause.

When numeric fields contain digits to the right of the decimal point, the COBOL compiler must be informed of the position of the decimal point within the field in order to perform the arithmetic and editing operations properly. Since in most applications the decimal point does not actually appear in the input record, the COBOL language allows the programmer to specify where the implied decimal point is located through the use of the character V within a Picture clause.

The Connect Time field in the input record is the only field that contains a digit to the right of the decimal point. The field contains one digit to the right of the decimal point (see Figure 4-10). The Picture clause used for the Connect Time field is PIC 9(4)V9. The nine, of course, indicates the field is to be treated as a numeric field. The value 4 in the parentheses specifies there are four digits to the left of the decimal point.

The V in the Picture clause indicates to the compiler the position of the assumed decimal point. Storage is not reserved for the V. It is used merely to provide the compiler with the implied position of the decimal point in the numeric field. The single character 9 to the right of the V in the Picture clause specifies there is one numeric digit to the right of the decimal point in the Connect Time field. This corresponds to the record format.

The Number of Calls field is zero suppressed on the report (see Figure 4-1). Therefore, it must also be defined as a numeric field. It can be seen from Figure 4-10 that the Number of Calls field is defined as a two digit numeric field with no digits to the right of the decimal point.

Add Statement

Business application programs often require adding or subtracting two numbers. Although the sample program does not require any addition or subtraction, these operations are explained in this chapter.

Figure 4-11 illustrates the use of the Add statement to add the values stored in two numeric fields.

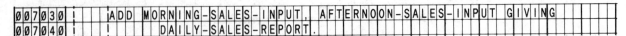

Figure 4-11 Example of the Add Statement

In the coding in Figure 4-11, the value in the MORNING-SALES-INPUT field is added to the value in the AFTERNOON-SALES-INPUT field, and the answer is stored in the DAILY-SALES-REPORT field. The format notation for the Add statement used in Figure 4-11 is illustrated in Figure 4-12.

The word ADD is the first word in the Add statement. It must begin in Area B on the coding form. The values in those fields specified as identifier-1, identifier-2, identifier-3... are added together, and the sum is placed in the field identified by identifier-m. The word GIVING following all of the fields to be added and preceding the field where the sum is to be stored is required. It will also be noted that more than one field can follow the word GIVING. Thus, the values in two or more fields can be added together and the sum placed in one or more fields.

```
ADD    {identifier-1}  ,  {identifier-2}  [, identifier-3] ...
       {literal-1   }     {literal-2   }  [, literal-3   ]

       GIVING identifier-m [ROUNDED] [, identifier-n [ROUNDED]] ...
```

Figure 4 - 12 Add Statement — Format Notation

The comma between identifiers is used merely for ease of readability and is not required.

Each of the fields specified by identifier-1, identifier-2, etc. in the format notation for the Add statement must be defined in the Data Division as elementary numeric fields. The fields specified in an Add statement cannot refer to an alphanumeric field (Picture X) or a group item. The total number of digits in all of the fields to be added cannot exceed 18.

When the Add statement is executed with the Giving clause, the answer is first developed in a work area set up by the compiler and then is moved to the area referenced by identifier-m following the word GIVING. Figure 4–13 illustrates this operation.

```
007030 |   |ADD MORNING-SALES-INPUT, AFTERNOON-SALES-INPUT GIVING
007040 |   |    DAILY-SALES-REPORT.
```

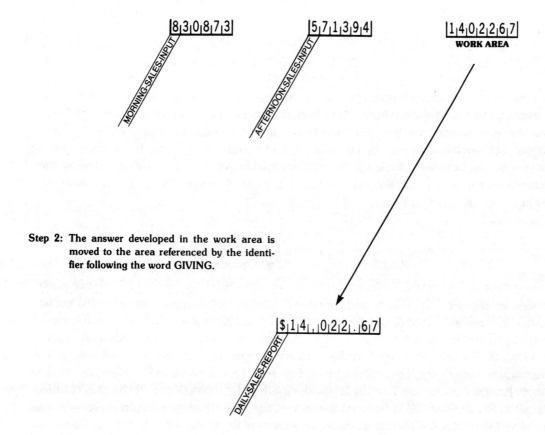

Step 1: When the Add Statement is executed, the values in the two fields are added, and the answer is stored in a work area.

Step 2: The answer developed in the work area is moved to the area referenced by the identifier following the word GIVING.

Figure 4 - 13 Operation of the Add Statement

The answer to the addition operation is first placed in a work area (Step 1), and then it is moved to the field specified following the word GIVING (Step 2). The answer is edited with a dollar sign, comma, and decimal point when it is placed in the DAILY-SALES-REPORT field.

More than one field may be specified following the word GIVING in an Add statement. Figure 4-14 illustrates an operation in which the values in four different fields are added together and placed in two result fields.

Figure 4-14 Example of Multiple Fields with Add Statement

The values in the fields WEEK1-INPUT, WEEK2-INPUT, WEEK3-INPUT, and WEEK4-INPUT would be added together, and the sum would be stored in both the MONTH1-REPORT and the MONTH2-REPORT fields. The contents of the WEEK1-INPUT, WEEK2-INPUT, WEEK3-INPUT, and WEEK4-INPUT fields will not be altered as a result of the execution of the Add statement.

Add Statement — Literals

In the format notation of the Add statement in Figure 4-12, a numeric literal, which is a number that may be used in an arithmetic statement rather than an identifier, can be used in place of identifier-1, identifier-2, identifier-3, etc. Figure 4-15 illustrates the use of a numeric literal.

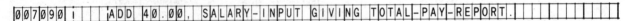

Figure 4-15 Example of Add Statement with Numeric Literal

The numeric literal 40.00 and the value in the area referenced by SALARY-INPUT are added together, and the answer is stored in the area referenced by TOTAL-PAY-REPORT.

A numeric literal must contain at least one, and not more than 18 digits, and may consist of the digits 0 through 9, one plus or minus sign, and one decimal point. If a numeric literal does not contain a minus sign or plus sign, it is assumed positive. A single decimal point may appear anywhere within the literal except as the rightmost character. If a numeric literal does not contain a decimal point, it is assumed to be a whole number.

Add Statement — "To" Option

The Add statement may also be written in a different format which uses the To option. Figure 4-16 illustrates the use of the To option in the Add statement.

When the To option is used in an Add statement, the values in the fields specified by identifier-1, identifier-2, ... , and identifier-m are added together, and the sum is placed in the field specified as identifier-m. In the example in Figure 4-16, the value in the BONUS-INPUT field (15000) is added to the value in the BONUS-ACCUM field (200000) and the sum (215000) is stored in the BONUS-ACCUM field. As a result of the execution of this Add statement, the value in the BONUS-INPUT field is unchanged, while the BONUS-ACCUM field contains the result of the addition operation.

```
008030 !    ADD BONUS-INPUT TO BONUS-ACCUM .
```

```
ADD  {identifier-1}  [, identifier-2]  ...  TO identifier-m  [ROUNDED]
     {literal-1   }  [, literal-2   ]

     [, identifier-n  [ROUNDED]]  ...  [; ON SIZE ERROR imperative-statement]
```

Before Execution

After Execution

Figure 4-16 Example of Add Statement with To Option

Following the word TO in the format notation of the Add statement in Figure 4-16 are identifier-m, identifier-n, etc. These identifiers indicate that more than one field can be specified as the field where the answer will be stored. Thus, the answer developed in the Add statement will be placed in each of the identifier names that follow the word TO in the Add statement. Figure 4-17 on page 4.14 illustrates multiple fields in an Add statement.

The values in SALES1-INPUT (30000) and SALES2-INPUT (20000) are added together, and this sum is then added to the value in SALES-TOTAL (060000). The answer (110000) is stored in the SALES-TOTAL field. In the same manner, the values in SALES1-INPUT and SALES2-INPUT are added to the value in SALES-ACCUM (450000), and the sum (500000) is stored in the SALES-ACCUM field. As a result of the execution of this Add statement, the values in the SALES1-INPUT field and the SALES2-INPUT field are unchanged, while the SALES-TOTAL field and the SALES-ACCUM field contain the answer from the addition operations.

`010020 |    |ADD SALES1-INPUT, SALES2-INPUT TO SALES-TOTAL, SALES-ACCUM. |`

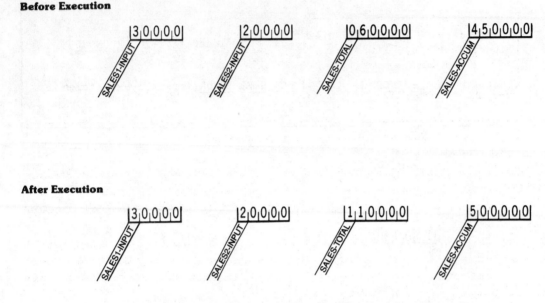

Before Execution

After Execution

Figure 4-17 Example of Multiple Identifiers with Add Statement

A numeric literal may also be used in the Add statement when using the To option. Figure 4-18 illustrates the use of a numeric literal in an Add statement using the To option.

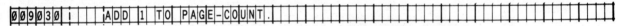

`009030 |    |ADD 1 TO PAGE-COUNT. |`

Figure 4-18 Example of Add Statement with Numeric Literal

The numeric literal 1 is added to the value in the PAGE-COUNT field, and the answer is stored in the PAGE-COUNT field. The Add statement with the To option is frequently used with numeric literals when a field must be incremented by a fixed value, such as when counting the number of pages on a report.

When using the Add statement, the value in the fields being added are aligned according to the decimal point within each field. When the values in the fields, which can be either positive or negative, are added, the result of the add operation can result in either a positive or negative value.

If the size of the area which is to contain the sum after the calculations are performed is not large enough to contain all of the digits in the answer, portions of the answer will be lost and an incorrect answer will develop. To prevent this condition, the programmer must ensure that the Picture clause of the field where the answer is to be stored specifies a sufficient number of digits to allow for the largest possible answer which can develop.

Subtract Statement

The Subtract statement subtracts the value in one numeric field (or a sum of two or more numeric fields) from the value in a specified field and sets the value of one or more fields equal to the difference. Figure 4-19 illustrates the use of the Subtract statement.

```
006040       SUBTRACT TAXES-INPUT FROM GROSS-PAY-INPUT GIVING
006050              NET-PAY-REPORT.
```

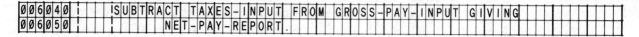

SUBTRACT $\left\{ \begin{array}{l} \text{identifier-1} \\ \text{literal-1} \end{array} \right\}$ $\left[\begin{array}{l} \text{, identifier-2} \\ \text{, literal-2} \end{array} \right]$ ... FROM $\left\{ \begin{array}{l} \text{identifier-m} \\ \text{literal-m} \end{array} \right\}$

GIVING identifier-n [ROUNDED] [, identifier-o [ROUNDED]] ...

Figure 4-19 Example of Subtract Statement

The value in the TAXES-INPUT field will be subtracted from the value in the GROSS-PAY-INPUT field and the answer will be stored in the NET-PAY-REPORT field. Note that the Giving option is used with the Subtract statement in the same manner as with the Add statement.

In the format notation for the Subtract statement with the Giving option, it can be seen that one or more fields can be added prior to being subtracted from the value in the identifier-m field. Also, the answer can be stored in more than one field since identifier-n, identifier-o, ... can be specified following the word GIVING.

The use of two or more fields before the word FROM and following the word GIVING is illustrated in Figure 4-20.

```
006070       SUBTRACT TAX1-INPUT, TAX2-INPUT FROM GROSS-PAY-INPUT GIVING
006080              NET-PAY-REPORT, NET-PAY-WORK.
```

Figure 4-20 Example of Multiple Identifiers with Subtract Statement

The values in the TAX1-INPUT field and the TAX2-INPUT field would be added together, and the sum would then be subtracted from the value in the GROSS-PAY-INPUT field. The answer would be stored in the NET-PAY-REPORT field and the NET-PAY-WORK field. All of this processing takes place automatically as a result of using the Subtract statement. The programmer need not be concerned with the intermediate results which are produced by the subtraction operation. The values in the TAX1-INPUT field, the TAX2-INPUT field, and the GROSS-PAY-INPUT field would be unchanged, while the values in the NET-PAY-REPORT field and NET-PAY-WORK field would be replaced with the answer from the subtraction operation.

Use of the word GIVING is optional in the Subtract statement. An example of the Subtract statement without the Giving option and the format notation are illustrated in Figure 4-21.

```
007030       SUBTRACT COMMISSION-INPUT FROM TOTAL-SALARY-WORK.
```

SUBTRACT $\left\{ \begin{array}{l} \text{identifier-1} \\ \text{literal-1} \end{array} \right\}$ $\left[\begin{array}{l} \text{, identifier-2} \\ \text{, literal-2} \end{array} \right]$ ... FROM identifier-m [ROUNDED]

[, identifier-n [ROUNDED]] ... [; ON SIZE ERROR imperative-statement]

Figure 4-21 Example of Subtract Statement Without the Giving Option

When the Subtract statement is executed, the value in the COMMISSION-INPUT field is subtracted from the value in the TOTAL-SALARY-WORK field, and the answer is stored in the TOTAL-SALARY-WORK field. After the execution of the Subtract statement, the value in the COMMISSION-INPUT field remains unchanged, while the value in the TOTAL-SALARY-WORK field is replaced with the answer from the subtraction operation.

Numeric literals can also be used in the Subtract statement, as illustrated in Figure 4-22.

```
008070    SUBTRACT 15.75 FROM SALARY-WORK.
```

Figure 4-22 Example of a Numeric Literal in Subtract Statement

The effect of the Subtract statement in Figure 4-22 is to subtract the numeric literal 15.75 from the value in the SALARY-WORK field and store the answer in the SALARY-WORK field.

The use of numeric literals in both the Add statement and the Subtract statement is discouraged unless the programmer is absolutely sure that the value represented by the literal will not change throughout the use of the program. If there is a possibility that a constant value could change, then it is better to define the constant with a data-name and Value clause in the Data Division. It is easier to make changes to data in the Data Division than to search the Procedure Division for all of the numeric literals which must be changed. Numeric literals should be used with discrimination by the programmer and only when a value is very unlikely to be changed later in the life of the program.

Multiplication

When performing multiplication operations, it is important that the programmer understands the procedure for determining the maximum size answer that may develop and to understand the method of rounding answers. These two topics are explained in the following paragraphs.

Determining Maximum Size Answers

When performing multiplication operations, manually or with a computer, the maximum size answer that may develop can be determined by adding the number of digits in the multiplier to the number of digits in the multiplicand. Figure 4-23 demonstrates that if a five digit Connect Time field is multiplied by a four digit Billing Rate field, the maximum size answer that may develop is nine digits in length.

```
    9 9 9 9.9    Connect Time (Multiplicand)
      .9 9 9 9    Billing Rate (Multiplier)
    8 9 9 9 9 1
    8 9 9 9 9 1
    8 9 9 9 9 1
    8 9 9 9 9 1
  9,9 9 8.9 0 0 0 1    (Maximum size answer—9 digits)
```

Figure 4-23 Example of Multiplication

Even when the largest possible numbers for the Connect Time and the Billing Rate are multiplied together, the largest number of digits which can be in the answer is nine (9). In addition, the number of positions to the right of the decimal point in the answer is the sum of the number of digits to the right of the decimal point in the multiplicand plus the number of digits to the right of the decimal point in the multiplier. In Figure 4-23, the number of digits to the right of the decimal point in the answer (9998.90001) is five since there is one digit to the right of the decimal point in the Connect Time field (9999.9) and four digits to the right of the decimal point in the Billing Rate field (.9999).

Rounding

When programming business applications involving decimal positions in the answer, it is frequently desirable to round off the answer. For example, if the answer in a problem is 675.869, it may be desirable to round the answer to 675.87 so the answer can be expressed in terms of dollars and cents. If the answer in a problem is developed as 675.864, then after rounding, the value expressed in dollars and cents would be 675.86. In either example, if the low order position (the digit on the far right) is less than 5, the amount is not rounded upward; if the low order position is five or more, the amount is rounded upward.

When programming in COBOL, rounding is accomplished by use of the Rounded option that is available with all arithmetic statements.

Multiply Statement

When multiplying in COBOL, the Multiply statement is used. The Multiply statement used in the sample program to multiply the Connect Time by the Billing Rate to obtain the Billing Amount is illustrated in Figure 4-24.

```
008010 |    DIVIDE NUMBER-OF-CALLS INTO CONNECT-TIME-INPUT GIVING
008020 |         AVERAGE-TIME-REPORT ROUNDED.
```

MULTIPLY {identifier-1 / literal-1} BY {identifier-2 / literal-2} GIVING identifier-3 [ROUNDED]

[, identifier-4 [ROUNDED]] ... [; ON SIZE ERROR imperative-statement]

Figure 4-24 Example of the Multiply Statement

The Multiply statement must begin with the word MULTIPLY. When the Giving option is used, as in Figure 4-24, the value in the identifier-1 field is multiplied by the value in the identifier-2 field, and the answer is stored in the identifier-3, identifier-4, . . . fields which follow the word GIVING. When the coding in Figure 4-24 is executed, the value in the CONNECT-TIME-INPUT field is multiplied by the value in the BILLING-RATE-CONSTANT field, and the answer is stored in the BILLING-AMOUNT-REPORT field. After the execution of the Multiply statement, the values in the CONNECT-TIME-INPUT field and the BILLING-RATE-CONSTANT field would be unchanged. The BILLING-AMOUNT-REPORT field would contain the answer from the multiplication operation.

The word ROUNDED is used following identifier-3 (BILLING-AMOUNT-REPORT) in Figure 4-24 to indicate that the answer to the multiplication operation should be rounded prior to being placed in the field. Rounding takes place as was discussed previously. If the word ROUNDED is not specified in the Multiply statement, truncation will occur on those digits for which there is not room in the identifier-3 Picture clause. The results after both rounding and truncation are illustrated in Figure 4-25.

| | Item to Receive Calculated Result | | |
Calculated Result	PICTURE	Value After Rounding	Value After Truncating
12.36	99V9	12▲4	12▲3
8.432	9V9	8▲4	8▲4
35.6	99V9	35▲6	35▲6
65.6	99V	66▲	65▲
.0055	V999	▲006	▲005

▲ = Assumed Decimal Point

Figure 4-25 Example of Rounding and Truncation

With most business application programs, rounding is performed instead of truncation. As a general rule, whenever it is possible that an answer will develop with more digits to the right of the decimal place than will be contained in the final answer, rounding should be specified in the Multiply statement.

The On Size Error entry in the Multiply statement is utilized when there is the possibility that the answer, as a result of the Multiply statement, will be larger than the field in which the answer is to be stored. The use of the On Size Error entry will be explained in detail in a later chapter.

As with the Add statement and the Subtract statement, use of the word GIVING in the Multiply statement is optional. Figure 4-26 illustrates the Multiply statement without the Giving option.

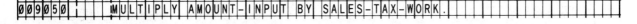

```
ØØ9Ø5Ø     MULTIPLY AMOUNT-INPUT BY SALES-TAX-WORK.
```

```
MULTIPLY  {identifier-1}  BY identifier-2 [ ROUNDED ]
          {literal-1   }

          [ , identifier-3 [ ROUNDED ] ] ...  [ ; ON SIZE ERROR imperative-statement ]
```

Figure 4-26 Example of Multiply Statement without the Giving Option

When the Multiply statement is used without the Giving option, the value in identifier-1 or literal-1 is multiplied by the value in the identifier-2 field, and the answer is stored in the identifier-2 field. In Figure 4-26, the value in the AMOUNT-INPUT field is multiplied by the value in the SALES-TAX-WORK field, and the answer is stored in the SALES-TAX-WORK field. If identifier-3,... is specified, it is treated the same as identifier-2. A literal cannot be specified for identifier-2, identifier-3, ..., but a literal can be used in place of identifier-1.

Division

When division is performed, the programmer must be aware of the sizes of the fields being used so that the quotient field and the remainder field can be properly defined. In a division operation, the maximum number of digits which may be found in the answer is equal to the number of digits in the dividend. This is illustrated in Figure 4-27.

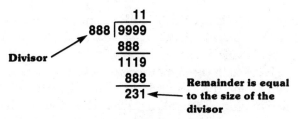

Figure 4-27 Example of Division Operation

The number of digits in the answer to the division operation (quotient size) is equal to the size of the dividend. The largest number of digits which can be generated in the remainder of a division operation is equal to the number of digits in the divisor. This is illustrated in Figure 4-28.

$$\begin{array}{r} 11 \\ 888 \overline{)9999} \\ 888 \\ \hline 1119 \\ 888 \\ \hline 231 \end{array}$$

Divisor →

Remainder is equal to the size of the divisor

Figure 4-28 Remainder Size

The remainder contains the same number of digits as the divisor. It is important that the programmer understand these functions of the division operation in order to properly use the Divide statement.

Divide Statement

To perform the division operation in COBOL, the Divide statement is used. Two examples of the Divide statement are contained in Figure 4-29, Example 1 and Example 2 (page 4.20).

The Divide statement with the Giving option can be specified in two formats. In Example 1, the value in the identifier-1 field is divided INTO the value in the identifier-2 field, and the answer to the division operation is stored in the identifier-3, identifier-4, . . . fields. Thus, the

EXAMPLE 1

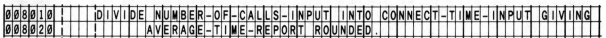

```
008010    DIVIDE NUMBER-OF-CALLS-INPUT INTO CONNECT-TIME-INPUT GIVING
008020           AVERAGE-TIME-REPORT ROUNDED.
```

```
DIVIDE {identifier-1}  INTO {identifier-2}  GIVING identifier-3 [ROUNDED]
       {literal-1   }       {literal-2   }

[, identifier-4 [ROUNDED]] ... [; ON SIZE ERROR imperative-statement]
```

Figure 4-29 Examples of the Divide Statement (Example 1)

EXAMPLE 2

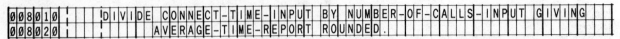

Figure 4-29 Examples of the Divide Statement (Example 2)

value in the NUMBER-OF-CALLS-INPUT field is divided into the value in the CONNECT-TIME-INPUT field, and the answer is stored in the AVERAGE-TIME-REPORT field.

In Example 2, the value in the identifier-1 field is divided BY the value in the identifier-2 field, and the answer is stored in the identifier-3, identifier-4, . . . fields. Thus, the value in the CONNECT-TIME-INPUT field will be divided by the value in the NUMBER-OF-CALLS-INPUT field.

The two Divide statements in Example 1 and Example 2 are equivalent to one another. The value in the AVERAGE-TIME-REPORT field after the division operation will be the same for both formats of the Divide statement. Either Example 1 or Example 2 is an appropriate Divide statement to be used in the sample program to calculate Average Time.

The Rounded option can be specified for either format of the Divide statement. It operates in the same manner as the rounding which takes place in the Multiply statement. The On Size Error entry in the Divide statement can be used when there is a possibility that the answer to the division operation will be too large for the field defined for it; or if the divisor of the division operation may be zero, which is not allowed. A detailed explanation of the use of the On Size Error option is contained in a later chapter.

As noted previously, a remainder may develop as a result of the division operation. If the program is to process the remainder, one of the two formats illustrated in Figure 4–30 (Example 1) and Figure 4–30 (Example 2) should be used.

The formats of the Divide statement when the remainder is to be retained are basically the same as when the remainder is not kept. Two differences exist. First, the word REMAINDER is required, followed by the data-name of the field into which the remainder will be placed. In both examples, the remainder after the division operation is performed will be stored in the MINUTES-REPORT field. Second, only one field (identifier-3) may be specified following the word GIVING instead of multiple fields, as when the Remainder option is not used.

EXAMPLE 1

Figure 4-30 Example of the Remainder Option with the Divide Statement (Example 1)

EXAMPLE 2

```
009100        DIVIDE TOTAL-MINUTES-INPUT BY 60 GIVING
009110        HOURS-REPORT
009120        REMAINDER MINUTES-REPORT.
```

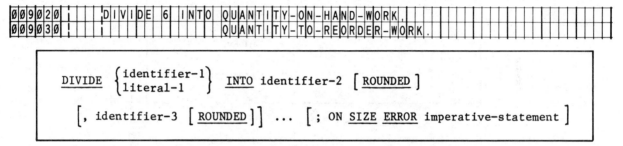

Figure 4-30 Example of the Remainder Option with the Divide Statement (Example 2)

The Divide statement can also be written without the Giving option, as illustrated in Figure 4–31.

```
009020        DIVIDE 6 INTO QUANTITY-ON-HAND-WORK,
009030        QUANTITY-TO-REORDER-WORK.
```

DIVIDE $\begin{Bmatrix} \text{identifier-1} \\ \text{literal-1} \end{Bmatrix}$ <u>INTO</u> identifier-2 [<u>ROUNDED</u>]

[, identifier-3 [<u>ROUNDED</u>]] ... [; ON <u>SIZE</u> <u>ERROR</u> imperative-statement]

Figure 4-31 Example of the Divide Statement without the Giving Option

The value in the identifier-1 field is divided into the value in the identifier-2, identifier-3, . . fields, and the answer is stored in identifier-2, identifier-3, etc. In Figure 4–31, the value 6 will be divided into the value in the QUANTITY-ON-HAND-WORK field, and the answer will be stored in the QUANTITY-ON-HAND-WORK field. Similarly, the value 6 will be divided into the value in the QUANTITY-TO-REORDER-WORK field and the answer will be stored in the QUANTITY-TO-REORDER-WORK field. The Rounded option may be specified if required.

Compute Statement

Although not utilized in the sample program in this chapter, in some applications it is necessary to perform a series of arithmetic calculations. With the Compute statement, arithmetic expressions can be used to specify one or a series of arithmetic operations. An example of the Compute statement and the format notation appears in Figure 4–32.

```
008100        COMPUTE PROFIT-REPORT = SALES-INPUT - COST-INPUT.
```

<u>COMPUTE</u> identifier-1 [<u>ROUNDED</u>] [, identifier-2 [<u>ROUNDED</u>]] ...

= arithmetic-expression [; ON <u>SIZE</u> <u>ERROR</u> imperative-statement]

Figure 4-32 Format of the Compute Statement

The arithmetic expression on the right side of the equal sign (=) is evaluated, and the answer is stored in the identifier-1, identifier-2, . . . fields. In the example in Figure 4–32, the value in the COST-INPUT field will be subtracted from the value in the SALES-INPUT field, and the result will be stored in the PROFIT-REPORT field.

Identifier-1, identifier-2, . . . must be defined as numeric or edited numeric fields in the Data Division. The arithmetic expression on the right side of the equal sign may consist of literals, identifiers, and arithmetic operators. The arithmetic operators which may be used in the Compute statement are listed in Figure 4–33.

Operator	Arithmetic Operation
+	Addition
–	Subtraction
*	Multiplication
/	Division
* *	Exponentiation

Figure 4 - 33 Arithmetic Operators

The equal sign and the arithmetic operators in a Compute Statement must always be preceded by and followed by a space. The seven examples that follow illustrate the use of the arithmetic operators in the Compute statement.

EXAMPLE 1: Addition

```
001050      COMPUTE EARNINGS-REPORT = SALARY-INPUT + BONUS-INPUT.
```
Figure 4 - 34 Example of Addition Arithmetic Operator

The value in the SALARY-INPUT field is added to the value in the BONUS-INPUT field, and the answer is stored in the EARNINGS-REPORT field.

EXAMPLE 2: Subtraction

```
009100      COMPUTE NET-SALES-REPORT = SALES-INPUT - RETURNS-INPUT.
```
Figure 4 - 35 Example of Subtraction Arithmetic Operator

The value in the RETURNS-INPUT field is subtracted from the value in the SALES-INPUT field, and the answer is stored in the NET-SALES-REPORT field.

EXAMPLE 3: Multiplication

```
010020      COMPUTE TOTAL-PAY-REPORT = RATE-INPUT * HOURS-INPUT.
```
Figure 4 - 36 Example of Multiplication Arithmetic Operator

The value in the RATE-INPUT field is multiplied by the value in the HOURS-INPUT field, and the answer is stored in the TOTAL-PAY-REPORT field.

EXAMPLE 4: Division

| 0 | 2 | 0 | 0 | 2 | 0 | | | | | | C | O | M | P | U | T | E | | G | R | A | D | E | - | P | O | I | N | T | - | R | E | P | O | R | T | | = | | T | O | T | A | L | - | P | O | I | N | T | S | - | W | O | R | K | | / | | U | N | I | T | S | - | I | N | P | U | T | . |

Figure 4-37 Division Arithmetic Operator

The value in the TOTAL-POINTS-WORK field is divided by the value in the UNITS-INPUT field, and the answer is stored in the GRADE-POINT-REPORT field.

EXAMPLE 5: Exponentiation

| 0 | 1 | 2 | 1 | 4 | 0 | | | | | | C | O | M | P | U | T | E | | V | O | L | U | M | E | - | O | F | - | C | U | B | E | - | R | E | P | O | R | T | | = | | L | E | N | G | T | H | - | O | F | - | S | I | D | E | - | I | N | P | U | T | | * | * | | 3 | . |

Figure 4-38 Exponentiation Arithmetic Operator

Exponentiation is the process of raising a value to a power. The value X^3 is equivalent to $X * X * X$.

A double asterisk (**) is used to indicate that a value is to be raised to a certain power. In the example, the value in the LENGTH-OF-SIDE-INPUT field will be raised to the third power. The answer will be stored in the VOLUME-OF-CUBE-REPORT field.

EXAMPLE 6: Numeric Literals

Numeric literals may be specified within the arithmetic expression used in the Compute statement. They cannot, however, be used on the left side of the equal sign. Figure 4–39 illustrates the use of a numeric literal in an arithmetic expression.

| 0 | 0 | 9 | 0 | 9 | 0 | | | | | | C | O | M | P | U | T | E | | N | U | M | B | E | R | - | O | F | - | D | A | Y | S | - | R | E | P | O | R | T | | = | | N | U | M | B | E | R | - | O | F | - | H | O | U | R | S | - | I | N | P | U | T | | / | | 2 | 4 | . |

Figure 4-39 Example of a Numeric Literal in the Arithmetic Expression

When the Compute statement is executed, the value in the NUMBER-OF-HOURS-INPUT field will be divided by 24, and the answer will be stored in the NUMBER-OF-DAYS-REPORT field.

EXAMPLE 7: Rounded Option

The Rounded option can be used to cause the answer to be rounded prior to being placed in the field to the left of the equal sign (Figure 4–40).

| 0 | 1 | 1 | 0 | 4 | 0 | | | | | | C | O | M | P | U | T | E | | A | M | O | U | N | T | - | R | E | P | O | R | T | | R | O | U | N | D | E | D | | = | | Q | U | A | N | T | I | T | Y | - | I | N | P | U | T | | * | | C | O | S | T | - | I | N | P | U | T | . |

Figure 4-40 Example of Rounded Option with Compute Statement

Evaluating Arithmetic Expressions

The way in which the arithmetic expressions which appear in a Compute statement are evaluated may be specified through the use of parentheses. This may be necessary when the expression might be ambiguous. For example, in the expression A * B + C, does the programmer mean (A * B) + C or A * (B + C)? In COBOL, the programmer may use pairs of parentheses in order to describe exactly the way in which a computation is to be performed when specified in a Compute statement.

If parentheses are NOT used to specify the order of computations, the COBOL compiler will generate instructions to evaluate an arithmetic expression using the following rules:

1. All exponentiation is performed first.

2. Then, multiplication and division are performed.

3. Finally, addition and subtraction are performed.

4. In each of the three above steps, computation starts at the left of the expression and proceeds to the right. Thus, A * B / C is computed as (A * B) / C, and A / B * C is computed as (A / B) * C.

If parentheses are present, computation begins with the innermost set and proceeds to the outermost set. Items grouped within parentheses will be evaluated in accordance with the above rules, and the result will then be treated as if the parentheses were removed.

Figure 4–41 illustrates the use of the Compute statement to compute the Overtime Earnings of an employee. The Overtime Earnings are calculated by subtracting 40 from the Hours Worked in order to determine the Overtime Hours. The Overtime Hours are then multiplied by 1.5 to determine the hours which will be used to calculate the Overtime Earnings. Those hours are then multiplied by the Pay Rate to determine the Overtime Earnings.

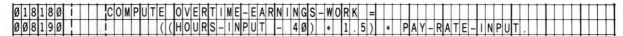

Figure 4-41 Example of the Use of Parentheses in Compute Statement

Parentheses are used to specify the sequence of operations which should take place within the arithmetic expression. The expressions within the innermost parentheses are evaluated first. Thus, the first operation performed is to subtract the value 40 from the value in the HOURS-INPUT field. Next, the result of this subtraction operation will be multiplied by the value 1.5. This result will in turn be multiplied by the value in the PAY-RATE-INPUT field.

Suppose that the HOURS-INPUT field contains the value 44, and the PAY-RATE-INPUT field contains the value 4.00. The result of the (HOURS-INPUT - 40) operation will be 4. This value is then multiplied by 1.5, yielding an answer of 6. The value in the PAY-RATE-INPUT field (4.00) is then multiplied by 6, giving an Overtime Earnings of 24.00.

The Compute statement is a valuable programming tool when complex arithmetic expressions must be evaluated. The programmer, however, must take care when writing the arithmetic expression to ensure that the correct computations will take place.

REPORT EDITING

Business reports normally require some form of report editing. Report editing consists of suppressing leading zeros in numeric fields and inserting punctuation within a field to make it more legible on the report. Report editing is easily accomplished through the use of special editing characters placed in the Picture clause. To edit a field with a dollar sign, comma, and decimal point, the dollar sign, comma, and period are inserted in the Picture clause as they are to appear when the field is printed. Figure 4–42 illustrates the use of editing characters.

```
004080       05   BALANCE-REPORT              PIC  $9,999.99.
```

Figure 4-42 Example of Report Editing

When the numeric data is moved to the BALANCE-REPORT field, it is edited according to the format established in the Picture clause. Figure 4-43 illustrates data as it appears in memory, a related Picture clause, and the printed output that would result.

DATA IN MEMORY	PICTURE	PRINTED OUTPUT
1325ᴧ50	PICTURE $9,999.99	$1,325.50

*The "ᴧ" indicates the location of the assumed decimal point

Figure 4-43 Picture Clause and Related Printed Output

The printed output contains the dollar sign, comma, and decimal point which are placed in the output in the same positions as they are contained in the Picture clause.

Zero Suppression

An important editing function which must often be performed in business applications is zero suppression. Zero suppression is the process of replacing leading, non-significant zeros in a numeric field with blanks or other chosen characters. To zero suppress a field with blanks, the letter "Z" is placed in the Picture clause in each position which is to be zero suppressed. Figure 4-44 illustrates zero suppression.

```
0 0 4 0 2 0     0 5     I N V O I C E - A M O U N T - R E P O R T     P I C   $ Z , Z Z Z . 9 9 .
```

DATA IN MEMORY	PICTURE	PRINTED OUTPUT
0325ᴧ95	PICTURE $Z,ZZZ.99	$ 325.95

Figure 4-44 Example of Zero Suppression

The leading zero in the data in memory is replaced by a blank when it is zero suppressed. The methods to accomplish the report editing illustrated in Figure 4-43 and Figure 4-44 are discussed in detail in the following paragraphs.

Zero Suppression — Blank Fill

The letter of the alphabet Z in the Picture clause represents numeric digits that are to be suppressed, meaning the characters will be replaced by blanks when they are zero. The only characters which can precede the Z in a Picture clause are the dollar sign and the comma. A Z in a Picture clause indicates that the leading zeros in the indicated positions are to be replaced with blanks. Figure 4–45 illustrates the use of the Z editing character.

DATA IN MEMORY	PICTURE	PRINTED OUTPUT
12595	PICTURE ZZZ99	12595
00123	PICTURE ZZZ99	123
00005	PICTURE ZZZ99	05
00000	PICTURE ZZZZZ	[blank]
00409	PICTURE ZZZZZ	409

Figure 4-45 Examples of Zero Suppression

Leading zeros are changed to blanks if the corresponding position in the Picture clause contains a Z. If the corresponding position in the Picture clause contains a 9, the zero is printed. After the first significant digit is printed, all following zeros are printed.

Zero Suppression — Asterisk Fill

The asterisk (*) can also be used in zero suppression. When the corresponding position in the Picture clause contains an asterisk, leading zeros are replaced by asterisks. This is illustrated in Figure 4–46.

DATA IN MEMORY	PICTURE	PRINTED OUTPUT
12345	PICTURE ***99	12345
00123	PICTURE ***99	**123
00100	PICTURE ***99	**100
00000	PICTURE ***99	***00
00000	PICTURE *****	*****

Figure 4-46 Example of Zero Suppression with Asterisk Fill

The use of asterisks in zero suppression is usually limited to cases where blanks are not desirable in front of dollar figures, such as on a payroll check.

Insertion Characters — Dollar Sign, Comma, and Decimal Point

The dollar sign, comma, and decimal point are referred to as insertion characters. An insertion character specified in a Picture clause will be placed in the corresponding position of the field when data is moved to that field. When insertion characters are used, the Picture must be large enough to hold both the data and the insertion character. The dollar sign, comma, and decimal point can be used only when the data in the field is numeric.

The appearance of a single symbol "$" in a Picture clause indicates that a dollar sign is to be inserted at the position occupied by the symbol. Several consecutive repetitions of the symbol "$" indicate that the data is to be edited with a floating dollar sign, which is a dollar sign that is to print to the left of and adjacent to the first significant character.

When a comma is placed in a Picture clause, the comma will be inserted in the same place as it appears in the Picture. If the zero to the left of the comma has been suppressed, then the comma will not be inserted in the position where it appears; rather, the comma will be replaced by the character which is replacing the zeros in the zero suppression operation.

When the decimal point appears in a Picture clause, a decimal point will be inserted at the position occupied by the decimal point in the Picture. The data in the field to be moved to the edited Picture will be aligned so that the assumed decimal point, as indicated by the character V in the numeric field being edited, corresponds to the actual decimal point. The decimal point can appear in the Picture clause only one time. Figure 4-47 illustrates the use of the dollar sign, comma, and decimal point in the Picture clause.

DATA IN MEMORY	PICTURE	PRINTED OUTPUT
0001,25	PICTURE $Z,ZZZ.99	$ 1.25
0000,00	PICTURE $Z,ZZZ.99	$ .00
0003,25	PICTURE $$,$$$.99	$3.25
0000,00	PICTURE $$,$$$.99	$.00
0005,50	PICTURE $*,***.99	$****5.50
0000,05	PICTURE $*,***.99	$*****.05
,1250	PICTURE $$,$$9.99	$0.12
1234,	PICTURE $Z,ZZZ.99	$1,234.00

Figure 4-47 Insertion of Dollar Sign, Comma, and Decimal Point

In addition to editing the output report using the Z character, asterisk (*) character, dollar sign ($), comma (,), and decimal point (.), additional insertion characters are available in COBOL for report editing. These insertion characters include the Minus Sign (-), floating Minus Sign, Plus Sign (+), floating Plus Sign, Credit Symbol (CR), Debit Symbol (DB), Implied Position Symbol (P), Blank Character, Zero (0) character, and Stroke character (/). These additional insertion characters are illustrated and explained in detail in a later chapter.

Editing in the Sample Program

The printer spacing chart for the sample program is illustrated in Figure 4-48.

PRINTER SPACING CHART

```
1  
2 NUMBER          NAME              TIME      CALLS   AVERAGE     RATE        AMOUNT
3  
4 ZZZZ9   XXXXXXXXXXXXXXXXXXXX   Z,ZZZ.9     Z9    Z,ZZZ.9   $.9999    $$,$$$.99
5 ZZZZ9   XXXXXXXXXXXXXXXXXXXX   Z,ZZZ.9     Z9    Z,ZZZ.9   $.9999    $$,$$$.99
6  
7  
```

Figure 4-48 Printer Spacing Chart for Sample Program

The Company Number, Connect Time, Number of Calls, and Average Time have the character Z within their specification. The character Z indicates that zero suppression is to take place. The Connect Time, Average Time, Billing Rate, and Billing Amount are edited using a decimal point; the Connect Time, Average Time, and Billing Amount use a comma; and the Billing Rate and Billing Amount use a dollar sign. The Billing Rate is edited using a fixed dollar sign, and the Billing Amount is edited using a floating dollar sign.

Figure 4-49 contains the file description and record description for the BILLING-REPORT-FILE from the sample program.

```
003120 FD  BILLING-REPORT-FILE                                    BILLRPT
003130 I       RECORD CONTAINS 133 CHARACTERS                     BILLRPT
003140 I       LABEL RECORDS ARE OMITTED                          BILLRPT
003150 I       DATA RECORD IS BILLING-REPORT-LINE.                BILLRPT
003160 01  BILLING-REPORT-LINE.                                   BILLRPT
003170 I       05  CARRIAGE-CONTROL       PIC X.                  BILLRPT
003180 I       05  FILLER                 PIC X.                  BILLRPT
003190 I       05  COMPANY-NUMBER-REPORT  PIC ZZZZ9.              BILLRPT
003200 I       05  FILLER                 PIC X(5).               BILLRPT
004010 I       05  COMPANY-NAME-REPORT    PIC X(20).              BILLRPT
004020 I       05  FILLER                 PIC X(5).               BILLRPT
004030 I       05  CONNECT-TIME-REPORT    PIC Z,ZZZ.9.            BILLRPT
004040 I       05  FILLER                 PIC X(5).               BILLRPT
004050 I       05  NUMBER-OF-CALLS-REPORT PIC Z9.                 BILLRPT
004060 I       05  FILLER                 PIC X(5).               BILLRPT
004070 I       05  AVERAGE-TIME-REPORT    PIC Z,ZZZ.9.            BILLRPT
004080 I       05  FILLER                 PIC X(4).               BILLRPT
004090 I       05  BILLING-RATE-REPORT    PIC $.9999.             BILLRPT
004100 I       05  FILLER                 PIC X(5).               BILLRPT
004110 I       05  BILLING-AMOUNT-REPORT  PIC $$,$$$.99.          BILLRPT
004120 I       05  FILLER                 PIC X(46).              BILLRPT
```

Figure 4-49 File and Record Description for Sample Program

In the record description for the BILLING-REPORT-FILE, the Company Number, Connect Time, Number of Calls, and Average Time have been zero suppressed using the edit character Z. A comma will be inserted in the appropriate location if the number is large enough. The edit character $ has been used to edit the Billing Rate and Billing Amount.

Program Constant

It will be recalled from the sample program that the Billing Rate must be defined in the Working-Storage Section as a constant. Its definition in the Working-Storage Section of the Data Division is illustrated in Figure 4-50.

```
004190 01  PROGRAM-CONSTANTS.
004200     05  BILLING-RATE-CONSTANT   PIC V9999   VALUE .2175.
```

Figure 4-50 Definition of Program Constant

The group item data-name is PROGRAM-CONSTANT, which indicates that all elementary items within the group are constants for use within the program. Whenever fields are defined within the Data Division, a group item should be used to indicate their function.

The BILLING-RATE-CONSTANT field has a Picture clause of PIC V9999. This indicates that it consists of four numeric digits, all of which are to the right of the decimal point. This is the desired result since Billing Rate is a decimal amount, not a whole number.

The Value clause is used to place a value in the field. The value specified for the BILLING-RATE-CONSTANT is .2175. The use of the decimal point in the value is to inform the compiler of the location of the decimal point. The decimal point will not be contained in the value which is stored in main memory.

Move Statement and Numeric Fields

When the source field and the receiving field specified in a Move statement are numeric by definition (Picture 9's or editing characters), then the data is aligned by the actual or assumed decimal. When numeric data is moved from one area to another, the field is edited according to the editing characters specified in the receiving field. Figure 4–51 illustrates the operation of the Move statement when numeric data is being moved and edited.

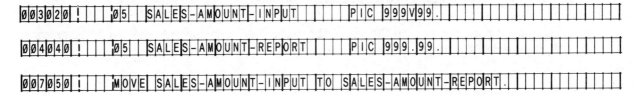

Before Execution

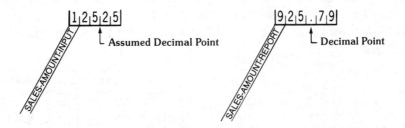

After Execution

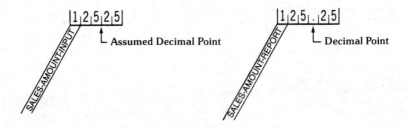

Figure 4-51 Example of the Move Statement and Numeric Data

When the data in the SALES-AMOUNT-INPUT field is moved to the SALES-AMOUNT-REPORT field, the data in the SALES-AMOUNT-INPUT field is aligned in the SALES-AMOUNT-REPORT field on the basis of the assumed and actual decimal points specified in the Picture clauses.

The sending field and the receiving field in Figure 4–51 each have the same number of digits to the left of the decimal point and the same number of digits to the right of the decimal point. To make the object program as efficient as possible, both the sending and receiving fields should have the same length. If, for some reason, the sending and receiving fields are of different lengths, COBOL will process the fields based upon these rules.

1. If the receiving field contains fewer digits to the left of the decimal point than the sending field, the extra leftmost digits of the sending field are truncated when moved to the receiving field because the receiving field does not contain space for the leftmost digits.

2. If the receiving field contains fewer digits to the right of the decimal point than are contained in the sending field, the rightmost extra digits are truncated.

3. If the receiving field contains more digits to the right of the decimal point than are contained in the sending field, then the receiving field is "zero-filled," meaning that zeros are placed in the extra rightmost positions.

4. If extra positions were to the left of the decimal point in the receiving field, the extra high-order (the digits on the left) positions would be filled with zeros.

REPORT HEADINGS

The sample program contains headings on the first page of the report. The headings are printed at the top of form on a new page of computer printer paper. Printing starts on the first printing line. The headings to be printed are illustrated in the printer spacing chart and program output in Figure 4–52.

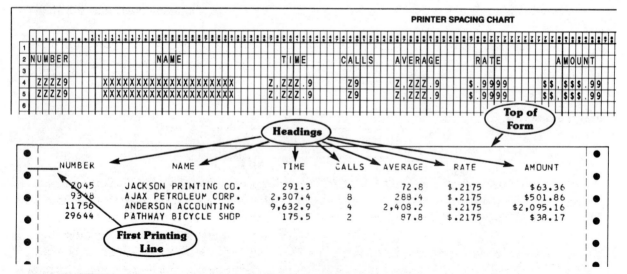

Figure 4-52 Example of Report Headings

Special-Names Paragraph

To cause the heading to print at the top of the page, it is necessary in the program to give a mnemonic-name to the code on the printer which represents the top of the page. This is accomplished through the use of the Special-Names paragraph within the Environment Division, as illustrated in Figure 4-53.

```
002020 ENVIRONMENT DIVISION.
002030
002040 CONFIGURATION SECTION.
002050
002060 SOURCE-COMPUTER. IBM-4381.
002070 OBJECT-COMPUTER. IBM-4381.
002080 SPECIAL-NAMES. C01 IS TO-TOP-OF-PAGE.
```

```
ENVIRONMENT DIVISION.

CONFIGURATION SECTION.

SOURCE-COMPUTER.    computer-name

OBJECT-COMPUTER.    computer-name

[ SPECIAL-NAMES. [ , implementor-name IS mnemonic-name ] ]
```

Figure 4-53 Example of Special-Names Paragraph

The Special-Names paragraph follows the Source-Computer and Object-Computer paragraphs within the Configuration Section. Following the Special-Names paragraph name is the sentence, "C01 IS TO-TOP-OF-PAGE." The C01 entry is a special implementor-name which indicates that a mnemonic-name is to be given to the code on the printer which represents the top of the page. The word IS is required. The mnemonic-name following it is a programmer-chosen symbolic name given to the code. In the sample program, the name chosen is TO-TOP-OF-PAGE.

On some computers, this entry in the Special-Names paragraph is not required. The COBOL users' manual for the particular computer and COBOL compiler being used should be consulted to determine if this paragraph is required.

Definition of the Heading Line

To print headings at the top of the page, it is necessary to define, in the Working-Storage Section of the Data Division, the heading line to be printed. The entries used in the sample program to define the heading line are illustrated in Figure 4-54 on page 4.32.

The group item 01 HEADING-LINE is used to give a name to the entire heading line. Each elementary item within the heading has FILLER in place of a data-name. The word FILLER is used as a data-name when the field being described will not be referenced within the program.

```
005070    01  HEADING-LINE.
005080        05  CARRIAGE-CONTROL          PIC X.
005090        05  FILLER                    PIC X(6)    VALUE 'NUMBER'.
005100        05  FILLER                    PIC X(13)   VALUE SPACES.
005110        05  FILLER                    PIC X(4)    VALUE 'NAME'.
005120        05  FILLER                    PIC X(15)   VALUE SPACES.
005130        05  FILLER                    PIC X(4)    VALUE 'TIME'.
005140        05  FILLER                    PIC X(5)    VALUE SPACES.
005150        05  FILLER                    PIC X(5)    VALUE 'CALLS'.
005160        05  FILLER                    PIC X(3)    VALUE SPACES.
005170        05  FILLER                    PIC X(7)    VALUE 'AVERAGE'.
005180        05  FILLER                    PIC X(5)    VALUE SPACES.
005190        05  FILLER                    PIC X(4)    VALUE 'RATE'.
005200        05  FILLER                    PIC X(8)    VALUE SPACES.
006010        05  FILLER                    PIC X(6)    VALUE 'AMOUNT'.
006020        05  FILLER                    PIC X(47)   VALUE SPACES.
```

Figure 4-54 Definition of Heading Line

The Pictures for each of the FILLER fields are alphanumeric and indicate the length of each of the entries. These lengths correspond to the format of the heading line (see Figure 4-52). The Value clauses give values to each of the fields and correspond to the entries for the heading line. The VALUE SPACES clause specifies that the entire field as defined by the Picture clause is to contain blanks or spaces.

Writing the Heading Line

As with other lines on the report, the Write statement is used to write the heading line. The Write statement used in the sample program is illustrated in Figure 4-55.

```
006200    WRITE BILLING-REPORT-LINE FROM HEADING-LINE
007010        AFTER ADVANCING TO-TOP-OF-PAGE.
```

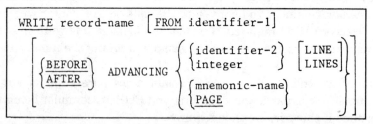

Figure 4-55 Example of Write Statement to Print Headings

BILLING-REPORT-LINE is the data-name used in the File Section of the Data Division to define the printer output area. The From option is used with the Write statement to write the heading. When the From option is used, the data in identifier-1 (HEADING-LINE) is moved to the record-name specified, BILLING-REPORT-LINE. The line is then written. Thus, as a result of the Write statement in Figure 4-55, the heading defined in HEADING-LINE (see Figure 4-54) will be printed on the report.

The After Advancing clause is used with the mnemonic name TO-TOP-OF-PAGE. The After Advancing clause with this entry, as defined in the Special-Names paragraph (Figure 4-53), causes the printer to advance to the beginning of a new page and print the heading on the first line of the new page.

Variable Line Spacing

After the heading is printed, the report is to be double-spaced; but all of the remaining lines on the report are to be single-spaced. The spacing of the report is illustrated in Figure 4–56.

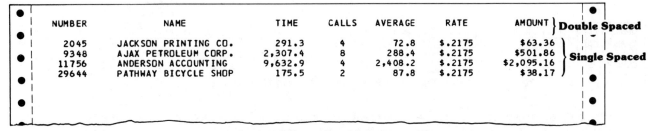

Figure 4 - 56 Example of Spacing on Report

The first detail line for Jackson Printing Co. is double-spaced following the report heading, but the remaining detail lines are single-spaced. For this to occur, a field must be defined which will contain a spacing control character used to indicate what spacing should occur. In addition, the specific spacing control characters must be defined in the Working-Storage Section of the Data Division. The definition of these characters is illustrated in Figure 4–57.

```
005020  01  PRINTER-CONTROL.
005030      05  PROPER-SPACING          PIC 9.
005040      05  SPACE-ONE-LINE          PIC 9    VALUE 1.
005050      05  SPACE-TWO-LINES         PIC 9    VALUE 2.
```

Figure 4 - 57 Printer Control Values

The PROPER-SPACING field is the field which will contain the spacing control character that indicates the spacing to occur when writing the report. It must be defined as a numeric field (Picture 9). If it contains the value 1, then the report will be single-spaced. If it contains the value 2, then the report will be double-spaced.

The SPACE-ONE-LINE field contains the constant value 1 (as a result of the VALUE 1 clause), which will be moved to the PROPER-SPACING field to cause single-spacing. The SPACE-TWO-LINES field contains the value 2, which will be moved to the PROPER-SPACING field when double-spacing is required. The values to be contained in the fields (1 and 2) are not contained within quotes as has been done previously when using the Value clause (see Figure 4–54). This is because when the Value clause is used with numeric fields (Picture 9), the values are not placed in quotes. Only when the fields are alphanumeric (Picture X) are the quotes required.

The values stored in the SPACE-ONE-LINE and SPACE-TWO-LINES fields must be moved to the PROPER-SPACING field prior to the Write statement so that the spacing will take place properly. The sequence which is followed in the program is illustrated in Figure 4–58 on page 4.34.

Immediately after the headings are written (lines 006200 and 007010), the value in the SPACE-TWO-LINES field (2) is moved to the PROPER-SPACING field (line 007020).

When the Write statement to print the detail record is encountered for the first time (line 008060 and line 008070), the PROPER-SPACING field will contain the value 2. For the first detail record to be printed, the printer will be spaced two lines, that is, double-spaced. This is the desired result according to the printer spacing chart.

```
006200     WRITE BILLING-REPORT-LINE FROM HEADING-LINE
007010             AFTER ADVANCING TO-TOP-OF-PAGE.
007020     MOVE SPACE-TWO-LINES TO PROPER-SPACING.
```

Set for Double Spacing

Set for Single Spacing

```
008060     WRITE BILLING-REPORT-LINE
008070             AFTER ADVANCING PROPER-SPACING.
008080     MOVE SPACE-ONE-LINE TO PROPER-SPACING.
```

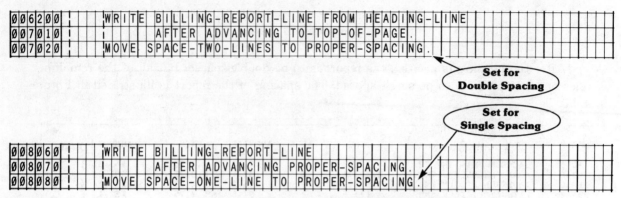

Figure 4-58 Example of Spacing Control

Immediately after the Write statement on lines 008060 and 008070, the value in the SPACE-ONE-LINE field is moved to the PROPER-SPACING field (line 008080). The SPACE-ONE-LINE field contains the value 1 (see Figure 4-57). Therefore, after the first Write statement for a detail line, the PROPER-SPACING field contains the value 1.

Since the remaining detail records will be written by the Write statement on lines 008060 and 008070, all of the records will be single-spaced. This is the desired result. Spacing on the report can be varied at any time by placing the proper value in the spacing control field. The maximum number of lines which can be spaced is 99. In the sample program, only single and double spacing are used.

SAMPLE PROGRAM

The following pages illustrate the Output, Input, IPO Chart, Pseudocode Specifications, Source Listing, and Printed Output of the sample program to create the Telephone Billing Report.

Output

PRINTER SPACING CHART

```
1
2 NUMBER            NAME                         TIME      CALLS    AVERAGE        RATE        AMOUNT
3
4  ZZZZ9     XXXXXXXXXXXXXXXXXXXXXXXXX          Z,ZZZ.9    Z9      Z,ZZZ.9      $.9999      $$,$$$.99
5  ZZZZ9     XXXXXXXXXXXXXXXXXXXXXXXXX          Z,ZZZ.9    Z9      Z,ZZZ.9      $.9999      $$,$$$.99
6
7
8
```

Figure 4-59 Printer Spacing Chart

Input

Billing Disk Record				
FIELD DESCRIPTION	POSITION	LENGTH	DEC	ATTRIBUTE
Company Number	1 – 5	5	0	Numeric
Company Name	6 – 25	20		Alphanumeric
Connect Time	26 – 30	5	1	Numeric
Number of Calls	31 – 32	2	0	Numeric
Record Length		32		

Figure 4-60 Billing Disk Record Report

IPO CHART				
PROGRAM: Billing Report		PROGRAMMER: Forsythe		DATE: Oct. 18
MODULE NAME: Create Billing Report	REF: A000	MODULE FUNCTION: Create Billing Report		
INPUT	PROCESSING		REF:	OUTPUT
1. Billing Disk File	1. Initialize			1. Billing Report
	2. Obtain the input data			
	3. Perform the calculations			
	4. Format the print line			
	5. Write the report			
	6. Terminate			

Figure 4-61 IPO Chart

PSEUDOCODE SPECIFICATIONS

PROGRAM: Billing Report	PROGRAMMER: Forsythe	DATE: Oct. 18
MODULE NAME: Create Billing Report	REF: A000	MODULE FUNCTION: Create Billing Report

PSEUDOCODE	REF:	DATA BASES, FILES, RECORDS, FIELDS REQUIRED

Open the files
Write the heading line
Set space control for double spacing
Read an input record
PERFORM UNTIL no more input records
    Clear the output area
    Move the company number, company name,
       connect time, and number of calls to the
       output area
    Calculate average time = connect time / number
       of calls
    Move the billing rate to the output area
    Calculate billing amount = connect time x
       billing rate
    Write the line on the report
    Set space control for single spacing
    Read an input record
ENDPERFORM
Close the files
Stop run
		Billing disk file
		Billing report file
		Heading line
		Printer spacing field
		Double space control character
		Input area for input record
		    Company number
		    Company name
		    Connect time
		    Number of calls
		No more records indicator
		Printer output area
		    Company number
		    Company name
		    Connect time
		    Number of calls
		    Average time
		    Billing rate
		    Billing amount
		Billing rate constant
		Single space control character

Figure 4 - 62 Pseudocode Specifications

Source Listing

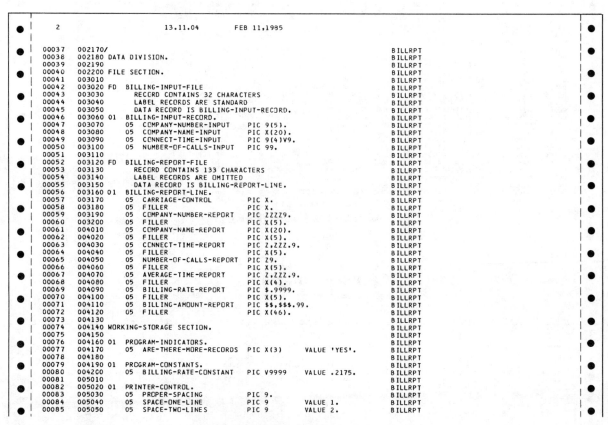

```
PP 5740-CB1 RELEASE 2.3 + PTF 8 - UP13477        IBM OS/VS COBOL  JULY 24, 1978        13.11.04  DATE FEB 11,1985

   1                    13.11.04      FEB 11,1985


00001   001010 IDENTIFICATION DIVISION.                                         BILLRPT
00002   001020                                                                  BILLRPT
00003   001030 PROGRAM-ID.    BILLRPT.                                          BILLRPT
00004   001040 AUTHOR.        FORSYTHE.                                         BILLRPT
00005   001050 INSTALLATION.  BREA.                                             BILLRPT
00006   001060 DATE-WRITTEN.  OCT 28,1984.                                      BILLRPT
00007   001070 DATE-COMPILED. FEB 11,1985.                                      BILLRPT
00008   001080 SECURITY.      UNCLASSIFIED.                                     BILLRPT
00009   001090                                                                  BILLRPT
00010   001100**********************************************************        BILLRPT
00011   001110*                                                        *        BILLRPT
00012   001120*  THIS PROGRAM PREPARES A MONTHLY TELEPHONE BILLING REPORT  *     BILLRPT
00013   001130*  THAT CALCULATES AVERAGE CONNECT TIME AND BILLING AMOUNT.  *     BILLRPT
00014   001140*  AVERAGE CONNECT TIME IS CALCULATED BY DIVIDING CONNECT TIME *   BILLRPT
00015   001150*  BY THE NUMBER OF CALLS. BILLING AMOUNT IS CALCULATED BY   *     BILLRPT
00016   001160*  MULTIPLYING CONNECT TIME BY BILLING RATE.               *       BILLRPT
00017   001170*                                                        *        BILLRPT
00018   001180**********************************************************        BILLRPT
00019   001190                                                                  BILLRPT
00020   001200                                                                  BILLRPT
00021   002010                                                                  BILLRPT
00022   002020 ENVIRONMENT DIVISION.                                            BILLRPT
00023   002030                                                                  BILLRPT
00024   002040 CONFIGURATION SECTION.                                           BILLRPT
00025   002050                                                                  BILLRPT
00026   002060 SOURCE-COMPUTER. IBM-4381.                                       BILLRPT
00027   002070 OBJECT-COMPUTER. IBM-4381.                                       BILLRPT
00028   002080 SPECIAL-NAMES.   C01 IS TO-TOP-OF-PAGE.                          BILLRPT
00029   002090                                                                  BILLRPT
00030   002100 INPUT-OUTPUT SECTION.                                            BILLRPT
00031   002110                                                                  BILLRPT
00032   002120 FILE-CONTROL.                                                    BILLRPT
00033   002130     SELECT BILLING-INPUT-FILE                                    BILLRPT
00034   002140         ASSIGN TO UT-S-BILLDATA.                                 BILLRPT
00035   002150     SELECT BILLING-REPORT-FILE                                   BILLRPT
00036   002160         ASSIGN TO UT-S-BILLPRNT.                                 BILLRPT
```

```
   2                    13.11.04      FEB 11,1985


00037   002170/                                                                 BILLRPT
00038   002180 DATA DIVISION.                                                   BILLRPT
00039   002190                                                                  BILLRPT
00040   002200 FILE SECTION.                                                    BILLRPT
00041   003010                                                                  BILLRPT
00042   003020 FD  BILLING-INPUT-FILE                                           BILLRPT
00043   003030     RECORD CONTAINS 32 CHARACTERS                                BILLRPT
00044   003040     LABEL RECORDS ARE STANDARD                                   BILLRPT
00045   003050     DATA RECORD IS BILLING-INPUT-RECORD.                         BILLRPT
00046   003060 01  BILLING-INPUT-RECORD.                                        BILLRPT
00047   003070     05  COMPANY-NUMBER-INPUT    PIC 9(5).                        BILLRPT
00048   003080     05  COMPANY-NAME-INPUT      PIC X(20).                       BILLRPT
00049   003090     05  CONNECT-TIME-INPUT      PIC 9(4)V9.                      BILLRPT
00050   003100     05  NUMBER-OF-CALLS-INPUT   PIC 99.                          BILLRPT
00051   003110                                                                  BILLRPT
00052   003120 FD  BILLING-REPORT-FILE                                          BILLRPT
00053   003130     RECORD CONTAINS 133 CHARACTERS                               BILLRPT
00054   003140     LABEL RECORDS ARE OMITTED                                    BILLRPT
00055   003150     DATA RECORD IS BILLING-REPORT-LINE.                          BILLRPT
00056   003160 01  BILLING-REPORT-LINE.                                         BILLRPT
00057   003170     05  CARRIAGE-CONTROL        PIC X.                           BILLRPT
00058   003180     05  FILLER                  PIC X.                           BILLRPT
00059   003190     05  COMPANY-NUMBER-REPORT   PIC ZZZZ9.                       BILLRPT
00060   003200     05  FILLER                  PIC X(5).                        BILLRPT
00061   004010     05  COMPANY-NAME-REPORT     PIC X(20).                       BILLRPT
00062   004020     05  FILLER                  PIC X(5).                        BILLRPT
00063   004030     05  CONNECT-TIME-REPORT     PIC Z,ZZZ.9.                     BILLRPT
00064   004040     05  FILLER                  PIC X(5).                        BILLRPT
00065   004050     05  NUMBER-OF-CALLS-REPORT  PIC Z9.                          BILLRPT
00066   004060     05  FILLER                  PIC X(5).                        BILLRPT
00067   004070     05  AVERAGE-TIME-REPORT     PIC Z,ZZZ.9.                     BILLRPT
00068   004080     05  FILLER                  PIC X(4).                        BILLRPT
00069   004090     05  BILLING-RATE-REPORT     PIC $.9999.                      BILLRPT
00070   004100     05  FILLER                  PIC X(5).                        BILLRPT
00071   004110     05  BILLING-AMOUNT-REPORT   PIC $$,$$$.99.                   BILLRPT
00072   004120     05  FILLER                  PIC X(46).                       BILLRPT
00073   004130                                                                  BILLRPT
00074   004140 WORKING-STORAGE SECTION.                                         BILLRPT
00075   004150                                                                  BILLRPT
00076   004160 01  PROGRAM-INDICATORS.                                          BILLRPT
00077   004170     05  ARE-THERE-MORE-RECORDS  PIC X(3)      VALUE 'YES'.       BILLRPT
00078   004180                                                                  BILLRPT
00079   004190 01  PROGRAM-CONSTANTS.                                           BILLRPT
00080   004200     05  BILLING-RATE-CONSTANT   PIC V9999     VALUE .2175.       BILLRPT
00081   005010                                                                  BILLRPT
00082   005020 01  PRINTER-CONTROL.                                             BILLRPT
00083   005030     05  PROPER-SPACING          PIC 9.                           BILLRPT
00084   005040     05  SPACE-ONE-LINE          PIC 9        VALUE 1.            BILLRPT
00085   005050     05  SPACE-TWO-LINES         PIC 9        VALUE 2.            BILLRPT
```

Figure 4-63 Source Listing (Part 1 of 2)

```
   3                      13.11.04      FEB 11,1985

 00086   005060                                                                    BILLRPT
 00087   005070 01  HEADING-LINE.                                                  BILLRPT
 00088   005080     05  CARRIAGE-CONTROL        PIC X.                             BILLRPT
 00089   005090     05  FILLER                  PIC X(6)     VALUE 'NUMBER'.        BILLRPT
 00090   005100     05  FILLER                  PIC X(13)    VALUE SPACES.          BILLRPT
 00091   005110     05  FILLER                  PIC X(4)     VALUE 'NAME'.          BILLRPT
 00092   005120     05  FILLER                  PIC X(15)    VALUE SPACES.          BILLRPT
 00093   005130     05  FILLER                  PIC X(4)     VALUE 'TIME'.          BILLRPT
 00094   005140     05  FILLER                  PIC X(5)     VALUE SPACES.          BILLRPT
 00095   005150     05  FILLER                  PIC X(5)     VALUE 'CALLS'.         BILLRPT
 00096   005160     05  FILLER                  PIC X(3)     VALUE SPACES.          BILLRPT
 00097   005170     05  FILLER                  PIC X(7)     VALUE 'AVERAGE'.       BILLRPT
 00098   005180     05  FILLER                  PIC X(5)     VALUE SPACES.          BILLRPT
 00099   005190     05  FILLER                  PIC X(4)     VALUE 'RATE'.          BILLRPT
 00100   005200     05  FILLER                  PIC X(8)     VALUE SPACES.          BILLRPT
 00101   006010     05  FILLER                  PIC X(6)     VALUE 'AMOUNT'.        BILLRPT
 00102   006020     05  FILLER                  PIC X(47)    VALUE SPACES.          BILLRPT
```

```
   4                      13.11.04      FEB 11,1985

 00103   006030/                                                                   BILLRPT
 00104   006040 PROCEDURE DIVISION.                                                BILLRPT
 00105   006050                                                                    BILLRPT
 00106   006060**************************************************************      BILLRPT
 00107   006070*                                                            *      BILLRPT
 00108   006080*  THIS PROGRAM READS THE INPUT RECORDS, PERFORMS CALCULATIONS *    BILLRPT
 00109   006090*  TO DETERMINE AVERAGE TIME (CONNECT TIME / NUMBER OF CALLS)  *    BILLRPT
 00110   006100*  AND BILLING AMOUNT (CONNECT TIME X BILLING RATE), AND       *    BILLRPT
 00111   006110*  FORMATS AND PRINTS THE TELEPHONE BILLING REPORT. IT IS      *    BILLRPT
 00112   006120*  ENTERED FROM AND EXITS TO THE OPERATING SYSTEM.             *    BILLRPT
 00113   006130*                                                            *      BILLRPT
 00114   006140**************************************************************      BILLRPT
 00115   006150                                                                    BILLRPT
 00116   006160 A000-CREATE-BILLING-REPORT.                                        BILLRPT
 00117   006170                                                                    BILLRPT
 00118   006180     OPEN INPUT  BILLING-INPUT-FILE                                 BILLRPT
 00119   006190          OUTPUT BILLING-REPORT-FILE                                BILLRPT
 00120   006200     WRITE BILLING-REPORT-LINE FROM HEADING-LINE                    BILLRPT
 00121   007010          AFTER ADVANCING TO-TOP-OF-PAGE.                           BILLRPT
 00122   007020     MOVE SPACE-TWO-LINES TO PROPER-SPACING.                        BILLRPT
 00123   007030     READ BILLING-INPUT-FILE                                        BILLRPT
 00124   007040          AT END                                                    BILLRPT
 00125   007050              MOVE 'NO ' TO ARE-THERE-MORE-RECORDS.                 BILLRPT
 00126   007060     PERFORM A001-FORMAT-PRINT-LINE                                 BILLRPT
 00127   007070          UNTIL ARE-THERE-MORE-RECORDS = 'NO '.                     BILLRPT
 00128   007080     CLOSE BILLING-INPUT-FILE                                       BILLRPT
 00129   007090           BILLING-REPORT-FILE.                                     BILLRPT
 00130   007100     STOP RUN.                                                      BILLRPT
 00131   007110                                                                    BILLRPT
 00132   007120                                                                    BILLRPT
 00133   007130                                                                    BILLRPT
 00134   007140 A001-FORMAT-PRINT-LINE.                                            BILLRPT
 00135   007150                                                                    BILLRPT
 00136   007160     MOVE SPACES TO BILLING-REPORT-LINE.                            BILLRPT
 00137   007170     MOVE COMPANY-NUMBER-INPUT TO COMPANY-NUMBER-REPORT.            BILLRPT
 00138   007180     MOVE COMPANY-NAME-INPUT TO COMPANY-NAME-REPORT.                BILLRPT
 00139   007190     MOVE CONNECT-TIME-INPUT TO CONNECT-TIME-REPORT.                BILLRPT
 00140   007200     MOVE NUMBER-OF-CALLS-INPUT TO NUMBER-OF-CALLS-REPORT.          BILLRPT
 00141   008010     DIVIDE CONNECT-TIME-INPUT BY NUMBER-OF-CALLS-INPUT GIVING      BILLRPT
 00142   008020          AVERAGE-TIME-REPORT ROUNDED.                              BILLRPT
 00143   008030     MOVE BILLING-RATE-CONSTANT TO BILLING-RATE-REPORT.             BILLRPT
 00144   008040     MULTIPLY CONNECT-TIME-INPUT BY BILLING-RATE-CONSTANT GIVING    BILLRPT
 00145   008050          BILLING-AMOUNT-REPORT ROUNDED.                            BILLRPT
 00146   008060     WRITE BILLING-REPORT-LINE                                      BILLRPT
 00147   008070          AFTER ADVANCING PROPER-SPACING.                           BILLRPT
 00148   008080     MOVE SPACE-ONE-LINE TO PROPER-SPACING.                         BILLRPT
 00149   008090     READ BILLING-INPUT-FILE                                        BILLRPT
 00150   008100          AT END                                                    BILLRPT
 00151   008110              MOVE 'NO ' TO ARE-THERE-MORE-RECORDS.                 BILLRPT
```

Figure 4-64 Source Listing (Part 2 of 2)

Printed Output

```
 NUMBER         NAME              TIME     CALLS   AVERAGE     RATE      AMOUNT

  2045     JACKSON PRINTING CO.    291.3     4       72.8      $.2175       $63.36
  9348     AJAX PETROLEUM CORP.  2,307.4     8      288.4      $.2175      $501.86
 11756     ANDERSON ACCOUNTING   9,632.9     4    2,408.2      $.2175    $2,095.16
 29644     PATHWAY BICYCLE SHOP    175.5     2       87.8      $.2175       $38.17
```

Figure 4-65 Printed Report

REVIEW QUESTIONS

1. When is a Picture clause with 9's required in a COBOL program?

2. What is the purpose of a "V" in a Picture clause?

3. What is the difference between an Add statement using the Giving option and an Add statement using the To option?

4. What type of field must be used with the Add statement?

5. What is a numeric literal? How can it be used in arithmetic statements?

6. What will occur in Add statements if the answer is larger than the area defined for it?

7. When should numeric literals be used in arithmetic statements? Why shouldn't they be used?

8. What is the rule for determining the maximum size answer that may develop when performing a multiplication operation?

9. For the following numbers, state the result obtained if they are rounded for a dollars and cents value: 567.988; 4.998765; 876.002; 21.644; 98.7660001.

10. Identify the difference between rounding a number and truncating a number. What are the advantages and disadvantages of each?

11. In a division operation, if the divisor contains 3 digits and the dividend 5 digits, what is the maximum size remainder that can develop? What is the basic rule for determining the size of a remainder in a division operation?

12. Briefly summarize the rules for evaluating arithmetic expressions when using the Compute statement. What effect do parentheses have on these rules?

13. Define zero suppression. Identify the results of the following fields being zero suppressed with the Picture clauses given: 8.009 — PIC Z.999.; 009.765 — PIC ZZZ.999.; 0043.9 — PIC ZZZZ.99; 976.33 — PIC ZZZ.99.

14. What occurs when insertion editing characters are used?

15. How are program constants defined in the Data Division of a program?

16. What is the Special-Names paragraph of the Environment Division used for when writing headings on the top line of a report?

17. What fields must be defined to cause variable spacing to occur on a printed report?

COBOL CODING EXERCISES

1. Write the COBOL statement to add the values in the fields HOURS1-INPUT, HOURS2-INPUT and HOURS3-INPUT, storing the answer in TOTAL-HOURS-REPORT.

2. Write the COBOL statement to add the value in the field COMM-BONUS-INPUT and 50.00, storing the answer in TOTAL-COMMISSION-REPORT.

3. Write the COBOL statement to add the values in the fields SALES1-INPUT and SALES2-INPUT, subtract that result from the value in the field TOTAL-SALES-INPUT, and store the answer in the field FINAL-SALES-REPORT.

4. Write the COBOL statement to multiply the value in the PRICE-INPUT field by the value in the QUANTITY-INPUT field, storing the answer in the TOTAL-PRICE-REPORT field.

5. Write the Compute statement to add the values in the fields CURRENT-SALES-INPUT and YTD-SALES-INPUT and divide the result by the value in the NO-OF-MONTHS-INPUT field. The answer should be stored in the AVERAGE-SALES-REPORT field.

6. Write the Picture clause to cause a five digit field to be printed with a floating dollar sign, a comma, and a decimal point. The field is to be zero suppressed up to the decimal point. There are two positions to the right of the decimal point in the edited field.

STRUCTURED WALKTHROUGH EXERCISES

The following portions of COBOL code contain one or more errors in program logic, in the use of the COBOL language itself, or in the programming standards which should be followed. Review the code in each exercise in the same manner used for structured walkthroughs. Identify the errors, and make the appropriate corrections.

1.

```
003010 01  BILLING-INPUT-RECORD.
003020     05  COMPANY-NUMBER-INPUT      PIC 5(9).
003030     05  COMPANY-NAME-INPUT        PIC X(20).
003040     05  CONNECT-TIME-INPUT        PIC 4(9)V9.
003050     05  NUMBER-OF-CALLS           PIC 99.
```

2.

```
005010 01  BILLING-REPORT-LINE.
005020     05  CARRIAGE-CONTROL          PIC X.
005030     05  COMPANY-NUMBER-REPORT     PIC XXXX99.
005040     05  FILLER                    PIC X(6).
005050     05  COMPANY-NAME              PIC X(20.
005060     05  FILLER                    PIC X(5).
005070     05  CONNECT-TIME              PIC Z.ZZZ,9.
005080     05  FILLER                    PIC X(5).
005090     05  NUMBER-OF-CALLS-REPORT    PIC Z9.
005100     05  FILLER                    PIC X(6).
005110     05  AVERAGE-TIME-REPORT       PIC ZZZ.9.
005120     05  FILLER                    PIC X(6).
005130     05  BILLING-RATE-REPORT       PIC $.9999.
005140     05  FILLER                    PIC X(4).
005150     05  BILLING-AMOUNT-REPORT     PIC $$$$,.9$.
005160     05  FILLER                    PIC 45.
```

3.

```
008090     ADD MORNING-SALES-INPUT, EVENING-SALES-INPUT TO TOTAL-SALES.
```

4.

```
009010     ADD FIELD-1 GIVING FIELD-2, FIELD-3.
```

5.

```
002060     COMPUTE AVERAGE-SCORE-REPORT = SCORE1-INPUT + SCORE2-INPUT +
002070         SCORE3-INPUT / 3.
```

PROGRAMMING ASSIGNMENT 1

INSTRUCTIONS

A Payroll Report is to be prepared. Write the COBOL program to prepare this report. An IPO Chart and Pseudocode Specifications should be used when designing the program. Use Test Data Set 1 in Appendix A.

INPUT

Input consists of Payroll Records that contain the Salesperson Number, Salesperson Name, Salary, and Commission. The format of the Payroll Disk Record is illustrated below.

Payroll Disk Record				
FIELD NAME	**POSITION**	**LENGTH**	**DEC**	**ATTRIBUTE**
UNUSED	1 – 5	5		Alphanumeric
Salesperson Number	6 – 8	3	0	Numeric
UNUSED	9	1		Alphanumeric
Salesperson Name	10 – 29	20		Alphanumeric
UNUSED	30 – 50	21		Alphanumeric
Salary	51 – 55	5	2	Numeric
UNUSED	56	1		Alphanumeric
Commission	57 – 61	5	2	Numeric
Record Length		**61**		

OUTPUT

Output consists of a Payroll Report listing the Salesperson Number, Salesperson Name, Salary, Commission, and Total Pay. Total Pay is calculated by adding Salary and Commission. Salesperson Number, Salary, and Commission are to be zero suppressed. Total Pay is to be printed using a floating dollar sign. The printer spacing chart for the report is illustrated below.

PRINTER SPACING CHART

```
1
2 NUMBER              NAME            SALARY      COMMISSION    TOTAL PAY
3
4 ZZ9        XXXXXXXXXXXXXXXXXXXX     ZZZ.99      ZZZ.99        $$,$$$.99
5 ZZ9        XXXXXXXXXXXXXXXXXXXX     ZZZ.99      ZZZ.99        $$,$$$.99
6
7
8
9
```

PROGRAMMING ASSIGNMENT 2

INSTRUCTIONS

A Credit Report is to be prepared. Write the COBOL program to prepare this report. An IPO Chart and Pseudocode Specifications should be used when designing the program. Use Test Data Set 2 in Appendix A.

INPUT

Input consists of Credit Records that contain the Account Number, Customer Name, Balance, and Purchases. The format of the Credit Disk Record is illustrated below.

Credit Disk Record				
FIELD NAME	POSITION	LENGTH	DEC	ATTRIBUTE
UNUSED	1 – 6	6		Alphanumeric
Account Number	7 – 12	6	0	Numeric
Customer Name	13 – 32	20		Alphanumeric
UNUSED	33 – 53	21		Alphanumeric
Balance	54 – 59	6	2	Numeric
Purchases	60 – 65	6	2	Numeric
UNUSED	66 – 67	2		Alphanumeric
Record Length		67		

OUTPUT

Output consists of a Credit Report listing the Account Number, Customer Name, Balance, Purchases, Credit Limit, and Available Credit. Available Credit is calculated by adding the Balance and Purchases and subtracting the result from the Credit Limit. The Credit Limit for all customers is $1500.00. Account Number, Balance, Purchases and Credit Limit are to be zero suppressed. Available Credit is to be printed using a floating dollar sign. The printer spacing chart for the report is illustrated below.

PRINTER SPACING CHART

```
   NUMBER           NAME           BALANCE    PURCHASES      LIMIT        CREDIT
   ZZZZ9    XXXXXXXXXXXXXXXXXXXX   Z,ZZZ.99   Z,ZZZ.99     Z,ZZZ.99    $$,$$$.99
   ZZZZ9    XXXXXXXXXXXXXXXXXXXX   Z,ZZZ.99   Z,ZZZ.99     Z,ZZZ.99    $$,$$$.99
```

PROGRAMMING ASSIGNMENT 3

INSTRUCTIONS

A Tax Report is to be prepared. Write the COBOL program to prepare this report. An IPO Chart and Pseudocode Specifications should be used when designing the program. Use Test Data Set 3 in Appendix A.

INPUT

Input consists of Tax Records that contain the Property Number, Property Owner, and Assessed Value. The format of the Tax Disk Record is given below.

Tax Disk Record				
FIELD NAME	POSITION	LENGTH	DEC	ATTRIBUTE
UNUSED	1 – 6	6		Alphanumeric
Property Number	7 – 10	4	0	Numeric
UNUSED	11 – 36	26		Alphanumeric
Property Owner	37 – 56	20		Alphanumeric
UNUSED	57 – 58	2		Alphanumeric
Assessed Value	59 – 64	6	0	Numeric
Record Length		64		

OUTPUT

Output consists of a Tax Report listing the Property Number, Property Owner, Assessed Value, Old Tax Rate, Old Taxes, New Tax Rate, and New Taxes. Old Taxes are calculated by multiplying the Assessed Value by the Old Rate. New Taxes are calculated by multiplying the Assessed Value by the New Rate. The Old Rate is .75 percent of the Assessed Value and the New Rate is 1.25 percent of the Assessed Value. The printer spacing chart is illustrated below.

PRINTER SPACING CHART

```
NUMBER          OWNER           VALUE    OLD RATE   OLD TAXES    NEW RATE   NEW TAXES
ZZZ9    XXXXXXXXXXXXXXXXXXXX    ZZZ,ZZ9   9.99%     $Z,ZZZ.99     9.99%    $ZZ,ZZZ.99
ZZZ9    XXXXXXXXXXXXXXXXXXXX    ZZZ,ZZ9   9.99%     $Z,ZZZ.99     9.99%    $ZZ,ZZZ.99
```

PROGRAMMING ASSIGNMENT 4

INSTRUCTIONS

A Customer Payment Report is to be prepared. Write the COBOL program to prepare this report. An IPO Chart and Pseudocode Specifications should be used when designing the program. Use Test Data Set 4 in Appendix A.

INPUT

Input consists of Customer Records that contain the Customer Number, Customer Name, Purchase Date, and Purchase Price. The format of the Customer Disk Record is given below.

Customer Disk Record				
FIELD NAME	POSITION	LENGTH	DEC	ATTRIBUTE
UNUSED	1 – 9	9		Alphanumeric
Customer Number	10 – 13	4	0	Numeric
Customer Name	14 – 33	20		Alphanumeric
Purchase Date	34 – 39	6		Alphanumeric
UNUSED	40 – 59	20		Alphanumeric
Purchase Price	60 – 65	6	2	Numeric
UNUSED	66 – 73	8		Alphanumeric
Record Length		73		

OUTPUT

Output consists of a Customer Payment Report listing Customer Number, Customer Name, Purchase Date, Purchase Price, Interest Rate, and Monthly Payment. Monthly payment is calculated by multiplying Interest Rate by Purchase Price, adding the result to the Purchase Price, and dividing that result by 12 (the number of months in the year). The Interest Rate is fixed at 12.5%. Notice on the printer spacing chart illustrated below that the month, day, and year of the date are separated by one blank space. In addition, there are two heading lines.

PRINTER SPACING CHART

```
     1234567891111111111222222222233333333334444444444555555555566666666667777777777
              0123456789012345678901234567890123456789012345678901234567890123456789

 2  CUSTOMER           CUSTOMER          PURCHASE        PURCHASE      INTEREST      MONTHLY
 3  NUMBER               NAME              DATE            PRICE         RATE        PAYMENT
 4
 5   ZZZ9      XXXXXXXXXXXXXXXXXXXX      XX XX XX        $Z,ZZZ.99      99.9%       $ZZZ.99
 6   ZZZ9      XXXXXXXXXXXXXXXXXXXX      XX XX XX        $Z,ZZZ.99      99.9%       $ZZZ.99
 7
 8
 9
10
11
12
```

CHAPTER FIVE

COMPARING; FINAL TOTALS

COMPARING; FINAL TOTALS

5

INTRODUCTION

One of the most powerful features of any programming language is the ability to compare numbers or letters of the alphabet and perform alternative statements based upon the results of the comparison. In Chapter 1, it was pointed out that three basic control structures (sequence, if-then-else, and looping) can be used to express the logic of any program. The control structure used for comparing is the if-then-else structure (Figure 5-1).

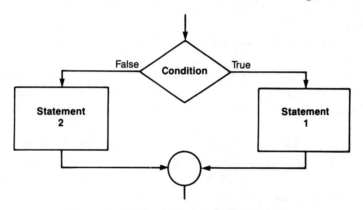

Figure 5-1 If-Then-Else Control Structure

The if-then-else control structure specifies that a condition is to be tested (the diamond-shaped symbol). If the condition is true, one statement or a series of statements will be executed. If the condition is false, a different statement or series of statements will be executed.

The ability to execute alternative statements based upon conditions which can be tested within the program is normally implemented in COBOL using the If statement. The If statement compares values stored in main memory and directs which statements should be executed based upon the results of the comparison. The comparisons determine if two values are equal or not equal; or if one value is greater than or less than another value. The if-then-else control structure and the If statement are explained in this chapter.

When arithmetic operations are performed within business programs, it is often necessary to accumulate totals. These totals reflect the accumulated values of a field or fields. Final totals are totals which are printed after all records have been processed by the program. The techniques for accumulating final totals are also explained in this chapter.

SAMPLE PROBLEM

To illustrate comparing operations and final totals, the sample problem in this chapter creates an Electricity Consumption Report. The printer spacing chart and program output for the Electricity Consumption Report is illustrated in Figure 5–2.

PRINTER SPACING CHART

METER	PREVIOUS	PRESENT	UNITS	DAYS	UNIT	BILLING	AVER. DAILY
NUMBER	READING	READING	CONSUMED	BILLED	COST	AMOUNT	CONSUMPTION
9999999	ZZZZ9	ZZZZ9	ZZ,ZZ9	Z9	.9999	ZZ,ZZZ.99	ZZ,ZZZ.9
9999999	ZZZZ9	ZZZZ9	ZZ,ZZ9	Z9	.9999	ZZ,ZZZ.99	ZZ,ZZZ.9
TOTAL RECORDS ZZ9			ZZZ,ZZ9			$$$$,$$$.99	

```
    METER    PREVIOUS  PRESENT    UNITS     DAYS    UNIT   BILLING  AVER. DAILY
    NUMBER    READING  READING  CONSUMED   BILLED   COST    AMOUNT  CONSUMPTION

    0348799    40050    41360     1,310      30    .0711     93.14      43.7
    2531928    13076    27158    14,082      31    .0711  1,001.23     454.3
    3456720    45006    45231       225      31    .0656     14.76       7.3
    6139596    23459    23698       239      28    .0656     15.68       8.5
    7123201    79010    80493     1,483      30    .0711    105.44      49.4

    TOTAL RECORDS    5             17,339            $1,230.25
```

Figure 5-2 Printer Spacing Chart for Sample Program

The report contains the Meter Number, Previous Reading, Present Reading, Units Consumed, Days Billed, Unit Cost, Billing Amount, and Average Daily Consumption. Final totals are accumulated and printed for the Total Records processed, the Units Consumed, and the Billing Amount.

The Units Consumed value is calculated by subtracting the Previous Reading from the Present Reading. The Billing Amount is calculated by multiplying the Units Consumed by .0656 if the Units Consumed are less than 240 units or multiplying the Units Consumed by .0711 if the Units Consumed are 240 units or more. Average Daily Consumption is calculated by dividing Units Consumed by Days Billed.

CONCEPTS OF COMPARING

Three major comparing operations can be performed on data stored in main memory: a comparison can be made to determine if the data in one field is greater than the data in another field; whether the data in one field is less than the data in another field; or whether the data in one field is equal to the data in another field. These types of comparing operations are called relation tests. The if-then-else control structure in Figure 5–3 illustrates the relation test to determine if the value in the Units Consumed field is less than the value 240.

The condition tested in Figure 5–3 is "Are Units Consumed Less Than 240." If the value in the Units Consumed field is less than the value 240, then the yes path is taken, and the Billing Amount is calculated by multiplying Units Consumed by the value .0656. If Units Consumed are not less than the value 240 (the Units Consumed would therefore be equal to or greater than 240), then the no path is taken, and the Billing Amount is calculated by multiplying Units Consumed by the value .0711.

In a similar manner using the same control structure, values can be tested to determine if they are equal or not, and to determine if one value is greater than another value. Alternative processing can be specified based upon the results of the comparison.

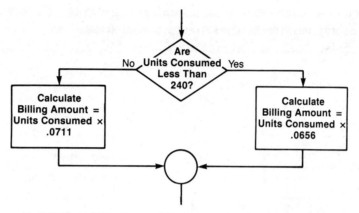

Figure 5 - 3 If-Then-Else Control Structure to Test Less Than Condition

Forms of the If-Then-Else Structure

The if-then-else structure can take several forms within a program. An if-then-else struc-ture can be developed in which no processing will occur when the condition is false. Similarly, a structure can be developed where no processing occurs when the condition is true. These two variations are illustrated in Figure 5–4 and Figure 5–5.

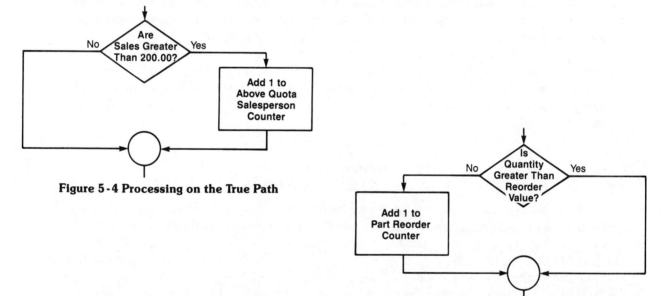

Figure 5 - 4 Processing on the True Path

Figure 5 - 5 Processing on the False Path

In Figure 5–4, if the value in the Sales field is greater than 200.00, the Above Quota Salesperson Counter is increased by 1. If the value in the Sales field is not greater than 200.00 (it is less than or equal to 200.00), no processing will occur. Processing will occur if the condi-tion is true, but no processing will occur if the condition is false.

In Figure 5–5, if the Quantity is greater than the Reorder Value, no processing will occur. If, however, the Quantity is not greater than the Reorder Value, the value 1 is added to the Part Reorder Counter. Processing occurs when the condition is false, but no processing occurs if the condition is true.

It is allowable to have one statement or a series of statements for either the true or false paths. In addition, there need not be the same number of statements for one path as there is for the other path. This is illustrated in Figure 5-6.

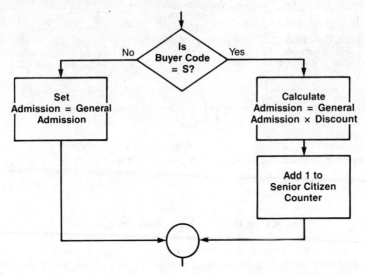

Figure 5 - 6 Multiple Statements in the If-Then-Else Control Structure

In Figure 5-6, if the Buyer Code is equal to the value S, the buyer is a senior citizen. Therefore, the Admission is calculated by multiplying the General Admission by a Discount. In addition, the value 1 is added to the Senior Citizen Counter. If the Buyer Code is not equal to the value S, then the Admission is set equal to the General Admission.

It is possible to test for conditions of NOT GREATER THAN, NOT LESS THAN, and NOT EQUAL as well as those illustrated previously. Thus, it is possible within a program to test for any relationship between two values stored in main memory, and to execute different statements based upon that relationship.

If Statement

In COBOL, the If statement is used to perform comparing operations. Figure 5-7 illustrates the use of the If statement to determine if two fields contain equal values.

0	1	2	1	0				I	F		P	A	Y	R	O	L	L	-	S	T	A	T	U	S	-	I	N	P	U	T		=		H	O	U	R	L	Y	-	C	O	N	S	T	A	N	T	
0	1	2	1	2	0						A	D	D		1		T	O		H	O	U	R	L	Y	-	E	M	P	L	O	Y	E	E	-	C	O	U	N	T	
0	1	2	1	3	0				E	L	S	E
0	1	2	1	4	0						A	D	D		1		T	O		S	A	L	A	R	I	E	D	-	E	M	P	L	O	Y	E	E	-	C	O	U	N	T	.

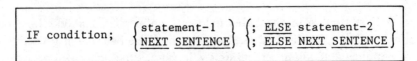

Figure 5 - 7 Example of If Statement and Format Notation

The If statement begins with the word IF. The word IF is followed by a condition to be tested. The condition tested in Figure 5-7 is whether the value in the field PAYROLL-STATUS-INPUT is equal to the value in the HOURLY-CONSTANT field. If the values are equal, then the Add statement on line 012120, which is immediately below the If condition line (line 012110), will be executed. If the values are not equal, then the Add statement on line 012140, which follows the ELSE word line, will be executed.

The If statement must be followed by a period. The period is used to indicate the end of the effect of the If statement. When programming in COBOL, the period must be specified following the last statement which is to be executed as a result of the If statement. In Figure 5–7, the period follows the Add statement on line 012140.

When writing an If statement, the words IF and ELSE are written to begin in the same columns. The statements which are to be executed as a result of the condition being true or not being true are indented three columns. This is the suggested standard to be used when writing the If statement, although it is not required in order for the If statement to function properly.

More than one statement can be specified following the IF or the ELSE words. Figure 5–8 illustrates an If statement containing several statements following the word IF and several statements following the word ELSE.

0 1 3 1 1 0			IF	EMPLOYEE-CODE-INPUT = FULL-TIME-CONSTANT
0 1 3 1 2 0				PERFORM C030-PROCESS-FULL-TIME-EMPLOY
0 1 3 1 3 0				ADD 1 TO FULL-TIME-COUNT
0 1 3 1 4 0			ELSE	
0 1 3 1 5 0				PERFORM C040-PROCESS-PART-TIME-EMPLOY
0 1 3 1 6 0				ADD 1 TO PART-TIME-COUNT.
0 1 3 1 7 0			MOVE EMPLOYEE-CODE-INPUT TO EMPLOYEE-CODE-REPORT.	

Figure 5-8 Example of Multiple Statements in the If Statement

In Figure 5–8, if the value in the EMPLOYEE-CODE-INPUT field is equal to the value in the FULL-TIME-CONSTANT field, the Perform statement on line 013120 and the Add statement on line 013130 will be executed. If the values are not equal, the Perform statement on line 013150 and the Add statement on line 013160 are executed.

It is important to recognize that after execution of the If statement, the statement following the period at the end of the If statement is executed. In Figure 5–8, after the If statement has been executed, that is, after the condition has been evaluated and the appropriate processing has occurred, the Move statement on line 013170 will be executed. It will be executed regardless of the condition which is found in the If statement because it follows the period which terminates the If statement.

The entry NEXT SENTENCE can be placed in an If statement to indicate that the next sentence in the program is to be executed based upon a given condition. The next sentence in a COBOL program is the statement following the period in the If statement. This is illustrated in Figure 5–9.

0 1 3 0 4 0			IF	QUANTITY-SOLD-INPUT IS LESS THAN MINIMUM-QUANTITY-CONSTANT
0 1 3 0 5 0				NEXT SENTENCE
0 1 3 0 6 0			ELSE	
0 1 3 0 7 0				PERFORM C020-PROCESS-OVER-QUOTA.
0 1 3 0 8 0			MOVE QUANTITY-SOLD-INPUT TO QUANTITY-SOLD-REPORT.	

Figure 5-9 Example of the Next Sentence Entry

In Figure 5–9, if the value in the QUANTITY-SOLD-INPUT field is less than the value in the MINIMUM-QUANTITY-CONSTANT field, the statement on line 013080, which follows the period in the If statement, is executed. In most instances, the NEXT SENTENCE entry will not be used in coding COBOL programs.

The Else clause in an If statement is not required. If the Else clause is omitted and the condition is true, the processing specified following the condition will be executed. If the condition is not true, then the next sentence will be executed. This is illustrated in Figure 5-10.

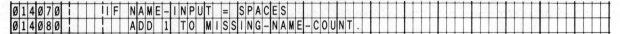

| Ø|1|4|Ø|7|Ø| | | | | |I|F| |N|A|M|E|-|I|N|P|U|T| |=| |S|P|A|C|E|S| | | | | | | | | | | | | | | | | | | | | | |
| Ø|1|4|Ø|8|Ø| | | | | | | | |A|D|D| |1| |T|O| |M|I|S|S|I|N|G|-|N|A|M|E|-|C|O|U|N|T|.| | | | | | | | | | | |

Figure 5-10 If Statement with No Else Clause

If the value in the NAME-INPUT field is equal to SPACES (the name field is blank) in Figure 5-10, then 1 will be added to MISSING-NAME-COUNT. If the field is not equal to spaces, the statement following the period in the If statement will be executed.

It is important that the programmer thoroughly understands the use of the If statement because it is used often when programming in COBOL and, if used improperly, can be the source of errors which are difficult to uncover when the program is being tested.

Relation Test

The If statement is used to test a condition. The most common type of condition tested is a relation test, where the values in two different fields are compared to one another. The general format of the relation condition is shown in Figure 5-11.

$$\begin{Bmatrix} \text{identifier-1} \\ \text{literal-1} \\ \text{arithmetic-expression-1} \\ \text{index-name-1} \end{Bmatrix} \begin{Bmatrix} \text{IS [NOT] GREATER THAN} \\ \text{IS [NOT] LESS THAN} \\ \text{IS [NOT] EQUAL TO} \\ \text{IS [NOT] >} \\ \text{IS [NOT] <} \\ \text{IS [NOT] =} \end{Bmatrix} \begin{Bmatrix} \text{identifier-2} \\ \text{literal-2} \\ \text{arithmetic-expression-2} \\ \text{index-name-2} \end{Bmatrix}$$

Figure 5-11 Format of Relation Conditions

The values in an identifier, a literal, an arithmetic-expression, or an index-name shown in Figure 5-11 can be compared to determine if one is greater than, less than, equal to, not greater than, not less than, or not equal to the other. Either the words (IS EQUAL TO, IS GREATER THAN, etc.) or the symbols ("=," ">," etc.) may be used to express the relation being tested. It is suggested that the words be used except when testing for an equal condition.

The three examples in Figure 5-12 illustrate the use of identifiers, literals, and arithmetic-expressions in If statements.

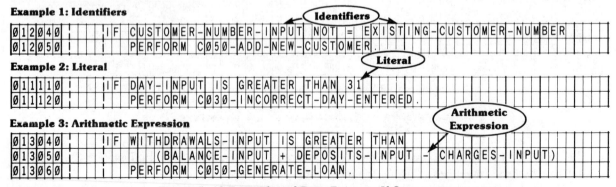

Example 1: Identifiers

Identifiers

| Ø|1|2|Ø|4|Ø| | | | | |I|F| |C|U|S|T|O|M|E|R|-|N|U|M|B|E|R|-|I|N|P|U|T| |N|O|T| |=| |E|X|I|S|T|I|N|G|-|C|U|S|T|O|M|E|R|-|N|U|M|B|E|R| | |
| Ø|1|2|Ø|5|Ø| | | | | | | | |P|E|R|F|O|R|M| |C|Ø|5|Ø|-|A|D|D|-|N|E|W|-|C|U|S|T|O|M|E|R|.| | | | | | | | | | | |

Example 2: Literal

Literal

| Ø|1|1|1|1|Ø| | | | | |I|F| |D|A|Y|-|I|N|P|U|T| |I|S| |G|R|E|A|T|E|R| |T|H|A|N| |3|1| | | | | | | | | | | |
| Ø|1|1|1|2|Ø| | | | | | | | |P|E|R|F|O|R|M| |C|Ø|3|Ø|-|I|N|C|O|R|R|E|C|T|-|D|A|Y|-|E|N|T|E|R|E|D|.| | | | | |

Example 3: Arithmetic Expression

Arithmetic Expression

Ø	1	3	Ø	4	Ø						I	F		W	I	T	H	D	R	A	W	A	L	S	-	I	N	P	U	T		I	S		G	R	E	A	T	E	R		T	H	A	N									
Ø	1	3	Ø	5	Ø									(	B	A	L	A	N	C	E	-	I	N	P	U	T		+		D	E	P	O	S	I	T	S	-	I	N	P	U	T		-		C	H	A	R	G	E	S	-	I	N	P	U	T	)	
Ø	1	3	Ø	6	Ø									P	E	R	F	O	R	M		C	Ø	5	Ø	-	G	E	N	E	R	A	T	E	-	L	O	A	N	.													

Figure 5-12 Examples of Data Types in If Statements

Identifiers, literals, and arithmetic expressions may be used in an If statement when using a relation test. An arithmetic expression is evaluated using the same rules as the Compute statement (see page 4.23). The resulting answer is then compared to the other identifier, literal, or arithmetic-expression in the statement.

Comparison of Numeric Items (Picture 9)

For numeric fields, a relation test determines if the value of one of the items is less than, equal to, or greater than the other, regardless of the length of the fields. When both fields are numeric, the comparison is based directly on their algebraic values. Length differences are ignored. For example, the algebraic value of 09.7000 is considered to be equal to the algebraic value of 00009.70. If no decimal points are indicated, the values are considered whole numbers. For example, 010000 would be considered 10,000 and 000100 would be considered 100.

Since zero is considered a unique value, neither positive nor negative, fields with zero values are considered equal regardless of length, decimal points, and signs.

Figure 5-13 illustrates the comparison of numeric fields.

Data Division

```
ØØ4Ø2Ø        Ø5  HOURS-WORKED-INPUT   PIC 99V9.
ØØ4Ø3Ø        Ø5  HOURS-LIMIT-INPUT    PIC 99.
```

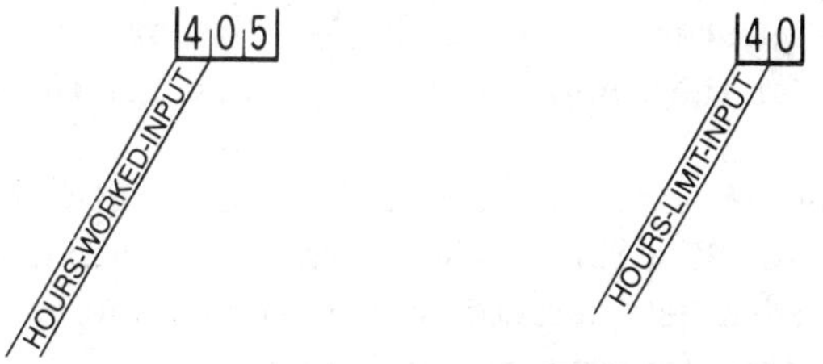

Procedure Division

```
Ø13Ø5Ø        IF HOURS-WORKED-INPUT IS GREATER THAN HOURS-LIMIT-INPUT
Ø13Ø6Ø           PERFORM BØ6Ø-PROCESS-OVERTIME.
```

Figure 5-13 Numeric Comparison using an If Statement

The condition tested in Figure 5-13 would be evaluated as true. The value in the HOURS-WORKED-INPUT field is greater than the value in the HOURS-LIMIT-INPUT field because the HOURS-LIMIT-INPUT field will be extended with a zero in the position to the right of the decimal point and then be compared. Thus, the values compared would be 40.5 and 40.0.

When comparing fields defined as numeric (Picture 9), the fields must contain valid plus or minus signs. As the sign of the field is considered in a numeric compare, any value other than a valid sign in the sign position may result in the abnormal termination of the program.

Comparison of Alphanumeric Data (Picture X)

For fields defined as alphanumeric (Picture X), a comparison results in the determination that the value in one of the fields is greater than, less than, or equal to the other.

The determination of which characters are greater than, less than, or equal to other characters is based upon the code used to store data in main memory. The characters that make up the code used and their relative values comprise what is called the collating sequence of the computer. On many computers, the collating sequence in Figure 5–14 is used for alphanumeric comparisons.

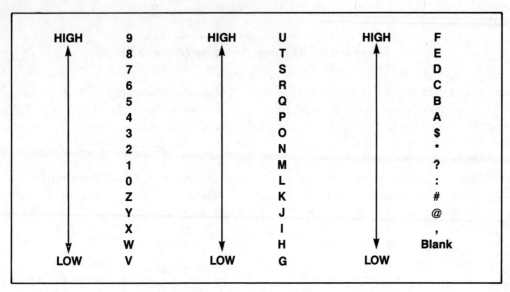

Figure 5-14 Commonly Used Collating Sequence

Although the collating sequence shown in Figure 5–14 is commonly used, the programmer should consult the manuals for the computer being used to determine the actual collating sequence.

If the alphanumeric fields to be compared are of the same length, the comparison proceeds from left to right one character at a time. When a character in one field is not equal to a character in another field or when all characters have been compared, the comparison terminates. Figure 5–15 illustrates the comparison of alphanumeric fields.

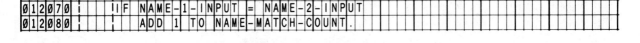

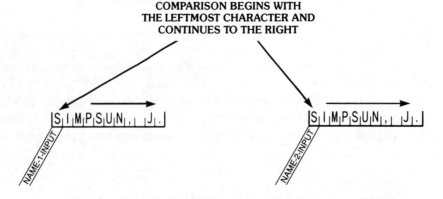

Figure 5-15 Alphanumeric Comparison using an If Statement

The values in the NAME-1-INPUT field and the NAME-2-INPUT field are equal in Figure 5–15. As a result of the condition "NAME-1-INPUT = NAME-2-INPUT" being true, the value 1 would be added to the NAME-MATCH-COUNT field.

When an unequal condition occurs when comparing alphanumeric fields, the first pair of unequal characters encountered is compared for relative position in the collating sequence. The field containing the character that is positioned higher in the collating sequence is considered the greater field. Figure 5–16 illustrates the comparison of alphanumeric data in which an unequal condition results.

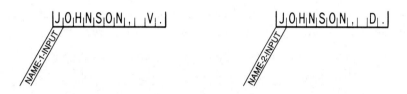

Figure 5 - 16 Unequal Alphanumeric Comparison

The value in the NAME-1-INPUT field in Figure 5–16 is greater than the value in the NAME-2-INPUT field because the letter "V" is higher than the letter "D" in the collating sequence (see Figure 5–14).

If the alphanumeric fields are of unequal length, the value in the shorter field is "extended" internally with blanks until it is the length of the longer field. The two fields are then compared as illustrated previously. A blank character is lower in the collating sequence than any letters or numbers. This process is illustrated in Figure 5–17.

Figure 5 - 17 Example of Alphanumeric Comparison with Different Length Fields

In Figure 5–17, the STATE-INPUT field is two characters in length, and the STATE-CONSTANT field is four characters in length. When they are compared, the STATE-INPUT field is extended two positions internally within main memory, so that it is the same length as the longer STATE-CONSTANT field. Then the values are compared.

Even though the first two characters are equal, the STATE-CONSTANT field contains the values "CH" in the last two positions, while the STATE-INPUT field contains the extended blanks. The value in the STATE-CONSTANT field is considered greater than the value in the STATE-INPUT field because all letters of the alphabet are greater than blanks in the collating sequence of the computer.

Combined If Statements

The previous discussions of the If statement have illustrated its use when testing a single condition. Through the use of combined If statements, two or more conditions can be combined by either the "AND" logical operator or the "OR" logical operator. The use of these logical operators is explained in the following paragraphs.

AND Logical Operator

The word AND is used to mean "both" when two or more conditions are specified in an If statement. The use of the AND logical operator is shown in Figure 5–18.

```
018120   IF AGE-INPUT IS LESS THAN AGE-CONSTANT AND
018130      SEX-INPUT = FEMALE-SEX-CONSTANT
018140      PERFORM C040-YOUNG-FEMALE-ROUTINE.
```

Figure 5 - 18 Use of AND Logical Operator

The If statement in Figure 5–18 checks two conditions — "AGE-INPUT IS LESS THAN AGE-CONSTANT" and "SEX-INPUT = FEMALE-SEX-CONSTANT." If BOTH of these conditions are true, then the C040-YOUNG-FEMALE-ROUTINE module will be performed. When the word AND is used, it means both conditions must be true. If either of the conditions is not true, the Else portion of the If statement will be executed; or if there is no Else clause, as in Figure 5–18, the next sentence in the program will be executed.

It is important to understand that when the program narrative indicates that BOTH conditions must be true before any processing is to take place, the logical operator AND can be used in the If statement.

OR Logical Operator

Two or more conditions can be combined with the logical operator OR to indicate that if EITHER or BOTH of the conditions are true, then the conditions tested are considered true. The use of the OR logical operator is illustrated in Figure 5–19.

```
019030   IF SALES-INPUT IS GREATER THAN SALES-QUOTA OR
019040      SALES-INPUT IS GREATER THAN PREVIOUS-SALES-INPUT
019050      PERFORM C030-PROCESS-COMMISSION
019060   ELSE
019070      PERFORM C040-PROCESS-SALARY.
```

Figure 5 - 19 Use of OR Logical Operator

Two conditions are tested in Figure 5–19. The first is "SALES-INPUT IS GREATER THAN SALES-QUOTA," and the second is "SALES-INPUT IS GREATER THAN PREVIOUS-SALES-INPUT." If EITHER of these conditions is true, then the entire If statement is considered true and the C030-PROCESS-COMMISSION module will be performed. If both of the conditions are not true, that is, if sales are not greater than sales quota and sales are not greater than previous sales, then the conditions tested are considered not true and the

C040-PROCESS-SALARY module will be performed.

When the word OR is used to combine two conditions in an If statement, it means if EITHER or BOTH of the conditions tested is true, then the entire If statement is considered true.

Complex If Statements

Two or more combined If statements can be put together to form a complex If statement. Figure 5–20 illustrates a program narrative and related complex If statement to solve the problem.

Narrative: If the class of a student is freshman or sophomore and the student has a grade point average (GPA) greater than 3.5, then the student should be placed on the honor roll.

011060	IF (STUDENT-CLASS-INPUT = FRESHMAN-CONSTANT OR
011070	STUDENT-CLASS-INPUT = SOPHOMORE-CONSTANT) AND
011080	STUDENT-GPA-INPUT IS GREATER THAN HONOR-GPA-CONSTANT
011090	PERFORM C060-PLACE-ON-HONOR-ROLL.

Figure 5-20 Example of a Complex If Statement

In the program narrative for Figure 5–20, there are two conditions, both of which have to be true, in order for a student to be placed on the honor roll. First, the student must be either a freshman or a sophomore. If the student is, then the first part of the two-part condition is satisfied. If the student is not, then the two-part condition cannot be satisfied, and the student should not be placed on the honor roll.

The second part of the condition is that the student has a grade point average greater than 3.5. If the first part and the second part of the two-part condition are true, then the student should be placed on the honor roll.

The complex If statement in Figure 5–20 is used to solve the problem stated in the narrative. Parentheses are used in the complex If statement to indicate the order in which the conditions are to be evaluated. From the use of the parentheses, the order of evaluation will be as follows:

> **Evaluation: 1 — STUDENT-CLASS-INPUT = FRESHMAN-CONSTANT OR**
> **STUDENT-CLASS-INPUT = SOPHOMORE-CONSTANT**
> **–AND–**
> **2 — STUDENT-GPA-INPUT IS GREATER THAN**
> **HONOR-GPA-CONSTANT**

The reason the first statement above is evaluated first and as a single unit is because of the parentheses around the statement in Figure 5–20. Whenever parentheses are placed around conditions within a complex If statement, these conditions are evaluated as a single unit, giving a true or not true indication. Thus, #1 above will be evaluated as to whether it is true or not true even though the word OR is present. Number 2 above would also be evaluated as to its being true or not true. If both #1 and #2 above are true, then the entire If statement will be considered true since the word AND is used to join them. If either #1 or #2 is not true, then the entire If statement will be considered not true.

Parentheses are not required in complex If statements. If they are not used, then the order of evaluation is as follows:

1. AND and its surrounding conditions are evaluated first, starting at the left of the expression and proceeding to the right.

2. OR and its surrounding conditions are then evaluated, also working from left to right.

The difference between using and not using parentheses is illustrated in Figure 5–21 and Figure 5–22.

```
017060        IF (JOB-CLASS-INPUT = POLICE-CONSTANT OR
017070           JOB-CLASS-INPUT = FIRE-CONSTANT) AND
017080           AGE-INPUT IS GREATER THAN RETIRE-AGE-CONSTANT
017090        PERFORM C020-PROCESS-RETIREMENT.
```

Evaluation: 1 — JOB-CLASS-INPUT = POLICE-CONSTANT OR
JOB-CLASS-INPUT = FIRE-CONSTANT
—AND—
2 — AGE-INPUT IS GREATER THAN RETIRE-AGE-CONSTANT

Figure 5 - 21 A Complex If Statement with Parentheses

Parentheses are used in Figure 5–21. The phrase within the parentheses is evaluated as a single condition, and both (JOB-CLASS-INPUT = POLICE-CONSTANT OR JOB-CLASS-INPUT = FIRE-CONSTANT) and AGE-INPUT IS GREATER THAN RETIRE-AGE-CONSTANT must be true in order for the If statement to be true.

The If statement in Figure 5–22 is the same as that in Figure 5–21 with the exception that no parentheses are used. Therefore, the If statement in Figure 5–22 is evaluated differently than the If statement in Figure 5–21.

```
017060        IF JOB-CLASS-INPUT = POLICE-CONSTANT OR
017070           JOB-CLASS-INPUT = FIRE-CONSTANT AND
017080           AGE-INPUT IS GREATER THAN RETIRE-AGE-CONSTANT
017090        PERFORM C020-PROCESS-RETIREMENT.
```

Evaluation: 1 — JOB-CLASS-INPUT = POLICE-CONSTANT
—OR—
2 — JOB-CLASS-INPUT = FIRE-CONSTANT AND
AGE-INPUT IS GREATER THAN RETIRE-AGE-CONSTANT

Figure 5 - 22 A Complex If Statement without Parentheses

In Figure 5–22, the conditions separated by the word AND are evaluated as a single unit; that is, JOB-CLASS-INPUT = FIRE-CONSTANT and AGE-INPUT IS GREATER THAN RETIRE-AGE-CONSTANT is evaluated as a single condition. The first condition JOB-CLASS-INPUT = POLICE-CONSTANT is evaluated in an OR (either or both) relationship with the two conditions joined by the word AND. Thus, in Figure 5–22, if JOB-CLASS-INPUT = POLICE-CONSTANT, the C020-PROCESS-RETIREMENT paragraph will be performed.

An entirely different result will occur when evaluating complex If statements depending upon whether or not parentheses are used. It is strongly suggested that whenever complex If statements are used, parentheses be specified in the coding whether they are needed or not. Even if the way COBOL analyzes the conditions without parentheses is correct, it is still a good idea for clarity and ease of reading to include the parentheses. In this manner, the reader has no doubts as to the order of evaluation of the conditions specified.

SAMPLE PROGRAM

The sample program in this chapter creates an Electricity Consumption Report. As in previous programs, the programmer must analyze the program narrative together with the format of the input records and printer spacing chart. The program narrative, printer spacing chart, and input are illustrated in Figure 5-23, Figure 5-24, and Figure 5-25.

PROGRAM NARRATIVE		
SUBJECT Electricity Consumption Report	**DATE** October 29	**PAGE** 1 OF 1
TO Programmer	**FROM** Systems Analyst	

A program is to be written to prepare an Electricity Consumption Report. The format of the input record and the printer spacing chart are included with this narrative. The program should be written to include the following processing:

1. The program should read the input records and create the Consumption Report as per the format illustrated on the printer spacing chart. The report shall contain the Meter Number, Previous Reading, Present Reading, Units Consumed, Days Billed, Unit Cost, Billing Amount, and Average Daily Consumption.

2. Headings should be printed on the first page to indicate the values contained in the columns of the report.

3. One line is to be printed on the report for each record which is read. The lines are to be single-spaced.

4. The calculations are as follows:
   a. Units Consumed is obtained by subtracting Previous Reading from Present Reading.
   b. If Units Consumed is less than 240 units, the Billing Amount is calculated by multiplying Units Consumed by .0656.
   c. If Units Consumed is 240 units or more, the Billing Amount is obtained by multiplying Units Consumed by .0711.
   d. Average Daily Consumption is obtained by dividing Units Consumed by Days Billed.

5. Final Totals are to be taken for Total Records processed, Units Consumed, and Billing Amount.

6. The program should be written in COBOL.

Figure 5-23 Program Narrative

Output

PRINTER SPACING CHART

1																																											
2	METER		PREVIOUS		PRESENT		UNITS		DAYS		UNIT		BILLING		AVER.	DAILY
3	NUMBER		READING		READING	CONSUMED		BILLED		COST		AMOUNT		CONSUMPTION
4														
5	9999999	ZZZZ9	ZZZZ9	ZZ,ZZ9	Z9	.9999	ZZ,ZZZ.99	ZZ,ZZZ.9
6	9999999	ZZZZ9	ZZZZ9	ZZ,ZZ9	Z9	.9999	ZZ,ZZZ.99	ZZ,ZZZ.9
7								
8	TOTAL RECORDS ZZ9		ZZZ,ZZ9			$$$$,$$$.99		
9								
10								
11								
12								
13								

Figure 5-24 Printer Spacing Chart for Electricity Consumption Report

Input

Consumption Disk Record				
FIELD DESCRIPTION	POSITION	LENGTH	DEC	ATTRIBUTE
Meter Number	1 – 7	7		Alphanumeric
Previous Reading	8 – 12	5	0	Numeric
Present Reading	13 – 17	5	0	Numeric
Days Billed	18 – 19	2	0	Numeric
Record Length		19		

Figure 5-25 Consumption Disk Record

In summary, the program narrative contains the processing required to transform the Consumption Disk Records into the Electricity Consumption Report. The program narrative specifies that headings should be printed, the report should be single spaced, and final totals should be printed. The program narrative further specifies the calculations and logical operations to be performed.

Processing Input Records

It is important that the programmer understands the basic processing which must take place on each individual input record to create the detailed print line prior to specifying what must occur within the program to transform the input to output. This is illustrated in Figure 5-26 through Figure 5-31.

The first processing step that occurs involves reading the input record into the input area and moving the fields from the input area to the output area. These operations are illustrated in Figure 5-26.

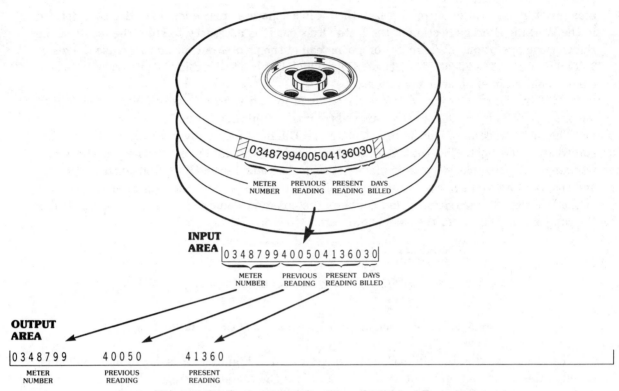

Figure 5-26 Output Area after Move Statement Execution

The input record is read into the input area, and the Meter Number, Previous Reading, and Present Reading are moved to the output area. The only field not moved from the input area, the Days Billed field, will be moved at a later time.

After the data is moved to the output area, the next processing step is to calculate the Units Consumed by subtracting the Previous Reading from the Present Reading and to move the Units Consumed to the output area (Figure 5-27).

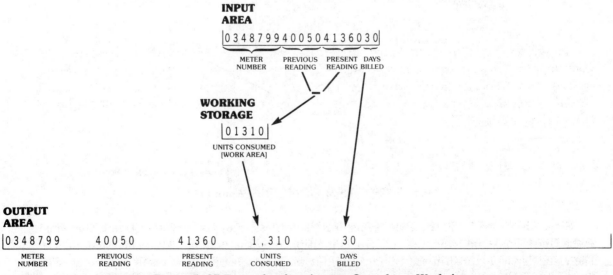

Figure 5-27 Example of an Answer Stored in a Work Area

In Figure 5-27, when the Units Consumed is calculated by subtracting the Previous Reading from the Present Reading, the answer is stored in a work area in main memory. The work area is not in the printer output area. Rather, it is a separate area which, in COBOL, is defined in the Working-Storage Section of the Data Division. It is necessary to store the result of the Subtraction operation in Working-Storage instead of the printer output area because the result will be used in subsequent calculations. Data which has been edited in the printer output area cannot be used in arithmetic operations.

After the Units Consumed is calculated, it is moved from the work area to the printer output area. The Days Billed is then moved from the input area to the output area.

The next processing step is to calculate the Billing Amount by multiplying Units Consumed by Unit Cost. The Unit Cost used (either .0656 or .0711) depends upon the Units Consumed. A comparison must be made between the value in the Units Consumed work area and the constant value in the Conservation Limit area. The Conservation Limit area is defined in the Working-Storage Section and contains the constant value 240. Figure 5–28 illustrates the comparison needed for the sample program.

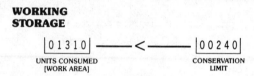

Figure 5-28 Comparison of Units Consumed and Conservation Limit

The value stored in the Units Consumed work area in Figure 5–28 is 01310 and the value stored in the Conservation Limit area is 00240. Since the condition being tested is "Are Units Consumed less than Conservation Limit," the condition being tested is false.

If the value stored in the Units Consumed work area is less than 240, then the Billing Amount is calculated by multiplying Units Consumed by the Conservation Cost (.0656). If the value in the Units Consumed work area is 240 or greater, then the Billing Amount is calculated by multiplying Units Consumed by the Standard Cost (.0711). Both the Conservation Cost and the Standard Cost are constants located in the Working-Storage Section. Figure 5–29 illustrates the necessary calculation for the sample program.

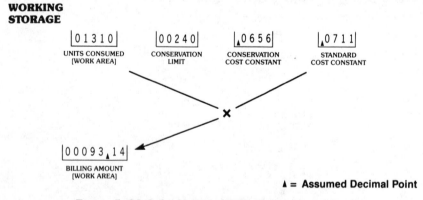

Figure 5-29 Calculation of Billing Amount

Since, in Figure 5–29, the Units Consumed is not less than Conservation Limit, the value in the Units Consumed work area (01310) is multiplied by the Standard Cost Constant (.0711). The result is then stored in the Billing Amount work area because the result will be used in another calculation.

The appropriate Unit Cost (the Standard Cost Constant) and the Billing Amount are then moved from the Working-Storage Section to the printer output area. This can be seen in Figure 5–30.

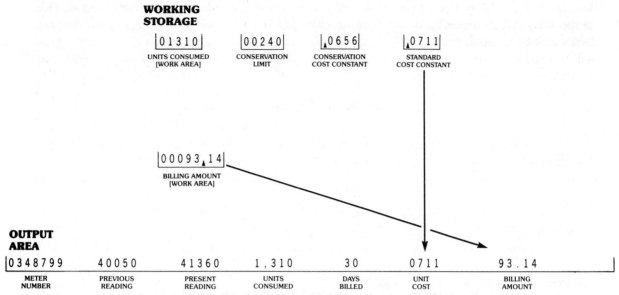

Figure 5-30 Moving Unit Cost and Billing Amount to Output Area

The output area now contains the Meter Number, Previous Reading, Present Reading, Units Consumed, Days Billed, Unit Cost, and Billing Amount.

The next processing step is to calculate the Average Daily Consumption by dividing Units Consumed by the Days Billed, as illustrated in Figure 5-31.

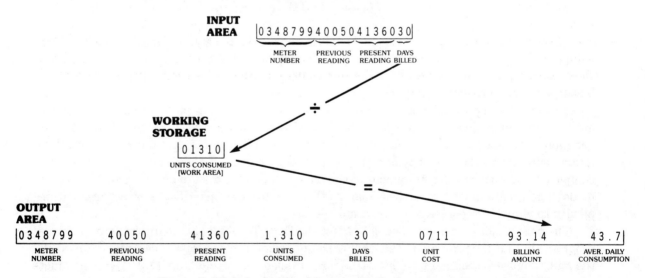

Figure 5-31 Calculation of Average Daily Consumption

The Average Daily Consumption is calculated in Figure 5-31 by dividing the Units Consumed, which is stored in a work area, by the Days Billed, which is stored in the input area. The answer is placed directly in the output area. It need not be placed in a work area because there are no further calculations which must be performed on it.

If the answer to a calculation is to be used in subsequent calculations, then it should be stored in a work area in the Working-Storage Section of the Data Division. If it is not to be used in another calculation, it can be placed directly in the output area.

After all values have been calculated and moved to the output area, the Units Consumed and Billing Amount values in Working-Storage are added to the accumulators to accumulate the final totals. Then, the line is printed on the report, and another input record is read. This processing will continue until there are no more records to process, at which time the final totals will be printed.

PROGRAM DESIGN

The first step in the design of the program is to complete the IPO Chart for the module whose function is to Create the Consumption Report. This is illustrated in Figure 5–32.

IPO CHART				
PROGRAM: Consumption Report		**PROGRAMMER:** Forsythe		**DATE:** Oct. 30
MODULE NAME: Create Consumption Report	**REF:** A000	**MODULE FUNCTION:** Create the Consumption Report		
INPUT	PROCESSING		REF:	OUTPUT
1. Consumption Disk	1. Initialize			1. Consumption Report
File	2. Obtain the input data			
	3. Process the detail records		B000	
	4. Print the final totals		B010	
	5. Terminate			

Figure 5-32 IPO Chart

There are five major processing tasks which must take place in order to create the Consumption Report — these are initialize, obtain the input data, process the detail records, print the final totals, and terminate. The tasks of initialize and obtain the input data are the same as have been used in previous programs.

The Process the Detail Records task differs from previous programs in that it is a more generalized statement of the task to be performed than has been used previously. It is more generalized because the processing which must be accomplished in order to perform the calculations and format the print line is more complex than in previous programs. Since it is more complex, a more generalized statement of the major processing task to be performed should be made. The programmer would then analyze the task to determine if it is of sufficient complexity to require a separate, lower-level module.

The next major processing task is to Print the Final Totals. This too differs from previous programs in that the program in this chapter requires not only the detail lines to be printed on the report but also the final total line. It is not sufficient to merely state that the report must be written. It is necessary to specify that two major areas must be processed — the detail record processing and the final total processing. The last major processing task is Terminate.

After the IPO Chart has been prepared by the programmer, the major processing tasks must be analyzed to determine if the module should be decomposed into lower-level modules. This determination is made by analyzing each major processing task with regard to the function it is to perform and also with regard to the amount of processing which is required in order to accomplish the task. In Figure 5–32, the tasks of Initialize and Obtain the Input Data do not require significant processing.

The task of Process the Detail Records, however, does require significant processing. In addition, it is a well-defined function which must be accomplished in order to transform the input to the output. Therefore, the major processing task of Process the Detail Records should be made into a lower-level module. A further review of the IPO Chart reveals that the major processing task of Print the Final Totals is also a specific, well-defined function which must be performed within the program and it may also contain a significant amount of processing. Thus, the major processing task of Print the Final Totals should be made into a separate, lower-level module.

The Terminate task does not require much processing, so it is not placed in a separate module.

When there is more than a single module in a program, a Hierarchy Chart is drawn to show the relationship between the modules within the program. Figure 5–33 illustrates the hierarchy chart for the sample program.

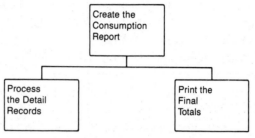

Figure 5 - 33 Hierarchy Chart

The modules which process the detail records and print the final totals are both under the module whose function is to create the consumption report. In the program, the Create the Consumption Report module will cause both the Process the Detail Records module and Print the Final Totals module to be executed. However, the two modules, Process the Detail Records and Print the Final Totals, will never reference one another; that is, no instructions in the Process the Detail Records module will cause any processing in the Print the Final Totals module to be executed, and vice versa. Thus, the hierarchy chart not only shows the relationships between modules but also shows which modules control other modules.

After the structure of the modules on the second level of the program has been defined through the use of a hierarchy chart, the next step is to define the major processing tasks for each of the modules on the second level. Thus, an IPO Chart for the module whose function is to process the detail records and an IPO Chart for the module whose function is to print the final totals must be developed by the programmer.

The IPO Chart for the module whose function is to process the detail records is illustrated in Figure 5–34.

IPO CHART				
PROGRAM: Consumption Report	**PROGRAMMER:** Forsythe			**DATE:** Oct. 30
MODULE NAME: Process Detail Records	**REF:** B000	**MODULE FUNCTION:** Process the Detail Records		
INPUT	**PROCESSING**		**REF:**	**OUTPUT**
1. Consumption Disk	1. Format print line			1. Detail Print Line
Record	2. Perform detail calculations			2. Updated Final Total
2. Final Total	3. Update final totals			Accumulators
Accumulators	4. Write the detail line			

Figure 5 - 34 IPO Chart for the Process the Detail Records Module

The same form is used for the module whose function is to Process the Detail Records as is used for the module whose function is to Create the Consumption Report. The program name is the same; however, the module name and module function are different.

The output from the module, which is either written on an external device or is used by other modules in the program, is the detail print line and the updated final total accumulators. The detail print line is printed on the printer, and the final total accumulators are used by another module within the program.

The input to the module, which is the data on which the module is to operate, is the consumption disk record and the final total accumulators. The consumption records contain the data to be used in formatting the report and performing the required calculations. The final total accumulators are input to the module because they contain data (the accumulated totals) which will be used in calculations within the module. Whenever data is required for calculations within the module, the data should be specified as input to the module.

The major processing tasks which are required to process the detail records are specified on the IPO Chart. They consist of formatting the print line, performing the detail calculations, updating the final totals, and writing the detail line. These are the tasks which are necessary in order to process the detail records.

In the IPO Chart in Figure 5-34, the reference number (REF) for the module is B000, whereas the reference number for the Create the Consumption Report module is A000 (see Figure 5-32). The reference number is used to indicate the hierarchy of the modules within a program and to illustrate their relationship to one another. The hierarchy chart for the program with the reference numbers included is illustrated in Figure 5-35.

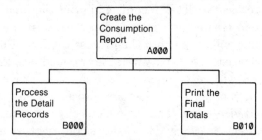

Figure 5-35 Hierarchy Chart with Reference Numbers

The highest level module (Create the Consumption Report) contains the prefix A in the reference number. The second level modules contain the prefix B in their reference numbers. In this manner, the prefix letter is used to indicate the level on which the particular module is found within the program. The numbers are incremented by 10 (ie., the first is 000 and the second is 010) so as to give a unique number to each module on a given level.

In order to illustrate on the IPO Chart that processing tasks are going to be accomplished in separate modules, the REF column is used to indicate the reference number of those tasks which are separate modules. In Figure 5-32, the entry for the task Process the Detail Records is B000, and the entry for the task Print the Final Totals is B010. In this manner, it is clear which tasks specified on the IPO Chart are going to be accomplished by separate modules within the program.

After the IPO Chart for the module whose function is to Process the Detail Records is completed, the programmer would then complete the IPO Chart for the module whose function is to Print the Final Totals. This IPO Chart is illustrated in Figure 5-36.

As with the previous IPO Charts, the IPO Chart for the Print the Final Totals module contains the standard identification material. The reference number is B010, which is the same as that contained on the hierarchy chart in Figure 5-35. The output from the module is the Final Total Line which is printed on the report. The input to the module is the Final Total Accumulators, which contain the totals accumulated in the module which processed the detail records. The major processing tasks are to Format the Final Total Line and to Print the Final

IPO CHART				
PROGRAM: Consumption Report	**PROGRAMMER:** Forsythe			**DATE:** Oct. 30
MODULE NAME: Print Final Totals	**REF:** B010	**MODULE FUNCTION:** Print the Final Totals		
INPUT	**PROCESSING**		**REF:**	**OUTPUT**
1. Final Total	1. Format final total line			1. Final Total Line
Accumulators	2. Print final total line			

Figure 5-36 IPO Chart for the Print the Final Totals Module

Total Line.

    After the modules on the second level within the hierarchy of the program are defined using IPO Charts, the programmer must once again review each of the modules to determine if further decomposition is required. For the module which processes the detail records (Figure 5-34), each of the major processing tasks is relatively simple and does not require extensive programming to accomplish. Therefore, the decision is that the module need not be decomposed further. An analysis of the module which is to print the final totals yields a similar result. Therefore, the modules for the program have been completely defined. Their relationship to one another is illustrated in Figure 5-37.

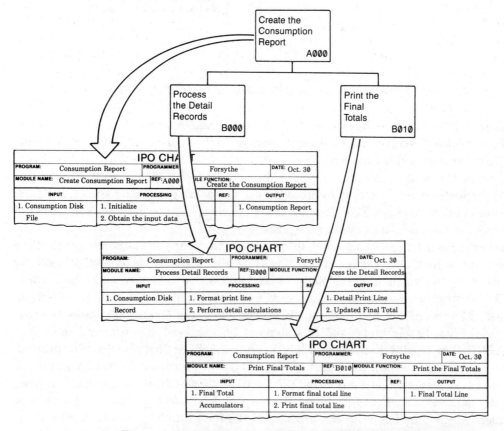

Figure 5-37 Relationship of Hierarchy Chart and IPO Charts

    Each module in the hierarchy chart has a corresponding definition on the IPO Chart. An IPO Chart is prepared for each module within the program.

Pseudocode Specifications

Once the IPO Charts and the related Hierarchy Chart are complete, the programmer must design the logic for the program. The logic is designed using pseudocode written on the Pseudocode Specifications form. The Pseudocode Specifications for the Create Consumption Report module are illustrated in Figure 5-38.

PSEUDOCODE SPECIFICATIONS

PROGRAM: Consumption Report	PROGRAMMER: Forsythe	DATE: Oct. 30

MODULE NAME: Create Consumption Report	REF: A000	MODULE FUNCTION: Create Consumption Report

PSEUDOCODE	REF:	DATA BASES, FILES, RECORDS, FIELDS REQUIRED
Open the files		Consumption disk file
Write the heading lines		Consumption report file
Set space control for double spacing		Heading lines
Read an input record		Printer spacing field
IF there is a record		Double space control character
PERFORM UNTIL no more input records		Input record area
Process detail records	B000	Meter number
Read an input record		Previous reading
ENDPERFORM		Present reading
Print the final totals	B010	Days billed
ENDIF		There is a record indicator
Close the files		No more records indicator
Stop run		

Figure 5-38 Hierarchy Chart and Pseudocode for A000 Module

The first step in the module is to open the files. The headings are then written on the report, and the spacing control is set for double spacing so the first detail line will be double spaced. The first input record is then read.

In some cases, there may not be any input records at all. Although this is unusual, it is a possibility. If there are no input records to process, then the detail processing and printing the final totals should not take place. Therefore, an If statement is used to determine if the detail processing and final total printing should take place.

An If statement is used to test for a condition which can occur within the program. If the specified condition occurs, then certain processing is to take place. If the condition does not occur, then other processing should take place. In the pseudocode in Figure 5-38, the If statement is used to test whether there are any records to process. This is specified by the statement, "If there is a record." When using an If statement, if the condition is true, the processing specified immediately under the If statement is processed. Therefore, if there is a record, the PERFORM UNTIL statement will be executed and the final totals will be printed.

If there is not an input record, these statements will not be processed. Instead, control will be passed to the statements following the ENDIF statement. The ENDIF statement indicates where the effect of the If statement terminates. In the pseudocode in Figure 5-38, the effect of the If statement terminates following the printing of the final totals. It will be recalled that when coding in COBOL, the effect of the If statement terminates where a period is specified.

The word IF will always be capitalized because it, like the word PERFORM, has special meaning within pseudocode. It is used to indicate that a condition within a program is to be tested. An If statement in pseudocode must always be terminated by an ENDIF statement.

The ENDIF statement will always be capitalized and should be vertically aligned with the If statement it terminates. In this manner, it is easy to see the beginning and end of the If statement. The processing which is to be accomplished if the condition tested is true should be indented, as in Figure 5-38, so it can be easily seen what processing will take place.

As noted, if there is a record, the detail records will be processed until there are no more records. Then the final totals will be printed, the files closed, and the program terminated.

The data bases, files, records, and fields required for the program are also shown in Figure 5-38. While most of the entries are similar to those shown in previous programs, it should be noted that two indicators are needed to implement the logic shown by the pseudocode. The first indicator, the "There is a Record" indicator, is used by the If statement to determine if there are any records to process. The second indicator, the "No More Records" indicator, is used by the PERFORM UNTIL statement to determine if there are more records to process.

Since separate modules and separate IPO Charts were designed for the functions of processing the detail records and printing the final totals, pseudocode must be developed to express the logic for these modules. The Pseudocode Specifications for the module whose function is to process the detail records is illustrated in Figure 5-39.

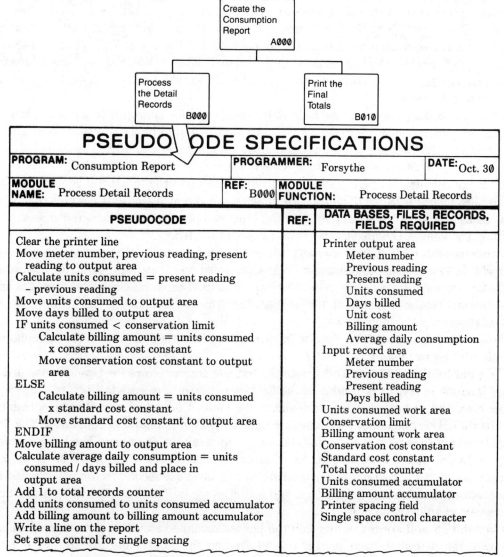

Figure 5-39 Hierarchy Chart and Pseudocode for B000 Module

The first step within the module is to clear the printer line. The next step is to move the Meter Number, Previous Reading, and Present Reading from the input area to the printer output area. Then, the Units Consumed are calculated by subtracting the Previous Reading from the Present Reading and moved to the output area. The Days Billed are then moved to the output area.

Next, the Billing Amount must be calculated. Since the Billing Amount depends upon the Units Consumed, the relationship checked to calculate the Billing Amount is whether the value in the Units Consumed field is less than the Conservation Limit or whether the Units Consumed field is not less than the Conservation Limit. This relationship is tested through the use of the If statement that specifies "If units consumed < conservation limit." When the condition stated in the If statement is true, the statements specified immediately below the If statement are executed. Therefore, if the Units Consumed is less than the Conservation Limit, the Billing Amount is calculated by multiplying Units Consumed by the Conservation Cost Constant. After calculating the Billing Amount, the Conservation Cost Constant is then moved to the output area.

When the condition stated in the If statement is false, the statements following the ELSE portion of the If statement will be executed. Therefore, if the Units Consumed are not less than the Conservation Limit, the Billing Amount will be calculated by multiplying Units Consumed by the Standard Cost Constant. The Standard Cost Constant is then moved to the output area.

The word ELSE is used to indicate the processing that will occur if the condition tested is not true. It is capitalized in the pseudocode because, like the word IF, it has special meaning within the pseudocode. In addition, the word ELSE should be vertically aligned with its corresponding IF word.

After the Billing Amount has been calculated and the appropriate constant has been moved to the printer output area, the Billing Amount is moved to the printer output area and the Average Daily Consumption is calculated by dividing the Units Consumed by the Days Billed.

After the calculation of the Average Daily Consumption, the final total counter and accumulators are incremented. A final total counter is a field which contains a count that is kept within the program. In the sample program, the number of records processed is counted. Therefore, the value 1 is added to the Total Records Counter.

An accumulator is a field in memory where a value is accumulated during the processing of records. In the sample program, the Units Consumed and the Billing Amount are accumulated to be printed after all records have been processed. Therefore, Units Consumed is added to the Units Consumed Accumulator, and Billing Amount is added to the Billing Amount Accumulator.

The processing which takes place to increment the final total counter and accumulators is illustrated in Figure 5-40.

The final total counter for Total Records and the accumulators for Units Consumed and Billing Amount are set to zero prior to the first record being processed. When the first record is processed, the values which are calculated for Units Consumed and Billing Amount are added to the Units Consumed Accumulator and the Billing Amount Accumulator. The literal value 1 is added to the Total Records Counter to indicate that one record has been processed. When the second record is processed, the same calculations occur. Thus, since the counter and accumulators contain the values from the first record, after the second record is processed they will contain the total values for the first and second records. These totals will be accumulated for each record which is processed.

After the Total Records Counter and the Units Consumed and Billing Amount Accumulators have been processed, the detail line is printed on the report, and the spacing is set for single spacing (see Figure 5-39).

First Record

Before Execution

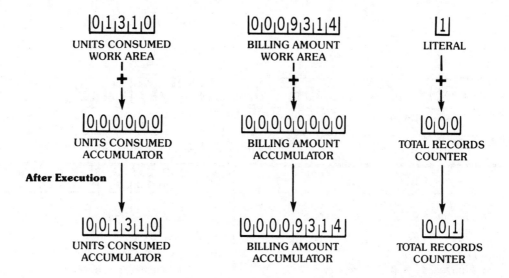

Second Record

Before Execution

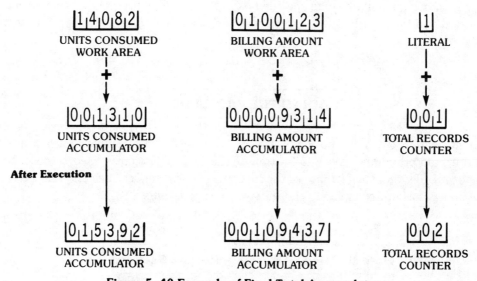

Figure 5-40 Example of Final Total Accumulators

The Pseudocode Specifications for the module which prints the final totals must also be prepared by the programmer. The Pseudocode Specifications together with the Hierarchy Chart are illustrated in Figure 5–41.

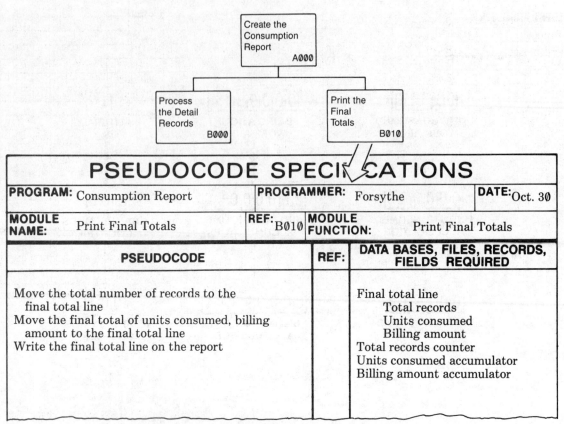

Figure 5-41 Hierarchy Chart and Pseudocode for B010 Module

Printing the final totals consists of moving the values in the total counter and accumulators to the final total print line and then printing the final total line.

On all of the Pseudocode Specifications forms, the Data Bases, Files, Records, and Fields required for processing should also be specified as in the previous programs. When this activity is completed and the pseudocode has been reviewed, then the programmer is ready to begin coding the program.

CODING THE PROGRAM

The Identification Division and Environment Division for the sample program are very similar to previous programs. The File Section of the Data Division is used to describe the input and output files and the formats of the input record and report line. The File Section in the sample program is quite similar to those in previous programs.

Data Division — Working-Storage Section

The Working-Storage Section of the Data Division contains several new entries, including the use of condition names, the use of work areas for the intermediate storage of answers resulting from arithmetic operations, and the use of final total counters and accumulators to store accumulated values. These entries are illustrated in Figure 5-42.

```
004170 WORKING-STORAGE SECTION.
004180
004190 01  PROGRAM-INDICATORS.
004200     05  ARE-THERE-MORE-RECORDS      PIC X(3)       VALUE 'YES'.
005010         88  THERE-IS-A-RECORD                      VALUE 'YES'.
005020         88  THERE-ARE-NO-MORE-RECORDS              VALUE 'NO '.
005030
005040 01  PROGRAM-CONSTANTS.
005050     05  CONSERVATION-COST-CONSTANT  PIC V9(4)      VALUE .0656.
005060     05  STANDARD-COST-CONSTANT      PIC V9(4)      VALUE .0711.
005070     05  CONSERVATION-LIMIT          PIC 9(5)       VALUE 00240.
005080
005090 01  WORK-AREAS.
005100     05  UNITS-CONSUMED-WORK         PIC S9(5).
005110     05  BILLING-AMOUNT-WORK         PIC S9(5)V99.
005120
005130 01  TOTAL-ACCUMULATORS-COUNTERS.
005140     05  TOTAL-RECORDS-COUNT         PIC S999       VALUE ZERO.
005150     05  UNITS-CONSUMED-ACCUM        PIC S9(6)      VALUE ZERO.
005160     05  BILLING-AMOUNT-ACCUM        PIC S9(6)V99 VALUE ZERO.
```

Figure 5-42 Working-Storage Section of Data Division

Condition Names

The first entry in the Working-Storage Section is 01 PROGRAM-INDICATORS. The group item (PROGRAM-INDICATORS) and the elementary item (ARE-THERE-MORE-RECORDS) are defined in exactly the same manner as in previous programs. However, two level-88 items (THERE-IS-A-RECORD and THERE-ARE-NO-MORE-RECORDS) are defined. Level-88 items assign a condition name to a value which can appear within a field. The condition name THERE-IS-A-RECORD is given to the value YES, and the condition name THERE-ARE-NO-MORE-RECORDS is given to the value NO within the field called ARE-THERE-MORE-RECORDS.

Referencing a condition name in a conditional statement within the Procedure Division is equivalent to testing to determine if the value represented by the condition name is stored in the associated field. Thus, the entry IF THERE-IS-A-RECORD is the same as specifying IF ARE-THERE-MORE-RECORDS = 'YES'.

The entries in the Data Division to define the condition names, together with the format notation for level-88 items, are illustrated in Figure 5-43.

```
004190 01  PROGRAM-INDICATORS.
004200     05  ARE-THERE-MORE-RECORDS      PIC X(3)       VALUE 'YES'.
005010         88  THERE-IS-A-RECORD                      VALUE 'YES'.
005020         88  THERE-ARE-NO-MORE-RECORDS             VALUE 'NO '.
```

$$88 \text{ condition-name; } \left\{ \begin{matrix} \text{VALUE IS} \\ \text{VALUES ARE} \end{matrix} \right\} \text{ literal-1} \left[\left\{ \begin{matrix} \text{THROUGH} \\ \text{THRU} \end{matrix} \right\} \text{ literal-2} \right.$$

$$\left. \left[\text{, literal-3} \left[\left\{ \begin{matrix} \text{THROUGH} \\ \text{THRU} \end{matrix} \right\} \text{ literal-4} \right] \right] \ldots \quad . \right]$$

Figure 5-43 Example of Condition Names

A condition name must be specified as a level-88 item. It immediately follows the definition of the field to which it applies. Thus, in Figure 5–43, the two level-88 items immediately follow the ARE-THERE-MORE-RECORDS field definition. The condition name entry must contain two parts — the condition name itself and the value which is to be associated with the condition name. The condition names are THERE-IS-A-RECORD and THERE-ARE-NO-MORE-RECORDS. The value to be associated with each of these condition names is indicated through the use of the Value clause. The clause VALUE 'YES' is included to indicate that referencing the condition name THERE-IS-A-RECORD is equivalent to testing the ARE-THERE-MORE-RECORDS field for the value YES. Similarly, the clause VALUE 'NO ' is specified with the condition name THERE-ARE-NO-MORE-RECORDS to indicate that referencing that condition name is the same as testing to determine if the ARE-THERE-MORE-RECORDS field contains the value NO .

Condition Names and the Perform Statement

In previous programs the Until clause within the Perform statement contained a condition which had to be satisfied in order for the loop to be stopped. This type of Perform statement is illustrated in Figure 5–44.

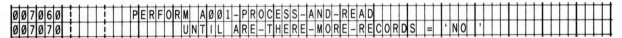

Figure 5 - 44 Perform Statement from Previous Program

The A001-PROCESS-AND-READ paragraph will be performed until such time as the field ARE-THERE-MORE-RECORDS contains the value NO . When the field does contain this value, the loop will be terminated. Although this Perform statement executes properly, the use of a condition name can make the statement clearer in terms of reading the program. In Figure 5–43, the condition name THERE-ARE-NO-MORE-RECORDS is given the value NO . The Perform statement illustrated in Figure 5–45 is written using this condition name.

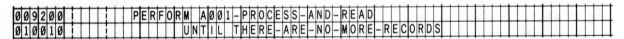

Figure 5 - 45 Use of a Condition Name in a Perform Statement

The Perform statement in Figure 5–45 will work exactly the same as the Perform statement in Figure 5–44 provided the condition name THERE-ARE-NO-MORE-RECORDS is equated to the value NO being in the field ARE-THERE-MORE-RECORDS. From the use of the condition name, the exact reason for ceasing the looping is specified. It is to be terminated when there are no more records. This is clearer than specifying the equal condition as in Figure 5–44 and should normally be used when a value in the field can be equated to a condition name.

Definition of Constants and Work Areas in Working Storage

Constant values are values which can be used in calculations or for other purposes within the program which will not change during the execution of the program. In the sample program in this chapter, three constant values are required. These constant values, together with the two work areas that are required in the program, are illustrated in Figure 5–46.

```
004170 WORKING-STORAGE SECTION.
       :
005040 01  PROGRAM-CONSTANTS.
005050     05  CONSERVATION-COST-CONSTANT      PIC V9(4)    VALUE .0656.
005060     05  STANDARD-COST-CONSTANT          PIC V9(4)    VALUE .0711.
005070     05  CONSERVATION-LIMIT              PIC 9(5)     VALUE 00240.
005080
005090 01  WORK-AREAS.
005100     05  UNITS-CONSUMED-WORK         PIC S9(5).
005110     05  BILLING-AMOUNT-WORK         PIC S9(5)V99.
```

Figure 5-46 Working-Storage Entries for Work Areas

The constants required for the program are the CONSERVATION-COST-CONSTANT containing the cost for each unit of electricity if the conservation limit is not exceeded; the STANDARD-COST-CONSTANT, which is the cost if the conservation limit is reached or exceeded; and the CONSERVATION-LIMIT, which is the number of units under which the conservation cost is used. The group item, PROGRAM-CONSTANTS, identifies all of the elementary items as constants used in the program. The use of the letter V as the first character in the Picture clauses for the cost fields indicates that there are no digits to the left of the number being defined (the costs are cents only). The Value clause numbers begin with a decimal point for the same reason.

In Figure 5–46, the two work areas required for the sample program are also defined. One work area is used to store the Units Consumed, and the other is used to store the Billing Amount. The group item WORK-AREAS is used to designate that the elementary items following it are to be used as work areas. The level numbers and data-names are utilized the same as in previous examples. There is, however, a new entry in specifying the attributes of the fields: the Sign clause.

The character S is used in the Picture clause to indicate the presence of an operational sign. It must be the leftmost character of the Picture clause. When the S is included with a Picture clause for numeric data, any data which is stored in the field as a result of a Move statement or an Arithmetic statement (Add, Subtract, Multiply, Divide, Compute) will be stored with the appropriate positive or negative sign. If the letter S is not included in the Picture clause, then the absolute value of the result of the calculation will be placed in the field regardless of the sign generated from the arithmetic operation.

Whenever the result of an arithmetic operation is to be placed into a work area or a numeric value moved to a work area, the S should always be included in the Picture clause unless a value without a positive or negative sign is desired. If the S is not included, additional code is generated by the compiler to ensure that the data in the field is stored as an absolute value; and this coding is generally unnecessary. Therefore, unless an absolute value is required, the S should always be included on any numeric field which will contain the result of an arithmetic operation or any numeric field to which a numeric value will be moved.

Definition of Total Accumulators

In order to accumulate final totals, areas within main memory must be defined in which to store the accumulated values. These areas are defined within the Working-Storage Section. The portion of the Working-Storage Section which includes the total accumulators and counters is illustrated in Figure 5–47.

0 0 4 1 7 0	WORKING-STORAGE SECTION.

. . .

0 0 5 1 3 0	0 1	TOTAL-ACCUMULATORS-COUNTERS.		
0 0 5 1 4 0		0 5	TOTAL-RECORDS-COUNT	PIC S999 VALUE ZERO.
0 0 5 1 5 0		0 5	UNITS-CONSUMED-ACCUM	PIC S9(6) VALUE ZERO.
0 0 5 1 6 0		0 5	BILLING-AMOUNT-ACCUM	PIC S9(6)V99 VALUE ZERO.

Figure 5-47 Definition of Total Accumulators

The group name TOTAL-ACCUMULATORS-COUNTERS is used to identify that the following elementary items will be used as final total accumulators and counters. The necessary fields for the sample program are the Total Records Counter, the Units Consumed Accumulator, and the Billing Amount Accumulator. Since all three fields will contain the result of an arithmetic operation, the S is included in the Picture clause of each field.

Whenever fields are to be used to accumulate values, they should have an initial value of zero. Therefore, the Value clause is used for all counters and accumulators to give them an initial value of zero. The word ZERO is a Figurative Constant which will cause the value zero to be placed in the field before execution of the program begins.

Defining the Final Total Line

The final total line must be defined in the Working-Storage Section. The coding to define the final total line is illustrated in Figure 5–48.

0 0 8 0 3 0	0 1	TOTAL-LINES.		
0 0 8 0 4 0		0 5	FINAL-TOTAL-LINE.	
0 0 8 0 5 0			1 0 CARRIAGE-CONTROL	PIC X.
0 0 8 0 6 0			1 0 FILLER	PIC X(13) VALUE
0 0 8 0 7 0				'TOTAL RECORDS'.
0 0 8 0 8 0			1 0 FILLER	PIC X VALUE SPACES.
0 0 8 0 9 0			1 0 TOTAL-RECORDS-FINAL	PIC ZZ9.
0 0 8 1 0 0			1 0 FILLER	PIC X(11) VALUE SPACES.
0 0 8 1 1 0			1 0 UNITS-CONSUMED-FINAL	PIC ZZZ,ZZ9.
0 0 8 1 2 0			1 0 FILLER	PIC X(19) VALUE SPACES.
0 0 8 1 3 0			1 0 BILLING-AMOUNT-FINAL	PIC $$$$,$$$.99.
0 0 8 1 4 0			1 0 FILLER	PIC X(67) VALUE SPACES.

PRINTER SPACING CHART

1							
2	METER	PREVIOUS	PRESENT	UNITS	DAYS	UNIT	BILLING	AVER. DAILY
3	NUMBER	READING	READING	CONSUMED	BILLED	COST	AMOUNT	CONSUMPTION
4								
5	9999999	ZZZZ9	ZZZZ9	ZZ,ZZ9	Z9	.9999	ZZ,ZZZ.99	ZZ,ZZZ.9
6	9999999	ZZZZ9	ZZZZ9	ZZ,ZZ9	Z9	.9999	ZZ,ZZZ.99	ZZ,ZZZ.9
7								
8	TOTAL RECORDS ZZ9			ZZZ,ZZ9			$$$,$$$.99	
9								

Figure 5-48 Definition of Final Total Line

The entries in the Working-Storage Section are used to define the Final Total Line. The constant "TOTAL READINGS" is defined, together with the fields which will contain the final totals. The spacing of the total line must correspond to the format illustrated on the printer spacing chart. The entire line should be 133 characters in length.

PROCEDURE DIVISION

The A000-CREATE-CONSUMPTION-REPORT module in the Procedure Division is illustrated in Figure 5-49.

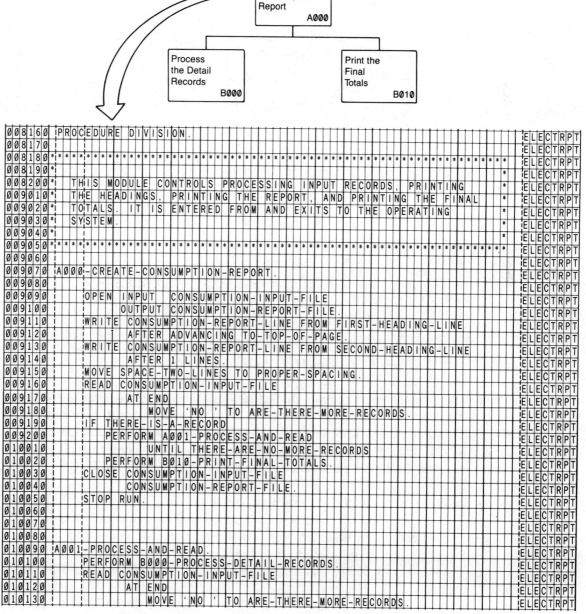

Figure 5-49 A000-CREATE-CONSUMPTION-REPORT Module

The A000-CREATE-CONSUMPTION-REPORT module opens the files, writes the report headings, and reads the first input record. If there is a record, the A001-PROCESS-AND-READ paragraph is performed until there are no more input records. The A001-PROCESS-AND-READ paragraph causes the detail record to be processed and then reads another input record. After all of the detail records have been read and processed, the final totals are printed, the files are closed, and the program is terminated.

Condition Names and the If Statement

As illustrated previously in this chapter, condition names can be used in the Perform Until statement. Condition names are also used in an If statement in the sample program (Figure 5-50).

```
004170  WORKING-STORAGE SECTION.
004180
004190  01  PROGRAM-INDICATORS.
004200      05  ARE-THERE-MORE-RECORDS    PIC X(3)    VALUE 'YES'.
005010          88  THERE-IS-A-RECORD                 VALUE 'YES'.
005020          88  THERE-ARE-NO-MORE-RECORDS         VALUE 'NO '.

          .
          .
          .

008160  PROCEDURE DIVISION.

          .
          .
          .

009160      READ CONSUMPTION-INPUT-FILE
009170          AT END
009180              MOVE 'NO ' TO ARE-THERE-MORE-RECORDS.
009190      IF THERE-IS-A-RECORD
009200          PERFORM A001-PROCESS-AND-READ
010010              UNTIL THERE-ARE-NO-MORE-RECORDS
010020      PERFORM B010-PRINT-FINAL-TOTALS.
```

Figure 5-50 Example of Condition Names

In the Procedure Division coding shown in Figure 5-50, the Read statement is used to read the first input record in the file. If an attempt is made to read an input record and no input record is read, meaning there is not one input record in the file, the value NO is moved to the indicator ARE-THERE-MORE-RECORDS. If there is an input record, the value YES will remain in the indicator field since the indicator was given an initial value of YES with the Value clause.

When the If statement on line 009190 is executed, the condition THERE-IS-A-RECORD will be true if an input record was read. Therefore, the processing for the detail records and final totals will be accomplished. If no input record was read, the condition THERE-IS-A-RECORD will be false, and control will pass to the statement following the period that ends the effect of the If statement (010030). This coding implements the logic expressed by the pseudocode in Figure 5-38.

When a detail record is read, it is processed by the B000-PROCESS-DETAIL-RECORDS module, which is illustrated in Figure 5-51.

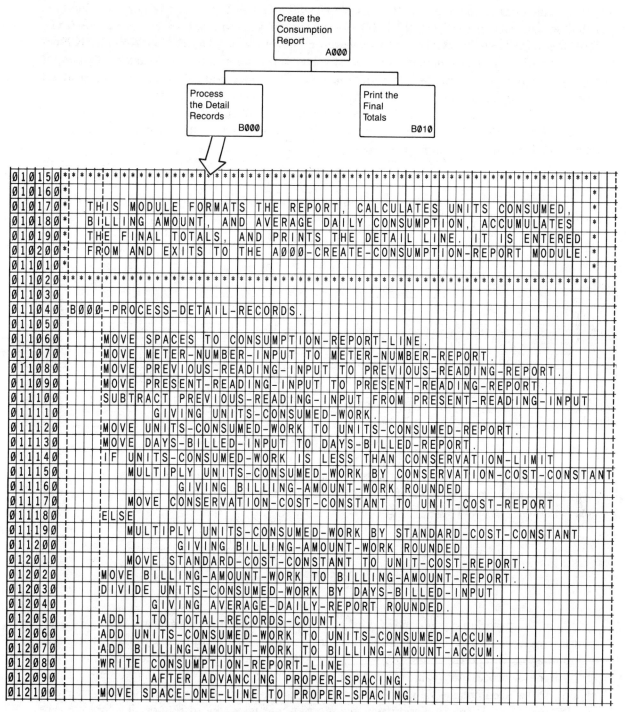

Figure 5-51 B000-PROCESS-DETAIL-RECORDS Module

The COBOL statements closely follow the pseudocode which was developed for this module (see Figure 5-39). The first portion of the coding clears the printer output area and moves the fields in the input record to the output area.

The Units Consumed value is then calculated and moved to the output area, along with the data in the DAYS-BILLED-INPUT field. If the value in the UNITS-CONSUMED-WORK field is less than the value in the CONSERVATION-LIMIT field, then the Billing Amount is calculated as illustrated previously and the CONSERVATION-COST-CONSTANT is moved to the output area. If the value in the UNITS-CONSUMED-WORK field is not less than the value in the CONSERVATION-LIMIT field, the Billing Amount is calculated and the STANDARD-COST-CONSTANT is moved to the output area. The Billing Amount is then moved to the output area, and the Average Daily Consumption is calculated. The Total Records Counter is incremented by 1, and the Units Consumed and Billing Amounts are added to the final total accumulators. A line is printed and the space control is set for single spacing. This completes the processing in the B000-PROCESS-DETAIL-RECORDS.

The B010-PRINT-FINAL-TOTALS module is used to print the final totals on the report. This module is illustrated in Figure 5-52.

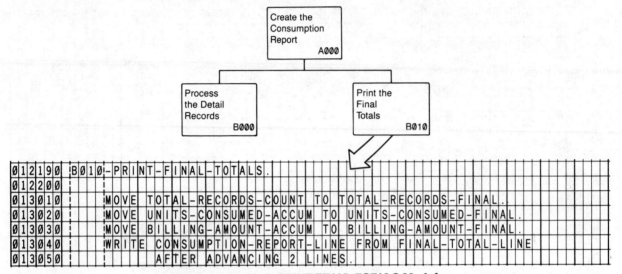

Figure 5-52 B010-PRINT-FINAL-TOTALS Module

In Figure 5-52, the values in the total counter and accumulators are moved to the final total line and the line is written on the report. This corresponds to the pseudocode which was developed for this module (see Figure 5-41).

Summary

From the program design and coding of the consumption report program, it can be seen that it is extremely important in the earliest design phases to carefully analyze the processing which must occur and the major processing tasks which are necessary; and to decompose each of these major processing tasks into individual modules if there is a significant amount of processing to be accomplished and if each task represents a specific function to be performed within a program. Using this approach, the programmer may concentrate on developing accurate, efficient processing in each individual module rather than trying to consider all aspects of the entire problem at one time.

Source Listing

The source listing for the sample program is contained on this and the following pages.

```
PP 5740-CB1 RELEASE 2.3 + PTF 8 - UP13477        IBM OS/VS COBOL   JULY 24, 1978        11.37.06  DATE FEB 22,1985

     1                      11.37.06       FEB 22,1985

00001   001010 IDENTIFICATION DIVISION.                                          ELECTRPT
00002   001020                                                                   ELECTRPT
00003   001030 PROGRAM-ID.      ELECTRPT.                                        ELECTRPT
00004   001040 AUTHOR.          FORSYTHE.                                        ELECTRPT
00005   001050 INSTALLATION.    BREA.                                           ELECTRPT
00006   001060 DATE-WRITTEN.    NOV  7,1984.                                    ELECTRPT
00007   001070 DATE-COMPILED.   FEB 22,1985.                                    ELECTRPT
00008   001080 SECURITY.        UNCLASSIFIED.                                   ELECTRPT
00009   001090                                                                   ELECTRPT
00010   001100******************************************************************  ELECTRPT
00011   001110*                                                               *  ELECTRPT
00012   001120*   THIS PROGRAM PRODUCES AN ELECTRICITY CONSUMPTION REPORT      *  ELECTRPT
00013   001130*   CALCULATING UNITS CONSUMED, BILLING AMOUNT, AND AVERAGE      *  ELECTRPT
00014   001140*   DAILY CONSUMPTION. UNITS CONSUMED IS CALCULATED BY           *  ELECTRPT
00015   001150*   SUBTRACTING PREVIOUS READING FROM PRESENT READING. BILLING   *  ELECTRPT
00016   001160*   AMOUNT IS CALCULATED BY MULTIPLYING UNIT COST BY UNITS       *  ELECTRPT
00017   001170*   CONSUMED. AVERAGE DAILY CONSUMPTION IS CALCULATED BY         *  ELECTRPT
00018   001180*   DIVIDING UNITS CONSUMED BY THE NUMBER OF DAYS BILLED.        *  ELECTRPT
00019   001190*                                                               *  ELECTRPT
00020   001200******************************************************************  ELECTRPT
00021   002010                                                                   ELECTRPT
00022   002020                                                                   ELECTRPT
00023   002030                                                                   ELECTRPT
00024   002040 ENVIRONMENT DIVISION.                                            ELECTRPT
00025   002050                                                                   ELECTRPT
00026   002060 CONFIGURATION SECTION.                                           ELECTRPT
00027   002070                                                                   ELECTRPT
00028   002080 SOURCE-COMPUTER. IBM-4381.                                       ELECTRPT
00029   002090 OBJECT-COMPUTER. IBM-4381.                                       ELECTRPT
00030   002100 SPECIAL-NAMES.   C01 IS TO-TOP-OF-PAGE.                          ELECTRPT
00031   002110                                                                   ELECTRPT
00032   002120 INPUT-OUTPUT SECTION.                                            ELECTRPT
00033   002130                                                                   ELECTRPT
00034   002140 FILE-CONTROL.                                                    ELECTRPT
00035   002150     SELECT CONSUMPTION-INPUT-FILE                                ELECTRPT
00036   002160         ASSIGN TO UT-S-ELECDATA.                                 ELECTRPT
00037   002170     SELECT CONSUMPTION-REPORT-FILE                               ELECTRPT
00038   002180         ASSIGN TO UT-S-ELECPRNT.                                 ELECTRPT
```

```
     2                      11.37.06       FEB 22,1985

00039   002190/                                                                  ELECTRPT
00040   002200 DATA DIVISION.                                                   ELECTRPT
00041   003010                                                                   ELECTRPT
00042   003020 FILE SECTION.                                                    ELECTRPT
00043   003030                                                                   ELECTRPT
00044   003040 FD  CONSUMPTION-INPUT-FILE                                       ELECTRPT
00045   003050     RECORD CONTAINS 19 CHARACTERS                                ELECTRPT
00046   003060     LABEL RECORDS ARE STANDARD                                   ELECTRPT
00047   003070     DATA RECORD IS CONSUMPTION-INPUT-RECORD.                     ELECTRPT
00048   003080 01  CONSUMPTION-INPUT-RECORD.                                    ELECTRPT
00049   003090     05   METER-NUMBER-INPUT       PIC 9(7).                      ELECTRPT
00050   003100     05   PREVIOUS-READING-INPUT   PIC 9(5).                      ELECTRPT
00051   003110     05   PRESENT-READING-INPUT    PIC 9(5).                      ELECTRPT
00052   003120     05   DAYS-BILLED-INPUT        PIC 99.                        ELECTRPT
00053   003130                                                                   ELECTRPT
00054   003140 FD  CONSUMPTION-REPORT-FILE                                      ELECTRPT
00055   003150     RECORD CONTAINS 133 CHARACTERS                               ELECTRPT
00056   003160     LABEL RECORDS ARE OMITTED                                    ELECTRPT
00057   003170     DATA RECORD IS CONSUMPTION-REPORT-LINE.                      ELECTRPT
00058   003180 01  CONSUMPTION-REPORT-LINE.                                     ELECTRPT
00059   003190     05   CARRIAGE-CONTROL         PIC X.                         ELECTRPT
00060   003200     05   METER-NUMBER-REPORT      PIC 9(7).                      ELECTRPT
00061   004010     05   FILLER                   PIC X(4).                      ELECTRPT
00062   004020     05   PREVIOUS-READING-REPORT PIC ZZZZ9.                      ELECTRPT
00063   004030     05   FILLER                   PIC X(5).                      ELECTRPT
00064   004040     05   PRESENT-READING-REPORT   PIC ZZZZ9.                     ELECTRPT
00065   004050     05   FILLER                   PIC X(3).                      ELECTRPT
00066   004060     05   UNITS-CONSUMED-REPORT    PIC ZZ,ZZ9.                    ELECTRPT
00067   004070     05   FILLER                   PIC X(6).                      ELECTRPT
00068   004080     05   DAYS-BILLED-REPORT       PIC Z9.                        ELECTRPT
00069   004090     05   FILLER                   PIC X(5).                      ELECTRPT
00070   004100     05   UNIT-COST-REPORT         PIC .9999.                     ELECTRPT
00071   004110     05   FILLER                   PIC X(3).                      ELECTRPT
00072   004120     05   BILLING-AMOUNT-REPORT    PIC ZZ,ZZZ.99.                 ELECTRPT
00073   004130     05   FILLER                   PIC X.                         ELECTRPT
00074   004140     05   AVERAGE-DAILY-REPORT     PIC ZZ,ZZZ.9.                  ELECTRPT
00075   004150     05   FILLER                   PIC X(58).                     ELECTRPT
00076   004160                                                                   ELECTRPT
```

Figure 5-53 Source Listing (Part 1 of 4)

```
         3                  11.37.06      FEB 22,1985

    00077   004170 WORKING-STORAGE SECTION.                                    ELECTRPT
    00078   004180                                                             ELECTRPT
    00079   004190 01  PROGRAM-INDICATORS.                                     ELECTRPT
    00080   004200     05  ARE-THERE-MORE-RECORDS  PIC X(3)     VALUE 'YES'.    ELECTRPT
    00081   005010         88  THERE-IS-A-RECORD               VALUE 'YES'.    ELECTRPT
    00082   005020         88  THERE-ARE-NO-MORE-RECORDS       VALUE 'NO '.    ELECTRPT
    00083   005030                                                             ELECTRPT
    00084   005040 01  PROGRAM-CONSTANTS.                                      ELECTRPT
    00085   005050     05  CONSERVATION-COST-CONSTANT  PIC V9(4)  VALUE .0656. ELECTRPT
    00086   005060     05  STANDARD-COST-CONSTANT      PIC V9(4)  VALUE .0711. ELECTRPT
    00087   005070     05  CONSERVATION-LIMIT          PIC 9(5)   VALUE 00240. ELECTRPT
    00088   005080                                                             ELECTRPT
    00089   005090 01  WORK-AREAS.                                             ELECTRPT
    00090   005100     05  UNITS-CONSUMED-WORK     PIC S9(5).                  ELECTRPT
    00091   005110     05  BILLING-AMOUNT-WORK     PIC S9(5)V99.               ELECTRPT
    00092   005120                                                             ELECTRPT
    00093   005130 01  TOTAL-ACCUMULATORS-COUNTERS.                            ELECTRPT
    00094   005140     05  TOTAL-RECORDS-COUNT     PIC S999    VALUE ZERO.     ELECTRPT
    00095   005150     05  UNITS-CONSUMED-ACCUM    PIC S9(6)   VALUE ZERO.     ELECTRPT
    00096   005160     05  BILLING-AMOUNT-ACCUM    PIC S9(6)V99 VALUE ZERO.    ELECTRPT
    00097   005170                                                             ELECTRPT
    00098   005180 01  PRINTER-CONTROL.                                        ELECTRPT
    00099   005190     05  PROPER-SPACING          PIC 9.                      ELECTRPT
    00100   005200     05  SPACE-ONE-LINE          PIC 9       VALUE 1.        ELECTRPT
    00101   006010     05  SPACE-TWO-LINES         PIC 9       VALUE 2.        ELECTRPT
    00102   006020                                                             ELECTRPT
    00103   006030 01  HEADING-LINES.                                          ELECTRPT
    00104   006040     05  FIRST-HEADING-LINE.                                 ELECTRPT
    00105   006050         10  CARRIAGE-CONTROL   PIC X.                       ELECTRPT
    00106   006060         10  FILLER             PIC X       VALUE SPACES.    ELECTRPT
    00107   006070         10  FILLER             PIC X(5)    VALUE 'METER'.   ELECTRPT
    00108   006080         10  FILLER             PIC X(4)    VALUE SPACES.    ELECTRPT
    00109   006090         10  FILLER             PIC X(8)    VALUE 'PREVIOUS'. ELECTRPT
    00110   006100         10  FILLER             PIC X(2)    VALUE SPACES.    ELECTRPT
    00111   006110         10  FILLER             PIC X(7)    VALUE 'PRESENT'. ELECTRPT
    00112   006120         10  FILLER             PIC X(4)    VALUE SPACES.    ELECTRPT
    00113   006130         10  FILLER             PIC X(5)    VALUE 'UNITS'.   ELECTRPT
    00114   006140         10  FILLER             PIC X(4)    VALUE SPACES.    ELECTRPT
    00115   006150         10  FILLER             PIC X(4)    VALUE 'DAYS'.    ELECTRPT
    00116   006160         10  FILLER             PIC X(5)    VALUE SPACES.    ELECTRPT
    00117   006170         10  FILLER             PIC X(4)    VALUE 'UNIT'.    ELECTRPT
    00118   006180         10  FILLER             PIC X(4)    VALUE SPACES.    ELECTRPT
    00119   006190         10  FILLER             PIC X(7)    VALUE 'BILLING'. ELECTRPT
    00120   006200         10  FILLER             PIC X(2)    VALUE SPACES.    ELECTRPT
    00121   007010         10  FILLER             PIC X(11)   VALUE 'AVER. DAILY'.ELECTRPT
    00122   007020         10  FILLER             PIC X(55)   VALUE SPACES.    ELECTRPT
    00123   007030     05  SECOND-HEADING-LINE.                                ELECTRPT
    00124   007040         10  CARRIAGE-CONTROL   PIC X.                       ELECTRPT
    00125   007050         10  FILLER             PIC X       VALUE SPACES.    ELECTRPT
    00126   007060         10  FILLER             PIC X(6)    VALUE 'NUMBER'.  ELECTRPT
    00127   007070         10  FILLER             PIC X(3)    VALUE SPACES.    ELECTRPT
    00128   007080         10  FILLER             PIC X(7)    VALUE 'READING'. ELECTRPT
    00129   007090         10  FILLER             PIC X(3)    VALUE SPACES.    ELECTRPT
    00130   007100         10  FILLER             PIC X(7)    VALUE 'READING'. ELECTRPT
    00131   007110         10  FILLER             PIC X(2)    VALUE SPACES.    ELECTRPT
    00132   007120         10  FILLER             PIC X(8)    VALUE 'CONSUMED'. ELECTRPT
    00133   007130         10  FILLER             PIC X(2)    VALUE SPACES.    ELECTRPT
    00134   007140         10  FILLER             PIC X(6)    VALUE 'BILLED'.  ELECTRPT
    00135   007150         10  FILLER             PIC X(4)    VALUE SPACES.    ELECTRPT
    00136   007160         10  FILLER             PIC X(4)    VALUE 'COST'.    ELECTRPT
    00137   007170         10  FILLER             PIC X(5)    VALUE SPACES.    ELECTRPT
    00138   007180         10  FILLER             PIC X(6)    VALUE 'AMOUNT'.  ELECTRPT
    00139   007190         10  FILLER             PIC X(2)    VALUE SPACES.    ELECTRPT
    00140   007200         10  FILLER             PIC X(11)   VALUE 'CONSUMPTION'.ELECTRPT
    00141   008010         10  FILLER             PIC X(55)   VALUE SPACES.    ELECTRPT
    00142   008020                                                             ELECTRPT
    00143   008030 01  TOTAL-LINES.                                            ELECTRPT
    00144   008040     05  FINAL-TOTAL-LINE.                                   ELECTRPT
    00145   008050         10  CARRIAGE-CONTROL   PIC X.                       ELECTRPT
    00146   008060         10  FILLER             PIC X(13)   VALUE            ELECTRPT
    00147   008070                                           'TOTAL RECORDS'. ELECTRPT
    00148   008080         10  FILLER             PIC X       VALUE SPACES.    ELECTRPT
    00149   008090         10  TOTAL-RECORDS-FINAL PIC ZZ9.                    ELECTRPT
    00150   008100         10  FILLER             PIC X(11)   VALUE SPACES.    ELECTRPT
    00151   008110         10  UNITS-CONSUMED-FINAL PIC ZZZ,ZZ9.               ELECTRPT
    00152   008120         10  FILLER             PIC X(19)   VALUE SPACES.    ELECTRPT
    00153   008130         10  BILLING-AMOUNT-FINAL PIC $$$$,$$$.99.           ELECTRPT
    00154   008140         10  FILLER             PIC X(67)   VALUE SPACES.    ELECTRPT
```

Figure 5 - 54 Source Listing (Part 2 of 4)

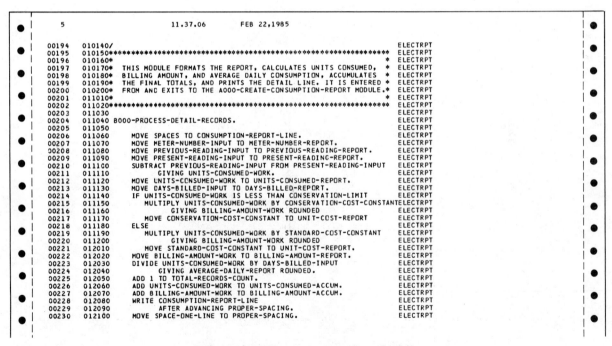

```
                    11.37.06        FEB 22,1985

00155    008150/                                                         ELECTRPT
00156    008160 PROCEDURE DIVISION.                                      ELECTRPT
00157    008170                                                         ELECTRPT
00158    008180*************************************************************** ELECTRPT
00159    008190*                                                     *  ELECTRPT
00160    008200*  THIS MODULE CONTROLS PROCESSING INPUT RECORDS, PRINTING  *  ELECTRPT
00161    009010*  THE HEADINGS, PRINTING THE REPORT, AND PRINTING THE FINAL *  ELECTRPT
00162    009020*  TOTALS. IT IS ENTERED FROM AND EXITS TO THE OPERATING   *  ELECTRPT
00163    009030*  SYSTEM.                                              *  ELECTRPT
00164    009040*                                                     *  ELECTRPT
00165    009050*************************************************************** ELECTRPT
00166    009060                                                         ELECTRPT
00167    009070 A000-CREATE-CONSUMPTION-REPORT.                           ELECTRPT
00168    009080                                                         ELECTRPT
00169    009090     OPEN INPUT  CONSUMPTION-INPUT-FILE                    ELECTRPT
00170    009100          OUTPUT CONSUMPTION-REPORT-FILE.                  ELECTRPT
00171    009110     WRITE CONSUMPTION-REPORT-LINE FROM FIRST-HEADING-LINE  ELECTRPT
00172    009120          AFTER ADVANCING TO-TOP-OF-PAGE.                  ELECTRPT
00173    009130     WRITE CONSUMPTION-REPORT-LINE FROM SECOND-HEADING-LINE ELECTRPT
00174    009140          AFTER 1 LINES.                                  ELECTRPT
00175    009150     MOVE SPACE-TWO-LINES TO PROPER-SPACING.               ELECTRPT
00176    009160     READ CONSUMPTION-INPUT-FILE                          ELECTRPT
00177    009170          AT END                                          ELECTRPT
00178    009180               MOVE 'NO ' TO ARE-THERE-MORE-RECORDS.       ELECTRPT
00179    009190     IF THERE-IS-A-RECORD                                 ELECTRPT
00180    009200          PERFORM A001-PROCESS-AND-READ                    ELECTRPT
00181    010010               UNTIL THERE-ARE-NO-MORE-RECORDS             ELECTRPT
00182    010020          PERFORM B010-PRINT-FINAL-TOTALS.                 ELECTRPT
00183    010030     CLOSE CONSUMPTION-INPUT-FILE                         ELECTRPT
00184    010040          CONSUMPTION-REPORT-FILE.                        ELECTRPT
00185    010050     STOP RUN.                                           ELECTRPT
00186    010060                                                         ELECTRPT
00187    010070                                                         ELECTRPT
00188    010080                                                         ELECTRPT
00189    010090 A001-PROCESS-AND-READ.                                   ELECTRPT
00190    010100     PERFORM B000-PROCESS-DETAIL-RECORDS.                  ELECTRPT
00191    010110     READ CONSUMPTION-INPUT-FILE                          ELECTRPT
00192    010120          AT END                                          ELECTRPT
00193    010130               MOVE 'NO ' TO ARE-THERE-MORE-RECORDS.       ELECTRPT
```

```
  5                 11.37.06        FEB 22,1985

00194    010140/                                                         ELECTRPT
00195    010150*************************************************************** ELECTRPT
00196    010160*                                                     *  ELECTRPT
00197    010170*  THIS MODULE FORMATS THE REPORT, CALCULATES UNITS CONSUMED, *  ELECTRPT
00198    010180*  BILLING AMOUNT, AND AVERAGE DAILY CONSUMPTION, ACCUMULATES  *  ELECTRPT
00199    010190*  THE FINAL TOTALS, AND PRINTS THE DETAIL LINE. IT IS ENTERED *  ELECTRPT
00200    010200*  FROM AND EXITS TO THE A000-CREATE-CONSUMPTION-REPORT MODULE.* ELECTRPT
00201    011010*                                                     *  ELECTRPT
00202    011020*************************************************************** ELECTRPT
00203    011030                                                         ELECTRPT
00204    011040 B000-PROCESS-DETAIL-RECORDS.                             ELECTRPT
00205    011050                                                         ELECTRPT
00206    011060     MOVE SPACES TO CONSUMPTION-REPORT-LINE.               ELECTRPT
00207    011070     MOVE METER-NUMBER-INPUT TO METER-NUMBER-REPORT.       ELECTRPT
00208    011080     MOVE PREVIOUS-READING-INPUT TO PREVIOUS-READING-REPORT. ELECTRPT
00209    011090     MOVE PRESENT-READING-INPUT TO PRESENT-READING-REPORT.  ELECTRPT
00210    011100     SUBTRACT PREVIOUS-READING-INPUT FROM PRESENT-READING-INPUT ELECTRPT
00211    011110          GIVING UNITS-CONSUMED-WORK.                      ELECTRPT
00212    011120     MOVE UNITS-CONSUMED-WORK TO UNITS-CONSUMED-REPORT.     ELECTRPT
00213    011130     MOVE DAYS-BILLED-INPUT TO DAYS-BILLED-REPORT.          ELECTRPT
00214    011140     IF UNITS-CONSUMED-WORK IS LESS THAN CONSERVATION-LIMIT  ELECTRPT
00215    011150          MULTIPLY UNITS-CONSUMED-WORK BY CONSERVATION-COST-CONSTANTELECTRPT
00216    011160               GIVING BILLING-AMOUNT-WORK ROUNDED          ELECTRPT
00217    011170          MOVE CONSERVATION-COST-CONSTANT TO UNIT-COST-REPORT  ELECTRPT
00218    011180     ELSE                                                ELECTRPT
00219    011190          MULTIPLY UNITS-CONSUMED-WORK BY STANDARD-COST-CONSTANT  ELECTRPT
00220    011200               GIVING BILLING-AMOUNT-WORK ROUNDED          ELECTRPT
00221    012010          MOVE STANDARD-COST-CONSTANT TO UNIT-COST-REPORT.   ELECTRPT
00222    012020     MOVE BILLING-AMOUNT-WORK TO BILLING-AMOUNT-REPORT.     ELECTRPT
00223    012030     DIVIDE UNITS-CONSUMED-WORK BY DAYS-BILLED-INPUT        ELECTRPT
00224    012040          GIVING AVERAGE-DAILY-REPORT ROUNDED.             ELECTRPT
00225    012050     ADD 1 TO TOTAL-RECORDS-COUNT.                         ELECTRPT
00226    012060     ADD UNITS-CONSUMED-WORK TO UNITS-CONSUMED-ACCUM.       ELECTRPT
00227    012070     ADD BILLING-AMOUNT-WORK TO BILLING-AMOUNT-ACCUM.       ELECTRPT
00228    012080     WRITE CONSUMPTION-REPORT-LINE                        ELECTRPT
00229    012090          AFTER ADVANCING PROPER-SPACING.                  ELECTRPT
00230    012100     MOVE SPACE-ONE-LINE TO PROPER-SPACING.                ELECTRPT
```

Figure 5-55 Source Listing (Part 3 of 4)

```
      6                    11.37.06      FEB 22,1985

   00231   012110/                                                                      ELECTRPT
   00232   012120*****************************************************************      ELECTRPT
   00233   012130*                                                                 *    ELECTRPT
   00234   012140*   THIS MODULE PRINTS THE FINAL TOTALS.  IT IS ENTERED FROM      *    ELECTRPT
   00235   012150*   AND EXITS TO THE A000-CREATE-CONSUMPTION-REPORT MODULE.       *    ELECTRPT
   00236   012160*                                                                 *    ELECTRPT
   00237   012170*****************************************************************      ELECTRPT
   00238   012180                                                                       ELECTRPT
   00239   012190 B010-PRINT-FINAL-TOTALS.                                              ELECTRPT
   00240   012200                                                                       ELECTRPT
   00241   013010     MOVE TOTAL-RECORDS-COUNT TO TOTAL-RECORDS-FINAL.                   ELECTRPT
   00242   013020     MOVE UNITS-CONSUMED-ACCUM TO UNITS-CONSUMED-FINAL.                 ELECTRPT
   00243   013030     MOVE BILLING-AMOUNT-ACCUM TO BILLING-AMOUNT-FINAL.                 ELECTRPT
   00244   013040     WRITE CONSUMPTION-REPORT-LINE FROM FINAL-TOTAL-LINE                ELECTRPT
   00245   013050         AFTER ADVANCING 2 LINES.                                       ELECTRPT
```

Figure 5-56 Source Listing (Part 4 of 4)

REVIEW QUESTIONS

1. What are the three major comparing operations that can be performed on data?

2. What is the if-then-else control structure? What type of operation does it implement?

3. What statement in COBOL is used to implement the if-then-else control structure? What is the role of the word ELSE in this statement?

4. What is the effect of the period in a COBOL If statement?

5. What does the entry NEXT SENTENCE do in a COBOL If statement?

6. What is a relation test? What conditions can be tested with a relation test?

7. What occurs in a COBOL comparison when one numeric field that is being compared contains more digits than the other field being compared?

8. What determines whether the value in one alphanumeric field is greater than the value in another alphanumeric field?

9. Explain the collating sequence found on computers.

10. How are the words AND and OR used in COBOL If statements?

11. In a complex If statement, what is the sequence of comparing followed by COBOL? How does the use of parentheses alter this sequence?

12. Explain how a work area is defined in the Working-Storage Section of the Data Division. When should a work area be used?

13. What is a hierarchy chart? Explain the manner in which modules in a program are numbered.

14. When is the word ENDIF used in pseudocode?

15. What is a final total accumulator? Through the use of a diagram, draw the processing that would occur for the first two records containing a BALANCE-INPUT field. The value in the first record is 556.89, and the value in the second record is 43.09.

16. How are condition names used in a COBOL program?

17. What is the effect of the "S" entry in a numeric Picture clause?

COBOL CODING EXERCISES

1. Write the If statement in COBOL to determine if the value in the field referenced by TEST-CODE-INPUT is equal to the value in the field GENIUS-CONSTANT. If the values are equal, add 1 to GENIUS-COUNT. If the fields are not equal, add 1 to AVERAGE-COUNT.

2. Write the If statement in COBOL to determine if the value in the HOURS-INPUT field is greater than the value in the REGULAR-TIME-CONSTANT field. If so, add 1 to the OVERTIME-COUNT field.

3. Write the COBOL code in the Working-Storage Section of the Data Division to define the condition name SENIOR-CITIZEN if the value in the BUYER-INPUT field is equal to the value "S."

4. Write the COBOL If statement to test whether the field BUYER-INPUT contains the value "S" using the condition name defined in Exercise #3. If so, multiply GENERAL-ADMISSION by DISCOUNT-PERCENT and add the result to TOTAL-ADMISSIONS-ACCUM. If the buyer is not a senior citizen, add the value in GENERAL-ADMISSION to TOTAL-ADMISSIONS-ACCUM.

5. Write a Perform statement to perform the paragraph C010-PROCESS-SENIOR-CITIZEN as long as the buyer is a senior citizen as defined in Exercise #3.

6. Define in the Working-Storage Section of the Data Division the Total Counter areas to accumulate the number of students, the number of students who passed a course, and the number of students who failed a course.

7. Write the COBOL If statement and other statements required in the Procedure Division to accumulate the number of students who took a course, the number of students who passed a course, and the number of students who did not pass a course. If the value in GRADE-INPUT is 70 or higher, the student passed the course. Otherwise, the student failed the course. Accumulate the counts in the fields defined in Exercise #6.

STRUCTURED WALKTHROUGH EXERCISES

The following portions of COBOL code contain one or more errors in program logic, in the use of the COBOL language itself, or in the programming standards which should be followed. Review the code in each exercise in the same manner used for structured walkthroughs. Identify the errors and make the appropriate corrections.

1.

```
013110        IF EMPLOYEE-CODE-INPUT = FULL-TIME-CONSTANT
013120           PERFORM C030-PROCESS-FULL-TIME-EMPLOYEE.
013130           ADD 1 TO FULL-TIME-COUNT.
013140        ELSE
013150           PERFORM C040-PROCESS-PART-TIME-EMPLOYEE
013160           ADD 1 TO PART-TIME-COUNT.
```

2.

```
011060        IF STUDENT-CLASS-INPUT = FRESHMAN-CONSTANT
011070           OR STUDENT-CLASS-INPUT = SOPHOMORE-CONSTANT)
011080           AND STUDENT-GPA-INPUT > HONOR-GPA-CONSTANT
011090           PERFORM C060-PLACE-ON-HONOR-ROLL.
```

3.

```
011140        IF UNITS-CONSUMED-WORK LESS CONSERVATION-LIMIT
011150           MULTIPLY UNITS-CONSUMED-WORK BY CONSERVATION-COST-CONSTANT
011160              GIVING ROUNDED BILLING-AMOUNT-WORK
011170           MOVE CONSERVATION-COST-CONSTANT TO UNIT-COST-REPORT
011180        ELSE
011190           MULTIPLY UNITS-CONSUMED-WORK BY STANDARD-COST-CONSTANT
011200              GIVING ROUNDED BILLING-AMOUNT-WORK
012010           MOVE STANDARD-COST-CONSTANT TO UNIT-COST-REPORT
012180
```

4.

```
003170 WORKING STORAGE SECTION.
003180
003190 01  PROGRAM-INDICATORS.
003200     05  ARE-THERE-MORE-RECORDS        PIC 999       VALUE YES.
004010         08  THERE-IS-A-RECORD                       VALUE YES.
004020         08  THERE-ARE-NO-MORE-RECORDS               VALUE NO.
004030
004040 01  PROGRAM-CONSTANTS.
004050     05  REGULAR-AMOUNT-CONSTANT       PIC 99.9  VALUE 83.78.
004060     05  IRREGULAR-AMOUNT-CONSTANT     PIC X(5)  VALUE 99.92.
004070     05  AREA-LIMIT                    PIC 999   VALUE 00123.
004080
004090 01  WORK-AREAS.
004100     05  INVOICE-TOTAL             PIC 9(5).99
004110     05  BILLING-AMOUNT            PIC 9(5).99
004120
004130 01  TOTAL-ACCUMULATORS-COUNTERS.
004140     05  TOTAL-RECORDS-ACCUM       PIC 999      ZERO.
004150     05  INVOICE-TOTAL-ACCUM       PIC 9(6)     ZERO.
004160     05  BILLING-AMOUNT-ACCUM      PIC 9(6)V99  ZERO.
```

5.

```
004170 WORKING-STORAGE SECTION.

008030 01  TOTAL-LINES.
008040     05  FINAL-TOTAL-LINE.
008060         10  FILLER                    PIC X(13)      VALUE
008070                                       'TOTAL RECORD'.
008080         10  FILLER                    PIC X.
008090         10  TOTAL-RECORDS-FINAL       PIC ZZ9.
008100         10  FILLER                    PIC X(11).
008110         10  PARTS-USED-FINAL          PIC ZZZ,ZZ9.
008120         10  FILLER                    PIC X(19).
008130         10  INVENTORY-AMOUNT-FINAL    PIC $$$$,$$$.99.
008140         10  FILLER                    PIC X(62).

008160 PROCEDURE DIVISION.

013010     MOVE TOTAL-RECORDS-COUNT TO TOTAL-RECORDSFINAL.
013020     MOVE PARTS-USED-ACCUM TO PARTS-USEDFINAL.
013030     MOVE INVENTORY-AMOUNT-ACCUM TO INVENTORY-AMOUNTFINAL.
013040     WRITE FINAL-TOTAL-LINE FROM INVENTORY-REPORT-LINE
013050         ADVANCING 2 LINES.
```

PROGRAMMING ASSIGNMENT 1

INSTRUCTIONS

A Shipping Report is to be prepared. Design and write the COBOL program to produce the required report. An IPO Chart and pseudocode should be used when designing the program. Use Test Data Set 1 in Appendix A.

INPUT

Input consists of Shipping Records that contain the Package Number, Package Contents, Shipment Weight, and Shipment Value. The format of the input record is illustrated below.

Shipping Disk Record				
FIELD DESCRIPTION	POSITION	LENGTH	DEC	ATTRIBUTE
UNUSED	1 – 5	5		Alphanumeric
Package Number	6 – 8	3	0	Numeric
UNUSED	9 – 29	21		Alphanumeric
Package Contents	30 – 49	20		Alphanumeric
UNUSED	50 – 53	4		Alphanumeric
Shipment Weight	54 – 55	2	0	Numeric
Shipment Value	56 – 61	6	2	Numeric
Record Length		61		

OUTPUT

Output consists of a Shipping Report listing the Package Number, Package Contents, Shipment Weight, Shipment Value, Shipping Cost, Insurance Cost, and Total Cost. If Shipment Weight is greater than 50 pounds, then Shipping Cost is calculated by multiplying Shipment Weight by .10. If Shipment Weight is 50 pounds or less, Shipping Cost is calculated by multiplying Shipment Weight by .07. Insurance Costs are calculated by multiplying Shipment Value by .005. Total Cost is the sum of Shipping Cost and Insurance Cost. Final Totals should be kept on Number of Shipments, Shipping Cost, Insurance Cost, and Total Cost. The printer spacing chart for the report is illustrated below.

PRINTER SPACING CHART

```
PACKAGE         PACKAGE          SHIPMENT   SHIPMENT    SHIPPING      INSURANCE        TOTAL
NUMBER          CONTENTS         WEIGHT     VALUE       COST          COST             COST

 ZZ9   XXXXXXXXXXXXXXXXXXXX        Z9      Z,ZZZ.99     Z.99         ZZ.99           ZZ.99
 ZZ9   XXXXXXXXXXXXXXXXXXXX        Z9      Z,ZZZ.99     Z.99         ZZ.99           ZZ.99

TOTAL SHIPMENTS   ZZ9                                $$$.99       $$$$.99         $$$$.99
```

PROGRAMMING ASSIGNMENT 2

INSTRUCTIONS

A Commodity Report is to be prepared. Write the COBOL program to prepare this report. An IPO Chart and Pseudocode Specifications should be used when designing the program. Use Test Data Set 2 in Appendix A.

INPUT

Input consists of Commodity Records that contain the Contract Number, Contract Owner, Number of Contracts, and Contract Cost. The format of the Commodity Record is illustrated below.

Commodity Disk Record				
FIELD DESCRIPTION	POSITION	LENGTH	DEC	ATTRIBUTE
UNUSED	1 – 6	6		Alphanumeric
Contract Number	7 – 12	6	0	Numeric
Contract Owner	13 – 32	20		Alphanumeric
UNUSED	33 – 57	25		Alphanumeric
Number of Contracts	58 – 59	2	0	Numeric
UNUSED	60 – 61	2		Alphanumeric
Contract Cost	62 – 65	4	2	Numeric
UNUSED	66 – 67	2		Alphanumeric
Record Length		67		

OUTPUT

Output consists of a Commodity Report listing the Contract Number, Contract Owner, Number of Contracts, Contract Cost, Contract Total, Commission, and Total Cost. Contract Total is calculated by multiplying Number of Contracts by Contract Cost. For Contract Totals equal to or less than $1000.00, a 7% commission is charged. For Contract Totals in excess of $1000.00, a 5% commission is charged on the amount in excess of $1000.00 in addition to the 7% commission on the first $1000.00. Thus, if the Contract total is $1200.00, the Commission would be (1000.00 X .07) + (200.00 X .05). Total Cost is calculated by adding the Contract Total to the Commission. The printer spacing chart is shown below.

PROGRAMMING ASSIGNMENT 3

INSTRUCTIONS

An Accounts Receivable Report is to be prepared. Write the COBOL program to prepare this report. An IPO Chart and Pseudocode Specifications should be used when designing the program. Use Test Data Set 3 in Appendix A.

INPUT

Input consists of Accounts Receivable Records that contain Account Number, Customer Name, Monthly Balance, and Age of Account. The format of the Accounts Receivable Record is illustrated below.

Accounts Receivable Disk Record				
FIELD DESCRIPTION	**POSITION**	**LENGTH**	**DEC**	**ATTRIBUTE**
UNUSED	1 – 6	6		Alphanumeric
Account Number	7 – 10	4	0	Numeric
UNUSED	11 – 36	26		Alphanumeric
Customer Name	37 – 56	20		Alphanumeric
UNUSED		57	1	Alphanumeric
Monthly Balance	58 – 62	5	2	Numeric
Age of Account	63 – 64	2	0	Numeric
Record Length		64		

OUTPUT

Output consists of a Receivables Report listing the Account Number, Customer Name, Monthly Balance, Finance Charge, Total Receivable, and Account Status. A Penalty Charge Percentage of 1.5% is charged on accounts with an Age of Account greater than 30 days. The Finance Charge is calculated by multiplying the Monthly Balance by the Penalty Charge Percentage. If the Age of Account is not greater than 30 days, there will be no Finance Charge. Total Receivable is calculated by adding the Finance Charge and the Monthly Balance. If the Age of Account is greater than 30 days, a message "PAST DUE" is to be printed in the Account Status field. If the Age of Account is not greater than 30 days, no message appears in the Account Status field. Final Totals are to be taken for the Monthly Balance, Finance Charge, and Total Receivable. In addition, the total number of accounts processed and the total number of accounts past due should be printed. The printer spacing chart is shown on the next page.

PRINTER SPACING CHART

```
   1         1111111112222222222333333333344444444445555555555666666666677777777778
   1234567890123456789012345678901234567890123456789012345678901234567890123456789 0
 1
 2 ACCOUNT       CUSTOMER        MONTHLY     FINANCE      TOTAL        ACCOUNT
 3  NUMBER         NAME          BALANCE     CHARGE     RECEIVABLE      STATUS
 4
 5    ZZZ9    XXXXXXXXXXXXXXXXXXXX  $$$$.99    $$$.99    $$,$$$.99
 6    ZZZ9    XXXXXXXXXXXXXXXXXXXX  $$$$.99    $$$.99    $$,$$$.99    PAST DUE
 7
 8               FINAL TOTALS    $$,$$$.99   $$$.99   $$,$$$.99
 9
10 TOTAL ACCOUNTS   ZZ9
11 TOTAL ACCOUNTS PAST DUE   ZZ9
```

PROGRAMMING ASSIGNMENT 4

INSTRUCTIONS

A Charity Report is to be prepared. Write the COBOL program to prepare this report. An IPO Chart and Pseudocode Specifications should be used when designing the program. Use Test Data Set 4 in Appendix A.

INPUT

Input consists of Charity Records that contain Contributor Number, Contributor Name, Last Year's Contribution, and This Year's Contribution. The format of the Charity Record is illustrated below.

Charity Disk Record				
FIELD DESCRIPTION	**POSITION**	**LENGTH**	**DEC**	**ATTRIBUTE**
UNUSED	1 – 9	9		Alphanumeric
Contributor Number	10 – 13	4	0	Numeric
Contributor Name	14 – 33	20		Alphanumeric
UNUSED	34 – 59	26		Alphanumeric
Last Year's Contribution	60 – 65	6	2	Numeric
This Year's Contribution	66 – 71	6	2	Numeric
UNUSED	72 – 73	2		Alphanumeric
Record Length		73		

OUTPUT

Output consists of a Charity Report and a Charity Leaders Report. The formats of these two reports are illustrated below and on the following page.

PRINTER SPACING CHART

Line 2: CHARITY REPORT

Line 4: CONTRIBUTOR   CONTRIBUTOR   LAST YEAR'S   THIS YEAR'S   AMOUNT OF   PERCENT OF
Line 5: NUMBER   NAME   CONTRIBUTION   CONTRIBUTION   INCREASE   INCREASE

Line 7: ZZZ9   XXXXXXXXXXXXXXXXXXXX   Z,ZZZ.99   Z,ZZZ.99   Z,ZZZ.99   Z9%
Line 8: ZZZ9   XXXXXXXXXXXXXXXXXXXX   Z,ZZZ.99   Z,ZZZ.99   Z,ZZZ.99   Z9%

Line 10: RESULTS OF CHARITY DRIVE $$$,$$$.99 $$$,$$$.99 $$$,$$$.99   Z9%

```
14                          (SEPARATE PAGE)
15
16                       CHARITY LEADERS REPORT
17
18        CHARITY                    CONTRIBUTOR              AMOUNT/
19       CATEGORIES                     NAME                 PERCENT
20
21  LARGEST CONTRIBUTION         XXXXXXXXXXXXXXXXXXXX    $Z,ZZZ.99
22
23  LARGEST PERCENT INCREASE     XXXXXXXXXXXXXXXXXXXX          Z9%
24
25
```

For the Charity Report, the Amount of Increase is calculated by subtracting Last Year's Contribution from This Year's Contribution. Percent of Increase is calculated by dividing the Amount of Increase by Last Year's Contribution. The Amount of Increase and Percent of Increase should be printed ONLY if there was an increase. If no increase exists, these fields should contain zeros.

After all records have been processed, the "RESULTS OF CHARITY DRIVE" line should be printed. This line on the Charity Report is a summary of the activities for the whole charity drive. The Amount of Increase is calculated by subtracting last year's contributions by all contributors from this year's contributions by all contributors. The Percent of Increase is calculated by dividing the amount of increase of all contributions by the total of last year's contributions by all contributors. If no increase exists, both the Amount of Increase for the charity drive and the Percent of Increase for the charity drive should contain zero.

Next, on a separate page, the Charity Leaders Report should be printed. This report contains the Contributor Name and Amount of Contribution for the largest contributor for the whole charity drive, and the Contributor Name and Percent Increase of the Contributor with the largest percent increase for the whole charity drive. If two contributors should have the same contribution or percent of increase, print the first contributor that is found. The report contains headings and is to be double spaced as illustrated.

CHAPTER
SIX

DATA EDITING
AND
NESTED IF STATEMENTS

DATA EDITING AND NESTED IF STATEMENTS

6

INTRODUCTION

The if-then-else logic structure and the If statement presented in Chapter 5 form an important basis for much of the programming that is performed on a computer. The use of the if-then-else structure can vary depending upon the application being programmed. In the sample program in this chapter, the if-then-else structure is used in a "nested" configuration, where an if-then-else structure is contained within another if-then-else structure.

In previous programs, headings have been printed on the first page of the report. This chapter will illustrate printing headings on the first, and subsequent, pages of a report.

In addition to the nested if-then-else structure and headings, this chapter will illustrate techniques to edit input data. One of the most likely causes for a program's failure to produce correct output is that fields in the input record contain invalid data. For example, fields which should contain alphabetic data may have been left blank; numeric fields may erroneously contain alphabetic data or may have been left blank; or the values recorded in numeric fields may be unreasonable. These problems may occur because of errors on the documents from which data is entered into a computer or because of errors made when data is entered.

With many programs, when an attempt is made to process invalid data, the program will either produce incorrect output (garbage in, garbage out), or the program will abnormally terminate. Therefore, one of the more important aspects of processing data using a computer is editing the data to be processed.

Editing refers to the process of including in the design of the program the necessary instructions to ensure that data entered into the computer conforms to predetermined criteria. Data which does not conform to predetermined criteria is identified on a report by printing an error message.

Editing can take many forms. Some common forms of editing include the following:

1. Checking for blank fields.
2. Checking to ensure fields contain only numeric data.
3. Checking the reasonableness of values contained in numeric fields.
4. Checking to ensure a field contains specific values.

Although there are other types of editing, these forms of editing are commonly used in computer programs to detect invalid data. They are illustrated in the sample program in this chapter.

SAMPLE PROGRAM

To illustrate Nested If statements, data editing, and printing headings on each page of the report, the sample program in this chapter will produce an Edit Report. A sample of the report is illustrated in Figure 6-1.

```
  02/27/85                        EDIT REPORT                        PAGE    1

        DEALER            PRODUCT      SHIPPING    SHIPPING              ERROR
         NAME              TYPE        METHOD      WEIGHT              MESSAGE

   ABC COMPUTER STCRES    SCFTWARE     AIR             5
   **MISSING DEALER**     HARDWARE     SURFACE       100        **ERROR IN RECORD**
   TECNI-COMPUTERS        SCFTWARE     AIR        *INVALID*     **ERROR IN RECORD**
   ALU SHOPS              HARDWARE     SURFACE        75
   BITS INCORPCRATED      HARDWARE     *INVALID*     350        **ERROR IN RECORD**
   INTEGRITY CIRCUITS     *INVALID*                   30        **ERROR IN RECORD**
   BOARDS UNLIMITEC       SCFTWARE     AIR             9
   AMERICAN COMPUTERS     HARDWARE     SURFACE    *INVALID*     **ERROR IN RECORD**

     8 TOTAL RECCRDS
     5 RECORDS IN ERRCR
```

Figure 6-1 Example of the Edit Report

The heading on the Edit Report contains the Date and the Page Number as well as the other headings. The report itself contains the Dealer Name, Product Type, Shipping Method, Shipping Weight, and Error Message. Notice that embedded in the body of the report are error messages used to identify fields that have been edited and found to contain invalid data. These error messages include: **MISSING DEALER**, *INVALID*, and **ERROR IN RECORD**. The error messages will be explained in detail later in this chapter. The input to create this report is illustrated in Figure 6-2.

Shipping Disk Record				
FIELD DESCRIPTION	POSITION	LENGTH	DEC	ATTRIBUTE
Dealer Name	1 – 20	20		Alphanumeric
Product Code	21	1		Alphanumeric
Shipping Code	22	1		Alphanumeric
Shipping Weight	23 – 25	3	0	Numeric
Record Length		25		

Figure 6-2 Input to the Sample Program

The input record contains the Dealer Name, Product Code, Shipping Code, and Shipping Weight. The Product Type, which appears on the report, is determined from the value contained in the Product Code field in the input record. The Product Type is determined in the following manner: If the Product Code in the input record is an S, then the product being shipped is a software product, and the word SOFTWARE will be printed on the report. If the Product Code on the input record is H, then the product being shipped is a hardware product, and the word HARDWARE will printed on the report. The only two codes that are valid for Product Code are S and H.

The Shipping Method, which appears on the report, is determined from the value contained in the Product Code field and the Shipping Code field in the input record. If the Product Code in the input record is H, and the Shipping Code in the input record is T (shipped by Truck) or R (shipped by Railroad), then the hardware is shipped by surface, and the word

SURFACE will be printed on the report. A hardware product must always be shipped by truck or railroad. Any shipping code other than T or R is invalid for a hardware product.

If the Product Code in the input record is S, then the product is shipped by air, and the word AIR will be printed on the report. All software products are shipped by air.

In addition, the Dealer Name field must not be blank, and the Shipping Weight field must contain valid numeric data and must not be greater than 400 pounds.

To properly process the editing conditions specified, Nested If statements are required. The use of Nested If statements is explained in the following sections.

NESTED IF-THEN-ELSE STRUCTURE

To understand the nested if-then-else structure, it is mandatory to first understand the if-then-else structure itself. The if-then-else structure explained in Chapter 5 is reviewed in Figure 6–3.

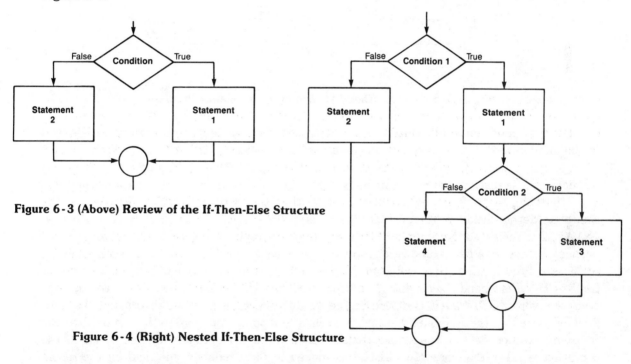

Figure 6-3 (Above) Review of the If-Then-Else Structure

Figure 6-4 (Right) Nested If-Then-Else Structure

When the condition tested in the if-then-else structure is true, Statement 1 is executed. If the condition is false, Statement 2 is executed. Statement 1 and Statement 2 can themselves be any set of instructions available on the computer. It is perfectly allowable, therefore, that the statement executed when the condition is true, or when the condition is false, can include another if-then-else structure. When this occurs, the second if-then-else structure is said to be nested within the first if-then-else structure. This is illustrated in Figure 6–4.

In Figure 6–4, the instructions to be executed when the first condition is true include Statement 1 and another if-then-else structure. This nested if-then-else structure, which tests condition 2, will be executed only if the first condition is true. If condition 2 is true, statement 3 is executed; while if it is not true, statement 4 is executed.

If condition 1 is false, statement 2 is executed and the if-then-else structure is exited.

A nested if-then-else structure is required in the sample program to determine the Shipping Method. This nested if-then-else structure is illustrated in Figure 6–5.

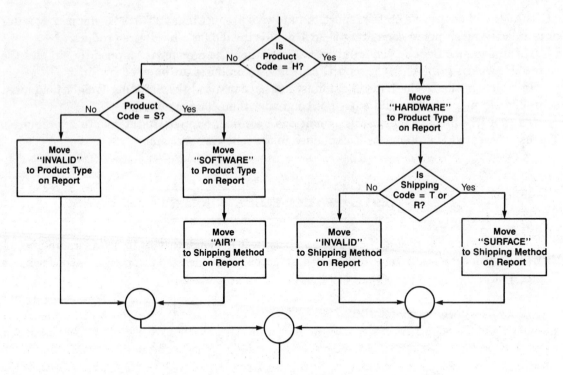

Figure 6-5 Nested If-Then-Else Structure for Sample Problem

The first condition, Is Product Code = H, tests for the value H in the Product Code field in the input record. If the Product Code field contains the value H, the first condition is true. Therefore, the word HARDWARE is moved to the Product Type field on the report, and a further check is made to determine if the Shipping Code in the input record contains the value T or the value R. If Shipping Code = T or R, then the word SURFACE is moved to the Shipping Method field on the report. If the Shipping Code is not equal to T or R, then the word INVALID is moved to the Shipping Method field on the report. The invalid message is moved because, as noted earlier, a hardware product must always be shipped by truck or railroad.

If the Product Code does not contain the value H, then the first condition, Is Product Code = H, is false; and the condition, Is Product Code = S, is then tested. If the condition is true, the word SOFTWARE is moved to the Product Type field on the report and the word AIR is moved to the Shipping Method field on the report. The word AIR is moved to the Shipping Method field on the report because all software products are shipped by air. If the condition is false, the word *INVALID* is moved to the Product Type field on the report because the Product Code field must contain either S or H. Any other code is considered invalid.

As can be seen from Figure 6–5, the nested if-then-else structure can be used when the first condition tested is false as well as when the first condition tested is true. In addition, the nested if-then-else structure may itself contain an if-then-else structure.

Implementing the Nested If-Then-Else Structure

The If statement is used to implement the if-then-else structure. If the condition is true, then one set of instructions is executed; if it is not true, then another set of statements is executed. This general format of the If statement is illustrated in Figure 6-6.

```
IF condition
    Execute statements if condition is true
ELSE
    Execute statements if condition is not true
```

Figure 6-6 General Format of the If Statement

A COBOL coding example of this general format is illustrated in Figure 6-7.

```
012030              IF BUILDING-TYPE-INPUT = 'B'
012040  Executed  {MOVE BUSINESS-CONSTANT TO BUILDING-TYPE-REPORT
012050  If        {ADD 1 TO BUSINESS-COUNT
        True
012060              ELSE
012070  Executed  {MOVE NON-BUSINESS-CONSTANT TO BUILDING-TYPE-REPORT
012080  If        {ADD 1 TO NON-BUSINESS-COUNT.
        False
```

Figure 6-7 Example of the If Statement

If the value B is contained in the BUILDING-TYPE-INPUT field, then the value in the BUSINESS-CONSTANT field is moved to the BUILDING-TYPE-REPORT field and the value 1 is added to BUSINESS-COUNT. If the value B is not contained in the BUILDING-TYPE-INPUT field, then the value in the NON-BUSINESS-CONSTANT field is moved to the BUILDING-TYPE-REPORT field and the value 1 is added to NON-BUSINESS-COUNT.

A Move statement and an Add statement are executed if the condition is true, and a Move statement and an Add statement are executed if the condition is not true. As noted previously, another If statement could be nested within the existing If statement. This is illustrated in Figure 6-8.

```
013020              IF BUILDING-TYPE-INPUT = 'B'
013030             {MOVE BUSINESS-CONSTANT TO BUILDING-TYPE-REPORT
013040             {IF PROPERTY-STATUS-INPUT = 'L'
013050  Executed  {   MOVE LEASED-CONSTANT TO PROPERTY-STATUS-REPORT
013060  If        {   ADD 1 TO LEASED-BUSINESS-COUNT
        True
013070             {ELSE
013080             {   MOVE OWNED-CONSTANT TO PROPERTY-STATUS-REPORT
013090             {   ADD 1 TO OWNED-BUSINESS-COUNT
013100              ELSE
013110             {MOVE NON-BUSINESS-CONSTANT TO BUILDING-TYPE-REPORT
013120             {IF PROPERTY-STATUS-INPUT = 'L'
013130  Executed  {   MOVE LEASED-CONSTANT TO PROPERTY-STATUS-REPORT
013140  If        {   ADD 1 TO LEASED-RESIDENCE-COUNT
        False
013150             {ELSE
013160             {   MOVE OWNED-CONSTANT TO PROPERTY-STATUS-REPORT
013170             {   ADD 1 TO OWNED-RESIDENCE-COUNT.
013180              ADD 1 TO TOTAL-RECORDS-COUNT.
```

Figure 6-8 Example of a Nested If Statement

In Figure 6-8, if the value B is contained in the BUILDING-TYPE-INPUT field, the Move statement (line 013030) and the If statement (lines 013040 through 013090) are executed. If the value B is not in the BUILDING-TYPE-INPUT field, a Move statement (line 013110) and an If statement (lines 013120 through 013170) are executed. The inner If statements which will be executed when the condition is true and when the condition is not true are merely statements, like the Add statements in Figure 6-7, which will be executed when the condition is true or not true. The fact that an If statement will be executed as a result of a condition's being true or not true does not change the way in which the If statement works, nor does it have any other effect on the program; it is merely another statement to be executed.

If each of the inner If statements is analyzed as individual if-then-else structures, the structure and logic of the Nested If statement becomes easy to understand. Thus, the If statements which will be executed upon a given condition are themselves evaluated in the same way as all If statements. This is illustrated in Figure 6-9.

```
013020      IF BUILDING-TYPE-INPUT = 'B'
013030          MOVE BUSINESS-CONSTANT TO BUILDING-TYPE-REPORT
013040          IF PROPERTY-STATUS-INPUT = 'L'
013050  Executed ⌠MOVE LEASED-CONSTANT TO PROPERTY-STATUS-REPORT
013060  If True  ⌡ADD 1 TO LEASED-BUSINESS-COUNT
013070          ELSE
013080  Executed ⌠MOVE OWNED-CONSTANT TO PROPERTY-STATUS-REPORT
013090  If False ⌡ADD 1 TO OWNED-BUSINESS-COUNT
013100      ELSE
013110          MOVE NON-BUSINESS-CONSTANT TO BUILDING-TYPE-REPORT
013120          IF PROPERTY-STATUS-INPUT = 'L'
013130  Executed ⌠MOVE LEASED-CONSTANT TO PROPERTY-STATUS-REPORT
013140  If True  ⌡ADD 1 TO LEASED-RESIDENCE-COUNT
013150          ELSE
013160  Executed ⌠MOVE OWNED-CONSTANT TO PROPERTY-STATUS-REPORT
013170  If False ⌡ADD 1 TO OWNED-RESIDENCE-COUNT.
013180      ADD 1 TO TOTAL-RECORDS-COUNT.
```

Figure 6-9 Example of Nested Ifs

The inner If statements in Figure 6-9, which are executed as a result of a prior condition being true or false, are evaluated in the same manner as If statements which are not a part of Nested If statements. The statements immediately following the If statement are executed if the condition is true, and the statements following the word ELSE are executed if the condition is false.

After statements have been executed as a result of the conditions found in the Nested If statement, the sentence which follows the period in the Nested If statement is executed. In Figure 6-9, if the value B is found in the BUILDING-TYPE-INPUT field and if the PROPERTY-STATUS-INPUT field contains the value L, the statements on lines 013050 and 013060 will be executed. After they are executed, the word ELSE is encountered; therefore, there are no more statements to be executed as a result of the condition's being true. Thus, the remaining statements within the Nested If statement are bypassed and the Add statement on line 013180, which follows the period for the Nested If statement, will be executed.

The same is true for all the other conditions which are tested within the Nested If statement. When the statements have been executed as a result of the condition's being true or false, the statement following the period in the Nested If statement is executed.

Nested If Statement Examples

Nested If statements may be used in a variety of forms. The example in Figure 6-10 illustrates a Nested If statement where the first If statement does not have an Else clause.

In Figure 6-10, the first condition tested is whether the value in the EMPLOYEE-TYPE-INPUT field is equal to T. If it is, then the value in the CLASS-SIZE-INPUT field is checked to determine if it is greater than the value in the CLASS-MAXIMUM-CONSTANT field. If the Size is greater than the Class Maximum, the Over Enrolled message is moved to the printer output area; if it is not, the Not Over Enrolled message is moved to the output area.

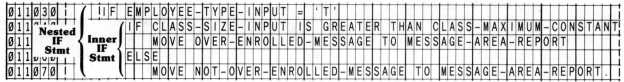

0 1 1 0 3 0			IF EMPLOYEE-TYPE-INPUT = 'T'
0 1 1	Nested IF Stmt	Inner IF Stmt	IF CLASS-SIZE-INPUT IS GREATER THAN CLASS-MAXIMUM-CONSTANT
0 1 1			MOVE OVER-ENROLLED-MESSAGE TO MESSAGE-AREA-REPORT
0 1 1			ELSE
0 1 1 0 7 0			MOVE NOT-OVER-ENROLLED-MESSAGE TO MESSAGE-AREA-REPORT.

Figure 6-10 Example of a Nested If Statement without an Else Clause

There is no Else clause for the first If statement. Thus, if the EMPLOYEE-TYPE-INPUT field does not contain the value T, no further processing will be done by the Nested If statement and the statement following line 011070 would be executed.

Figure 6-11 illustrates a Nested If statement in which both If statements contain a related Else clause.

0 1 1 0 6 0			IF ACCOUNT-IS-OVERDUE
0 1 1 0 7 0		Inner IF Stmt	IF BALANCE-INPUT IS GREATER THAN MAXIMUM-ACCOUNT-BALANCE
0 1 1	Nested IF Stmt		PERFORM C010-CALL-CUSTOMER
0 1 1			ELSE
0 1 1			PERFORM C020-SEND-LATE-NOTICE
0 1 1 1 1 0			ELSE
0 1 1 1 2 0			PERFORM C030-SEND-STATEMENT.

Figure 6-11 Example of Nested If Statements with Else Clauses

In Figure 6-11, the inner If statement (line 011070) is executed if the account is overdue. If the account is overdue, the BALANCE-INPUT field is tested to determine if the balance is greater than the maximum account balance. If the balance is greater than the maximum account balance, then the customer is called. If the balance is not greater than the maximum account balance, then a late notice is sent.

If the account is not overdue, then the Perform statement on line 011120 is executed and the customer is sent a statement.

Figure 6-12 illustrates a Nested If statement in which the inner If statement follows the Else portion of the first If statement.

0 1 3 1 0 0			IF PRODUCT-CODE-INPUT = 'H'
0 1 3 1 1 0			MOVE HARDWARE-CONSTANT TO PRODUCT-TYPE-REPORT
0 1 3	Nested IF Stmt		ELSE
0 1 3		Inner IF Stmt	IF PRODUCT-CODE-INPUT = 'S'
0 1 3 1 4 0			MOVE SOFTWARE-CONSTANT TO PRODUCT-TYPE-REPORT
0 1 3 1 5 0			ELSE
0 1 3 1 6 0			MOVE INVALID-CONSTANT TO PRODUCT-TYPE-REPORT.

Figure 6-12 Nested If Statement Following an Else Clause

In Figure 6-12, if the value in the PRODUCT-CODE-INPUT field is equal to H, then the value in the HARDWARE-CONSTANT field is moved to the PRODUCT-TYPE-REPORT field. If the value in the PRODUCT-CODE-INPUT field is not equal to H, then the Else portion of the If statement is executed.

In the Else portion, the value in the PRODUCT-CODE-INPUT field is compared to S. If it is equal to S, the value in the SOFTWARE-CONSTANT field is moved to the PRODUCT-TYPE-REPORT field. If the value is not equal to S, then the value in the INVALID-CONSTANT field is moved to the PRODUCT-TYPE-REPORT field.

Thus, the inner If statement need not be specified after the first If statement but may also be specified as part of the Else clause associated with the first If statement. The determination of where the second If statement should be placed in the Nested If statement is made from the requirements of the logic of the program.

In some applications, there may be a requirement to test for certain conditions; but unless those conditions occur, no processing is to be done. In these cases, the NEXT SENTENCE statement is useful. To illustrate the use of the NEXT SENTENCE statement, assume the following conditions must be tested:

1. If the Last Name field and the First Name field both contain all spaces, normal processing is to occur.
2. If the Last Name field contains all spaces but the First Name field contains data, an error message is to be printed.
3. If the Last Name field contains data but the First Name field contains all spaces, an error message is to be printed.
4. If the Last Name field and First Name field both contain data, normal processing is to occur.

In summary, both fields must contain spaces or both fields must contain data in order for normal processing to occur. If one of the fields contains data and the other field contains just spaces, an error message is to be printed. The Nested If statement to process these conditions is illustrated in Figure 6–13.

```
013040      IF LAST-NAME-INPUT = SPACES
013050          IF FIRST-NAME-INPUT = SPACES
013060              NEXT SENTENCE
013          ELSE
013              MOVE ERROR-CONSTANT TO MESSAGE-AREA-REPORT
013090      ELSE
013100          IF FIRST-NAME-INPUT = SPACES
013110              MOVE ERROR-CONSTANT TO MESSAGE-AREA-REPORT.
```

Figure 6-13 Example of Next Sentence Statement

In Figure 6–13, the LAST-NAME-INPUT field is first checked for spaces. If the LAST-NAME-INPUT field contains all spaces, then the FIRST-NAME-INPUT field is checked for spaces. If the FIRST-NAME-INPUT field contains all spaces, NEXT SENTENCE is specified. The use of the NEXT SENTENCE statement will cause the remaining statements in the If statement to be bypassed, and the statement following line 013110 will be executed. If, however, the LAST-NAME-INPUT contains all spaces but the FIRST-NAME-INPUT field does not contain all spaces (the field contains data), then an error message is moved to the output area.

The Else portion of the first If statement (line 013090) is executed when the LAST-NAME-INPUT field does not contain all spaces (the field contains data). When this occurs and the FIRST-NAME-INPUT field contains all spaces, then an error message is written. Lastly, if neither the LAST-NAME-INPUT field nor the FIRST-NAME-INPUT field contains all spaces (both contain data), the statement following line 013110 would be executed, providing for normal processing.

Nested If statements are not restricted to two levels. The example in Figure 6–14 illustrates a Nested If statement with three levels.

In Figure 6–14, a Check Cashing application is illustrated. The problem states that if there is enough money in the Checking Account to cover the check, then the check is cashed. If there is not enough money in the Checking Account, then the Savings Account is examined. If there is enough money in the Savings Account to cover the Check, then money is transferred from the Savings Account to the Checking Account. If there is not enough money in the Savings Account to cover the check, then if the customer is a credit card holder, the Check Amount is charged to the customer's credit card. If the customer is not a credit card holder, the check is returned.

| 0 1 4 0 4 0 | | | | IF | CHECK-AMOUNT-INPUT | IS | GREATER | THAN | CHECKING-BALANCE-INPUT |
| 0 1 4 0 5 0 | | | | | IF | SAVINGS-BALANCE-INPUT | IS | LESS | THAN | CHECK-AMOUNT-INPUT |

Figure 6-14 Example of a Three-Level Nested If Statement

The If statement on line 014040 determines if the Check Amount is greater than the Checking Account Balance. If so, then the check cannot be cashed using the funds in the Checking Account. If it is not greater, then the Else clause on line 014120 will be executed and the check will be cashed. If the check cannot be cashed using money in the Checking Account, the If statement on line 014050 tests if the Savings Account Balance is less than the Check Amount. If it is, the check cannot be cashed using money in the Savings Account. If it is not, the Else clause on line 014100 is executed and the money needed to cash the check is transferred from the Savings Account to the Checking Account.

If the Savings Account Balance is less than the Check Amount, the next question to be asked is whether the customer is a Credit Card Holder. If the customer is a Credit Card Holder, the Check Amount is charged to the Credit Card Account. If not, the Check is returned. Thus, on line 014060, the If statement tests if the Customer is a Credit Card Holder. If so, the charge to the credit card account will be processed by the Perform statement on line 014070; otherwise, the C020-RETURN-CHECK module will be performed by the Perform statement on line 014090.

It is important to realize how the analysis of the Nested If statement in Figure 6-14 took place. The first If statement within the group is analyzed. If the condition tested is true, then the statement immediately following the If statement is analyzed. In the example, this is another If statement; but it should be noted that it could be any permissible COBOL statement. If the condition tested is not true, then the processing following the Else clause is analyzed. Again, it can be any allowable COBOL statement; in the example, it is a Perform statement. It is critical to realize that the first If statement operates just as if there were no other If statements in the entire sentence. It is only when the processing which is to take place if the condition is true is analyzed that another If statement is found.

When inner If statement #1 is found, then it too is analyzed just as if it were the only If statement in the sentence. If the condition tested is true, then the statements immediately following the If statement are executed. If the condition is not true, then the statements following the Else clause are executed. Again, the If statement is treated as though it were a single If statement instead of an If statement contained within a Nested If statement. Inner If statement #2 is treated the same way. Thus, even though an inner If statement will be executed only upon a particular condition, it still should be analyzed as if it were the only If statement in the sentence. In this manner, the reader will not become confused in trying to remember all of the possible conditions which must occur in order to have a statement executed.

When is a Nested If Statement Required

When designing a program, the programmer must be aware of when a Nested If statement is required. Although every condition under which a Nested If statement is used cannot be covered, two general rules can be applied to determine if a Nested If statement is required:

Rule 1: If a given condition must be tested only when a previous condition has been tested, AND alternative actions are required for one or more of the conditions, then a Nested If statement must be used.

The example in Figure 6-15 illustrates the application of this rule.

```
011060        IF ACCOUNT-IS-OVERDUE
011070            IF BALANCE-INPUT IS GREATER THAN MAXIMUM-ACCOUNT-BALANCE
011080                PERFORM C010-CALL-CUSTOMER
011090            ELSE
011100                PERFORM C020-SEND-LATE-NOTICE
011110        ELSE
011120            PERFORM C030-SEND-STATEMENT.
```
Figure 6-15 Example of Nested If Rule 1

In Figure 6-15, testing for the condition of whether the Balance is Greater than the Maximum Account Balance is to take place only if the Account Is Overdue. Thus, the first part of the rule stating that a condition is to be tested only when a previous condition has been tested is satisfied. In addition, both of the conditions tested (Account Is Overdue and Balance is greater than Maximum Account Balance) require alternative actions, that is, actions which will take place when they are true and actions which will take place when they are not true. This is indicated by the Else clauses. Therefore, the second portion of the rule is satisfied and the Nested If statement should be used.

Rule 2: If a given condition must be tested only when a previous condition has been tested, AND one or more statements are to be executed before or after the second if-then-else structure, then a Nested If statement should be used.

The example in Figure 6-16 illustrates the application of Rule 2.

```
020090        IF HOURLY-EMPLOYEE
020100            MOVE HOURLY-CONSTANT TO WAGE-TYPE-REPORT
020110            IF HOURS-INPUT IS GREATER THAN OVERTIME-HOURS-CONSTANT
020120                PERFORM C000-CALC-REGULAR-OVERTIME-PAY
020130            ELSE
020140                PERFORM C010-CALC-REGULAR-PAY.
```
Figure 6-16 Example of Nested If Rule 2

In Figure 6-16, the first condition tested is whether the Employee Is Hourly. If the employee is not hourly, then the test for Hours being greater than the Overtime Hours constant has no meaning; therefore, the first part of the rule is satisfied. If the Employee Is Hourly, then the Hourly constant will be moved to the output area regardless of whether the Hours are greater than the Overtime Hours constant. Thus, the second part of the rule which states that one or more statements are to be executed before or after the second if-then-else structure is satisfied. Therefore, the Nested If statement should be used.

Special Nested If Conditions — Condition 1

There are several conditions which logically require Nested If statements of the kind illustrated previously but which cannot be written as shown previously because of limitations in the COBOL language. Consider the following program narrative:

The Total Payroll for all authors in a company is to be accumulated and printed on a report. If the author receives royalties and the books sold (dollars received from the sale of books) are greater than a quota, then royalties are 6% of the books sold; if books sold are equal to or less than the quota, the royalties are 4% of the books sold. An author who does not receive royalties receives a salary in place of royalties. The Total Payroll for all authors is calculated by accumulating both the royalties and the salaries.

An analysis of the program narrative reveals that this processing should be handled by a Nested If statement because one condition (books sold over quota) is to be tested only if another condition (author receives royalties) is true; and there are alternative actions to perform based upon both conditions.

The Nested If statement in Figure 6-17, which is INCORRECT, might be developed by a programmer to solve the problem.

```
016090          IF ROYALTY-AUTHOR
016100             IF BOOKS-SOLD-INPUT IS GREATER THAN MINIMUM-BOOKS-CONSTANT
016110                COMPUTE ROYALTY-WORK = BOOKS-SOLD-INPUT * HIGH-PCT
016120             ELSE
016130                COMPUTE ROYALTY-WORK = BOOKS-SOLD-INPUT * LOW-PCT
016140             ADD ROYALTY-WORK TO TOTAL-PAYROLL-ACCUM
016150          ELSE
016160             ADD SALARY-INPUT TO TOTAL-PAYROLL-ACCUM.
```

Figure 6-17 Example of INCORRECT Nested If Statement

The sequence of statements in Figure 6-17 logically satisfies the programming specifications. If the author receives royalties and if the books sold are greater than the minimum books constant, then the royalty is computed by multiplying the books sold by the high percent constant; else, the royalty is computed by multiplying the books sold by the low percent constant. After the royalty is computed and stored in the ROYALTY-WORK field, it is added to the Total Payroll Accumulator. If the author does not receive royalties, then the salary from the input record is added to the Total Payroll Accumulator.

The reason this If statement is incorrect is the Add statement on line 016140. Although it is intended that this Add statement will add the calculated royalties regardless of whether the books sold are greater than or not greater than the minimum books constant, in fact it will add the royalties only if the books sold are not greater than the minimum books constant. This is because it follows the Else clause for the If statement which determines if the books sold are greater than the minimum books constant. It MUST be noted that any statement following an Else clause will be executed only when the condition tested is not true. In addition, all statements within the Else clause, which is terminated by either another Else statement or a period, will be executed when the condition is not true. Thus, as a result of the Else statement on line 016120, the two statements on line 016130 and 016140 are executed when the condition tested on line 016100 is false.

There are three methods with which to solve this difficulty imposed by the Nested If statement. The first method is illustrated in Figure 6-18.

```
016090        IF ROYALTY-AUTHOR
016100            IF BOOKS-SOLD-INPUT IS GREATER THAN MINIMUM-BOOKS-CONSTANT
016110                COMPUTE ROYALTY-WORK = BOOKS-SOLD-INPUT * HIGH-PCT
016120            ELSE
016130                COMPUTE ROYALTY-WORK = BOOKS-SOLD-INPUT * LOW-PCT
016140            END-IF
016150            ADD ROYALTY-WORK TO TOTAL-PAYROLL-ACCUM
016160        ELSE
016170            ADD SALARY-INPUT TO TOTAL-PAYROLL-ACCUM.
```

Figure 6-18 Example of End-If Clause

The Nested If statement in Figure 6-18 is written in the same manner as the statement in Figure 6-17 until line 016140. On this line is inserted the COBOL END-IF statement. This statement, which is not available on all COBOL compilers, ends the scope of the preceding If statement in the same manner that the ENDIF word when using pseudocode ends the scope of an If statement. Since, in Figure 6-18, the scope of the If statement on line 016100 is ended by the END-IF statement on line 016140, the Add statement on line 016150 will be executed regardless of whether the books sold are greater than the minimum books constant. This, of course, is the desired result.

Many COBOL compilers do not allow the END-IF statement. For those programs which will be compiled using a compiler which does not allow the END-IF statement, a second or third method should be used. The second method to solve the problem is shown in Figure 6-19.

```
016090        IF ROYALTY-AUTHOR
016100            IF BOOKS-SOLD-INPUT IS GREATER THAN MINIMUM-BOOKS-CONSTANT
016110                COMPUTE ROYALTY-WORK = BOOKS-SOLD-INPUT * HIGH-PCT
016120                ADD ROYALTY-WORK TO TOTAL-PAYROLL-ACCUM
016130            ELSE
016140                COMPUTE ROYALTY-WORK = BOOKS-SOLD-INPUT * LOW-PCT
016150                ADD ROYALTY-WORK TO TOTAL-PAYROLL-ACCUM
016160        ELSE
016170            ADD SALARY-INPUT TO TOTAL-PAYROLL-ACCUM.
```

Figure 6-19 Example of a Second Method to Solve the Problem

In Figure 6-19, the Add statement to add the calculated royalties to the Total Payroll Accumulator is duplicated on line 016120 and line 016150. Therefore, regardless of whether the books sold are greater than or not greater than the minimum books constant, the computed royalty will be added to the Total Payroll Accumulator. This solution is best used if there are a few statements that must be duplicated.

If there are numerous statements that must be duplicated, the method illustrated in Figure 6-20 is normally used.

The If statement on line 012010 in Figure 6-20 determines if the author receives a royalty. If so, the paragraph B001-CHECK-BOOKS-SOLD is performed. This paragraph consists of the If statement (to determine if the books sold are greater than the minimum books constant) and the Compute statements (to calculate the royalty).

After the royalty has been calculated, control will return to the Add statement on line 012030, which will add the royalty to the accumulated payroll. The addition of the royalty to the accumulated payroll is not dependent upon any condition other than the fact that the author receives royalties. The If statement and related Else clause to determine the royalty percentage is placed in the performed paragraph.

0 1 2 0 1 0			I F	R O Y A L T Y - A U T H O R												
0 1 2 0 2 0				P E R F O R M	B 0 0 1 - C H E C K - B O O K S - S O L D											
0 1 2 0 3 0				A D D	R O Y A L T Y - W O R K	T O	T O T A L - P A Y R O L L - A C C U M								
0 1 2 0 4 0		E L S E														
0 1 2 0 5 0				A D D	S A L A R Y - I N P U T	T O	T O T A L - P A Y R O L L - A C C U M .								
0 1 2 0 6 0																
0 1 2 0 7 0																
0 1 2 0 8 0	B 0 0 1 - C H E C K - B O O K S - S O L D .															
0 1 2 0 9 0																
0 1 2 1 0 0			I F	B O O K S - S O L D - I N P U T	I S	G R E A T E R	T H A N	M I N I M U M - B O O K S - C O N S T A N T							
0 1 2 1 1 0				C O M P U T E	R O Y A L T Y - W O R K	=	B O O K S - S O L D - I N P U T	*	H I G H - P C T						
0 1 2 1 2 0			E L S E													
0 1 2 1 3 0				C O M P U T E	R O Y A L T Y - W O R K	=	B O O K S - S O L D - I N P U T	*	L O W - P C T .						

Figure 6-20 Example of a Third Method to Solve the Problem

Special Nested If Conditions — Condition 2

Another condition which must be handled properly is illustrated by the following program narrative:

> If the books sold for an author are above the minimum books constant, the over minimum message is to be moved to the printer output area. If the books sold are above the minimum books constant and the author has been employed more than 3 years, then a bonus amount should be added to the royalty. If the books sold are not above the minimum books constant, then the below minimum message should be moved to the printer output area.

This statement of a problem should be handled with a Nested If statement since the employment period of an author is to be checked only if the book sales are above the minimum books constant; and an alternative action is required for the first condition tested. The Nested If statement in Figure 6-21 is an INCORRECT METHOD to solve the problem.

0 1 5 0 6 0			I F	B O O K S - S O L D - I N P U T	I S	G R E A T E R	T H A N	M I N I M U M - B O O K S - C O N S T A N T				
0 1 5 0 7 0				M O V E	O V E R - M I N I M U M - M E S S A G E	T O	M E S S A G E - A R E A - R E P O R T					
0 1 5 0 8 0				I F	Y E A R S - E M P L O Y E D - I N P U T	I S	G R E A T E R	T H A N	B O N U S - Y R S - C O N S T A N T			
0 1 5 0 9 0					A D D	B O N U S - A M O U N T - C O N S T A N T	T O	R O Y A L T Y - W O R K				
0 1 5 1 0 0		E L S E										
0 1 5 1 1 0				M O V E	U N D E R - M I N I M U M - M E S S A G E	T O	M E S S A G E - A R E A - R E P O R T .					

Figure 6-21 Example of INCORRECT Use of a Nested If Statement

The books sold are compared to the minimum books constant on line 015060. If the value in the BOOKS-SOLD-INPUT field is greater than the value in the MINIMUM-BOOKS-CONSTANT field, an over minimum message is moved to the output area. The years employed are then checked to determine if the author has worked more than three years. If so, the bonus amount is added to the royalty.

The error in the Nested If statement occurs on line 015100. The Else clause is intended by the programmer to pertain to the If statement on line 015060. Instead, it pertains to the If statement on line 015080. As a result of the Nested If statement in Figure 6-21, if the books sold are not greater than the minimum books constant, nothing will take place.

In addition, if the years employed are less than or equal to three years when the books sold are greater than the minimum books constant, an under minimum message will be printed, which is not the proper processing.

The reason the Else clause on line 015100 pertains to the If statement on line 015080 is that If statements and Else clauses are matched with one another. This is illustrated in Figure 6-22.

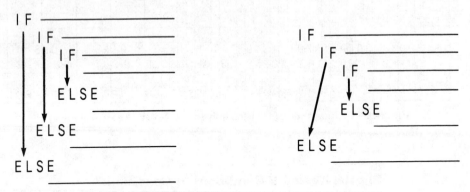

Figure 6-22 Example of Matching If...Else Statements

On the left side of Figure 6-22, each of the If statements is matched by an Else clause. The rule is that in a Nested If statement, the first Else clause corresponds to the innermost If statement. The second Else clause corresponds to the next innermost If statement, and so on. As demonstrated by the right side of Figure 6-22, indentation has no effect whatsoever on the Nested If statement.

Figure 6-23 illustrates a correct solution to the problem using an If statement and a matching Else clause.

015060	IF BOOKS-SOLD-INPUT IS GREATER THAN MINIMUM-BOOKS-CONSTANT
015070	MOVE OVER-MINIMUM-MESSAGE TO MESSAGE-AREA-REPORT
015080	IF YEARS-EMPLOYED-INPUT IS GREATER THAN BONUS-YRS-CONSTANT
015090	ADD BONUS-AMOUNT-CONSTANT TO ROYALTY-WORK
015100	ELSE
015110	NEXT SENTENCE
015120	ELSE
015130	MOVE UNDER-MINIMUM-MESSAGE TO MESSAGE-AREA-REPORT.

Figure 6-23 Example of a Correct Nested If Statement

In Figure 6-23, the Else clause on line 015100 corresponds to the If statement on line 015080, and the Else clause on line 015120 corresponds to the If statement on line 015060. In order to obtain the intended result, it is necessary that the innermost If statement, on line 015080, has a corresponding Else clause. Since nothing is to take place if the books sold are greater than the minimum books constant but the author is employed three years or less, the NEXT SENTENCE clause should be used. Thus, as is required, each If statement has a matching Else clause.

A second method which can be used with those COBOL compilers allowing the use of the END-IF statement is shown in Figure 6-24.

The Nested If statement in Figure 6-24 includes the END-IF statement on line 015100. This statement terminates the effect of the If statement on line 015080. Therefore, the Else clause on line 015110 pertains to the If statement on line 015060, as intended by the programmer. It should be noted again, however, that many COBOL compilers do not allow the use of the END-IF statement.


```
015060        IF BOOKS-SOLD-INPUT IS GREATER THAN MINIMUM-BOOKS-CONSTANT
015070           MOVE OVER-MINIMUM-MESSAGE TO MESSAGE-AREA-REPORT
015080           IF YEARS-EMPLOYED-INPUT IS GREATER THAN BONUS-YRS-CONSTANT
015090              ADD BONUS-AMOUNT-CONSTANT TO ROYALTY-WORK
015100           END-IF
015110        ELSE
015120           MOVE UNDER-MINIMUM-MESSAGE TO MESSAGE-AREA-REPORT.
```

Figure 6-24 Example of End-If Clause

SAMPLE PROGRAM

To illustrate the use of the Nested If statement and to show typical data editing within a program, the sample program in this chapter is designed and programmed to create an Edit Report. As noted previously, data which is invalid or incorrect is normally printed on the Edit Report and identified with the printing of an error message. The printer spacing chart, which illustrates the Edit Report, is shown in Figure 6-25.

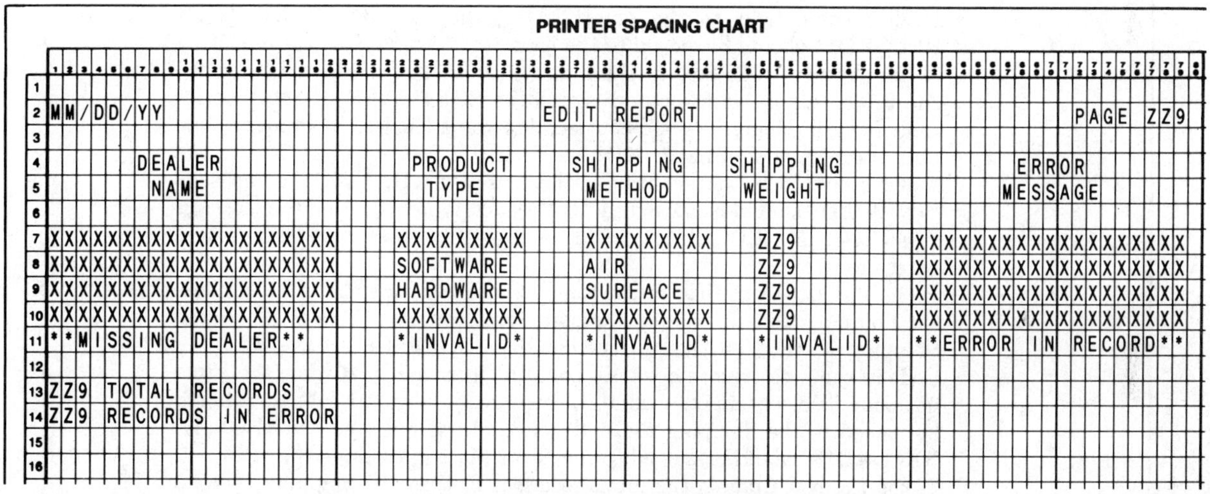

Figure 6-25 Printer Spacing Chart

The input to the program is a disk file of Shipping Records. The format of the input records is illustrated in Figure 6-26.

Shipping Disk Record				
FIELD DESCRIPTION	POSITION	LENGTH	DEC	ATTRIBUTE
Dealer Name	1 – 20	20		Alphanumeric
Product Code	21	1		Alphanumeric
Shipping Code	22	1		Alphanumeric
Shipping Weight	23 – 25	3	0	Numeric
Record Length		25		

Figure 6-26 Program Input

The program narrative for the sample problem is illustrated in Figure 6–27.

PROGRAM NARRATIVE

SUBJECT	Edit Report	DATE	October 14	PAGE 1 OF 1
TO	Programmer	FROM	Systems Analyst	

A program is to be written to prepare an Edit Report. The format of the input record and the printer spacing chart are included with this narrative. The program should be written to include the following processing:

1. The program should read the input records from the disk input file and create the Edit Report as per the format illustrated on the printer spacing chart. The report shall contain the Dealer Name, Product Type, Shipping Method, Shipping Weight, and an Error Message area.

2. The following editing of the input record should occur:

   a. The Dealer Name must be present. If the field is all blanks, it is in error and the message **MISSING DEALER** should be moved to the Dealer Name field on the report. Also, the message **ERROR IN RECORD** should be moved to the Error Message area on the report.

   b. If the Product Code field in the input record contains the value S, then the Product Type on the report should be SOFTWARE. If the Product Code field in the input record contains the value H then the Product Type on the report should be HARDWARE. If the Product Code field in the input record does not contain either an S or H, then the message *INVALID* should be moved to the Product Type Field, and the message **ERROR IN RECORD** should be moved to the Error Message area on the report.

   c. If the Product Code field in the input record contains the value H, then the Shipping Code in the input record must contain a T or R. If so, the Shipping Method on the report should be SURFACE. If the Shipping Code in the input record does not contain either a T or R when the Product Code field contains the value H, then the message *INVALID* should be moved to the Shipping Method field and the message **ERROR IN RECORD** should be moved to the Error Message area on the report.

   d. If the Product Code in the input record is S, then the Shipping Method AIR should be printed on the report.

   e. The Shipping Weight must contain numeric data and must not be greater than 400 pounds. If the Shipping Weight is not numeric or is greater than 400 pounds, the message *INVALID* should be moved to the Shipping Weight field on the report. Also, the message **ERROR IN RECORD** should be moved to the Error Message area on the report.

3. Final totals should be printed for the number of records processed and the number of records in error.

4. Headings are to be printed on the top of each new page of the report. The report is to have a total of 55 lines per page. The date and page number should appear in the heading. The page number should begin at 1, and be incremented by 1 for each new page.

5. The program should be written in COBOL.

Figure 6-27 Program Narrative

EDITING INPUT FIELDS

It is important that the fields within the input record be edited prior to being processed to ensure that they contain valid data. In many cases, allowing invalid data to be processed will result in either the production of invalid output (garbage in, garbage out) or the abnormal termination of the program. The program narrative for the sample program listed the types of editing which are to take place on each of the input fields. The following sections explain the methods used to edit the input records.

Checking for Blank Fields and Missing Data

It is commonly required that a field should contain some data, even though it is not possible to determine exactly what the value of the data should be. For example, in the sample program, it is specified that the Dealer Name must be present; that is, the field cannot contain all blanks. When programming in COBOL, this test can be performed by testing the field for SPACES, as illustrated in Figure 6-28.

```
015110        IF DEALER-NAME-INPUT = SPACES
015120           MOVE MISSING-DEALER-CONSTANT TO DEALER-NAME-REPORT
015130           MOVE ERROR-IN-RECORD-CONSTANT TO MESSAGE-AREA-REPORT
015140           MOVE 'NO' TO IS-THE-RECORD-VALID
015150        ELSE
015160           MOVE DEALER-NAME-INPUT TO DEALER-NAME-REPORT.
```

Figure 6-28 Example of Checking for Missing Data

In Figure 6-28, the value in the DEALER-NAME-INPUT field is compared to the figurative constant SPACES. If the Dealer Name field is equal to spaces, it means there is no data in the Dealer Name field, which constitutes an error. Therefore, if the condition is true, the MISSING-DEALER-CONSTANT (**MISSING DEALER**) and the ERROR-IN-RECORD-CONSTANT (**ERROR IN RECORD**) are moved to the printer output area. In addition, the value NO is moved to the indicator IS-THE-RECORD-VALID to indicate the record is not valid. This indicator can be checked by other modules in the program to determine if a field was not valid. If the value in the DEALER-NAME-INPUT field is not equal to SPACES, then the Dealer Name is moved to the output area.

The field being compared to the figurative constant, SPACES, must be defined as an alphanumeric field (Pic X). A field defined as a numeric field (Pic 9) cannot be checked for spaces using the figurative constant, SPACES. A numeric field to be checked for spaces must be redefined as an alphanumeric field using the Redefines clause (see page 6.30).

Checking for Numeric Data

In some applications, it is necessary to check not only for the presence of data, but also that the data present is numeric. This is the case, for example, with the Shipping Weight field in the sample program. The program narrative states that the Shipping Weight field must contain numeric data. The COBOL statement to check that the Shipping Weight field contains numeric data is illustrated in Figure 6-29.

016130			IF	SHIPPING-WEIGHT-INPUT	IS	NOT	NUMERIC			
016140				MOVE	INVALID-CONSTANT	TO	INVALID-WEIGHT-REPORT			
016150				MOVE	ERROR-IN-RECORD-CONSTANT	TO	MESSAGE-AREA-REPORT			
016160				MOVE	'NO '	TO	IS-THE-RECORD-VALID			
016170		ELSE								
016180				MOVE	SHIPPING-WEIGHT-INPUT	TO	SHIPPING-WEIGHT-REPORT.			

Figure 6-29 Example of If Numeric Test

The value in the SHIPPING-WEIGHT-INPUT field is checked for a numeric value through the use of the If statement and the Numeric Class Test. If the field does not contain numeric data, then the INVALID-CONSTANT (**INVALID**) and the ERROR-IN-RECORD-CONSTANT (**ERROR IN RECORD**) are moved to the output area, and the indicator IS-THE-RECORD-VALID is set to NO to indicate that the record is not valid.

The Numeric Class Test performs several functions. First, it tests to determine if there is a value in the field, since a field which contains all blanks would contain nonnumeric data. Secondly, it tests to ensure that all data in the field is numeric data.

The following rules apply when testing fields for numeric data:

1. If the field being tested for numeric is defined as an Alphanumeric field (Pic X), then the presence of a positive or negative sign in the field would cause the field to be nonnumeric. The numeric value must be an unsigned absolute value.
2. If the field being tested for numeric is defined as a Numeric field (Pic 9) without the Sign Indication (S), then the presence of a positive or negative sign in the field would cause the field to be nonnumeric.
3. If the field being tested for numeric is defined as a Numeric field with a sign (Pic S9), then the presence of a positive or negative sign in the field is valid and will not affect the determination of whether the field is numeric.

Testing for Reasonableness in a Numeric Field

It is common to edit the contents of a numeric field for reasonable values. In the sample program, in addition to editing the Shipping Weight field for valid numeric data, the program narrative states that the field must also be edited to ensure that the value contained in the field is not greater than 400 pounds. The nested If statement to check that the Shipping Weight field contains numeric data and is not greater than 400 pounds is illustrated in Figure 6-30.

016130			IF	SHIPPING-WEIGHT-INPUT	IS	NOT	NUMERIC			
016140				MOVE	INVALID-CONSTANT	TO	INVALID-WEIGHT-REPORT			
016150				MOVE	ERROR-IN-RECORD-CONSTANT	TO	MESSAGE-AREA-REPORT			
016160				MOVE	'NO '	TO	IS-THE-RECORD-VALID			
016170		ELSE								
016180			IF	SHIPPING-WEIGHT-INPUT	IS	GREATER	THAN			
016190				MAX-SHIPPING-WEIGHT-CONSTANT						
016200				MOVE	INVALID-CONSTANT	TO	INVALID-WEIGHT-REPORT			
017010				MOVE	ERROR-IN-RECORD-CONSTANT	TO	MESSAGE-AREA-REPORT			
017020				MOVE	'NO '	TO	IS-THE-RECORD-VALID			
017030		ELSE								
017040				MOVE	SHIPPING-WEIGHT-INPUT	TO	SHIPPING-WEIGHT-REPORT.			

Figure 6-30 Example of a Reasonableness Test

In Figure 6–30, the SHIPPING-WEIGHT-INPUT field is checked for nonnumeric data and unreasonable data using a Nested If statement. If the SHIPPING-WEIGHT-INPUT field does not contain numeric data, then the INVALID-CONSTANT (**INVALID**) and the ERROR-IN-RECORD-CONSTANT (**ERROR IN RECORD**) will be moved to the printer output area, and the indicator IS-THE-RECORD-VALID will be set to NO to indicate that the record is not valid.

If the value in the SHIPPING-WEIGHT-INPUT field is numeric, then an If statement (line 016180) is performed to test the contents of the field for a value greater than 400. If the value in the SHIPPING-WEIGHT-INPUT field is greater than MAX-SHIPPING-WEIGHT-CONSTANT (400), then the INVALID-CONSTANT (**INVALID**) and the ERROR-IN-RECORD-CONSTANT (**ERROR IN RECORD**) will be moved to the output area, and the indicator IS-THE-RECORD-VALID will be set to NO to indicate that the record is not valid.

Testing for Specific Values in a Field

In some cases, it is necessary to determine if a field contains specific values. If it does not, then the data in the field is in error. This is the case with the Shipping Code field in the sample program. The Shipping Code field in the input record must contain the specific values T or R to be valid. Figure 6–31 illustrates one method that can be used to test for specific values in the Shipping Code field.

Data Division

```
003150        05  SHIPPING-CODE-INPUT          PIC X.
003160        88  SHIPPING-BY-TRUCK-OR-RAILROAD      VALUE 'T', 'R'.
```

Procedure Division

```
015190              IF SHIPPING-BY-TRUCK-OR-RAILROAD
015200                  MOVE SURFACE-CONSTANT TO SHIPPING-METHOD-REPORT
016010              ELSE
016020                  MOVE INVALID-CONSTANT TO SHIPPING-METHOD-REPORT
016030                  MOVE ERROR-IN-RECORD-CONSTANT TO MESSAGE-AREA-REPORT
016040                  MOVE 'NO ' TO IS-THE-RECORD-VALID
```

Figure 6-31 Example of Specific Value Testing

In Figure 6–31, the SHIPPING-CODE-INPUT field is defined in the Data Division as an alphanumeric (Pic X) field. Immediately following the definition of the SHIPPING-CODE-INPUT field is the condition name SHIPPING-BY-TRUCK-OR-RAILROAD (identified by level 88), followed by the two values which are valid for the Shipping Code field (T and R). The values are each contained within quotation marks and are separated by a comma. Any number of individual values that could appear in the SHIPPING-CODE-INPUT field can be associated with a condition-name in this manner.

In the Procedure Division, the If statement containing the condition name SHIPPING-BY-TRUCK-OR-RAILROAD is used to determine if any of the valid values (T or R) are present in the SHIPPING-CODE-INPUT field. If any of the valid values are in the field, then the condition will be considered true and the SURFACE-CONSTANT will be moved to the printer output area. If the condition is not true, then the INVALID-CONSTANT and the ERROR-IN-RECORD-CONSTANT will be moved to the printer output area, and the value NO will be moved to the indicator field IS-THE-RECORD-VALID.

Summary — Editing Input Fields

The previous examples have illustrated some of the techniques which can be used to edit input data in an attempt to ensure that only valid data enters the computer. Editing is an important part of the programming process, and the programmer should be familiar with editing techniques and when they should be used.

PROGRAM DESIGN

After thoroughly analyzing the program narrative, the programmer would set about to design the program. The first step is to develop the structure of the program through the use of IPO Charts. The IPO Chart for the module to create the edit report is illustrated in Figure 6-32.

IPO CHART

PROGRAM: Edit Report	PROGRAMMER: Forsythe		DATE: Oct. 24
MODULE NAME: Create Edit Report	REF: A000	MODULE FUNCTION:	Create the Edit Report

INPUT	PROCESSING	REF:	OUTPUT
1. Shipping Disk File	1. Initialize		1. Edit Report
	2. Obtain the input data		
	3. Process the detail records	B000	
	4. Print the final totals	B010	
	5. Terminate		

Figure 6-32 IPO Chart for Create the Edit Report Module

As in previous programs, the major processing tasks of the module whose function is to create the edit report are specified, together with the input to the module and the output from the module. After the major processing tasks are listed, each of them is analyzed to determine if it represents a specific function to be performed that is of sufficient size and/or complexity to justify another module. In this program, the major processing tasks of Process the Detail Records and Print the Final Totals each define specific tasks to be accomplished that are potentially of such size and difficulty to justify separate modules.

Once this determination is made, the hierarchy chart for the first and second levels is drawn, as illustrated in Figure 6-33.

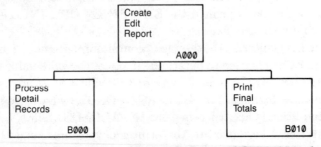

Figure 6-33 Hierarchy Chart with First and Second Levels

After drawing the Hierarchy chart, the programmer should design the IPO Charts for the modules identified on the Hierarchy Chart. The IPO Charts for the Process the Detail Records module and the Print the Final Totals module are illustrated in Figure 6-34.

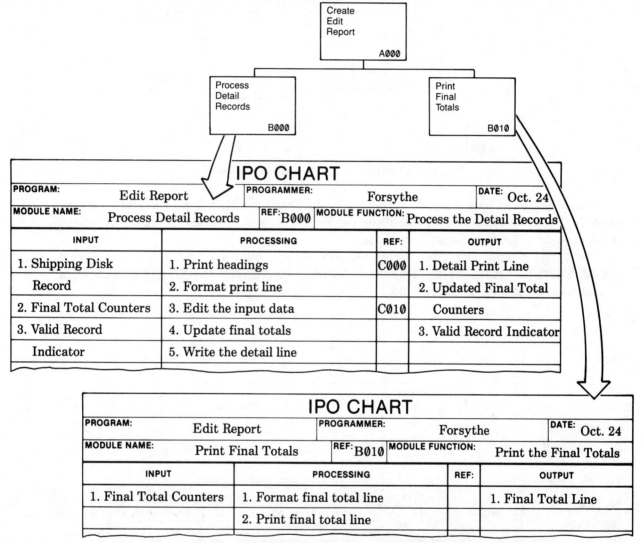

Figure 6-34 IPO Charts for Second Level Modules

The major processing tasks, together with the input and the output, are listed for the two modules (B000 and B010) on the second level of the hierarchy chart. When the IPO Charts are complete, the programmer would again analyze each major processing task in each of the modules to determine if it represents a specific function to be accomplished that is of such size and/or complexity to justify another module.

An analysis of the module whose function is to process the detail records reveals that the first major processing task, Print the Headings, specifies a unique function that is probably of such a size as to justify another module. Continued analysis reveals that the third major processing task, Edit the Input Data, is also a unique function that is probably complex enough to justify another module. Further analysis of the remaining major processing tasks in this module and the module whose function is to print the final totals does not reveal any other processing which would justify another module. Thus, after this analysis, the programmer would continue the hierarchy chart as illustrated in Figure 6-35.

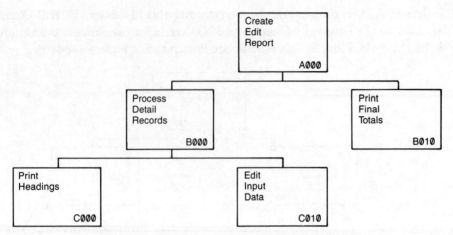

Figure 6-35 Hierarchy Chart with Third Level

The Hierarchy Chart shows five modules — the Create the Edit Report module, the Process the Detail Records module, the Print the Final Totals module, the Print the Headings module, and the Edit the Input Data module.

Next, the programmer must design the IPO Charts for the new modules which were added. The IPO Charts for the Print the Headings module and the Edit the Input Data modules are illustrated in Figure 6–36.

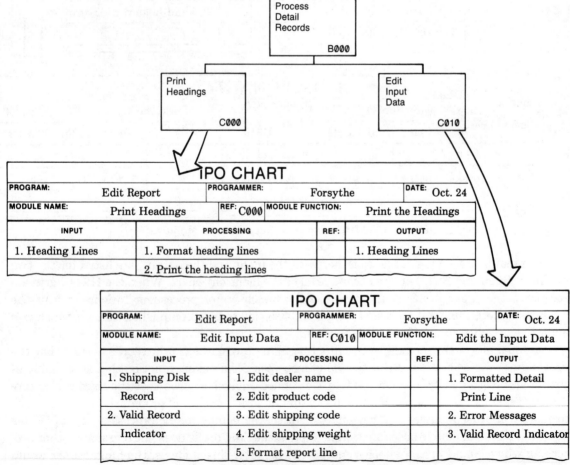

Figure 6-36 IPO Charts for Third Level Modules

An analysis of the IPO Charts for the modules to print the headings and edit the input data reveals there are no major processing tasks which appear to require another module. Therefore, the programmer would review the design of the program as specified on the IPO Charts and the Hierarchy Chart (the final hierarchy chart is shown in Figure 6–35) and then begin the design of the logic.

Pseudocode Specifications

The pseudocode for each of the modules is written on the Pseudocode Specifications form. In general, the pseudocode is prepared for the modules in top-down fashion, which means the logic for the highest level module is designed first, and then the logic for the modules on the second level is designed, and so on. In this manner, any problems which may arise in the method of solving the problem will be detected early in the design process. Thus, in the sample program, the first module for which to design the logic is the module whose function is to Create the Edit Report. The Pseudocode Specifications for this module are illustrated in Figure 6–37.

PSEUDOCODE SPECIFICATIONS

PROGRAM: Edit Report	PROGRAMMER: Forsythe	DATE: Oct. 24

MODULE NAME: Create Edit Report	REF: A000	MODULE FUNCTION: Create the Edit Report

PSEUDOCODE	REF:	DATA BASES, FILES, RECORDS, FIELDS REQUIRED

Open the files
Read an input record
IF there is a record
    PERFORM UNTIL no more input records
        Process detail records
        Read an input record
    ENDPERFORM
    Print the final totals
ENDIF
Close the files
Stop run
	
	B000
	
	B010
		Shipping disk file
		Edit report file
		Input record area
		    Dealer name
		    Product code
		    Shipping code
		    Shipping weight
		There is a record indicator
		No more records indicator

Figure 6-37 Pseudocode for the Highest Level Module

In Figure 6–37, the logic for the module which creates the Edit Report is basically the same as was seen for the highest level module in Chapter 5. The only difference is that no headings are written from this module. The headings will be produced from the module whose function is to write the headings.

The Reference Numbers for the modules which are called from the Create Edit Report module are contained in the REF column to indicate the fact that lower level modules are to be called to perform the function specified in the pseudocode. In this manner, the programmer is able to follow the processing which will take place within the program by following the reference numbers.

After the top level module is designed and reviewed, the next level of modules would be designed. The Pseudocode Specifications for the module whose function is to process the detail records is illustrated in Figure 6–38.

PSEUDOCODE SPECIFICATIONS

PROGRAM: Edit Report	PROGRAMMER: Forsythe	DATE: Oct. 24
MODULE NAME: Process Detail Records	REF: B000	MODULE FUNCTION: Process the Detail Records

PSEUDOCODE	REF:	DATA BASES, FILES, RECORDS, FIELDS REQUIRED

IF number of lines printed is = or > page size or first page
    Print the headings
ENDIF
Clear the printer area
Set valid record indicator to yes
Edit the input data
IF record is not valid
    Add 1 to records in error counter
ENDIF
Add 1 to total records counter
Write the line on the report
Add 1 to lines printed
Set spacing to single spacing
	C000
	
	C010
		Number of lines printed counter
		Page size constant
		First page indicator
		Printer output area
		    Dealer name
		    Product type
		    Shipping method
		    Shipping weight
		    Error message area
		Valid record indicator
		Record is not valid indicator
		Records in error counter
		Total records counter
		Spacing control area
		Single spacing constant

Figure 6-38 Pseudocode for the Detail Record Module

The first If statement in the pseudocode in Figure 6-38 is used to determine when the headings should be printed. There are two conditions that determine when they should be printed — first, when the first page of the report is to be printed; and second, when the number of lines actually printed on the page are equal to or greater than the number of lines that are supposed to be printed on the page. The If statement in Figure 6-38 checks if the number of lines printed are equal to or greater than the page size, or if the first page is to be printed. If either of these conditions is true, then the headings will be printed. Because of this checking, a counter for the number of lines printed, the page size constant, and a first page indicator must be defined in the program. The method for defining these fields will be illustrated later in this chapter.

After the headings are printed when required, the printer area is cleared. Next, the indicator used to indicate whether fields in the input record are valid is set to the value YES. Although editing the input data is performed in another module, it is necessary for the purpose of accumulating the number of records in error to know whether the record being edited contains errors. Thus, prior to passing control to the module that will edit the input record, the valid record indicator is set to YES to indicate that the record about to be edited is assumed valid prior to the editing process.

The input data is then edited by the Edit Input Data module. After the editing, the valid record indicator will contain the value YES if all fields contained valid data, or the value NO if the data in any of the fields being edited was found to be invalid.

After editing is complete, an If statement is used to test the valid record indicator. If, when the record was edited, any fields were found to contain invalid data, the value 1 will be added to the records in error counter.

The value 1 is then added to the total records counter, and the line is written on the report.

The number of lines printed is then incremented by 1. This is necessary because the manner in which page overflow is detected is by the number of lines which have been printed on a page. Therefore, after each line is printed on the report, the count must be incremented to reflect this. The spacing is then set for single spacing, and the processing of the detail record is complete.

The other module on the second level of the Hierarchy Chart is the module whose function is to print the final totals. The pseudocode for this module is illustrated in Figure 6-39.

PSEUDOCODE SPECIFICATIONS

PROGRAM: Edit Report	PROGRAMMER: Forsythe	DATE: Oct. 24
MODULE NAME: Print Final Totals	REF: B010 MODULE FUNCTION:	Print the Final Totals

PSEUDOCODE	REF:	DATA BASES, FILES, RECORDS, FIELDS REQUIRED
Move the total records to the final total line Write the total records total line on the report Move the total records in error to the final total line Write the total records in error final total line on the report		Total records counter Total records total line Total records in error counter Total records in error total line

Figure 6-39 Pseudocode for the Final Total Module

The processing in the Final Total module consists of moving the final totals to the final total lines and printing the final total lines.

Once the pseudocode for the second level modules has been designed, the programmer would begin the design of the logic for the modules on the third level. As illustrated in the Hierarchy Chart (see Figure 6-35), there are two modules on the third level — the module whose function is to print the headings, and the module whose function is to edit the input data. The pseudocode for the module which prints the headings is illustrated in Figure 6-40.

PSEUDOCODE SPECIFICATIONS

PROGRAM: Edit Report	PROGRAMMER: Forsythe	DATE: Oct. 24
MODULE NAME: Print Headings	REF: C000 MODULE FUNCTION:	Print the Headings on the report

PSEUDOCODE	REF:	DATA BASES, FILES, RECORDS, FIELDS REQUIRED
Obtain the date from memory Move the date to the heading line Move the page count to the heading line Write the first heading line Write the second heading line Write the third heading line Add 1 to page count Set lines printed counter to five Set spacing for double spacing		Date work area Page count counter First heading line Second heading line Third heading line Number of lines printed counter Spacing control area Double spacing constant

Figure 6-40 Pseudocode for the Heading Module

The first step in writing the headings is to obtain the date from memory and move it to the heading line. The date is stored in computer memory by the operating system. The technique for accessing the current date using COBOL is illustrated later in this chapter.

The page count must also be moved to the heading line. The page count begins with the value one and is incremented by one for each page which is written on the report.

After the first heading line is formatted, the three heading lines are printed on the report. The page count is then incremented by one so that the next time the page number is printed, it will be the proper value. The counter for the number of lines is then set to the value 5, which is the number of lines in the heading, including the blank line following the column headings. This is necessary because when each new page is started, the lines will be counted on that page. If the counter were not set, there would be no way to determine that page overflow had occurred. The spacing is then set for double spacing so that the first line following the heading will be double spaced.

The pseudocode for the module which edits the fields in the input record is illustrated in Figure 6-41.

PSEUDOCODE SPECIFICATIONS

PROGRAM: Edit Report	PROGRAMMER: Forsythe	DATE: Oct. 24

MODULE NAME: Edit Input Data	REF: C010	MODULE FUNCTION: Edit the Input Data

PSEUDOCODE	REF:	DATA BASES, FILES, RECORDS, FIELDS REQUIRED

IF dealer name = spaces
    Move "missing dealer" to printer output area
    Move "error in record" to printer output area
    Indicate invalid record
ELSE
    Move dealer name to printer output area
ENDIF
IF product is hardware
    Move "hardware" to printer output area
    IF shipping by truck or railroad
        Move "surface" to printer output area
    ELSE
        Move "invalid" to printer output area
        Move "error in record" to printer
          output area
        Indicate invalid record
    ENDIF
ELSE
    IF product is software
        Move "software" to printer output area
        Move "air" to printer output area
    ELSE
        Move "invalid" to printer output area
        Move "error in record" to printer
          output area
        Indicate invalid record
    ENDIF
ENDIF
IF shipping weight is not numeric
    Move "invalid" to printer output area
    Move "error in record" to printer output area
    Indicate invalid record
ELSE
    IF shipping weight is greater than maximum
      shipping weight
        Move "invalid" to printer output area
        Move "error in record" to printer
          output area
        Indicate invalid record
    ELSE
        Move shipping weight to printer output
          area
    ENDIF
ENDIF
		Dealer name
		"Missing dealer" constant
		"Error in record" constant
		Printer output area
		    Dealer name
		    Product type
		    Shipping method
		    Shipping weight
		    Error message area
		Valid record indicator
		Product code
		"Hardware" constant
		Shipping code
		"Surface" constant
		"Invalid" constant
		"Software" constant
		"Air" constant
		Shipping weight
		Maximum shipping weight
		   constant

Figure 6-41 Pseudocode for the Edit Input Data Module

In Figure 6-41, an If statement is used to test the Dealer Name field for spaces. If the Dealer Name is equal to spaces, the missing dealer and error in record constants are moved to the printer output area, and the valid record indicator is set to indicate the record is not valid. If the Dealer Name is not equal to spaces, the dealer name is moved from the input area to the printer output area. Following the Else clause is the word ENDIF, indicating the end of the scope of the If statement.

After the Dealer Name field is edited, a Nested If statement is encountered. The first condition tested is whether the product is hardware. If the product being shipped is a hardware product, the hardware constant is moved to the printer output area. An If statement is then used to determine if shipping of the hardware product is by truck or railroad. If the hardware product is shipped by truck or railroad, then the surface constant is moved to the printer output area.

If the hardware product is not shipped by truck or railroad, the invalid constant and the error in record constant are moved to the printer output area, and the indicator is set to indicate the record is not valid. It will be recalled from the program narrative (Figure 6-27) that hardware products can only be shipped by truck or railroad. Shipment of a hardware product by any other method is invalid. Following these statements the word ENDIF indicates that the statements following it are not dependent upon the condition tested in the If statement.

If the product is not hardware, the next condition tested is whether the product is software. If the product is software, the software and air constants are moved to the printer output area because, as specified in the program narrative (Figure 6-27), all software products are shipped by air.

As indicated in the program narrative, a product is either a hardware product or a software product. If the product code in the input record specifies neither a hardware product nor a software product, the product code is invalid. Thus, the invalid constant and the error in record constant are moved to the printer output area to indicate an error in the input record, and the indicator is to set to show that the input record is not valid.

Next, a nested If statement is used to test the Shipping Weight field for reasonable, numeric data. If the data in the shipping weight field is not numeric, the invalid constant and the error in record constant are moved to the printer output area, and the indicator is set to show an invalid record. If the shipping weight is numeric, the If statement following the Else clause determines if the shipping weight is greater than the maximum shipping weight (400). If so, the invalid and error in record constants are moved to the printer output area, and the indicator is set to show an invalid record. If the shipping weight is not greater than 400, then it is moved to the printer output area.

After the pseudocode has been prepared for all modules in the program, it should be very carefully reviewed in a structured walkthrough. When there is a consensus that the program structure and the logic expressed in the pseudocode is correct, the programmer can begin the program coding.

DATA DIVISION

In previous programs, a condition name has been used in the Working-Storage Section of the Data Division. A condition name can also be used in the File Section when defining an input record. The use of a condition name in the sample program to indicate whether a product is software or hardware and to indicate whether shipping is by truck or railroad is illustrated in Figure 6-42.

```
003060 FD  SHIPPING-INPUT-FILE
003070         RECORD CONTAINS 25 CHARACTERS
003080         LABEL RECORDS ARE STANDARD
003090         DATA RECORD IS SHIPPING-INPUT-RECORD.
003100 01  SHIPPING-INPUT-RECORD.
003110     05  DEALER-NAME-INPUT            PIC X(20).
003120     05  PRODUCT-CODE-INPUT           PIC X.
003130         88  PRODUCT-IS-SOFTWARE                      VALUE 'S'.
003140         88  PRODUCT-IS-HARDWARE                      VALUE 'H'.
003150     05  SHIPPING-CODE-INPUT          PIC X.
003160         88  SHIPPING-BY-TRUCK-OR-RAILROAD            VALUE 'T', 'R'.
003170     05  SHIPPING-WEIGHT-INPUT        PIC 9(3).
```

Figure 6-42 Definition of the Input File

In Figure 6-42, the Shipping Input File is defined together with the input area to be used for the Shipping Input Record. The field which contains the code indicating whether the product is software or hardware is called PRODUCT-CODE-INPUT. Immediately following the definition of the field are the condition names which are used to identify if the product is software or hardware. On line 003130, the condition name PRODUCT-IS-SOFTWARE is given the value S. Thus, testing the condition name PRODUCT-IS-SOFTWARE is equivalent to testing for the value S in the field. Similarly, testing the condition name PRODUCT-IS-HARDWARE tests for the value H in the field.

The field which contains a code indicating whether shipping is by mail or truck was explained in Figure 6-31.

Program Constants and the Redefines Clause

The printer spacing chart for the sample program is shown again in Figure 6-43.

PRINTER SPACING CHART

	DEALER NAME	PRODUCT TYPE	SHIPPING METHOD	SHIPPING WEIGHT	ERROR MESSAGE
2	MM/DD/YY	EDIT REPORT			PAGE ZZ9
7	XXXXXXXXXXXXXXXXXXXX	XXXXXXXXX	XXXXXXXXX	ZZ9	XXXXXXXXXXXXXXXXXXXX
8	XXXXXXXXXXXXXXXXXXXX	SOFTWARE	AIR	ZZ9	XXXXXXXXXXXXXXXXXXXX
9	XXXXXXXXXXXXXXXXXXXX	HARDWARE	SURFACE	ZZ9	XXXXXXXXXXXXXXXXXXXX
10	XXXXXXXXXXXXXXXXXXXX	XXXXXXXXX	XXXXXXXXX	ZZ9	XXXXXXXXXXXXXXXXXXXX
11	**MISSING DEALER**	*INVALID*	*INVALID*	*INVALID*	**ERROR IN RECORD**
13	ZZ9 TOTAL RECORDS				
14	ZZ9 RECORDS IN ERROR				

Figure 6-43 Printer Spacing Chart for the Sample Program

Several constants are printed on the Edit report: SOFTWARE, HARDWARE, AIR, and SURFACE. Several error constants are also printed on the Edit Report: **MISSING DEALER**, *INVALID*, and **ERROR IN RECORD**. These program constants must be defined in the Working-Storage Section. Their definition is illustrated in Figure 6-44.

```
005090  01  PROGRAM-CONSTANTS.
005100      05  PRINT-CONSTANTS.
005110          10  SOFTWARE-CONSTANT    PIC X(9)     VALUE 'SOFTWARE '.
005120          10  HARDWARE-CONSTANT    PIC X(9)     VALUE 'HARDWARE '.
005130          10  SURFACE-CONSTANT     PIC X(9)     VALUE 'SURFACE '.
005140          10  AIR-CONSTANT         PIC X(9)     VALUE 'AIR      '.
005150
005160      05  ERROR-CONSTANTS.
005170          10  MISSING-DEALER-CONSTANT    PIC X(20)    VALUE
005180                                      '**MISSING DEALER**  '.
005190          10  INVALID-CONSTANT           PIC X(9)     VALUE
005200                                      '*INVALID*'.
006010          10  ERROR-IN-RECORD-CONSTANT   PIC X(19)    VALUE
006020                                      '**ERROR IN RECORD**'.
006030
006040      05  COMPARE-CONSTANTS.
006050          10  MAX-SHIPPING-WEIGHT-CONSTANT PIC 9(3) VALUE 400.
```

Figure 6-44 Definition of Program Constants

In Figure 6-44, three types of program constants are defined: print constants, error constants, and compare constants. The print constants are moved to the printer output area if the particular field in the input record contains valid data. The error constants are moved to the printer output area if the field contains invalid data. The compare constant, MAX-SHIPPING-WEIGHT-CONSTANT, is used to compare the contents of the Shipping Weight field to the value 400.

The printer spacing chart in Figure 6-43 shows that the Dealer Name, Product Type, Shipping Method, and Shipping Weight fields may contain an error message indicating that the data in the field is invalid. The Dealer Name field, in Figure 6-43, and the error constant, MISSING-DEALER-CONSTANT, in Figure 6-44, are both alphanumeric fields of the same length (20 positions). Thus, the Move statement in the Procedure Division that moves the error constant to the Dealer Name field in the output area is moving fields of the same type and the same length. It will be recalled from Chapter 3 that when both the sending and receiving fields in a move statement have the same length, the object program is more efficient. The program constants have been designed with this in mind.

Similarly, both the Product Type field and the Shipping Method field will contain either a print constant or an error message indicating invalid data. The Product Type field will contain either the constant SOFTWARE, the constant HARDWARE, or the error constant *INVALID*. All three constants, SOFTWARE-CONSTANT, HARDWARE-CONSTANT, and INVALID-CONSTANT, are alphanumeric; and all are the same length (9 positions) as the Product Type field.

Likewise, the Shipping Method field will contain either the constant AIR, the constant SURFACE, or the error constant *INVALID*. In Figure 6-44, all three constants, SURFACE-CONSTANT, AIR-CONSTANT, and INVALID-CONSTANT, are alphanumeric and are the same length as the Shipping Method field.

The Shipping Weight field on the report will contain either the valid shipping weight from the input record or the error constant *INVALID*. Shipping weight is an edited numeric field because it is zero suppressed (see Figure 6-43). The field INVALID-CONSTANT as defined in Figure 6-44 is an alphanumeric field. Since an alphanumeric field cannot be moved to an edited numeric field, the Shipping Weight field in the printer output area must be redefined as an alphanumeric field. The EDIT-REPORT-LINE and the redefinition of the Shipping Weight field are illustrated in Figure 6-45.

004030	01	EDIT-REPORT-LINE.			
004040		05	CARRIAGE-CONTROL	PIC	X.
004050		05	DEALER-NAME-REPORT	PIC	X(20).
004060		05	FILLER	PIC	X(4).
004070		05	PRODUCT-TYPE-REPORT	PIC	X(9).
004080		05	FILLER	PIC	X(4).
004090		05	SHIPPING-METHOD-REPORT	PIC	X(9).
004100		05	FILLER	PIC	X(3).
004110		05	VALID-WEIGHT-REPORT.		
004120			10 SHIPPING-WEIGHT-REPORT	PIC	ZZ9.
004130			10 FILLER	PIC	X(6).
004140		05	INVALID-WEIGHT-REPORT REDEFINES VALID-WEIGHT-REPORT		
004150				PIC	X(9).
004160		05	FILLER	PIC	X(2).
004170		05	MESSAGE-AREA-REPORT	PIC	X(19).
004180		05	FILLER	PIC	X(53).

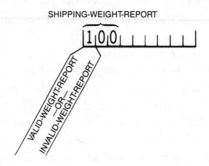

Figure 6-45 Redefinition of the Shipping Weight Field

In Figure 6–45, the Edit Report Line is defined. The field which is to contain either the shipping weight or the error constant *INVALID* is defined on line 004110 as the group item VALID-WEIGHT-REPORT. The two elementary item fields into which VALID-WEIGHT-REPORT is divided are the three character edited numeric field, SHIPPING-WEIGHT-REPORT, and the FILLER field on line 004130, which is a six character alphanumeric field.

The VALID-WEIGHT-REPORT field is then redefined on line 004140 and is given the name INVALID-WEIGHT-REPORT. The Redefines clause is used to give the same area of computer memory a different name, different attributes (numeric or alphanumeric), or both. Thus, the nine positions in computer memory can be referenced in the Procedure Division both by the name VALID-WEIGHT-REPORT and by the name INVALID-WEIGHT-REPORT. In addition, the first three positions can be referenced by the name SHIPPING-WEIGHT-REPORT. In the example in Figure 6–45, a shipping weight of 100 is stored in the first three positions of the field.

If, when the shipping weight data in the input record is edited, the shipping weight is found to be nonnumeric or is greater than 400, the value in the INVALID-CONSTANT field (*INVALID*) will be moved to the INVALID-WEIGHT-REPORT field. Both the INVALID-CONSTANT field and the INVALID-WEIGHT-REPORT field are defined as nine position alphanumeric fields. Therefore, an alphanumeric field of 9 characters is being moved to a similarly defined field.

If the shipping weight is found to be numeric and not greater than the value 400, the shipping weight from the input record will be moved to the SHIPPING-WEIGHT-REPORT field. Therefore, a numeric field 3 characters in length (SHIPPING-WEIGHT-INPUT) is being moved to an edited numeric field (SHIPPING-WEIGHT-REPORT) of equal length.

When using the Redefines clause, the programmer must follow two rules. First, the field being redefined and the redefined field should be the same length. Second, the statement that performs the redefinition should immediately follow the area being redefined and both the redefining statement and the redefined area should have the same level number.

Valid Record Indicator

In the sample program in this chapter, an indicator is needed to indicate whether a record being edited is valid or invalid. Figure 6–46 illustrates the definition of the indicator and its usage in the Procedure Division.

Working-Storage Section

```
005020  01   PROGRAM-INDICATORS.
005030       05  ARE-THERE-MORE-RECORDS      PIC X(3)      VALUE 'YES'.
005040           88  THERE-IS-A-RECORD                     VALUE 'YES'.
005050           88  THERE-ARE-NO-MORE-RECORDS             VALUE 'NO '.
005060       05  IS-THE-RECORD-VALID          PIC X(3)      VALUE 'YES'.
005070           88  THE-RECORD-IS-NOT-VALID               VALUE 'NO '.
```

Procedure Division

```
012120       MOVE 'YES' TO IS-THE-RECORD-VALID.
012130       PERFORM C010-EDIT-INPUT-DATA.
012140       IF THE-RECORD-IS-NOT-VALID
012150           ADD 1 TO RECORDS-IN-ERROR-COUNT.
                       .
                       .
                       .
015090  C010-EDIT-INPUT-DATA.
015100
015110       IF DEALER-NAME-INPUT = SPACES
015120           MOVE MISSING-DEALER-CONSTANT TO DEALER-NAME-REPORT
015130           MOVE ERROR-IN-RECORD-CONSTANT TO MESSAGE-AREA-REPORT
015140           MOVE 'NO ' TO IS-THE-RECORD-VALID
```

Figure 6-46 Example of an Indicator

In the Working-Storage Section in Figure 6–46, the condition name THE-RECORD-IS-NOT-VALID is equated to the value NO being in the indicator (line 005070). In the Procedure Division, the value YES is moved to the IS-THE-RECORD-VALID indicator (line 012120) prior to performing the edit input data module.

In the C010-EDIT-INPUT-DATA module (line 015090), several input fields are edited for invalid data. Among those fields being edited is the Dealer Name field. The Dealer Name is checked for all spaces. If it contains all spaces, the appropriate error messages are moved to the printer output area, and the value NO is moved to the IS-THE-RECORD-VALID indicator.

After checking all fields in the C010-EDIT-INPUT-DATA module, control is passed back to the If statement (line 012140) to see if the record is not valid. If any fields were found to contain invalid data, then the condition IF THE-RECORD-IS-NOT-VALID is true and the value 1 will be added to the records in error counter.

Printer Control

The page count, the page size, and the number of lines printed are required fields in order to print headings on each page. These fields, together with the spacing control fields which have appeared in previous programs, are illustrated in Figure 6–47.

006170	01	PRINTER-CONTROL.			
006180		05	PROPER-SPACING	PIC 9.	
006190		05	SPACE-ONE-LINE	PIC 9	VALUE 1.
006200		05	SPACE-TWO-LINES	PIC 9	VALUE 2.
007010		05	PAGE-COUNT	PIC S999	VALUE +1.
007020		88	FIRST-PAGE		VALUE +1.
007030		05	PAGE-SIZE	PIC 999	VALUE 55.
007040		05	LINES-PRINTED	PIC S999	VALUE ZERO.

Figure 6-47 Definition of the Printer Control Fields

In the Printer Control group, the first three fields for printer spacing control are the same as have been seen in previous programs. The three additional fields, PAGE-COUNT, PAGE-SIZE, and LINES-PRINTED, are required in order to print headings on each page of the report.

The PAGE-COUNT field is used to count the number of pages in the report and to supply the Page Number to be printed on the report. It is given the initial value of +1 because the first page on the report will be numbered 1. The plus sign is used because the numeric field is specified as a signed field (PIC S999).

The condition name FIRST-PAGE is used to identify the first page of the report. If the PAGE-COUNT field contains the value +1, then the first page on the report has not yet been printed, and the module to print the headings will be invoked to print the headings on the first page.

The PAGE-SIZE field is a constant field which is used to determine if a complete page has been printed. It is given the value 55, which is the number of lines to be printed on each page of the report. The value 55 is chosen by the programmer and may be any value which is required for the particular report.

The LINES-PRINTED field is used to count the number of lines which have been printed on a page of the report. It is given the initial value zero. As each line is printed on the page, the value 1 will be added to this field. Prior to printing a detail line, the value in this field is checked against the Page Size. If it is equal to or greater than the page size, then headings will be printed.

Defining the Date Work Area

On most computers, the current date is stored in computer memory as a 6 character field (Year, Month, Day). In the sample program, the date, which will be printed in the report heading, is obtained from computer memory and is placed in a work area within the Working-Storage Section of the Data Division. The work area and the method used in the Procedure Division of the sample program to place the date in the work area are shown in Figure 6-48.

In Figure 6-48, the DATE-WORK field is defined on line 006080. The DATE-WORK field is then subdivided into three 2-digit numeric fields — the YEAR-WORK field, the MONTH-WORK field, and the DAY-WORK field. The date is six characters in length and is stored in

Data Division

```
006070 01  WORK-AREAS.
006080     05  DATE-WORK.
006090         10  YEAR-WORK           PIC 99.
006100         10  MONTH-WORK          PIC 99.
006110         10  DAY-WORK            PIC 99.
```

Procedure Division

```
014070     ACCEPT DATE-WORK FROM DATE.
014080     MOVE MONTH-WORK TO MONTH-HEADING.
014090     MOVE DAY-WORK TO DAY-HEADING.
014100     MOVE YEAR-WORK TO YEAR-HEADING.
```

$$\text{ACCEPT identifier FROM} \left\{ \begin{array}{l} \text{DATE} \\ \text{DAY} \\ \text{TIME} \end{array} \right\}$$

Figure 6-48 Definition of the Date Work Area and the Accept Statement

YYMMDD format (ie. — January 25, 1987 would be stored as 870125).

The date is obtained from computer memory using the Accept statement. When the Accept statement is executed, the reserved word DATE identifies that the current date is to be copied from the area in main computer memory where it is stored by the operating system to the field DATE-WORK which has been defined in the program.

The Accept statement can also be used to retrieve the day of the year and the time of day. The day of the year is returned in a Julian date format. The first two numeric characters are the year and the next three numeric characters are the day of the year. Thus, the value returned for January 25, 1987 would be 87025. The time is returned as a two-digit numeric hour, a two-digit numeric minute, a two-digit numeric second, and a two-digit numeric hundredths of a second. Thus, the time 9:15 a.m. would be returned as 09150000.

Defining the Heading Line

The first heading line on the report contains the date and the page number (see Figure 6-43). These fields must be defined in the heading line. The definition of the heading line for the sample program is illustrated in Figure 6-49.

```
007060 01  HEADING-LINES.
007070     05  FIRST-HEADING-LINE.
007080         10  CARRIAGE-CONTROL        PIC X.
007090         10  DATE-HEADING.
007100             15  MONTH-HEADING       PIC 99.
007110             15  FILLER              PIC X     VALUE '/'.
007120             15  DAY-HEADING         PIC 99.
007130             15  FILLER              PIC X     VALUE '/'.
007140             15  YEAR-HEADING        PIC 99.
007150         10  FILLER                  PIC X(26) VALUE SPACES.
007160         10  FILLER                  PIC X(12) VALUE
007170                                               'EDIT REPORT'.
007180         10  FILLER                  PIC X(25) VALUE SPACES.
007190         10  FILLER                  PIC X(5)  VALUE 'PAGE '.
007200         10  PAGE-NUMBER-HEADING     PIC ZZ9.
008010         10  FILLER                  PIC X(53) VALUE SPACES.
```

Figure 6-49 Definition of the Heading Line

In Figure 6-49, the DATE-HEADING field for the date which will be printed in the heading is defined on line 007090. Since the date on the report is printed in the form MM/DD/ YY and the date in the work area is in the form YYMMDD (see Figure 6-48), the DATE-HEADING field must be subdivided so the Month, Day, and Year may be moved from the work area to the heading line. Thus, the date is subdivided into the MONTH-HEADING, DAY-HEADING, and YEAR-HEADING fields. The field DATE-HEADING is 8 characters in length, and the month, day, and year are separated by slashes.

PROCEDURE DIVISION

The top-level module which creates the edit report contains coding similar to that seen in previous programs. It is shown with the complete program in Figure 6-55.

The module which processes the detail records contains the coding to determine when headings should be printed. The coding for this module is illustrated in Figure 6-50.

```
012050  B000-PROCESS-DETAIL-RECORDS.
012060
012070      IF LINES-PRINTED IS EQUAL TO PAGE-SIZE OR
012080          LINES-PRINTED IS GREATER THAN PAGE-SIZE OR
012090          FIRST-PAGE
012100          PERFORM C000-PRINT-HEADINGS.
012110      MOVE SPACES TO EDIT-REPORT-LINE.
012120      MOVE 'YES' TO IS-THE-RECORD-VALID.
012130      PERFORM C010-EDIT-INPUT-DATA.
012140      IF THE-RECORD-IS-NOT-VALID
012150          ADD 1 TO RECORDS-IN-ERROR-COUNT.
012160      ADD 1 TO TOTAL-RECORDS-COUNT.
012170      WRITE EDIT-REPORT-LINE
012180          AFTER ADVANCING PROPER-SPACING.
012190      ADD 1 TO LINES-PRINTED.
012200      MOVE SPACE-ONE-LINE TO PROPER-SPACING.
```

Figure 6-50 Detail Processing Module

In Figure 6-50, the coding on lines 012070, 012080, and 012090 checks for the conditions upon which the headings will be printed on the report. On line 012070 the number of lines which have been printed on the page are compared to the page size to determine if the number of lines printed are equal to or greater than the number of lines to be printed on the page. If so, the heading module will be performed. The reason the equal to or greater than condition is specified instead of just equal to is that in some programs several lines may be printed in a module and the value in the lines printed counter may exceed the page count. If the greater than test were not included, page overflow would never occur. Therefore, as a matter of convention, it is suggested that whenever page overflow is checked, the test should be equal to or greater than.

The Add statement on line 012190 increments the line counter by one. Whenever page overflow is to be checked by counting the number of lines printed on a page, a statement must be included to increment the line counter by the number of lines which were printed. In the sample problem, the report is single spaced, so the line counter is incremented by one. If the report is to be double spaced, the line counter should be incremented by 2 each time a line is printed.

The module which prints the headings on the report is illustrated in Figure 6-51.

```
013180 *****************************************************************
013190 *                                                               *
013200 * THIS MODULE PRINTS THE HEADINGS.  IT IS ENTERED FROM AND      *
014010 * EXITS TO THE B000-PROCESS-DETAIL-RECORDS MODULE.             *
014020 *                                                               *
014030 *****************************************************************
014040
014050  C000-PRINT-HEADINGS.
014060
014070      ACCEPT DATE-WORK FROM DATE.
014080      MOVE MONTH-WORK TO MONTH-HEADING.
014090      MOVE DAY-WORK TO DAY-HEADING.
014100      MOVE YEAR-WORK TO YEAR-HEADING.
014110      MOVE PAGE-COUNT TO PAGE-NUMBER-HEADING.
014120      WRITE EDIT-REPORT-LINE FROM FIRST-HEADING-LINE
014130          AFTER ADVANCING TO-TOP-OF-PAGE.
014140      WRITE EDIT-REPORT-LINE FROM SECOND-HEADING-LINE
014150          AFTER ADVANCING 2 LINES
014160      WRITE EDIT-REPORT-LINE FROM THIRD-HEADING-LINE
014170          AFTER ADVANCING 1 LINES.
014180      ADD 1 TO PAGE-COUNT.
014190      MOVE 5 TO LINES-PRINTED.
014200      MOVE SPACE-TWO-LINES TO PROPER-SPACING.
```

Figure 6-51 Heading Module

On lines 014080 through 014100, the values in the date work area are moved to the heading line. On line 014110, the value in the PAGE-COUNT field is moved to the PAGE-NUMBER-HEADING field. This places the page number in the heading.

After the headings are printed, the page count is incremented by one and the number of lines printed counter (LINES-PRINTED) is set to five. This is done so that the number of lines printed on the page will be counted properly. The spacing is then set for double spacing, and the module is completed.

SAMPLE PROGRAM

The sample program prepares an Edit Report. The output, input, and source listing of the sample program are illustrated on the following pages.

Output

```
02/27/85                    EDIT REPORT                    PAGE   1

          DEALER        PRODUCT    SHIPPING    SHIPPING       ERROR
          NAME          TYPE       METHOD      WEIGHT         MESSAGE

   ABC COMPUTER STORES  SOFTWARE   AIR            5
   **MISSING DEALER**   HARDWARE   SURFACE      100           **ERROR IN RECORD**
   TECNI-COMPUTERS      SOFTWARE   AIR        *INVALID*       **ERROR IN RECORD**
   ALU SHOPS            HARDWARE   SURFACE       75
   BITS INCORPORATED    HARDWARE   *INVALID*    350           **ERROR IN RECORD**
   INTEGRITY CIRCUITS   *INVALID*                30           **ERROR IN RECORD**
   BOARDS UNLIMITED     SOFTWARE   AIR            9
   AMERICAN COMPUTERS   HARDWARE   SURFACE    *INVALID*       **ERROR IN RECORD**

      8 TOTAL RECORDS
      5 RECORDS IN ERROR
```

Figure 6-52 Edit Report

Input

Shipping Disk Record				
FIELD DESCRIPTION	**POSITION**	**LENGTH**	**DEC**	**ATTRIBUTE**
Dealer Name	1 – 20	20		Alphanumeric
Product Code	21	1		Alphanumeric
Shipping Code	22	1		Alphanumeric
Shipping Weight	23 – 25	3	0	Numeric
Record Length		25		

Figure 6-53 Input

Source Listing

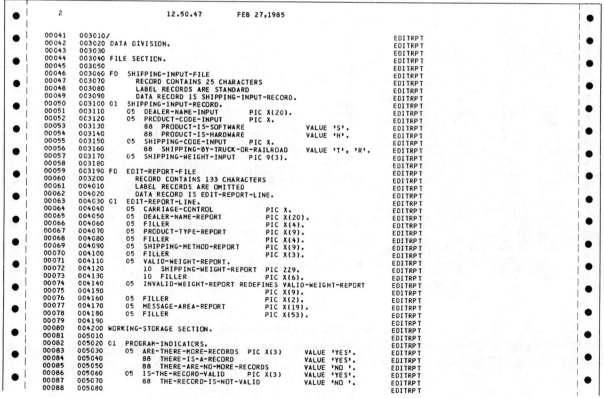

```
PP 5740-CB1 RELEASE 2.3 + PTF 8 - UP13477          IBM OS/VS COBOL  JULY 24, 1978        12.50.47  DATE FEB 27,1985


     1                           12.50.47      FEB 27,1985


00001   001010 IDENTIFICATION DIVISION.                                              EDITRPT
00002   001020                                                                       EDITRPT
00003   001030 PROGRAM-ID.      EDITRPT.                                             EDITRPT
00004   001040 AUTHOR.          FORSYTHE.                                            EDITRPT
00005   001050 INSTALLATION.  BREA.                                                  EDITRPT
00006   001060 DATE-WRITTEN.  DEC 21,1984.                                           EDITRPT
00007   001070 DATE-COMPILED. FEB 27,1985.                                           EDITRPT
00008   001080 SECURITY.       UNCLASSIFIED.                                         EDITRPT
00009   001090                                                                       EDITRPT
00010   001100******************************************************************     EDITRPT
00011   001110*                                                                 *    EDITRPT
00012   001120*   THIS PROGRAM PRODUCES AN EDIT REPORT EDITING DEALER NAME      *    EDITRPT
00013   001130*   FOR BLANKS, PRODUCT CODE AND SHIPPING CODE FOR VALID          *    EDITRPT
00014   001140*   CODES, AND THE SHIPPING WEIGHT FOR NUMERIC, REASONABLE        *    EDITRPT
00015   001150*   DATA. IF ALL FIELDS IN THE RECORD ARE VALID, A LINE IS        *    EDITRPT
00016   001160*   WRITTEN ON THE EDIT REPORT. IF ANY ERRORS ARE FOUND, A LINE   *    EDITRPT
00017   001170*   IS WRITTEN ON THE REPORT NOTING THAT THE RECORD IS IN ERROR   *    EDITRPT
00018   001180*   AND IDENTIFYING THE FIELD IN ERROR. FINAL TOTALS ARE          *    EDITRPT
00019   001190*   PRINTED FOR THE NUMBER OF RECORDS PROCESSED AND THE NUMBER    *    EDITRPT
00020   001200*   OF RECORDS IN ERROR.                                          *    EDITRPT
00021   002010*                                                                 *    EDITRPT
00022   002020******************************************************************     EDITRPT
00023   002030                                                                       EDITRPT
00024   002040                                                                       EDITRPT
00025   002050                                                                       EDITRPT
00026   002060 ENVIRONMENT DIVISION.                                                 EDITRPT
00027   002070                                                                       EDITRPT
00028   002080 CONFIGURATION SECTION.                                                EDITRPT
00029   002090                                                                       EDITRPT
00030   002100 SOURCE-COMPUTER. IBM-4381.                                            EDITRPT
00031   002110 OBJECT-COMPUTER. IBM-4381.                                            EDITRPT
00032   002120 SPECIAL-NAMES.   C01 IS TO-TOP-OF-PAGE.                               EDITRPT
00033   002130                                                                       EDITRPT
00034   002140 INPUT-OUTPUT SECTION.                                                 EDITRPT
00035   002150                                                                       EDITRPT
00036   002160 FILE-CONTROL.                                                         EDITRPT
00037   002170     SELECT SHIPPING-INPUT-FILE                                        EDITRPT
00038   002180         ASSIGN TO UT-S-EDITDATA.                                      EDITRPT
00039   002190     SELECT EDIT-REPORT-FILE                                           EDITRPT
00040   002200         ASSIGN TO UT-S-EDITPRNT.                                      EDITRPT


     2                           12.50.47      FEB 27,1985


00041   003010/                                                                      EDITRPT
00042   003020 DATA DIVISION.                                                        EDITRPT
00043   003030                                                                       EDITRPT
00044   003040 FILE SECTION.                                                         EDITRPT
00045   003050                                                                       EDITRPT
00046   003060 FD  SHIPPING-INPUT-FILE                                               EDITRPT
00047   003070     RECORD CONTAINS 25 CHARACTERS                                     EDITRPT
00048   003080     LABEL RECORDS ARE STANDARD                                        EDITRPT
00049   003090     DATA RECORD IS SHIPPING-INPUT-RECORD.                             EDITRPT
00050   003100 01  SHIPPING-INPUT-RECORD.                                            EDITRPT
00051   003110     05  DEALER-NAME-INPUT       PIC X(20).                            EDITRPT
00052   003120     05  PRODUCT-CODE-INPUT      PIC X.                                EDITRPT
00053   003130         88  PRODUCT-IS-SOFTWARE           VALUE 'S'.                  EDITRPT
00054   003140         88  PRODUCT-IS-HARDWARE           VALUE 'H'.                  EDITRPT
00055   003150     05  SHIPPING-CODE-INPUT     PIC X.                                EDITRPT
00056   003160         88  SHIPPING-BY-TRUCK-OR-RAILROAD VALUE 'T', 'R'.            EDITRPT
00057   003170     05  SHIPPING-WEIGHT-INPUT   PIC 9(3).                             EDITRPT
00058   003180                                                                       EDITRPT
00059   003190 FD  EDIT-REPORT-FILE                                                  EDITRPT
00060   003200     RECORD CONTAINS 133 CHARACTERS                                    EDITRPT
00061   004010     LABEL RECORDS ARE OMITTED                                         EDITRPT
00062   004020     DATA RECORD IS EDIT-REPORT-LINE.                                  EDITRPT
00063   004030 01  EDIT-REPORT-LINE.                                                 EDITRPT
00064   004040     05  CARRIAGE-CONTROL        PIC X.                                EDITRPT
00065   004050     05  DEALER-NAME-REPORT      PIC X(20).                            EDITRPT
00066   004060     05  FILLER                  PIC X(4).                             EDITRPT
00067   004070     05  PRODUCT-TYPE-REPORT     PIC X(9).                             EDITRPT
00068   004080     05  FILLER                  PIC X(4).                             EDITRPT
00069   004090     05  SHIPPING-METHOD-REPORT  PIC X(9).                             EDITRPT
00070   004100     05  FILLER                  PIC X(3).                             EDITRPT
00071   004110     05  VALID-WEIGHT-REPORT.                                          EDITRPT
00072   004120         10  SHIPPING-WEIGHT-REPORT PIC ZZ9.                           EDITRPT
00073   004130         10  FILLER              PIC X(6).                             EDITRPT
00074   004140     05  INVALID-WEIGHT-REPORT REDEFINES VALID-WEIGHT-REPORT           EDITRPT
00075   004150                                 PIC X(9).                             EDITRPT
00076   004160     05  FILLER                  PIC X(2).                             EDITRPT
00077   004170     05  MESSAGE-AREA-REPORT     PIC X(19).                            EDITRPT
00078   004180     05  FILLER                  PIC X(53).                            EDITRPT
00079   004190                                                                       EDITRPT
00080   004200 WORKING-STORAGE SECTION.                                              EDITRPT
00081   005010                                                                       EDITRPT
00082   005020 01  PROGRAM-INDICATORS.                                               EDITRPT
00083   005030     05  ARE-THERE-MORE-RECORDS  PIC X(3)    VALUE 'YES'.             EDITRPT
00084   005040         88  THERE-IS-A-RECORD               VALUE 'YES'.             EDITRPT
00085   005050         88  THERE-ARE-NO-MORE-RECORDS       VALUE 'NO '.             EDITRPT
00086   005060     05  IS-THE-RECORD-VALID     PIC X(3)    VALUE 'YES'.             EDITRPT
00087   005070         88  THE-RECORD-IS-NOT-VALID         VALUE 'NO '.             EDITRPT
00088   005080                                                                       EDITRPT
```

Figure 6-54 Source Listing (Part 1 of 4)

```
    3                    12.50.47      FEB 27,1985

00089  005090 01  PROGRAM-CONSTANTS.                                      EDITRPT
00090  005100     05  PRINT-CONSTANTS.                                    EDITRPT
00091  005110         10  SOFTWARE-CONSTANT    PIC X(9)      VALUE 'SOFTWARE '.  EDITRPT
00092  005120         10  HARDWARE-CONSTANT    PIC X(9)      VALUE 'HARDWARE '.  EDITRPT
00093  005130         10  SURFACE-CONSTANT     PIC X(9)      VALUE 'SURFACE  '.  EDITRPT
00094  005140         10  AIR-CONSTANT         PIC X(9)      VALUE 'AIR      '.  EDITRPT
00095  005150                                                            EDITRPT
00096  005160     05  ERROR-CONSTANTS.                                   EDITRPT
00097  005170         10  MISSING-DEALER-CONSTANT     PIC X(20)   VALUE  EDITRPT
00098  005180                                            '**MISSING DEALER** '.EDITRPT
00099  005190         10  INVALID-CONSTANT            PIC X(9)    VALUE  EDITRPT
00100  005200                                            '*INVALID*'.    EDITRPT
00101  006010         10  ERROR-IN-RECORD-CONSTANT    PIC X(19)   VALUE  EDITRPT
00102  006020                                            '**ERROR IN RECORD**'.EDITRPT
00103  006030                                                            EDITRPT
00104  006040     05  COMPARE-CONSTANTS.                                 EDITRPT
00105  006050         10  MAX-SHIPPING-WEIGHT-CONSTANT PIC 9(3) VALUE 400. EDITRPT
00106  006060                                                            EDITRPT
00107  006070 01  WORK-AREAS.                                            EDITRPT
00108  006080     05  DATE-WORK.                                         EDITRPT
00109  006090         10  YEAR-WORK            PIC 99.                    EDITRPT
00110  006100         10  MONTH-WORK           PIC 99.                    EDITRPT
00111  006110         10  DAY-WORK             PIC 99.                    EDITRPT
00112  006120                                                            EDITRPT
00113  006130 01  TOTAL-ACCUMULATORS-COUNTERS.                           EDITRPT
00114  006140     05  TOTAL-RECORDS-COUNT      PIC S999     VALUE ZERO.   EDITRPT
00115  006150     05  RECORDS-IN-ERROR-COUNT   PIC S999     VALUE ZERO.   EDITRPT
00116  006160                                                            EDITRPT
00117  006170 01  PRINTER-CONTROL.                                       EDITRPT
00118  006180     05  PROPER-SPACING           PIC 9.                     EDITRPT
00119  006190     05  SPACE-ONE-LINE           PIC 9        VALUE 1.      EDITRPT
00120  006200     05  SPACE-TWO-LINES          PIC 9        VALUE 2.      EDITRPT
00121  007010     05  PAGE-COUNT               PIC S999     VALUE +1.     EDITRPT
00122  007020         88  FIRST-PAGE                        VALUE +1.     EDITRPT
00123  007030     05  PAGE-SIZE                PIC 999      VALUE 55.     EDITRPT
00124  007040     05  LINES-PRINTED            PIC S999     VALUE ZERO.   EDITRPT
00125  007050                                                            EDITRPT
00126  007060 01  HEADING-LINES.                                         EDITRPT
00127  007070     05  FIRST-HEADING-LINE.                                EDITRPT
00128  007080         10  CARRIAGE-CONTROL     PIC X.                     EDITRPT
00129  007090         10  DATE-HEADING.                                  EDITRPT
00130  007100             15  MONTH-HEADING    PIC 99.                    EDITRPT
00131  007110             15  FILLER           PIC X        VALUE '/'.    EDITRPT
00132  007120             15  DAY-HEADING      PIC 99.                    EDITRPT
00133  007130             15  FILLER           PIC X        VALUE '/'.    EDITRPT
00134  007140             15  YEAR-HEADING     PIC 99.                    EDITRPT
00135  007150         10  FILLER               PIC X(26)    VALUE SPACES. EDITRPT
00136  007160         10  FILLER               PIC X(12)    VALUE         EDITRPT
00137  007170                                            'EDIT REPORT'.   EDITRPT
00138  007180         10  FILLER               PIC X(25)    VALUE SPACES. EDITRPT
00139  007190         10  FILLER               PIC X(5)     VALUE 'PAGE '. EDITRPT
00140  007200         10  PAGE-NUMBER-HEADING  PIC ZZ9.                   EDITRPT
00141  008010         10  FILLER               PIC X(53)    VALUE SPACES. EDITRPT
00142  008020     05  SECOND-HEADING-LINE.                               EDITRPT
00143  008030         10  CARRIAGE-CONTROL     PIC X.                     EDITRPT
00144  008040         10  FILLER               PIC X(6)     VALUE SPACES. EDITRPT
00145  008050         10  FILLER               PIC X(6)     VALUE 'DEALER'. EDITRPT
00146  008060         10  FILLER               PIC X(13)    VALUE SPACES. EDITRPT
00147  008070         10  FILLER               PIC X(7)     VALUE 'PRODUCT'. EDITRPT
00148  008080         10  FILLER               PIC X(4)     VALUE SPACES. EDITRPT
00149  008090         10  FILLER               PIC X(8)     VALUE 'SHIPPING'. EDITRPT
00150  008100         10  FILLER               PIC X(3)     VALUE SPACES. EDITRPT
00151  008110         10  FILLER               PIC X(8)     VALUE 'SHIPPING'. EDITRPT
00152  008120         10  FILLER               PIC X(12)    VALUE SPACES. EDITRPT
00153  008130         10  FILLER               PIC X(5)     VALUE 'ERROR'. EDITRPT
00154  008140         10  FILLER               PIC X(60)    VALUE SPACES. EDITRPT
00155  008150     05  THIRD-HEADING-LINE.                                EDITRPT
00156  008160         10  CARRIAGE-CONTROL     PIC X.                     EDITRPT
00157  008170         10  FILLER               PIC X(7)     VALUE SPACES. EDITRPT
00158  008180         10  FILLER               PIC X(4)     VALUE 'NAME'.  EDITRPT
00159  008190         10  FILLER               PIC X(15)    VALUE SPACES. EDITRPT
00160  008200         10  FILLER               PIC X(4)     VALUE 'TYPE'.  EDITRPT
00161  009010         10  FILLER               PIC X(7)     VALUE SPACES. EDITRPT
00162  009020         10  FILLER               PIC X(7)     VALUE 'METHOD'. EDITRPT
00163  009030         10  FILLER               PIC X(4)     VALUE SPACES. EDITRPT
00164  009040         10  FILLER               PIC X(6)     VALUE 'WEIGHT'. EDITRPT
00165  009050         10  FILLER               PIC X(12)    VALUE SPACES. EDITRPT
00166  009060         10  FILLER               PIC X(7)     VALUE 'MESSAGE'. EDITRPT
00167  009070         10  FILLER               PIC X(59)    VALUE SPACES. EDITRPT
00168  009080                                                            EDITRPT
00169  009090 01  TOTAL-LINES.                                           EDITRPT
00170  009100     05  FIRST-TOTAL-LINE.                                  EDITRPT
00171  009110         10  CARRIAGE-CONTROL     PIC X.                     EDITRPT
00172  009120         10  TOTAL-RECORDS-FINAL  PIC ZZ9.                   EDITRPT
00173  009130         10  FILLER               PIC X(14)    VALUE         EDITRPT
00174  009140                                            ' TOTAL RECORDS'. EDITRPT
00175  009150         10  FILLER               PIC X(115)   VALUE SPACES. EDITRPT
00176  009160     05  SECOND-TOTAL-LINE.                                 EDITRPT
00177  009170         10  CARRIAGE-CONTROL     PIC X.                     EDITRPT
00178  009180         10  RECORDS-IN-ERROR-FINAL PIC ZZ9.                 EDITRPT
00179  009190         10  FILLER               PIC X(17)    VALUE         EDITRPT
00180  009200                                            ' RECORDS IN ERROR'.EDITRPT
00181  010010         10  FILLER               PIC X(112)   VALUE SPACES. EDITRPT
```

Figure 6-55 Source Listing (Part 2 of 4)

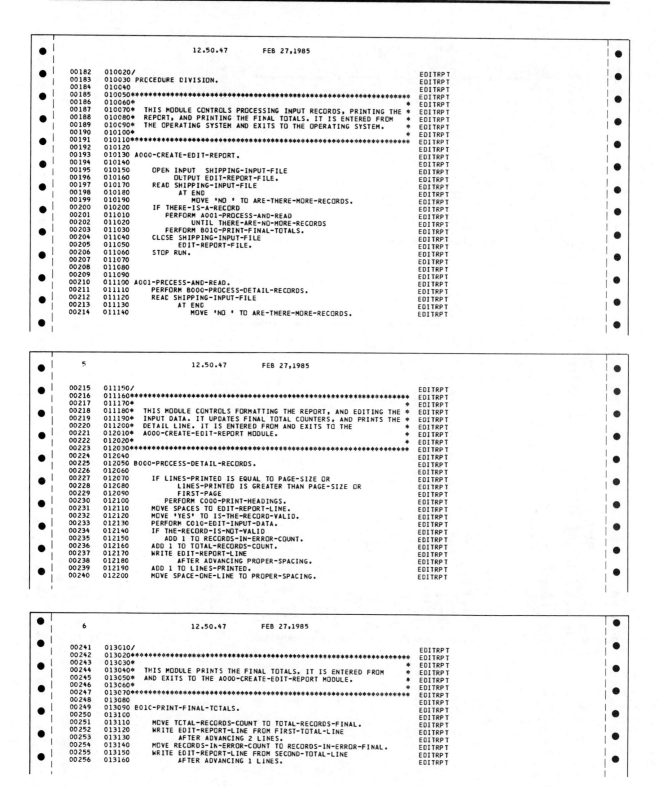

```
                        12.50.47      FEB 27,1985

00182   010020/                                                        EDITRPT
00183   010030 PROCEDURE DIVISION.                                     EDITRPT
00184   010040                                                         EDITRPT
00185   010050**********************************************************EDITRPT
00186   010060*                                                       *EDITRPT
00187   010070*  THIS MODULE CONTROLS PROCESSING INPUT RECORDS, PRINTING THE *EDITRPT
00188   010080*  REPORT, AND PRINTING THE FINAL TOTALS. IT IS ENTERED FROM  *EDITRPT
00189   010090*  THE OPERATING SYSTEM AND EXITS TO THE OPERATING SYSTEM.    *EDITRPT
00190   010100*                                                       *EDITRPT
00191   010110**********************************************************EDITRPT
00192   010120                                                         EDITRPT
00193   010130 A000-CREATE-EDIT-REPORT.                                EDITRPT
00194   010140                                                         EDITRPT
00195   010150     OPEN INPUT  SHIPPING-INPUT-FILE                      EDITRPT
00196   010160          OUTPUT EDIT-REPORT-FILE.                        EDITRPT
00197   010170     READ SHIPPING-INPUT-FILE                             EDITRPT
00198   010180          AT END                                         EDITRPT
00199   010190              MOVE 'NO ' TO ARE-THERE-MORE-RECORDS.       EDITRPT
00200   010200     IF THERE-IS-A-RECORD                                 EDITRPT
00201   011010          PERFORM A001-PROCESS-AND-READ                   EDITRPT
00202   011020              UNTIL THERE-ARE-NO-MORE-RECORDS             EDITRPT
00203   011030          PERFORM B010-PRINT-FINAL-TOTALS.                EDITRPT
00204   011040     CLOSE SHIPPING-INPUT-FILE                            EDITRPT
00205   011050          EDIT-REPORT-FILE.                               EDITRPT
00206   011060     STOP RUN.                                            EDITRPT
00207   011070                                                         EDITRPT
00208   011080                                                         EDITRPT
00209   011090                                                         EDITRPT
00210   011100 A001-PROCESS-AND-READ.                                   EDITRPT
00211   011110     PERFORM B000-PROCESS-DETAIL-RECORDS.                 EDITRPT
00212   011120     READ SHIPPING-INPUT-FILE                             EDITRPT
00213   011130          AT END                                         EDITRPT
00214   011140              MOVE 'NO ' TO ARE-THERE-MORE-RECORDS.       EDITRPT
```

```
   5                    12.50.47      FEB 27,1985

00215   011150/                                                        EDITRPT
00216   011160**********************************************************EDITRPT
00217   011170*                                                       *EDITRPT
00218   011180*  THIS MODULE CONTROLS FORMATTING THE REPORT, AND EDITING THE *EDITRPT
00219   011190*  INPUT DATA. IT UPDATES FINAL TOTAL COUNTERS, AND PRINTS THE *EDITRPT
00220   011200*  DETAIL LINE. IT IS ENTERED FROM AND EXITS TO THE    *EDITRPT
00221   012010*  A000-CREATE-EDIT-REPORT MODULE.                     *EDITRPT
00222   012020*                                                       *EDITRPT
00223   012030**********************************************************EDITRPT
00224   012040                                                         EDITRPT
00225   012050 B000-PROCESS-DETAIL-RECORDS.                            EDITRPT
00226   012060                                                         EDITRPT
00227   012070     IF LINES-PRINTED IS EQUAL TO PAGE-SIZE OR           EDITRPT
00228   012080          LINES-PRINTED IS GREATER THAN PAGE-SIZE OR     EDITRPT
00229   012090          FIRST-PAGE                                     EDITRPT
00230   012100          PERFORM C000-PRINT-HEADINGS.                   EDITRPT
00231   012110     MOVE SPACES TO EDIT-REPORT-LINE.                    EDITRPT
00232   012120     MOVE 'YES' TO IS-THE-RECORD-VALID.                  EDITRPT
00233   012130     PERFORM C010-EDIT-THE-INPUT-DATA.                   EDITRPT
00234   012140     IF THE-RECORD-IS-NOT-VALID                          EDITRPT
00235   012150          ADD 1 TO RECORDS-IN-ERROR-COUNT.               EDITRPT
00236   012160     ADD 1 TO TOTAL-RECORDS-COUNT.                       EDITRPT
00237   012170     WRITE EDIT-REPORT-LINE                              EDITRPT
00238   012180          AFTER ADVANCING PROPER-SPACING.                EDITRPT
00239   012190     ADD 1 TO LINES-PRINTED.                             EDITRPT
00240   012200     MOVE SPACE-ONE-LINE TO PROPER-SPACING.              EDITRPT
```

```
   6                    12.50.47      FEB 27,1985

00241   013010/                                                        EDITRPT
00242   013020**********************************************************EDITRPT
00243   013030*                                                       *EDITRPT
00244   013040*  THIS MODULE PRINTS THE FINAL TOTALS. IT IS ENTERED FROM *EDITRPT
00245   013050*  AND EXITS TO THE A000-CREATE-EDIT-REPORT MODULE.     *EDITRPT
00246   013060*                                                       *EDITRPT
00247   013070**********************************************************EDITRPT
00248   013080                                                         EDITRPT
00249   013090 B010-PRINT-FINAL-TOTALS.                                EDITRPT
00250   013100                                                         EDITRPT
00251   013110     MOVE TOTAL-RECORDS-COUNT TO TOTAL-RECORDS-FINAL.    EDITRPT
00252   013120     WRITE EDIT-REPORT-LINE FROM FIRST-TOTAL-LINE        EDITRPT
00253   013130          AFTER ADVANCING 2 LINES.                       EDITRPT
00254   013140     MOVE RECORDS-IN-ERROR-COUNT TO RECORDS-IN-ERROR-FINAL. EDITRPT
00255   013150     WRITE EDIT-REPORT-LINE FROM SECOND-TOTAL-LINE       EDITRPT
00256   013160          AFTER ADVANCING 1 LINES.                       EDITRPT
```

Figure 6-56 Source Listing (Part 3 of 4)

```
      7                    12.50.47      FEB 27,1985

00257  013170/                                                         EDITRPT
00258  013180*************************************************************  * EDITRPT
00259  013190*                                                         * EDITRPT
00260  013200*  THIS MODULE PRINTS THE HEADINGS. IT IS ENTERED FROM AND  * EDITRPT
00261  014010*  EXITS TO THE B000-PROCESS-DETAIL-RECORDS MODULE.        * EDITRPT
00262  014020*                                                         * EDITRPT
00263  014030*************************************************************  * EDITRPT
00264  014040                                                            EDITRPT
00265  014050 C000-PRINT-HEADINGS.                                       EDITRPT
00266  014060                                                            EDITRPT
00267  014070     ACCEPT DATE-WORK FROM DATE.                            EDITRPT
00268  014080     MOVE MONTH-WORK TO MONTH-HEADING.                      EDITRPT
00269  014090     MOVE DAY-WORK TO DAY-HEADING.                          EDITRPT
00270  014100     MOVE YEAR-WORK TO YEAR-HEADING.                        EDITRPT
00271  014110     MOVE PAGE-COUNT TO PAGE-NUMBER-HEADING.                EDITRPT
00272  014120     WRITE EDIT-REPORT-LINE FROM FIRST-HEADING-LINE         EDITRPT
00273  014130         AFTER ADVANCING TO-TOP-OF-PAGE.                    EDITRPT
00274  014140     WRITE EDIT-REPORT-LINE FROM SECOND-HEADING-LINE        EDITRPT
00275  014150         AFTER ADVANCING 2 LINES                            EDITRPT
00276  014160     WRITE EDIT-REPORT-LINE FROM THIRD-HEADING-LINE         EDITRPT
00277  014170         AFTER ADVANCING 1 LINES.                           EDITRPT
00278  014180     ADD 1 TO PAGE-COUNT.                                   EDITRPT
00279  014190     MOVE 5 TO LINES-PRINTED.                               EDITRPT
00280  014200     MOVE SPACE-TWO-LINES TO PROPER-SPACING.                EDITRPT
```

```
      8                    12.50.47      FEB 27,1985

00281  015010/                                                         EDITRPT
00282  015020*************************************************************  * EDITRPT
00283  015030*                                                         * EDITRPT
00284  015040*  THIS MODULE EDITS THE INPUT DATA. IT IS ENTERED FROM AND  * EDITRPT
00285  015050*  EXITS TO THE B000-PROCESS-DETAIL-RECORDS MODULE.        * EDITRPT
00286  015060*                                                         * EDITRPT
00287  015070*************************************************************  * EDITRPT
00288  015080                                                            EDITRPT
00289  015090 C010-EDIT-INPUT-DATA.                                      EDITRPT
00290  015100                                                            EDITRPT
00291  015110     IF DEALER-NAME-INPUT = SPACES                          EDITRPT
00292  015120         MOVE MISSING-DEALER-CONSTANT TO DEALER-NAME-REPORT EDITRPT
00293  015130         MOVE ERROR-IN-RECORD-CONSTANT TO MESSAGE-AREA-REPORT EDITRPT
00294  015140         MOVE 'NO ' TO IS-THE-RECORD-VALID                  EDITRPT
00295  015150     ELSE                                                   EDITRPT
00296  015160         MOVE DEALER-NAME-INPUT TO DEALER-NAME-REPORT.      EDITRPT
00297  015170     IF PRODUCT-IS-HARDWARE                                 EDITRPT
00298  015180         MOVE HARDWARE-CONSTANT TO PRODUCT-TYPE-REPORT      EDITRPT
00299  015190         IF SHIPPING-BY-TRUCK-OR-RAILROAD                   EDITRPT
00300  015200             MOVE SURFACE-CONSTANT TO SHIPPING-METHOD-REPORT EDITRPT
00301  016010         ELSE                                               EDITRPT
00302  016020             MOVE INVALID-CONSTANT TO SHIPPING-METHOD-REPORT EDITRPT
00303  016030             MOVE ERROR-IN-RECORD-CONSTANT TO MESSAGE-AREA-REPORT EDITRPT
00304  016040             MOVE 'NO ' TO IS-THE-RECORD-VALID              EDITRPT
00305  016050     ELSE                                                   EDITRPT
00306  016060         IF PRODUCT-IS-SOFTWARE                             EDITRPT
00307  016070             MOVE SOFTWARE-CONSTANT TO PRODUCT-TYPE-REPORT  EDITRPT
00308  016080             MOVE AIR-CONSTANT TO SHIPPING-METHOD-REPORT    EDITRPT
00309  016090         ELSE                                               EDITRPT
00310  016100             MOVE INVALID-CONSTANT TO PRODUCT-TYPE-REPORT   EDITRPT
00311  016110             MOVE ERROR-IN-RECORD-CONSTANT TO MESSAGE-AREA-REPORT EDITRPT
00312  016120             MOVE 'NO ' TO IS-THE-RECORD-VALID.             EDITRPT
00313  016130     IF SHIPPING-WEIGHT-INPUT IS NOT NUMERIC                EDITRPT
00314  016140         MOVE INVALID-CONSTANT TO INVALID-WEIGHT-REPORT     EDITRPT
00315  016150         MOVE ERROR-IN-RECORD-CONSTANT TO MESSAGE-AREA-REPORT EDITRPT
00316  016160         MOVE 'NO ' TO IS-THE-RECORD-VALID                  EDITRPT
00317  016170     ELSE                                                   EDITRPT
00318  016180         IF SHIPPING-WEIGHT-INPUT IS GREATER THAN           EDITRPT
00319  016190             MAX-SHIPPING-WEIGHT-CONSTANT                   EDITRPT
00320  016200             MOVE INVALID-CONSTANT TO INVALID-WEIGHT-REPORT EDITRPT
00321  017010             MOVE ERROR-IN-RECORD-CONSTANT TO MESSAGE-AREA-REPORT EDITRPT
00322  017020             MOVE 'NO ' TO IS-THE-RECORD-VALID              EDITRPT
00323  017030         ELSE                                               EDITRPT
00324  017040             MOVE SHIPPING-WEIGHT-INPUT TO SHIPPING-WEIGHT-REPORT. EDITRPT
```

Figure 6-57 Source Listing (Part 4 of 4)

REVIEW QUESTIONS

1. What is meant by the term Nested If statements?

2. What is meant by the term Editing?

3. Identify four common forms of input data editing.

4. Draw the flowchart for the if-then-else structure. Draw the flowchart for a nested if-then-else structure where a condition is tested when the first condition is true, and a condition is tested when the first condition is false. Each of the nested conditions have processing both when the condition is true and when the condition is false.

5. Write the two rules governing when a Nested If statement is required. Give an example of each.

6. Describe the two special Nested If conditions discussed in the text. Develop an original program problem for each of the conditions and then write the COBOL code to solve the problem.

7. What is the END-IF statement? Why isn't it always used in Nested If statements?

8. State the rule concerning matching If statements and Else clauses.

9. How can a field be checked to determine if it contains all spaces? Why would this check be performed?

10. How can a field be checked to determine if it contains numeric data?

11. What are the rules when an alphanumeric (Picture X) field is checked for numeric data using the numeric class test? What are the rules when an unsigned numeric field is checked? What are the rules when a signed numeric field is checked?

12. How is the Redefines clause used?

13. In what format is the current date stored on most computers? What instruction is used to obtain the current date?

COBOL CODING EXERCISES

1. Design and write the Nested If statement using both pseudocode and COBOL to perform the following:

   If the student is a NEW-STUDENT and the grade point average is greater than the MINIMUM-GRADE-POINT, move PASSING-CONSTANT to MESSAGE-REPORT. If the student is a NEW-STUDENT and the grade point average is equal to or less than MINIMUM-GRADE-POINT, move FAILING-CONSTANT to MESSAGE-REPORT. If the student is not a NEW-STUDENT, no special processing is to occur.

2. Design and write the Nested If statement using both pseudocode and COBOL to perform the following:

   If a home is a NEW-HOME and has a SECURITY-SYSTEM, multiply INSURANCE-AMOUNT-INPUT by GOOD-SECURITY-RATE and store the answer in AMOUNT-DUE-REPORT. If a home is a NEW-HOME and does not have a SECURITY-SYSTEM, multiply INSURANCE-AMOUNT-INPUT by STANDARD-RATE, storing the answer in AMOUNT-DUE-REPORT. If a home is not a NEW-HOME, multiply INSURANCE-AMOUNT-INPUT by NOT-NEW-RATE and store the answer in AMOUNT-DUE-REPORT.

3. Design and write the Nested If statement using both pseudocode and COBOL to perform the following:

   If the taxpayer is SINGLE, the field INCOME-AMOUNT-INPUT is to be multiplied by 35%, with the answer stored in TAX-AMOUNT-REPORT. If the taxpayer is MARRIED, files a JOINT-TAX-RETURN, and the NUMBER-OF-DEPENDENTS is greater than 10, then the field INCOME-AMOUNT-INPUT is to be multiplied by 25%, with the answer stored in TAX-AMOUNT-REPORT. If the taxpayer is MARRIED, files a JOINT-TAX-RETURN, and the NUMBER-OF-DEPENDENTS is equal to or less than 10, then the field INCOME-AMOUNT-INPUT is to be multiplied by 27% and the answer is stored in TAX-AMOUNT-REPORT. If the taxpayer is MARRIED, does not file a JOINT-TAX-RETURN, and the NUMBER-OF-DEPENDENTS is greater than 10, the field INCOME-AMOUNT-INPUT is to be multiplied by 28%, with the answer stored in TAX-AMOUNT-REPORT. If the taxpayer is MARRIED, does not file a JOINT-TAX-RETURN, and the NUMBER-OF-DEPENDENTS is equal to or less than 10, then the field INCOME-AMOUNT-INPUT is to be multiplied by 29%, with the answer stored in TAX-AMOUNT-REPORT.

4. Design and write the Nested If statement using both pseudocode and COBOL to perform the following:

   If a company uses the STANDARD-PHONE-COMPANY for local calls and uses a LONG-DISTANCE-COMPANY for long distance calls, then perform the C010-ROUTINE-ONE-BILLING module. If a company uses the STANDARD-PHONE-COMPANY for local calls and does not use a LONG-DISTANCE-COMPANY for long distance calls then perform C020-ROUTINE-TWO-BILLING module. If a company does not use a STANDARD-PHONE-COMPANY for local calls and the company is given a QUANTITY-DISCOUNT on the number of local calls made and the company does use a LONG-DISTANCE-COMPANY for long distance calls, then perform the C030-ROUTINE-THREE-BILLING module. If a

QUANTITY-DISCOUNT on the number of local calls made is given and the company does use a LONG-DISTANCE-COMPANY for long distance calls, then perform the C040-ROUTINE-FOUR-BILLING module.

5. Design and write the Nested If statement using both pseudocode and COBOL to perform the following:

If a customer has PREFERRED-CREDIT-RATING and AMOUNT-PURCHASED-INPUT is less than $1,500, move the message, CREDIT REMAINING to INVOICE-MESSAGE-REPORT. If a customer has a PREFERRED-CREDIT-RATING and the AMOUNT-PURCHASED-INPUT is equal to or greater than $1,500, move the message PREFERRED STATUS — NET 45 DAYS to INVOICE-MESSAGE-REPORT unless the AMOUNT-PURCHASED-INPUT is greater than $5,000. If it is, move the message PREFERRED STATUS — NET 20 DAYS to INVOICE-MESSAGE-REPORT. If the customer has an ACCEPTABLE-CREDIT-RATING and the AMOUNT-PURCHASED-INPUT is less than or equal to $500, move the message NET 30 DAYS to INVOICE-MESSAGE-REPORT. If the AMOUNT-PURCHASED-INPUT is greater than $500, move the message CONTACT CREDIT OFFICE to INVOICE-MESSAGE-REPORT. If there is NO-CREDIT-RATING the message CONTACT CREDIT OFFICE should be moved to INVOICE-MESSAGE-REPORT. In all cases except when a customer with an ACCEPTABLE-CREDIT-RATING has an AMOUNT-PURCHASED-INPUT greater than $500 or when there is NO-CREDIT-RATING, move the message THANK YOU FOR YOUR BUSINESS to COURTESY-MESSAGE-REPORT. Write the invoice for all customers by performing the D020-WRITE-INVOICE module.

6. Write the COBOL statement to edit the field STUDENT-NAME to determine if the field contains all spaces. If the field contains all spaces, the message MISSING-NAME should be moved to the printer output area, and the literal NO should be moved to IS-THE-RECORD-VALID.

7. Write the COBOL statement to determine if data in the field STUDENT-NUMBER is numeric. If the data contained in the field is not numeric, the message NOT NUMERIC should be moved to the printer output area, and the literal NO should be moved to IS-THE-RECORD-VALID.

STRUCTURED WALKTHROUGH EXERCISES

The following portions of COBOL code contain one or more errors in program logic, in the use of the COBOL language itself, or in the programming standards which should be followed. Review the code in each exercise in the same manner used for structured walkthroughs. Identify the errors and make the appropriate corrections.

1.

```
003100 01  SHIPPING-INPUT-RECORD.
003110     05  DEALER-NAME-INPUT              PIC X(20).
003120     05  PRODUCT-CODE-INPUT            PIC 9.
003130         88  PRODUCT-IS-SOFTWARE       VALUE 'S'.
003140         88  PRODUCT-IS-HARDWARE       VALUE 'H'.
003150     05  SHIPPING-CODE-INPUT          PIC X.
003160         88  SHIPPING-BY-TRUCK-OR-RAILROAD  PIC X   VALUE 'T', 'R'.
003170     05  SHIPPING-WEIGHT-INPUT        PIC 9(3).
```

2.

```
004110     05  VALID-WEIGHT-REPORT.
004120         10  SHIPPING-WEIGHT-REPORT    PIC ZZ9.
004130         10  FILLER                    PIC 9(6).
004140     05  INVALID-WEIGHT-REPORT REDEFINES SHIPPING-WEIGHT-REPORT
004150                                        PIC X(3).
```

3.

```
006070 01  WORK-AREAS.
006080     05  DAY-WORK.
006090         10  MONTH-WORK                PIC Z9.
006100         10  DAY-WORK                  PIC Z9.
006110         10  YEAR-WORK                 PIC Z9.
```

4.

```
007070     05  FIRST-HEADING-LINE.
007080         10  CARRIAGE-CONTROL          PIC X.
007090         10  DATE-HEADING.
007100         10  MONTH-HEADING             PIC 99.
007110         10  FILLER                    PIC 9      VALUE '/'.
007120         10  DAY-HEADING               PIC 99.
007130         10  FILLER                    PIC 9      VALUE '/'.
007140         10  YEAR-HEADING              PIC 99.
```

5.

```
012070    IF LINES-PRINTED IS EQUAL TO PAGE-SIZE AND
012080       LINES-PRINTED IS GREATER THAN PAGE-SIZE AND
012090       FIRST-PAGE
012100       PERFORM C000-PRINT-HEADINGS.
```

6.

```
012030    IF BUILDING-TYPE-INPUT = 'B
012040       MOVE BUSINESS-CONSTANT TO BUILDING TYPE-REPORT.
012050       ADD 1 TO BUSINESS-COUNT.
012060    ELSE
012070       MOVE NON-BUSINESS-CONSTANT TO BUILDING-TYPE-REPORT.
012080       ADD 1 TO NON-BUSINESS-COUNT.
```

7.

```
016090    IF ROYALTY-AUTHOR
016100       IF BOOKS-SOLD-INPUT IS GREATER THAN MINIMUM-BOOKS-CONSTANT
016110          COMPUTE ROYALTY-WORK = BOOKS-SOLD-INPUT * HIGH-PCT
016120       ELSE
016130          COMPUTE ROYALTY-WORK = BOOKS-SOLD-INPUT * LOW-PCT
016140       END-IF
016150       ADD ROYALTY-WORK TO TOTAL-PAYROLL-ACCUM
016160    END-IF
016170    ELSE
016180       ADD SALARY-INPUT TO TOTAL-PAYROLL-ACCUM.
```

PROGRAMMING ASSIGNMENT 1

INSTRUCTIONS

An Edit Report is to be prepared. Design and write the COBOL program to produce the required report. An IPO Chart and Pseudocode Specifications should be used when designing the program. Use Test Data Set 5 in Appendix A.

INPUT

Input consists of Police Records that contain the Motorist Name, Violation Code, Motorist Action Code, and Fine Amount. The format of the input record is illustrated below.

Police Disk Record				
FIELD NAME	**POSITION**	**LENGTH**	**DEC**	**ATTRIBUTE**
Motorist Name	1 – 20	20		Alphanumeric
UNUSED	21 – 24	4		Alphanumeric
Violation Code	25	1		Alphanumeric
Motorist Action Code	26	1		Alphanumeric
UNUSED	27 – 33	7		Alphanumeric
Fine Amount	34 – 38	5	2	Numeric
UNUSED	39 – 40	2		Alphanumeric
Record Length		**40**		

OUTPUT

Output consists of an Edit Report containing the Motorist Name, Violation Type, Motorist Action, Fine Amount, and Error Message. The heading for the Edit Report should contain the date and the page number. Following the processing of all records, the total number of records and the total number of records in error should be printed. The printer spacing chart for the report is illustrated below.

PRINTER SPACING CHART

```
 1
 2 MM/DD/YY                    EDIT REPORT                                      PAGE ZZ9
 3
 4    MOTORIST              VIOLATION        MOTORIST        FINE              ERROR
 5      NAME                  TYPE            ACTION        AMOUNT            MESSAGE
 6
 7 XXXXXXXXXXXXXXXXXXXX    XXXXXXXXXX     XXXXXXXXXXX     $ZZZ.99      XXXXXXXXXXXXXXXXXXXXX
 8 XXXXXXXXXXXXXXXXXXXX    MOVING         COURT           $ZZZ.99      XXXXXXXXXXXXXXXXXXXXX
 9 XXXXXXXXXXXXXXXXXXXX    NON-MOVING     PAY BY MAIL     $ZZZ.99      XXXXXXXXXXXXXXXXXXXXX
10 XXXXXXXXXXXXXXXXXXXX    XXXXXXXXXX     **INVALID**     $ZZZ.99      XXXXXXXXXXXXXXXXXXXXX
11 **MISSING MOTORIST**    **INVALID**                   **INVALID**  **ERROR IN RECORD**
12
13 ZZ9 TOTAL RECORDS
14 ZZ9 RECORDS IN ERROR
```

EDITING

The Motorist Name in the input record should be edited for blanks. If the Motorist Name field contains all spaces, then the message **MISSING MOTORIST** should be printed on the report.

The Violation Code in the input record should be edited for the values M or N. If the Violation Code is M, then the message MOVING should be printed on the report. If the Violation Code is N, then the message NON-MOVING should be printed on the report. If the Violation Code is not an M or N, then the message **INVALID** should be printed on the report.

The Motorist Action Code field on the report is determined in the following manner: If the Violation Code in the input record is M and the Motorist Action Code in the input record is A (Accident) or D (Drunk Driver), then the message COURT should be printed on the report. Any other Motorist Action Code is invalid and the message **INVALID** should be printed on the report. If the Violation Code is N, then the message PAY BY MAIL should be printed on the report. All non-moving violations are paid by mail. If the Violation Code is not M or N, the Motorist Action field should be left blank on the report.

The Fine Amount field should be edited for valid numeric data and must not be greater than $400.00. If invalid, the message **INVALID** should be printed on the report instead of the Fine Amount.

When any field within the input record is found to contain invalid data, the message **ERROR IN RECORD** should be printed on the report in the Error Message field.

PROGRAMMING ASSIGNMENT 2

INSTRUCTIONS

An Edit Report is to be prepared. Design and write the COBOL program to produce the required report. An IPO Chart and Pseudocode Specifications should be used when designing the program. Use Test Data Set 5 in Appendix A.

INPUT

Input consists of Membership Records that contain the Membership Name, Membership Code, Order Code, Credit Limit, and Length of Membership. The format of the Membership Disk Record is illustrated below.

Membership Disk Record				
FIELD NAME	POSITION	LENGTH	DEC	ATTRIBUTE
Membership Name	1 – 20	20		Alphanumeric
UNUSED	21 – 26	6		Alphanumeric
Membership Code	27	1		Alphanumeric
Order Code	28	1		Alphanumeric
UNUSED	29 – 33	5		Alphanumeric
Credit Limit	34 – 38	5	2	Numeric
Length of Membership	39 – 40	2	0	Numeric
Record Length		40		

OUTPUT

Output consists of an Edit Report containing the Membership Name, Membership Type, Order Type, Credit Limit, Membership Length, and Error Message. The heading of the Edit Report should contain the date and the page number. Following the processing of all records, the total number of records and the total number of records in error should be printed. The printer spacing chart is illustrated below.

PRINTER SPACING CHART

```
MM/DD/YY                        EDIT REPORT                              PAGE ZZ9

    MEMBERSHIP        MEMBERSHIP    ORDER        CREDIT   MEMBERSHIP        ERROR
       NAME              TYPE        TYPE         LIMIT    LENGTH          MESSAGE

XXXXXXXXXXXXXXXXXXXX   XXXXXXXXX   XXXXXXXXX   $ZZZ.99      XX        XXXXXXXXXXXXXXXXXXXXX
XXXXXXXXXXXXXXXXXXXX   BUSINESS    SPECIAL     $ZZZ.99      XX        XXXXXXXXXXXXXXXXXXXXX
XXXXXXXXXXXXXXXXXXXX   PERSONAL    REGULAR     $ZZZ.99      XX        XXXXXXXXXXXXXXXXXXXXX
***MISSING MEMBER***  *INVALID*   *INVALID*  *INVALID*  *INVALID*  **ERROR IN RECORD**

ZZ9 TOTAL RECORDS
ZZ9 RECORDS IN ERROR
```

EDITING

The Membership Name in the input record should be edited for blanks. If the Membership Name field contains all spaces, then the message ***MISSING MEMBER*** should be printed on the report.

The Membership Code in the input record should be edited for the values B or P. If the Membership Code is B, then the message BUSINESS should be printed on the report. If the Membership Code is P, then the message PERSONAL should be printed on the report. If the Membership Code is not B or P, then the message *INVALID* should be printed on the report.

The Order Type field on the report is determined in the following manner. If the Membership Code in the input record is B and the Order Code in the input record is M (Mail), P (Phone), or C (Computer), then the message SPECIAL should be printed on the report. Any other Order Code is invalid and the message *INVALID* should appear on the report.

If the Membership Code in the input record is P and the Order Code in the input record is M (Mail) or P (Phone), then the message REGULAR should be printed on the report. Any other Order Code is invalid and the message *INVALID* should be printed on the report.

If the Membership Code is neither M nor P, the Order Type field on the report should be left blank.

The Credit Limit field should be edited for valid numeric data and must not be greater than $400.00. If invalid, the message *INVALID* should be printed on the report instead of the Credit Limit.

The Length of Membership field should be edited for valid numeric data and must not be greater than 15. If invalid, the message *INVALID* should be printed on the report instead of the Membership Length.

When any field within the input record is found to contain invalid data, the message **ERROR IN RECORD** should be printed on the report in the Error Message field.

PROGRAMMING ASSIGNMENT 3

INSTRUCTIONS

A Construction Edit Report is to be prepared. Write the COBOL program to prepare this report. An IPO Chart and Pseudocode Specifications should be used when designing the program. Use Test Data Set 5 in Appendix A.

INPUT

Input consists of Construction Records that contain the Permit Holder's Name, Permit Number, Construction Code, and Building Code. The format of the Construction Disk Record is illustrated below.

Construction Disk Record				
FIELD NAME	POSITION	LENGTH	DEC	ATTRIBUTE
Permit Holder's Name	1 – 20	20		Alphanumeric
Permit Number	21 – 24	4		Alphanumeric
UNUSED	25 – 28	4		Alphanumeric
Construction Code	29	1	0	Numeric
Building Code	30	1	0	Numeric
UNUSED	31 – 40	10		Alphanumeric
Record Length		40		

OUTPUT

Output consists of a Construction Edit Report containing the Permit Holder's Name, Permit Number, Construction Type, Building Type, and Error Message. The heading of the Construction Edit Report should contain the date and the page number. Following the processing of all records, the total number of residential records, the total number of commercial records, the total number of records, and the total number of records in error should be printed. The printer spacing chart is illustrated below.

PRINTER SPACING CHART

```
1
2  MM/DD/YY                    CONSTRUCTION EDIT REPORT                              PAGE ZZ9
3
4     PERMIT HOLDER'S        PERMIT    CONSTRUCTION          BUILDING              ERROR
5        NAME                NUMBER       TYPE                 TYPE               MESSAGE
6
7  XXXXXXXXXXXXXXXXXXXX      XXXX     XXXXXXXXXXXXX         XXXXXXXXXXXXX      XXXXXXXXXXXXXXXXXXXX
8  XXXXXXXXXXXXXXXXXXXX      XXXX     RESIDENTIAL           SINGLE-FAMILY      XXXXXXXXXXXXXXXXXXXX
9  XXXXXXXXXXXXXXXXXXXX      XXXX     COMMERCIAL            OFFICE             XXXXXXXXXXXXXXXXXXXX
10 XXXXXXXXXXXXXXXXXXXX      XXXX     *NOT NUMERIC*         *NOT NUMERIC*      XXXXXXXXXXXXXXXXXXXX
11 ***MISSING NAME AND NUMBER***     ***INVALID***         ***INVALID***      **ERROR IN RECORD**
12
13 ZZ9 TOTAL RESIDENTIAL RECORDS                           ZZ9 TOTAL RECORDS
14 ZZ9 TOTAL COMMERCIAL RECORDS                            ZZ9 TOTAL RECORDS IN ERROR
```

EDITING

The Permit Holder's Name and the Permit Number in the input record should be edited in the following manner: If the Permit Holder's Name field contains all spaces and the Permit Number contains a valid permit number, the Permit Holder's Name on the report should be blank and the Permit Number should be printed. If the Permit Number field contains all spaces and the Permit Holder's Name contains a valid name, the Permit Holder's Name should be printed on the report and the Permit Number should be blank. If both fields contain data, the contents of both fields should be printed on the report. If both the Permit Holder's Name field and the Permit Number field contain all spaces, the message ***MISSING NAME AND NUMBER*** should be printed on the report.

The Construction Code should be edited for the valid numeric values 1 or 2. If the Construction Code is not numeric, the message *NOT NUMERIC* should be printed in the Construction Type field on the report. If the Construction Code is 1, then the message RESIDENTIAL should be printed on the report. If the Construction Code is 2, then the message COMMERCIAL should be printed on the report. If the Construction Code is numeric but is not 1 or 2, the message ***INVALID*** should be printed on the report.

If the Building Code in the input record is not numeric, the message *NOT NUMERIC* should be printed in the Building Type field on the report. If the Building Code is numeric, the Building Type field on the report is determined in the following manner: If the Construction Code in the input record is 1 and the Building Code in the input record is 1 (House) or 2 (Condo), then the message SINGLE-FAMILY should be printed on the report. If the Building Code is not 1 or 2, the message ***INVALID*** should be printed on the report. If the Construction Code is 2, then the message OFFICE should be printed on the report in the Building Type field.

If the Construction Code field in the input record is invalid, the Building Type field should be blank on the report.

When any field within the input record is found to contain invalid data, the message **ERROR IN RECORD** should be printed on the report in the Error Message field.

PROGRAMMING ASSIGNMENT 4

INSTRUCTIONS

A U. S. Government Edit Report and U. S. Government Summary Report are to be prepared. Write the COBOL program to prepare these reports. An IPO Chart and Pseudocode Specifications should be used when designing the program. Use Test Data Set 5 in Appendix A.

INPUT

Input consists of Military Records that contain the Personnel Name, Military Type Code, Military Rank Code, Military Status Code, and Length of Service. The format of the Military Disk Record is illustrated below.

Military Disk Record				
FIELD NAME	**POSITION**	**LENGTH**	**DEC**	**ATTRIBUTE**
Personnel Name	1 – 20	20		Alphanumeric
UNUSED	21 – 30	10		Alphanumeric
Military Type Code	31	1		Alphanumeric
Military Rank Code	32	1		Alphanumeric
Military Status Code	33	1		Alphanumeric
UNUSED	34 – 38	5		Alphanumeric
Length of Service	39 – 40	2	0	Numeric
Record Length		**40**		

OUTPUT

Output consists of a U. S. Government Edit Report and a U. S. Government Summary Report. The Edit Report contains the Personnel Name, Military Type, Military Rank, Military Status, Length of Service, and an Error Message. After all records have been processed, the U. S. Government Summary Report is to be printed at the top of a new page and contains Total Records, Total Records in Error, Total Active Personnel, Total Retired Personnel, Total Army Personnel, Total Navy Personnel, Total Air Force Personnel, and Total Marine Personnel. The heading on both reports should contain the date and the page number. The date consists of the month of the year and the last two digits of the year. For example: If the date is 09/23/87, then the date in the heading should be: SEPTEMBER - 87. The printer spacing charts for both reports are illustrated on the following page.

PRINTER SPACING CHART

```
 2 XXXXXXXX - YY                    U. S. GOVERNMENT                          PAGE ZZ9
 3                                     EDIT REPORT
 5      PERSONNEL         MILITARY      MILITARY      MILITARY     LENGTH OF            ERROR
 6        NAME              TYPE          RANK          STATUS      SERVICE            MESSAGE
 8 XXXXXXXXXXXXXXXXXXXX    XXXXXXXXX    XXXXXXXXXX    XXXXXXXXX       Z9      XXXXXXXXXXXXXXXXXXXXXX
 9 XXXXXXXXXXXXXXXXXXXX    ARMY         PRIVATE       ACTIVE          Z9      XXXXXXXXXXXXXXXXXXXXXX
10 XXXXXXXXXXXXXXXXXXXX    ARMY         LIEUTENANT    RETIRED         Z9      XXXXXXXXXXXXXXXXXXXXXX
11 XXXXXXXXXXXXXXXXXXXX    NAVY         ENSIGN        ACTIVE          Z9      XXXXXXXXXXXXXXXXXXXXXX
12 XXXXXXXXXXXXXXXXXXXX    NAVY         CAPTAIN       RETIRED         Z9      XXXXXXXXXXXXXXXXXXXXXX
13 XXXXXXXXXXXXXXXXXXXX    AIR FORCE    AIRMAN        ACTIVE          Z9      XXXXXXXXXXXXXXXXXXXXXX
14 XXXXXXXXXXXXXXXXXXXX    AIR FORCE    MAJOR         RETIRED         Z9      XXXXXXXXXXXXXXXXXXXXXX
15 XXXXXXXXXXXXXXXXXXXX    MARINES      GENERAL       ACTIVE          Z9      XXXXXXXXXXXXXXXXXXXXXX
16 XXXXXXXXXXXXXXXXXXXX    MARINES      COLONEL       RETIRED         Z9      XXXXXXXXXXXXXXXXXXXXXX
17 *MISSING PERSONNEL*     *INVALID*    *INVALID*     *INVALID*     *INVALID*  **ERROR IN RECORD**

20                                    (SEPARATE PAGE)

22 XXXXXXXX - YY                    U. S. GOVERNMENT                   PAGE ZZ9
23                                    SUMMARY REPORT

26 ZZ9 TOTAL RECORDS                                 ZZ9 TOTAL ARMY PERSONNEL
27 ZZ9 TOTAL RECORDS IN ERROR                        ZZ9 TOTAL NAVY PERSONNEL
28 ZZ9 TOTAL ACTIVE PERSONNEL                        ZZ9 TOTAL AIR FORCE PERSONNEL
29 ZZ9 TOTAL RETIRED PERSONNEL                       ZZ9 TOTAL MARINE PERSONNEL
```

EDITING

If the Personnel Name field contains all spaces, then the message *MISSING PERSONNEL* should be printed on the report.

The Military Type Code in the input record should be edited for the values A, N, F, or M. If the Military Type Code is A, the message ARMY should be printed on the report in the Military Type field. If the Military Type Code is N, the message NAVY should be printed. If the Military Type Code is F, the message AIR FORCE should be printed. If the Military Type Code is M, the message MARINES should be printed. If the Military Type Code is not an A, N, F, or M, the message *INVALID* should be printed on the report.

The Military Rank field on the report is determined in the following manner: If the Military Type Code is A in the input record and the Military Rank Code in the input record is P (Private), the message PRIVATE should be printed. If the Military Rank Code is L (Lieutenant), the message LIEUTENANT should be printed. Any other Military Rank Code is invalid and the message *INVALID* should be printed on the report.

If the Military Type Code is N and the Military Rank Code is E (Ensign), the message ENSIGN should be printed. If the Military Rank Code is C (Captain), the message CAPTAIN should be printed. Any other Military Rank Code is invalid and the message *INVALID* should be printed on the report.

If the Military Type Code is F and the Military Rank Code is A (Airman), the message AIRMAN should be printed. If the Military Rank Code is M (Major), the message MAJOR should be printed. Any other Military Rank Code is invalid and the message *INVALID* should be printed on the report.

If the Military Type Code is M and the Military Rank Code is G (General), the message GENERAL should be printed. If the Military Rank Code is C (Colonel), the message COLONEL should be printed. Any other Military Rank Code is invalid and the message *INVALID* should be printed on the report.

If the Military Type Code is invalid, the Military Rank field on the report should be blank.

The Military Status Code should be edited for the values A (Active) or R (Retired). If the status is A, the message ACTIVE should be printed. If the status is R, the message RETIRED should be printed. Any other Military Status Code is invalid and the message *INVALID* should be printed on the report.

The Length of Service field should be edited for valid numeric data and must not be less than 7 nor greater than 15. If invalid, the message *INVALID* should be printed on the report instead of the Length of Service.

When any field within the input record is found to contain invalid data, the message **ERROR IN RECORD** should be printed on the report in the Error Message field.

CHAPTER SEVEN

CONTROL BREAKS; TABLE PROCESSING

CONTROL BREAKS; TABLE PROCESSING

7

INTRODUCTION

In previous programs illustrated in this text, the data which was read from an input record was formatted in the output area, one or more calculations or comparing operations were performed, and a line was printed. This process, where one line of printed information is generated from one input record, is commonly called detail printing. In many business applications, it is necessary to print intermediate information generated from the detail processing, such as totals on the report. Printing this information occurs under control of the program.

In addition, the COBOL language provides the ability to process data stored in the form of lists of adjacent data fields which have similar characteristics. These lists are commonly called tables; and the techniques for defining and processing tables is called table processing.

Table processing and printing intermediate information generated from detail processing will be illustrated and explained in this chapter.

CONTROL BREAKS

To illustrate printing intermediate information generated from detail processing, the sample program in this chapter creates a Rent Report. The input to the program is a file of Property Disk Records. The format of these records is illustrated in Figure 7-1.

Property Disk Record				
FIELD DESCRIPTION	**POSITION**	**LENGTH**	**DEC**	**ATTRIBUTE**
Property Number	1 – 4	4	0	Numeric
Apartment Number	5 – 7	3	0	Numeric
Last Month Code	8 – 9	2	0	Numeric
Rent Amount	10 – 14	5	2	Numeric
Record Length		14		

Figure 7-1 Format of Input Records

The input record contains the Property Number, Apartment Number, Last Month Code, and Rent Amount.

A control break occurs during the processing of input records when the value in a given field in the record, called a control field, changes from the value found in that field in the previous input record. When a control break occurs, normally some type of unique processing, such as printing a total, will take place. A control break in the input records for the sample program is illustrated in Figure 7-2.

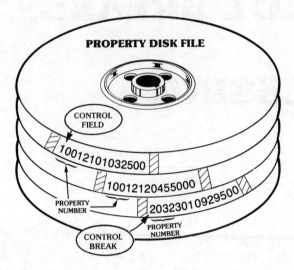

Figure 7-2 Control Breaks Based Upon a Change in Property Number

In Figure 7-2, the Property Number is found in the first four positions of each disk input record. The first two records contain Property Number 1001. The third record, however, contains Property Number 2032. When the third record is read, a control break occurs because the value in the control field, in this case the Property Number, has changed from 1001 to 2032.

When a control break occurs in the sample program which creates the Rent Report, the total rent for the property together with the property number is printed. This is illustrated in Figure 7-3.

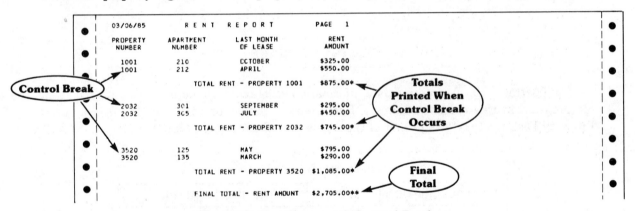

Figure 7-3 Rent Report with Control Breaks

In Figure 7-3, the report contains the Property Number, Apartment Number, Last Month of Lease, and Rent Amount. Whenever the Property Number changes (a control break occurs), the previous property number and the total rent for the previous property is printed. Thus, when the Property Number changed from 1001 to 2032, the total rent for Property 1001 ($875.00) was printed prior to processing the first record with Property Number 2032. In addition, a final total is printed after all of the input records have been processed.

Control Break Processing

Prior to designing and writing programs which require control breaks, it is essential to understand the processing that takes place for detail records, control breaks, and final totals.

The diagrams on the following pages illustrate the processing which must be understood in order to create a program that prints totals when a control break occurs.

Initial Processing

After the first record has been read into main computer memory, several steps must be accomplished before the record is processed. These steps are illustrated in Figure 7–4.

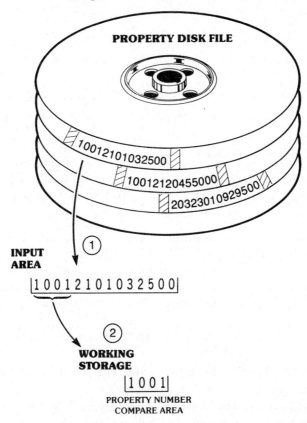

Figure 7 - 4 Initial Steps in Control Break Processing

The numbered steps in Figure 7–4 correspond to the following processing:

Step 1: The first input record in the file is read into the input area.
Step 2: The Property Number from the first input record is moved to a compare area in Working Storage. The value in the compare area is compared to the Property Number on subsequent input records to determine if a control break has occurred.

Detail Record Processing

After the first detail record is read into the input area and the Property Number is moved to the compare area, the detail record processing will occur. The steps in the processing of the first detail record are illustrated in Figure 7–5.

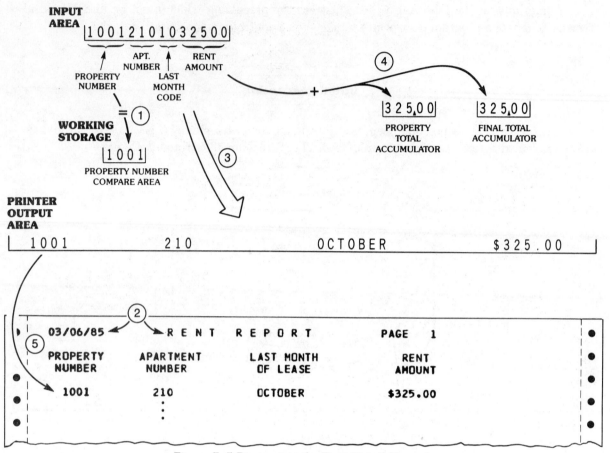

Figure 7-5 Processing the First Detail Record

The numbered steps in Figure 7-5 correspond to the following processing:

Step 1: The Property Number in the input area is compared to the Property Number in the compare area. Since the Property Number in the compare area was moved from the input area for the first record (see Figure 7-4), they are equal. Since they are equal, no control break processing should occur.

Step 2: Since it is the first page on the report, the page headings are printed.

Step 3: After the headings are printed, the input record data is moved from the input area to the printer output area. The Last Month Code (10) in the input record is changed to the name of the 10th month (OCTOBER) when it is moved to the printer output area. The technique to accomplish this is explained in detail later in this chapter.

Step 4: The Rent Amount from the input record is added to the Property Total Accumulator and the Final Total Accumulator. The Property Total Accumulator is used to accumulate the total rent amount for each piece of property with the same Property Number. The Final Total Accumulator is used to accumulate the total rent amount for all of the records processed. After this addition step for the first record, both accumulators contain the value 325.00.

Step 5: The detail line is printed on the report.

After the processing for the first record is completed, the second record is read and processed. The steps that occur for the second record are illustrated in Figure 7-6.

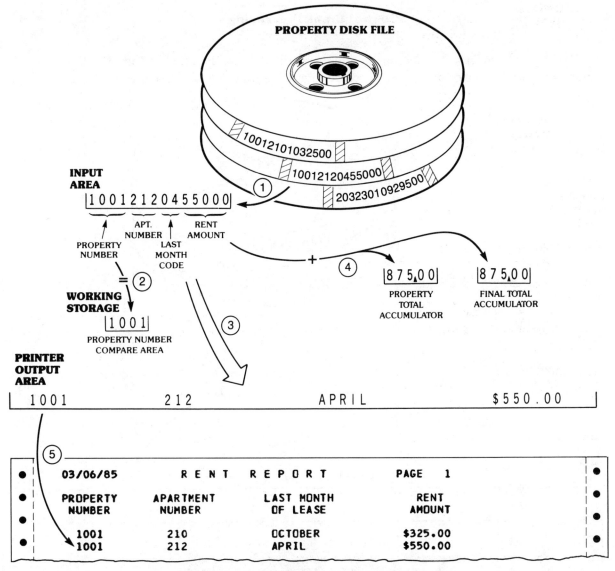

Figure 7-6 Processing the Second Detail Record

The numbered steps in Figure 7-6 accomplish the following processing:

Step 1: The second record is read into the input area.

Step 2: The Property Number from the second input record is compared to the Property Number in the compare area. The Property Number in the compare area, 1001, is from the first record. Since the Property Numbers are equal, no control break has occurred.

Step 3: The fields in the input area are moved to the printer output area.

Step 4: The Rent Amount from the second record is added to the Property Total Accumulator and the Final Total Accumulator. Both accumulators now contain the value 875.00 (325.00 from the first record plus 550.00 from the second record).

Step 5: The second detail line is printed.

The processing shown for the second input record in Figure 7-6 will continue for each subsequent input record until a control break occurs.

Control Break Processing

When the Property Number in the input record just read is different than the Property Number stored in the compare area, a control break has occurred, as illustrated in Figure 7–7.

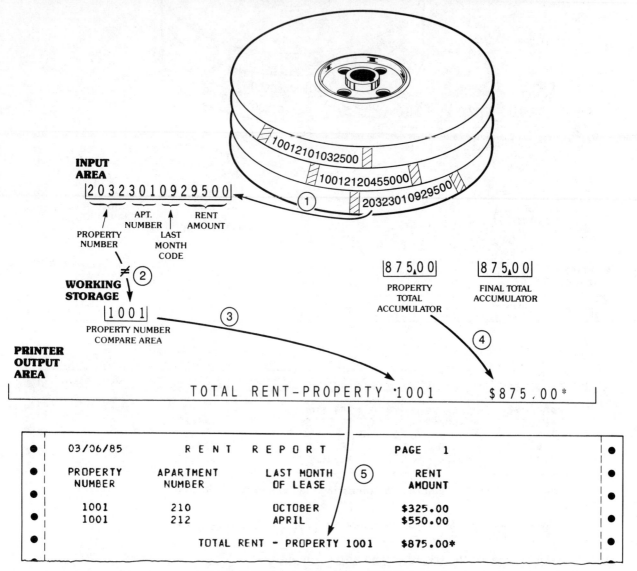

Figure 7-7 Processing a Control Break

The control break processing in Figure 7-7 is explained by the following steps:

Step 1: The third record is read into the input area.

Step 2: The Property Number from the third record is compared to the Property Number in the compare area. The Property Number from the third record is 2032 and the Property Number in the compare area is 1001. Since the Property Numbers are not equal, a control break has occurred.

Step 3: When a control break has occurred, the Property Number from the compare area, which is the Property Number for the group of records just processed, is moved to the Property Total Line. In the example, Property Number 1001 is moved to the

Property Total Line. The Property Number is moved from the compare area and not the input area because the total is for the group of records just processed, not for the new group of property records.

Step 4: The value in the Property Total Accumulator (875.00) is moved from its position in working storage to the Property Total Line. This value has been accumulated for each detail record previously processed and reflects the total rent amount for all of the apartments in Property 1001.

Step 5: The Property Total Line containing the Property Number 1001 and the value 875.00 from the Property Total Accumulator is printed on the report.

The control break processing shown in Figure 7–7 takes place before any detail processing for the record which causes the control break. The detail record processing for the new property, Property Number 2032, occurs only after all control break processing has been completed for Property Number 1001.

After the total has been printed, several other steps must be accomplished before the control break processing for Property Number 1001 is complete. The compare area in Figure 7–7 still contains the value 1001, which is the property number for the previous group of records; and the Property Total Accumulator still contains the accumulated Rent Amount for Property 1001. Therefore, the Property Number for the new group of records (2032) must be moved to the compare area; and the Property Total Accumulator must be reset to zero so that the property total will reflect the total for the new property, 2032. These steps are illustrated in Figure 7–8.

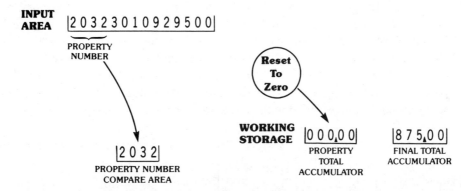

Figure 7-8 Resetting the Property Number Compare Area and Property Total Accumulator

After the Property Number which caused the control break (2032) is moved to the Property Number compare area and the Property Total Accumulator has been reset to zero, the detail record processing necessary to process Property Number 2032 would take place as illustrated previously. These basic steps of reading records, comparing the Property Numbers, processing the control break if required, and processing the detail records will continue until all of the records have been processed, at which time the Final Total processing will occur.

Final Total Processing

After all records have been read, the control break processing for the last group of records must be accomplished. After the last control break is processed, the final totals are processed. A segment of the report illustrating the last Property Total and the Final Total is contained in Figure 7–9.

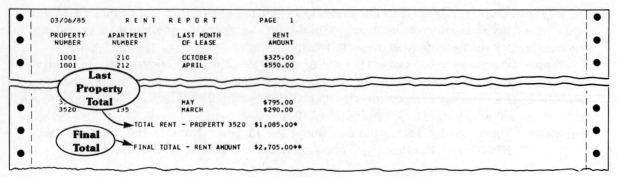

Figure 7-9 Last Property Total and Final Total

In Figure 7-9, the Property Total for Property Number 3520 is printed and then the Final Total ($2,705.00) is printed, together with double asterisks to identify the line.

It is extremely important to understand the basic steps required when processing control breaks in order to be able to properly design and code a control break program.

TABLE PROCESSING

In the sample program, the Last Month Code in the input record contains a two-digit numeric value representing the number of a month (01 for January, 02 for February, etc.). The Rent Report contains the actual name of the Last Month of the Lease (see Figure 7-3). To determine the name of the month from the number of the month, tables are used.

A table is a series of related fields with the same attributes stored in consecutive locations in main memory. Data stored in a table may be extracted from the table and used within a computer program. In the sample program, the name of the month is extracted from a table based upon the number of the month found in the input record, as illustrated below.

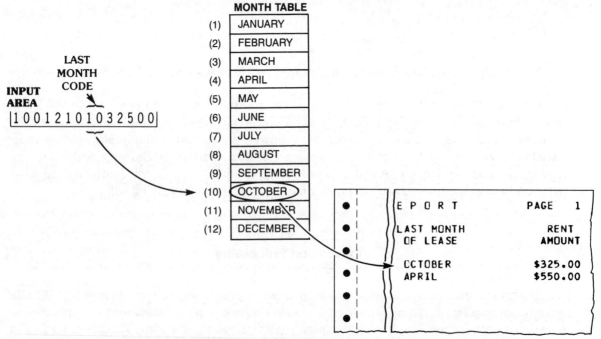

Figure 7-10 Example of Extracting Data from a Table

In Figure 7-10, the input record contains the value 10 in the Last Month Code field. This value indicates the Last Month is October. In order to print the month name on the report, this number is used to extract the tenth month name (October) from the Month Table.

The values 01 through 12 in the Last Month Code field are used to extract the corresponding month name from the Month Table. In order for this processing to occur, the Month Table must be defined in the Working-Storage Section of the Data Division and corresponding instructions in the Procedure Division must be used to extract the Month Name. These techniques are explained in the following paragraphs.

Definition of Tables

In the sample program, the Month Table is defined in the Working-Storage Section of the Data Division. The coding to define the table is shown in Figure 7-11.

```
005160 01  PROGRAM-TABLES.
005170     05  MONTHS-TABLE.
005180         10  MONTH-CONSTANTS.
005190             15  FILLER        PIC X(9)  VALUE 'JANUARY   '.
005200             15  FILLER        PIC X(9)  VALUE 'FEBRUARY  '.
006010             15  FILLER        PIC X(9)  VALUE 'MARCH     '.
006020             15  FILLER        PIC X(9)  VALUE 'APRIL     '.
006030             15  FILLER        PIC X(9)  VALUE 'MAY       '.
006040             15  FILLER        PIC X(9)  VALUE 'JUNE      '.
006050             15  FILLER        PIC X(9)  VALUE 'JULY      '.
006060             15  FILLER        PIC X(9)  VALUE 'AUGUST    '.
006070             15  FILLER        PIC X(9)  VALUE 'SEPTEMBER'.
006080             15  FILLER        PIC X(9)  VALUE 'OCTOBER   '.
006090             15  FILLER        PIC X(9)  VALUE 'NOVEMBER  '.
006100             15  FILLER        PIC X(9)  VALUE 'DECEMBER  '.
006110         10  MONTH-TABLE REDEFINES MONTH-CONSTANTS
006120                            PIC X(9)  OCCURS 12 TIMES.
```

```
OCCURS   integer-2 TIMES
```

Figure 7-11 Coding to Define the Month Table

In Figure 7-11, the level 01 entry, PROGRAM-TABLES, is used to document that the lower level entries following it comprise the tables to be used in the program. The level 05 entry, MONTHS-TABLE, states that the following table is for the month names.

A table for which the values are defined within the program (sometimes called an internal table) normally consists of two separate entities. The first entity is the constant values which are to be stored in the table. This entity must be specified as a group item. In Figure 7-11, the group name given to the constant values which are stored in the table is MONTH-CONSTANTS. Within this group are the level 15 entries that define the actual constant values. In the sample program, these constant values are the names of the months. Each of the names are defined using a Filler data-name.

The names of the months cannot be referenced using the Filler data-name. Therefore, a Redefines clause together with an Occurs clause must be used. This is the second entity required when defining the table. As seen in Chapter 6, the Redefines clause is used to give a single area in main computer memory a different name, different attributes, or both. In Figure 7-11, the statement MONTH-TABLE REDEFINES MONTH-CONSTANTS specifies that the area in main memory with the name MONTH-CONSTANTS can also be referenced by the name MONTH-TABLE. This concept is shown in Figure 7-12.

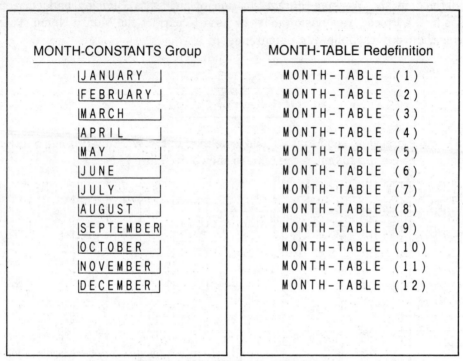

Figure 7-12 Illustration of the Effect of the Redefines Statement

In Figure 7-12, the MONTH-CONSTANTS group consists of twelve areas, each of which is nine characters in length. Each of the areas contains the name of a month. The use of the Redefines clause together with the Occurs clause allows the same areas of main memory to be referenced using the MONTH-TABLE name.

The Occurs clause specifies the number of times a field is repeated. In the example in Figure 7-11, the entry OCCURS 12 TIMES is specified. This means that the MONTH-TABLE field, which is a nine-position alphanumeric field (PIC X(9)), is repeated twelve times. This corresponds to the number of Filler data-names that are found in the group item MONTH-CONSTANTS. Thus, the area in memory consisting of 108 positions (9 characters x 12 entries) is identified by the group item MONTH-CONSTANTS and by the elementary item MONTH-TABLE, which occurs 12 times. Each of the twelve fields is called an element within the table.

Subscripts

In Figure 7-12, since the field MONTH-TABLE occurs 12 times, the data-name MONTH-TABLE by itself does not identify which of the twelve elements is to be referenced. Therefore, the particular 9-position element to be referenced must be identified through the use of a subscript. A subscript is a numeric value which identifies which element within the table is to be referenced. For example, to reference the first element within the table, which contains the month name JANUARY, the Move statement in Figure 7-13 could be used.

```
Ø15Ø2Ø      MOVE MONTH-TABLE (1) TO LAST-MONTH-REPORT.
```

Figure 7-13 Example of Subscript Usage

In Figure 7-13, the subscript value 1 is used to specify that the first element of the table MONTH-TABLE is to be moved to the LAST-MONTH-REPORT field. The subscript value must be contained within parentheses. There is a space between the table name and the left parenthesis and there is a space after the right parenthesis. There are no spaces within the parentheses. The data-name used with a subscript must be the name that includes an Occurs clause. Thus, from Figure 7-11, the MONTH-TABLE name can be used with a subscript, but the MONTH-CONSTANTS name cannot. As a result of the statement in Figure 7-13, the value JANUARY, which is stored in the first element of MONTH-TABLE, would be moved to the LAST-MONTH-REPORT field.

In order to move the month name MAY (the value in the fifth element) to the report output area, the Move statement in Figure 7-14 could be used.

```
Ø15Ø9Ø      MOVE MONTH-TABLE (5) TO LAST-MONTH-REPORT.
```

Figure 7-14 Use of Subscript

In Figure 7-14, the value 5 is used as the subscript for the table MONTH-TABLE. As a result, the fifth element within the table will be extracted and moved to the LAST-MONTH-REPORT field. Since the fifth element of the table contains the value MAY, the month name MAY would be moved to the printer output area.

Although the literal subscripts used in Figure 7-13 and Figure 7-14 allow elements within a table to be referenced properly, a more practical method for specifying subscripts is the use of a data-name within parentheses. The value in the field identified by the data-name acts as the subscript. The Move statement in the sample program which uses a data-name as the subscript to extract the proper name of the month from the MONTH-TABLE is illustrated in Figure 7-15.

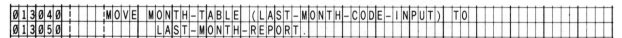

```
Ø13Ø4Ø      MOVE MONTH-TABLE (LAST-MONTH-CODE-INPUT) TO
Ø13Ø5Ø          LAST-MONTH-REPORT.
```

Figure 7-15 Use of a Data-Name as a Subscript

In Figure 7-15, the element to be moved from the MONTH-TABLE to the LAST-MONTH-REPORT field depends upon the value found in the field LAST-MONTH-CODE-INPUT. If the value is equal to 1, then the first element from the table (JANUARY) is moved. If the value in the LAST-MONTH-CODE-INPUT field is equal to 2, then the second element (FEBRUARY) is moved from the table to the LAST-MONTH-REPORT field. Similarly, if the value in the subscript field is equal to 12, then the twelfth element in the table (DECEMBER) is moved. Since the value in a field identified by a data-name can be altered, depending upon the processing within the program, subscripts are normally specified as data-names rather than literals.

Fields which are used as subscripts must be defined as elementary numeric items. Because subscripts are used to refer to the position of elements within a table, the use of the value zero as a subscript is invalid. The highest permissible subscript value is the maximum number of elements in the table as specified by the Occurs clause.

Tables are quite useful tools when performing business application programming using the COBOL language. Programmers should be very comfortable with their use.

SAMPLE PROGRAM

To illustrate the design and programming of an application requiring control breaks and tables, the problem previously described, involving the preparation of a Rent Report, will be explained. The input to the program is the Property Disk File (see Figure 7–1).

The printer spacing chart for the Rent Report is illustrated in Figure 7–16.

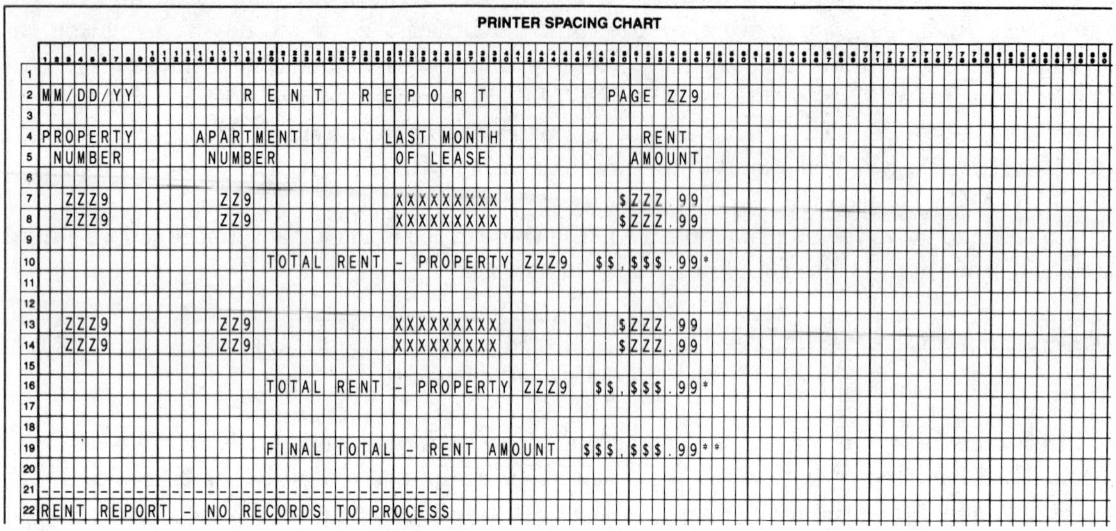

Figure 7-16 Printer Spacing Chart for Sample Program

In Figure 7–16, the Rent Report contains the Property Number, Apartment Number, Last Month of Lease, and Rent Amount. When there is a change in Property Number, the Total Rent Amount for that property, together with the Property Number, is printed. After all the input records have been processed, the Total Rent Amount for all properties is printed. If no input records are read, the no records to process message is printed.

Program Narrative

The Program Narrative for the sample program is illustrated in Figure 7–17.

PROGRAM NARRATIVE

SUBJECT	Rent Report	DATE	January 4	PAGE 1 OF 1
TO	Programmer	FROM	Systems Analyst	

A program is to be written to prepare a Rent Report. The format of the input record and the printer spacing chart are included with this narrative. The program should include the following processing:

1. The program should read the input records and create the Rent Report as per the format illustrated on the printer spacing chart. The report shall contain the Property Number, Apartment Number, Last Month of Lease, and Rent Amount.

Figure 7-17 Program Narrative (Part 1 of 2)

2. The Last Month of Lease is to be extracted from a table based upon the Last Month Code contained in the input record.

3. Headings are to be printed on the first page of the report. The heading is to contain the date and page number. Subsequent pages are also to include report and column headings. Fifty-five (55) lines are to appear on each page before skipping to a new page.

4. One line is to be printed on the report for each input record that is read. The lines are to be single spaced.

5. Editing on the report is to occur as illustrated on the printer spacing chart.

6. When there is a change in Property Number, the Property Number and Rent Amount are to be printed. A final total of the Rent Amount is to be printed after all input records have been processed. Spacing for the total lines should correspond to the printer spacing chart.

7. All input records have been edited prior to running this program.

8. The program is to be written in COBOL.

Figure 7 - 17 Program Narrative (Part 2 of 2)

PROGRAM DESIGN

Once the program narrative, input, and output are reviewed, the programmer would begin the process of designing the program. The following section shows the design process for the program which produces the Rent Report.

IPO Charts and Hierarchy Charts

As with previous problems, the programmer must analyze the program narrative, together with the format of the input records and the printer spacing chart, to determine the major processing tasks necessary to transform the input to output; and then record the tasks on an IPO Chart. The IPO Chart for the module whose function is to Create the Rent Report is illustrated in Figure 7-18.

IPO CHART				
PROGRAM: Rent Report	**PROGRAMMER:** Forsythe			**DATE:** Jan. 4
MODULE NAME: Create Rent Report	**REF:** A000	**MODULE FUNCTION:** Create the Rent Report		
INPUT	**PROCESSING**		**REF:**	**OUTPUT**
1. Property Disk File	1. Initialize			1. Rent Report
	2. Obtain the input data			
	3. Process the detail records		B000	
	4. Process a property change		B010	
	5. Print the final totals		B020	
	6. Terminate			

Figure 7 - 18 IPO Chart for Create Rent Report Module

The major processing tasks to produce the Rent Report from the Property Disk File are Initialize, Obtain the input data, Process the detail records, Process property changes, Print the final totals, and Terminate.

Initialize and obtain the input data are basically the same functions seen in previous programs. The major processing task of processing the detail records corresponds to the processing shown in Figure 7-5 and Figure 7-6.

The task of processing the property changes consists of those operations which must be performed when a control break occurs. A control break occurs in the sample program when the Property Number in the input record just read is not equal to the Property Number from the previous record. This processing was illustrated in Figure 7-7 and Figure 7-8.

The task of printing the final totals was illustrated in Figure 7-9. The terminate task is the same as in previous programs.

The next step in the design process is to analyze each of the major processing tasks on the IPO Chart and determine if any of them is of such a size or complexity as to justify another module.

The Initialize and Obtain the input data tasks are simple tasks and, as in previous programs, do not justify separate modules. The task of processing the detail records, however, is a specific function which is large enough and complex enough to require a separate module.

The task of processing property changes also appears to be large enough and complex enough to require a separate module. Printing the final totals may also require some significant processing; therefore, it too should be a separate module. The Terminate task is straightforward and simple and would not require another module.

As a result of this analysis, three separate modules have been identified. The programmer would document them on the hierarchy chart for the program, as illustrated in Figure 7-19.

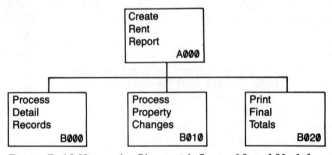

Figure 7-19 Hierarchy Chart with Second Level Modules

The IPO Chart for the module whose function is to process the detail records is illustrated in Figure 7-20.

IPO CHART				
PROGRAM: Rent Report	**PROGRAMMER:** Forsythe		**DATE:** Jan. 4	
MODULE NAME: Process Detail Records	**REF:** B000	**MODULE FUNCTION:** Process the Detail Records		
INPUT	**PROCESSING**	**REF:**	**OUTPUT**	
1. Property Disk Record	1. Print headings	C000	1. Detail Print Line	
2. Property Total	2. Format print line		2. Updated Property	
Accumulator	3. Update accumulators		Total Accumulator	
3. Final Total	4. Write the detail line		3. Updated Final	
Accumulator			Total Accumulator	

Figure 7-20 IPO Chart for Detail Processing Module

Of the major processing tasks specified on the IPO Chart in Figure 7-20, the task of printing the headings, as was seen in Chapter 6, requires a separate module. The remaining major processing tasks are not large enough nor complex enough to justify any lower-level modules. The hierarchy chart developed from this analysis is shown in Figure 7-21.

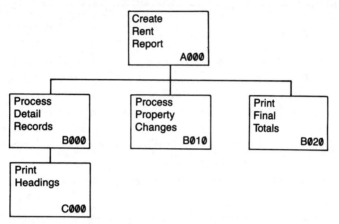

Figure 7-21 Hierarchy Chart with Print Headings Module

The IPO Chart for the module which processes the property changes is illustrated below.

IPO CHART					
PROGRAM: Rent Report		**PROGRAMMER:** Forsythe			**DATE:** Jan. 4
MODULE NAME: Process Property Change		**REF:** B010	**MODULE FUNCTION:** Process Property Change		
INPUT	**PROCESSING**		**REF:**	**OUTPUT**	
1. Old Property Number	1. Format property total line			1. Property Total Line	
2. New Property	2. Write the property total line			2. Property Total	
Number	3. Reset property total			Accumulator	
3. Property Total	accumulator			3. Property Number	
Accumulator	4. Reset property number			Compare Area	
	compare area				

Figure 7-22 IPO Chart for Process a Property Change Module

In Figure 7-22, the output from the module is the Property Total Line, Property Total Accumulator, and Property Number Compare Area. The property total line is printed on the report; the property total accumulator is reset and is used in another module for accumulating the property total; and the compare area is reset to the new property number and used in another module. Therefore, these fields constitute the output of the module.

The input to the module are the Old Property Number, New Property Number, and Property Total Accumulator. The old property number is printed on the property total line; the new property number is placed in the property number compare area; and the property total accumulator contains the value which will be printed on the property total line.

The major processing tasks accomplish the processing identified previously in Figure 7-7 and Figure 7-8. An analysis of these tasks reveals that none of them are of such size or complexity to justify another module.

The third module on the second level is the module whose function is to print the final totals. The IPO Chart for this module is illustrated in Figure 7-23.

IPO CHART

PROGRAM: Rent Report	PROGRAMMER: Forsythe	DATE: Jan. 4
MODULE NAME: Print Final Totals	REF: B020 MODULE FUNCTION: Print the Final Totals	

INPUT	PROCESSING	REF:	OUTPUT
1. Final Total Accumulator	1. Format total line 2. Write the final total line		1. Final Total Line

Figure 7-23 IPO Chart for Print Final Totals Module

Neither of the major processing tasks required in this module are large or complex, so no further decomposition of the module is required.

The IPO Chart for the module whose function is to print the headings is illustrated in Figure 7-24.

IPO CHART

PROGRAM: Rent Report	PROGRAMMER: Forsythe	DATE: Jan. 4
MODULE NAME: Print Headings	REF: C000 MODULE FUNCTION: Print the Headings	

INPUT	PROCESSING	REF:	OUTPUT
1. Heading Lines	1. Format heading lines 2. Print the heading lines		1. Heading Lines

Figure 7-24 IPO Chart for Print the Headings Module

The major processing tasks required to print the headings are not large enough or complex enough to require separate modules.

The hierarchy chart for the completed program structure is illustrated in Figure 7-25.

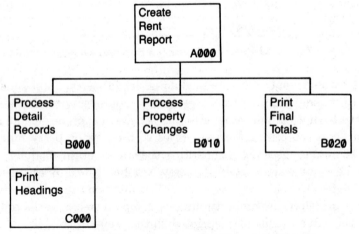

Figure 7-25 Hierarchy Chart for Complete Program

Once the IPO Charts and hierarchy chart are completed and have been reviewed, the programmer may move on to designing the logic for each of the modules through the use of pseudocode.

Pseudocode Specifications

The logic for the module whose function is to create the rent report is shown in Figure 7-26, together with the data bases, files, records, and fields required for the module.

PSEUDOCODE SPECIFICATIONS		
PROGRAM: Rent Report	**PROGRAMMER:** Forsythe	**DATE:** Jan. 4
MODULE NAME: Create Rent Report	**REF:** A000 **MODULE FUNCTION:**	Create the Rent Report

PSEUDOCODE	REF:	DATA BASES, FILES, RECORDS, FIELDS REQUIRED
Open the files		Property disk file
Read an input record		Rent report file
IF there is a record		Input record area
Move property number to compare area		Property number
PERFORM UNTIL no more input records		Apartment number
IF property number not = property		Last month code
number in compare area		Rent amount
Process property change	B010	There is a record indicator
ENDIF		Property number compare area
Process detail records	B000	No more records indicator
Read an input record		No records message
ENDPERFORM		
Process property change	B010	
Print final totals	B020	
ELSE		
Print no records message		
ENDIF		
Close the files		
Stop run		

Figure 7-26 Pseudocode for Create Rent Report Module

The logic expressed in the pseudocode in Figure 7-26 is basically the same as has been seen in previous programs. There are, however, several significant differences. If there is an input record, the Property Number from the input record is moved to the compare area. This initializes the compare area with the Property Number of the first input record (see Figure 7-4 for a detailed drawing of this process). A loop is then entered to process the input records.

The first statement in the loop compares the property number in the input record with the property number in the compare area. If they are not equal, a control break has occurred and the property change module is executed. For the first record, they will be equal since the property number is moved to the compare area just prior to entering the loop; subsequent records will be compared each time a new input record is read.

Regardless of whether there is a control break, the detail record is then processed. After the detail record is processed, another input record is read. This loop will continue until there are no more input records.

When the loop terminates, the first step is to process a property change. This is necessary because the property total for the last group of records must be printed. The final totals are then printed by the final totals module, the files are closed, and the program is terminated.

If a record is not read when the first read statement in the program is executed, a message is printed on the report (see Figure 7-16). This message informs the computer operator that no input records were read. In many applications, this precaution should be taken to ensure that the correct input file was read by the program.

After the pseudocode for the top-level module has been designed, the programmer would normally continue the design of the program by writing the pseudocode for the lower-level modules. The pseudocode for the module which processes the detail records is illustrated in Figure 7-27.

PSEUDOCODE SPECIFICATIONS

PROGRAM: Rent Report   **PROGRAMMER:** Forsythe   **DATE:** Jan. 4

MODULE NAME: Process Detail Records   **REF:** B000   **MODULE FUNCTION:** Process the Detail Records

PSEUDOCODE	REF:	DATA BASES, FILES, RECORDS, FIELDS REQUIRED

IF number of lines printed is = or > page size or first page
    Print the headings
ENDIF
Clear the printer line
Move property number, apartment number, last month of lease from table, and rent amount to output area
Add rent amount to property total and final total accumulators
Write the detail line on the report
Add 1 to lines printed counter
Set spacing to single spacing
	C000	Lines printed counter
		Page size constant
		First page indicator
		Printer output area
		    Property number
		    Apartment number
		    Last month of lease
		    Rent amount
		Input area
		    Property number
		    Apartment number
		    Last month code
		    Rent amount
		Months table
		Property total accumulator
		Final total accumulator
		Spacing control field
		Single space control character

Figure 7-27 Pseudocode for Detail Processing Module

The first step is to print the headings if required. Then the data is moved to the printer output area and the total accumulators are incremented by the rent amount in the input record. Finally, the detail line is printed, the number of lines printed is incremented by 1, and the spacing is set for single spacing.

The logic for the module which processes a property change is illustrated in Figure 7-28.

PSEUDOCODE SPECIFICATIONS

PROGRAM: Rent Report   **PROGRAMMER:** Forsythe   **DATE:** Jan. 4

MODULE NAME: Process Property Change   **REF:** B010   **MODULE FUNCTION:** Process the Property Change

PSEUDOCODE	REF:	DATA BASES, FILES, RECORDS, FIELDS REQUIRED
Move previous property number to property total line Move property total to property total line Write the property total line on the report Add 4 to the number of lines printed Set spacing for triple spacing Set the property total accumulator to zero Move the new property number to the compare area		Previous property number from compare area Property total accumulator Property total line Lines printed counter Spacing control field Triple space control character New property number from input record Property number compare area

Figure 7-28 Pseudocode for Process a Property Change Module

In Figure 7-28, the logic expressed by the pseudocode implements the processing previously illustrated in Figure 7-7 and Figure 7-8. The property number and property total are moved to the property total line, and the line is written on the report. The line count is then incremented by 4 because printing the property total line accounts for four lines on the report — one blank line before the line is printed, the line itself, and two blank lines following the property total line. The spacing is set for triple spacing, since there are two blank lines between the property total line and the first detail line for the next property (see Figure 7-16).

The accumulator for the property total is then set to zero so that the total for the next property will begin with zero. The Property Number from the input record which was just read and which caused the control break is moved from the input area to the compare area so that all records with the same property number in subsequent records will not cause a control break. Control is then relinquished by this module back to the module which called it.

The pseudocode for the module which prints the final totals is illustrated in Figure 7-29.

PSEUDOCODE SPECIFICATIONS

PROGRAM: Rent Report	PROGRAMMER: Forsythe	DATE: Jan. 4
MODULE NAME: Print Final Totals	REF: B020	MODULE FUNCTION: Print the Final Totals

PSEUDOCODE	REF:	DATA BASES, FILES, RECORDS, FIELDS REQUIRED
Move the final total amount to the final total line Write the final total line on the report		Final total accumulator Final total line

Figure 7-29 Pseudocode for Print the Final Totals Module

Printing the final totals consists of moving the final total amount to the final total line and printing the line.

The last module to be designed is the module whose function is to print the headings. The pseudocode for this module is illustrated in Figure 7-30.

PSEUDOCODE SPECIFICATIONS

PROGRAM: Rent Report	PROGRAMMER: Forsythe	DATE: Jan. 4
MODULE NAME: Print Headings	REF: C000	MODULE FUNCTION: Print the Headings

PSEUDOCODE	REF:	DATA BASES, FILES, RECORDS, FIELDS REQUIRED
Obtain the date Move the date to the heading line Move the page count to the heading line Write the first heading line Add 1 to page count Write the second heading line Write the third heading line Set spacing for double spacing Move 5 to lines printer counter		Date work area First heading line Page count Second heading line Third heading line Spacing control area Double spacing control character Lines printed counter

Figure 7-30 Pseudocode for Print the Headings Module

The processing in the module whose function is to print the headings is the same as seen in Chapter 6. The date is obtained from memory and is moved, together with the page number, to the first heading line. The line is then printed on the report. After the page count is incremented by 1, the second and third heading lines are printed. The spacing is then set for double spacing and the counter for the number of lines printed on the page is set to five because the heading requires five lines.

DATA DIVISION

Although the majority of the Data Division coding in this program is similar to that in previous programs, it is necessary in order to process the control break to define a compare area for the property number. The compare area for the Property Number must be defined in the Working-Storage Section of the Data Division. The compare area defined in the sample program is illustrated in Figure 7-31.

```
004160 01   PROGRAM-COMPARE-AREAS.
004170       05   PREVIOUS-PROPERTY-NUMBER  PIC  9(4).
```

Figure 7-31 Definition of Compare Area

The compare area is called PREVIOUS-PROPERTY-NUMBER because the value which is stored in this field is the Property Number from the previous records which have been processed. The field is defined as a numeric field four digits in length to correspond to the type and length of the property number field as described in the input record format (see Figure 7-1).

PROCEDURE DIVISION

The Procedure Division consists of the coding to implement the pseudocode which has been described. Two modules contain processing which is seen for the first time in this program — the module to Create the rent report and the module to Process a property change.

Module to Create the Rent Report

The coding for the module whose function is to Create the rent report is illustrated in Figure 7-32.

In Figure 7-32, the files are opened and the first input record is read. If there is an input record, the property number is moved from the input area to the property compare area. The A001-COMPARE-AND-PROCESS routine is then performed until there are no more input records, at which time the property total and final totals are printed, the files are closed, and the program is terminated.

If there is not an input record when the first Read statement is executed, a message is printed on the report to identify the condition (lines 011080 and 011090). The files are then closed and the program is terminated.

In the A001-COMPARE-AND-PROCESS routine, the property number in the input record is compared to the property number in the compare area (PREVIOUS-PROPERTY-NUMBER). If they are not equal, then the B010-PROCESS-PROPERTY-CHANGE module is

```
010140  A000-CREATE-RENT-REPORT.
010150
010160      OPEN INPUT    PROPERTY-INPUT-FILE
010170           OUTPUT RENT-REPORT-FILE.
010180      READ PROPERTY-INPUT-FILE
010190           AT END
010200               MOVE 'NO ' TO ARE-THERE-MORE-RECORDS.
011010      IF THERE-IS-A-RECORD
011020          MOVE PROPERTY-NUMBER-INPUT TO PREVIOUS-PROPERTY-NUMBER
011030          PERFORM A001-COMPARE-AND-PROCESS
011040              UNTIL THERE-ARE-NO-MORE-RECORDS
011050          PERFORM B010-PROCESS-PROPERTY-CHANGE
011060          PERFORM B020-PRINT-FINAL-TOTALS
011070      ELSE
011080          WRITE RENT-REPORT-LINE FROM NO-RECORDS-MESSAGE
011090              AFTER ADVANCING TO-TOP-OF-PAGE.
011100      CLOSE PROPERTY-INPUT-FILE
011110            RENT-REPORT-FILE.
011120      STOP RUN.
011130
011140
011150
011160  A001-COMPARE-AND-PROCESS.
011170
011180      IF PROPERTY-NUMBER-INPUT IS NOT = PREVIOUS-PROPERTY-NUMBER
011190          PERFORM B010-PROCESS-PROPERTY-CHANGE.
011200      PERFORM B000-PROCESS-DETAIL-RECORDS.
012010      READ PROPERTY-INPUT-FILE
012020           AT END
012030               MOVE 'NO ' TO ARE-THERE-MORE-RECORDS.
```

Figure 7-32 Coding for Create the Rent Report Module

performed. Regardless of whether the property numbers are equal or not, the detail record processing module (B000-PROCESS-DETAIL-RECORDS) is performed to process the detail record. Another record is then read and, so long as there are more records, the A001-COMPARE-AND-PROCESS routine will be repeated.

Module to Process a Property Change

The module which processes a property change is shown in Figure 7-33.

```
014030  B010-PROCESS-PROPERTY-CHANGE.
014040
014050      MOVE PREVIOUS-PROPERTY-NUMBER TO PROPERTY-NUMBER-TOTAL-LINE.
014060      MOVE PROPERTY-TOTAL-ACCUM TO PROPERTY-AMOUNT-TOTAL-LINE.
014070      WRITE RENT-REPORT-LINE FROM PROPERTY-TOTAL-LINE
014080           AFTER ADVANCING 2 LINES.
014090      ADD 4 TO LINES-PRINTED.
014100      MOVE SPACE-THREE-LINES TO PROPER-SPACING.
014110      MOVE ZEROS TO PROPERTY-TOTAL-ACCUM.
014120      MOVE PROPERTY-NUMBER-INPUT TO PREVIOUS-PROPERTY-NUMBER.
```

Figure 7-33 Coding for Process a Property Change Module

In Figure 7-33, the property total line is formatted and printed. The value 4 is added to the line count because printing the property total requires four lines. The spacing is set for triple spacing, the property total accumulator is reset to zero, and the property number from the input record is moved to the compare area. The logic in this module follows the pseudocode which was developed in Figure 7-28.

SAMPLE PROGRAM

The following pages contain the Input, Output, and Source Listing of the program to create the Rent Report.

Input

Property Disk Record				
FIELD DESCRIPTION	POSITION	LENGTH	DEC	ATTRIBUTE
Property Number	1 – 4	4	0	Numeric
Apartment Number	5 – 7	3	0	Numeric
Last Month Code	8 – 9	2	0	Numeric
Rent Amount	10 – 14	5	2	Numeric
Record Length		14		

Figure 7-34 Input

Output

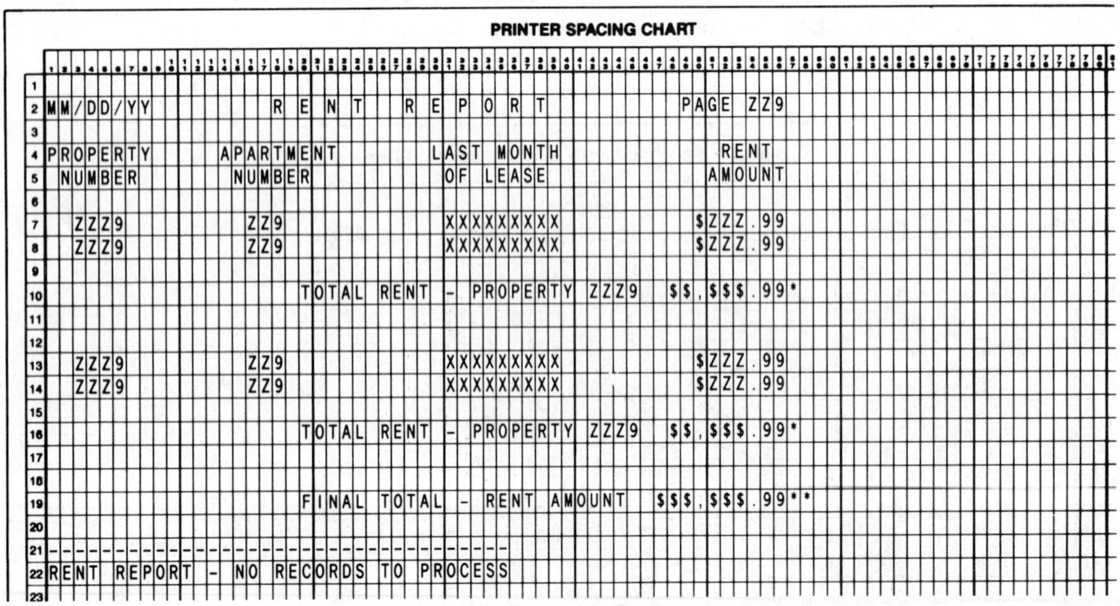

Figure 7-35 Output

Source Listing

```
PP 5740-CB1 RELEASE 2.3 + PTF 8 - UP13477          IBM OS/VS COBOL  JULY 24, 1978          12.46.26  DATE MAR  6,1985


     1                     12.46.26       MAR  6,1985


   00001   001010 IDENTIFICATION DIVISION.                                              RENTRPT
   00002   001020                                                                       RENTRPT
   00003   001030 PROGRAM-ID.    RENTRPT.                                               RENTRPT
   00004   001040 AUTHOR.        FORSYTHE.                                              RENTRPT
   00005   001050 INSTALLATION.  BREA.                                                  RENTRPT
   00006   001060 DATE-WRITTEN.  JAN 10,1985.                                           RENTRPT
   00007   001070 DATE-COMPILED. MAR  6,1985.                                           RENTRPT
   00008   001080 SECURITY.      UNCLASSIFIED.                                          RENTRPT
   00009   001090                                                                       RENTRPT
   00010   001100************************************************************           RENTRPT
   00011   001110*                                                          *           RENTRPT
   00012   001120*    THIS PROGRAM PRODUCES A RENT REPORT LISTING PROPERTY   *           RENTRPT
   00013   001130*    NUMBER, APARTMENT NUMBER, LAST MONTH OF LEASE, AND RENT *          RENTRPT
   00014   001140*    AMOUNT. WHEN THERE IS A CHANGE IN PROPERTY NUMBER, A TOTAL *       RENTRPT
   00015   001150*    IS PRINTED LISTING THE RENT AMOUNT FOR THE PROPERTY. AFTER *       RENTRPT
   00016   001160*    ALL RECORDS HAVE BEEN PROCESSED, A FINAL TOTAL WILL BE   *         RENTRPT
   00017   001170*    PRINTED.                                               *           RENTRPT
   00018   001180*                                                          *           RENTRPT
   00019   001190************************************************************           RENTRPT
   00020   001200                                                                       RENTRPT
   00021   002010                                                                       RENTRPT
   00022   002020                                                                       RENTRPT
   00023   002030 ENVIRONMENT DIVISION.                                                 RENTRPT
   00024   002040                                                                       RENTRPT
   00025   002050 CONFIGURATION SECTION.                                                RENTRPT
   00026   002060                                                                       RENTRPT
   00027   002070 SOURCE-COMPUTER. IBM-4381.                                            RENTRPT
   00028   002080 OBJECT-COMPUTER. IBM-4381.                                            RENTRPT
   00029   002090 SPECIAL-NAMES.   C01 IS TO-TOP-OF-PAGE.                               RENTRPT
   00030   002100                                                                       RENTRPT
   00031   002110 INPUT-OUTPUT SECTION.                                                 RENTRPT
   00032   002120                                                                       RENTRPT
   00033   002130 FILE-CONTROL.                                                         RENTRPT
   00034   002140     SELECT PROPERTY-INPUT-FILE                                        RENTRPT
   00035   002150         ASSIGN TO UT-S-RENTDATA.                                      RENTRPT
   00036   002160     SELECT RENT-REPORT-FILE                                           RENTRPT
   00037   002170         ASSIGN TO UT-S-RENTPRNT.                                      RENTRPT


     2                     12.46.26       MAR  6,1985


   00038   002180/                                                                      RENTRPT
   00039   002190 DATA DIVISION.                                                        RENTRPT
   00040   002200                                                                       RENTRPT
   00041   003010 FILE SECTION.                                                         RENTRPT
   00042   003020                                                                       RENTRPT
   00043   003030 FD  PROPERTY-INPUT-FILE                                               RENTRPT
   00044   003040     RECORD CONTAINS 14 CHARACTERS                                     RENTRPT
   00045   003050     LABEL RECORDS ARE STANDARD                                        RENTRPT
   00046   003060     DATA RECORD IS PROPERTY-INPUT-RECORD.                             RENTRPT
   00047   003070 01  PROPERTY-INPUT-RECORD.                                            RENTRPT
   00048   003080     05  PROPERTY-NUMBER-INPUT    PIC 9(4).                            RENTRPT
   00049   003090     05  APARTMENT-NUMBER-INPUT   PIC 9(3).                            RENTRPT
   00050   003100     05  LAST-MONTH-CODE-INPUT    PIC 9(2).                            RENTRPT
   00051   003110     05  RENT-AMOUNT-INPUT        PIC 9(3)V99.                         RENTRPT
   00052   003120                                                                       RENTRPT
   00053   003130 FD  RENT-REPORT-FILE                                                  RENTRPT
   00054   003140     RECORD CONTAINS 133 CHARACTERS                                    RENTRPT
   00055   003150     LABEL RECORDS ARE OMITTED                                         RENTRPT
   00056   003160     DATA RECORD IS RENT-REPORT-LINE.                                  RENTRPT
   00057   003170 01  RENT-REPORT-LINE.                                                 RENTRPT
   00058   003180     05  CARRIAGE-CONTROL         PIC X.                               RENTRPT
   00059   003190     05  FILLER                   PIC XX.                              RENTRPT
   00060   003200     05  PROPERTY-NUMBER-REPORT   PIC ZZZ9.                            RENTRPT
   00061   004010     05  FILLER                   PIC X(9).                            RENTRPT
   00062   004020     05  APARTMENT-NUMBER-REPORT  PIC ZZ9.                             RENTRPT
   00063   004030     05  FILLER                   PIC X(12).                           RENTRPT
   00064   004040     05  LAST-MONTH-REPORT        PIC X(9).                            RENTRPT
   00065   004050     05  FILLER                   PIC X(10).                           RENTRPT
   00066   004060     05  RENT-AMOUNT-REPORT       PIC $ZZZ.99.                         RENTRPT
   00067   004070     05  FILLER                   PIC X(76).                           RENTRPT
   00068   004080                                                                       RENTRPT
   00069   004090 WORKING-STORAGE SECTION.                                              RENTRPT
   00070   004100                                                                       RENTRPT
   00071   004110 01  PROGRAM-INDICATORS.                                               RENTRPT
   00072   004120     05  ARE-THERE-MORE-RECORDS PIC X(3)     VALUE 'YES'.              RENTRPT
   00073   004130         88  THERE-IS-A-RECORD               VALUE 'YES'.              RENTRPT
   00074   004140         88  THERE-ARE-NO-MORE-RECORDS       VALUE 'NO '.              RENTRPT
   00075   004150                                                                       RENTRPT
   00076   004160 01  PROGRAM-COMPARE-AREAS.                                            RENTRPT
   00077   004170     05  PREVIOUS-PROPERTY-NUMBER PIC 9(4).                            RENTRPT
   00078   004180                                                                       RENTRPT
   00079   004190 01  WORK-AREAS.                                                       RENTRPT
   00080   004200     05  DATE-WORK.                                                    RENTRPT
   00081   005010         10  YEAR-WORK            PIC 99.                              RENTRPT
   00082   005020         10  MONTH-WORK           PIC 99.                              RENTRPT
   00083   005030         10  DAY-WORK             PIC 99.                              RENTRPT
   00084   005040                                                                       RENTRPT
   00085   005050 01  PROGRAM-CONSTANTS.                                                RENTRPT
   00086   005060     05  NO-RECORDS-MESSAGE.                                           RENTRPT
   00087   005070         10  CARRIAGE-CONTROL     PIC X.                               RENTRPT
   00088   005080         10  FILLER               PIC X(35)   VALUE                    RENTRPT
   00089   005090             'RENT REPORT - NO RECORDS TO PROCESS'.RENTRPT
```

Figure 7-36 Sample Program (Part 1 of 4)

```
       3                    12.46.26      MAR 6,1985

  00090  005100        10  FILLER            PIC X(97)     VALUE SPACES.      RENTRPT
  00091  005110                                                              RENTRPT
  00092  005120 01 TOTAL-ACCUMULATORS-COUNTERS.                              RENTRPT
  00093  005130    05  PROPERTY-TOTAL-ACCUM  PIC S9(4)V99 VALUE ZERO.        RENTRPT
  00094  005140    05  FINAL-TOTAL-ACCUM     PIC S9(5)V99 VALUE ZERO.        RENTRPT
  00095  005150                                                              RENTRPT
  00096  005160 01 PROGRAM-TABLES.                                           RENTRPT
  00097  005170    05  MONTHS-TABLE.                                         RENTRPT
  00098  005180        10  MONTH-CONSTANTS.                                  RENTRPT
  00099  005190            15  FILLER        PIC X(9)      VALUE 'JANUARY  '. RENTRPT
  00100  005200            15  FILLER        PIC X(9)      VALUE 'FEBRUARY '. RENTRPT
  00101  006010            15  FILLER        PIC X(9)      VALUE 'MARCH    '. RENTRPT
  00102  006020            15  FILLER        PIC X(9)      VALUE 'APRIL    '. RENTRPT
  00103  006030            15  FILLER        PIC X(9)      VALUE 'MAY      '. RENTRPT
  00104  006040            15  FILLER        PIC X(9)      VALUE 'JUNE     '. RENTRPT
  00105  006050            15  FILLER        PIC X(9)      VALUE 'JULY     '. RENTRPT
  00106  006060            15  FILLER        PIC X(9)      VALUE 'AUGUST   '. RENTRPT
  00107  006070            15  FILLER        PIC X(9)      VALUE 'SEPTEMBER'. RENTRPT
  00108  006080            15  FILLER        PIC X(9)      VALUE 'OCTOBER  '. RENTRPT
  00109  006090            15  FILLER        PIC X(9)      VALUE 'NOVEMBER '. RENTRPT
  00110  006100            15  FILLER        PIC X(9)      VALUE 'DECEMBER '. RENTRPT
  00111  006110        10  MONTH-TABLE REDEFINES MONTH-CONSTANTS             RENTRPT
  00112  006120                              PIC X(9)      OCCURS 12 TIMES.   RENTRPT
  00113  006130                                                              RENTRPT
  00114  006140 01 PRINTER-CONTROL.                                          RENTRPT
  00115  006150    05  PROPER-SPACING        PIC 9.                          RENTRPT
  00116  006160    05  SPACE-ONE-LINE        PIC 9         VALUE 1.          RENTRPT
  00117  006170    05  SPACE-TWO-LINES       PIC 9         VALUE 2.          RENTRPT
  00118  006180    05  SPACE-THREE-LINES     PIC 9         VALUE 3.          RENTRPT
  00119  006190    05  PAGE-COUNT            PIC S999      VALUE +1.         RENTRPT
  00120  006200        88  FIRST-PAGE                      VALUE +1.         RENTRPT
  00121  007010    05  PAGE-SIZE             PIC 999       VALUE 55.         RENTRPT
  00122  007020    05  LINES-PRINTED         PIC S999      VALUE ZERO.       RENTRPT
  00123  007030                                                              RENTRPT
  00124  007040 01 HEADING-LINES.                                            RENTRPT
  00125  007050    05  FIRST-HEADING-LINE.                                   RENTRPT
  00126  007060        10  CARRIAGE-CONTROL  PIC X.                          RENTRPT
  00127  007070        10  DATE-HEADING.                                     RENTRPT
  00128  007080            15  MONTH-HEADING PIC 99.                         RENTRPT
  00129  007090            15  FILLER        PIC X         VALUE '/'.        RENTRPT
  00130  007100            15  DAY-HEADING   PIC 99.                         RENTRPT
  00131  007110            15  FILLER        PIC X         VALUE '/'.        RENTRPT
  00132  007120            15  YEAR-HEADING  PIC 99.                         RENTRPT
  00133  007130        10  FILLER            PIC X(9)      VALUE SPACES.      RENTRPT
  00134  007140        10  FILLER            PIC X(21)     VALUE             RENTRPT
  00135  007150                                     'R E N T   R E P O R T'.RENTRPT
  00136  007160        10  FILLER            PIC X(10)     VALUE SPACES.      RENTRPT
  00137  007170        10  FILLER            PIC X(5)      VALUE 'PAGE '.    RENTRPT
  00138  007180        10  PAGE-HEADING      PIC ZZ9.                        RENTRPT
  00139  007190        10  FILLER            PIC X(76).                      RENTRPT
  00140  007200    05  SECOND-HEADING-LINE.                                  RENTRPT
  00141  008010        10  CARRIAGE-CONTROL  PIC X.                          RENTRPT
  00142  008020        10  FILLER            PIC X(8)      VALUE 'PROPERTY'.  RENTRPT
  00143  008030        10  FILLER            PIC X(5)      VALUE SPACES.      RENTRPT
  00144  008040        10  FILLER            PIC X(9)      VALUE 'APARTMENT'. RENTRPT
  00145  008050        10  FILLER            PIC X(7)      VALUE SPACES.      RENTRPT
  00146  008060        10  FILLER            PIC X(10)     VALUE 'LAST MONTH'.RENTRPT
  00147  008070        10  FILLER            PIC X(12)     VALUE SPACES.      RENTRPT
  00148  008080        10  FILLER            PIC X(4)      VALUE 'RENT'.      RENTRPT
  00149  008090        10  FILLER            PIC X(77)     VALUE SPACES.      RENTRPT
  00150  008100    05  THIRD-HEADING-LINE.                                   RENTRPT
  00151  008110        10  CARRIAGE-CONTROL  PIC X.                          RENTRPT
  00152  008120        10  FILLER            PIC X         VALUE SPACES.      RENTRPT
  00153  008130        10  FILLER            PIC X(6)      VALUE 'NUMBER'.    RENTRPT
  00154  008140        10  FILLER            PIC X(7)      VALUE SPACES.      RENTRPT
  00155  008150        10  FILLER            PIC X(6)      VALUE 'NUMBER'.    RENTRPT
  00156  008160        10  FILLER            PIC X(10)     VALUE SPACES.      RENTRPT
  00157  008170        10  FILLER            PIC X(8)      VALUE 'OF LEASE'.  RENTRPT
  00158  008180        10  FILLER            PIC X(12)     VALUE SPACES.      RENTRPT
  00159  008190        10  FILLER            PIC X(6)      VALUE 'AMOUNT'.    RENTRPT
  00160  008200        10  FILLER            PIC X(76)     VALUE SPACES.      RENTRPT
  00161  009010                                                              RENTRPT
  00162  009020 01 TOTAL-LINES.                                              RENTRPT
  00163  009030    05  PROPERTY-TOTAL-LINE.                                  RENTRPT
  00164  009040        10  CARRIAGE-CONTROL        PIC X.                    RENTRPT
  00165  009050        10  FILLER                  PIC X(19) VALUE SPACES.   RENTRPT
  00166  009060        10  FILLER                  PIC X(22) VALUE           RENTRPT
  00167  009070                                   'TOTAL RENT - PROPERTY '.  RENTRPT
  00168  009080        10  PROPERTY-NUMBER-TOTAL-LINE PIC ZZZ9.              RENTRPT
  00169  009090        10  FILLER                  PIC X(2)  VALUE SPACES.   RENTRPT
  00170  009100        10  PROPERTY-AMOUNT-TOTAL-LINE PIC $$,$$$.99.         RENTRPT
  00171  009110        10  FILLER                  PIC X     VALUE '*'.      RENTRPT
  00172  009120        10  FILLER                  PIC X(75) VALUE SPACES.   RENTRPT
  00173  009130    05  FINAL-TOTAL-LINE.                                     RENTRPT
  00174  009140        10  CARRIAGE-CONTROL        PIC X.                    RENTRPT
  00175  009150        10  FILLER                  PIC X(19) VALUE SPACES.   RENTRPT
  00176  009160        10  FILLER                  PIC X(27) VALUE           RENTRPT
  00177  009170                                   'FINAL TOTAL - RENT AMOUNT '.RENTRPT
  00178  009180        10  PROPERTY-AMOUNT-FINAL-TOTAL PIC $$$,$$$.99.       RENTRPT
  00179  009190        10  FILLER                  PIC XX    VALUE '**'.     RENTRPT
  00180  009200        10  FILLER                  PIC X(74) VALUE SPACES.   RENTRPT
```

Figure 7-37 Sample Program (Part 2 of 4)

```
    4                    12.46.26      MAR  6,1985

00181   010010/                                                                RENTRPT
00182   010020 PROCEDURE DIVISION.                                             RENTRPT
00183   010030                                                                 RENTRPT
00184   010040*****************************************************************RENTRPT
00185   010050*                                                              * RENTRPT
00186   010060*    THIS MODULE CONTROLS PROCESSING THE RECORDS. WHEN A CONTROL * RENTRPT
00187   010070*    BREAK OCCURS ON PROPERTY NUMBER, CONTROL IS TRANSFERRED TO * RENTRPT
00188   010080*    A MODULE TO PRINT THE PROPERTY TOTALS. FINAL TOTALS ARE    * RENTRPT
00189   010090*    PRINTED AFTER ALL RECORDS HAVE BEEN PROCESSED. THIS MODULE * RENTRPT
00190   010100*    IS ENTERED FROM AND EXITS TO THE OPERATING SYSTEM.         * RENTRPT
00191   010110*                                                              * RENTRPT
00192   010120*****************************************************************RENTRPT
00193   010130                                                                 RENTRPT
00194   010140 A000-CREATE-RENT-REPORT.                                        RENTRPT
00195   010150                                                                 RENTRPT
00196   010160     OPEN INPUT  PROPERTY-INPUT-FILE                             RENTRPT
00197   010170          OUTPUT RENT-REPORT-FILE.                               RENTRPT
00198   010180     READ PROPERTY-INPUT-FILE                                    RENTRPT
00199   010190        AT END                                                   RENTRPT
00200   010200           MOVE 'NO ' TO ARE-THERE-MORE-RECORDS.                 RENTRPT
00201   011010     IF THERE-IS-A-RECORD                                        RENTRPT
00202   011020        MOVE PROPERTY-NUMBER-INPUT TO PREVIOUS-PROPERTY-NUMBER   RENTRPT
00203   011030        PERFORM A001-COMPARE-AND-PROCESS                         RENTRPT
00204   011040           UNTIL THERE-ARE-NO-MORE-RECORDS                       RENTRPT
00205   011050        PERFORM B010-PROCESS-PROPERTY-CHANGE                     RENTRPT
00206   011060        PERFORM B020-PRINT-FINAL-TOTALS                          RENTRPT
00207   011070     ELSE                                                        RENTRPT
00208   011080        WRITE RENT-REPORT-LINE FROM NO-RECORDS-MESSAGE           RENTRPT
00209   011090           AFTER ADVANCING TO-TOP-OF-PAGE.                       RENTRPT
00210   011100     CLOSE PROPERTY-INPUT-FILE                                   RENTRPT
00211   011110           RENT-REPORT-FILE.                                     RENTRPT
00212   011120     STOP RUN.                                                   RENTRPT
00213   011130                                                                 RENTRPT
00214   011140                                                                 RENTRPT
00215   011150                                                                 RENTRPT
00216   011160 A001-COMPARE-AND-PROCESS.                                       RENTRPT
00217   011170                                                                 RENTRPT
00218   011180     IF PROPERTY-NUMBER-INPUT IS NOT = PREVIOUS-PROPERTY-NUMBER  RENTRPT
00219   011190        PERFORM B010-PROCESS-PROPERTY-CHANGE.                    RENTRPT
00220   011200     PERFORM B000-PROCESS-DETAIL-RECORDS.                        RENTRPT
00221   012010     READ PROPERTY-INPUT-FILE                                    RENTRPT
00222   012020        AT END                                                   RENTRPT
00223   012030           MOVE 'NO ' TO ARE-THERE-MORE-RECORDS.                 RENTRPT
```

```
    5                    12.46.26      MAR  6,1985

00224   012040/                                                                RENTRPT
00225   012050*****************************************************************RENTRPT
00226   012060*                                                              * RENTRPT
00227   012070*    THIS MODULE PRINTS THE DETAIL LINE FOR THE REPORT.         * RENTRPT
00228   012080*    IF NECESSARY, IT CAUSES THE HEADINGS TO BE PRINTED AND THEN* RENTRPT
00229   012090*    FORMATS AND PRINTS THE DETAIL LINE. PROPERTY AND FINAL     * RENTRPT
00230   012100*    TOTALS ARE ALSO ACCUMULATED. THIS MODULE IS ENTERED FROM   * RENTRPT
00231   012110*    AND EXITS TO THE A000-CREATE-RENT-REPORT MODULE.           * RENTRPT
00232   012120*                                                              * RENTRPT
00233   012130*****************************************************************RENTRPT
00234   012140                                                                 RENTRPT
00235   012150 B000-PROCESS-DETAIL-RECORDS.                                    RENTRPT
00236   012160                                                                 RENTRPT
00237   012170     IF LINES-PRINTED IS EQUAL TO PAGE-SIZE OR                   RENTRPT
00238   012180        LINES-PRINTED IS GREATER THAN PAGE-SIZE OR              RENTRPT
00239   012190        FIRST-PAGE                                               RENTRPT
00240   012200        PERFORM C000-PRINT-HEADINGS.                             RENTRPT
00241   013010     MOVE SPACES TO RENT-REPORT-LINE.                            RENTRPT
00242   013020     MOVE PROPERTY-NUMBER-INPUT TO PROPERTY-NUMBER-REPORT.       RENTRPT
00243   013030     MOVE APARTMENT-NUMBER-INPUT TO APARTMENT-NUMBER-REPORT.     RENTRPT
00244   013040     MOVE MONTH-TABLE (LAST-MONTH-CODE-INPUT) TO                 RENTRPT
00245   013050        LAST-MONTH-REPORT.                                       RENTRPT
00246   013060     MOVE RENT-AMOUNT-INPUT TO RENT-AMOUNT-REPORT.               RENTRPT
00247   013070     ADD RENT-AMOUNT-INPUT TO PROPERTY-TOTAL-ACCUM.              RENTRPT
00248   013080     ADD RENT-AMOUNT-INPUT TO FINAL-TOTAL-ACCUM.                 RENTRPT
00249   013090     WRITE RENT-REPORT-LINE                                      RENTRPT
00250   013100        AFTER ADVANCING PROPER-SPACING.                          RENTRPT
00251   013120     ADD 1 TO LINES-PRINTED.                                     RENTRPT
00252   013121     MOVE SPACE-ONE-LINE TO PROPER-SPACING.                      RENTRPT
```

```
    6                    12.46.26      MAR  6,1985

00253   013130/                                                                RENTRPT
00254   013140*****************************************************************RENTRPT
00255   013150*                                                              * RENTRPT
00256   013160*    THIS MODULE PROCESSES A CHANGE IN PROPERTY NUMBER. THE     * RENTRPT
00257   013170*    PROPERTY NUMBER TOTAL IS PRINTED AND THE ACCUMULATOR AND   * RENTRPT
00258   013180*    COMPARE AREAS ARE RESET. THIS MODULE IS ENTERED FROM AND   * RENTRPT
00259   013190*    EXITS TO THE A000-CREATE-RENT-REPORT MODULE.               * RENTRPT
00260   013200*                                                              * RENTRPT
00261   014010*****************************************************************RENTRPT
00262   014020                                                                 RENTRPT
00263   014030 B010-PROCESS-PROPERTY-CHANGE.                                   RENTRPT
00264   014040                                                                 RENTRPT
00265   014050     MOVE PREVIOUS-PROPERTY-NUMBER TO PROPERTY-NUMBER-TOTAL-LINE.RENTRPT
00266   014060     MOVE PROPERTY-TOTAL-ACCUM TO PROPERTY-AMOUNT-TOTAL-LINE.    RENTRPT
00267   014070     WRITE RENT-REPORT-LINE FROM PROPERTY-TOTAL-LINE             RENTRPT
00268   014080        AFTER ADVANCING 2 LINES.                                 RENTRPT
00269   014090     ADD 4 TO LINES-PRINTED.                                     RENTRPT
00270   014100     MOVE SPACE-THREE-LINES TO PROPER-SPACING.                   RENTRPT
00271   014110     MOVE ZEROS TO PROPERTY-TOTAL-ACCUM.                         RENTRPT
00272   014120     MOVE PROPERTY-NUMBER-INPUT TO PREVIOUS-PROPERTY-NUMBER.     RENTRPT
```

Figure 7-38 Sample Program (Part 3 of 4)

```
     7                     12.46.26      MAR  6,1985

00273  014130/                                                                RENTRPT
00274  014140*******************************************************************   RENTRPT
00275  014150*                                                               *    RENTRPT
00276  014160*   THIS MODULE PRINTS THE FINAL TOTALS. IT IS ENTERED FROM AND *    RENTRPT
00277  014170*   EXITS TO THE A000-CREATE-RENT-REPORT MODULE.                *    RENTRPT
00278  014180*                                                               *    RENTRPT
00279  014190*******************************************************************   RENTRPT
00280  014200                                                                RENTRPT
00281  015010 B020-PRINT-FINAL-TOTALS.                                       RENTRPT
00282  015020                                                                RENTRPT
00283  015030     MOVE FINAL-TOTAL-ACCUM TO PROPERTY-AMOUNT-FINAL-TOTAL.     RENTRPT
00284  015040     WRITE RENT-REPORT-LINE FROM FINAL-TOTAL-LINE               RENTRPT
00285  015050         AFTER ADVANCING 3 LINES.                               RENTRPT
```

```
     8                     12.46.26      MAR  6,1985

00286  015060/                                                                RENTRPT
00287  015070*******************************************************************   RENTRPT
00288  015080*                                                               *    RENTRPT
00289  015090*   THIS MODULE PRINTS THE HEADINGS ON THE REPORT. IT IS        *    RENTRPT
00290  015100*   ENTERED FROM AND EXITS TO THE B000-PROCESS-DETAIL-RECORD    *    RENTRPT
00291  015110*   MODULE.                                                     *    RENTRPT
00292  015120*                                                               *    RENTRPT
00293  015130*******************************************************************   RENTRPT
00294  015140                                                                RENTRPT
00295  015150 C000-PRINT-HEADINGS.                                           RENTRPT
00296  015160                                                                RENTRPT
00297  015170     ACCEPT DATE-WORK FROM DATE.                                RENTRPT
00298  015180     MOVE MONTH-WORK TO MONTH-HEADING.                          RENTRPT
00299  015190     MOVE DAY-WORK TO DAY-HEADING.                              RENTRPT
00300  015200     MOVE YEAR-WORK TO YEAR-HEADING.                            RENTRPT
00301  016010     MOVE PAGE-COUNT TO PAGE-HEADING.                           RENTRPT
00302  016020     WRITE RENT-REPORT-LINE FROM FIRST-HEADING-LINE             RENTRPT
00303  016030         AFTER ADVANCING TO-TOP-OF-PAGE.                        RENTRPT
00304  016040     ADD 1 TO PAGE-COUNT.                                       RENTRPT
00305  016050     WRITE RENT-REPORT-LINE FROM SECOND-HEADING-LINE            RENTRPT
00306  016060         AFTER ADVANCING 2 LINES.                               RENTRPT
00307  016070     WRITE RENT-REPORT-LINE FROM THIRD-HEADING-LINE             RENTRPT
00308  016080         AFTER ADVANCING 1 LINES.                               RENTRPT
00309  016090     MOVE SPACE-TWO-LINES TO PROPER-SPACING.                    RENTRPT
00310  016100     MOVE 5 TO LINES-PRINTED.                                   RENTRPT
```

Figure 7-39 Sample Program (Part 4 of 4)

REVIEW QUESTIONS

1. What is meant by detail printing?

2. Explain the term control break.

3. Briefly explain the processing that must occur when the first record is read in a program involving a control break.

4. Briefly explain the processing that must occur in a program involving a control break when a control break occurs.

5. When should a compare area be defined?

6. What is a table in a computer program? What type of processing can be performed on data stored in a table?

7. Why must a Redefines clause be used when defining a table?

8. What is the purpose of the Occurs clause?

9. What is a subscript? How is it used?

10. What are the advantages of using a data-name instead of a numeric literal for a subscript.

11. What are the major processing tasks required when a program is to process a control break and print final totals?

12. Why doesn't the first record read in a file cause a control break?

COBOL CODING EXERCISES

1. Write the COBOL code to define the input file record area and the program compare area needed to produce a report containing a control break. The control break is based upon a change in Vehicle Number. The format of the input records in the disk file for the problem is as follows: Vehicle Number, positions 1-7; Vehicle Make, positions 8-17; Vehicle Model, positions 18-27; and Registration Amount, positions 28-32. Vehicle Number and Registration Amount are numeric fields.

2. Write the COBOL code required in the Working-Storage Section of the Data Division to define the program constant needed to print the message VEHICLE REPORT — NO RECORDS TO PROCESS if the disk input file described in problem #1 should contain no records.

3. Write the COBOL code required in the Working-Storage Section of the Data Division to define a table containing the following list of U. S. presidents:

>   HERBERT HOOVER
>   FRANKLIN ROOSEVELT
>   HARRY TRUMAN
>   DWIGHT EISENHOWER
>   JOHN KENNEDY
>   LYNDON JOHNSON
>   RICHARD NIXON
>   GERALD FORD
>   JIMMY CARTER
>   RONALD REAGAN

4. Write the COBOL Move statement required to move the name of the fifth president from the table defined in problem #3 above to the field PRESIDENT-REPORT.

5. Write the COBOL Move statement required to move the name of any president from the table defined in problem #3 above to the field PRESIDENT-REPORT. Use the PRESIDENT-CODE-INPUT field as a subscript.

STRUCTURED WALKTHROUGH EXERCISES

The following portions of COBOL code contain one or more errors in program logic, in the use of the COBOL language itself, or in the programming standards which should be followed. Review the code in each exercise in the same manner used for structured walkthroughs. Identify the errors and make the appropriate corrections.

1.

```
005050  01  PROGRAM-CONSTANTS.
005060      05  NO-RECORDS-MESSAGE.
005070          10  FILLER                    PIC X(35)     VALUE
005080                        'GOLF REPORT - NO RECORDS TO PROCESS'.
```

2.

```
006010  WORKING-STORAGE SECTION.

007160  01  PROGRAM-TABLES.
007170      05  INSTRUCTORS-TABLE.
007180          10  INSTRUCTORS-CONSTANTS.
007190              10  FILLER        PIC X(11)    VALUE 'JONES STEVE'.
007200              10  FILLER        PIC X(11)    VALUE 'MARCUS, BOB'.
008010              10  FILLER        PIC X(11)    VALUE 'SMITH, JOE '.
008020              10  FILLER        PIC X(11)    VALUE 'TOWER, JILL'.
008030              10  FILLER        PIC X(11)    VALUE 'WENDEL, SUE'.
008040          10  INSTRUCTOR-TABLE DEFINES INSTRUCTORS-TABLE
008050                              PIC X((1)    OCURS 6 TIMES.

012030  PROCEDURE DIVISION.

013040      MOVE INSTRUCTOR-CONSTANTS (7) TO INSTRUCTOR-REPORT.
013050      MOVE INSTRUCTOR-TABLE INSTRUCTOR-CODE-INPUT TO
                INSTRUCTOR-REPORT.
```

3.

```
008040  A000-CREATE-STORE-REPORT.

009010      IF THERE-IS-A-RECORD
009020          MOVE STORE-NUMBER-INPUT TO PREVIOUS-STORE-REPORT.
009030          PERFORM A001-COMPARE-AND-PROCESS.
009040              UNTIL THERE-ARE-NO-MORE-RECORDS.
009050          PERFORM B010-PRINT-FINAL-TOTALS.
009060          PERFORM B020-PROCESS-STORE-CHANGE.
009070      ELSE
009080          WRITE NO-RECORDS-MESSAGE FROM STORE-REPORT-LINE
009090              AFTER ADVANCING TO-TOP-OF-PAGE.

011160  A001-COMPARE-AND-PROCESS.
011170
011180      IF STORE-NUMBER-INPUT = PREVIOUS-STORE-NUMBER
011190          PERFORM B010-PROCESS-STORE-CHANGE.

014030  B010-PROCESS-STORE-CHANGE.
014040
014050      MOVE STORE-NUMBER-INPUT TO STORE-NUMBER-TOTAL-LINE.
014060      WRITE STORE-REPORT-LINE FROM STORE-TOTAL-LINE
014070          AFTER ADVANCING 2 LINES.
014080      MOVE STORE-NUMBER-INPUT TO PREVIOUS-STORE-NUMBER.
```

PROGRAMMING ASSIGNMENT 1

INSTRUCTIONS

A Fast Food Sales Report is to be prepared. Design and write the COBOL program to produce the required report. An IPO Chart and Pseudocode Specifications should be used when designing the program. Use Test Data Set 1 in Appendix A.

INPUT

Input consists of Fast Food Records that contain the District Number, Franchise Number, Franchise Owner, Sales Code, and Daily Sales. The input records have been sorted in ascending sequence by District Number prior to processing. The format of the input record is illustrated below.

Fast Food Disk Record				
FIELD DESCRIPTION	**POSITION**	**LENGTH**	**DEC**	**ATTRIBUTE**
District Number	1 – 4	4	0	Numeric
UNUSED	5 – 6	2		Alphanumeric
Franchise Number	7 – 9	3	0	Numeric
Franchise Owner	10 – 29	20		Alphanumeric
UNUSED	30 – 50	21		Alphanumeric
Sales Code	51	1	0	Numeric
UNUSED	52 – 55	4		Alphanumeric
Daily Sales	56 – 61	6	2	Numeric
Record Length		61		

OUTPUT

Output consists of a Fast Food Sales Report containing the District Number, Franchise Number, Franchise Owner, Sales Category, and Daily Sales. When there is a change in District Number, the district number and the total sales for that district are to be printed. After all records have been processed, a final total for all districts is to be printed. The printer spacing chart for the report is illustrated on the following page. If no records are read from the input file, the no records to process message shown on the printer spacing chart should be printed.

PRINTER SPACING CHART

```
 1
 2 MM/DD/YY                    FAST FOOD SALES                      PAGE  ZZ9
 3
 4 DISTRICT    FRANCHISE       FRANCHISE                SALES            DAILY
 5 NUMBER      NUMBER            OWNER                 CATEGORY           SALES
 6
 7   ZZZ9        ZZ9      XXXXXXXXXXXXXXXXXXXX    XXXXXXXXXXXXXXXXXXXX   Z,ZZZ.99
 8   ZZZ9        ZZ9      XXXXXXXXXXXXXXXXXXXX    XXXXXXXXXXXXXXXXXXXX   Z,ZZZ.99
 9
10                               TOTAL SALES - DISTRICT ZZZ9        ZZ,ZZZ.99*
11
12   ZZZ9        ZZ9      XXXXXXXXXXXXXXXXXXXX    XXXXXXXXXXXXXXXXXXXX   Z,ZZZ.99
13   ZZZ9        ZZ9      XXXXXXXXXXXXXXXXXXXX    XXXXXXXXXXXXXXXXXXXX   Z,ZZZ.99
14
15                               TOTAL SALES - DISTRICT ZZZ9        ZZ,ZZZ.99*
16
17                               FINAL TOTAL - ALL DISTRICTS   $ZZZ,ZZZ.99**
18
19 ---------------------------------------------------------
20 FAST FOOD SALES REPORT - NO RECORDS TO PROCESS
```

TABLE PROCESSING

The Sales Category printed on the report is extracted from the following table, based upon the Sales Code in the input record.

SALES CATEGORY

	(1)	OVER 1 MILLION SOLD
	(2)	OVER 2 MILLION SOLD
SALES	(3)	OVER 3 MILLION SOLD
CODE	(4)	OVER 4 MILLION SOLD
	(5)	OVER 5 MILLION SOLD
	(6)	OVER 6 MILLION SOLD

PROGRAMMING ASSIGNMENT 2

INSTRUCTIONS

A Job Assembly Report is to be prepared. Design and write the COBOL program to produce the required report. An IPO Chart and Pseudocode Specifications should be used when designing the program. Use Test Data Set 2 in Appendix A.

INPUT

Input consists of Job Records that contain the Job Number, Sub-Assembly Number, Sub-Assembly Code, Quantity Needed, and Sub-Assembly Cost. The format of the input record is illustrated below.

Job Disk Record				
FIELD DESCRIPTION	POSITION	LENGTH	DEC	ATTRIBUTE
UNUSED	1 – 8	8		Alphanumeric
Job Number	9 – 10	2		Alphanumeric
Sub-Assembly Number	11 – 12	2		Alphanumeric
UNUSED	13 – 52	40		Alphanumeric
Sub-Assembly Code	53	1	0	Numeric
UNUSED	54 – 57	4		Alphanumeric
Quantity Needed	58 – 59	2	0	Numeric
UNUSED	60 – 63	4		Alphanumeric
Sub-Assembly Cost	64 – 67	4	2	Numeric
Record Length		67		

OUTPUT

Output consists of a Job Assembly Report containing the Job Number, Sub-Assembly Number, Sub-Assembly Status, Quantity Needed, Sub-Assembly Cost, and Total Cost. Total Cost is obtained by multiplying Quantity Needed by Sub-Assembly Cost. When there is a change in Job Number, the Job Number and the Total Cost for that job are to be printed. After all records are processed, a final total of the costs for all jobs is to be printed. The printer spacing chart is illustrated on the following page. If no records are read from the input file, the no records to process message shown on the printer spacing chart should be printed.

PRINTER SPACING CHART

```
1
2  MM/DD/YY                    JOB ASSEMBLY REPORT                      PAGE ZZ9
3
4    JOB      SUB-ASSEMBLY     SUB-ASSEMBLY       QUANTITY   SUB-ASSEMBLY    TOTAL
5  NUMBER       NUMBER           STATUS           NEEDED         COST        COST
6
7    XX          XX          XXXXXXXXXXXXX          Z9          ZZ.99     Z,ZZZ.99
8    XX          XX          XXXXXXXXXXXXX          Z9          ZZ.99     Z,ZZZ.99
9
10                           JOB NUMBER XX - TOTAL COST          ZZ,ZZZ.99*
11
12   XX          XX          XXXXXXXXXXXXX          Z9          ZZ.99     Z,ZZZ.99
13   XX          XX          XXXXXXXXXXXXX          Z9          ZZ.99     Z,ZZZ.99
14
15                           JOB NUMBER XX - TOTAL COST          ZZ,ZZZ.99*
16
17                           FINAL TOTAL - ALL JOBS             ZZZ,ZZZ.99**
18
19
20 JOB ASSEMBLY REPORT - NO RECORDS TO PROCESS
```

TABLE PROCESSING

The Sub-Assembly Status printed on the report is extracted from the following table, based upon the Sub-Assembly Code in the input record.

		SUB-ASSEMBLY STATUS
	(1)	IN WAREHOUSE
SUB-ASSEMBLY	(2)	NOT AVAILABLE
CODE	(3)	ON ORDER
	(4)	ON BACKORDER

PROGRAMMING ASSIGNMENT 3

INSTRUCTIONS

An Airfare Report is to be prepared. Write the COBOL program to prepare this report. An IPO Chart and Pseudocode Specifications should be used when designing the program. Use Test Data Set 3 in Appendix A.

INPUT

Input consists of Flight Records that contain the Flight Number, Flight Date, and Number of Passengers. The flight date is in the format MMDDYY. The input records have been sorted in ascending sequence by Flight Date prior to processing. The format of the input record is illustrated below.

Flight Disk Record				
FIELD DESCRIPTION	POSITION	LENGTH	DEC	ATTRIBUTE
UNUSED	1 – 6	6		Alphanumeric
Flight Number	7 – 10	4	0	Numeric
Flight Date	11 – 16	6		Alphanumeric
UNUSED	17 – 58	42		Alphanumeric
Number of Passengers	59 – 60	2	0	Numeric
UNUSED	61 – 64	4		Alphanumeric
Record Length		64		

OUTPUT

Output consists of an Airfare Report. The report is to be GROUP PRINTED; that is, one line is to be printed for each flight date (there is more than one record for each flight date). When there is a change in Flight Date, the accumulated number of passengers and the accumulated airfares for that Flight Date are to be printed. Airfares are calculated based upon the table data discussed in the Table Processing section of this assignment. If the accumulated airfares for any flight date are less than $20,000.00, the message * FLIGHT BELOW AVERAGE * should be printed. After all records have been processed, the total number of passengers and the total airfares for all flight dates should be printed. The printer spacing chart is illustrated on the following page. If no records are read from the input file, the no records to process message shown on the printer spacing chart should be printed.

PRINTER SPACING CHART

```
   1234567890112131415161718192021222324252627282930313233343536373839404142434445464748495051525354555657585960616263646566676869707172737475767778
 1
 2 MM/DD/YY                    AIRFARE REPORT                      PAGE ZZ9
 3
 4 FLIGHT
 5   DATE          PASSENGERS        AIRFARES
 6
 7 MM/DD/YY            ZZ9        $ZZ,ZZZ.99
 8 MM/DD/YY            ZZ9        $ZZ,ZZZ.99    * FLIGHT BELOW AVERAGE *
 9 MM/DD/YY            ZZ9        $ZZ,ZZZ.99
10 MM/DD/YY            ZZ9        $ZZ,ZZZ.99    * FLIGHT BELOW AVERAGE *
11
12 TOTAL PASSENGERS  =    Z,ZZ9
13 TOTAL FARES       =  $ZZZ,ZZZ.99
14
15 ------------------------------------------------
16 AIRFARE REPORT - NO RECORDS TO PROCESS
```

TABLE PROCESSING

The airfare for one flight is calculated by multiplying the Number of Passengers from the input record by the passenger airfare extracted from a table. The last digit of the Flight Number in the input record is used to extract the passenger airfare from the table. The airfares printed on the report are a result of accumulating the airfare for each flight for that date.

	AIRFARE
(1)	120.00
(2)	131.00
LAST DIGIT OF (3)	150.00
PASSENGER	
FLIGHT NUMBER (4)	179.00
(5)	203.00
(6)	215.00

PROGRAMMING ASSIGNMENT 4

INSTRUCTIONS

A Telephone Rebate Report is to be prepared. Write the COBOL program to prepare this report. The IPO Chart and Pseudocode Specifications should be used when designing the program. Use Test Data Set 4 in Appendix A.

INPUT

Input consists of Telephone Records that contain the Customer Number, Type of Call Code, and Length of Call Code. The input records have been sorted in ascending sequence by Customer Number prior to processing. The Type of Call Code indicates whether the phone call was an Intrastate Call or an Interstate Call. The Length of Call Code indicates whether the phone call was under or equal to 5 minutes or over 5 minutes in length. The format of the input record is illustrated below.

Telephone Disk Record				
FIELD DESCRIPTION	POSITION	LENGTH	DEC	ATTRIBUTE
UNUSED	1 – 2	2		Alphanumeric
Customer Number	3 – 6	4		Alphanumeric
UNUSED	7 – 71	65		Alphanumeric
Type of Call Code	72	1	0	Numeric
Length of Call Code	73	1	0	Numeric
Record Length		73		

Note that for the Type of Call Code in position 72, the value 1 indicates an intrastate call. The value 2 indicates an interstate call. The value 1 in the Length of Call Code field indicates a call under or equal to 5 minutes, and the value 2 indicates a call over 5 minutes.

OUTPUT

The output of the program is the Telephone Rebate Report. The report contains the Customer Number, the Type of Call (INTRASTATE or INTERSTATE), and the Length of Call (UNDER 5 MIN. or OVER 5 MIN.). The messages INTRASTATE and INTERSTATE should be extracted from a table based upon the value in the Type of Call Code field in the input record. The messages UNDER 5 MIN. and OVER 5 MIN. should be extracted from a table based upon the value in the Length of Call Code field in the input record. These two tables are explained in the Table Processing section of this assignment. The format of the report is illustrated on the following page. If no records are read from the input file, the no records to process message shown on the printer spacing chart should be printed.

PRINTER SPACING CHART

```
 1
 2 MM/DD/YY                    TELEPHONE REBATE REPORT                              PAGE ZZ9
 3
 4 CUSTOMER      TYPE OF        LENGTH
 5  NUMBER        CALL          OF CALL
 6
 7   XXXX      XXXXXXXXXX     XXXXXXXXXXXX
 8             XXXXXXXXXX     XXXXXXXXXXXX
 9             INTRASTATE     UNDER 5 MIN.
10             INTRASTATE     OVER 5 MIN.
11             INTERSTATE     UNDER 5 MIN.
12             INTERSTATE     OVER 5 MIN.
13
14             INTRASTATE CALLS -      TOTAL ZZ9    UNDER 5 MIN. ZZ9    OVER 5 MIN. ZZ9
15             INTERSTATE CALLS -      TOTAL ZZ9    UNDER 5 MIN. ZZ9    OVER 5 MIN. ZZ9
16
17             TOTAL CREDITS ISSUED ZZ9     REBATE EARNED = XXXXXXXXX
18
19   XXXX      XXXXXXXXXX     XXXXXXXXXXXX
20             XXXXXXXXXX     XXXXXXXXXXXX
21
22             INTRASTATE CALLS  -     TOTAL ZZ9    UNDER 5 MIN. ZZ9    OVER 5 MIN. ZZ9
23             INTERSTATE CALLS  -     TOTAL ZZ9    UNDER 5 MIN. ZZ9    OVER 5 MIN. ZZ9
24
25             TOTAL CREDITS ISSUED ZZ9     REBATE EARNED = XXXXXXXXX
26
27                          (SEPARATE PAGE)
28
29 MM/DD/YY                    TELEPHONE REBATE REPORT                              PAGE ZZ9
30                              FINAL TOTALS
31
32 INTRASTATE CALLS -
33                    TOTAL CALLS  Z,ZZ9
34                    UNDER 5 MIN. Z,ZZ9
35                    OVER 5 MIN.  Z,ZZ9
36
37 INTERSTATE CALLS -
38                    TOTAL CALLS  Z,ZZ9
39                    UNDER 5 MIN. Z,ZZ9
40                    OVER 5 MIN.  Z,ZZ9
41
42 TOTAL REBATES EARNED -
43                    $5  REBATES EARNED ZZ9
44                    $10 REBATES EARNED ZZ9
45                    $15 REBATES EARNED ZZ9
46
47 - - - - - - - - - - - - - - - - - - - - - - - - -
48 TELEPHONE REBATE REPORT - NO RECORDS TO PROCESS
```

TABLE PROCESSING

The two tables used to obtain the messages on the report are illustrated below.

		TYPE OF CALL
TYPE OF	(1)	INTRASTATE
CALL CODE	(2)	INTERSTATE

		LENGTH OF CALL
LENGTH OF	(1)	UNDER 5 MIN.
CALL CODE	(2)	OVER 5 MIN.

In addition, the total intrastate calls, total intrastate calls under 5 minutes, total intrastate calls over 5 minutes, total interstate calls, total interstate calls under 5 minutes, total interstate calls over 5 minutes, total credits issued, and the rebate earned are to be printed for each customer.

For each customer, the total credits and the rebate earned are to be printed. Credits are calculated for interstate calls in the following manner: 2 credits for each call under 5 minutes; 4 credits for each call over 5 minutes. Intrastate calls do not count in the credit calculation. Based upon the total credits, one of the following messages should be printed in the Rebate Earned position:

		REBATE EARNED MESSAGE
	Under 5	$ 5 REBATE
CREDITS	6 — 10	$10 REBATE
	Over 10	$15 REBATE

CHAPTER EIGHT

MULTIPLE LEVEL CONTROL BREAKS; TABLE PROCESSING

MULTIPLE LEVEL CONTROL BREAKS; TABLE PROCESSING

8

INTRODUCTION

The sample program in Chapter 7 introduced printing totals when a control break occurred. In some applications, it may be necessary to print more than one level of totals when processing records. For example, in the Unsold Lots Report in Figure 8-1, when there is a change in Tract Number, the total for the tract is printed; when there is a change in City Number, the total for the tract and the total for the city are printed; and when there is a change in Developer Number, the total for the tract, the total for the city, and the total for the developer are printed.

03/14/85		UNSOLD LOTS REPORT			PAGE 1		
DEVELOPER NUMBER	CITY NUMBER	TRACT NUMBER	LOT NUMBER	BUILDING STYLE	SELLING PRICE		
10	38	1	1	SIERRA	165,000		
			3	BIG OAKS	198,000		
			7	RANCHERO	187,000		
					550,000*		
		11	2	WOODLAND	179,000		
			3	BIG OAKS	198,000		
			8	SEVILLE	193,000		
					570,000*		
				TOTAL CITY NO 38	1,120,000**		
	152	7	2	WOODLAND	179,000		
			4	SUNRISE	212,000		
					391,000*		
				TOTAL CITY NO 152	391,000**		
				TOTAL DEVELOPER NO 10	1,511,000***		

38	115	14	3	BIG OAKS	198,000		
			5	MEADOWS	206,000		
					404,000*		
				TOTAL CITY NO 115	404,000**		
				TOTAL DEVELOPER NO 38	404,000***		
				FINAL TOTAL	$3,790,000****		

Figure 8-1 Multiple Level Control Breaks with Group Indication

In Figure 8-1, Developer Number, City Number, and Tract Number are group indicated, meaning that these numbers are printed only for the first record of the group. Group indication refers to suppressing the printing of repetitive information and is used to improve readability.

Whenever a control break occurs on City Number, a control break automatically occurs on Tract Number because a change in city will mean that a new tract is being processed also. Thus, when there is a change in City Number, both the tract total and the city total are printed.

Similarly, whenever a change occurs on Developer Number, a control break automatically occurs on City Number and Tract Number as well. Therefore, on a change in Developer

Number, the tract total, city total, and developer total are printed.

When processing records containing multiple level control breaks, the records must be properly sorted prior to processing. In Figure 8–1, the Tract Numbers (lowest level control break) are arranged in an ascending sequence within each City (middle level control break), the City Numbers are arranged in an ascending sequence within each Developer (highest level control break), and all of the Developer Numbers are arranged in an ascending sequence. This sorting sequence, from the lowest level control break field to the highest level control break field, must always be followed when multiple level control break processing is to occur.

The sample program in Chapter 7 also introduced the concept of storing and extracting data from a table. It is also possible to extract multiple items of data from a table using one subscript. In Figure 8–1, Building Style and Selling Price both relate to the Lot Number. A lot is built with a particular building style and selling price. As such, the Lot Number becomes the subscript to extract the building style and selling price from a table.

SAMPLE PROGRAM

The sample program in this chapter illustrates the technique of designing and programming an application requiring table processing and multiple level control breaks. The format of the input records and the printer spacing chart are illustrated in Figure 8–2.

Developer Disk Record				
FIELD DESCRIPTION	POSITION	LENGTH	DEC	ATTRIBUTE
Developer Number	1 – 2	2	0	Numeric
City Number	3 – 5	3	0	Numeric
Tract Number	6 – 7	2	0	Numeric
Lot Number	8 – 9	2	0	Numeric
Record Length		9		

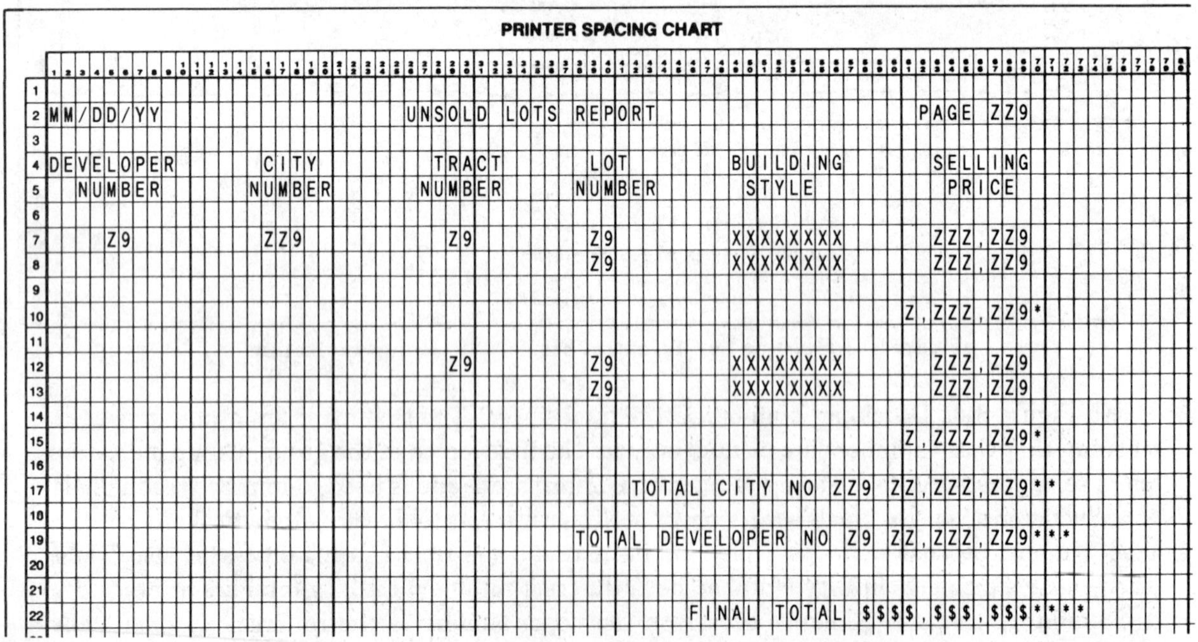

Figure 8-2 Record Format and Printer Spacing Chart

In Figure 8-2, the input records contain Developer Number, City Number, Tract Number, and Lot Number. The report produced contains Tract Totals, City Totals, Developer Totals, and a Final Total.

The program narrative for the sample problem is illustrated in Figure 8-3.

PROGRAM NARRATIVE			
SUBJECT Unsold Lots Report	**DATE** January 9		**PAGE** 1 **OF** 1
TO Programmer	**FROM**	Systems Analyst	

A program is to be written to prepare an Unsold Lots Report. The format of the input record and the printer spacing chart are included with this narrative. The program should include the following processing:

1. The program should read the input records and create the Unsold Lots Report as per the format illustrated on the printer spacing chart. The report shall contain Developer Number, City Number, Tract Number, Lot Number, Building Style, and Selling Price.

2. The building style and the selling price are to be extracted from a table based upon the Lot Number contained in the input record. Lots numbers 01 through 15 are valid.

3. Headings are to be printed on the first and subsequent pages of the report. The heading is to contain the date and page number. Fifty-five lines are to appear on each page before skipping to a new page.

4. One line is to be printed on the report for each input record that is read. The lines are to be single spaced.

5. Editing on the report is to occur as illustrated on the printer spacing chart.

6. When there is a change in Tract Number, a Tract Total is to be printed. When there is a change in City Number, a Tract Total, and a City Total are to be printed; and when there is a change in Developer Number, a Tract, a City, and a Developer Total are to be printed. A Final Total is to be printed after all input records have been processed.

7. All input records have been edited prior to running this program.

8. Input records have been sorted by Tract Number within City Number within Developer Number prior to processing.

9. The program is to be written in COBOL.

Figure 8-3 Program Narrative

MULTIPLE LEVEL CONTROL BREAK PROCESSING

Prior to beginning the design of a program involving the use of multiple level control breaks, it is important to have an overall understanding of the processing that must take place. The processing of multiple level control breaks is similar to the processing for single level control breaks as illustrated in Chapter 7 — the records are read, the control fields are moved to a compare area, and the control fields on subsequent input records are compared to the values in the compare area. If the values are equal, a detail record is processed and printed. If the values are not equal, control break processing occurs to print the appropriate totals. The following paragraphs examine this processing in more detail.

Initial Processing

The processing that occurs for the first record in an application involving multiple level control breaks is illustrated in Figure 8-4.

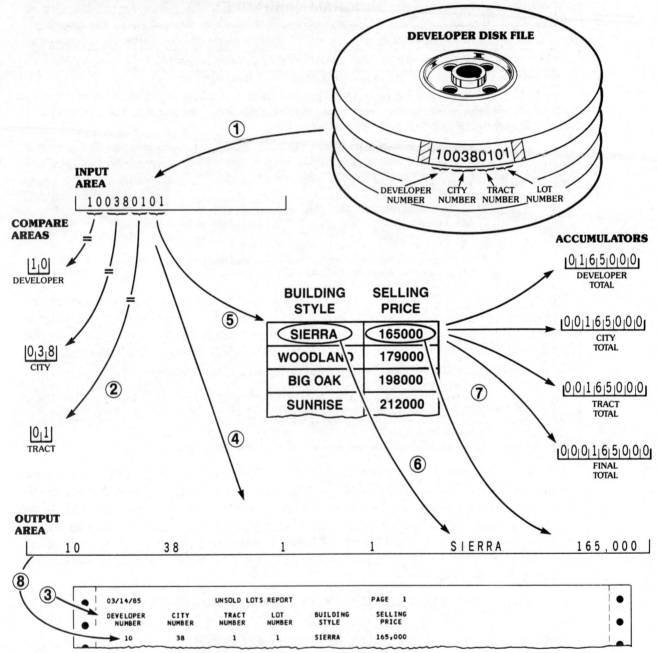

Figure 8-4 Processing the First Record

In step 1, the first record is read into the input area. Then in step 2, the Developer Number, City Number, and Tract Number are moved to individual compare areas. Each of the values in the compare areas are then compared to the corresponding fields in the input area. When processing the first record, all fields will be equal and processing the first detail record will occur.

Processing Detail Records

When processing the detail record, a heading is printed on the first page of the report (step 3). Then, the fields in the input area are moved to the output area (step 4). In step 5, the Building Style and Selling Price are identified in the Lot Table by using the Lot Number as the subscript. In the example, the Lot Number is 01. Using Lot Number 01 as the subscript, the first Building Style (SIERRA) and the first Selling Price (165,000) are extracted from the table and are moved to the output area (step 6). In the sample program, Lot Numbers 01 – 15 can be used to extract Building Style and Selling Price from the table.

In step 7, the Selling Price from the table is added to the Developer Total Accumulator, the City Total Accumulator, the Tract Total Accumulator, and the Final Total Accumulator. Then, in step 8, the detail line is printed on the report.

As long as each subsequent record read contains a Developer Number, City Number, and Tract Number that are equal to the related numbers in the compare areas, processing of the detail records will continue. When a change in any of the control fields is found, a control break has occurred and the following processing takes place.

Control Break — Tract Number

When the Tract Number in an input record is not equal to the Tract Number in the compare area, a control break has occurred on the Track Number. Therefore, the Tract Total in the Tract Total Accumulator is printed, the Tract Total Accumulator is set to zero, and the Tract Number in the input record that caused the control break is moved to the Tract Number compare area. The record that caused the control break is then processed.

Control Break — City Number

When the City Number in an input record is not equal to the City Number in the compare area, a control break has occurred on the City Number. It will be recalled that this automatically means a control break has also occurred on the Tract Number. Therefore, the Tract Total and City Total are both printed. The Tract Total and City Total Accumulators are then set to zero, and the Tract Number and the City Number from the input record that caused the control break are moved to their respective compare areas. The record that caused the control break is then processed.

Control Break — Developer Number

When a record is read in which the Developer Number is not equal to the Developer Number in the compare area, control breaks have occurred on the Tract Number and the City Number as well as the Developer Number. As a result, the Tract Total, the City Total, and the Developer Total are printed. The Developer, City, and Tract Accumulators are then set to zero, and the Developer Number, City Number, and Tract Number are moved from the input record to their respective compare areas. The record that caused the control break is then processed.

Control Break — End of Job and Final Totals

After all records have been read, a control break effectively occurs. Therefore, the Tract Total, City Total, and Developer Total for the last group of records must be printed. Then, a Final Total is printed and the program is terminated.

It is important for the programmer to have a thorough understanding of the processing of records that contain multiple level control breaks in order to be able to properly design a program which includes multiple level control break processing.

PROGRAM DESIGN

An analysis of the format of the input records, the printer spacing chart, and the program narrative provides the programmer with the information needed for the design of the program. The IPO Chart for the module which creates the unsold lots report is illustrated in Figure 8-5.

IPO CHART

PROGRAM: Unsold Lots Report			PROGRAMMER: Forsythe		DATE: Jan. 9
MODULE NAME: Create Unsold Lots Report		REF: A000	MODULE FUNCTION: Create Unsold Lots Report		

INPUT	PROCESSING	REF:	OUTPUT
1. Developer Disk File	1. Initialize		1. Unsold Lots Report
	2. Obtain the input data		
	3. Process the detail records	B000	
	4. Process a tract change	B010	
	5. Process a city change	B020	
	6. Process a developer change	B030	
	7. Print the final totals	B040	
	8. Terminate		

Figure 8-5 IPO Chart for the Create the Unsold Lots Report Module

In the IPO Chart in Figure 8-5, the output is the Unsold Lots Report and the input is the Developer Disk File. In addition to initialize, obtain the input data, process the detail records, print the final totals, and terminate, other major processing tasks include the processing that must occur when there is a change in Tract Number, City Number, and Developer Number.

An analysis of the major processing tasks specified on the IPO Chart in Figure 8-5 determines that the program should contain five additional modules. These modules are illustrated in the hierarchy chart in Figure 8-6.

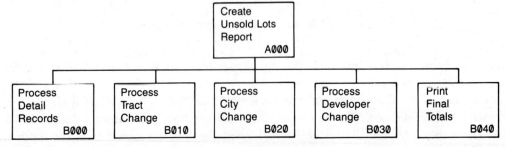

Figure 8-6 Hierarchy Chart

The major processing tasks which warrant separate modules include processing the detail records, processing a tract change, processing a city change, processing a developer change, and printing the final totals.

After the relationship of the modules has been defined through the hierarchy chart, the next step in the design of the program is to define the major processing tasks associated with each module. The IPO Chart for the module which processes the detail records is shown in Figure 8-7.

IPO CHART				
PROGRAM: Unsold Lots Report		**PROGRAMMER:** Forsythe		**DATE:** Jan. 9
MODULE NAME: Process Detail Records	**REF:** B000	**MODULE FUNCTION:** Process the Detail Records		
INPUT	**PROCESSING**		**REF:**	**OUTPUT**
1. Developer Disk	1. Print headings		C000	1. Detail Print Line
Record	2. Format print line			2. Updated
2. Accumulators	3. Update accumulators			Accumulators
	4. Write the detail line			

Figure 8-7 IPO Chart for the Process the Detail Records Module

The output of the module is the detail print line and the updated accumulators. The accumulators are considered output because they are used in another module of the program.

The input to the module consists of the developer disk record and the accumulators. The major processing tasks include printing the headings, formatting the print line, updating the accumulators, and writing the detail line.

As with all IPO Charts, the major processing tasks must be analyzed to determine if any of the tasks justifies the creation of an additional module. For this module, printing the headings on the report contains significant enough processing to justify a separate module. The module to print the headings should be shown on the hierarchy chart, as illustrated in Figure 8-8.

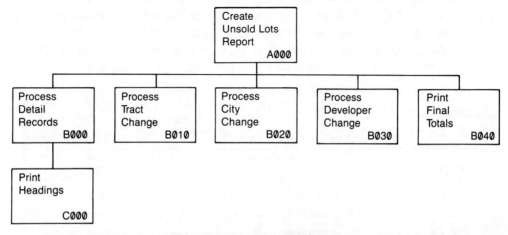

Figure 8-8 Hierarchy Chart

The next IPO Chart which must be prepared defines the major processing tasks when there is a change in Tract Number. This IPO Chart is illustrated in Figure 8-9.

IPO CHART				
PROGRAM: Unsold Lots Report		**PROGRAMMER:** Forsythe		**DATE:** Jan. 9
MODULE NAME: Process Tract Change		**REF:** B010 **MODULE FUNCTION:**		Process Tract Change
INPUT	**PROCESSING**	**REF:**	**OUTPUT**	
1. New Tract Number	1. Format the tract total line		1. Tract Total Line	
2. Tract Total	2. Write the tract total line		2. Tract Total	
Accumulator	3. Reset the tract accumulator		Accumulator	
	4. Reset the tract number		3. Tract Number	
	compare area		Compare Area	

Figure 8-9 IPO Chart for the Process a Tract Change Module

The output of this module consists of the tract total line, the tract total accumulator, and the tract number compare area. The input is the new tract number from the input record that must be placed in the compare area and the tract total accumulator. An analysis of the major processing tasks required reveals that none is of such size or complexity to justify a separate module.

The IPO Chart for the module which processes a city change is illustrated in Figure 8-10.

IPO CHART				
PROGRAM: Unsold Lots Report		**PROGRAMMER:** Forsythe		**DATE:** Jan. 9
MODULE NAME: Process City Change		**REF:** B020 **MODULE FUNCTION:**		Process City Change
INPUT	**PROCESSING**	**REF:**	**OUTPUT**	
1. Old City Number	1. Format city total line		1. City Total Line	
2. New City Number	2. Write the city total line		2. City Total	
3. City Total	3. Reset the city total		Accumulator	
Accumulator	accumulator		3. City Number	
	4. Reset the city number		Compare Area	
	compare area			

Figure 8-10 IPO Chart for the Process a City Change Module

The output, input, and major processing tasks of the module which processes a city change are quite similar to those of the module which processes a tract change. None of the major processing tasks of this module requires a separate module.

The IPO Chart for the module which processes a developer change is illustrated in Figure 8-11.

IPO CHART				
PROGRAM: Unsold Lots Report		**PROGRAMMER:** Forsythe		**DATE:** Jan. 9
MODULE NAME: Process Developer Change		**REF:** B030 **MODULE FUNCTION:**		Process Developer Change
INPUT	**PROCESSING**	**REF:**	**OUTPUT**	
1. Old Developer	1. Format the developer total line		1. Developer Total Line	
Number	2. Write the developer total line		2. Developer Total	
2. New Developer	3. Reset the developer total		Accumulator	
Number	accumulator		3. Developer Number	
3. Developer Total	4. Reset the developer number		Compare Area	
Accumulator	compare area			

Figure 8-11 IPO Chart for the Process a Developer Change Module

None of the major processing tasks in the module requires a separate module.

The IPO Chart for the module whose function is to print the final totals is illustrated in Figure 8-12.

IPO CHART

PROGRAM: Unsold Lots Report		PROGRAMMER: Forsythe		DATE: Jan. 9
MODULE NAME: Print Final Totals		REF: B040	MODULE FUNCTION: Print the Final Totals	
INPUT	PROCESSING		REF:	OUTPUT
1. Final Total	1. Format the total line			1. Final Total Line
Accumulator	2. Write the final total line			

Figure 8-12 IPO Chart for the Print the Final Totals Module

The output from the module is the Final Total Line. The input is the Final Total Accumulator. Neither of the major processing tasks justifies a lower-level module.

After the IPO Charts for the modules on the second level of the program have been designed, the programmer would review them and then design the modules on the third level. In the sample program, there is only one module on the third level — the module to print the headings. The IPO Chart for this module is illustrated in Figure 8-13.

IPO CHART

PROGRAM: Unsold Lots Report		PROGRAMMER: Forsythe		DATE: Jan. 9
MODULE NAME: Print Headings		REF: C000	MODULE FUNCTION: Print the Headings	
INPUT	PROCESSING		REF:	OUTPUT
1. Heading Lines	1. Format the heading lines			1. Heading Lines
	2. Write the heading lines			

Figure 8-13 IPO Chart for the Print the Headings Module

Neither of the major processing tasks justifies a lower-level module. Since there is not a lower-level module required for this module, the design of the structure of the program is completed (the hierarchy chart for the program is shown in Figure 8-8). The programmer would normally review this design with analysts and other programmers to ensure that a viable solution to the problem has been designed. After everyone is agreed that the solution is correct, the programmer would proceed to the next level of design — that of developing the logic for the program through the use of pseudocode.

PSEUDOCODE SPECIFICATIONS

Although the program in this chapter is more complex than previous programs, the decomposition of the program through the use of the IPO Charts results in a program made up of small, reasonably easy to understand modules. The logic for the program, which is expressed using pseudocode, must specify only the processing which is to take place within each of the relatively simple modules, not the entire program.

The pseudocode for the module whose function is to create the unsold lots report is illustrated in Figure 8-14.

PSEUDOCODE SPECIFICATIONS

PROGRAM: Unsold Lots Report	PROGRAMMER: Forsythe	DATE: Jan. 9
MODULE NAME: Create Unsold Lots Report	REF: A000	MODULE FUNCTION: Create the Unsold Lots Report

PSEUDOCODE	REF:	DATA BASES, FILES, RECORDS, FIELDS REQUIRED
Open the files		Developer disk file
Read an input record		Unsold lots report file
IF there is a record		Input record area
Move tract number to compare area		Developer number
Move city number to compare area		City number
Move developer number to compare area		Tract number
PERFORM UNTIL no more input records		Lot number
IF developer number not = developer		There is a record indicator
number in compare area		Tract number compare area
Process tract change	B010	City number compare area
Process city change	B020	Developer number compare area
Process developer change	B030	No more records indicator
Indicate a change in developer number		Developer number change
ELSE		indicator
IF city number not = city		City number change indicator
number in compare area		Tract number change indicator
Process tract change	B010	No records message
Process city change	B020	
Indicate a change in city number		
ELSE		
IF tract number not = tract		
number in compare area		
Process tract change	B010	
Indicate a change in tract		
number		
ENDIF		
ENDIF		
ENDIF		
Process detail records	B000	
Read an input record		
ENDPERFORM		
Process tract change	B010	
Process city change	B020	
Process developer change	B030	
Print final totals	B040	
ELSE		
Print no records message		
ENDIF		
Close the files		
Stop run		

Figure 8-14 Pseudocode for the Create the Unsold Lots Report Module

In the pseudocode in Figure 8-14, the files are opened and the first record is read. If there is no record to process, a message is written on the report, the files are closed, and the program is terminated.

If there is a record to be processed, the Tract Number, City Number, and Developer Number are moved to individual compare areas. When subsequent input records are read, the values in the control fields of the record will be compared to the values stored in the compare area to determine if a control break has occurred.

The loop to process the input records is then entered. The first step is to check for a control break. When comparing to determine if a control break has occurred, the Developer Number is compared first because when there is a change in Developer Number, there is also a change in Tract Number and City Number. Thus, when there is is a change in the Developer Number, the module which processes a tract change will be executed first, followed by the module which processes the city change, and then the module which processes the developer change. Therefore, when there is a change in the Developer Number, the tract total will be printed first, followed by the city total, and then the developer total.

Similarly, when there is a change in the City Number, the module which processes a tract change and the module which process a city change are both executed. Lastly, when there is a change in the Tract Number, the module which processes a tract change is executed to print the total for the tract.

In each case, when there is a control break, an indicator is set to indicate that a control break has occurred on the particular field. This indicator is used in the module which processes detail records in order to group indicate the report.

Regardless of whether a control break occurs, the detail record is then processed by the B000 module, and another input record is read.

After all input records have been read and processed, the tract, city, and developer totals for the last group of records must be printed. Therefore, the modules for accomplishing this printing are performed followed by the module to print the final total.

In addition to the pseudocode, the entries for the Data Bases, Files, Records, and Fields required are specified in Figure 8-14. Also, the REF column includes the reference numbers for the lower-level modules. These reference numbers correspond to the reference numbers given to the modules when the hierarchy chart was designed.

The pseudocode for the module whose function is to process the detail records is illustrated in Figure 8-15.

PSEUDOCODE SPECIFICATIONS

PROGRAM: Unsold Lots Report	PROGRAMMER: Forsythe	DATE: Jan. 9
MODULE NAME: Process Detail Records	REF: B000	MODULE FUNCTION: Process the Detail Records

PSEUDOCODE	REF:	DATA BASES, FILES, RECORDS, FIELDS REQUIRED

IF lines printed is = or > page size or first page
    Print the headings
    Move developer number to output area
    Move city number to output area
    Move tract number to output area
ENDIF
IF there was a change in developer number
    Move developer number to output area
    Move city number to output area
    Move tract number to output area
    Reset developer change indicator
ELSE
    IF there was a change in city number
        Move city number to output area
        Move tract number to output area
        Reset city change indicator
    ELSE
        IF there was a change in tract number
            Move tract number to output area
            Reset tract change indicator
        ENDIF
    ENDIF
ENDIF
Move lot number, building style from table, and
    selling price from table to output area
Add selling price from table to tract total
    accumulator, city total accumulator,
    developer total accumulator, and final
    total accumulator
Write a line on the report
Add lines printed to lines printed counter
Set spacing to single spacing
Clear printer output area
	C000	Lines printed counter
		Page size constant
		First page indicator
		Printer output area
		    Developer number
		    City number
		    Tract number
		    Lot number
		    Building style
		    Selling price
		Developer number compare area
		City number compare area
		Tract number compare area
		Developer change indicator
		Input record area
		    Developer number
		    City number
		    Tract number
		    Lot number
		City change indicator
		Tract change indicator
		Lot table
		    Building style & price
		Tract total accumulator
		City total accumulator
		Developer total accumulator
		Final total accumulator
		Spacing control field
		Single space control character

Figure 8-15 Pseudocode for the Process the Detail Records Module

The logic shown in Figure 8-15 is intended to produce a multiple level control break report which is group indicated. The report produced from the logic in Figure 8-15 is illustrated in Figure 8-16.

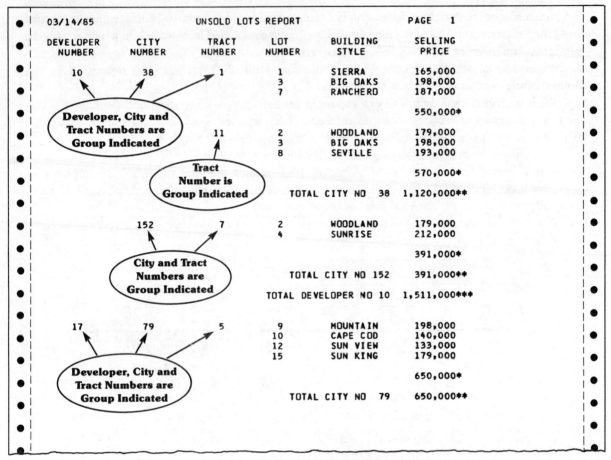

Figure 8-16 Group Indicated Report

In the report shown in Figure 8-16, the Developer Number, City Number, and Tract Number are printed for the first record processed, but are not printed again until a change in one of the fields has occurred or until a new page is printed on the report. Thus, after the first line on the page, the developer number is printed when there is a change in developer number; the city number is printed when there is a change in developer number or when there is a change in city number; and the tract number is printed when there is a change in developer number, city number, or tract number. In addition, they are all three printed on the first line of each new page regardless of whether a control break occurred.

In the logic shown by the pseudocode in Figure 8-15, the headings are printed for the first page of the report and then the Developer Number, City Number, and Tract Number are moved to the output area. A test is then performed to determine if there were any control breaks. This test is performed by checking the indicator set in the module which creates the unsold lots report (see Figure 8-14).

If a control break has occurred for any of the three fields, the respective fields are moved to the output area so they can be group indicated. In addition, the indicator showing a control break is reset so on the next pass through the module, the fields will not be printed unless another control break has occurred.

After group indicating the report, the lot number, the building style from the table, and the selling price from the table are moved to the output area, the total accumulators are incremented by the selling price from the table, and the line is printed. The number of lines printed is then added to the lines printed counter and the spacing is set for single spacing.

The last statement is to clear the printer output area. It will be recalled that in previous programs, the printer output area was cleared to spaces before any data was moved to it. In this program, the printer output area is cleared to spaces after the first line is printed. This is necessary because the report is group indicated. The technique in COBOL to cause the printer output area to be initialized to spaces before processing the first record, which involves the Value Clause, is illustrated later in this chapter.

The logic for the module which processes a tract change is illustrated in Figure 8–17.

PSEUDOCODE SPECIFICATIONS

PROGRAM: Unsold Lots Report	PROGRAMMER: Forsythe	DATE: Jan. 9
MODULE NAME: Process Tract Change	REF: B010 MODULE FUNCTION: Process the Tract Change	

PSEUDOCODE	REF:	DATA BASES, FILES, RECORDS, FIELDS REQUIRED
Move tract total to tract total line Write tract total line on the report Add 2 to the lines printed counter Set spacing for double spacing Set tract total accumulator to zero Move the new tract number to compare area		Tract total accumulator Tract total line New tract number from input record Tract number compare area Lines printed counter Spacing control field Double space control character

Figure 8-17 Pseudocode for the Process a Tract Change Module

In Figure 8–17, the tract total is moved to the tract total line. The line is then printed. The value 2 is added to the lines printed counter because the total line is double spaced on the printer, and the spacing is set for double spacing. The tract total accumulator is then set to zero, and the Tract Number which caused the control break is moved from the input area to the tract number compare area.

The logic expressed in pseudocode for the module which processes a city change is illustrated in Figure 8–18.

PSEUDOCODE SPECIFICATIONS

PROGRAM: Unsold Lots Report	PROGRAMMER: Forsythe	DATE: Jan. 9
MODULE NAME: Process City Changes	REF: B020 MODULE FUNCTION: Process the City Changes	

PSEUDOCODE	REF:	DATA BASES, FILES, RECORDS, FIELDS REQUIRED
Move previous city number to city total line Move city total to city total line Write city total line on the report Add 2 to lines printed counter Set spacing for triple spacing Set city total accumulator to zero Move the new city number to the compare area		Previous city number from compare area City total accumulator City total line New city number from input record City number compare area Lines printed counter Spacing control field Triple space control character

Figure 8-18 Pseudocode for the Process a City Change Module

In the first statement in Figure 8–18, the City Number in the compare area (the previous city number) is moved to the City Total Line. The remaining statements are virtually identical to those found in the module which processes a tract change. They include writing the city total line, adding the value 2 to the lines printed counter, setting the spacing for triple spacing, setting the city total accumulator to zero, and moving the City Number which caused the control break to the city number compare area.

Figure 8-19 illustrates the pseudocode for the module which processes a change in Developer Number.

PSEUDOCODE SPECIFICATIONS

PROGRAM: Unsold Lots Report		PROGRAMMER: Forsythe	DATE: Jan. 9
MODULE NAME: Process Developer Change	REF: B030	MODULE FUNCTION: Process the Developer Change	

PSEUDOCODE	REF:	DATA BASES, FILES, RECORDS, FIELDS REQUIRED
Move previous developer number to developer total line Move developer total to developer total line Write developer total line on the report Add 2 to lines printed counter Set spacing for triple spacing Set developer total accumulator to zero Move the new developer number to the compare area		Previous developer number from compare area Developer total accumulator Developer total line New developer number from input record Developer number compare area Number of lines printed counter Spacing control field Triple space control character

Figure 8-19 Pseudocode for the Process a Developer Change Module

In the pseudocode in Figure 8-19, the processing required when the Developer Number changes is essentially the same as the processing which occurs when the City Number changes.

The Pseudocode Specifications for the module which prints the final totals is shown in Figure 8-20.

PSEUDOCODE SPECIFICATIONS

PROGRAM: Unsold Lots Report		PROGRAMMER: Forsythe	DATE: Jan. 9
MODULE NAME: Print Final Totals	REF: B040	MODULE FUNCTION: Print the Final Totals	

PSEUDOCODE	REF:	DATA BASES, FILES, RECORDS, FIELDS REQUIRED
Move the final total to the final total line Write the final total line on the report		Final total accumulator Final total line

Figure 8-20 Pseudocode for the Print the Final Totals Module

In order to print the final totals, the final total value is moved from the final total accumulator to the final total line and then the line is printed. This is similar to the processing which has been seen in previous programs.

After the pseudocode for the modules on the second level of the program has been completed, the programmer would normally begin the pseudocode for modules on the third level of the hierarchy chart. The only module on the third level in this program is the module whose function is to print the headings. The pseudocode for this module is illustrated in Figure 8-21.

PSEUDOCODE SPECIFICATIONS

PROGRAM: Unsold Lots Report		PROGRAMMER: Forsythe		DATE: Jan. 9
MODULE NAME: Print Headings		REF: C000	MODULE FUNCTION: Print the Headings	

PSEUDOCODE	REF:	DATA BASES, FILES, RECORDS, FIELDS REQUIRED
Obtain the date Move the date to the heading line Move the page count to the heading line Write the first heading line Add 1 to page count Write the second heading line Write the third heading line Set spacing for double spacing Set lines printed counter to four		Date work area First heading line Page count Second heading line Third heading line Spacing control field Double spacing control character Lines printed counter

Figure 8-21 Pseudocode for the Print the Headings Module

Note from Figure 8-21 that the headings are formatted and printed in the same manner as has been seen in previous programs.

Summary — Program Design

As can be seen from the program design of the sample problem in this chapter, when the major processing tasks of a module are decomposed into lower-level modules, the development of the logical steps to accomplish the task is not an overly difficult job. If at first the design of a program seems difficult, the seemingly complex task of designing the program becomes simpler as the more complex modules are decomposed into lower-level modules and IPO Charts and Pseudocode Specifications are written for these modules. Through the decomposition process and attention to detail when writing the IPO Charts and Pseudocode Specifications, any problem, no matter how complex, can be made simpler and easier to design, resulting in a well-designed program that can and should work the first time it is placed on the computer.

DATA DIVISION

The Data Division in the sample program for this chapter contains several entries which have not been seen in previous programs. These entries are described in the following paragraphs.

Definition of Indicators, Compare Areas, and Accumulators

A series of indicators is required in the sample program to indicate when a change occurs in the Developer Number, City Number, and Tract Number. The required Working-Storage entries for these indicators, together with the compare areas and accumulators used in the sample program, are illustrated in Figure 8-22.

```
003180  WORKING-STORAGE SECTION.
003190
003200  01  PROGRAM-INDICATORS.
004010      05  ARE-THERE-MORE-RECORDS              PIC XXX   VALUE 'YES'.
004020          88  THERE-IS-A-RECORD                        VALUE 'YES'.
004030          88  THERE-ARE-NO-MORE-RECORDS                VALUE 'NO '.
004040      05  WAS-THERE-A-DEVELOPER-CHANGE       PIC XXX   VALUE 'NO '.
004050          88  THERE-WAS-A-DEVELOPER-CHANGE             VALUE 'YES'.
004060      05  WAS-THERE-A-CITY-CHANGE            PIC XXX   VALUE 'NO '.
004070          88  THERE-WAS-A-CITY-CHANGE                  VALUE 'YES'.
004080      05  WAS-THERE-A-TRACT-CHANGE           PIC XXX   VALUE 'NO '.
004090          88  THERE-WAS-A-TRACT-CHANGE                 VALUE 'YES'.
004100
004110  01  PROGRAM-COMPARE-AREAS.
004120      05  PREVIOUS-DEVELOPER-NUMBER      PIC 99.
004130      05  PREVIOUS-CITY-NUMBER           PIC 9(3).
004140      05  PREVIOUS-TRACT-NUMBER          PIC 99.
          .
          .
          .
005090  01  TOTAL-ACCUMULATORS-COUNTERS.
005100      05  TRACT-TOTAL-ACCUM          PIC S9(7)    VALUE ZERO.
005110      05  CITY-TOTAL-ACCUM           PIC S9(8)    VALUE ZERO.
005120      05  DEVELOPER-TOTAL-ACCUM      PIC S9(8)    VALUE ZERO.
005130      05  FINAL-TOTAL-ACCUM          PIC S9(9)    VALUE ZERO.
```

Figure 8-22 Working-Storage Coding

In Figure 8-22, the indicators are defined together with the condition names which can be tested in the Procedure Division. In addition, the compare areas and accumulators for the tract, city, developer, and final totals are shown.

Definition of the Lot Table

In the sample program, the building style and selling price are printed on the report. The input record contains the Lot Number, which is used as the subscript to extract the building style and selling price from the lot table. The COBOL code to define the lot table in the Working-Storage Section of the Data Division is illustrated in Figure 8-23.

In Figure 8-23, the name of the entire table is LOTS-TABLE (line 005160). The group item STYLE-PRICE-CONSTANTS on line 005170 contains all of the constants for the table. Each elementary item (15 FILLER) is an element in the table and has a PIC X(14) entry. The fourteen alphanumeric characters in each element of the table consist of 8 characters for the building style and 6 characters for the selling price. There are fifteen elements in the table.

The entries to redefine the table so that each element in the table may be referenced in the Procedure Division begin on line 007080. The group item LOT-CONSTANTS-TABLE redefines STYLE-PRICE-CONSTANTS and occurs 15 times. Thus, each element within the table is defined by the group item LOT-CONSTANTS-TABLE.

The group item LOT-CONSTANTS-TABLE is followed by two elementary items — STYLE-TABLE and PRICE-TABLE. These two items reference each of the elements within the table. The first eight characters of each element within the table will be referenced by the name STYLE-TABLE, and the next six characters of each element within the table will be referenced by the name PRICE-TABLE. For example, if the subscript LOT-NUMBER-INPUT contained the value 1, the entry STYLE-TABLE (LOT-NUMBER-INPUT) in the Procedure Division would reference the first eight characters of the first element of the table (SIERRA). In the same manner, the entry PRICE-TABLE (LOT-NUMBER-INPUT) would reference the next six characters of the first element of the table (165000). Similarly, if the subscript LOT-NUMBER-INPUT contained the value 12, the entry STYLE-TABLE (LOT-NUMBER-INPUT) would reference the first eight characters of the 12th element in the table (SUN VIEW), and the entry PRICE-TABLE (LOT-NUMBER-INPUT) would reference the next six characters of the 12th element in the table (133000).

```
005150 01  PROGRAM-TABLES.
005160     05  LOTS-TABLE.
005170         10  STYLE-PRICE-CONSTANTS.
005180             15  FILLER              PIC X(14)  VALUE
005190                                                'SIERRA  165000'.
005200             15  FILLER              PIC X(14)  VALUE
006010                                                'WOODLAND179000'.
006020             15  FILLER              PIC X(14)  VALUE
006030                                                'BIG OAKS198000'.
006040             15  FILLER              PIC X(14)  VALUE
006050                                                'SUNRISE 212000'.
006060             15  FILLER              PIC X(14)  VALUE
006070                                                'MEADOWS 206000'.
006080             15  FILLER              PIC X(14)  VALUE
006090                                                'WESTLAKE079000'.
006100             15  FILLER              PIC X(14)  VALUE
006110                                                'RANCHERO187000'.
006120             15  FILLER              PIC X(14)  VALUE
006130                                                'SEVILLE 193000'.
006140             15  FILLER              PIC X(14)  VALUE
006150                                                'MOUNTAIN198000'.
006160             15  FILLER              PIC X(14)  VALUE
006170                                                'CAPE COD140000'.
006180             15  FILLER              PIC X(14)  VALUE
006190                                                'HILL TOP121000'.
006200             15  FILLER              PIC X(14)  VALUE
007010                                                'SUN VIEW133000'.
007020             15  FILLER              PIC X(14)  VALUE
007030                                                'KNIGHTLY145000'.
007040             15  FILLER              PIC X(14)  VALUE
007050                                                'ROYALTY 163000'.
007060             15  FILLER              PIC X(14)  VALUE
007070                                                'SUN KING179000'.
007080         10  LOT-CONSTANTS-TABLE REDEFINES STYLE-PRICE-CONSTANTS
007090                                                OCCURS 15 TIMES.
007100             15  STYLE-TABLE         PIC X(8).
007110             15  PRICE-TABLE         PIC 9(6).
```

Figure 8-23 Coding to Define a Table

The first eight characters of each element (referenced by STYLE-TABLE) comprise an alphanumeric field (PIC X(8)), while the next six characters (referenced by PRICE-TABLE) comprise a numeric field (PIC 9(6)). It is not uncommon for tables such as the one illustrated in Figure 8–23 to contain elements which are subdivided into fields that can be numeric or alphanumeric. A numeric element within a table is treated the same as a numeric field defined elsewhere in Working Storage. It may contain decimal places and be used in calculations in the Procedure Division.

The statements which reference the building style and selling price elements in the table are shown in the Procedure Division coding in Figure 8-25 on page 8.19.

PROCEDURE DIVISION

The Procedure Division coding for the modules which create the unsold lots report and process the detail records are similar to the sample program in Chapter 7, but they do contain some differences. These two modules are illustrated and explained on the following pages.

COBOL Coding — Create the Unsold Lots Report

The coding for the create the unsold lots report module is illustrated in Figure 8-24.

```
013130  A000-CREATE-UNSOLD-LOTS-REPORT.                                           LOTRPT
013140                                                                            LOTRPT
013150      OPEN INPUT    DEVELOPER-INPUT-FILE                                     LOTRPT
013160           OUTPUT UNSOLD-LOTS-REPORT-FILE.                                  LOTRPT
013170      READ DEVELOPER-INPUT-FILE                                             LOTRPT
013180           AT END                                                           LOTRPT
013190               MOVE 'NO ' TO ARE-THERE-MORE-RECORDS.                        LOTRPT
013200      IF THERE-IS-A-RECORD                                                  LOTRPT
014010          MOVE TRACT-NUMBER-INPUT TO PREVIOUS-TRACT-NUMBER                  LOTRPT
014020          MOVE CITY-NUMBER-INPUT TO PREVIOUS-CITY-NUMBER                    LOTRPT
014030          MOVE DEVELOPER-NUMBER-INPUT TO PREVIOUS-DEVELOPER-NUMBER          LOTRPT
014040          PERFORM A001-PROCESS-AND-READ                                     LOTRPT
014050              UNTIL THERE-ARE-NO-MORE-RECORDS                               LOTRPT
014060          PERFORM B010-PROCESS-TRACT-CHANGE                                 LOTRPT
014070          PERFORM B020-PROCESS-CITY-CHANGE                                  LOTRPT
014080          PERFORM B030-PROCESS-DEVELOPER-CHANGE                             LOTRPT
014090          PERFORM B040-PRINT-FINAL-TOTALS                                   LOTRPT
014100      ELSE                                                                  LOTRPT
014110          WRITE UNSOLD-LOTS-REPORT-LINE FROM NO-RECORDS-MESSAGE             LOTRPT
014120              AFTER ADVANCING TO-TOP-OF-PAGE.                               LOTRPT
014130      CLOSE DEVELOPER-INPUT-FILE                                            LOTRPT
014140            UNSOLD-LOTS-REPORT-FILE.                                        LOTRPT
014150      STOP RUN.                                                             LOTRPT
014160                                                                            LOTRPT
014170                                                                            LOTRPT
014190  A001-PROCESS-AND-READ.                                                    LOTRPT
014200                                                                            LOTRPT
015010      IF DEVELOPER-NUMBER-INPUT IS NOT = PREVIOUS-DEVELOPER-NUMBER          LOTRPT
015020          PERFORM B010-PROCESS-TRACT-CHANGE                                 LOTRPT
015030          PERFORM B020-PROCESS-CITY-CHANGE                                  LOTRPT
015040          PERFORM B030-PROCESS-DEVELOPER-CHANGE                             LOTRPT
015050          MOVE 'YES' TO WAS-THERE-A-DEVELOPER-CHANGE                        LOTRPT
015060      ELSE                                                                  LOTRPT
015070          IF CITY-NUMBER-INPUT NOT = PREVIOUS-CITY-NUMBER                   LOTRPT
015080              PERFORM B010-PROCESS-TRACT-CHANGE                             LOTRPT
015090              PERFORM B020-PROCESS-CITY-CHANGE                             LOTRPT
015100              MOVE 'YES' TO WAS-THERE-A-CITY-CHANGE                         LOTRPT
015110          ELSE                                                             LOTRPT
015120              IF TRACT-NUMBER-INPUT NOT = PREVIOUS-TRACT-NUMBER             LOTRPT
015130                  PERFORM B010-PROCESS-TRACT-CHANGE                         LOTRPT
015140                  MOVE 'YES' TO WAS-THERE-A-TRACT-CHANGE.                   LOTRPT
015150      PERFORM B000-PROCESS-DETAIL-RECORDS.                                  LOTRPT
015160      READ DEVELOPER-INPUT-FILE                                             LOTRPT
015170           AT END.                                                          LOTRPT
015180               MOVE 'NO ' TO ARE-THERE-MORE-RECORDS.                        LOTRPT
```

Figure 8-24 COBOL Coding for the Create the Unsold Lots Report Module

After the files are opened and the Read statement on line 013070 is executed, a test is made to determine if there is a record to process (line 013200). If there is, the Tract Number, City Number, and Developer Number are moved to their compare areas (see Figure 8–22).

Then, the A001-PROCESS-AND-READ routine is performed until there are no more records. The statements in the A001-PROCESS-AND-READ routine determine if a control break has occurred. When the first record is processed, no control break will occur because the Developer Number, City Number, and Tract Number for the first record were moved to their respective compare areas by the statements on lines 014010 through 014030. For each input record after the first record, if a control break occurs, the appropriate modules are performed, and the appropriate indicator is set to indicate a control break occurred.

After processing any control breaks, the module which processes the detail records is performed, and another input record is read. This processing will continue until there are no more input records. When there are no more input records, the modules to print the control break totals will be performed so that the totals for the last group of records will be printed; and the final totals will be printed. The files are then closed, and the program is terminated.

The module which creates the unsold lots report controls when processing is to occur within the program. This is normally the function of the highest level module in a program.

COBOL Coding – Process Detail Records Module

The module which processes the detail records is illustrated in Figure 8–25.

```
016100  B000-PROCESS-DETAIL-RECORDS.                                           LOTRPT
016110                                                                         LOTRPT
016120      IF LINES-PRINTED IS EQUAL TO PAGE-SIZE OR                          LOTRPT
016130         LINES-PRINTED IS GREATER THAN PAGE-SIZE OR                      LOTRPT
016140         FIRST-PAGE                                                      LOTRPT
016150      PERFORM C000-PRINT-HEADINGS                                        LOTRPT
016160      MOVE PREVIOUS-DEVELOPER-NUMBER TO DEVELOPER-NUMBER-REPORT          LOTRPT
016170      MOVE PREVIOUS-CITY-NUMBER TO CITY-NUMBER-REPORT                    LOTRPT
016180      MOVE PREVIOUS-TRACT-NUMBER TO TRACT-NUMBER-REPORT.                 LOTRPT
016190      IF THERE-WAS-A-DEVELOPER-CHANGE                                    LOTRPT
016200      MOVE DEVELOPER-NUMBER-INPUT TO DEVELOPER-NUMBER-REPORT             LOTRPT
017010      MOVE CITY-NUMBER-INPUT TO CITY-NUMBER-REPORT                       LOTRPT
017020      MOVE TRACT-NUMBER-INPUT TO TRACT-NUMBER-REPORT                     LOTRPT
017030      MOVE 'NO ' TO WAS-THERE-A-DEVELOPER-CHANGE                         LOTRPT
017040  ELSE                                                                   LOTRPT
017050      IF THERE-WAS-A-CITY-CHANGE                                         LOTRPT
017060      MOVE CITY-NUMBER-INPUT TO CITY-NUMBER-REPORT                       LOTRPT
017070      MOVE TRACT-NUMBER-INPUT TO TRACT-NUMBER-REPORT                     LOTRPT
017080      MOVE 'NO ' TO WAS-THERE-A-CITY-CHANGE                              LOTRPT
017090      ELSE                                                               LOTRPT
017100          IF THERE-WAS-A-TRACT-CHANGE                                    LOTRPT
017110          MOVE TRACT-NUMBER-INPUT TO TRACT-NUMBER-REPORT                 LOTRPT
017120          MOVE 'NO ' TO WAS-THERE-A-TRACT-CHANGE.                        LOTRPT
017130  MOVE LOT-NUMBER-INPUT TO LOT-NUMBER-REPORT.                            LOTRPT
017140  MOVE STYLE-TABLE (LOT-NUMBER-INPUT) TO BUILDING-STYLE-REPORT.          LOTRPT
017150  MOVE PRICE-TABLE (LOT-NUMBER-INPUT) TO SELLING-PRICE-REPORT.           LOTRPT
017160  ADD PRICE-TABLE (LOT-NUMBER-INPUT) TO TRACT-TOTAL-ACCUM.               LOTRPT
017170  ADD PRICE-TABLE (LOT-NUMBER-INPUT) TO CITY-TOTAL-ACCUM.                LOTRPT
017180  ADD PRICE-TABLE (LOT-NUMBER-INPUT) TO DEVELOPER-TOTAL-ACCUM.           LOTRPT
017190  ADD PRICE-TABLE (LOT-NUMBER-INPUT) TO FINAL-TOTAL-ACCUM.               LOTRPT
017200  WRITE UNSOLD-LOTS-REPORT-LINE FROM DETAIL-LINE                         LOTRPT
018010          AFTER ADVANCING PROPER-SPACING.                               LOTRPT
018020  ADD PROPER-SPACING TO LINES-PRINTED.                                   LOTRPT
018030  MOVE SPACE-ONE-LINE TO PROPER-SPACING.                                 LOTRPT
018040  MOVE SPACES TO DETAIL-LINE.                                            LOTRPT
```

Figure 8-25 COBOL Coding for the Process the Detail Records Module

The first entries in the module in Figure 8–25 determine if a heading should be printed. If so, the headings are printed, and then the Developer Number, City Number, and Tract Number are moved to the printer output area so they will appear on the first line of a new page regardless of whether a control break has occurred. Normally, group indicated fields will be printed on the first line of a new page.

The next statements test if a control break has occurred for any of the control fields (Developer Number, City Number, or Tract Number). If so, the data in the input area is moved to the output area so that the value will print for the first record. In addition, the indicator for the control break is reset because the processing that is to occur in this module when there is a control break (moving the values to the report output area) has been completed.

It should be noted that all of the checks for a control break are a part of a nested If statement. If any one of the tests is true, the remaining tests will not be performed.

Prior to writing the detail line on the report, the Lot Number is moved to the output area and, using the LOT-NUMBER-INPUT field as the subscript, the Building Style and Selling Price are extracted from the table and moved to the output area. The fields STYLE-TABLE and PRICE-TABLE were previously defined in the Working-Storage Section (see Figure 8–23).

The Selling Price from the table is then added to the values in the Tract Total Accumulator, the City Total Accumulator, the Developer Total Accumulator, and the Final Total Accumulator. The subscript LOT-NUMBER-INPUT is used to extract the Selling Price from the table using the entry PRICE-TABLE (LOT-NUMBER-INPUT).

After the addition of the selling price to the proper accumulators, each detail record will be printed. The Write statement on line 017200 uses the "Write ... From" form of the Write verb. Thus, DETAIL-LINE must be defined in the Working-Storage Section of the Data Division rather than the File Section of the Data Division. The field UNSOLD-LOTS-REPORT-LINE, however, must be defined in the File Section. This coding is illustrated in Figure 8–26.

File Section

```
003120  FD   UNSOLD-LOTS-REPORT-FILE
003130            RECORD CONTAINS 133 CHARACTERS
003140            LABEL RECORDS ARE OMITTED
003150            DATA RECORD IS UNSOLD-LOTS-REPORT-LINE.
003160  01   UNSOLD-LOTS-REPORT-LINE          PIC X(133).
```

Working-Storage Section

```
008030  01   DETAIL-LINE.
008040       05   CARRIAGE-CONTROL              PIC X.
008050       05   FILLER                        PIC X(4)       VALUE SPACES.
008060       05   DEVELOPER-NUMBER-REPORT       PIC Z9.
008070       05   FILLER                        PIC X(9)       VALUE SPACES.
008080       05   CITY-NUMBER-REPORT            PIC ZZ9.
008090       05   FILLER                        PIC X(10)      VALUE SPACES.
008100       05   TRACT-NUMBER-REPORT           PIC Z9.
008110       05   FILLER                        PIC X(8)       VALUE SPACES.
008120       05   LOT-NUMBER-REPORT             PIC Z9.
008130       05   FILLER                        PIC X(8)       VALUE SPACES.
008140       05   BUILDING-STYLE-REPORT         PIC X(8).
008150       05   FILLER                        PIC X(6)       VALUE SPACES.
008160       05   SELLING-PRICE-REPORT          PIC ZZZ,ZZ9.
008170       05   FILLER                        PIC X(63)      VALUE SPACES.
```

Procedure Division

```
017200       WRITE UNSOLD-LOTS-REPORT-LINE FROM DETAIL-LINE
018010            AFTER ADVANCING PROPER-SPACING.
```

Figure 8-26 COBOL Coding of Report Detail Line

In the coding of the File Section of the Data Division, the UNSOLD-LOTS-REPORT-FILE is defined in the same manner as in previous programs. The output area, however, is defined with a PIC X(133), instead of each individual field, because each individual field is defined in the Working-Storage Section of the Data Division as a part of the output record.

In Working-Storage, the group item DETAIL-LINE is defined, together with each elementary item comprising the print line. The FILLER elementary items which do not contain data are given the value Spaces through the use of the Value Clause. This is necessary so that the first time the line is printed, these Filler fields will not contain extraneous data. After the first line is printed, spaces will be moved to the DETAIL-LINE so subsequent lines will contain only valid data. This technique is required when the report is group indicated.

When preparing a report involving multiple level control breaks, it is important to keep an accurate count of the number of detail and total lines printed, including the spaces before and after these lines, so that proper page overflow will take place. Figure 8–27 illustrates the report from the sample program and the spacing with which the programmer must be concerned.

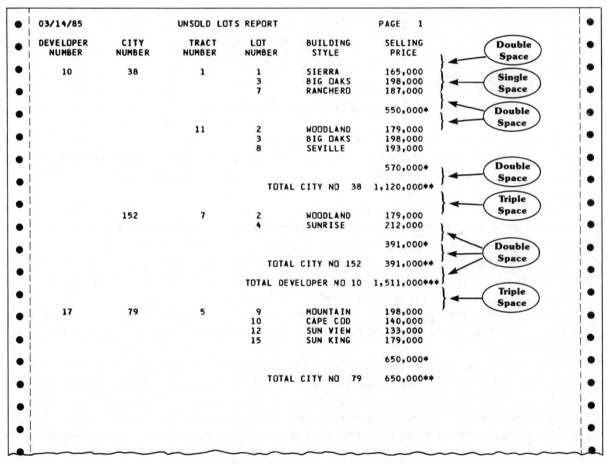

Figure 8-27 Spacing on the Unsold Lots Report

After the heading is printed, the report is double spaced. Double spacing means there is one blank line with the data printed on the second line. The detail lines are single spaced. There is double spacing before and after the tract total is printed, and before the city total is printed. There is triple spacing after the city total unless the developer total is printed immediately after it, in which case there is double spacing following the city total and triple spacing following the developer total. Triple spacing means there are two blank lines with the data printed on the third line.

It is important that the lines printed be counted properly. Figure 8–28 illustrates segments of coding from the sample program and how the lines printed counter is updated after printing the headings on a page.

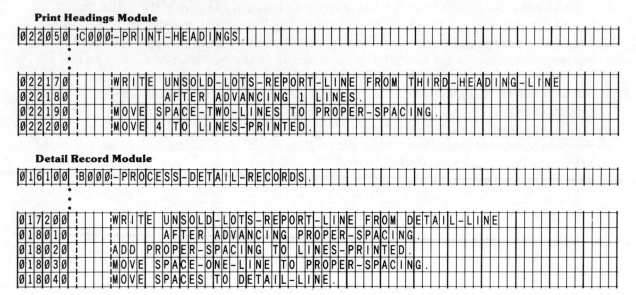

Print Headings Module

| 0 2 2 0 5 0 | C000-PRINT-HEADINGS. |

0 2 2 1 7 0	WRITE UNSOLD-LOTS-REPORT-LINE FROM THIRD-HEADING-LINE
0 2 2 1 8 0	AFTER ADVANCING 1 LINES.
0 2 2 1 9 0	MOVE SPACE-TWO-LINES TO PROPER-SPACING.
0 2 2 2 0 0	MOVE 4 TO LINES-PRINTED.

Detail Record Module

| 0 1 6 1 0 0 | B000-PROCESS-DETAIL-RECORDS. |

0 1 7 2 0 0	WRITE UNSOLD-LOTS-REPORT-LINE FROM DETAIL-LINE
0 1 8 0 1 0	AFTER ADVANCING PROPER-SPACING.
0 1 8 0 2 0	ADD PROPER-SPACING TO LINES-PRINTED.
0 1 8 0 3 0	MOVE SPACE-ONE-LINE TO PROPER-SPACING.
0 1 8 0 4 0	MOVE SPACES TO DETAIL-LINE.

Figure 8-28 Coding for Line Counting

In Figure 8–28, after the third heading line is written (line 022170), the statement MOVE SPACE-TWO-LINES TO PROPER-SPACING results in the value 2 being moved to the PROPER-SPACING field. The value 4 is then moved to the lines printed counter (LINES-PRINTED) because the heading consists of four lines.

When the first detail line is written in the Detail Record Module (line 017200), the line is written after advancing PROPER-SPACING. Since the field PROPER-SPACING contains the value 2, the first detail line is double spaced. The next statement, ADD PROPER-SPACING TO LINES-PRINTED, adds the value 2 to the LINES-PRINTED counter. Thus, the two lines on the page which were used for double spacing are accounted for in the count of the number of lines printed on the page. After the first detail line is printed on the report and the coding in the detail record module is complete for the first record, the lines printed counter will contain the value 6, which accounts for the four lines in the heading and the double spacing for the first detail record.

The statement on line 018030, MOVE SPACE-ONE-LINE TO PROPER-SPACING, moves the value 1 to the PROPER-SPACING field so that when the next detail line is printed, the line will be single spaced. The one will subsequently be added to the lines printed counter each time a detail line is printed, accounting for the single spacing of the detail lines. This coding technique results in the proper number of lines being accumulated in the lines printed counter.

This same basic technique is utilized to handle the variable spacing that occurs when there is a change in Developer Number, City Number, and Tract Number.

Source Listing

The following pages contain the source listing of the sample program in this chapter.

```
PP 5740-CB1 RELEASE 2.3 + PTF 8 - UP13477        IBM OS/VS COBOL  JULY 24, 1978        9.09.51  DATE MAR 14,1985

    1                        9.09.51      MAR 14,1985

00001   001010 IDENTIFICATION DIVISION.                                    LOTRPT
00002   001020                                                             LOTRPT
00003   001030 PROGRAM-ID.     LOTRPT.                                      LOTRPT
00004   001040 AUTHOR.         FORSYTHE.                                    LOTRPT
00005   001050 INSTALLATION.   BREA.                                        LOTRPT
00006   001060 DATE-WRITTEN.   JAN 16,1985.                                 LOTRPT
00007   001070 DATE-COMPILED.  MAR 14,1985.                                 LOTRPT
00008   001080 SECURITY.       UNCLASSIFIED.                                LOTRPT
00009   001090                                                             LOTRPT
00010   001100*************************************************************  LOTRPT
00011   001110*                                                          *  LOTRPT
00012   001120*  THIS PROGRAM PRODUCES AN UNSOLD LOTS REPORT. THE REPORT  *  LOTRPT
00013   001130*  CONTAINS LOT NUMBER, BUILDING STYLE, AND SELLING PRICE FOR *  LOTRPT
00014   001140*  EACH DEVELOPER, CITY, AND TRACT. TOTALS ARE TAKEN FOR A  *  LOTRPT
00015   001150*  CHANGE IN TRACT NUMBER, A CHANGE IN CITY NUMBER, AND A   *  LOTRPT
00016   001160*  CHANGE IN DEVELOPER NUMBER. FINAL TOTALS ARE ALSO PRINTED. *  LOTRPT
00017   001170*                                                          *  LOTRPT
00018   001180*************************************************************  LOTRPT
00019   001190                                                             LOTRPT
00020   001200                                                             LOTRPT
00021   002010                                                             LOTRPT
00022   002020 ENVIRONMENT DIVISION.                                       LOTRPT
00023   002030                                                             LOTRPT
00024   002040 CONFIGURATION SECTION.                                      LOTRPT
00025   002050                                                             LOTRPT
00026   002060 SOURCE-COMPUTER. IBM-4381.                                  LOTRPT
00027   002070 OBJECT-COMPUTER. IBM-4381.                                  LOTRPT
00028   002080 SPECIAL-NAMES.   C01 IS TO-TOP-OF-PAGE.                     LOTRPT
00029   002090                                                             LOTRPT
00030   002100 INPUT-OUTPUT SECTION.                                       LOTRPT
00031   002110                                                             LOTRPT
00032   002120 FILE-CONTROL.                                              LOTRPT
00033   002130     SELECT DEVELOPER-INPUT-FILE                            LOTRPT
00034   002140         ASSIGN TO UT-S-LOTDATA.                            LOTRPT
00035   002150     SELECT UNSOLD-LOTS-REPORT-FILE                         LOTRPT
00036   002160         ASSIGN TO UT-S-LOTPRINT.                           LOTRPT

    2                        9.09.51      MAR 14,1985

00037   002170/                                                           LOTRPT
00038   002180 DATA DIVISION.                                             LOTRPT
00039   002190                                                            LOTRPT
00040   002200 FILE SECTION.                                              LOTRPT
00041   003010                                                            LOTRPT
00042   003020 FD  DEVELOPER-INPUT-FILE                                   LOTRPT
00043   003030     RECORD CONTAINS 9 CHARACTERS                          LOTRPT
00044   003040     LABEL RECORDS ARE STANDARD                            LOTRPT
00045   003050     DATA RECORD IS DEVELOPER-INPUT-RECORD.                LOTRPT
00046   003060 01  DEVELOPER-INPUT-RECORD.                               LOTRPT
00047   003070     05  DEVELOPER-NUMBER-INPUT   PIC 99.                  LOTRPT
00048   003080     05  CITY-NUMBER-INPUT        PIC 9(3).                LOTRPT
00049   003090     05  TRACT-NUMBER-INPUT       PIC 99.                  LOTRPT
00050   003100     05  LOT-NUMBER-INPUT         PIC 99.                  LOTRPT
00051   003110                                                           LOTRPT
00052   003120 FD  UNSOLD-LOTS-REPORT-FILE                               LOTRPT
00053   003130     RECORD CONTAINS 133 CHARACTERS                        LOTRPT
00054   003140     LABEL RECORDS ARE OMITTED                             LOTRPT
00055   003150     DATA RECORD IS UNSOLD-LOTS-REPORT-LINE.               LOTRPT
00056   003160 01  UNSOLD-LOTS-REPORT-LINE    PIC X(133).                LOTRPT
00057   003170                                                           LOTRPT
00058   003180 WORKING-STORAGE SECTION.                                  LOTRPT
00059   003190                                                           LOTRPT
00060   003200 01  PROGRAM-INDICATORS.                                   LOTRPT
00061   004010     05  ARE-THERE-MORE-RECORDS       PIC XXX  VALUE 'YES'. LOTRPT
00062   004020         88  THERE-IS-A-RECORD                 VALUE 'YES'. LOTRPT
00063   004030         88  THERE-ARE-NO-MORE-RECORDS         VALUE 'NO '. LOTRPT
00064   004040     05  WAS-THERE-A-DEVELOPER-CHANGE PIC XXX  VALUE 'NO '. LOTRPT
00065   004050         88  THERE-WAS-A-DEVELOPER-CHANGE      VALUE 'YES'. LOTRPT
00066   004060     05  WAS-THERE-A-CITY-CHANGE      PIC XXX  VALUE 'NO '. LOTRPT
00067   004070         88  THERE-WAS-A-CITY-CHANGE           VALUE 'YES'. LOTRPT
00068   004080     05  WAS-THERE-A-TRACT-CHANGE     PIC XXX  VALUE 'NO '. LOTRPT
00069   004090         88  THERE-WAS-A-TRACT-CHANGE          VALUE 'YES'. LOTRPT
00070   004100                                                           LOTRPT
00071   004110 01  PROGRAM-COMPARE-AREAS.                                LOTRPT
00072   004120     05  PREVIOUS-DEVELOPER-NUMBER  PIC 99.                LOTRPT
00073   004130     05  PREVIOUS-CITY-NUMBER       PIC 9(3).              LOTRPT
00074   004140     05  PREVIOUS-TRACT-NUMBER      PIC 99.                LOTRPT
00075   004150                                                           LOTRPT
00076   004160 01  WORK-AREAS.                                           LOTRPT
00077   004170     05  DATE-WORK.                                        LOTRPT
00078   004180         10  YEAR-WORK        PIC 99.                      LOTRPT
00079   004190         10  MONTH-WORK       PIC 99.                      LOTRPT
00080   004200         10  DAY-WORK         PIC 99.                      LOTRPT
00081   005010                                                           LOTRPT
```

Figure 8-29 Source Listing (1 of 5)

```
  3                 9.09.51     MAR 14,1985

00082  005020 01  PROGRAM-CONSTANTS.                                      LOTRPT
00083  005030    05  NO-RECORDS-MESSAGE.                                  LOTRPT
00084  005040        10  CARRIAGE-CONTROL    PIC X.                       LOTRPT
00085  005050        10  FILLER              PIC X(34)    VALUE           LOTRPT
00086  005060                      'LOT REPORT - NO RECORDS TO PROCESS'.  LOTRPT
00087  005070        10  FILLER              PIC X(98)    VALUE SPACES.   LOTRPT
00088  005080                                                            LOTRPT
00089  005090 01  TOTAL-ACCUMULATORS-COUNTERS.                           LOTRPT
00090  005100    05  TRACT-TOTAL-ACCUM       PIC S9(7)    VALUE ZERO.     LOTRPT
00091  005110    05  CITY-TOTAL-ACCUM        PIC S9(8)    VALUE ZERO.     LOTRPT
00092  005120    05  DEVELOPER-TOTAL-ACCUM   PIC S9(8)    VALUE ZERO.     LOTRPT
00093  005130    05  FINAL-TOTAL-ACCUM       PIC S9(9)    VALUE ZERO.     LOTRPT
00094  005140                                                            LOTRPT
00095  005150 01  PROGRAM-TABLES.                                        LOTRPT
00096  005160    05  LOTS-TABLE.                                         LOTRPT
00097  005170        10  STYLE-PRICE-CONSTANTS.                          LOTRPT
00098  005180            15  FILLER          PIC X(14)    VALUE           LOTRPT
00099  005190                                      'SIERRA  165000'.     LOTRPT
00100  005200            15  FILLER          PIC X(14)    VALUE           LOTRPT
00101  006010                                      'WOODLAND179000'.     LOTRPT
00102  006020            15  FILLER          PIC X(14)    VALUE           LOTRPT
00103  006030                                      'BIG OAKS198000'.     LOTRPT
00104  006040            15  FILLER          PIC X(14)    VALUE           LOTRPT
00105  006050                                      'SUNRISE 212000'.     LOTRPT
00106  006060            15  FILLER          PIC X(14)    VALUE           LOTRPT
00107  006070                                      'MEADOWS 206000'.     LOTRPT
00108  006080            15  FILLER          PIC X(14)    VALUE           LOTRPT
00109  006090                                      'WESTLAKE079000'.     LOTRPT
00110  006100            15  FILLER          PIC X(14)    VALUE           LOTRPT
00111  006110                                      'RANCHERO187000'.     LOTRPT
00112  006120            15  FILLER          PIC X(14)    VALUE           LOTRPT
00113  006130                                      'SEVILLE 193000'.     LOTRPT
00114  006140            15  FILLER          PIC X(14)    VALUE           LOTRPT
00115  006150                                      'MOUNTAIN198000'.     LOTRPT
00116  006160            15  FILLER          PIC X(14)    VALUE           LOTRPT
00117  006170                                      'CAPE COD140000'.     LOTRPT
00118  006180            15  FILLER          PIC X(14)    VALUE           LOTRPT
00119  006190                                      'HILL TOP121000'.     LOTRPT
00120  006200            15  FILLER          PIC X(14)    VALUE           LOTRPT
00121  007010                                      'SUN VIEW133000'.     LOTRPT
00122  007020            15  FILLER          PIC X(14)    VALUE           LOTRPT
00123  007030                                      'KNIGHTLY145000'.     LOTRPT
00124  007040            15  FILLER          PIC X(14)    VALUE           LOTRPT
00125  007050                                      'ROYALTY 163000'.     LOTRPT
00126  007060            15  FILLER          PIC X(14)    VALUE           LOTRPT
00127  007070                                      'SUN KING179000'.     LOTRPT
00128  007080        10  LOT-CONSTANTS-TABLE REDEFINES STYLE-PRICE-CONSTANTS LOTRPT
00129  007090                                      OCCURS 15 TIMES.      LOTRPT
00130  007100            15  STYLE-TABLE      PIC X(8).                  LOTRPT
00131  007110            15  PRICE-TABLE      PIC 9(6).                  LOTRPT
00132  007120                                                            LOTRPT
00133  007130 01  PRINTER-CONTROL.                                       LOTRPT
00134  007140    05  PROPER-SPACING          PIC 9.                      LOTRPT
00135  007150    05  SPACE-ONE-LINE          PIC 9        VALUE 1.       LOTRPT
00136  007160    05  SPACE-TWO-LINES         PIC 9        VALUE 2.       LOTRPT
00137  007170    05  SPACE-THREE-LINES       PIC 9        VALUE 3.       LOTRPT
00138  007180    05  LINES-PRINTED           PIC S999     VALUE ZERO.    LOTRPT
00139  007190    05  PAGE-SIZE               PIC 999      VALUE 55.      LOTRPT
00140  007200    05  PAGE-COUNT              PIC S999     VALUE +1.      LOTRPT
00141  008010        88  FIRST-PAGE                       VALUE +1.      LOTRPT
00142  008020                                                            LOTRPT
00143  008030 01  DETAIL-LINE.                                           LOTRPT
00144  008040    05  CARRIAGE-CONTROL        PIC X.                      LOTRPT
00145  008050    05  FILLER                  PIC X(4)     VALUE SPACES.  LOTRPT
00146  008060    05  DEVELOPER-NUMBER-REPORT PIC Z9.                     LOTRPT
00147  008070    05  FILLER                  PIC X(9)     VALUE SPACES.  LOTRPT
00148  008080    05  CITY-NUMBER-REPORT      PIC ZZ9.                    LOTRPT
00149  008090    05  FILLER                  PIC X(10)    VALUE SPACES.  LOTRPT
00150  008100    05  TRACT-NUMBER-REPORT     PIC Z9.                     LOTRPT
00151  008110    05  FILLER                  PIC X(8)     VALUE SPACES.  LOTRPT
00152  008120    05  LOT-NUMBER-REPORT       PIC Z9.                     LOTRPT
00153  008130    05  FILLER                  PIC X(8)     VALUE SPACES.  LOTRPT
00154  008140    05  BUILDING-STYLE-REPORT   PIC X(8).                   LOTRPT
00155  008150    05  FILLER                  PIC X(6)     VALUE SPACES.  LOTRPT
00156  008160    05  SELLING-PRICE-REPORT    PIC ZZZ,ZZ9.                LOTRPT
00157  008170    05  FILLER                  PIC X(63)    VALUE SPACES.  LOTRPT
00158  008180                                                            LOTRPT
00159  008190 01  HEADING-LINES.                                         LOTRPT
00160  008200    05  FIRST-HEADING-LINE.                                 LOTRPT
00161  009010        10  CARRIAGE-CONTROL    PIC X.                      LOTRPT
00162  009020        10  DATE-HEADING.                                   LOTRPT
00163  009030            15  MONTH-HEADING    PIC 99.                    LOTRPT
00164  009040            15  FILLER           PIC X        VALUE '/'.    LOTRPT
00165  009050            15  DAY-HEADING      PIC 99.                    LOTRPT
00166  009060            15  FILLER           PIC X        VALUE '/'.    LOTRPT
00167  009070            15  YEAR-HEADING     PIC 99.                    LOTRPT
00168  009080        10  FILLER              PIC X(17)    VALUE SPACES.  LOTRPT
00169  009090        10  FILLER              PIC X(18)    VALUE          LOTRPT
00170  009100                                      'UNSOLD LOTS REPORT'. LOTRPT
00171  009110        10  FILLER              PIC X(18)    VALUE SPACES.  LOTRPT
00172  009120        10  FILLER              PIC X(5)     VALUE 'PAGE '. LOTRPT
00173  009130        10  PAGE-HEADING        PIC ZZ9.                    LOTRPT
00174  009140        10  FILLER              PIC X(63).                  LOTRPT
00175  009150    05  SECOND-HEADING-LINE.                               LOTRPT
00176  009160        10  CARRIAGE-CONTROL    PIC X.                      LOTRPT
00177  009170        10  FILLER              PIC X(9)     VALUE 'DEVELOPER'. LOTRPT
00178  009180        10  FILLER              PIC X(6)     VALUE SPACES.  LOTRPT
00179  009190        10  FILLER              PIC X(4)     VALUE 'CITY'.  LOTRPT
00180  009200        10  FILLER              PIC X(4)     VALUE SPACES.  LOTRPT
00181  010010        10  FILLER              PIC X(5)     VALUE 'TRACT'. LOTRPT
00182  010020        10  FILLER              PIC X(4)     VALUE SPACES.  LOTRPT
00183  010030        10  FILLER              PIC X(3)     VALUE 'LOT'.   LOTRPT
00184  010040        10  FILLER              PIC X(7)     VALUE SPACES.  LOTRPT
00185  010050        10  FILLER              PIC X(8)     VALUE 'BUILDING'. LOTRPT
00186  010060        10  FILLER              PIC X(6)     VALUE SPACES.  LOTRPT
00187  010070        10  FILLER              PIC X(7)     VALUE 'SELLING'. LOTRPT
00188  010080        10  FILLER              PIC X(63)    VALUE SPACES.  LOTRPT
```

Figure 8-30 Source Listing (2 of 5)

```
   4                    9.09.51      MAR 14,1985

00189  010090    05   THIRD-HEADING-LINE.                              LOTRPT
00190  010100       10   CARRIAGE-CONTROL     PIC X.                   LOTRPT
00191  010110       10   FILLER               PIC XX       VALUE SPACES.  LOTRPT
00192  010120       10   FILLER               PIC X(6)     VALUE 'NUMBER'. LOTRPT
00193  010130       10   FILLER               PIC X(6)     VALUE SPACES.  LOTRPT
00194  010140       10   FILLER               PIC X(6)     VALUE 'NUMBER'. LOTRPT
00195  010150       10   FILLER               PIC X(6)     VALUE SPACES.  LOTRPT
00196  010160       10   FILLER               PIC X(6)     VALUE 'NUMBER'. LOTRPT
00197  010170       10   FILLER               PIC X(5)     VALUE SPACES.  LOTRPT
00198  010180       10   FILLER               PIC X(6)     VALUE 'NUMBER'. LOTRPT
00199  010190       10   FILLER               PIC X(6)     VALUE SPACES.  LOTRPT
00200  010200       10   FILLER               PIC X(5)     VALUE 'STYLE'.  LOTRPT
00201  011010       10   FILLER               PIC X(9)     VALUE SPACES.  LOTRPT
00202  011020       10   FILLER               PIC X(5)     VALUE 'PRICE'.  LOTRPT
00203  011030       10   FILLER               PIC X(64)    VALUE SPACES.  LOTRPT
00204  011040                                                          LOTRPT
00205  011050  01   TOTAL-LINES.                                       LOTRPT
00206  011060    05   TRACT-TOTAL-LINE.                                LOTRPT
00207  011070       10   CARRIAGE-CONTROL     PIC X.                   LOTRPT
00208  011080       10   FILLER               PIC X(60)    VALUE SPACES.  LOTRPT
00209  011090       10   TRACT-TOTAL-TRACTOT  PIC Z,ZZZ,ZZ9.           LOTRPT
00210  011100       10   FILLER               PIC X        VALUE '*'.    LOTRPT
00211  011110       10   FILLER               PIC X(62)    VALUE SPACES.  LOTRPT
00212  011120    05   CITY-TOTAL-LINE.                                 LOTRPT
00213  011130       10   CARRIAGE-CONTROL     PIC X.                   LOTRPT
00214  011140       10   FILLER               PIC X(41)    VALUE SPACES.  LOTRPT
00215  011150       10   FILLER               PIC X(14)    VALUE         LOTRPT
00216  011160                                       'TOTAL CITY NO '.    LOTRPT
00217  011170       10   CITY-NUMBER-CITYTOT  PIC ZZ9.                 LOTRPT
00218  011180       10   FILLER               PIC X        VALUE SPACES.  LOTRPT
00219  011190       10   CITY-TOTAL-CITYTOT   PIC ZZ,ZZZ,ZZ9.          LOTRPT
00220  011200       10   FILLER               PIC X(2)     VALUE '**'.   LOTRPT
00221  012010       10   FILLER               PIC X(61).               LOTRPT
00222  012020    05   DEVELOPER-TOTAL-LINE.                            LOTRPT
00223  012030       10   CARRIAGE-CONTROL     PIC X.                   LOTRPT
00224  012040       10   FILLER               PIC X(37)    VALUE SPACES.  LOTRPT
00225  012050       10   FILLER               PIC X(19)    VALUE         LOTRPT
00226  012060                                       'TOTAL DEVELOPER NO '.LOTRPT
00227  012070       10   DEVELOPER-NUMBER-DEVTOT PIC Z9.               LOTRPT
00228  012080       10   FILLER               PIC X        VALUE SPACES.  LOTRPT
00229  012090       10   DEVELOPER-TOTAL-DEVTOT  PIC ZZ,ZZZ,ZZ9.       LOTRPT
00230  012100       10   FILLER               PIC X(3)     VALUE '***'.  LOTRPT
00231  012110       10   FILLER               PIC X(60)    VALUE SPACES.  LOTRPT
00232  012120    05   FINAL-TOTAL-LINE.                                LOTRPT
00233  012130       10   CARRIAGE-CONTROL     PIC X.                   LOTRPT
00234  012140       10   FILLER               PIC X(45)    VALUE SPACES.  LOTRPT
00235  012150       10   FILLER               PIC X(12)    VALUE         LOTRPT
00236  012160                                       'FINAL TOTAL '.      LOTRPT
00237  012170       10   FINAL-TOTAL-FINTOT   PIC $$$$,$$$,$$$.         LOTRPT
00238  012180       10   FILLER               PIC X(4)     VALUE '****'. LOTRPT
00239  012190       10   FILLER               PIC X(59)    VALUE SPACES.  LOTRPT
```

```
   5                    9.09.51      MAR 14,1985

00240  012200/                                                        LOTRPT
00241  013010  PROCEDURE DIVISION.                                    LOTRPT
00242  013020                                                         LOTRPT
00243  013030**************************************************************LOTRPT
00244  013040*                                                      * LOTRPT
00245  013050*   THIS MODULE INITIALIZES THE FILES AND THEN DETERMINES WHEN * LOTRPT
00246  013060*   CONTROL BREAKS HAVE OCCURRED AND CAUSES THE APPROPRIATE  * LOTRPT
00247  013070*   PROCESSING TO OCCUR. IT ALSO CAUSES THE DETAIL LINES TO  * LOTRPT
00248  013080*   BE PRINTED. IT IS ENTERED FROM THE OPERATING SYSTEM AND  * LOTRPT
00249  013090*   EXITS TO THE OPERATING SYSTEM.                       * LOTRPT
00250  013100*                                                      * LOTRPT
00251  013110**************************************************************LOTRPT
00252  013120                                                         LOTRPT
00253  013130  A000-CREATE-UNSOLD-LOTS-REPORT.                        LOTRPT
00254  013140                                                         LOTRPT
00255  013150       OPEN INPUT  DEVELOPER-INPUT-FILE                  LOTRPT
00256  013160            OUTPUT UNSOLD-LOTS-REPORT-FILE.              LOTRPT
00257  013170       READ DEVELOPER-INPUT-FILE                         LOTRPT
00258  013180            AT END                                       LOTRPT
00259  013190            MOVE 'NO ' TO ARE-THERE-MORE-RECORDS.        LOTRPT
00260  013200       IF THERE-IS-A-RECORD                              LOTRPT
00261  014010            MOVE TRACT-NUMBER-INPUT TO PREVIOUS-TRACT-NUMBER   LOTRPT
00262  014020            MOVE CITY-NUMBER-INPUT TO PREVIOUS-CITY-NUMBER     LOTRPT
00263  014030            MOVE DEVELOPER-NUMBER-INPUT TO PREVIOUS-DEVELOPER-NUMBER LOTRPT
00264  014040            PERFORM A001-PROCESS-AND-READ                LOTRPT
00265  014050                 UNTIL THERE-ARE-NO-MORE-RECORDS         LOTRPT
00266  014060            PERFORM B010-PROCESS-TRACT-CHANGE            LOTRPT
00267  014070            PERFORM B020-PROCESS-CITY-CHANGE             LOTRPT
00268  014080            PERFORM B030-PROCESS-DEVELOPER-CHANGE        LOTRPT
00269  014090            PERFORM B040-PRINT-FINAL-TOTALS              LOTRPT
00270  014100       ELSE                                              LOTRPT
00271  014110            WRITE UNSOLD-LOTS-REPORT-LINE FROM NO-RECORDS-MESSAGE LOTRPT
00272  014120                 AFTER ADVANCING TO-TOP-OF-PAGE.         LOTRPT
00273  014130       CLOSE DEVELOPER-INPUT-FILE                        LOTRPT
00274  014140             UNSOLD-LOTS-REPORT-FILE.                    LOTRPT
00275  014150       STOP RUN.                                         LOTRPT
00276  014160                                                         LOTRPT
00277  014170                                                         LOTRPT
00278  014180                                                         LOTRPT
```

Figure 8-31 Source Listing (3 of 5)

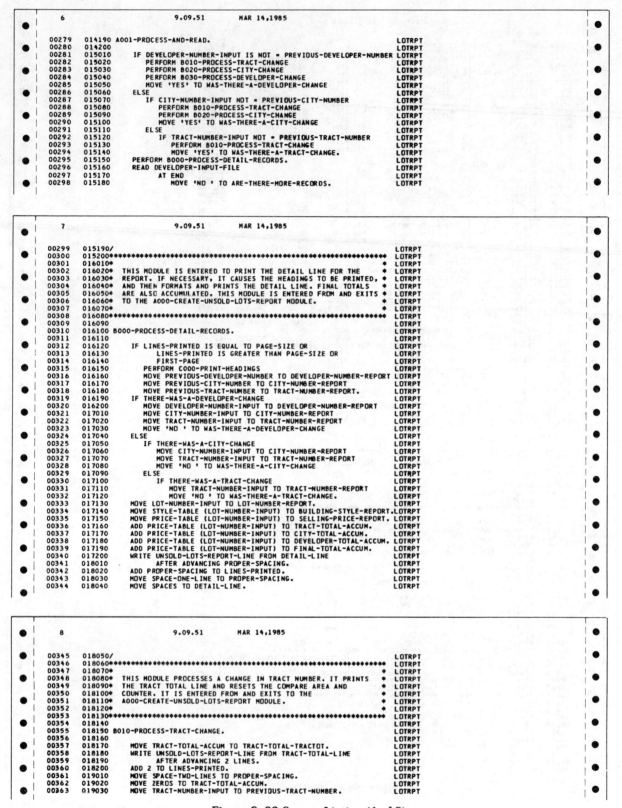

```
     6                    9.09.51     MAR 14,1985

  00279   014190  A001-PROCESS-AND-READ.                                        LOTRPT
  00280   014200                                                               LOTRPT
  00281   015010          IF DEVELOPER-NUMBER-INPUT IS NOT = PREVIOUS-DEVELOPER-NUMBER LOTRPT
  00282   015020              PERFORM B010-PROCESS-TRACT-CHANGE                 LOTRPT
  00283   015030              PERFORM B020-PROCESS-CITY-CHANGE                  LOTRPT
  00284   015040              PERFORM B030-PROCESS-DEVELOPER-CHANGE             LOTRPT
  00285   015050              MOVE 'YES' TO WAS-THERE-A-DEVELOPER-CHANGE        LOTRPT
  00286   015060          ELSE                                                  LOTRPT
  00287   015070              IF CITY-NUMBER-INPUT NOT = PREVIOUS-CITY-NUMBER   LOTRPT
  00288   015080                  PERFORM B010-PROCESS-TRACT-CHANGE            LOTRPT
  00289   015090                  PERFORM B020-PROCESS-CITY-CHANGE             LOTRPT
  00290   015100                  MOVE 'YES' TO WAS-THERE-A-CITY-CHANGE        LOTRPT
  00291   015110              ELSE                                              LOTRPT
  00292   015120                  IF TRACT-NUMBER-INPUT NOT = PREVIOUS-TRACT-NUMBER LOTRPT
  00293   015130                      PERFORM B010-PROCESS-TRACT-CHANGE        LOTRPT
  00294   015140                      MOVE 'YES' TO WAS-THERE-A-TRACT-CHANGE.  LOTRPT
  00295   015150          PERFORM B000-PROCESS-DETAIL-RECORDS.                 LOTRPT
  00296   015160          READ DEVELOPER-INPUT-FILE                            LOTRPT
  00297   015170              AT END                                           LOTRPT
  00298   015180                  MOVE 'NO ' TO ARE-THERE-MORE-RECORDS.        LOTRPT


     7                    9.09.51     MAR 14,1985

  00299   015190/                                                              LOTRPT
  00300   015200************************************************************    LOTRPT
  00301   016010*                                                         *    LOTRPT
  00302   016020*   THIS MODULE IS ENTERED TO PRINT THE DETAIL LINE FOR THE *  LOTRPT
  00303   016030*   REPORT. IF NECESSARY, IT CAUSES THE HEADINGS TO BE PRINTED, * LOTRPT
  00304   016040*   AND THEN FORMATS AND PRINTS THE DETAIL LINE. FINAL TOTALS * LOTRPT
  00305   016050*   ARE ALSO ACCUMULATED. THIS MODULE IS ENTERED FROM AND EXITS * LOTRPT
  00306   016060*   TO THE A000-CREATE-UNSOLD-LOTS-REPORT MODULE.          *    LOTRPT
  00307   016070*                                                         *    LOTRPT
  00308   016080************************************************************    LOTRPT
  00309   016090                                                               LOTRPT
  00310   016100  B000-PROCESS-DETAIL-RECORDS.                                 LOTRPT
  00311   016110                                                               LOTRPT
  00312   016120          IF LINES-PRINTED IS EQUAL TO PAGE-SIZE OR            LOTRPT
  00313   016130              LINES-PRINTED IS GREATER THAN PAGE-SIZE OR       LOTRPT
  00314   016140              FIRST-PAGE                                       LOTRPT
  00315   016150              PERFORM C000-PRINT-HEADINGS                      LOTRPT
  00316   016160              MOVE PREVIOUS-DEVELOPER-NUMBER TO DEVELOPER-NUMBER-REPORT LOTRPT
  00317   016170              MOVE PREVIOUS-CITY-NUMBER TO CITY-NUMBER-REPORT  LOTRPT
  00318   016180              MOVE PREVIOUS-TRACT-NUMBER TO TRACT-NUMBER-REPORT. LOTRPT
  00319   016190          IF THERE-WAS-A-DEVELOPER-CHANGE                      LOTRPT
  00320   016200              MOVE DEVELOPER-NUMBER-INPUT TO DEVELOPER-NUMBER-REPORT LOTRPT
  00321   017010              MOVE CITY-NUMBER-INPUT TO CITY-NUMBER-REPORT     LOTRPT
  00322   017020              MOVE TRACT-NUMBER-INPUT TO TRACT-NUMBER-REPORT   LOTRPT
  00323   017030              MOVE 'NO ' TO WAS-THERE-A-DEVELOPER-CHANGE       LOTRPT
  00324   017040          ELSE                                                 LOTRPT
  00325   017050              IF THERE-WAS-A-CITY-CHANGE                       LOTRPT
  00326   017060                  MOVE CITY-NUMBER-INPUT TO CITY-NUMBER-REPORT LOTRPT
  00327   017070                  MOVE TRACT-NUMBER-INPUT TO TRACT-NUMBER-REPORT LOTRPT
  00328   017080                  MOVE 'NO ' TO WAS-THERE-A-CITY-CHANGE        LOTRPT
  00329   017090              ELSE                                             LOTRPT
  00330   017100                  IF THERE-WAS-A-TRACT-CHANGE                  LOTRPT
  00331   017110                      MOVE TRACT-NUMBER-INPUT TO TRACT-NUMBER-REPORT LOTRPT
  00332   017120                      MOVE 'NO ' TO WAS-THERE-A-TRACT-CHANGE.  LOTRPT
  00333   017130          MOVE LOT-NUMBER-INPUT TO LOT-NUMBER-REPORT.          LOTRPT
  00334   017140          MOVE STYLE-TABLE (LOT-NUMBER-INPUT) TO BUILDING-STYLE-REPORT. LOTRPT
  00335   017150          MOVE PRICE-TABLE (LOT-NUMBER-INPUT) TO SELLING-PRICE-REPORT. LOTRPT
  00336   017160          ADD PRICE-TABLE (LOT-NUMBER-INPUT) TO TRACT-TOTAL-ACCUM. LOTRPT
  00337   017170          ADD PRICE-TABLE (LOT-NUMBER-INPUT) TO CITY-TOTAL-ACCUM. LOTRPT
  00338   017180          ADD PRICE-TABLE (LOT-NUMBER-INPUT) TO DEVELOPER-TOTAL-ACCUM. LOTRPT
  00339   017190          ADD PRICE-TABLE (LOT-NUMBER-INPUT) TO FINAL-TOTAL-ACCUM. LOTRPT
  00340   017200          WRITE UNSOLD-LOTS-REPORT-LINE FROM DETAIL-LINE       LOTRPT
  00341   018010              AFTER ADVANCING PROPER-SPACING.                  LOTRPT
  00342   018020          ADD PROPER-SPACING TO LINES-PRINTED.                 LOTRPT
  00343   018030          MOVE SPACE-ONE-LINE TO PROPER-SPACING.               LOTRPT
  00344   018040          MOVE SPACES TO DETAIL-LINE.                          LOTRPT


     8                    9.09.51     MAR 14,1985

  00345   018050/                                                              LOTRPT
  00346   018060************************************************************    LOTRPT
  00347   018070*                                                         *    LOTRPT
  00348   018080*   THIS MODULE PROCESSES A CHANGE IN TRACT NUMBER. IT PRINTS * LOTRPT
  00349   018090*   THE TRACT TOTAL LINE AND RESETS THE COMPARE AREA AND    * LOTRPT
  00350   018100*   COUNTER. IT IS ENTERED FROM AND EXITS TO THE           *  LOTRPT
  00351   018110*   A000-CREATE-UNSOLD-LOTS-REPORT MODULE.                 *    LOTRPT
  00352   018120*                                                         *    LOTRPT
  00353   018130************************************************************    LOTRPT
  00354   018140                                                               LOTRPT
  00355   018150  B010-PROCESS-TRACT-CHANGE.                                   LOTRPT
  00356   018160                                                               LOTRPT
  00357   018170          MOVE TRACT-TOTAL-ACCUM TO TRACT-TOTAL-TRACTOT.       LOTRPT
  00358   018180          WRITE UNSOLD-LOTS-REPORT-LINE FROM TRACT-TOTAL-LINE  LOTRPT
  00359   018190              AFTER ADVANCING 2 LINES.                         LOTRPT
  00360   018200          ADD 2 TO LINES-PRINTED.                              LOTRPT
  00361   019010          MOVE SPACE-TWO-LINES TO PROPER-SPACING.              LOTRPT
  00362   019020          MOVE ZEROS TO TRACT-TOTAL-ACCUM.                     LOTRPT
  00363   019030          MOVE TRACT-NUMBER-INPUT TO PREVIOUS-TRACT-NUMBER.    LOTRPT
```

Figure 8-32 Source Listing (4 of 5)

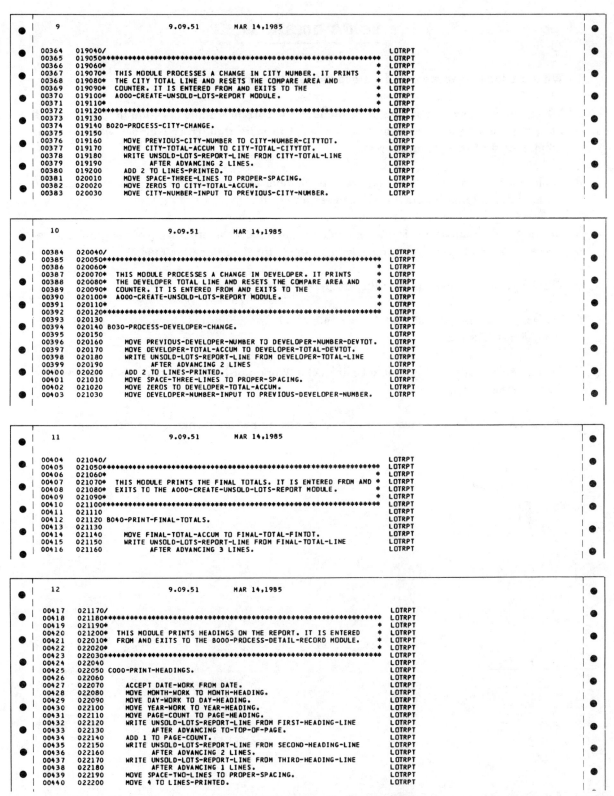

```
   9                9.09.51      MAR 14,1985

00364  019040/                                                              LOTRPT
00365  019050**********************************************************     LOTRPT
00366  019060*                                                         *    LOTRPT
00367  019070*  THIS MODULE PROCESSES A CHANGE IN CITY NUMBER. IT PRINTS *  LOTRPT
00368  019080*  THE CITY TOTAL LINE AND RESETS THE COMPARE AREA AND      *  LOTRPT
00369  019090*  COUNTER. IT IS ENTERED FROM AND EXITS TO THE             *  LOTRPT
00370  019100*  A000-CREATE-UNSOLD-LOTS-REPORT MODULE.                   *  LOTRPT
00371  019110*                                                         *    LOTRPT
00372  019120**********************************************************     LOTRPT
00373  019130  B020-PROCESS-CITY-CHANGE.                                    LOTRPT
00374  019140                                                               LOTRPT
00375  019150                                                               LOTRPT
00376  019160      MOVE PREVIOUS-CITY-NUMBER TO CITY-NUMBER-CITYTOT.         LOTRPT
00377  019170      MOVE CITY-TOTAL-ACCUM TO CITY-TOTAL-CITYTOT.              LOTRPT
00378  019180      WRITE UNSOLD-LOTS-REPORT-LINE FROM CITY-TOTAL-LINE        LOTRPT
00379  019190          AFTER ADVANCING 2 LINES.                             LOTRPT
00380  019200      ADD 2 TO LINES-PRINTED.                                  LOTRPT
00381  020010      MOVE SPACE-THREE-LINES TO PROPER-SPACING.                LOTRPT
00382  020020      MOVE ZEROS TO CITY-TOTAL-ACCUM.                          LOTRPT
00383  020030      MOVE CITY-NUMBER-INPUT TO PREVIOUS-CITY-NUMBER.          LOTRPT
```

```
   10               9.09.51      MAR 14,1985

00384  020040/                                                              LOTRPT
00385  020050**********************************************************     LOTRPT
00386  020060*                                                         *    LOTRPT
00387  020070*  THIS MODULE PROCESSES A CHANGE IN DEVELOPER. IT PRINTS  *   LOTRPT
00388  020080*  THE DEVELOPER TOTAL LINE AND RESETS THE COMPARE AREA AND*   LOTRPT
00389  020090*  COUNTER. IT IS ENTERED FROM AND EXITS TO THE            *   LOTRPT
00390  020100*  A000-CREATE-UNSOLD-LOTS-REPORT MODULE.                  *   LOTRPT
00391  020110*                                                         *    LOTRPT
00392  020120**********************************************************     LOTRPT
00393  020130                                                               LOTRPT
00394  020140  B030-PROCESS-DEVELOPER-CHANGE.                               LOTRPT
00395  020150                                                               LOTRPT
00396  020160      MOVE PREVIOUS-DEVELOPER-NUMBER TO DEVELOPER-NUMBER-DEVTOT.LOTRPT
00397  020170      MOVE DEVELOPER-TOTAL-ACCUM TO DEVELOPER-TOTAL-DEVTOT.     LOTRPT
00398  020180      WRITE UNSOLD-LOTS-REPORT-LINE FROM DEVELOPER-TOTAL-LINE   LOTRPT
00399  020190          AFTER ADVANCING 2 LINES                              LOTRPT
00400  020200      ADD 2 TO LINES-PRINTED.                                  LOTRPT
00401  021010      MOVE SPACE-THREE-LINES TO PROPER-SPACING.                LOTRPT
00402  021020      MOVE ZEROS TO DEVELOPER-TOTAL-ACCUM.                     LOTRPT
00403  021030      MOVE DEVELOPER-NUMBER-INPUT TO PREVIOUS-DEVELOPER-NUMBER. LOTRPT
```

```
   11               9.09.51      MAR 14,1985

00404  021040/                                                              LOTRPT
00405  021050**********************************************************     LOTRPT
00406  021060*                                                         *    LOTRPT
00407  021070*  THIS MODULE PRINTS THE FINAL TOTALS. IT IS ENTERED FROM AND*LOTRPT
00408  021080*  EXITS TO THE A000-CREATE-UNSOLD-LOTS-REPORT MODULE.     *   LOTRPT
00409  021090*                                                         *    LOTRPT
00410  021100**********************************************************     LOTRPT
00411  021110                                                               LOTRPT
00412  021120  B040-PRINT-FINAL-TOTALS.                                     LOTRPT
00413  021130                                                               LOTRPT
00414  021140      MOVE FINAL-TOTAL-ACCUM TO FINAL-TOTAL-FINTOT.            LOTRPT
00415  021150      WRITE UNSOLD-LOTS-REPORT-LINE FROM FINAL-TOTAL-LINE      LOTRPT
00416  021160          AFTER ADVANCING 3 LINES.                             LOTRPT
```

```
   12               9.09.51      MAR 14,1985

00417  021170/                                                              LOTRPT
00418  021180**********************************************************     LOTRPT
00419  021190*                                                         *    LOTRPT
00420  021200*  THIS MODULE PRINTS HEADINGS ON THE REPORT. IT IS ENTERED*   LOTRPT
00421  022010*  FROM AND EXITS TO THE B000-PROCESS-DETAIL-RECORD MODULE.*   LOTRPT
00422  022020*                                                         *    LOTRPT
00423  022030**********************************************************     LOTRPT
00424  022040                                                               LOTRPT
00425  022050  C000-PRINT-HEADINGS.                                         LOTRPT
00426  022060                                                               LOTRPT
00427  022070      ACCEPT DATE-WORK FROM DATE.                              LOTRPT
00428  022080      MOVE MONTH-WORK TO MONTH-HEADING.                        LOTRPT
00429  022090      MOVE DAY-WORK TO DAY-HEADING.                            LOTRPT
00430  022100      MOVE YEAR-WORK TO YEAR-HEADING.                          LOTRPT
00431  022110      MOVE PAGE-COUNT TO PAGE-HEADING.                         LOTRPT
00432  022120      WRITE UNSOLD-LOTS-REPORT-LINE FROM FIRST-HEADING-LINE    LOTRPT
00433  022130          AFTER ADVANCING TO-TOP-OF-PAGE.                      LOTRPT
00434  022140      ADD 1 TO PAGE-COUNT.                                     LOTRPT
00435  022150      WRITE UNSOLD-LOTS-REPORT-LINE FROM SECOND-HEADING-LINE   LOTRPT
00436  022160          AFTER ADVANCING 2 LINES.                             LOTRPT
00437  022170      WRITE UNSOLD-LOTS-REPORT-LINE FROM THIRD-HEADING-LINE    LOTRPT
00438  022180          AFTER ADVANCING 1 LINES.                             LOTRPT
00439  022190      MOVE SPACE-TWO-LINES TO PROPER-SPACING.                  LOTRPT
00440  022200      MOVE 4 TO LINES-PRINTED.                                 LOTRPT
```

Figure 8-33 Source Listing (5 of 5)

REVIEW QUESTIONS

1. What are the characteristics of a group indicated report?

2. What modifications would have to be made to the current sample program in this chapter if the programming specifications were changed to state that Tract Number was not to be group indicated on subsequent reports?

3. Explain the difference between an Old City Number and a New City Number as it relates to the sample program on the IPO Chart in Figure 8-10.

4. How is the determination of which module should handle the processing of the group indication made? Upon what program design concept is the determination made?

5. What is the role of indicators in the sample program?

6. Tables can be defined that contain elements which are subdivided into numeric and alphanumeric fields. Explain.

7. Explain how the detail line should be defined in Working-Storage when group indication is to occur on the report.

8. Explain how the Value Clause is used to clear the output area when group indicating.

COBOL CODING EXERCISES

1. A COBOL program is to be prepared that will contain three control breaks based upon a change in Hospital Number, Doctor Number, and Room Number. The format of the input records in the disk file for the problem is as follows: Hospital Number, positions 1 - 4; Doctor Number, positions 5 - 8; Room Number, positions 9 - 12; Patient Name, positions 13 - 32; and Hospital Bill, positions 33 - 38. Hospital Number, Doctor Number, Room Number, and Hospital Bill should be defined as numeric fields. The Hospital Bill field contains dollars and cents. Write the COBOL code to define the Hospital Input File and the associated input area for this problem.

2. The format of the detail line to be printed on the printer for the program specified in problem # 1 above is as follows: Hospital Number, positions 2 - 5; Doctor Number, positions 11 - 14; Room Number, positions 20 - 23; Patient Name, positions 29 - 48; Hospital Bill, positions 54 - 62. The Hospital Number, Doctor Number, and Room Number fields should all be edited using the Picture clause PIC ZZZ9. The Hospital Bill field should have PIC $Z,ZZZ.99 as its Picture clause. Write the COBOL code required to define the detail line in the Working-Storage Section of the Data Division.

3. Write the COBOL Write statement required to write a line on the printer using the detail line designed in problem #2 and the file output area HOSPITAL-REPORT-LINE.

4. Write the COBOL code required in the Working-Storage Section to define the program indicators needed for the three control breaks described in problems #1 and #2 above, assuming the three fields, Hospital Number, Doctor Number, and Patient Number, are to be group indicated on the report.

5. Write the COBOL code required in the Working-Storage Section to define the compare areas needed for the three control breaks described in problems #1 and #2 above.

6. Write the COBOL code required in the Working-Storage Section to define a table containing the following data:

CITY	AVERAGE YEARLY TEMPERATURE
ATLANTA	67
BOSTON	55
CLEVELAND	51
DES MOINES	59
FORT LAUDERDALE	70
SAN FRANCISCO	52
TEMPE	71

7. Write the COBOL Move statement required to move the City Name from the table defined in problem #6 above to the field CITY-NAME-REPORT. Use the WEATHER-CODE-INPUT field as a subscript.

8. Write the COBOL Move statement required to move the Average Yearly Temperature from the table defined in problem #6 above to the field AVERAGE-TEMPERATURE-REPORT. Use the WEATHER-CODE-INPUT field as a subscript.

STRUCTURED WALKTHROUGH EXERCISES

The following portions of COBOL code contain one or more errors in program logic, in the use of the COBOL language itself, or in the programming standards which should be followed. Review the code in each exercise in the same manner used for structured walkthroughs. Identify the errors and make the appropriate corrections.

1.

```
004010 FD  BUDGET-REPORT-FILE
004020         RECORD CONTAINS 132 CHARACTERS
004030         DATA RECORD IS BUDGET-REPORT-LINE
004040         LABEL RECORDS ARE STANDARD.
004050 01  BUDGET-REPORT-LINE                PIC X(133).

006030 01  DETAIL-LINE.
006040     05  FILLER                        PIC X(4).
006050     05  STORE-NUMBER-DETAIL           PIC ZZX.
006060     05  FILLER                        PIC X(9).
006070     05  BUILDING-NUMBER-DETAIL        PIC Z9.
006080     05  FILLER                        PIC X(10).
006090     05  ACCOUNT-NUMBER-DETAIL         PIC ZZZ9.
006100     05  FILLER                        PIC X(8).
006110     05  ACCOUNT-ENTRY-DETAIL          PIC ZZ,ZZ9.
006120     05  FILLER                        PIC X(75).

012070     WRITE DETAIL-LINE FROM BUDGET-REPORT-LINE
012080         AFTER ADVANCING PROPER-SPACING.
012090     ADD PROPER-SPACING TO LINES-PRINTED.
012100     MOVE SPACE-ONE-LINE TO PROPER-SPACING.
012110     MOVE SPACES TO BUDGET-REPORT-LINE.
```

2.

```
007020 01  PROGRAM-TABLES.
007030     10  MILEAGE-TABLE.
007040         10  CITY-MILES-CONSTANTS.
007050             15  FILLER            PIC X(11)  VALUE 'ANAHEIM   12.
007060             15  FILLER            PIC X(11)  VALUE 'RIVERSIDE07.
007070             15  FILLER            PIC X(11)  VALUE 'FULLERTON05.
007080             15  FILLER            PIC X(11)  VALUE 'LA HABRA 03.
007090             15  FILLER            PIC X(11)  VALUE 'WHITTIER 04.
007100             15  FILLER            PIC X(11)  VALUE 'IRVINE   35.
007110         15  MILEAGE-CONSTANT-TABLE DEFINES CITY-MILES-CONSTANTS
007120             OCCURS 7 TIMES.
007130             20  CITY-TABLE        PIC X(10).
007140             20  MILES-TABLE       PIC Z9.
```

3.

```
011010  A000-CREATE-REPORT.

011050      IF  THERE-ARE-NO-RECORDS
011060          MOVE  STORE-NUMBER-INPUT  TO  STORE-NUMBER-REPORT
011070          MOVE  BUILDING-NUMBER-INPUT  TO  BUILDING-NUMBER-REPORT
011080          MOVE  ACCOUNT-NUMBER-INPUT  TO  ACCOUNT-NUMBER-REPORT
011090      PERFORM  A001-PROCESS-AND-READ
011100          UNTIL  THERE-ARE-NO-MORE-RECORDS
011110      PERFORM  B030-PROCESS-STORE-CHANGE
011120      PERFORM  B020-PROCESS-BUILDING-CHANGE
011130      PERFORM  B010-PROCESS-ACCOUNT-CHANGE
011140      PERFORM  B040-PRINT-FINAL-TOTALS.

012030  A001-PROCESS-AND-READ.
012040
012050      IF  STORE-NUMBER-INPUT  =  PREVIOUS-STORE-NUMBER
012060          PERFORM  B010-PROCESS-ACCOUNT-CHANGE
012070          PERFORM  B030-PROCESS-STORE-CHANGE
012080      ELSE
012090      IF  BUILDING-NUMBER-INPUT  =  PREVIOUS-BUILDING-NUMBER
012100          PERFORM  B010-PROCESS-ACCOUNT-CHANGE
012110          PERFORM  B020-PROCESS-BUILDING-CHANGE
012120      ELSE
012130          IF  ACCOUNT-NUMBER-INPUT  =  PREVIOUS-ACCOUNT-NUMBER            .
012140              PERFORM  B010-PROCESS-ACCOUNT-CHANGE.
012150      B000-PROCESS-DETAIL-RECORDS.

015010  B000-PROCESS-DETAIL-RECORDS.

015180      IF  THERE-WAS-A-STORE-CHANGE
015190          MOVE  STORE-NUMBER-INPUT  TO  STORE-NUMBER-REPORT
015200          MOVE  BUILDING-NUMBER-INPUT  TO  BUILDING-NUMBER-REPORT
016010          MOVE  ACCOUNT-NUMBER-INPUT  TO  ACCOUNT-NUMBER-REPORT
016020      ELSE
016030      IF  THERE-WAS-A-BUILDING-CHANGE
016040          MOVE  BUILDING-NUMBER-INPUT  TO  BUILDING-NUMBER-REPORT
016050          MOVE  ACCOUNT-NUMBER-INPUT  TO  TRACT-NUMBER-REPORT
016060      ELSE
016070      IF  THERE-WAS-AN-ACCOUNT-CHANGE
016080          MOVE  ACCOUNT-NUMBER-INPUT  TO  ACCOUNT-NUMBER-REPORT.
```

PROGRAMMING ASSIGNMENT 1

INSTRUCTIONS

A Proposed Bond Issues Report is to be prepared. Design and write the COBOL program to produce the required report. An IPO Chart and Pseudocode Specifications should be used when designing the program. Use Test Data Set 1 in Appendix A.

INPUT

Input consists of Bond Issue Records that contain District Number, County Number, City Number, and Account Number. The input records have been sorted in ascending sequence by City Number within County Number within District Number prior to processing. All input records contain valid data. The format of the input record is illustrated below.

Bond Issue Disk Record				
FIELD DESCRIPTION	POSITION	LENGTH	DEC	ATTRIBUTE
District Number	1 – 2	2	0	Numeric
County Number	3 – 4	2	0	Numeric
City Number	5 – 6	2	0	Numeric
UNUSED	7 – 50	44		Alphanumeric
Account Number	51	1	0	Numeric
UNUSED	52 – 61	10		Alphanumeric
Record Length		61		

OUTPUT

Output consists of a Proposed Bond Issues Report containing the District Number, County Number, City Number, Account Number, Account Name, and Bond Amount. When there is a change in City Number, the total bond amount for that city is to be printed. When there is a change in County Number, the total bond amounts for County and City are to be printed. When there is a change in District Number, the total bond amounts for the City, County, and District are to be printed. The report is group indicated. After all records have been processed, a final total is to be printed. The printer spacing chart for the report is illustrated on the following page.

PRINTER SPACING CHART

```
 1  
 2  MM/DD/YY              PROPOSED BOND ISSUES                    PAGE ZZ9
 3  
 4  DISTRICT    COUNTY      CITY      ACCOUNT          ACCOUNT         BOND
 5  NUMBER      NUMBER      NUMBER    NUMBER           NAME            AMOUNT
 6  
 7    Z9          Z9          Z9         9   XXXXXXXXXXXXXXXXXXXX       ZZZ,ZZ9
 8                                      9   XXXXXXXXXXXXXXXXXXXX       ZZZ,ZZ9
 9  
10                                           CITY Z9 TOTAL       Z,ZZZ,ZZ9*
11  
12                          Z9         9   XXXXXXXXXXXXXXXXXXXX       ZZZ,ZZ9
13  
14                                           CITY Z9 TOTAL       Z,ZZZ,ZZ9*
15  
16                                         COUNTY Z9 TOTAL       Z,ZZZ,ZZ9**
17  
18              Z9          Z9         9   XXXXXXXXXXXXXXXXXXXX       ZZZ,ZZ9
19  
20                                           CITY Z9 TOTAL       Z,ZZZ,ZZ9*
21  
22                                         COUNTY Z9 TOTAL       Z,ZZZ,ZZ9**
23  
24                                        DISTRICT Z9 TOTAL      Z,ZZZ,ZZ9***
25  
26  
27    Z9          Z9          Z9         9   XXXXXXXXXXXXXXXXXXXX       ZZZ,ZZ9
28  
29                                           CITY Z9 TOTAL       Z,ZZZ,ZZ9*
30  
31                                         COUNTY Z9 TOTAL       Z,ZZZ,ZZ9**
32  
33                                        DISTRICT Z9 TOTAL      Z,ZZZ,ZZ9***
34  
35  
36                                           FINAL TOTAL       $$,$$$,$$9
```

TABLE PROCESSING

The Account Name and Bond Amount printed on the report are to be extracted from the following table, based upon the Account Number in the input record. The Account Name is a maximum of 20 alphanumeric characters, and the Bond Amount is six numeric digits in length.

		ACCOUNT NAME	BOND AMOUNT
ACCOUNT NUMBER	(1)	HIGHWAY CONSTRUCTION	300000
	(2)	PARKS & RECREATION	270000
	(3)	MENTAL HEALTH	150000
	(4)	SECONDARY SCHOOLS	450000
	(5)	COLLEGE & UNIVERSITY	325000
	(6)	POLICE - FIRE	450000

PROGRAMMING ASSIGNMENT 2

INSTRUCTIONS

A Sales Report is to be prepared. Design and write the COBOL program to produce the required report. An IPO Chart and Pseudocode Specifications should be used when designing the program. Use Test Data Set 2 in Appendix A.

INPUT

Input consists of Salesperson Records that contain the Date in MMDDYY format, the Store Number, Department Number, Salesperson Number, Salesperson Name, Sales Code, and Sales Amount. The input records have been sorted in ascending sequence by Department Number within Store Number within Date. All input records contain valid data. The format of the input record is illustrated below.

Salesperson Disk Record				
FIELD DESCRIPTION	**POSITION**	**LENGTH**	**DEC**	**ATTRIBUTE**
Date	1 – 6	6		Alphanumeric
Store Number	7 – 8	2	0	Numeric
Department Number	9 – 10	2	0	Numeric
Salesperson Number	11 – 12	2	0	Numeric
Salesperson Name	13 – 32	20		Alphanumeric
UNUSED	33 – 52	20		
Sales Code	53	1	0	Numeric
UNUSED	54 – 60	7		Alphanumeric
Sales Amount	61 – 66	6	2	Numeric
UNUSED	67	1		Alphanumeric
Record Length		67		

OUTPUT

Output consists of a Sales Report containing Date, Store Number, Department Number, Salesperson Number, Salesperson Name, Sales Amount, and a Sales Message. When there is a change in Department Number, the total sales for the department are printed. When there is a change in Store Number, the total sales for the department and the total sales for the store are printed. When there is a change in Date, the total sales for the department, store, and date are printed. After all records are processed, the total salespeople below range, the total salespeople above range, and the total sales for all dates are printed. The report is group indicated. The printer spacing chart is illustrated on the following page.

PRINTER SPACING CHART

```
 2  MM/DD/YY                                      SALES REPORT                                    PAGE ZZ9
 4          STORE     DEPART.   SALESPERSON        SALESPERSON              SALES
 5  DATE    NUMBER    NUMBER    NUMBER               NAME                   AMOUNT
 7  MM/DD/YY   Z9        Z9         Z9     XXXXXXXXXXXXXXXXXXXXX   Z,ZZZ.99   Z,ZZZ.99 BELOW RANGE
 8                                 Z9     XXXXXXXXXXXXXXXXXXXXX   Z,ZZZ.99   Z,ZZZ.99 ABOVE RANGE
10                                        DEPARTMENT Z9 TOTAL    ZZ,ZZZ.99
12                      Z9         Z9     XXXXXXXXXXXXXXXXXXXXX   Z,ZZZ.99
13                                 Z9     XXXXXXXXXXXXXXXXXXXXX   Z,ZZZ.99
15                                        DEPARTMENT Z9 TOTAL    ZZ,ZZZ.99
17                                          STORE Z9 TOTAL       ZZ,ZZZ.99
19            Z9        Z9         Z9     XXXXXXXXXXXXXXXXXXXXX   Z,ZZZ.99
21                                        DEPARTMENT Z9 TOTAL    ZZ,ZZZ.99
23                                          STORE Z9 TOTAL       ZZ,ZZZ.99
25                                        DATE MM/DD/YY TOTAL    ZZZ,ZZZ.99
28  MM/DD/YY   Z9        Z9         Z9     XXXXXXXXXXXXXXXXXXXXX   Z,ZZZ.99
30                                        DEPARTMENT Z9 TOTAL    ZZ,ZZZ.99
32                                          STORE Z9 TOTAL       ZZ,ZZZ.99
34                                        DATE MM/DD/YY TOTAL    ZZZ,ZZZ.99
37  TOTAL SALESPEOPLE BELOW RANGE       ZZ9
38  TOTAL SALESPEOPLE ABOVE RANGE       ZZ9
39  FINAL SALES AMOUNT TOTAL          ZZZ,ZZZ.99
```

TABLE PROCESSING

The Sales Amount of each salesperson is expected to fall within a range of acceptable sales amounts as obtained by the Lower Sales Limit and Upper Sales Limit in the table below. The messages BELOW RANGE and ABOVE RANGE are printed on the report based upon the salesperson's sales amount and the Lower Sales Limit and Upper Sales Limit amounts extracted from the table based upon the Sales Code in the input record. If the salesperson's sales amount is less than the Lower Sales Limit extracted from the table based upon the value in the Sales Code in the input record, then the message BELOW RANGE and the amount below the Lower Sales Limit is printed on the report. If the salesperson's sales amount is greater than the Upper Sales Limit extracted from the table, then the message ABOVE RANGE and the amount above the Upper Sales Limit is printed on the report. If the salesperson's sales amount falls within the range of acceptable sales amounts, then no message is printed on the report.

		LOWER SALES LIMIT	HIGHER SALES LIMIT
	(1)	400.00	1300.00
SALES	(2)	500.00	3500.00
CODE	(3)	300.00	4000.00
	(4)	400.00	4000.00

PROGRAMMING ASSIGNMENT 3

INSTRUCTIONS

A Test Results Report is to be prepared. Write the COBOL program to prepare this report. An IPO Chart and Pseudocode Specifications should be used when designing the program. Use Test Data Set 3 in Appendix A.

INPUT

Input consists of Test Records that contain School Number, Test Type, Test Date (MMDDYY format), and Test Score. The input records have been sorted in ascending sequence by Test Type within School Number. All records contain valid data. The format of the input record is illustrated below.

Test Disk Record				
FIELD DESCRIPTION	POSITION	LENGTH	DEC	ATTRIBUTE
School Number	1 – 4	4	0	Numeric
Test Type	5	1	0	Numeric
UNUSED	6 – 10	5		Alphanumeric
Test Date	11 – 16	6		Alphanumeric
UNUSED	17 – 61	45		Alphanumeric
Test Score	62 – 64	3	0	Numeric
Record Length		64		

OUTPUT

Output consists of a Test Results Report containing School Number, Test Name, Test Date, and Test Score. The Test Name on the report is extracted from a table based upon the value in the Test Type field in the input record.

When there is a change in Test Type in the input record, the Test Name and the Standard Score (extracted from a table based upon Test Type) are printed, and scores for that test type are to be divided by the number of tests in the group to determine the average score of that test type. When there is a change in school, the processing occurring when there is a change in test type must take place; and then the scores of all tests in that school are to be divided by the number of tests taken in that school to determine the average score of all tests taken in that school.

If the score recorded in the input record is greater than 950 or less than 300, the message ** SCORE NOT IN RANGE ** is to be printed on the report, and these scores are not to be included when computing the average score.

The table that contains the Test Name and Standard Score is illustrated on the next page.

	TEST NAME	STANDARD SCORE
(1)	MATH	467
(2)	PHYSICS	601
(3)	READING	613
TEST (4)	WRITING	763
TYPE (5)	CHEMISTRY	594
(6)	GEOLOGY	735
(7)	SPEECH	852
(8)	GEOGRAPHY	613
(9)	HISTORY	700

The School Number and Test Name are group indicated on the report. After all records have been processed, the total number of tests taken and the average score for all tests are to be printed.

The printer spacing chart is illustrated below.

PRINTER SPACING CHART

```
 1 
 2 MM/DD/YY                        TEST RESULTS                    PAGE ZZ9
 3 
 4 SCHOOL        TEST          TEST           TEST
 5 NUMBER        NAME          DATE           SCORE
 6 
 7 ZZZ9      XXXXXXXXX     MM/DD/YY        ZZ9
 8                        MM/DD/YY        ZZ9
 9                        MM/DD/YY        ZZ9   ** SCORE NOT IN RANGE **
10                        MM/DD/YY        ZZ9
11 
12       XXXXXXXXX TEST - STANDARD SCORE ZZ9
13                        AVERAGE SCORE ZZ9
14 
15           XXXXXXXXX     MM/DD/YY        ZZ9
16                        MM/DD/YY        ZZ9
17 
18      XXXXXXXXX TEST - STANDARD SCORE ZZ9
19                        AVERAGE SCORE ZZ9
20 
21          SCHOOL ZZZ9 - AVERAGE SCORE ZZ9
22 
23 
24 ZZZ9      XXXXXXXXX     MM/DD/YY        ZZ9
25 
26       XXXXXXXXX TEST - STANDARD SCORE ZZ9
27                        AVERAGE SCORE ZZ9
28 
29          SCHOOL ZZZ9 - AVERAGE SCORE ZZ9
30 
31 
32       TOTAL TESTS ZZ9 - AVERAGE SCORE ZZ9
33 
```

PROGRAMMING ASSIGNMENT 4

INSTRUCTIONS

An Automotive Profit Report is to be prepared. Write the COBOL program to prepare this report. The IPO Chart and Pseudocode Specifications should be used when designing the program. Use Test Data Set 4 in Appendix A.

INPUT

Input consists of Automotive Records that contain Division Number, Plant Number, Car Number, and Quantity Produced. The input records have been sorted in ascending sequence by Plant Number within Division Number. All input records contain valid data. The format of the input record is illustrated below.

Automotive Disk Record				
FIELD DESCRIPTION	POSITION	LENGTH	DEC	ATTRIBUTE
UNUSED	1 – 2	2		Alphanumeric
Division Number	3 – 5	3	0	Numeric
Plant Number	6 – 7	2	0	Numeric
Car Number	8 – 9	2	0	Numeric
UNUSED	10 – 11	2		Alphanumeric
Quantity Produced	12 – 13	2	0	Numeric
UNUSED	14 – 73	60		Alphanumeric
Record Length		73		

OUTPUT

Output consists of an Automotive Profit Report containing Division Name, Plant Name, Car Name, Factory Cost, Sticker Price, Quantity Produced, and Potential Profit. The Division Name and the Plant Name on the report are extracted from tables based upon the Division Number and the Plant Number, respectively, in the input record. The Car Name, Factory Cost, and Sticker Price on the report are extracted from a table based upon the Car Number in the input record.

When there is a change in Plant Number in the input record, the Plant Name is to be printed together with the total quantity produced and total potential profit for that plant. When there is a change in Division Number in the input record, the processing occurring when there is a change in plant number must take place; and then the Division Name is to be printed together with the total quantity produced and the total potential profit for that division.

The necessary tables are illustrated on the following page.

	DIVISION NAME
DIVISION NUMBER 050	EAST COAST
100	WEST COAST

	PLANT NAME
10	ELKS GLENN
20	GRAND BEND
PLANT NUMBER 30	CLEVELAND
40	TRAVERSE
50	STERLING
60	YPSILANTI

	CAR NAME	FACTORY COST	STICKER PRICE
(1)	ELEPHANT	6789.34	7805.00
(2)	ROVER	7928.89	9100.00
CAR (3)	PANTHER	3939.44	4590.00
NUMBER (4)	COBRA	8900.34	9899.00
(5)	FASTBACK	7893.28	9070.00
(6)	CLIMBER	6834.93	8760.00

The Division Name and Plant Name are to be group indicated on the report. Potential profit is calculated by subtracting the Factory Cost from the Sticker Price and multiplying the result by the Quantity Produced.

After all records have been processed, the total quantity produced and the total potential profit for all divisions are to be printed.

The printer spacing chart is illustrated on the following page.

PRINTER SPACING CHART

	DIVISION NAME	PLANT NAME	CAR NAME	FACTORY COST	STICKER PRICE	QUANTITY PRODUCED	POTENTIAL PROFIT
2	MM/DD/YY		AUTOMOTIVE PROFIT REPORT				PAGE ZZ9
7	XXXXXXXXXX	XXXXXXXXXX	XXXXXXXX	Z,ZZ9.99	Z,ZZ9.99	Z9	ZZ,ZZ9.99
8			XXXXXXXX	Z,ZZ9.99	Z,ZZ9.99	Z9	ZZ,ZZ9.99
10		TOTALS FOR PLANT XXXXXXXXX -				ZZ9	ZZZ,ZZ9.99*
12		XXXXXXXXXX	XXXXXXXX	Z,ZZ9.99	Z,ZZ9.99	Z9	ZZ,ZZ9.99
13			XXXXXXXX	Z,ZZ9.99	Z,ZZ9.99	Z9	ZZ,ZZ9.99
15		TOTALS FOR PLANT XXXXXXXXX -				ZZ9	ZZZ,ZZ9.99*
17		TOTALS FOR DIVISION XXXXXXXXX -				Z,ZZ9	Z,ZZZ,ZZ9.99**
19	XXXXXXXXXX	XXXXXXXXXX	XXXXXXXX	Z,ZZ9.99	Z,ZZ9.99	Z9	ZZ,ZZ9.99
20			XXXXXXXX	Z,ZZ9.99	Z,ZZ9.99	Z9	ZZ,ZZ9.99
22		TOTALS FOR PLANT XXXXXXXXX -				ZZ9	ZZZ,ZZ9.99*
24		TOTALS FOR DIVISION XXXXXXXXX -				Z,ZZ9	Z,ZZZ,ZZ9.99**
26		FINAL TOTALS -				ZZ,ZZ9	ZZ,ZZZ,ZZ9.99***

CHAPTER NINE

TABLE SEARCHING; MULTIPLE LEVEL TABLES

TABLE SEARCHING; MULTIPLE LEVEL TABLES

9

INTRODUCTION

In Chapter 7, the concept of storing related items of data in a table and extracting data from the table was introduced. The table illustrated in Chapter 7 contained alphanumeric elements, the months from JANUARY to DECEMBER. The subscript used to reference and extract elements from the table was a number from 1 to 12. In this application, there was a direct relationship between the value in the subscript and the element which was to be extracted from the table. For example, the subscript 1 referenced the first element of the table (JANUARY), the subscript 2 referenced the second element in the table (FEBRUARY), and so on.

In Chapter 8, a table was defined which contained two entries for each element. The table contained both alphanumeric data (building style) and numeric data (selling price). The subscript to reference and extract these elements was a lot number that ranged from the value 1 to the value 15. Again, there was a direct relationship between the value in the subscript and the element which was to be extracted from the table. The subscript 1 referenced the first element of the table, which was the first building style and the first selling price.

In many applications, there is not a direct relationship between the subscript used to reference an element within a table and the actual element within the table. When this type of problem occurs, a procedure called table searching is commonly used. This chapter will illustrate the technique of table searching.

In addition, both the tables used thus far were one dimensional tables, meaning that each element within the table was identified by a single subscript. In some applications it is necessary to process multiple level tables, which are tables where multiple subscripts are required to locate a specific element within the table. This chapter will demonstrate the technique for processing multiple level tables.

In order to illustrate table searching and multiple level tables, a sample program is illustrated in this chapter which prepares a Faculty Salary Report from a file of Faculty Disk Records. The format of the input data and a sample of the report are illustrated in Figure 9-1.

Faculty Disk Record				
FIELD DESCRIPTION	**POSITION**	**LENGTH**	**DEC**	**ATTRIBUTE**
Faculty Number	1 – 4	4	0	Numeric
Faculty Name	5 – 24	20		Alphanumeric
Education Code	25	1	0	Numeric
Salary Grade	26	1	0	Numeric
Record Length		26		

Figure 9-1 Input Record Format (Part 1 of 2)

```
04/02/85                    FACULTY SALARY REPORT                    PAGE   1

FACULTY      FACULTY         DEPARTMENT        SALARY    EDUCATION    FACULTY
NUMBER       NAME            NAME              GRADE     LEVEL        SALARY

 0323     RAYMOND PETERS     DATA PROCESSING     3       MASTERS      $19,911.00
 0731     MARTHA GOODIN      MATHEMATICS         2       BACHELOR     $17,461.00
 1042     MICHAEL LORD       OFFICE EDUCATION    4       DOCTORATE    $25,252.00
 1154     JERRY LEICHTY      **** UNKNOWN ****   2       DOCTORATE    $23,231.00
 1567     CLAUDIA COLLINS    CULINARY ARTS       4       BACHELOR     $19,479.00
 2088     EDWARD LANDLESS    SOCIAL SCIENCE      1       MASTERS      $17,893.00


FINAL TOTALS:

TOTAL SALARY      $123,227.00
AVERAGE SALARY     $20,537.83
```

Figure 9-1 Faculty Salary Report (Part 2 of 2)

In Figure 9-1, the input record contains the Faculty Number, Faculty Name, Education Code, and Salary Grade. The first two digits of the Faculty Number are the Department Number.

The Faculty Salary Report contains the Faculty Number, Faculty Name, Department Name, Salary Grade, Education Level, and Faculty Salary. The Department Name is extracted from a table based upon the first two digits of the Faculty Number (Department Number). The Education Level that appears on the report is extracted from a table based upon the Education Code in the input record. The Faculty Salary is extracted from a table based upon the Education Code and the Salary Grade fields in the input record.

After all records have been processed, a final total of the faculty salary is printed, and the average salary of all faculty is calculated and printed. The average faculty salary is obtained by accumulating the faculty salaries and dividing the total by the number of faculty members processed.

TABLES

In the sample program in this chapter, three tables are needed. The first one, the Education Table, is similar to the tables in previous chapters. Figure 9-2 illustrates the use of the Education Table.

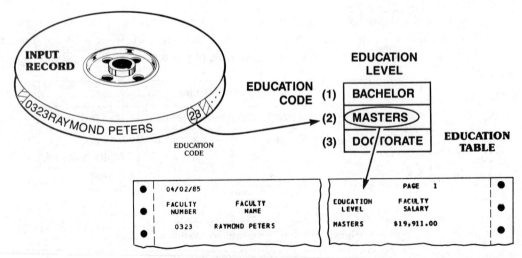

Figure 9-2 Education Table

The subscript used to extract the correct education level from the table is the Education Code found in the input record. The input record in Figure 9-2 contains the value 2 in the Education Code field. This value indicates which education level is to be extracted from the table (MASTERS) and printed on the report.

The values 1 through 3 in the Education Code field are valid values to extract the corresponding education level from the Education Table. The Education Table is a table with a direct relationship between the value in the subscript (Education Code) and the element which is extracted from the table (Education Level).

Figure 9-3 shows the definition of the Education Table as it appears in the Working-Storage Section of the Data Division.

```
007030        05  EDUCATION-LEVEL-TABLE.
007040            10  EDUCATION-LEVEL-CONSTANTS.
007050                15  FILLER          PIC X(9)    VALUE 'BACHELOR '.
007060                15  FILLER          PIC X(9)    VALUE 'MASTERS  '.
007070                15  FILLER          PIC X(9)    VALUE 'DOCTORATE'.
007080            10  EDUCATION-TABLE REDEFINES
007090                EDUCATION-LEVEL-CONSTANTS
007100                                    PIC X(9)    OCCURS 3 TIMES.
```

Figure 9-3 COBOL Coding to Define the Education Table

In Figure 9-3, EDUCATION-LEVEL-TABLE is the name of the table. The name given to the group item containing the constant values stored in the table is EDUCATION-LEVEL-CONSTANTS. Within this group are the level 15 entries which define the constant values in the table. The Redefines clause on line 007080 redefines EDUCATION-LEVEL-CONSTANTS as EDUCATION-TABLE. EDUCATION-TABLE consists of 3 elements (OCCURS 3 TIMES).

Sequential Table Search

Another table used in the sample program is the Department Table. The Department Table contains six department numbers (03, 07, 10, 15, 18, 20) and six associated department names (Data Processing, Mathematics, Office Education, Culinary Arts, Physical Education, and Social Science), as shown in Figure 9-4.

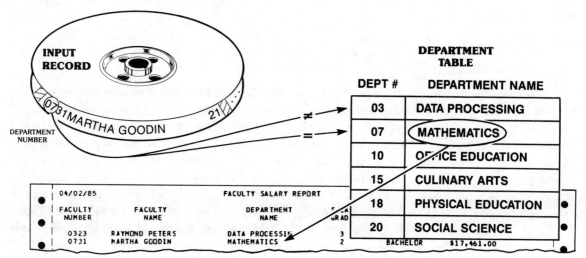

Figure 9-4 Table Search Illustration

The first two digits of the Faculty Number in the input record represent the department in which the faculty member teaches. This number is used to extract the corresponding department name from the table. There is not a direct relationship between the department numbers used to extract the department name and the position of the corresponding department name within the table. When this type of problem occurs, a procedure called Table Search is commonly used.

In Figure 9-4, the Department Table consists of department numbers and their related department names. The input record contains the Department Number (first two digits of the Faculty Number). Since there is no relationship between the department number itself and the position of the department number in the table, the department table must be searched to determine the proper department name to extract and print on the report.

One method of performing a table search involves comparing the Department Number in the input record to the first department number in the table to determine if they are equal. If the numbers are equal, the corresponding Department Name would be extracted from the table. If the numbers are not equal, the next department number in the table would be examined to determine if this number is equal to the department number in the input record. If the second department number in the table is not equal to the department number in the input record, then the third element of the table would be examined. This process will continue until either an equal department number is found in the table or until all elements in the table have been examined and none of the department numbers in the table is equal to the department number in the input record. If no equal department number is found in the table, then an error message (**** UNKNOWN ****) is printed on the report in place of the department name.

In Figure 9-4, the Department Number in the input record is 07. The first step in the table search procedure is to compare the entry in the input record to the first entry in the table. The first entry in the table (03) is not equal to the Department Number 07 found in the input record; therefore, the next entry in the table is examined.

The second entry in the table is Department Number 07. Since this number is equal to the Department Number in the input record, the related department name is extracted from the table and moved to the output area for printing on the report. The table search procedure is now complete. The remainder of the processing of the detail record will occur.

In this table search illustration, the comparison of the department number in the input record began with the first entry in the table, followed by a comparison with the second entry in the table, etc., until an equal condition was found or until all of the entries in the table had been compared. This method of table searching is called a sequential table search.

Binary Table Search

Another technique, called a binary table search, is often used when searching a table. When a binary search is used, the elements for which a search is being made must be in either an ascending or a descending sequence. When the binary search begins, the element in the middle of the table is examined first, rather than the first entry as with the sequential search. If the element in the middle of a table stored in ascending sequence is lower than the value in the input record, then the table element being searched for must reside in the upper half of the table. By the same token, if the element in the middle of the table is higher than the value in the input record, then the element being searched for must reside in the lower half of the table.

The middle entry in the proper half of the table is then examined to determine if it is greater than, less than, or equal to the value in the input record. Depending upon the result of the comparison, the table is again split in half and the middle entry of the remaining "half" is examined. This process of reducing the size of the table in half each time a comparison is made continues until the desired entry in the table is located.

When searching large tables, the binary search technique can substantially reduce the search time compared to the sequential search technique. As noted, when the binary search technique is used, the values in the table which are searched must be arranged in either an ascending or descending sequence; while with the sequential search technique, the values do not have to be in a particular sequence.

Defining a Table — Table Search

The COBOL coding to define a table containing the Department Number and Department Name is illustrated in Figure 9-5.

```
006010 01  PROGRAM-TABLES.
006020     05   DEPARTMENTS-TABLE.
006030          10   DEPARTMENT-CONSTANTS.
006040               15   FILLER                PIC X(20)     VALUE
006050                                          '03DATA PROCESSING        '.
006060               15   FILLER                PIC X(20)     VALUE
006070                                          '07MATHEMATICS            '.
006080               15   FILLER                PIC X(20)     VALUE
006090                                          '10OFFICE EDUCATION       '.
006100               15   FILLER                PIC X(20)     VALUE
006110                                          '15CULINARY ARTS          '.
006120               15   FILLER                PIC X(20)     VALUE
006130                                          '18PHYSICAL EDUCATION'.
006140               15   FILLER                PIC X(20)     VALUE
006150                                          '20SOCIAL SCIENCE         '.
006160          10   DEPARTMENT-CONSTANTS-TABLE REDEFINES
006170               DEPARTMENT-CONSTANTS OCCURS 6 TIMES
006180                                          ASCENDING KEY IS
006190                                          DEPARTMENT-NUMBER-TABLE
006200                                          INDEXED BY DEPT-IND.
007010               15   DEPARTMENT-NUMBER-TABLE PIC 99.
007020               15   DEPARTMENT-NAME-TABLE   PIC X(18).
```

Figure 9-5 COBOL Coding to Define Department Table

In Figure 9-5, the name of the entire table is DEPARTMENTS-TABLE (line 006020). The group item DEPARTMENT-CONSTANTS contains all of the constants which are in the table. Each level 15 Filler entry has a Pic X(20) clause. The constant for each Filler contains 2 characters for the Department Number and 18 characters for the Department Name. There are six separate elements in the table.

The entries to redefine the table so that each element in the table may be referenced in the Procedure Division begin on line 006160. The group item DEPARTMENT-CONSTANTS-TABLE redefines DEPARTMENT-CONSTANTS and occurs 6 times. Thus, each element within the table is defined with the group item DEPARTMENT-CONSTANTS-TABLE. Two other phrases are included for the DEPARTMENT-CONSTANTS-TABLE group item. The first phrase is ASCENDING KEY IS DEPARTMENT-NUMBER-TABLE. The words ASCENDING KEY IS are required to define the value in the table which is to be compared and which must be in an ascending sequence. In Figure 9-5, this field is the Department Number field defined on line 007010. Therefore, the data-name DEPARTMENT-NUMBER-

TABLE must be specified.

The second phrase is INDEXED BY. This phrase specifies the data-name of a field which will be used as the index for the table search. An index operates in the same fashion as a subscript; that is, it contains a value which references a particular element within the table. When a table is to be searched, the index must be defined by using the INDEXED BY phrase. The name chosen for the index, in this case DEPT-IND, is a programmer-chosen name. The index should not be defined elsewhere in the program. The only place it should appear in the Data Division is in the INDEXED BY phrase.

The group item DEPARTMENT-CONSTANTS-TABLE is followed by two elementary items — DEPARTMENT-NUMBER-TABLE and DEPARTMENT-NAME-TABLE. These two items reference the Department Number and the Department Name within the table. The first two characters of each element within the table are referenced by the name DEPARTMENT-NUMBER-TABLE, and the next eighteen characters of each element are referenced by the name DEPARTMENT-NAME-TABLE.

For example, if the index DEPT-IND contained the value 1, the entry DEPARTMENT-NUMBER-TABLE (DEPT-IND) would reference the first two characters of the first element of the table (03); while the entry DEPARTMENT-NAME-TABLE (DEPT-IND) would reference the next eighteen characters of the first element of the table (DATA PROCESSING). Similarly, if the index DEPT-IND contained the value 5, the entry DEPARTMENT-NUMBER-TABLE (DEPT-IND) would reference the first two characters of the 5th element in the table (18), and the entry DEPARTMENT-NAME-TABLE (DEPT-IND) would reference the next eighteen characters of the 5th element in the table (PHYSICAL EDUCATION).

Search All Statement

After the table is defined in the Working-Storage Section of the Data Division, statements in the Procedure Division must be executed in order to search the table. COBOL provides two verbs to perform the search activity — the SEARCH ALL verb is used when a binary search is to be performed, and the SEARCH verb is used when a sequential search is to be performed.

The general format of the Search All statement used in the sample program to search the Department Table is illustrated in Figure 9-6.

```
SEARCH ALL identifier-1  [ ; AT END imperative-statement-1]

              ⎧               ⎧IS EQUAL TO⎫  ⎧identifier-3           ⎫⎫
  ; WHEN      ⎨ data-name-1   ⎨IS =       ⎬  ⎨literal-1              ⎬⎬
              ⎩ condition-name-1           ⎩arithmetic-expression-1⎭⎭

        ⎡       ⎧               ⎧IS EQUAL TO⎫  ⎧identifier-4           ⎫⎫⎤
        ⎢ AND   ⎨ data-name-2   ⎨IS =       ⎬  ⎨literal-2              ⎬⎬⎥ ...
        ⎣       ⎩ condition-name-2           ⎩arithmetic-expression-2⎭⎭⎦

  ⎧imperative-statement-2⎫
  ⎨NEXT SENTENCE          ⎬
  ⎩                      ⎭
```

Figure 9-6 Format of the Search All Statement

In the format notation of the Search statement, the words SEARCH ALL are required. Identifier-1 must be the name of the item in the Data Division which contains the Occurs clause, the Indexed By clause, and the Ascending Key Is clause. The AT END portion of the Search All statement specifies the processing which is to occur if the entire table is searched and no match is found. The statements following the word WHEN specify the conditions which must be satisfied in order to successfully complete the table search operation. The condition-name-1 entry should be an expression which uses the equal to condition operator.

In the sample program, a binary search is to be conducted. The Search All statement used in the sample program to search the Department Table is illustrated in Figure 9-7.

```
015020        SEARCH ALL DEPARTMENT-CONSTANTS-TABLE
015030            AT END
015040                MOVE UNKNOWN-CONSTANT TO DEPARTMENT-NAME-REPORT
015050            WHEN DEPARTMENT-NUMBER-TABLE (DEPT-IND) =
015060                 DEPARTMENT-NUMBER-INPUT
015070                MOVE DEPARTMENT-NAME-TABLE (DEPT-IND) TO
015080                     DEPARTMENT-NAME-REPORT.
```

Figure 9-7 Example of Search All Statement

The Search All statement is used to search the table that contains a Department Number and a related Department Name. The coding for this table was previously illustrated in Figure 9-5. As a result of the search, the Department Name corresponding to the Department Number found in the input record will be extracted from the table and moved to the report output area. If a Department Number equal to the Department Number in the input record is not found in the table, an error message will be moved to the report output area.

The words SEARCH ALL are required. The name DEPARTMENT-CONSTANTS-TABLE follows the words SEARCH ALL. DEPARTMENT-CONSTANTS-TABLE is the name of the item in the definition of the table which contains the Occurs clause, the Indexed By clause, and the Ascending Key Is clause. The coding on lines 015030 and 015040 contains the AT END clause and the processing to occur if the table is searched and no match is found. Thus, if the Department Number from the input record is not found in the Department Table, the value in the field UNKNOWN-CONSTANT is moved to the Department Name field on the report. Any imperative statement could have been specified following the AT END portion of the Search All statement.

Following the word WHEN on line 015050 are the statements that specify the conditions which are to be satisfied in order to successfully complete the table search operation. In Figure 9-7, the condition DEPARTMENT-NUMBER-TABLE (DEPT-IND) = DEPARTMENT-NUMBER-INPUT is specified. When this condition occurs, the Move statement that moves the Department Name from the table to the report will be executed. Some compilers require the data-name with the index to be on the left of the equal sign, while it does not matter with other compilers. Therefore, the safest way to write the condition in the When clause is to place the table name with the index name on the left side of the equal sign.

Set and Search Statements

In the previous example, the Search All statement was used to conduct a binary search of the table. If a sequential search of the table is required, the Search statement is used. In conjunction with the Search statement, however, the Set statement must be used to give the index an initial value before the table search begins. Figure 9-8 illustrates the Set and Search statements which could be used to perform a sequential search on the Department Table, together with the format notation for the statements.

```
015030      SET DEPT-IND TO 1.
015040      SEARCH DEPARTMENT-CONSTANTS-TABLE
015050          AT END
015060              MOVE UNKNOWN-CONSTANT TO DEPARTMENT-NAME-REPORT
015070          WHEN DEPARTMENT-NUMBER-TABLE (DEPT-IND) =
015080              DEPARTMENT-NUMBER-INPUT
015090              MOVE DEPARTMENT-NAME-TABLE (DEPT-IND) TO
015100              DEPARTMENT-NAME-REPORT.
```

$$\underline{\text{SET}} \left\{ \begin{array}{l} \text{identifier-1} \quad [\text{, identifier-2}] \quad \ldots \\ \text{index-name-1} \quad [\text{, index-name-2}] \quad \ldots \end{array} \right\} \underline{\text{TO}} \left\{ \begin{array}{l} \text{identifier-3} \\ \text{index-name-3} \\ \text{integer-1} \end{array} \right\}$$

$$\underline{\text{SET}} \text{ index-name-4} \quad [\text{, index-name-5}] \quad \ldots \left\{ \begin{array}{l} \underline{\text{UP BY}} \\ \underline{\text{DOWN BY}} \end{array} \right\} \left\{ \begin{array}{l} \text{identifier-4} \\ \text{integer-2} \end{array} \right\}$$

$$\underline{\text{SEARCH}} \text{ identifier-1} \left[\underline{\text{VARYING}} \left\{ \begin{array}{l} \text{identifier-2} \\ \text{index-name-1} \end{array} \right\} \right] \left[\text{; AT } \underline{\text{END}} \text{ imperative-statement-1} \right]$$

$$\text{; } \underline{\text{WHEN}} \text{ condition-1} \left\{ \begin{array}{l} \text{imperative-statement-2} \\ \underline{\text{NEXT SENTENCE}} \end{array} \right\}$$

$$\left[\text{; } \underline{\text{WHEN}} \text{ condition-2} \left\{ \begin{array}{l} \text{imperative-statement-3} \\ \underline{\text{NEXT SENTENCE}} \end{array} \right\} \right] \quad \ldots$$

Figure 9-8 Set and Search Statements

In Figure 9–8, the Set statement on line 015030 is used to set the index DEPT-IND to the value 1. The Set statement will set the fields, identifier-1, identifier-2, . . . or the index fields, index-name-1, index-name-2, . . . to the value in either identifier-3, index-name-3, or integer-1. In Figure 9–8, a numeric integer is used in the Set statement.

Before the Search statement can be used to perform a table search, the index associated with the table must be set to the number of the element in the table where the search is to begin. If the search is to begin with the first element in the table, then the index must be set to the value 1, as in Figure 9–8. If the program required that the search begin with the fourth element in the table, then the index must be set to the value 4 prior to beginning the search operation. Setting the index is not required for the Search All statement because it searches the entire table using the binary search technique.

The Search statement itself appears to be the same as the Search All statement except that the word ALL is not used. There are, however, several differences. First, when using the Search statement, the conditions specified for the termination of the search (condition-1, condition-2, etc.) do not have to be equal conditions; they can be any allowable relation conditions.

Secondly, in the format notation for the Search All statement in Figure 9–6, more than one condition can be specified, indicating that two or more conditions have to be true before the search is terminated. In the Search All statement, these conditions are in an AND relationship, meaning that all the conditions specified must be true before the Search All statement will be stopped and the "When" portion of the statement executed.

With the Search statement, on the other hand, the multiple conditions specified are in an OR relationship, which means that if any of the conditions specified is true, the search is terminated and the "When" portion of the statement is executed.

MULTIPLE LEVEL TABLES

The tables used so far have been one dimensional tables, which means that each element within the table was identified by a single subscript or index value. It is often necessary within a program to process multiple level tables, which are tables where two reference points are required to locate a specific element within the table. Figure 9-9 illustrates the Faculty Salary Table, which is a multiple level table used in the sample program.

EDUCATIONAL LEVEL

	BACHELOR (1)	MASTERS (2)	DOCTORATE (3)
(1)	16448.00	17893.00	22222.00
(2)	17461.00	18902.00	23231.00
(3)	18469.00	19911.00	24240.00
(4)	19479.00	20921.00	25252.00

SALARY GRADE (down the side, rows (1)-(4))

Figure 9-9 Faculty Salary Table

In Figure 9-9, the three education levels are listed across the top of the chart, and the four salary grades are listed down the side of the chart. There are three levels of education associated with each salary grade. In order to find the proper salary, it is necessary to know both the salary grade and the education level. For example, a faculty member in salary grade three who has a masters degree receives a salary of $19911.00 per year. This is determined by first locating the third Salary Grade row and then looking along that row until the Masters column is located. Thus, two points of reference are required — one for the salary grade and one for the education level.

In the sample program, the two references needed to extract the faculty salary from the Faculty Salary Table are obtained from the input record.

The Data Division entries to define the Faculty Salary Table described in Figure 9-9 are contained in Figure 9-10.

```
007110      05  FACULTY-SALARY-TABLE.
007120          10  FACULTY-SALARY-CONSTANTS.
007130              15  FILLER          PIC 9(5)V99  VALUE 16448.00.
007140              15  FILLER          PIC 9(5)V99  VALUE 17893.00.
007150              15  FILLER          PIC 9(5)V99  VALUE 22222.00.
007160              15  FILLER          PIC 9(5)V99  VALUE 17461.00.
007170              15  FILLER          PIC 9(5)V99  VALUE 18902.00.
007180              15  FILLER          PIC 9(5)V99  VALUE 23231.00.
007190              15  FILLER          PIC 9(5)V99  VALUE 18469.00.
007200              15  FILLER          PIC 9(5)V99  VALUE 19911.00.
008010              15  FILLER          PIC 9(5)V99  VALUE 24240.00.
008020              15  FILLER          PIC 9(5)V99  VALUE 19479.00.
008030              15  FILLER          PIC 9(5)V99  VALUE 20921.00.
008040              15  FILLER          PIC 9(5)V99  VALUE 25252.00.
008050          10  SALARY-GRADE-TABLE REDEFINES FACULTY-SALARY-CONSTANTS
008060                                               OCCURS 4 TIMES.
008070              15  SALARY-TABLE    PIC 9(5)V99  OCCURS 3 TIMES.
```

Figure 9-10 Definition of Two-Dimensional Faculty Salary Table

In Figure 9–10, the constant values for the table are defined in the same manner as a single level table. The name of the entire table is FACULTY-SALARY-TABLE (line 007110). The group item FACULTY-SALARY-CONSTANTS contains all the constants which are in the table. Each level 15 Filler has a Pic 9(5)V99 clause which defines the dollar amount for the faculty salary.

The entries to redefine the table so that each element in the table may be referenced in the Procedure Division begin on line 008050. The group item SALARY-GRADE-TABLE redefines FACULTY-SALARY-CONSTANTS and is specified as occurring four times (OCCURS 4 TIMES). Through this entry, the table is divided into four groups. Within the SALARY-GRADE-TABLE group is the elementary item SALARY-TABLE. This elementary item, with a Picture 9(5)V99, occurs three times. Thus, within each occurrence of the group item SALARY-GRADE-TABLE, the elementary item SALARY-TABLE occurs three times. As a result of this definition in the Data Division, the twelve constants defined in FACULTY-SALARY-CONSTANTS are organized into four groups, each containing three constants. This organization of the table is shown in Figure 9–11.

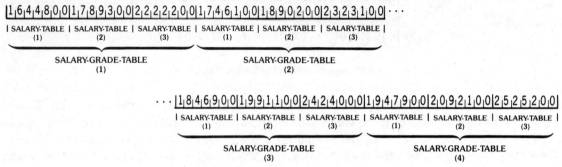

Figure 9-11 Faculty Salary Table Layout

In Figure 9–11, the group item SALARY-GRADE-TABLE occurs four times. Within each occurrence, the elementary item SALARY-TABLE occurs three times. To reference an element within the Faculty Salary Table, a double subscript must be used. The first subscript references the group item (SALARY-GRADE-TABLE), and the second subscript references the elementary item (SALARY-TABLE).

The first subscript specifies which of the four groups from SALARY-GRADE-TABLE is to be referenced, and the second subscript specifies which of the three elements of SALARY-TABLE within the specific SALARY-GRADE-TABLE group is to be referenced. This is illustrated in Figure 9–12.

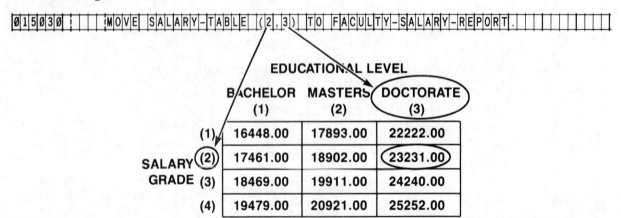

Figure 9-12 Move Statement to Reference Two-Dimensional Faculty Salary Table

When a multiple level table is referenced in any statement in the Procedure Division, the data-name of the elementary item must be specified. The name specified must be associated with an Occurs clause. In Figure 9-12, the data-name SALARY-TABLE is specified because it is the name of the elementary item.

The first subscript (2) in the Move statement in Figure 9-12 references the second Salary Grade row of the table. The second subscript (3) references the Doctorate column of the table. Thus, the first subscript specifies which Salary Grade group is to be referenced, and the second subscript specifies which Educational Level within the desired Salary Grade group is to be referenced. Therefore, the Move statement in Figure 9-12 will move the value 23231.00 from the table to the FACULTY-SALARY-REPORT field.

In Figure 9-12, literal subscripts are used to specify which element is to be processed. Variable names can also be used as subscripts to reference the elements within the Faculty Salary Table. The Move statement which extracts the faculty salary from the Faculty Salary Table in the sample program is illustrated in Figure 9-13.

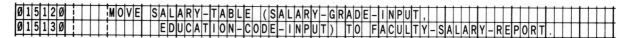

Figure 9-13 Move Statement to Reference Faculty Salary Table

In Figure 9-13, the SALARY-GRADE-INPUT field contains the first subscript, and the EDUCATION-CODE-INPUT field contains the second subscript. The value in the SALARY-GRADE-INPUT field specifies which Salary Grade group is to be referenced, and the value in the EDUCATION-CODE-INPUT field specifies which Educational Level within the desired Salary Group is to be referenced. Depending upon the value in these fields in the input record, the faculty salary will be extracted from the Faculty Salary Table and moved to the output area.

Most COBOL compilers also allow three dimensional tables to be defined. In most applications, however, three dimensional tables are not required; and their use is discouraged in many installations.

SAMPLE PROGRAM

The design of the sample program which produces the Faculty Salary Report illustrated in Figure 9-1 on page 9.2 is explained on the following pages. The format of the input records and the printer spacing chart are illustrated in Figure 9-14.

Faculty Disk Record				
FIELD DESCRIPTION	**POSITION**	**LENGTH**	**DEC**	**ATTRIBUTE**
Faculty Number	1 – 4	4	0	Numeric
Faculty Name	5 – 24	20		Alphanumeric
Education Code	25	1	0	Numeric
Salary Grade	26	1	0	Numeric
Record Length		26		

Figure 9-14 Program Input (Part 1 of 2)

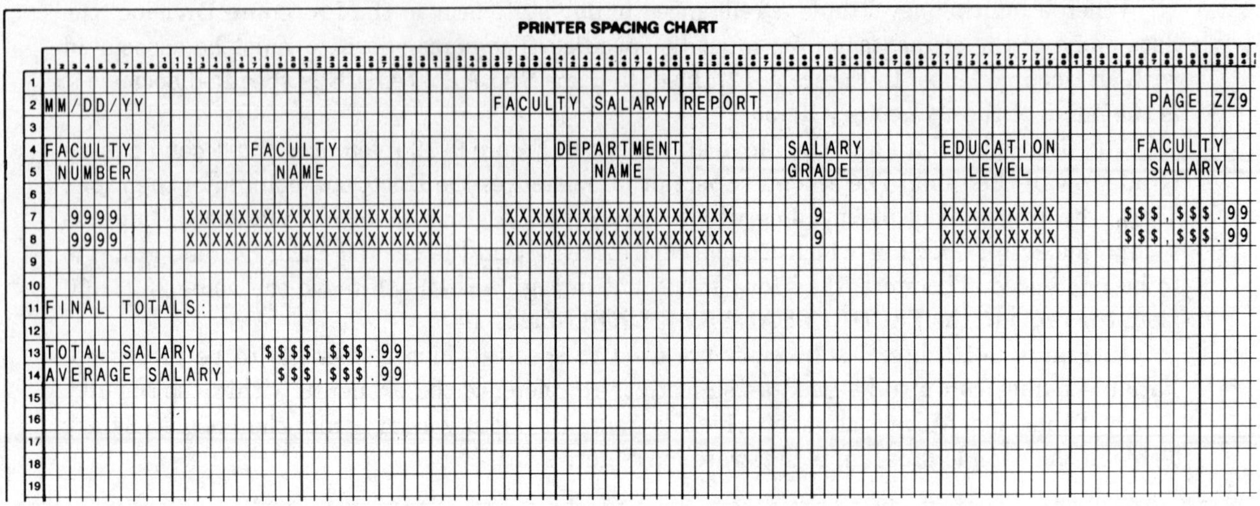

PRINTER SPACING CHART

Figure 9-14 Printer Spacing Chart (Part 2 of 2)

The program narrative for the sample program is contained in Figure 9-15.

PROGRAM NARRATIVE

SUBJECT	Faculty Salary Report	DATE	January 12	PAGE 1 OF 1
TO	Programmer	FROM		Systems Analyst

A program is to be written to prepare a Faculty Salary Report. The format of the input record and the printer spacing chart are included with this narrative. The program should include the following processing.

1. The program should read the input records and create the Faculty Salary Report as per the format illustrated on the printer spacing chart.

2. The department name of the department in which the faculty member works is to be extracted from a table based upon the first two digits of the faculty number.

3. The education level of the faculty member is to be extracted from a table based upon the education code in the input record.

4. The salary of the faculty member is to be extracted from a table based upon the salary grade and the education code, both found in the input record.

5. Headings are to be printed on the first and subsequent pages of the report. The heading is to contain the date and page number. Fifty-five lines are to appear on each page.

6. Final totals for the total salary and also the average salary for all faculty members are to be printed after all input records have been processed. The average salary is calculated by dividing the total salary for all faculty members by the total number of faculty members processed.

7. All input records have been edited prior to running this program.

8. The program is to be written in COBOL.

Figure 9-15 Program Narrative

Program Design

As with all programs, the first step in the program design is to analyze the output, input, and program narrative and determine the major processing tasks that are necessary to transform the input to output. The IPO Chart in Figure 9–16 illustrates the major processing tasks for the module which creates the salary report.

IPO CHART				
PROGRAM: Faculty Salary Report		**PROGRAMMER:** Forsythe		**DATE:** Jan. 15
MODULE NAME: Create Salary Report	**REF:** A000	**MODULE FUNCTION:** Create the Salary Report		
INPUT	**PROCESSING**		**REF:**	**OUTPUT**
1. Faculty Disk File	1. Initialize			1. Faculty Salary Report
	2. Obtain the input data			
	3. Process the detail records		B000	
	4. Print the final totals		B010	
	5. Terminate			

Figure 9-16 IPO Chart for Create Salary Report Module

In the IPO Chart in Figure 9–16, the output is the Faculty Salary Report, and the input is the Faculty Disk File. The major processing tasks, initialize, obtain the input data, process the detail records, print the final totals, and terminate, are similar to those found in previous programs. From an analysis of the major processing tasks, it would appear that the tasks of process the detail records and print the final totals should be accomplished in separate modules. Thus, the B000 reference number appears on the IPO Chart next to the process the detail records task, and the B010 reference number appears next to the print the final totals task.

The hierarchy chart showing the relationship of these modules, which should be developed at this time, is illustrated in Figure 9–17.

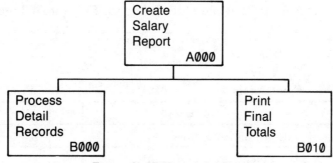

Figure 9-17 Hierarchy Chart

The hierarchy chart, at this point in the design process, consists of three modules, Create Salary Report, Process Detail Records, and Print Final Totals. The next step in the design process is to use the IPO Charts to develop the major processing tasks for the modules on the second level of the hierarchy chart.

The IPO Chart for the module whose function is to process the detail records is illustrated in Figure 9–18.

IPO CHART

PROGRAM: Faculty Salary Report	PROGRAMMER: Forsythe		DATE: Jan. 15

MODULE NAME: Process Detail Records	REF: B000	MODULE FUNCTION: Process the Detail Records

INPUT	PROCESSING	REF:	OUTPUT
1. Faculty Disk Record	1. Print headings	C000	1. Detail Print Line
2. Department Table	2. Format print line		2. Updated Total Salary
3. Education Table	3. Update accumulators and		Accumulator
4. Faculty Salary Table	counter		3. Updated Total
5. Total Salary	4. Write the detail line		Faculty Counter
Accumulator			
6. Total Faculty Counter			

Figure 9-18 IPO Chart for Process Detail Records Module

An analysis of the major processing tasks for the module in Figure 9-18 determines that the function of printing the headings should be in a separate module. The other tasks do not require separate modules. The hierarchy chart after this analysis is shown in Figure 9-19.

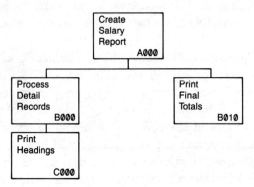

Figure 9-19 Hierarchy Chart

The next IPO Chart is for the module which prints the final totals (Figure 9-20).

IPO CHART

PROGRAM: Faculty Salary Report	PROGRAMMER: Forsythe		DATE: Jan. 15

MODULE NAME: Print Final Totals	REF: B010	MODULE FUNCTION: Print the Final Totals

INPUT	PROCESSING	REF:	OUTPUT
1. Total Salary	1. Format total lines		1. Final Total Lines
Accumulator	2. Calculate average salary		
2. Total Faculty Counter	3. Write the final total lines		

Figure 9-20 IPO Chart for Print Final Totals Module

None of the major processing tasks in Figure 9-20 requires a separate module. Therefore, the hierarchy chart as shown in Figure 9-19 would not be altered.

The IPO Chart for the only module on the third level of the hierarchy chart, which prints the headings, is illustrated in Figure 9-21.

IPO CHART

PROGRAM: Faculty Salary Report		PROGRAMMER: Forsythe		DATE: Jan. 15
MODULE NAME: Print Headings	REF: C000	MODULE FUNCTION: Print the Headings		

INPUT	PROCESSING	REF:	OUTPUT
1. Heading Lines	1. Format heading lines		1. Heading Lines
	2. Print the heading lines		

Figure 9-21 IPO Chart — Print the Headings

Neither of the major processing tasks in the module which prints the headings requires a lower-level module. Therefore, the design of the structure of the program is complete. The complete hierarchy chart is shown in Figure 9-19. Once the structure of the program is determined, the logic must be developed.

Design of Program Logic

The design of the program logic is accomplished through the use of pseudocode recorded on the pseudocode specifications. The pseudocode for each of the modules in the program is contained in Figures 9-22 through 9-25.

PSEUDOCODE SPECIFICATIONS

PROGRAM: Faculty Salary Report		PROGRAMMER: Forsythe		DATE: Jan. 15
MODULE NAME: Create Salary Report	REF: A000	MODULE FUNCTION: Create the Salary Report		

PSEUDOCODE	REF:	DATA BASES, FILES, RECORDS, FIELDS REQUIRED

Open the files
Read an input record
IF there is a record
    PERFORM UNTIL no more input records
        Process detail records
        Read an input record
    ENDPERFORM
    Print final totals
ELSE
    Print no records to process message
ENDIF
Close the files
Stop run
	
	B000
	
	B010
		Faculty disk file
		Faculty salary report file
		Input area
		    Faculty number
		    Faculty name
		    Education code
		    Salary grade
		More records indicator
		No more records indicator

Figure 9-22 Pseudocode Specifications for Create Salary Report Module

PSEUDOCODE SPECIFICATIONS

PROGRAM: Faculty Salary Report		PROGRAMMER: Forsythe	DATE: Jan. 15
MODULE NAME: Process Detail Records	REF: BØØØ	MODULE FUNCTION: Process the Detail Records	

PSEUDOCODE	REF:	DATA BASES, FILES, RECORDS, FIELDS REQUIRED
IF lines printed is = or > page size or		Lines printed counter
first page		Page size constant
Print the headings	CØØØ	First page indicator
ENDIF		Printer output area
Clear the output area		Faculty number
Move the faculty number and faculty		Faculty name
name to the output area		Department name
Search the department table for the department		Salary grade
name		Education level
IF department number in the record =		Faculty salary
department number in the table		Input area
Move the department name from the table		Faculty number
to the output area		Faculty name
ELSE		Education code
Move the unknown constant to the output		Salary grade
area		Tables
ENDIF		Department table
Move the salary grade, education level from the		Department number
table, and faculty salary from the table to the		Department name
output area		Education level table
Add the faculty salary from the table to the		Faculty salary table
total salary accumulator		Unknown constant
Add 1 to total faculty counter		Total salary accumulator
Write the line on the report		Total faculty counter
Add 1 to lines printed		Spacing control field
Set spacing to single spacing		Single space control

Figure 9-23 Pseudocode Specifications for Process Detail Records Module

PSEUDOCODE SPECIFICATIONS

PROGRAM: Faculty Salary Report		PROGRAMMER: Forsythe	DATE: Jan. 15
MODULE NAME: Print Final Totals	REF: BØ1Ø	MODULE FUNCTION: Print the Final Totals	

PSEUDOCODE	REF:	DATA BASES, FILES, RECORDS, FIELDS REQUIRED
Write the final total constant line		Final total constant line
Move final total salary to final total line		Final total salary line
Write the final total salary line		Final total average line
Calculate average salary = total salary / total		Total salary accumulator
faculty		Total faculty counter
Write the average salary line		

Figure 9-24 Pseudocode Specifications for Print Final Totals Module

PSEUDOCODE SPECIFICATIONS			
PROGRAM: Faculty Salary Report	**PROGRAMMER:** Forsythe		**DATE:** Jan. 15
MODULE NAME: Print Headings	**REF:** C000	**MODULE FUNCTION:** Print Headings on the Report	
PSEUDOCODE	**REF:**	**DATA BASES, FILES, RECORDS, FIELDS REQUIRED**	
Obtain the date Move the date to the heading line Move the page count to the heading line Write the first heading line Add 1 to page count Write the second heading line Write the third heading line Set spacing for double spacing Set lines printed counter to five		Date work area First heading line Page number (page count) Second heading line Third heading line Spacing control area Double spacing control character Number of lines printed counter	

Figure 9-25 Pseudocode Specifications for Print Headings Module

In Figure 9-23, the pseudocode for searching the Department Table involves a Search statement and an If statement. The Search statement describes the table to be searched and the object of the search. In the sample program, the Department Table is being searched for a Department Number equal to the Department Number in the input record in order to obtain the Department Name. When an equal Department Number is found, the corresponding Department Name from the table is moved to the printer output area. If an equal Department Number is not found in the table, the unknown constant (**** UNKNOWN ****) is moved to the printer output area. The If statement in the pseudocode illustrates the test that takes place when the table is searched.

Summary

The use of table searching and multiple level tables is quite common in installations where COBOL programming is performed. The programmer should have a firm understanding of these programming tools.

Source Listing

The following pages contain the source listing of the sample program.

```
PP 5740-CB1 RELEASE 2.3 + PTF 8 - UP13477        IBM OS/VS COBOL   JULY 24, 1978      13.11.42  DATE APR  2,1985


    1                        13.11.42       APR  2,1985


00001   001010 IDENTIFICATION DIVISION.                                    SALRPT
00002   001020                                                             SALRPT
00003   001030 PROGRAM-ID.    SALRPT.                                      SALRPT
00004   001040 AUTHOR.        FORSYTHE.                                     SALRPT
00005   001050 INSTALLATION.  BREA.                                        SALRPT
00006   001060 DATE-WRITTEN.  JAN 23,1985.                                 SALRPT
00007   001070 DATE-COMPILED. APR  2,1985.                                 SALRPT
00008   001080 SECURITY.      UNCLASSIFIED.                                SALRPT
00009   001090                                                             SALRPT
00010   001100****************************************************** SALRPT
00011   001110*                                                    * SALRPT
00012   001120*   THIS PROGRAM PRODUCES A FACULTY SALARY REPORT LISTING  * SALRPT
00013   001130*   FACULTY NUMBER, FACULTY NAME, DEPARTMENT NAME, SALARY   * SALRPT
00014   001140*   GRADE, EDUCATION LEVEL, AND FACULTY SALARY. AFTER ALL   * SALRPT
00015   001150*   RECORDS HAVE BEEN PROCESSED, THE TOTAL OF ALL SALARIES, AND * SALRPT
00016   001160*   THE AVERAGE SALARY IS PRINTED.                    * SALRPT
00017   001170*                                                    * SALRPT
00018   001180****************************************************** SALRPT
00019   001190                                                             SALRPT
00020   001200                                                             SALRPT
00021   002010                                                             SALRPT
00022   002020 ENVIRONMENT DIVISION.                                       SALRPT
00023   002030                                                             SALRPT
00024   002040 CONFIGURATION SECTION.                                      SALRPT
00025   002050                                                             SALRPT
00026   002060 SOURCE-COMPUTER. IBM-4381.                                  SALRPT
00027   002070 OBJECT-COMPUTER. IBM-4381.                                  SALRPT
00028   002080 SPECIAL-NAMES.   C01 IS TO-TOP-OF-PAGE.                     SALRPT
00029   002090                                                             SALRPT
00030   002100 INPUT-OUTPUT SECTION.                                       SALRPT
00031   002110                                                             SALRPT
00032   002120 FILE-CONTROL.                                               SALRPT
00033   002130     SELECT FACULTY-INPUT-FILE                               SALRPT
00034   002140         ASSIGN TO UT-S-SALDATA.                             SALRPT
00035   002150     SELECT SALARY-REPORT-FILE                               SALRPT
00036   002160         ASSIGN TO UT-S-SALPRINT.                            SALRPT


    2                        13.11.42       APR  2,1985


00037   002170/                                                            SALRPT
00038   002180 DATA DIVISION.                                              SALRPT
00039   002190                                                             SALRPT
00040   002200 FILE SECTION.                                               SALRPT
00041   003010                                                             SALRPT
00042   003020 FD  FACULTY-INPUT-FILE                                      SALRPT
00043   003030     RECORD CONTAINS 26 CHARACTERS                           SALRPT
00044   003040     LABEL RECORDS ARE STANDARD                              SALRPT
00045   003050     DATA RECORD IS FACULTY-INPUT-RECORD.                    SALRPT
00046   003060 01  FACULTY-INPUT-RECORD.                                   SALRPT
00047   003070     05  FACULTY-NUMBER-INPUT.                               SALRPT
00048   003080         10  DEPARTMENT-NUMBER-INPUT PIC 99.                 SALRPT
00049   003090         10  EMPLOYEE-NUMBER-INPUT   PIC 99.                 SALRPT
00050   003100     05  FACULTY-NAME-INPUT          PIC X(20).              SALRPT
00051   003110     05  EDUCATION-CODE-INPUT        PIC 9.                  SALRPT
00052   003120     05  SALARY-GRADE-INPUT          PIC 9.                  SALRPT
00053   003130                                                             SALRPT
00054   003140 FD  SALARY-REPORT-FILE                                      SALRPT
00055   003150     RECORD CONTAINS 133 CHARACTERS                          SALRPT
00056   003160     LABEL RECORDS ARE OMITTED                               SALRPT
00057   003170     DATA RECORD IS SALARY-REPORT-LINE.                      SALRPT
00058   003180 01  SALARY-REPORT-LINE.                                     SALRPT
00059   003190     05  CARRIAGE-CONTROL        PIC X.                      SALRPT
00060   003200     05  FILLER                  PIC XX.                     SALRPT
00061   004010     05  FACULTY-NUMBER-REPORT   PIC 9(4).                   SALRPT
00062   004020     05  FILLER                  PIC X(5).                   SALRPT
00063   004030     05  FACULTY-NAME-REPORT     PIC X(20).                  SALRPT
00064   004040     05  FILLER                  PIC X(5).                   SALRPT
00065   004050     05  DEPARTMENT-NAME-REPORT  PIC X(18).                  SALRPT
00066   004060     05  FILLER                  PIC X(6).                   SALRPT
00067   004070     05  SALARY-GRADE-REPORT     PIC 9.                      SALRPT
00068   004080     05  FILLER                  PIC X(9).                   SALRPT
00069   004090     05  EDUCATION-LEVEL-REPORT  PIC X(9).                   SALRPT
00070   004100     05  FILLER                  PIC X(5).                   SALRPT
00071   004110     05  FACULTY-SALARY-REPORT   PIC $$$,$$$.99.             SALRPT
00072   004120     05  FILLER                  PIC X(38).                  SALRPT
00073   004130                                                             SALRPT
00074   004140 WORKING-STORAGE SECTION.                                    SALRPT
00075   004150                                                             SALRPT
00076   004160 01  PROGRAM-INDICATORS.                                     SALRPT
00077   004170     05  ARE-THERE-MORE-RECORDS PIC X(3)   VALUE 'YES'.      SALRPT
00078   004180         88  THERE-IS-A-RECORD             VALUE 'YES'.      SALRPT
00079   004190         88  THERE-ARE-NO-MORE-RECORDS     VALUE 'NO '.      SALRPT
00080   004200                                                             SALRPT
```

Figure 9-26 Source Listing (Part 1 of 4)

```
   3              13.11.42      APR  2,1985

00081   005010 01  PROGRAM-CONSTANTS.                                      SALRPT
00082   005020 05   PRINT-CONSTANTS.                                       SALRPT
00083   005030      10   UNKNOWN-CONSTANT   PIC X(18)     VALUE            SALRPT
00084   005040                                  '**** UNKNOWN **** '.SALRPT
00085   005050 05   NO-RECORDS-MESSAGE.                                    SALRPT
00086   005060      10   CARRIAGE-CONTROL   PIC X.                         SALRPT
00087   005070      10   FILLER             PIC X(37)     VALUE            SALRPT
00088   005080              'SALARY REPORT - NO RECORDS TO PROCESS'.SALRPT
00089   005090      10   FILLER             PIC X(95)     VALUE SPACES.    SALRPT
00090   005100                                                            SALRPT
00091   005110 01  WORK-AREAS.                                            SALRPT
00092   005120 05   DATE-WORK.                                            SALRPT
00093   005130      10   YEAR-WORK          PIC 99.                       SALRPT
00094   005140      10   MONTH-WORK         PIC 99.                       SALRPT
00095   005150      10   DAY-WORK           PIC 99.                       SALRPT
00096   005160                                                            SALRPT
00097   005170 01  TOTAL-ACCUMULATORS-COUNTERS.                          SALRPT
00098   005180 05   TOTAL-SALARY-ACCUM      PIC S9(6)V99 VALUE ZERO.      SALRPT
00099   005190 05   TOTAL-FACULTY-COUNT     PIC S9(3)    VALUE ZERO.      SALRPT
00100   005200                                                            SALRPT
00101   006010 01  PROGRAM-TABLES.                                       SALRPT
00102   006020 05   DEPARTMENTS-TABLE.                                    SALRPT
00103   006030      10   DEPARTMENT-CONSTANTS.                            SALRPT
00104   006040          15   FILLER         PIC X(20)     VALUE           SALRPT
00105   006050                                  '03DATA PROCESSING   '.SALRPT
00106   006060          15   FILLER         PIC X(20)     VALUE           SALRPT
00107   006070                                  '07MATHEMATICS       '.SALRPT
00108   006080          15   FILLER         PIC X(20)     VALUE           SALRPT
00109   006090                                  '10OFFICE EDUCATION  '.SALRPT
00110   006100          15   FILLER         PIC X(20)     VALUE           SALRPT
00111   006110                                  '15CULINARY ARTS     '.SALRPT
00112   006120          15   FILLER         PIC X(20)     VALUE           SALRPT
00113   006130                                  '18PHYSICAL EDUCATION'.SALRPT
00114   006140          15   FILLER         PIC X(20)     VALUE           SALRPT
00115   006150                                  '20SOCIAL SCIENCE    '.SALRPT
00116   006160      10   DEPARTMENT-CONSTANTS-TABLE REDEFINES             SALRPT
00117   006170              DEPARTMENT-CONSTANTS OCCURS 6 TIMES           SALRPT
00118   006180                         ASCENDING KEY IS                  SALRPT
00119   006190                             DEPARTMENT-NUMBER-TABLESALRPT
00120   006200                         INDEXED BY DEPT-IND.              SALRPT
00121   007010          15   DEPARTMENT-NUMBER-TABLE PIC 99.             SALRPT
00122   007020          15   DEPARTMENT-NAME-TABLE   PIC X(18).          SALRPT
00123   007030 05   EDUCATION-LEVEL-TABLE.                               SALRPT
00124   007040      10   EDUCATION-LEVEL-CONSTANTS.                      SALRPT
00125   007050          15   FILLER         PIC X(9)     VALUE 'BACHELOR '.SALRPT
00126   007060          15   FILLER         PIC X(9)     VALUE 'MASTERS  '.SALRPT
00127   007070          15   FILLER         PIC X(9)     VALUE 'DOCTORATE'.SALRPT
00128   007080      10   EDUCATION-TABLE REDEFINES                       SALRPT
00129   007090              EDUCATION-LEVEL-CONSTANTS                    SALRPT
00130   007100                             PIC X(9)     OCCURS 3 TIMES.  SALRPT
00131   007110 05   FACULTY-SALARY-TABLE.                               SALRPT
00132   007120      10   FACULTY-SALARY-CONSTANTS.                       SALRPT
00133   007130          15   FILLER         PIC 9(5)V99 VALUE 16448.00.  SALRPT
00134   007140          15   FILLER         PIC 9(5)V99 VALUE 17893.00.  SALRPT
00135   007150          15   FILLER         PIC 9(5)V99 VALUE 22222.00.  SALRPT
00136   007160          15   FILLER         PIC 9(5)V99 VALUE 17461.00.  SALRPT
00137   007170          15   FILLER         PIC 9(5)V99 VALUE 18902.00.  SALRPT
00138   007180          15   FILLER         PIC 9(5)V99 VALUE 23231.00.  SALRPT
00139   007190          15   FILLER         PIC 9(5)V99 VALUE 18469.00.  SALRPT
00140   007200          15   FILLER         PIC 9(5)V99 VALUE 19911.00.  SALRPT
00141   008010          15   FILLER         PIC 9(5)V99 VALUE 24240.00.  SALRPT
00142   008020          15   FILLER         PIC 9(5)V99 VALUE 19479.00.  SALRPT
00143   008030          15   FILLER         PIC 9(5)V99 VALUE 20921.00.  SALRPT
00144   008040          15   FILLER         PIC 9(5)V99 VALUE 25252.00.  SALRPT
00145   008050      10   SALARY-GRADE-TABLE REDEFINES FACULTY-SALARY-CONSTANTSSALRPT
00146   008060                                        OCCURS 4 TIMES.    SALRPT
00147   008070          15   SALARY-TABLE   PIC 9(5)V99 OCCURS 3 TIMES.  SALRPT
00148   008080                                                          SALRPT
00149   008090 01  PRINTER-CONTROL.                                     SALRPT
00150   008100 05   PROPER-SPACING          PIC 9.                      SALRPT
00151   008110 05   SPACE-ONE-LINE          PIC 9       VALUE 1.        SALRPT
00152   008120 05   SPACE-TWO-LINES         PIC 9       VALUE 2.        SALRPT
00153   008130 05   PAGE-COUNT              PIC S999    VALUE +1.       SALRPT
00154   008140      88   FIRST-PAGE                     VALUE +1.       SALRPT
00155   008150 05   PAGE-SIZE               PIC 999     VALUE 55.       SALRPT
00156   008160 05   LINES-PRINTED           PIC S999    VALUE ZERO.     SALRPT
00157   008170                                                          SALRPT
00158   008180 01  HEADING-LINES.                                       SALRPT
00159   008190 05   FIRST-HEADING-LINE.                                 SALRPT
00160   008200      10   CARRIAGE-CONTROL   PIC X.                      SALRPT
00161   009010      10   DATE-HEADING.                                  SALRPT
00162   009020          15   MONTH-HEADING  PIC 99.                     SALRPT
00163   009030          15   FILLER         PIC X       VALUE '/'.      SALRPT
00164   009040          15   DAY-HEADING    PIC 99.                     SALRPT
00165   009050          15   FILLER         PIC X       VALUE '/'.      SALRPT
00166   009060          15   YEAR-HEADING   PIC 99.                     SALRPT
00167   009070      10   FILLER             PIC X(27)   VALUE SPACES.   SALRPT
00168   009080      10   FILLER             PIC X(21)   VALUE           SALRPT
00169   009090                                  'FACULTY SALARY REPORT'.SALRPT
00170   009100      10   FILLER             PIC X(30)   VALUE SPACES.   SALRPT
00171   009110      10   FILLER             PIC X(5)    VALUE 'PAGE '.  SALRPT
00172   009120      10   PAGE-HEADING       PIC ZZ9.                    SALRPT
00173   009130      10   FILLER             PIC X(38).                  SALRPT
```

Figure 9-27 Source Listing (Part 2 of 4)

```
    4                    13.11.42      APR  2,1985

00174  009140   05  SECOND-HEADING-LINE.                              SALRPT
00175  009150       1C  CARRIAGE-CONTROL   PIC X.                      SALRPT
00176  009160       10  FILLER             PIC X(7)    VALUE 'FACULTY'.    SALRPT
00177  009170       10  FILLER             PIC X(9)    VALUE SPACES.   SALRPT
00178  009180       10  FILLER             PIC X(7)    VALUE 'FACULTY'.    SALRPT
00179  009190       10  FILLER             PIC X(17)   VALUE SPACES.   SALRPT
00180  0092C0       1C  FILLER             PIC X(10)   VALUE 'DEPARTMENT'. SALRPT
00181  010010       10  FILLER             PIC X(8)    VALUE SPACES.   SALRPT
00182  010020       10  FILLER             PIC X(6)    VALUE 'SALARY'. SALRPT
00183  010030       10  FILLER             PIC X(6)    VALUE SPACES.   SALRPT
00184  010C40       10  FILLER             PIC X(9)    VALUE 'EDUCATION'.  SALRPT
00185  010050       10  FILLER             PIC X(6)    VALUE SPACES.   SALRPT
00186  010060       10  FILLER             PIC X(7)    VALUE 'FACULTY'. SALRPT
00187  010070       1C  FILLER             PIC X(40)   VALUE SPACES.   SALRPT
00188  010080   05  THIRD-HEADING-LINE.                               SALRPT
00189  010090       1C  CARRIAGE-CONTROL   PIC X.                      SALRPT
0019C  0101C0       1C  FILLER             PIC X       VALUE SPACES.   SALRPT
00191  010110       1C  FILLER             PIC X(6)    VALUE 'NUMBER'. SALRPT
00192  010120       10  FILLER             PIC X(11)   VALUE SPACES.   SALRPT
00193  010130       10  FILLER             PIC X(4)    VALUE 'NAME'.   SALRPT
00194  010140       1C  FILLER             PIC X(21)   VALUE SPACES.   SALRPT
00195  010150       1C  FILLER             PIC X(4)    VALUE 'NAME'.   SALRPT
00196  010160       10  FILLER             PIC X(11)   VALUE SPACES.   SALRPT
00197  010170       10  FILLER             PIC X(5)    VALUE 'GRADE'.  SALRPT
00198  010180       10  FILLER             PIC X(9)    VALUE SPACES.   SALRPT
00199  010190       10  FILLER             PIC X(5)    VALUE 'LEVEL'.  SALRPT
00200  0102C0       10  FILLER             PIC X(9)    VALUE SPACES.   SALRPT
00201  011010       10  FILLER             PIC X(6)    VALUE 'SALARY'. SALRPT
00202  011020       10  FILLER             PIC X(40)   VALUE SPACES.   SALRPT
00203  011030                                                         SALRPT
00204  011040 01  FINAL-TOTAL-LINES.                                  SALRPT
00205  011050   05  FINAL-TOTAL-CONSTANT-LINE.                        SALRPT
00206  011060       1C  CARRIAGE-CONTROL   PIC X.                      SALRPT
00207  011070       10  FILLER             PIC X(13)   VALUE          SALRPT
00208  011080                                    'FINAL TOTALS:'.     SALRPT
00209  011090       10  FILLER             PIC X(119)  VALUE SPACES.  SALRPT
00210  0111C0   05  TOTAL-SALARY-LINE.                                SALRPT
00211  011110       1C  CARRIAGE-CONTROL   PIC X.                      SALRPT
00212  011120       10  FILLER             PIC X(12)   VALUE          SALRPT
00213  011130                                    'TOTAL SALARY'.      SALRPT
00214  011140       10  FILLER             PIC X(5)    VALUE SPACES.  SALRPT
00215  011150       1C  TOTAL-SALARY-FINAL PIC $$$$,$$$.99.           SALRPT
00216  011160       1C  FILLER             PIC X(104)  VALUE SPACES.  SALRPT
00217  011170   05  AVERAGE-SALARY-LINE.                              SALRPT
00218  011180       10  CARRIAGE-CONTROL   PIC X.                      SALRPT
00219  011190       1C  FILLER             PIC X(14)   VALUE          SALRPT
00220  0112C0                                    'AVERAGE SALARY'.SALRPT
00221  012010       10  FILLER             PIC X(4)    VALUE SPACES.  SALRPT
00222  012020       10  AVERAGE-SALARY-FINAL PIC $$$,$$$.99.          SALRPT
00223  012030       10  FILLER             PIC X(104)  VALUE SPACES.  SALRPT
```

```
    5                    13.11.42      APR  2,1985

00224  012040/                                                        SALRPT
00225  012050 PROCEDURE DIVISION.                                     SALRPT
00226  012060                                                         SALRPT
00227  012070**************************************************************  SALRPT
00228  012080*                                                      * SALRPT
00229  012090*   THIS MODULE OBTAINS THE INPUT DATA AND CAUSES THE DETAIL   * SALRPT
00230  0121C0*   PROCESSING AND FINAL TOTAL PROCESSING TO OCCUR. IT IS      * SALRPT
00231  012110*   ENTERED FROM AND EXITS TO THE OPERATING SYSTEM.    * SALRPT
00232  012120*                                                      * SALRPT
00233  012130**************************************************************  SALRPT
00234  012140                                                         SALRPT
00235  012150 A000-CREATE-SALARY-REPORT.                              SALRPT
00236  012160                                                         SALRPT
00237  012170       OPEN INPUT  FACULTY-INPUT-FILE                    SALRPT
00238  012180            OUTPUT SALARY-REPORT-FILE.                   SALRPT
00239  012190       READ FACULTY-INPUT-FILE                           SALRPT
00240  0122C0            AT END                                       SALRPT
00241  013010            MOVE 'NO ' TO ARE-THERE-MORE-RECORDS.        SALRPT
00242  013020       IF THERE-IS-A-RECORD                              SALRPT
00243  013030            PERFORM A001-PROCESS-AND-READ                SALRPT
00244  013040                UNTIL THERE-ARE-NO-MORE-RECORDS          SALRPT
00245  013050            PERFORM B010-PRINT-FINAL-TOTALS              SALRPT
00246  013060       ELSE                                              SALRPT
00247  013070            WRITE SALARY-REPORT-LINE FROM NO-RECORDS-MESSAGE  SALRPT
00248  013080                AFTER ADVANCING TO-TOP-OF-PAGE.          SALRPT
00249  013090       CLOSE FACULTY-INPUT-FILE                          SALRPT
00250  0131C0             SALARY-REPORT-FILE.                         SALRPT
00251  013110       STOP RUN.                                         SALRPT
00252  013120                                                         SALRPT
00253  013130                                                         SALRPT
00254  013140                                                         SALRPT
00255  013150 A001-PROCESS-AND-READ.                                  SALRPT
00256  013160                                                         SALRPT
00257  013170       PERFORM B000-PROCESS-DETAIL-RECORDS.              SALRPT
00258  013180       READ FACULTY-INPUT-FILE                           SALRPT
00259  013190            AT END                                       SALRPT
0026C  0132C0            MOVE 'NO ' TO ARE-THERE-MORE-RECORDS.        SALRPT
```

Figure 9-28 Source Listing (Part 3 of 4)

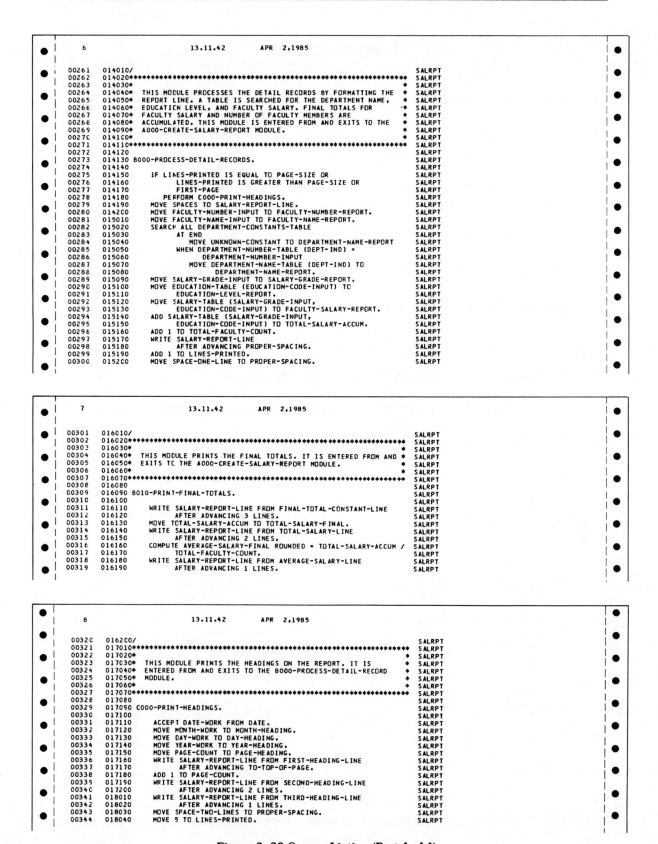

```
    6                13.11.42      APR  2,1985

00261  014010/                                                          SALRPT
00262  014020***********************************************************SALRPT
00263  014030*                                                        * SALRPT
00264  014040*  THIS MODULE PROCESSES THE DETAIL RECORDS BY FORMATTING THE * SALRPT
00265  014050*  REPORT LINE. A TABLE IS SEARCHED FOR THE DEPARTMENT NAME, * SALRPT
00266  014060*  EDUCATION LEVEL, AND FACULTY SALARY. FINAL TOTALS FOR   * SALRPT
00267  014070*  FACULTY SALARY AND NUMBER OF FACULTY MEMBERS ARE        * SALRPT
00268  014080*  ACCUMULATED. THIS MODULE IS ENTERED FROM AND EXITS TO THE * SALRPT
00269  014090*  A000-CREATE-SALARY-REPORT MODULE.                       * SALRPT
0027C  0141C0*                                                        * SALRPT
00271  014110***********************************************************SALRPT
00272  014120                                                           SALRPT
00273  014130 B000-PROCESS-DETAIL-RECORDS.                              SALRPT
00274  014140                                                           SALRPT
00275  014150      IF LINES-PRINTED IS EQUAL TO PAGE-SIZE OR            SALRPT
00276  014160            LINES-PRINTED IS GREATER THAN PAGE-SIZE OR     SALRPT
00277  014170            FIRST-PAGE                                     SALRPT
00278  014180         PERFORM C000-PRINT-HEADINGS.                      SALRPT
00279  014190      MOVE SPACES TO SALARY-REPORT-LINE.                   SALRPT
00280  0142C0      MOVE FACULTY-NUMBER-INPUT TO FACULTY-NUMBER-REPORT.  SALRPT
00281  015010      MOVE FACULTY-NAME-INPUT TO FACULTY-NAME-REPORT.      SALRPT
00282  015020      SEARCH ALL DEPARTMENT-CONSTANTS-TABLE                SALRPT
00283  015030         AT END                                           SALRPT
00284  015040            MOVE UNKNOWN-CONSTANT TO DEPARTMENT-NAME-REPORT SALRPT
00285  015050         WHEN DEPARTMENT-NUMBER-TABLE (DEPT-IND) =         SALRPT
00286  015060            DEPARTMENT-NUMBER-INPUT                        SALRPT
00287  015070            MOVE DEPARTMENT-NAME-TABLE (DEPT-IND) TO       SALRPT
00288  015080            DEPARTMENT-NAME-REPORT.                        SALRPT
00289  015090      MOVE SALARY-GRADE-INPUT TO SALARY-GRADE-REPORT.      SALRPT
00290  015100      MOVE EDUCATION-TABLE (EDUCATION-CODE-INPUT) TO       SALRPT
00291  015110            EDUCATION-LEVEL-REPORT.                        SALRPT
00292  015120      MOVE SALARY-TABLE (SALARY-GRADE-INPUT,              SALRPT
00293  015130            EDUCATION-CODE-INPUT) TO FACULTY-SALARY-REPORT. SALRPT
00294  015140      ADD SALARY-TABLE (SALARY-GRADE-INPUT,               SALRPT
00295  015150            EDUCATION-CODE-INPUT) TO TOTAL-SALARY-ACCUM.   SALRPT
00296  015160      ADD 1 TO TOTAL-FACULTY-COUNT.                        SALRPT
00297  015170      WRITE SALARY-REPORT-LINE                             SALRPT
00298  015180            AFTER ADVANCING PROPER-SPACING.                SALRPT
00299  015190      ADD 1 TO LINES-PRINTED.                              SALRPT
00300  0152C0      MOVE SPACE-ONE-LINE TO PROPER-SPACING.               SALRPT
```

```
    7                13.11.42      APR  2,1985

00301  016010/                                                          SALRPT
00302  016020***********************************************************SALRPT
00303  016030*                                                        * SALRPT
00304  016040*  THIS MODULE PRINTS THE FINAL TOTALS. IT IS ENTERED FROM AND * SALRPT
00305  016050*  EXITS TO THE A000-CREATE-SALARY-REPORT MODULE.          * SALRPT
00306  016060*                                                        * SALRPT
00307  016070***********************************************************SALRPT
00308  016080                                                           SALRPT
00309  016090 B010-PRINT-FINAL-TOTALS.                                  SALRPT
00310  016100                                                           SALRPT
00311  016110      WRITE SALARY-REPORT-LINE FROM FINAL-TOTAL-CONSTANT-LINE SALRPT
00312  016120            AFTER ADVANCING 3 LINES.                       SALRPT
00313  016130      MOVE TOTAL-SALARY-ACCUM TO TOTAL-SALARY-FINAL.       SALRPT
00314  016140      WRITE SALARY-REPORT-LINE FROM TOTAL-SALARY-LINE      SALRPT
00315  016150            AFTER ADVANCING 2 LINES.                       SALRPT
00316  016160      COMPUTE AVERAGE-SALARY-FINAL ROUNDED = TOTAL-SALARY-ACCUM / SALRPT
00317  016170            TOTAL-FACULTY-COUNT.                           SALRPT
00318  016180      WRITE SALARY-REPORT-LINE FROM AVERAGE-SALARY-LINE    SALRPT
00319  016190            AFTER ADVANCING 1 LINES.                       SALRPT
```

```
    8                13.11.42      APR  2,1985

0032C  0162C0/                                                          SALRPT
00321  017010***********************************************************SALRPT
00322  017020*                                                        * SALRPT
00323  017030*  THIS MODULE PRINTS THE HEADINGS ON THE REPORT. IT IS   * SALRPT
00324  017040*  ENTERED FROM AND EXITS TO THE B000-PROCESS-DETAIL-RECORD * SALRPT
00325  017050*  MODULE.                                                 * SALRPT
00326  017060*                                                        * SALRPT
00327  017070***********************************************************SALRPT
00328  017080                                                           SALRPT
00329  017090 C000-PRINT-HEADINGS.                                      SALRPT
00330  017100                                                           SALRPT
00331  017110      ACCEPT DATE-WORK FROM DATE.                          SALRPT
00332  017120      MOVE MONTH-WORK TO MONTH-HEADING.                    SALRPT
00333  017130      MOVE DAY-WORK TO DAY-HEADING.                        SALRPT
00334  017140      MOVE YEAR-WORK TO YEAR-HEADING.                      SALRPT
00335  017150      MOVE PAGE-COUNT TO PAGE-HEADING.                     SALRPT
00336  017160      WRITE SALARY-REPORT-LINE FROM FIRST-HEADING-LINE     SALRPT
00337  017170            AFTER ADVANCING TO-TOP-OF-PAGE.                SALRPT
00338  017180      ADD 1 TO PAGE-COUNT.                                 SALRPT
0034C  017190      WRITE SALARY-REPORT-LINE FROM SECOND-HEADING-LINE    SALRPT
00340  017200            AFTER ADVANCING 2 LINES.                       SALRPT
00341  018010      WRITE SALARY-REPORT-LINE FROM THIRD-HEADING-LINE     SALRPT
00342  018020            AFTER ADVANCING 2 LINES.                       SALRPT
00343  018030      MOVE SPACE-TWO-LINES TO PROPER-SPACING.              SALRPT
00344  018040      MOVE 5 TO LINES-PRINTED.                             SALRPT
```

Figure 9-29 Source Listing (Part 4 of 4)

REVIEW QUESTIONS

1. What is meant by the term table searching?

2. Briefly explain a table in which there is a direct relationship between a subscript and the position of the associated element in the table.

3. Briefly explain a table in which there is not a direct relationship between a subscript and the position of the associated element in the table.

4. Explain why a table search must be performed.

5. Explain the difference between sequential table searching and binary table searching.

6. Explain the purpose of the Ascending Key Is and Indexed By phrases.

7. What is the difference between an index and a subscript?

8. Summarize when the Search All statement should be used.

9. Explain the function of the AT END and WHEN phrases in the Search All statement.

10. Summarize when the Search statement should be used.

11. What is the function of the Set statement when used with the Search statement?

12. What are the differences between single dimension tables and multiple dimension tables?

COBOL CODING EXERCISES
---

1. Write the COBOL coding required in the Working-Storage Section to define a table containing a Player Number and the corresponding Player Name. The names PLAYER-NUMBER-TABLE and PLAYER-NAME-TABLE should be used to access the data within the table. The table is in ascending order by player number and the index used to access elements within the table is named PLAYER-IND.

PLAYER NUMBER	PLAYER NAME
07	FRAN SAMUELSON
11	ART WALDENSON
23	CHARLIE TOMLIN
38	ARTHUR RAMSEY
44	BENJAMIN BEAN
68	TURT COSELL
71	HANK WAYLON

2. Write the COBOL Set and Search statements required to sequentially search the table described in problem #1 above, beginning with the first player in the table. The table should be searched using the value in the PLAYER-NUMBER-INPUT field. When a match is found, the Player Name from the table should be moved to the PLAYER-NAME-REPORT field. If no match is found, then the contents of the UNKNOWN-CONSTANT field should be moved to the PLAYER-NAME-REPORT field.

3. Write the COBOL Search All statement required to perform a binary search of the table described in problem #1 above. The table should be searched using the value in the PLAYER-NUMBER-INPUT field. When a match is found, the Player Name from the table should be moved to the PLAYER-NAME-REPORT field. If no match is found, then the contents of the UNKNOWN-CONSTANT field should be moved to the PLAYER-NAME-REPORT field.

4. Write the COBOL coding required in the Working-Storage Section to define a multiple-level Oil Production Table containing the number of barrels produced from four different oil wells on each of the seven days of the week. The table contents are summarized below:

OIL WELL NUMBER

		1	2	3	4
	1	304	494	850	465
	2	756	273	745	947
DAYS	3	287	937	749	347
OF	4	847	483	873	837
THE					
WEEK	5	349	392	838	429
	6	834	837	383	923
	7	394	393	387	383

5. Write the COBOL Move statement to move the oil production of oil well #3 on the 5th day of the week from the table described in problem #4 on page 9.23 to the OIL-PRODUCTION-REPORT field.

6. Write the COBOL Move statement to move the oil production for any well and for any day from the table described in problem #4 on page 9.23 to the field OIL-PRODUCTION-REPORT. Use the OIL-WELL-NUMBER-INPUT field and the DAY-NUMBER-INPUT field as subscripts.

STRUCTURED WALKTHROUGH EXERCISES

The following portions of COBOL code contain one or more errors in program logic, in the use of the COBOL language itself, or in the programming standards which should be followed. Review the code in each exercise in the same manner used for structured walkthroughs. Identify the errors and make the appropriate corrections.

1.

```
003030  01   PROGRAM-TABLES.
003040       05   FREEWAYS-TABLE.
003050            10   FREEWAY-CONSTANTS.
003060                 15   FILLER          PIC X(11)      VALUE
003070                                                     '05SANTA ANA'.
003080                 15   FILLER          PIC X(12)      VALUE
003090                                                     '07LONG BEACH'.
003100                 15   FILLER          PIC X(15)      VALUE
003110                                                     '10SAN BERNARDINO'.
003120                 15   FILLER          PIC X(8)       VALUE
003130                                                     '11HARBOR'.
003140                 15   FILLER          PIC X(14)      VALUE
003150                                                     '22GARDEN GROVE'.
003160                 15   FILLER          PIC X(9)       VALUE
003170                                                     '55NEWPORT'.
003180                 15   FILLER          PIC X(8)       VALUE
003190                                                     '57ORANGE'.
003200                 15   FILLER          PIC X(11)      VALUE
004010                                                     '91RIVERSIDE'.
004020
004030            10   FREEWAY-CONSTANTS-TABLE REDEFINES
004040                 FREEWAY-CONSTANTS OCCURS 7 TIMES
004050                      KEY IS FREEWAY-NO-TABLE
004060                      INDEX IS FREEWAY-IND.
004070                 15   FREEWAY-NO-TABLE         PIC 9.
004080                 15   FREEWAY-NAME-TABLE       PIC X(14).
```

2.

```
014040       SEARCH ALL FREEWAY-CONSTANTS
014050            AT END
014060                 MOVE UNKNOWN-CONSTANT TO FREEWAY-NAME-REPORT.
014070       IF FREEWAY-NO (FREEWAY-NO-TABLE) = FREEWAY-NUMBER-INPUT
014080            MOVE FREEWAY-NAME (FREEWAY-IND) TO FREEWAY-NAME-REPORT.
```

3.

```
006050       05  BATTING-AVERAGE-CONSTANT.
006060           10  BATTING-AVERAGE-CONSTANTS.
006070               15  FILLER              PIC 999      VALUE 164.
006080               15  FILLER              PIC 999      VALUE 178.
006090               15  FILLER              PIC 999      VALUE 222.
006100               15  FILLER              PIC 999      VALUE 374.
006120               15  FILLER              PIC 999      VALUE 232.
006130               15  FILLER              PIC 999      VALUE 184.
006140               15  FILLER              PIC 999      VALUE 199.
006160               15  FILLER              PIC 999      VALUE 325.
006170               15  FILLER              PIC 999      VALUE 209.
006180               15  FILLER              PIC 999      VALUE 206.
006190           10  TEAM-TABLE REDEFINES BATTING-AVERAGE-CONSTANT
006200                                               OCCURS 2 TIMES.
007010               15  AVERAGE-TABLE  PIC 99     5 TIMES.
```

4.

```
014140       MOVE TEAM-TABLE (TEAM-NUMBER-INPUT, STARTING-POSITION-INPUT)
014150           TO BATTING-AVERAGE-REPORT.

014170       ADD AVERAGE-TABLE ( TEAM-NUMBER-INPUT,
014180           STARTING-POSITION-INPUT ) TO TOTAL-AVERAGE-ACCUM.
```

PROGRAMMING ASSIGNMENT 1

INSTRUCTIONS

A Railroad Passenger List is to be prepared. Design and write the COBOL program to produce the required report. An IPO Chart and Pseudocode Specifications should be used when designing the program. Use Test Data Set 1 in Appendix A.

INPUT

Input consists of Passenger Records that contain the Ticket Number, Passenger Name, Origination Code, and Destination Code. The format of the input record is illustrated below.

Passenger Disk Record				
FIELD DESCRIPTION	POSITION	LENGTH	DEC	ATTRIBUTE
UNUSED	1 – 3	3		Alphanumeric
Ticket Number	4 – 9	6	0	Numeric
Passenger Name	10 – 29	20		Alphanumeric
UNUSED	30 – 49	20		Alphanumeric
Origination Code	50	1	0	Numeric
Destination Code	51	1	0	Numeric
UNUSED	52 – 61	10		Alphanumeric
Record Length		61		

OUTPUT

Output is a Railroad Passenger List containing the Ticket Number, Railroad Line (extracted from a table based upon the first two digits of the Ticket Number), Passenger Name, Origination Point (extracted from a table based upon Origination Code), Destination Point (extracted from a table based upon Destination Code), and Ticket Amount (extracted from a table based upon Origination Code and Destination Code). After all records have been processed, a final total of the number of passengers and the ticket amount are to be printed. The printer spacing chart for the report is illustrated below.

PRINTER SPACING CHART

```
MM/DD/YY                        RAILROAD PASSENGER LIST                        PAGE ZZ9

TICKET          RAILROAD          PASSENGER          ORIGINATION     DESTINATION     TICKET
NUMBER           LINE              NAME                POINT            POINT         AMOUNT

ZZZZZ9      XXXXXXXX      XXXXXXXXXXXXXXXXXXXX      XXXXXXXXXX      XXXXXXXXXX      $ZZ.99
ZZZZZ9      *UNKNOWN      XXXXXXXXXXXXXXXXXXXX      XXXXXXXXXX      XXXXXXXXXX      $ZZ.99
ZZZZZ9      XXXXXXXX      XXXXXXXXXXXXXXXXXXXX      XXXXXXXXXX      XXXXXXXXXX      $ZZ.99

FINAL TOTALS -

TOTAL PASSENGERS          -    ZZ9
TOTAL TICKET AMOUNT       -    $Z,ZZZ.99
```

TABLE PROCESSING

The Railroad Line printed on the report is extracted from a table based upon the first two digits of the Ticket Number. The table appearing below must be searched to find the appropriate Railroad Line. If the first two digits of the Ticket Number in the input record are not found in the table, then the message *UNKNOWN should be printed on the report instead of the Railroad Line.

TICKET NUMBER (FIRST 2 DIGITS)	RAILROAD LINE
10	WESTERN
30	EXPRESS
50	FARGO
60	NORTHERN
70	UPSTATE
80	BULLET

The Origination Point printed on the report is extracted from a table based upon the Origination Code in the input record, and the Destination Point printed on the report is extracted from a table based upon the Destination Code in the input record. The appropriate tables appear below.

ORIGINATION POINT

CODE	
(1)	PORT HURON
(2)	DETROIT
(3)	ANN ARBOR
(4)	MARSHALL
(5)	LOWELL
(6)	LANSING

DESTINATION POINT

CODE	
(1)	FLINT
(2)	BAY CITY
(3)	MIDLAND
(4)	MUSKEGON
(5)	BENZONIA
(6)	MACKINAC

The Ticket Amount printed on the report is extracted from the following table, based upon the Origination Code and the Destination Code in the input record. The Origination Code and the Destination Code in the input record have been edited and contain valid values.

DESTINATION CODE

ORIGINATION CODE	(1)	(2)	(3)	(4)	(5)	(6)
(1)	25.73	45.67	47.35	63.51	79.34	89.45
(2)	26.34	47.83	53.84	61.45	67.98	94.83
(3)	25.67	49.87	51.47	65.03	81.40	91.40
(4)	43.43	51.45	53.98	57.98	63.33	81.83
(5)	44.56	44.87	43.99	13.98	51.49	62.90
(6)	31.99	31.88	33.57	23.87	50.00	63.45

PROGRAMMING ASSIGNMENT 2

INSTRUCTIONS

A Concert Ticket Report is to be prepared. Design and write the COBOL program to produce the required report. An IPO Chart and Pseudocode Specifications should be used when designing the program. Use Test Data Set 2 in Appendix A.

INPUT

Input consists of Ticket Records that contain the Ticket Number, Ticket Holder, Section Number, Quantity Purchased, and Row Number. The format of the input record is illustrated below.

Ticket Disk Record				
FIELD DESCRIPTION	POSITION	LENGTH	DEC	ATTRIBUTE
UNUSED	1 – 8	8		Alphanumeric
Ticket Number	9 – 12	4	0	Numeric
Ticket Holder	13 – 32	20		Alphanumeric
UNUSED	33 – 52	20		Alphanumeric
Section Number	53	1	0	Numeric
UNUSED	54 – 58	5		Alphanumeric
Quantity Purchased	59	1	0	Numeric
UNUSED	60 – 66	7		Alphanumeric
Row Number	67	1	0	Numeric
Record Length		67		

OUTPUT

Output is a Concert Ticket Report containing the Ticket Number, Ticket Holder, Concert Name (extracted from a table based upon the first two digits of the Ticket Number), Section Number, Row Number, Quantity Purchased, Ticket Amount (extracted from a table based upon Section Number and Row Number), and Total Amount. The Total Amount is calculated by multiplying the Ticket Amount by the Quantity Purchased. After all records have been processed, the total quantity of tickets purchased, the total amount, and the average ticket amount should be printed for each of the five concerts. The final total should then be printed containing the total quantity of tickets purchased, the total ticket amount, and the average ticket amount for all concerts. The printer spacing chart is illustrated on page 9.30.

PRINTER SPACING CHART

```
MM/DD/YY                          CONCERT TICKET REPORT                          PAGE ZZ9

TICKET              TICKET                  CONCERT      SECTION    ROW    QUANTITY   TICKET    TOTAL
NUMBER              HOLDER                  NAME         NUMBER    NUMBER PURCHASED  AMOUNT    AMOUNT

ZZZ9   XXXXXXXXXXXXXXXXXXXX   XXXXXXXXXXXXXX     9          9         9      $ZZ.99   $ZZZ.99
ZZZ9   XXXXXXXXXXXXXXXXXXXX   *** UNKNOWN ***
ZZZ9   XXXXXXXXXXXXXXXXXXXX   XXXXXXXXXXXXXX     9          9         9      $ZZ.99   $ZZZ.99

CONCERT TOTALS -

XXXXXXXXXXXXXX -
      TOTAL TICKETS PURCHASED    -   ZZ9
      TOTAL AMOUNT               -   $$,$$$.99
      AVERAGE TICKET AMOUNT      -   $ZZ.99

XXXXXXXXXXXXXX -
      TOTAL TICKETS PURCHASED    -   ZZ9
      TOTAL AMOUNT               -   $$,$$$.99
      AVERAGE TICKET AMOUNT      -   $ZZ.99

FINAL TOTALS -

      TOTAL TICKETS PURCHASED    -   Z,ZZ9
      TOTAL AMOUNT               -   $$$,$$$.99
      AVERAGE TICKET AMOUNT      -   $ZZ.99
```

TABLE PROCESSING

The Concert Name on the report is extracted from a table based upon the first two digits of the Ticket Number. The table appearing below must be searched to find the appropriate Concert Name. If the search is performed and the first two digits of the Ticket Number in the input record are not found in the table, then the message *** UNKNOWN *** should be printed instead of the Concert Name. If the Concert Name cannot be determined, none of the processing to determine ticket price, etc. should be performed, and no totals should be added to the final total accumulators.

TICKET NUMBER (FIRST 2 DIGITS)	CONCERT NAME
01	WILD ANGELS
03	HOT SHOT BAND
05	WESTERN ATTIRE
07	JAZZ O' HILL
09	THE AUTOMATICS

The Ticket Amount printed on the report is extracted from the following table based upon the Section Number and the Row Number in the input record. The Section Number and the Row Number in the input record have been edited and contain valid values.

ROW NUMBER

		(1)	(2)	(3)	(4)	(5)	(6)
	(1)	28.00	28.00	27.00	26.00	20.00	18.00
SECTION	(2)	23.00	23.00	22.00	21.00	15.00	13.00
NUMBER	(3)	18.00	18.00	17.00	16.00	10.00	08.00
	(4)	13.00	13.00	12.00	11.00	05.00	05.00

PROGRAMMING ASSIGNMENT 3

INSTRUCTIONS

An Optometric Order Report is to be prepared. Write the COBOL program to prepare this report. An IPO Chart and Pseudocode Specifications should be used when designing the program. Use Test Data Set 3 in Appendix A.

INPUT

Input consists of Order Records that contain the Store Number, Frame Number, and Quantity Ordered. The input records have been sorted in ascending sequence by Store Number. All input records contain valid data. The format of the input record is illustrated below.

Order Disk Record				
FIELD DESCRIPTION	POSITION	LENGTH	DEC	ATTRIBUTE
UNUSED	1 – 3	3		Alphanumeric
Store Number	4 – 6	3	0	Numeric
UNUSED	7 – 9	3		Alphanumeric
Frame Number	10 – 12	3	0	Numeric
UNUSED	13 – 62	50		Alphanumeric
Quantity Ordered	63 – 64	2	0	Numeric
Record Length		64		

OUTPUT

Output is an Optometric Order Report containing the Store Number, Frame Number, Frame Style (extracted from a table based upon Frame Number), Quantity Ordered, Frame Cost (extracted from a table based upon Frame Number), Total Cost, Discount Percent (extracted from a table based upon Frame Number and Quantity Ordered), Discount Amount, and Discount Cost.

Total Cost is calculated by multiplying Quantity Ordered by Frame Cost. Discount Percent is extracted from a table based upon the first digit of the Frame Number and the Quantity Ordered. Discount Amount is calculated by multiplying Total Cost by Discount Percent. Discount Cost is calculated by subtracting Discount Amount from Total Cost.

When there is a change in Store Number, the Store Number, Total Cost, Discount Amount, and Discount Cost for that store are to be printed. Store Number is to be group indicated on the report.

After all records have been processed, a final total of Total Cost, Discount Amount, and Discount Cost are to be printed.

The printer spacing chart is illustrated on the following page.

PRINTER SPACING CHART

```
MM/DD/YY                    OPTOMETRIC ORDERS                              PAGE ZZ9

STORE   FRAME       FRAME        QUANTITY   FRAME           TOTAL      DISCOUNT   DISCOUT     DISCOUNT
NUMBER  NUMBER      STYLE        ORDERED    COST            COST       PERCENT    AMOUNT      COST

ZZ9     ZZ9     XXXXXXXXXXXXXXXXXX    Z9      ZZ.99      Z,ZZZ.99      Z9%    Z,ZZZ.99   Z,ZZZ.99
        ZZ9     ****  UNKNOWN  ****    Z9      ZZ.99      Z,ZZZ.99      Z9%    Z,ZZZ.99   Z,ZZZ.99

                             STORE  ZZ9  -  ZZ,ZZZ.99            ZZ,ZZZ.99  ZZ,ZZZ.99

ZZ9     ZZ9     XXXXXXXXXXXXXXXXXX    Z9      ZZ.99      Z,ZZZ.99      Z9%    Z,ZZZ.99   Z,ZZZ.99

                             STORE  ZZ9  -  ZZ,ZZZ.99            ZZ,ZZZ.99  ZZ,ZZZ.99

                         FINAL TOTAL  -  ZZZ,ZZZ.99          ZZZ,ZZZ.99 ZZZ,ZZZ.99
```

TABLE PROCESSING

The Frame Style and Frame Cost printed on the report are extracted from a table based upon the Frame Number. The table appearing below must be searched to find the appropriate Frame Style and Frame Cost. If the Frame Number in the input record is not found in the table, then the message **** UNKNOWN **** should be printed on the report instead of the Frame Style, and the Frame Cost should be zero.

FRAME NUMBER	FRAME STYLE	FRAME COST
110	KATRINA SHADES	12.45
210	DESIGNER EYES	14.56
310	OFFICE SPECTACLES	19.67
410	COOL ACCENTUATORS	23.00
510	LIBRARY READERS	13.69
610	RAINBOW LOOKERS	15.88

The Discount Percent printed on the report is extracted from the following table, based upon the first digit of Frame Number and the Quantity Ordered in the input record.

QUANTITY ORDERED

		(1 – 15)	(16 – 30)	(31 – 45)	(46 – 60)	(61 – 75)	(76 – 90)
	(1)	03	05	10	12	14	15
	(2)	01	02	03	05	07	09
FRAME NUMBER (FIRST DIGIT)	(3)	02	04	06	08	10	12
	(4)	00	00	00	10	10	10
	(5)	07	09	11	13	15	20
	(6)	00	05	05	10	10	10

PROGRAMMING ASSIGNMENT 4

INSTRUCTIONS

An Art Gallery Auction Report is to be prepared. Write the COBOL program to prepare this report. The IPO Chart and Pseudocode Specifications should be used when designing the program. Use Test Data Set 4 in Appendix A.

INPUT

Input consists of Bid Records that contain the Gallery Number, Print Number, Bid Number, Bidder's Name, and Bid Amount. The input records have been sorted in ascending sequence by Print Number within Gallery Number. All input records contain valid data. The format of the input record is illustrated below.

Bid Disk Record				
FIELD DESCRIPTION	POSITION	LENGTH	DEC	ATTRIBUTE
UNUSED	1 – 2	2		Alphanumeric
Gallery Number	3 – 5	3	0	Numeric
Print Number	6 – 8	3	0	Numeric
UNUSED	9	1		Alphanumeric
Bid Number	10 – 13	4	0	Numeric
Bidder's Name	14 – 33	20		Alphanumeric
UNUSED	34 – 59	26		Alphanumeric
Bid Amount	60 – 64	5	0	Numeric
UNUSED	65 – 73	9		Alphanumeric
Record Length		73		

OUTPUT

Output is an Art Gallery Auction Report containing Gallery Number, Print Number, Print Name (extracted from a table based upon Print Number), Appraised Value (extracted from a table based upon Print Number), Bid Number, Bidder's Name, and Bid Amount.

The printer spacing chart is illustrated on the following page.

PRINTER SPACING CHART

```
     MM/DD/YY              ART GALLERY AUCTION REPORT                          PAGE  ZZ9

     GALLERY  PRINT     PRINT         APPRAISED        BID          BIDDER'S              BID
     NUMBER   NUMBER    NAME          VALUE            NUMBER       NAME                  AMOUNT

     ZZ9      ZZ9    XXXXXXXXX     $ZZ,ZZ9          ZZZ9      XXXXXXXXXXXXXXXXXXXX    $ZZ,ZZ9
                                                    ZZZ9      XXXXXXXXXXXXXXXXXX      $ZZ,ZZ9

                      PRINT ZZ9 SUMMARY    -    APPRAISED VALUE        -    $ZZ,ZZ9
                                                HIGHEST BID            -    $ZZ,ZZ9
                                                BID NUMBER             -    ZZZ9
                                                BID (ACCEPT/REJECT)    -    ACCEPTED

              ZZ9   **UNKNOWN*     $ZZ,ZZ9          ZZZ9      XXXXXXXXXXXXXXXXXXXX    $ZZ,ZZ9
                                                    ZZZ9      XXXXXXXXXXXXXXXXXX      $ZZ,ZZ9

                      PRINT ZZ9 SUMMARY    -    APPRAISED VALUE        -    $ZZ,ZZ9
                                                HIGHEST BID            -    $ZZ,ZZ9
                                                BID NUMBER             -    ZZZ9
                                                BID (ACCEPT/REJECT)    -    REJECTED

                      GALLERY ZZ9 SUMMARY  -    TOTAL BIDS ACCEPTED    -    ZZ9
                                           -    TOTAL BID AMOUNT       -    $ZZZZ,ZZ9

                      FINAL TOTAL          -    TOTAL BIDS ACCEPTED    -    ZZ9
                                           -    TOTAL BID AMOUNT       -    $Z,ZZZ,ZZ9
```

TABLE PROCESSING

The Print Name and Appraised Value can be found by searching the following table using the Print Number. If the Print Number in the input record is not found in the table, then the message **UNKNOWN* should be printed on the report instead of the Print Name, and the Appraised Value should be zero.

PRINT NUMBER	PRINT NAME	APPRAISED VALUE
100	WOODWARD	90,000
200	EXILED MAN	98,000
300	CITY LIFE	85,000
400	BEACH SIDE	82,000
500	OLDER DAYS	91,000
600	THE HEROES	94,000

When there is a change in Print Number, the Print Summary is to be printed. The Print Summary contains the Appraised Value, Highest Bid, Bid Number of the highest bid, and the message ACCEPTED or REJECTED. If the Print Number was not found in the table, the Highest Bid and the Bid Number should be printed, together with the message REJECTED. If the Print Number was found in the table, then whether the bid is accepted or rejected depends upon the print being auctioned and the gallery. Each gallery has rules for accepting bids or rejecting bids. All galleries accept the highest bid if the bid is over the appraised value. Galleries may accept or reject the highest bid if the bid is less than the appraised value. The multiple level table on page 9.36 summarizes the rules for accepting or rejecting high bids that are lower than the appraised value and is referenced using the first digit of the Print Number and the Gallery Number.

GALLERY NUMBER

		(050)	(100)
	(1)	YES	NO
PRINT	(2)	NO	YES
NUMBER	(3)	YES	NO
(FIRST DIGIT)	(4)	NO	NO
	(5)	YES	NO
	(6)	NO	YES

For example, if the highest bid for print number 100 is lower than the appraised value and gallery 050 is auctioning the print, the value YES is found in the table and means the gallery will accept the bid that is lower than the appraised value. If the highest bid for print number 300 is lower than the appraised value and gallery 100 is auctioning the print, then the value NO is found in the table and means the gallery will reject the highest bid.

When there is a change in Gallery Number, the processing which occurs when there is a change in print number must take place; and then the total number of bids accepted and the total of the bid amounts accepted for the gallery are to be printed.

After all records have been processed, the total number of bids accepted and the total bid amount for all records are to be printed.

CHAPTER TEN

SORTING; EXTERNAL TABLES

SORTING; EXTERNAL TABLES

10

INTRODUCTION

In many applications, reports are generated from records which are in a specific sequence. To place the input records in the desired sequence, they must be sorted prior to printing the report. Sorting is the process of placing records in an ascending or descending sequence based upon the value in a field or fields within the record. Records can be sorted in sequence based upon a numeric value in a field and can also be sorted in alphabetical sequence based upon an alphabetic value in a field. The fields upon which the records are sorted are called keys.

When programming using the COBOL language, input records can be sorted using the COBOL Sort statement. Sorting and the use of the Sort statement are explained in this chapter.

Previous chapters have explained the use of single level and multiple level tables. The data in the tables was specified during the coding process through the use of the Value clause and became part of the compiled COBOL program. In this chapter, the techniques for dynamically placing data in tables and then using the data in the tables will be explained.

SAMPLE PROGRAM

The sample program in this chapter produces a Cable Report which lists the customers of a cable TV service and their monthly charges. A sample of the Cable Report is illustrated in Figure 10-1.

```
APRIL 10, 1985              CALIFORNIA CABLE CO.                    PAGE   1

   CITY           CUSTOMER         BASE    NEWS    MOVIE   SPORTS   MUSIC   TOTAL
   NAME             NAME          CHARGE  CHARGE  CHARGE   CHARGE  CHARGE   CHARGE

ANAHEIM        LEVENSON, STEVEN    7.36    6.16   23.00     .00     .00    36.52
               METZEN, ARNOLD      7.36    6.16     .00   16.00    9.00    38.52
               YARBOURGH, PAMELA   7.36     .00     .00     .00     .00     7.36

RIVERSIDE      JONES, BARNABY      9.18     .00     .00     .00     .00     9.18
               SMITH, CHARLENE     9.18    7.05   19.00   17.00   11.00    63.23
               SMITH, CHARLES      9.18    7.05     .00   17.00     .00    33.23

SANTA ANA      ANDREWS, BETSY      8.47    6.93     .00   15.00   10.00    40.40
               FINDLATER, ROBERT   8.47    6.93   18.00   15.00   10.00    58.40

CHARGES BY CITY -

ANAHEIM    -      82.40
RIVERSIDE  -     105.64
SANTA ANA  -      98.80

TOTAL CHARGES   -    $286.84
```

Figure 10-1 California Cable Co. Report

The heading lines resemble those of previous programs except the date is printed in its longer form. That is, the date 04/10/85 appears in the heading as APRIL 10, 1985.

The report contains the City Name, Customer Name, Base Charge, News Charge, Movie Charge, Sports Charge, Music Charge, and Total Charge. The City Name is where the customer receives the cable TV service. Each of the charges pertains to a service used by the customer. All customers must pay the Base Charge. The News Charge, Movie Charge, Sports Charge, and Music Charge are optional. The Total Charge is the sum of the various charges for each customer.

A control break occurs when the City Name changes. A blank line appears when a control break occurs. For each city, the City Name is group indicated.

After all records have been processed, each City Name and the Total Charges for the city are printed, followed by the total charges for all cities.

The report is printed in ascending alphabetical order by City Name; and within each city, the records are in ascending alphabetical order by Customer Name. Thus, the records used to prepare this report must be sorted on Customer Name within City Name prior to printing the report.

The input to the program is a file of Cable Disk Records. The format of these records is illustrated in Figure 10-2.

Cable Disk Record				
FIELD DESCRIPTION	POSITION	LENGTH	DEC	ATTRIBUTE
City Name	1 – 10	10		Alphanumeric
Customer Name	11 – 30	20		Alphanumeric
Base Charge	31 – 34	4	2	Numeric
News Charge	35 – 38	4	2	Numeric
Movie Charge	39 – 42	4	2	Numeric
Sports Charge	43 – 46	4	2	Numeric
Music Charge	47 – 50	4	2	Numeric
Record Length		50		

Figure 10-2 Format of Cable Disk Records

The input record contains the City Name, Customer Name, Base Charge, News Charge, Movie Charge, Sports Charge, and Music Charge. A control break is taken upon a change in City Name. The file must be sorted based upon the key fields, City Name and Customer Name, found in the input record.

SORTING DATA

One of the requirements within the program is to sort the input records in an ascending sequence based upon the Customer Name within City Name. When programming in COBOL, a common method of sorting records within a file is to use the Sort statement. The processing which will be accomplished by the Sort statement is illustrated in Figures 10-3 and 10-4.

In step 1 in Figure 10-3, the records stored in the Cable Input File are read by the COBOL program one record at a time and are placed in a disk work file called the Sort Work File.

The records in the Cable Input File are read by the COBOL program and stored on disk in a Sort Work File in the same sequence in which they are read. After this step, the records in the Cable Input File and the records in the Sort Work File are identical. As with the Cable Input File, the Sort Work File must be defined in the COBOL program. After the data is placed in the Sort Work File, it is available to be sorted.

STEP 1

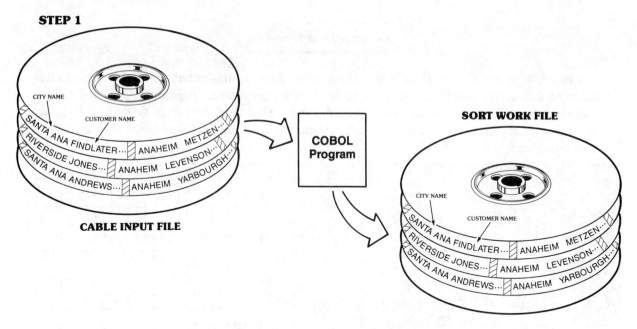

Figure 10-3 Placing Data in the Sort Work File

In step 2 in Figure 10-4, the Sort program, activated by the Sort statement, is invoked to sort the records in the Sort Work File and place them in the Sorted Cable File, which contains the output from the sort.

STEP 2

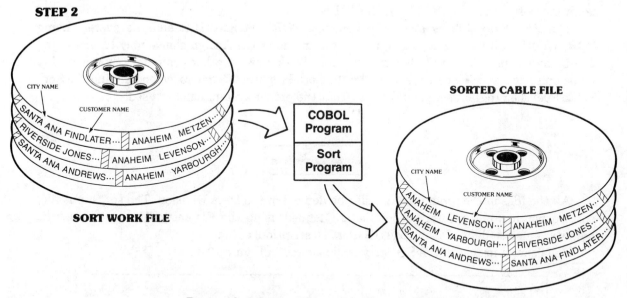

Figure 10-4 Sorting Data in the Sort Work File

The data stored in the Sort Work File is read by the Sort Program and is sorted into the desired sequence. In the sample program in this chapter, the data is sorted into ascending sequence based upon Customer Name within City Name. After the sorting is complete, the Sorted Cable File contains the records in an ascending sequence by Customer Name within City Name.

The Sorted Cable File must be defined within the COBOL program. After it has been created, it can be opened as an input file and be processed by the COBOL program to produce the Cable Report in the requested sequence.

Environment Division

In order to use the Sort statement to sort the data as illustrated, the Cable Input File must be defined so that it can be input to the sorting process. In addition, the Sorted Cable File must be defined to hold the sorted records, and a Sort Work File must be defined to hold the unsorted records. The entries in the Environment Division to define these files are illustrated in Figure 10–5.

```
002110  INPUT-OUTPUT SECTION.
002120
002130  FILE-CONTROL.
002140      SELECT CABLE-INPUT-FILE
002150          ASSIGN TO UT-S-CABLEIN.
002160      SELECT SORTED-CABLE-FILE
002170          ASSIGN TO UT-S-CABLESRT.
002180      SELECT CABLE-REPORT-FILE
002190          ASSIGN TO UT-S-CABLEPRT.
002200      SELECT SORT-WORK-FILE
003010          ASSIGN TO UT-S-SORTWORK.
```

Figure 10 - 5 Environment Division Entries for the Program Files

In Figure 10–5, the Select and Assign clauses for all of the files to be used in the sample program are illustrated. The Cable Input File is given the file-name CABLE-INPUT-FILE, the Sorted Cable File is given the file-name SORTED-CABLE-FILE, and the Printer Output File is given the file-name CABLE-REPORT-FILE.

The Sort Work File is given the file-name SORT-WORK-FILE and the system name SORTWORK. On some computers, the system name in the Assign clause may be any name chosen by the programmer to identify the Sort Work File; on other computers, however, this name must be a specific name required by the Sort Program. Therefore, when defining the Sort Work File, the programmer should ensure that the proper system name is used.

Data Division

All the files in the program must also be defined in the Data Division. The sort input file, sort output file, and printer output file are defined using the FD entry. The sort work file, however, must be defined using the SD (Sort Description) entry.

The general format of the SD entry is illustrated in Figure 10–6.

```
[SD  file-name

    [; RECORD CONTAINS [integer-1 TO] integer-2 CHARACTERS]

    [; DATA  {RECORD IS  }  data-name-1 [, data-name-2] ...] .
             {RECORDS ARE}
```

Figure 10 - 6 General Format of the SD Entry

The rules for constructing the SD entry are similar to those for the FD entries. Instead of coding the two characters FD in Area A of the coding form, the characters SD are coded.

Thus, in Figure 10–7, the two characters SD are specified together with the sort file-name SORT-WORK-FILE (line 004080).

```
003070 FD  CABLE-INPUT-FILE
003080         RECORD CONTAINS 50 CHARACTERS
003090         LABEL RECORDS ARE STANDARD
003100         DATA RECORD IS CABLE-INPUT-RECORD.
003110 01  CABLE-INPUT-RECORD.              PIC X(50).

003130 FD  SORTED-CABLE-FILE
003140         RECORD CONTAINS 50 CHARACTERS
003150         LABEL RECORDS ARE STANDARD
003160         DATA RECORD IS SORTED-CABLE-RECORD.
003170 01  SORTED-CABLE-RECORD.
003180     05  CITY-NAME-SORTCAB            PIC X(10).
003190     05  CUSTOMER-NAME-SORTCAB        PIC X(20).
003200     05  CABLE-USE-CHARGE-SORTCAB     PIC 99V99  OCCURS 5 TIMES.

004080 SD  SORT-WORK-FILE
004090         RECORD CONTAINS 50 CHARACTERS
004100         DATA RECORD IS SORT-WORK-RECORD.
004110 01  SORT-WORK-RECORD.
004120     05  CITY-NAME-SORTWRK            PIC X(10).
004130     05  CUSTOMER-NAME-SORTWRK        PIC X(20).
004140     05  FILLER                       PIC X(20).
```

Figure 10-7 Data Division File Definitions

Although the Record Contains clause and the Data Records clause are optional in the SD entry, it is suggested that these clauses be included for documentation purposes. Therefore, in Figure 10–7, these clauses are included to document that the record contains 50 characters and that the record name is SORT-WORK-RECORD.

Within SORT-WORK-RECORD, two fields are defined, CITY-NAME-SORTWRK and CUSTOMER-NAME-SORTWRK. The rest of the record is specified as Filler. The reason that the City Name and Customer Name are specified is that these are the fields, or keys, on which the sort is to take place. The only fields which must be specified in the sort work record are the fields which are to act as the keys when sorting. Since the City Name and Customer Name are the fields on which the sort is to take place, they must be specified in the Sort Work Record.

The input file to the sort is the CABLE-INPUT-FILE, as defined in Figure 10–7. The input area for this file (CABLE-INPUT-RECORD) is specified as 50 characters in length (Pic X(50)), but there are no detailed field definitions. This is because the fields within the record are not going to be referenced in the program; the fields will be referenced only in the sorted output file.

The output file from the sort is the SORTED-CABLE-FILE. This is the file which will be produced as a result of the sorting process, as illustrated in Figure 10–4. It contains the same number of characters in each record as the CABLE-INPUT-FILE because the same records are contained in this file as are contained in the CABLE-INPUT-FILE. The only difference between the two files is that the records in the CABLE-INPUT-FILE are unsorted, while the records in the SORTED-CABLE-FILE will be in sequence by Customer Name within City Name as a result of the sorting process.

The record description for the SORTED-CABLE-FILE contains a detailed definition of each of the fields because the records in this file will be processed by the instructions in the Procedure Division to produce the Cable Report. The use of the Occurs clause in the record definition will be explained later in this chapter.

SORT Statement

The Sort statement is used in the Procedure Division to cause the records in the input file to be read and placed into the sort work file, to cause the records in the sort work file to be sorted, and to create the sorted output file. The Sort statement in the sample program, together with the general format of the Sort statement, is illustrated in Figure 10-8.

```
021020        SORT SORT-WORK-FILE
021030             ASCENDING KEY CITY-NAME-SORTWRK, CUSTOMER-NAME-SORTWRK
021040             USING CABLE-INPUT-FILE
021050             GIVING SORTED-CABLE-FILE.
```

```
    SORT file-name-1 ON  {ASCENDING / DESCENDING}  KEY data-name-1  [, data-name-2]  ...

    USING file-name-2  [, file-name-3]  ...

    GIVING file-name-4
```

Figure 10-8 Sort Statement for the Sample Program and the General Format

The Sort statement begins with word SORT and is followed by the file-name-1 entry. The file-name-1 entry is always the name of the Sort Work File defined by the SD entry in the Data Division. In the coding for the sample program, the file-name specified is SORT-WORK-FILE, which is the name used for the SD entry (see Figure 10-7).

The next entry is the optional word ON followed by one of the required words, ASCENDING or DESCENDING. These words are used to indicate the sequence in which the particular field specified by data-name-1 is to be sorted. The word ASCENDING specifies that the data is to be sorted in an ascending sequence. Most sort programs will also allow the data to be sorted in a descending sequence, as specified by the word DESCENDING. The optional word KEY can then be specified to make the statement easier to read. In the sample program, the data is to be sorted in ascending sequence.

The data-name entry following either ASCENDING or DESCENDING specifies the data-name of the key field in the record to be sorted as specified in the File Section for the SD file. More than one field may be specified as a key field by using the data-name-2, etc. entries. The fields specified for the data-name-2, etc. are minor to the previous data-name; that is, the field specified first with data-name-1 is the major field in the sort, the field specified second with data-name-2 is the next major field in the sort, and so on. Different sort programs for different computers have varying maximums concerning the number of key fields which may be specified.

In the coding in Figure 10-8, the first field specified is CITY-NAME-SORTWRK, and the second name is CUSTOMER-NAME-SORTWRK. Thus, when the records are sorted, the major sort field is the City Name and the minor sort field is the Customer Name. After the records are sorted, they will be in Customer Name sequence within City Name sequence.

The entries described so far have specified the file to be sorted and the method and keys on which the records are to be sorted. It remains to specify which file(s) are input to the sort and what file is output from the sort. In order to specify the input file, the name of the file must be specified following the keyword USING. For the sample program, the file specified is CABLE-INPUT-FILE since this file contains the records to be sorted.

To specify the output file to be created by the sorting process, the GIVING keyword is used. The name of the file specified after the word GIVING is the file where the sorted records will be stored. In the coding in Figure 10–8, the file-name SORTED-CABLE-FILE is specified.

When the Sort statement is used with the USING and GIVING keywords, the input and output files specified are automatically opened prior to sorting and are closed after sorting by the Sort statement. After the output file is closed, the program can open the file as an input file and process the sorted data. This is the processing which takes place within the sample program. Thus, the CABLE-INPUT-FILE, SORTED-CABLE-FILE and SORT-WORK-FILE will be opened and closed by the Sort statement. After the sorting is complete, the SORTED-CABLE-FILE will contain the sorted data and is opened as an input file so the records can be read to produce the Cable Report.

TABLE PROCESSING

In previous chapters, single level and multiple level tables were used. The tables, together with the data they contained, were defined during the coding process and became part of the compiled source program. To change the data within one of the tables, the source program would have to be changed and recompiled. As a result, the data placed in the tables was data which would not change frequently.

In some applications, however, the data to be processed using tables is not known at the time the program is coded. Indeed, it may change dynamically based upon the data which is read from files or the processing which takes place within the program. When these types of tables (sometimes called external tables) are required, the COBOL program must reserve computer memory for the tables during the compilation process, but load the tables during program execution. As a result, these tables can be used to store and process data that changes frequently.

In the sample program, five different cable charges are found in the input record. All of these charges have the same attributes; that is, they are numeric, have the same number of characters in the fields, and have the same number of decimal positions. When a series of fields has the same attributes, it can be processed in a table rather than as separate fields. The definition of the table to contain the cable use charges is illustrated in Figure 10–9.

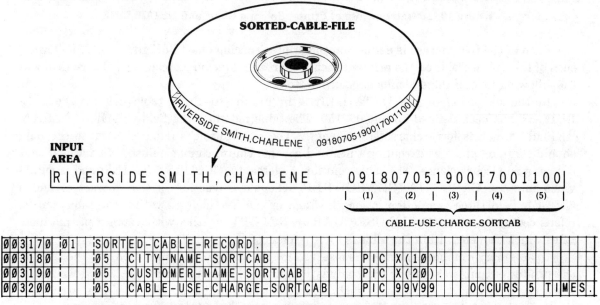

Figure 10-9 CABLE-USE-CHARGE-SORTCAB Table Defined in the Input Record

The input area contains the table named CABLE-USE-CHARGE-SORTCAB which is defined on line 003200. The Occurs clause specifies that the table contains five elements, one for each of the charges. Each element within the table can be referenced by the name CABLE-USE-CHARGE-SORTCAB plus a subscript that identifies which element within the table is to be referenced. This table is dynamically loaded with data since each time a new input record is read, the data in the table changes.

Since a table has been created to store the five cable charges associated with each input record, and since all five charge fields also appear on the Cable Report, a table is also defined in the printer output area. Figure 10–10 contains the printer spacing chart for the sample program and the coding for the printer output area in Working-Storage.

PRINTER SPACING CHART

XXXXXXXXXXXXXXXXX	CALIFORNIA CABLE CO.				PAGE ZZ9
CITY	CUSTOMER	BASE	NEWS	MOVIE	SPORTS	MUSIC	TOTAL
NAME	NAME	CHARGE	CHARGE	CHARGE	CHARGE	CHARGE	CHARGE
XXXXXXXXXX	XXXXXXXXXXXXXXXXXXXX	ZZ.99	ZZ.99	ZZ.99	ZZ.99	ZZ.99	ZZZ.99

| (1) | (2) | (3) | (4) | (5) |

CHARGE-REPORT

```
008070 01   DETAIL-LINE.
008080      05  CARRIAGE-CONTROL              PIC X.
008090      05  CITY-NAME-REPORT              PIC X(10).
008100      05  FILLER                        PIC X(3)    VALUE SPACES.
008110      05  CUSTOMER-NAME-REPORT          PIC X(20).
008120      05  FILLER                        PIC X(4)    VALUE SPACES.
008130      05  CHARGE-ALPHA-REPORT.
008140          10  FILLER                    PIC X(40)   VALUE SPACES.
008150      05  CHARGE-REPORT REDEFINES CHARGE-ALPHA-REPORT
008160                                                    OCCURS 5 TIMES.
008170          10  CABLE-USE-CHARGE-REPORT   PIC ZZ.99.
008180          10  FILLER                    PIC X(3).
008190      05  TOTAL-CHARGES-REPORT          PIC ZZZ.99.
008200      05  FILLER                        PIC X(49)   VALUE SPACES.
```

Figure 10-10 Relationship of Printer Spacing Chart and DETAIL-LINE

Each of the five charges is defined on the printer spacing chart in Figure 10–10. Following each of the charge fields on the printer spacing chart are three blank spaces. A charge field and the following field of three blanks appear five times.

In the definition of the DETAIL-LINE in Figure 10–10, a table called CHARGE-REPORT has been defined on line 008150. The table redefines the field CHARGE-ALPHA-REPORT which is forty characters in length. The redefinition is required because the field should contain spaces at execution time, and a Value clause cannot be used with a field that contains an Occurs clause. The table contains 5 elements (OCCURS 5 TIMES) and is subdivided into the CABLE-USE-CHARGE-REPORT field consisting of five characters and a FILLER field three characters in length. Each of the five charges within the table can be referenced by the name CABLE-USE-CHARGE-REPORT together with a subscript that identifies which element within the table is to be referenced.

In summary, computer memory is reserved for the table in the input area and the table in the printer output area during the compilation process, and the tables are loaded with data when the program is executed. As such, these tables are unlike other tables seen previously that were defined during the coding process and became part of the compiled source program.

Perform Varying Statement

In the sample program, the five charge fields contained in the input area are defined in a table called CABLE-USE-CHARGE-SORTCAB. The five charge fields contained in the output area are defined in a table called CABLE-USE-CHARGE-REPORT. One of the requirements of the sample program is that these charges be moved from the input area to the output area prior to printing the detail line. To move a series of fields which have been defined in a table to another series of fields defined in a table, the Perform Varying statement may be used. The Perform Varying statement used to move the charge fields in the sample program and the general format of the Perform Varying statement are illustrated in Figure 10-11.

```
016070        PERFORM B001-MOVE-CHARGES
016080            VARYING MOVE-CHARGES-SUBSCRIPT FROM 1 BY 1
016090            UNTIL MOVE-CHARGES-SUBSCRIPT IS GREATER THAN 5.

017050 B001-MOVE-CHARGES.
017060
017070        MOVE CABLE-USE-CHARGE-SORTCAB (MOVE-CHARGES-SUBSCRIPT) TO
017080            CABLE-USE-CHARGE-REPORT (MOVE-CHARGES-SUBSCRIPT).
```

$$\underline{\text{PERFORM}}\ \text{procedure-name-1}\ \left[\begin{Bmatrix}\underline{\text{THROUGH}}\\\underline{\text{THRU}}\end{Bmatrix}\ \text{procedure-name-2}\right]$$

$$\underline{\text{VARYING}}\ \begin{Bmatrix}\text{identifier-2}\\\text{index-name-1}\end{Bmatrix}\ \underline{\text{FROM}}\ \begin{Bmatrix}\text{identifier-3}\\\text{index-name-2}\\\text{literal-1}\end{Bmatrix}$$

$$\underline{\text{BY}}\ \begin{Bmatrix}\text{identifier-4}\\\text{literal-3}\end{Bmatrix}\ \underline{\text{UNTIL}}\ \text{condition-1}$$

Figure 10-11 Example of Perform Varying Statement

Procedure-name-1 in the general format of the Perform Varying statement specifies the name of the paragraph to be performed. The Varying clause is used to vary the value in a field FROM a given value BY a given value. The From value is the initial value to which the subscript identified by identifier-2 or index-name-1 will be set. The By value is the value which will be added to the value in the subscript each time the Perform Varying statement is executed.

In the coding in Figure 10-11, the value in the field MOVE-CHARGES-SUBSCRIPT will be varied from the value 1 by the value 1. This means that the first time the B001-MOVE-CHARGES paragraph is performed, the value in MOVE-CHARGES-SUBSCRIPT will be set to 1 ("From 1"). The second time the paragraph is performed by the Perform Varying statement, the value in MOVE-CHARGES-SUBSCRIPT will be 2, since the value 1 has been added to the subscript ("By 1"). The third time the paragraph is performed by the Perform Varying statement, the value in MOVE-CHARGES-SUBSCRIPT will be 3. The "By" value may be negative as well as positive, so that the effect would be to subtract a value from the subscript rather than add a value to the subscript.

When the Perform Varying statement is used, there must be a condition specified which indicates when the looping is to be terminated. This condition is indicated through the use of the Until clause. In the coding in Figure 10–11, the loop will be executed until the value in the MOVE-CHARGES-SUBSCRIPT field is greater than 5. When that condition occurs, performing the B001-MOVE-CHARGES paragraph will be terminated, and the statement on line 016100 which follows the Perform statement will be executed. After each execution of the loop, the arithmetic specified in the Varying clause through the use of the word BY takes place prior to the condition specified in the Until clause being checked.

The effect of the Perform Varying statement and the Move statement in the performed paragraph in Figure 10–11 is to move all five elements from the CABLE-USE-CHARGE-SORTCAB table in the input area to the five elements in the CABLE-USE-CHARGE-REPORT table in output area. This occurs in the following manner: The first time the B001-MOVE-CHARGES paragraph is performed, the value in the subscript field MOVE-CHARGES-SUBSCRIPT will be 1 because it was initially set to the value 1 ("From 1"). Therefore, the first element of the input table CABLE-USE-CHARGE-SORTCAB will be moved to the first element of the output table CABLE-USE-CHARGE-REPORT by the Move statement on line 017070. After the paragraph is performed one time, the value in the MOVE-CHARGES-SUBSCRIPT will be incremented "By 1," and then the condition specified by the Until clause will be tested. Since the value in MOVE-CHARGES-SUBSCRIPT is not greater than 5, the B001-MOVE-CHARGES paragraph will be performed again.

The second time, the value in MOVE-CHARGES-SUBSCRIPT is 2; therefore, the second element in the CABLE-USE-CHARGE-SORTCAB table will be moved to the second element in the CABLE-USE-CHARGE-REPORT table. After the paragraph is performed, the value in MOVE-CHARGES-SUBSCRIPT will incremented "By 1" and then the value in the MOVE-CHARGES-SUBSCRIPT field is compared to the value 5 by the Until clause. It will again be found that the value is not greater than 5. Therefore, the B001-MOVE-CHARGES paragraph will be performed a third time, with the value in MOVE-CHARGES-SUBSCRIPT equal to 3. Thus, the third element in the CABLE-USE-CHARGE-SORTCAB table will be moved to the third element in the CABLE-USE-CHARGE-REPORT table. This processing would continue until all five elements in the CABLE-USE-CHARGE-SORTCAB table are moved to the five elements in the CABLE-USE-CHARGE-REPORT table.

The Perform Varying statement is commonly used in problems involving tables. In the sample program, the five charges in the input area must be added together in order to obtain the Total Charge which is printed on the report. The Perform Varying statement and the performed paragraph used in the sample program to add the five charges is illustrated in Figure 10–12.

```
016100 |    MOVE ZERO TO TOTAL-CHARGES-WORK.
016110 |    PERFORM B002-CALCULATE-TOTAL-CHARGE
016120 |        VARYING ADD-CHARGES-SUBSCRIPT FROM 1 BY 1
016130 |        UNTIL ADD-CHARGES-SUBSCRIPT IS GREATER THAN 5.

017120 | B002-CALCULATE-TOTAL-CHARGE.
017130 |
017140 |    ADD CABLE-USE-CHARGE-SORTCAB (ADD-CHARGES-SUBSCRIPT) TO
017150 |        TOTAL-CHARGES-WORK.
```

Figure 10-12 Perform Varying Statement to Add Charges

The effect of the Perform statement and the Add statement in Figure 10–12 is to add all the charges stored in the CABLE-USE-CHARGE-SORTCAB table and store the sum in the TOTAL-CHARGES-WORK field. The processing involved is similar to the processing described earlier to move the five elements of the charge table from the input area to the output area. Prior to executing the Perform Varying statement that causes the addition of the charges, the TOTAL-CHARGES-WORK field must be set to zero to guarantee that the work area contains the value zero prior to beginning the addition operation.

After the five charges for each customer have been added together and stored in the Total Charges work area, the value in TOTAL-CHARGES-WORK is moved to the Total Charge field on the report. Then, the value in TOTAL-CHARGES-WORK is added to the City Total accumulator which contains the Total Charges for all customers within a city. When a control break occurs and all customers for a city have been processed, the name of the city from the Previous City Name field and the value in the City Total accumulator are moved to a table so they can be printed after all records have been processed. The use of a table to store the city name and the total city charge is illustrated in Figure 10–13.

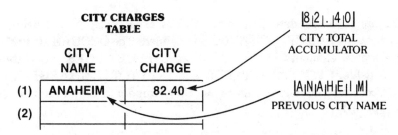

Figure 10-13 Use of a Table to Store City Name and Total Charges

Placing data in the City Charges Table will continue until all control breaks and all records have been processed. The data in the City Charges Table is then used to print the final totals as illustrated in Figure 10–14.

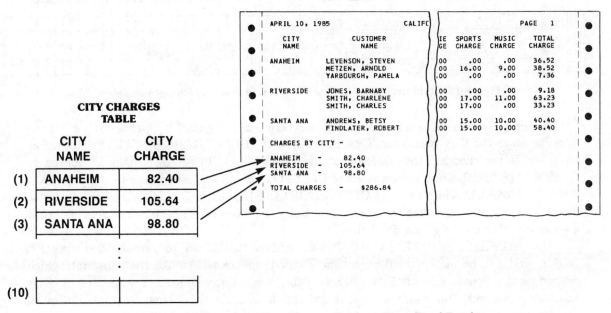

Figure 10-14 Use of the City Charges Table to Print Final Totals

After all records have been processed, each City Name and its Charges are moved from the City Charges Table to the final total line and are printed on the report.

At the time of programming, the number of cities to be processed is unknown, and that number may increase or decrease depending upon the data processed. Thus, the exact number of elements in the City Charges Table is unknown. Although the exact number of cities is unknown, a reasonable estimate of the number of cities must be made by the programmer in coordination with the systems analyst at the time of programming. This estimate should be based on the number of cities now serviced by the California Cable Company and an estimate of the number of cities that may be added in the future. Three cities are now serviced by the California Cable Company, and a reasonable estimate is determined to be 10 cities. Therefore, the City Charges Table should contain ten elements.

The definition of the City Charges Table appears in Figure 10–15.

```
007120          05  CITY-CHARGES-TABLE.
007130              10  CITY-CHARGES                      OCCURS 10 TIMES.
007140                  15  CITY-NAME-TABLE          PIC X(10).
007150                  15  CITY-TOTAL-CHARGE-TABLE  PIC 9(4)V99.
```

Figure 10-15 Definition of a Table to Store City Name and City Charges

The table in Figure 10–15 is identified as the CITY-CHARGES-TABLE using a level 05 entry. Within this entry, the field CITY-CHARGES is defined. The OCCURS 10 TIMES clause signifies that there are 10 elements in the table. The CITY-CHARGES group item is then subdivided into two fields, CITY-NAME-TABLE and CITY-TOTAL-CHARGE-TABLE. The instructions in the Procedure Division to store the City Name and City Charges in the table are illustrated in Figure 10–16.

```
018060  B020-PROCESS-CITY-CHANGE.
018070
018080      MOVE PREVIOUS-CITY-NAME TO
018090          CITY-NAME-TABLE (CITY-CHARGES-SUBSCRIPT).
018100      MOVE CITY-TOTAL-ACCUM TO
018110          CITY-TOTAL-CHARGE-TABLE (CITY-CHARGES-SUBSCRIPT).
018120      ADD 1 TO CITY-CHARGES-SUBSCRIPT.
018130      ADD 1 TO NUMBER-OF-CITIES-COUNT.
018140      MOVE ZEROS TO CITY-TOTAL-ACCUM.
018150      MOVE CITY-NAME-SORTCAB TO PREVIOUS-CITY-NAME.
018160      MOVE SPACE-TWO-LINES TO PROPER-SPACING.
```

Figure 10-16 Instructions to Store City Name and City Charges in Table

Within the module which is executed when there is a change in City Name are the instructions to store the City Name and City Charges in the CITY-CHARGES-TABLE. Each time the City Name changes, the contents of the PREVIOUS-CITY-NAME field are moved to CITY-NAME-TABLE and the contents of CITY-TOTAL-ACCUM are moved to CITY-TOTAL-CHARGE-TABLE. The subscript CITY-CHARGES-SUBSCRIPT is initialized to 1 prior to execution and is incremented by 1 each time a city is processed. This subscript references the elements within the City Charges Table.

The NUMBER-OF-CITIES-COUNT field will be initialized to zero before execution begins, and will be incremented each time a city is processed. Unlike the subscript, which references the elements in the City Charges Table, the counter contains the number of cities that are processed. This count is used to indicate how many cities must be printed after all records have been processed.

After all records have been processed and the table has been loaded with the City Name and City Charges for all cities, the contents of the City Charges Table will be printed as part of the final total lines. The Perform Varying statement used to print the elements of the CITY-CHARGES-TABLE appears in Figure 10–17.

```
019120        PERFORM B031-PRINT-CITY-TOTAL-LINES
019130            VARYING PRINT-CITY-SUBSCRIPT FROM 1 BY 1
019140            UNTIL PRINT-CITY-SUBSCRIPT IS GREATER THAN
019150            NUMBER-OF-CITIES-COUNT.

020020  B031-PRINT-CITY-TOTAL-LINES.
020030
020040      MOVE CITY-NAME-TABLE (PRINT-CITY-SUBSCRIPT) TO
020050          CITY-NAME-FINTOT.
020060      MOVE CITY-TOTAL-CHARGE-TABLE (PRINT-CITY-SUBSCRIPT) TO
020070          CITY-TOTAL-CHARGE-FINTOT.
020080      WRITE CABLE-REPORT-LINE FROM CITY-CHARGE-LINE
020090          AFTER ADVANCING PROPER-SPACING.
020100      MOVE SPACE-ONE-LINE TO PROPER-SPACING.
```

Figure 10-17 Perform Varying Statement to Print City Names and City Charges

The Perform Varying statement in Figure 10–17 performs the B031-PRINT-CITY-TOTAL-LINES paragraph one time for each city stored in the CITY-CHARGES-TABLE. The subscript PRINT-CITY-SUBSCRIPT is set to the value 1 ("From 1") and is incremented by 1 ("By 1") until the value in the PRINT-CITY-SUBSCRIPT field is greater than the value in the NUMBER-OF-CITIES-COUNT field. The NUMBER-OF-CITIES-COUNT field contains the number of cities processed (see Figure 10–16). Therefore, the Perform statement will terminate processing when one final total line has been printed for each city stored in the City Charges Table.

In the B031-PRINT-CITY-TOTAL-LINES paragraph, the City Name is moved from the City Charges Table to the field CITY-NAME-FINTOT located in the total line, and the City Charge is moved to the CITY-TOTAL-CHARGE-FINTOT field located in the same final total line. The line is then written on the report, the spacing is set for single spacing, and control is returned to the Perform Varying statement.

String Statement

In the sample programs illustrated thus far, the date for the heading line was obtained using the Accept statement. The date was stored in three fields, YEAR-WORK, MONTH-WORK, and DAY-WORK. The date was moved from these three work areas to the heading line in the form MM/DD/YY. For example, if the date was January 25, 1987, then the date appeared on the report as 01/25/87.

The date on the Cable Report created by the sample program in this chapter appears in its longer form (see Figure 10–1). Thus, the same date described above would appear on the report as JANUARY 25, 1987. Since the date is obtained in the same fashion as in previous programs, it must be manipulated in order to obtain the longer form.

Data which is stored in different fields, such as the three date work areas, can be concatenated, or joined, into a single field (in this case, the field to contain the longer date) using the String statement. The String statement to concatenate the data in the three work areas into a single field is illustrated in Figure 10–18.

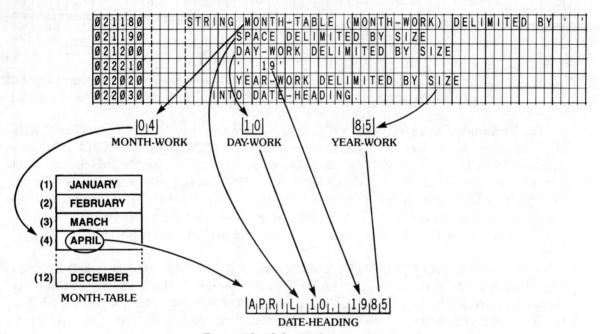

Figure 10-18 String Statement

The word STRING must be specified first. Next comes the name of the field or fields whose contents are to be placed into a single field. The first field specified in Figure 10-18 is MONTH-TABLE (MONTH-WORK). The MONTH-TABLE contains the names of the twelve months. The MONTH-WORK field contains a month number from 1 to 12 that is obtained using the Accept statement. The value in the MONTH-WORK field is used as a subscript to MONTH-TABLE to obtain the name of the month. The entry MONTH-TABLE (MONTH-WORK) will retrieve the name of the month associated with the value contained in the field MONTH-WORK. Thus, if MONTH-WORK contained the value 01, the first element of the table containing the month name JANUARY would be referenced. If, as in Figure 10-18, MONTH-WORK contained the value 04, the fourth element containing the month name APRIL would be referenced.

The Delimited clause in the String statement specifies the manner in which the number of characters to be included from a particular field is determined. The entry DELIMITED BY ' ' indicates that the element of the MONTH-TABLE is to be included until the first blank space is found in the element, until all the characters in the sending field have been moved, or until the receiving field has been filled, whichever occurs first. The space will not be moved. Thus, if the table element contains the value JANUARY, seven characters are included, whereas if the table element contains the value APRIL, five characters are included.

The data is moved to the field identified by the INTO phrase. In the coding in Figure 10–18, the data is concatenated into the DATE-HEADING field (line 022030).

The entry on line 021190, SPACE DELIMITED BY SIZE, contains the figurative constant SPACE, which refers to a single character field that contains a blank. The DELIMITED BY SIZE entry causes the full length of the field to be moved. In this case, the size of the field is one character, so a single blank character is moved to DATE-HEADING, following the name of the month.

Next, the DAY-WORK DELIMITED BY SIZE entry causes the full contents of the DAY-WORK field to be moved to the DATE-HEADING field. The DAY-WORK field is two characters in length, so the BY SIZE entry causes the two characters in the field, 10, to be moved to the DATE-HEADING field. The literal ', 19' is then moved to the DATE-HEADING field, followed by the contents of the YEAR-WORK field (85).

As a result of the String statement, data from a variety of fields has been joined together to produce the date in its long form for the heading line. The String statement can be used whenever data from different fields must be joined together into one field.

Unstring Statement

The Unstring statement will distribute data which is in a single field to two or more other fields. It is the opposite of the String statement. Figure 10–19 illustrates the use of the Unstring statement.

```
UNSTRING identifier-1

    [DELIMITED BY [ALL] {identifier-2}  [, OR [ALL] {identifier-3}] ...
                        {literal-1   }               {literal-2  }

    INTO identifier-4 [, DELIMITER IN identifier-5] [, COUNT IN identifier-6]

        [, identifier-7 [, DELIMITER IN identifier-8] [, COUNT IN identifier-9]] ...

    [WITH POINTER identifier-10] [TALLYING IN identifier-11]

    [; ON OVERFLOW imperative-statement]
```

```
010010        UNSTRING NAME-INPUT DELIMITED BY ' '
010020            INTO FIRST-NAME-WORK
010030                 LAST-NAME-WORK.
```

NAME-INPUT |H|E|R|B|E|R|T| |A|D|A|M|S| | | | | | | |

FIRST-NAME-WORK |H|E|R|B|E|R|T| | | | LAST-NAME-WORK |A|D|A|M|S| | | | |

Figure 10-19 Unstring Statement

The field which contains the data to be separated is specified as identifier-1. In Figure

10–19, the field is NAME-INPUT. The DELIMITED BY phrase is used to specify the characters which, when found in the identifier-1 field, will terminate the search and cause the data to be moved from the identifier-1 field to the identifier-4, identifier-7, . . . fields. The search is terminated by finding the delimiter character, when all of the sending field has been moved, or when the receiving field has been filled. In the coding in Figure 10–19, when a blank space is encountered in the NAME-INPUT field, the characters to the left of the blank will be moved to the first identifier (FIRST-NAME-WORK) following the word INTO in the Unstring statement. The blank occurs after the "T" in the name HERBERT in the NAME-INPUT field. Therefore, the characters H-E-R-B-E-R-T are moved to the FIRST-NAME-WORK field.

The search then continues for the next blank character in the NAME-INPUT field. It is found after the name ADAMS. Therefore, the letters A-D-A-M-S are moved to the next field specified in the Unstring statement (LAST-NAME-WORK). This type of search and move activity will continue until either there are no more receiving fields or until the last character in the sending field has been moved.

SAMPLE PROGRAM

The printer spacing chart and the format of the input records for the sample program are illustrated in Figure 10–20.

Output

```
                                                          PRINTER SPACING CHART

 1
 2 XXXXXXXXXXXXXXXXX          CALIFORNIA CABLE CO.                       PAGE ZZ9
 3
 4   CITY              CUSTOMER          BASE    NEWS    MOVIE   SPORTS  MUSIC    TOTAL
 5   NAME              NAME              CHARGE  CHARGE  CHARGE  CHARGE  CHARGE   CHARGE
 6
 7 XXXXXXXXX     XXXXXXXXXXXXXXXXXXXX    ZZ.99   ZZ.99   ZZ.99   ZZ.99   ZZ.99   ZZZ.99
 8               XXXXXXXXXXXXXXXXXXXX    ZZ.99   ZZ.99   ZZ.99   ZZ.99   ZZ.99   ZZZ.99
 9
10 XXXXXXXXX     XXXXXXXXXXXXXXXXXXXX    ZZ.99   ZZ.99   ZZ.99   ZZ.99   ZZ.99   ZZZ.99
11               XXXXXXXXXXXXXXXXXXXX    ZZ.99   ZZ.99   ZZ.99   ZZ.99   ZZ.99   ZZZ.99
12
13 CHARGES BY CITY -
14
15 XXXXXXXXXX -  Z,ZZZ.99
16 XXXXXXXXXX -  Z,ZZZ.99
17
18 TOTAL CHARGES    - $$$,$$$.99
19 - - - - - - - - - - - - - - - - - - - - -
20 CABLE REPORT - NO RECORDS TO PROCESS
```

Figure 10-20 Printer Spacing Chart (Part 1 of 2)

Input

Cable Disk Record				
FIELD DESCRIPTION	POSITION	LENGTH	DEC	ATTRIBUTE
City Name	1 – 10	10		Alphanumeric
Customer Name	11 – 30	20		Alphanumeric
Base Charge	31 – 34	4	2	Numeric
News Charge	35 – 38	4	2	Numeric
Movie Charge	39 – 42	4	2	Numeric
Sports Charge	43 – 46	4	2	Numeric
Music Charge	47 – 50	4	2	Numeric
Record Length		50		

Figure 10-20 Program Input (Part 2 of 2)

Program Narrative

PROGRAM NARRATIVE			
SUBJECT Cable Report	DATE January 21		PAGE 1 OF 1
TO Programmer	FROM Systems Analyst		

A program is to be written to prepare a Cable Report. The format of the input record and the printer spacing chart are included with this narrative. The program should include the following processing:

1. The program should read the input records and create the Cable Report as per the format illustrated on the printer spacing chart. The report contains the City Name, Customer Name, Base Charge, News Charge, Movie Charge, Sports Charge, Music Charge, and Total Charges.

2. Headings are printed on the first and subsequent pages of the report. The heading contains the date and page number. The date should contain the month (written out), the day, and the year (ex. — January 23, 1986). Fifty-five lines are to appear on each page before skipping to a new page.

3. One line is printed on the report for each input record that is read. The lines are single spaced. The report should be group indicated on City Name.

4. When there is a change in City Name, a blank line should be printed.

5. Final Total lines are printed after all input records have been processed. The Final Totals should include a list of all cities and their charges and a total of charges for all cities.

6. The program is to be written in COBOL.

7. Input records must be sorted by Customer Name within City Name.

Figure 10-21 Program Narrative

Program Design

As with all programs, the first step in the design of the sample program is to analyze the output, input, and program narrative, and then determine the structure of the program by determining the major processing tasks necessary to transform the input to output. The structure of the sample program is shown by the Hierarchy Chart in Figure 10-22. The IPO Charts which were used to determine the structure of the program are illustrated in Figure 10-23 through Figure 10-29.

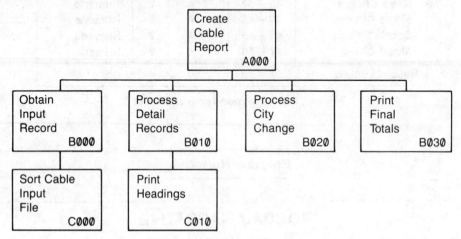

Figure 10-22 Hierarchy Chart

IPO CHART				
PROGRAM: Cable Report		**PROGRAMMER:** Forsythe		**DATE:** Jan. 23
MODULE NAME: Create Cable Report	**REF:** A000	**MODULE FUNCTION:** Create the Cable Report		
INPUT	**PROCESSING**	**REF:**		**OUTPUT**
1. Cable Disk File	1. Initialize			1. Cable Report
	2. Obtain an input record	B000		
	3. Process the detail records	B010		
	4. Process city change	B020		
	5. Print the final totals	B030		
	6. Terminate			

Figure 10-23 IPO Chart for Create Cable Report Module

IPO CHART

PROGRAM: Cable Report	PROGRAMMER: Forsythe	DATE: Jan. 23
MODULE NAME: Obtain Input Record	REF: B000	MODULE FUNCTION: Obtain an Input Record

INPUT	PROCESSING	REF:	OUTPUT
1. Sorted Cable Disk	1. Sort the cable records	C000	1. Input Record
File	2. Read sorted input records		

Figure 10-24 IPO Chart for Obtain Input Record Module

IPO CHART

PROGRAM: Cable Report	PROGRAMMER: Forsythe	DATE: Jan. 23
MODULE NAME: Process Detail Records	REF: B010	MODULE FUNCTION: Process the Detail Records

INPUT	PROCESSING	REF:	OUTPUT
1. Sorted Cable Disk	1. Print headings	C010	1. Detail Print Line
Record	2. Format print line		2. Updated Accumu-
2. Accumulators and	3. Calculate total charges		lators and Counters
Counters	4. Update counters and		
	accumulators		
	5. Write the detail line		

Figure 10-25 IPO Chart for Process Detail Records Module

IPO CHART

PROGRAM: Cable Report	PROGRAMMER: Forsythe	DATE: Jan. 23
MODULE NAME: Process City Change	REF: B020	MODULE FUNCTION: Process City Change

INPUT	PROCESSING	REF:	OUTPUT
1. Old City Name	1. Update city charges table		1. City Total
2. New City Name	2. Increment number of cities		Accumulator
3. City Total	counter		2. Number of Cities
Accumulator	3. Reset city total accumulator		Counter
4. Number of Cities	4. Reset city compare area		3. City Charges Table
Counter			4. City Name Compare
5. City Charges Table			Area

Figure 10-26 IPO Chart for Process City Change Module

IPO CHART

PROGRAM: Cable Report	PROGRAMMER: Forsythe	DATE: Jan. 23
MODULE NAME: Print Final Totals	REF: B030 MODULE FUNCTION:	Print the Final Totals

INPUT	PROCESSING	REF:	OUTPUT
1. Final Total	1. Format final total lines		1. Final Total Lines
Accumulator	2. Write final total lines		
2. Number of Cities			
Counter			
3. City Charges Table			

Figure 10-27 IPO Chart for Print Final Totals Module

IPO CHART

PROGRAM: Cable Report	PROGRAMMER: Forsythe	DATE: Jan. 23
MODULE NAME: Sort Cable File	REF: C000 MODULE FUNCTION:	Sort the Cable File

INPUT	PROCESSING	REF:	OUTPUT
1. Unsorted Cable Disk	1. Sort cable file on city name,		1. Sorted Cable Disk File
File	customer name		

Figure 10-28 IPO Chart for Sort Cable Input File Module

IPO CHART

PROGRAM: Cable Report	PROGRAMMER: Forsythe	DATE: Jan. 23
MODULE NAME: Print Headings	REF: C010 MODULE FUNCTION:	Print the Headings

INPUT	PROCESSING	REF:	OUTPUT
1. Heading Lines	1. Format the heading lines		1. Heading Lines
	2. Print the heading lines		

Figure 10-29 IPO Chart for Print Headings Module

Most of the modules in the sample program are the same as those found in previous programs. The major difference is that, as can be seen in Figure 10-23, obtaining an input record is large and complex enough to require a separate module. This is because as part of obtaining the input record, the records must be in the proper sequence. This, in turn, requires that the input records be sorted into the proper sequence — customer name within city name. This process is a part of obtaining an input record and, therefore, makes the major processing task of obtaining an input record large enough to justify a separate module.

An examination of the module which obtains an input record (Figure 10-24) reveals that the sorting task will take place in a separate module (C000). This is done because sorting is a single function which may require some significant processing.

The remainder of the major processing tasks for the program, and the resulting modules, are quite similar to prior programs.

Program Logic

The program logic is developed using pseudocode. The pseudocode specifications for the program are shown in Figure 10-30 thorough Figure 10-36.

PSEUDOCODE SPECIFICATIONS

PROGRAM: Cable Report	PROGRAMMER: Forsythe	DATE: Jan. 23
MODULE NAME: Create Cable Report	REF: A000	MODULE FUNCTION: Create the Cable Report

PSEUDOCODE	REF:	DATA BASES, FILES, RECORDS, FIELDS REQUIRED
Open cable report file		Cable report file
Obtain an input record	B000	Input record area
IF there is a record		City name
Move city name to compare area		Customer name
PERFORM UNTIL no more input		Charge fields
records		There is a record indicator
IF city name not = city name		City name compare area
in compare area		No more records indicator
Process city change	B020	City change indicator
Indicate a change in city		No records message
ENDIF		
Process detail records	B010	
Obtain an input record	B000	
ENDPERFORM		
Process city change	B020	
Print final totals	B030	
ELSE		
Print no records message		
ENDIF		
Close the files		
Stop run		

Figure 10-30 Pseudocode Specifications for Create Cable Report Module

PSEUDOCODE SPECIFICATIONS

PROGRAM: Cable Report	PROGRAMMER: Forsythe	DATE: Jan. 23
MODULE NAME: Obtain Input Record	REF: B000	MODULE FUNCTION: Obtain an Input Record

PSEUDOCODE	REF:	DATA BASES, FILES, RECORDS, FIELDS REQUIRED
IF cable input file not sorted		Cable input file sorted indicator
Sort cable records	C000	Sorted cable file
Indicate cable input file is sorted		Input area for sorted cable file
Open sorted cable file		No more records indicator
ENDIF		
Read a sorted cable input record		
IF there are no more records		
Close the sorted cable file		
ENDIF		

Figure 10-31 Pseudocode Specifications for Obtain Input Record Module

PSEUDOCODE SPECIFICATIONS

PROGRAM: Cable Report	PROGRAMMER: Forsythe	DATE: Jan. 23

MODULE NAME: Process Detail Records	REF: B010	MODULE FUNCTION: Process the Detail Records

PSEUDOCODE	REF:	DATA BASES, FILES, RECORDS, FIELDS REQUIRED

IF lines printed is = or > page size or
  first page
    Print the headings
    Move city name in compare area to output
      area
ENDIF
IF there was a change in city
    Move city name to output area
    Reset city change indicator
ENDIF
Move customer name to output area
PERFORM UNTIL all charges are moved
    Move charge to output area
ENDPERFORM
Set total charge work area to zero
PERFORM UNTIL all charges are added
    Add charge to total charges
ENDPERFORM
Move total charges to output area
Add total charges to city total accumulator
Add total charges to final total accumulator
Write a line on the report
Add proper spacing to lines printed
Set spacing to single spacing
Clear the output area
	C010	Lines printed counter
		Page size constant
		First page indicator
		City name compare area
		Printer output area
		    City name
		    Customer name
		    Base charge
		    News charge
		    Movie charge
		    Sports charge
		    Music charge
		    Total charge
		City change indicator
		Input area
		    City name
		    Customer name
		    Charges
		Move charges subscript
		Total charge work area
		Add charges subscript
		City total accumulator
		Final total accumulator
		Spacing control field
		Single space control character

Figure 10-32 Pseudocode Specifications for Process Detail Records Module

PSEUDOCODE SPECIFICATIONS

PROGRAM: Cable Report	PROGRAMMER: Forsythe	DATE: Jan. 23

MODULE NAME: Process City Change	REF: B020	MODULE FUNCTION: Process the City Change

PSEUDOCODE	REF:	DATA BASES, FILES, RECORDS, FIELDS REQUIRED

Move city name in compare area to city charge table
Move city total accumulator to city charge table
Add 1 to city charges subscript
Add 1 to number of cities counter
Set city total accumulator to zero
Move the new city name to compare area
Set spacing for double spacing
		City name compare area
		City charges table —
		    City name
		    City charges
		City total accumulator
		City charges subscript
		Number of cities counter
		New city from input area
		Spacing control field
		Double space control character

Figure 10-33 Pseudocode Specifications for Process City Change Module

PSEUDOCODE SPECIFICATIONS

PROGRAM: Cable Report	PROGRAMMER: Forsythe	DATE: Jan. 23
MODULE NAME: Print Final Totals	REF: B030	MODULE FUNCTION: Print the Final Totals

PSEUDOCODE	REF:	DATA BASES, FILES, RECORDS, FIELDS REQUIRED

Write final total heading line
Set spacing for double spacing
PERFORM UNTIL all table elements are printed
   Move city name from table to city total line
   Move city charges from table to city total line
   Write the city total line
   Set spacing for single spacing
ENDPERFORM
Move final total accumulator to final total line
Write final total line
		Final heading line
		Spacing control field
		Double space control character
		Print city subscript
		City charges table —
		   City name
		   City charges
		City total line
		Single space control character
		Final total accumulator
		Final total line

Figure 10-34 Pseudocode Specifications for Print Final Totals Module

PSEUDOCODE SPECIFICATIONS

PROGRAM: Cable Report	PROGRAMMER: Forsythe	DATE: Jan. 23
MODULE NAME: Sort Cable File	REF: C000	MODULE FUNCTION: Sort the Cable File

PSEUDOCODE	REF:	DATA BASES, FILES, RECORDS, FIELDS REQUIRED
Sort the cable disk file		City name Customer name Cable disk input file Sort work file Sort output file

Figure 10-35 Pseudocode Specifications for Sort Cable Input File Module

PSEUDOCODE SPECIFICATIONS

PROGRAM: Cable Report	PROGRAMMER: Forsythe	DATE: Jan. 23
MODULE NAME: Print Headings	REF: C010 MODULE FUNCTION:	Print the Headings

PSEUDOCODE	REF:	DATA BASES, FILES, RECORDS, FIELDS REQUIRED
Obtain the date Determine month and move date to first heading line Move the page number to the heading line Write the first heading line Add 1 to page count Write the second heading line Write the third heading line Set spacing for double spacing Set lines printed counter to four		Date work area Day Month Year Month table First heading line Page count Second heading line Third heading line Spacing control field Double spacing control character Lines printed counter

Figure 10-36 Pseudocode Specifications for Print Headings Module

DEFINITION OF SUBSCRIPTS

When moving, adding, and printing elements of a table, subscripts defined as numeric fields must be used. Any numeric field defining a whole number will suffice for a subscript field. The subscripts used in the sample program are illustrated in Figure 10-37.

```
006090  01   SUBSCRIPTS.
006100       05   ADD-CHARGES-SUBSCRIPT      PIC S9.
006110       05   MOVE-CHARGES-SUBSCRIPT     PIC S9.
006120       05   CITY-CHARGES-SUBSCRIPT     PIC S99      VALUE +1.
006130       05   PRINT-CITY-SUBSCRIPT       PIC S99.
```

Figure 10-37 Definition of Subscripts

The ADD-CHARGES-SUBSCRIPT and MOVE-CHARGES-SUBSCRIPT are used in the sample program to add and move the elements of the table which contains the five charges found in the input record.

The CITY-CHARGES-SUBSCRIPT and PRINT-CITY-SUBSCRIPT are used to load and print the elements of a table defined to contain a maximum of 10 elements. Since there may be as many as ten elements in this table, the subscripts are defined using PIC S99. The sample program requires that the CITY-CHARGES-SUBSCRIPT be initialized to 1 prior to the execution of the program. Thus, the VALUE +1 clause appears with this subscript.

SUMMARY

Sorting data files to place the data in the proper sequence and the use of dynamically loaded tables for the storage and manipulation of data are common and widespread practices in business application programming.

Source Listing

The following pages contain the source listing of the sample program.

```
PP 5740-CB1 RELEASE 2.3 + PTF 8 - UP13477        IBM OS/VS COBOL   JULY 24, 1978        16.19.01  DATE APR 10,1985

     1                        16.19.01       APR 10,1985

 00001    001010 IDENTIFICATION DIVISION.                                    CABLERPT
 00002    001020                                                             CABLERPT
 00003    001030 PROGRAM-ID.    CABLERPT.                                     CABLERPT
 00004    001040 AUTHOR.        FORSYTHE.                                     CABLERPT
 00005    001050 INSTALLATION.  BREA.                                         CABLERPT
 00006    001060 DATE-WRITTEN.  JAN 30,1985.                                  CABLERPT
 00007    001070 DATE-COMPILED. APR 10,1985.                                  CABLERPT
 00008    001080 SECURITY.      UNCLASSIFIED.                                 CABLERPT
 00009    001090                                                             CABLERPT
 00010    001100**********************************************************   CABLERPT
 00011    001110*                                                        *   CABLERPT
 00012    001120*  THIS PROGRAM PRODUCES A CABLE REPORT. THE REPORT CONTAINS  *   CABLERPT
 00013    001130*  CITY NAME, CUSTOMER NAME, BASE CHARGE, NEWS CHARGE, MOVIE  *   CABLERPT
 00014    001140*  CHARGE, SPORTS CHARGE, MUSIC CHARGE, AND TOTAL CHARGE.  *   CABLERPT
 00015    001150*  THE CABLE FILE IS SORTED BY CUSTOMER NAME WITHIN CITY NAME. *   CABLERPT
 00016    001160*  FINAL TOTALS INCLUDING CITY NAME AND CITY CHARGES ARE  *   CABLERPT
 00017    001170*  PRINTED.                                               *   CABLERPT
 00018    001180*                                                        *   CABLERPT
 00019    001190**********************************************************   CABLERPT
 00020    001200                                                             CABLERPT
 00021    002010                                                             CABLERPT
 00022    002020                                                             CABLERPT
 00023    002030 ENVIRONMENT DIVISION.                                        CABLERPT
 00024    002040                                                             CABLERPT
 00025    002050 CONFIGURATION SECTION.                                       CABLERPT
 00026    002060                                                             CABLERPT
 00027    002070 SOURCE-COMPUTER. IBM-4381.                                   CABLERPT
 00028    002080 OBJECT-COMPUTER. IBM-4381.                                   CABLERPT
 00029    002090 SPECIAL-NAMES.   C01 IS TO-TOP-OF-PAGE.                      CABLERPT
 00030    002100                                                             CABLERPT
 00031    002110 INPUT-OUTPUT SECTION.                                        CABLERPT
 00032    002120                                                             CABLERPT
 00033    002130 FILE-CONTROL.                                                CABLERPT
 00034    002140     SELECT CABLE-INPUT-FILE                                  CABLERPT
 00035    002150         ASSIGN TO UT-S-CABLEIN.                              CABLERPT
 00036    002160     SELECT SORTED-CABLE-FILE                                 CABLERPT
 00037    002170         ASSIGN TO UT-S-CABLESRT.                             CABLERPT
 00038    002180     SELECT CABLE-REPORT-FILE                                 CABLERPT
 00039    002190         ASSIGN TO UT-S-CABLEPRT.                             CABLERPT
 00040    002200     SELECT SORT-WORK-FILE                                    CABLERPT
 00041    003010         ASSIGN TO UT-S-SORTWORK.                             CABLERPT
```

```
     2                        16.19.01       APR 10,1985

 00042    003020/                                                            CABLERPT
 00043    003030 DATA DIVISION.                                               CABLERPT
 00044    003040                                                             CABLERPT
 00045    003050 FILE SECTION.                                                CABLERPT
 00046    003060                                                             CABLERPT
 00047    003070 FD   CABLE-INPUT-FILE                                        CABLERPT
 00048    003080      RECORD CONTAINS 50 CHARACTERS                           CABLERPT
 00049    003090      LABEL RECORDS ARE STANDARD                              CABLERPT
 00050    003100      DATA RECORD IS CABLE-INPUT-RECORD.                      CABLERPT
 00051    003110 01  CABLE-INPUT-RECORD            PIC X(50).                 CABLERPT
 00052    003120                                                             CABLERPT
 00053    003130 FD   SORTED-CABLE-FILE                                       CABLERPT
 00054    003140      RECORD CONTAINS 50 CHARACTERS                           CABLERPT
 00055    003150      LABEL RECORDS ARE STANDARD                              CABLERPT
 00056    003160      DATA RECORD IS SORTED-CABLE-RECORD.                     CABLERPT
 00057    003170 01  SORTED-CABLE-RECORD.                                     CABLERPT
 00058    003180     05  CITY-NAME-SORTCAB          PIC X(10).                CABLERPT
 00059    003190     05  CUSTOMER-NAME-SORTCAB      PIC X(20).                CABLERPT
 00060    003200     05  CABLE-USE-CHARGE-SORTCAB   PIC 99V99   OCCURS 5 TIMES. CABLERPT
 00061    004010                                                             CABLERPT
 00062    004020 FD   CABLE-REPORT-FILE                                       CABLERPT
 00063    004030      RECORD CONTAINS 133 CHARACTERS                          CABLERPT
 00064    004040      LABEL RECORDS ARE OMITTED                               CABLERPT
 00065    004050      DATA RECORD IS CABLE-REPORT-LINE.                       CABLERPT
 00066    004060 01  CABLE-REPORT-LINE             PIC X(133).                CABLERPT
 00067    004070                                                             CABLERPT
 00068    004080 SD   SORT-WORK-FILE                                          CABLERPT
 00069    004090      RECORD CONTAINS 50 CHARACTERS                           CABLERPT
 00070    004100      DATA RECORD IS SORT-WORK-RECORD.                        CABLERPT
 00071    004110 01  SORT-WORK-RECORD.                                        CABLERPT
 00072    004120     05  CITY-NAME-SORTWRK          PIC X(10).                CABLERPT
 00073    004130     05  CUSTOMER-NAME-SORTWRK      PIC X(20).                CABLERPT
 00074    004140     05  FILLER                     PIC X(20).                CABLERPT
 00075    004150                                                             CABLERPT
 00076    004160 WORKING-STORAGE SECTION.                                     CABLERPT
 00077    004170                                                             CABLERPT
 00078    004180 01  PROGRAM-INDICATORS.                                      CABLERPT
 00079    004190     05  ARE-THERE-MORE-RECORDS     PIC XXX  VALUE 'YES'.     CABLERPT
 00080    004200         88  THERE-IS-A-RECORD               VALUE 'YES'.     CABLERPT
 00081    005010         88  THERE-ARE-NO-MORE-RECORDS       VALUE 'NO '.     CABLERPT
 00082    005020     05  WAS-THERE-A-CITY-CHANGE     PIC XXX  VALUE 'NO '.    CABLERPT
 00083    005030         88  THERE-WAS-A-CITY-CHANGE          VALUE 'YES'.    CABLERPT
 00084    005040     05  IS-CABLE-INPUT-FILE-SORTED PIC XXX  VALUE 'NO '.     CABLERPT
 00085    005050         88  CABLE-INPUT-FILE-NOT-SORTED     VALUE 'NO '.     CABLERPT
 00086    005060                                                             CABLERPT
```

Figure 10-38 Source Listing (Part 1 of 5)

```
   3                    16.19.01      APR 10,1985

00087  005070 01  PROGRAM-CONSTANTS.                                      CABLERPT
00088  005080     05  NO-RECORDS-MESSAGE.                                 CABLERPT
00089  005090         10  CARRIAGE-CONTROL      PIC X.                    CABLERPT
00090  005100         10  FILLER               PIC X(36)    VALUE         CABLERPT
00091  005110                   'CABLE REPORT - NO RECORDS TO PROCESS'.CABLERPT
00092  005120         10  FILLER               PIC X(96)    VALUE SPACES. CABLERPT
00093  005130                                                            CABLERPT
00094  005140 01  PROGRAM-COMPARE-AREAS.                                  CABLERPT
00095  005150     05  PREVIOUS-CITY-NAME       PIC X(10).                 CABLERPT
00096  005160                                                            CABLERPT
00097  005170 01  WORK-AREAS.                                             CABLERPT
00098  005180     05  DATE-WORK.                                          CABLERPT
00099  005190         10  YEAR-WORK             PIC 99.                   CABLERPT
00100  005200         10  MONTH-WORK            PIC 99.                   CABLERPT
00101  006010         10  DAY-WORK              PIC 99.                   CABLERPT
00102  006020     05  TOTAL-CHARGES-WORK       PIC 9(3)V99 VALUE ZERO.    CABLERPT
00103  006030                                                            CABLERPT
00104  006040 01  TOTAL-ACCUMULATORS-COUNTERS.                           CABLERPT
00105  006050     05  NUMBER-OF-CITIES-COUNT   PIC S99      VALUE ZERO.   CABLERPT
00106  006060     05  CITY-TOTAL-ACCUM         PIC S9(4)V99 VALUE ZERO.   CABLERPT
00107  006070     05  FINAL-TOTAL-ACCUM        PIC S9(5)V99 VALUE ZERO.   CABLERPT
00108  006080                                                            CABLERPT
00109  006090 01  SUBSCRIPTS.                                             CABLERPT
00110  006100     05  ADD-CHARGES-SUBSCRIPT    PIC S9.                    CABLERPT
00111  006110     05  MOVE-CHARGES-SUBSCRIPT   PIC S9.                    CABLERPT
00112  006120     05  CITY-CHARGES-SUBSCRIPT   PIC S99      VALUE +1.     CABLERPT
00113  006130     05  PRINT-CITY-SUBSCRIPT     PIC S99.                   CABLERPT
00114  006140                                                            CABLERPT
00115  006150 01  PROGRAM-TABLES.                                        CABLERPT
00116  006160     05  MONTHS-TABLE.                                       CABLERPT
00117  006170         10  MONTH-CONSTANTS.                                CABLERPT
00118  006180             15  FILLER   PIC X(9)   VALUE 'JANUARY  '.      CABLERPT
00119  006190             15  FILLER   PIC X(9)   VALUE 'FEBRUARY '.      CABLERPT
00120  006200             15  FILLER   PIC X(9)   VALUE 'MARCH    '.      CABLERPT
00121  007010             15  FILLER   PIC X(9)   VALUE 'APRIL    '.      CABLERPT
00122  007020             15  FILLER   PIC X(9)   VALUE 'MAY      '.      CABLERPT
00123  007030             15  FILLER   PIC X(9)   VALUE 'JUNE     '.      CABLERPT
00124  007040             15  FILLER   PIC X(9)   VALUE 'JULY     '.      CABLERPT
00125  007050             15  FILLER   PIC X(9)   VALUE 'AUGUST   '.      CABLERPT
00126  007060             15  FILLER   PIC X(9)   VALUE 'SEPTEMBER'.      CABLERPT
00127  007070             15  FILLER   PIC X(9)   VALUE 'OCTOBER  '.      CABLERPT
00128  007080             15  FILLER   PIC X(9)   VALUE 'NOVEMBER '.      CABLERPT
00129  007090             15  FILLER   PIC X(9)   VALUE 'DECEMBER '.      CABLERPT
00130  007100         10  MONTH-TABLE REDEFINES MONTH-CONSTANTS           CABLERPT
00131  007110                          PIC X(9)   OCCURS 12 TIMES.        CABLERPT
00132  007120     05  CITY-CHARGES-TABLE.                                 CABLERPT
00133  007130         10  CITY-CHARGES           OCCURS 10 TIMES.         CABLERPT
00134  007140             15  CITY-NAME-TABLE      PIC X(10).             CABLERPT
00135  007150             15  CITY-TOTAL-CHARGE-TABLE PIC 9(4)V99.        CABLERPT
00136  007160                                                            CABLERPT
00137  007170 01  PRINTER-CONTROL.                                       CABLERPT
00138  007180     05  PROPER-SPACING           PIC 9.                     CABLERPT
00139  007190     05  SPACE-ONE-LINE           PIC 9        VALUE 1.      CABLERPT
00140  007200     05  SPACE-TWO-LINES          PIC 9        VALUE 2.      CABLERPT
00141  008010     05  SPACE-THREE-LINES        PIC 9        VALUE 3.      CABLERPT
00142  008020     05  LINES-PRINTED            PIC S999     VALUE ZERO.   CABLERPT
00143  008030     05  PAGE-SIZE                PIC 999      VALUE 55.     CABLERPT
00144  008040     05  PAGE-COUNT               PIC S999     VALUE +1.     CABLERPT
00145  008050         88  FIRST-PAGE                        VALUE +1.     CABLERPT
00146  008060                                                            CABLERPT
00147  008070 01  DETAIL-LINE.                                           CABLERPT
00148  008080     05  CARRIAGE-CONTROL         PIC X.                     CABLERPT
00149  008090     05  CITY-NAME-REPORT         PIC X(10).                 CABLERPT
00150  008100     05  FILLER                   PIC X(3)     VALUE SPACES. CABLERPT
00151  008110     05  CUSTOMER-NAME-REPORT     PIC X(20).                 CABLERPT
00152  008120     05  FILLER                   PIC X(4)     VALUE SPACES. CABLERPT
00153  008130     05  CHARGE-ALPHA-REPORT.                               CABLERPT
00154  008140         10  FILLER               PIC X(40)    VALUE SPACES. CABLERPT
00155  008150     05  CHARGE-REPORT REDEFINES CHARGE-ALPHA-REPORT         CABLERPT
00156  008160                                       OCCURS 5 TIMES.      CABLERPT
00157  008170         10  CABLE-USE-CHARGE-REPORT PIC ZZ.99.             CABLERPT
00158  008180         10  FILLER               PIC X(3).                  CABLERPT
00159  008190     05  TOTAL-CHARGES-REPORT     PIC ZZZ.99.                CABLERPT
00160  008200     05  FILLER                   PIC X(49)    VALUE SPACES. CABLERPT
00161  009010                                                            CABLERPT
00162  009020 01  HEADING-LINES.                                         CABLERPT
00163  009030     05  FIRST-HEADING-LINE.                                CABLERPT
00164  009040         10  CARRIAGE-CONTROL     PIC X.                     CABLERPT
00165  009050         10  DATE-HEADING         PIC X(18)    VALUE SPACES. CABLERPT
00166  009060         10  FILLER               PIC X(13)    VALUE SPACES. CABLERPT
00167  009070         10  FILLER               PIC X(20)    VALUE         CABLERPT
00168  009080                     'CALIFORNIA CABLE CO.'.CABLERPT
00169  009090         10  FILLER               PIC X(24)    VALUE SPACES. CABLERPT
00170  009100         10  FILLER               PIC X(5)     VALUE 'PAGE '.CABLERPT
00171  009110         10  PAGE-HEADING         PIC ZZ9.                   CABLERPT
00172  009120         10  FILLER               PIC X(49)    VALUE SPACES. CABLERPT
00173  009130     05  SECOND-HEADING-LINE.                               CABLERPT
00174  009140         10  CARRIAGE-CONTROL     PIC X.                     CABLERPT
00175  009150         10  FILLER               PIC X(3)     VALUE SPACES. CABLERPT
00176  009160         10  FILLER               PIC X(4)     VALUE 'CITY'. CABLERPT
00177  009170         10  FILLER               PIC X(12)    VALUE SPACES. CABLERPT
00178  009180         10  FILLER               PIC X(8)     VALUE 'CUSTOMER'.CABLERPT
00179  009190         10  FILLER               PIC X(10)    VALUE SPACES. CABLERPT
00180  009200         10  FILLER               PIC X(4)     VALUE 'BASE'. CABLERPT
00181  010010         10  FILLER               PIC X(4)     VALUE SPACES. CABLERPT
00182  010020         10  FILLER               PIC X(4)     VALUE 'NEWS'. CABLERPT
00183  010030         10  FILLER               PIC X(4)     VALUE SPACES. CABLERPT
00184  010040         10  FILLER               PIC X(5)     VALUE 'MOVIE'.CABLERPT
00185  010050         10  FILLER               PIC X(2)     VALUE SPACES. CABLERPT
00186  010060         10  FILLER               PIC X(6)     VALUE 'SPORTS'.CABLERPT
00187  010070         10  FILLER               PIC X(3)     VALUE SPACES. CABLERPT
00188  010080         10  FILLER               PIC X(5)     VALUE 'MUSIC'.CABLERPT
00189  010090         10  FILLER               PIC X(4)     VALUE SPACES. CABLERPT
00190  010100         10  FILLER               PIC X(5)     VALUE 'TOTAL'.CABLERPT
00191  010110         10  FILLER               PIC X(49)    VALUE SPACES. CABLERPT
```

Figure 10-39 Source Listing (Part 2 of 5)

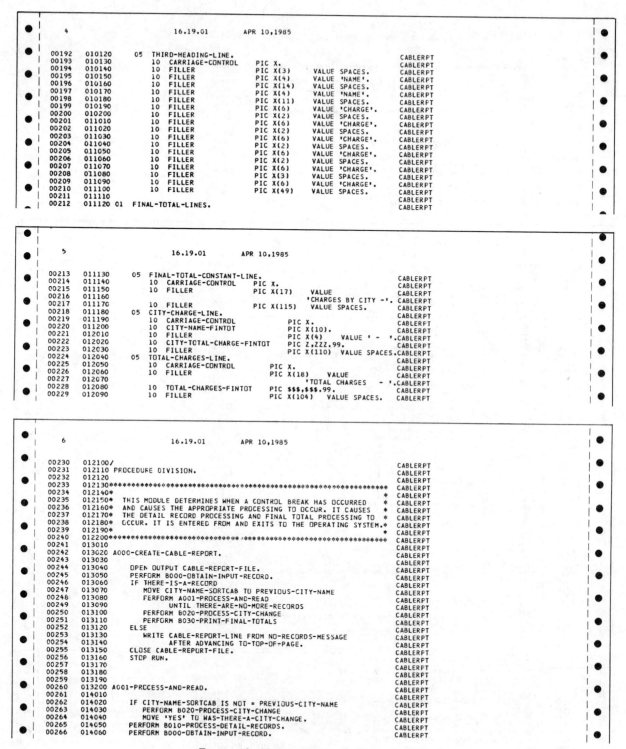

```
   4                    16.19.01      APR 10,1985

00192  010120     05  THIRD-HEADING-LINE.                                CABLERPT
00193  010130          10  CARRIAGE-CONTROL   PIC X.                     CABLERPT
00194  010140          10  FILLER             PIC X(3)     VALUE SPACES. CABLERPT
00195  010150          10  FILLER             PIC X(4)     VALUE 'NAME'. CABLERPT
00196  010160          10  FILLER             PIC X(14)    VALUE SPACES. CABLERPT
00197  010170          10  FILLER             PIC X(4)     VALUE 'NAME'. CABLERPT
00198  010180          10  FILLER             PIC X(11)    VALUE SPACES. CABLERPT
00199  010190          10  FILLER             PIC X(6)     VALUE 'CHARGE'.CABLERPT
00200  010200          10  FILLER             PIC X(2)     VALUE SPACES. CABLERPT
00201  011010          10  FILLER             PIC X(6)     VALUE 'CHARGE'.CABLERPT
00202  011020          10  FILLER             PIC X(2)     VALUE SPACES. CABLERPT
00203  011030          10  FILLER             PIC X(6)     VALUE 'CHARGE'.CABLERPT
00204  011040          10  FILLER             PIC X(2)     VALUE SPACES. CABLERPT
00205  011050          10  FILLER             PIC X(6)     VALUE 'CHARGE'.CABLERPT
00206  011060          10  FILLER             PIC X(2)     VALUE SPACES. CABLERPT
00207  011070          10  FILLER             PIC X(6)     VALUE 'CHARGE'.CABLERPT
00208  011080          10  FILLER             PIC X(3)     VALUE SPACES. CABLERPT
00209  011090          10  FILLER             PIC X(6)     VALUE 'CHARGE'.CABLERPT
00210  011100          10  FILLER             PIC X(49)    VALUE SPACES. CABLERPT
00211  011110                                                            CABLERPT
00212  011120 01  FINAL-TOTAL-LINES.                                     CABLERPT


   5                    16.19.01      APR 10,1985

00213  011130     05  FINAL-TOTAL-CONSTANT-LINE.                         CABLERPT
00214  011140          10  CARRIAGE-CONTROL   PIC X.                     CABLERPT
00215  011150          10  FILLER             PIC X(17)    VALUE         CABLERPT
00216  011160                                       'CHARGES BY CITY - ',CABLERPT
00217  011170          10  FILLER             PIC X(115)   VALUE SPACES. CABLERPT
00218  011180     05  CITY-CHARGE-LINE.                                  CABLERPT
00219  011190          10  CARRIAGE-CONTROL          PIC X.             CABLERPT
00220  011200          10  CITY-NAME-FINTOT          PIC X(10).         CABLERPT
00221  012010          10  FILLER                    PIC X(4)   VALUE ' - '.CABLERPT
00222  012020          10  CITY-TOTAL-CHARGE-FINTOT  PIC Z,ZZZ.99.      CABLERPT
00223  012030          10  FILLER                    PIC X(110) VALUE SPACES.CABLERPT
00224  012040     05  TOTAL-CHARGES-LINE.                                CABLERPT
00225  012050          10  CARRIAGE-CONTROL          PIC X.             CABLERPT
00226  012060          10  FILLER                    PIC X(18)  VALUE   CABLERPT
00227  012070                                             'TOTAL CHARGES  - '.CABLERPT
00228  012080          10  TOTAL-CHARGES-FINTOT      PIC $$$,$$$.99.    CABLERPT
00229  012090          10  FILLER                    PIC X(104) VALUE SPACES.CABLERPT


   6                    16.19.01      APR 10,1985

00230  012100/                                                           CABLERPT
00231  012110 PROCEDURE DIVISION.                                        CABLERPT
00232  012120                                                            CABLERPT
00233  012130****************************************************************CABLERPT
00234  012140*                                                        *  CABLERPT
00235  012150*  THIS MODULE DETERMINES WHEN A CONTROL BREAK HAS OCCURRED *CABLERPT
00236  012160*  AND CAUSES THE APPROPRIATE PROCESSING TO OCCUR. IT CAUSES *CABLERPT
00237  012170*  THE DETAIL RECORD PROCESSING AND FINAL TOTAL PROCESSING TO *CABLERPT
00238  012180*  OCCUR. IT IS ENTERED FROM AND EXITS TO THE OPERATING SYSTEM.*CABLERPT
00239  012190*                                                        *  CABLERPT
00240  012200****************************************************************CABLERPT
00241  013010                                                            CABLERPT
00242  013020 A000-CREATE-CABLE-REPORT.                                  CABLERPT
00243  013030                                                            CABLERPT
00244  013040     OPEN OUTPUT CABLE-REPORT-FILE.                         CABLERPT
00245  013050     PERFORM B000-OBTAIN-INPUT-RECORD.                      CABLERPT
00246  013060     IF THERE-IS-A-RECORD                                   CABLERPT
00247  013070        MOVE CITY-NAME-SORTCAB TO PREVIOUS-CITY-NAME        CABLERPT
00248  013080        PERFORM A001-PROCESS-AND-READ                       CABLERPT
00249  013090           UNTIL THERE-ARE-NO-MORE-RECORDS                  CABLERPT
00250  013100        PERFORM B020-PROCESS-CITY-CHANGE                    CABLERPT
00251  013110        PERFORM B030-PRINT-FINAL-TOTALS                     CABLERPT
00252  013120     ELSE                                                   CABLERPT
00253  013130        WRITE CABLE-REPORT-LINE FROM NO-RECORDS-MESSAGE     CABLERPT
00254  013140           AFTER ADVANCING TO-TOP-OF-PAGE.                  CABLERPT
00255  013150     CLOSE CABLE-REPORT-FILE.                               CABLERPT
00256  013160     STOP RUN.                                              CABLERPT
00257  013170                                                            CABLERPT
00258  013180                                                            CABLERPT
00259  013190                                                            CABLERPT
00260  013200 A001-PROCESS-AND-READ.                                     CABLERPT
00261  014010                                                            CABLERPT
00262  014020     IF CITY-NAME-SORTCAB IS NOT = PREVIOUS-CITY-NAME       CABLERPT
00263  014030        PERFORM B020-PROCESS-CITY-CHANGE                    CABLERPT
00264  014040        MOVE 'YES' TO WAS-THERE-A-CITY-CHANGE.              CABLERPT
00265  014050     PERFORM B010-PROCESS-DETAIL-RECORDS.                   CABLERPT
00266  014060     PERFORM B000-OBTAIN-INPUT-RECORD.                      CABLERPT
```

Figure 10-40 Source Listing (Part 3 of 5)

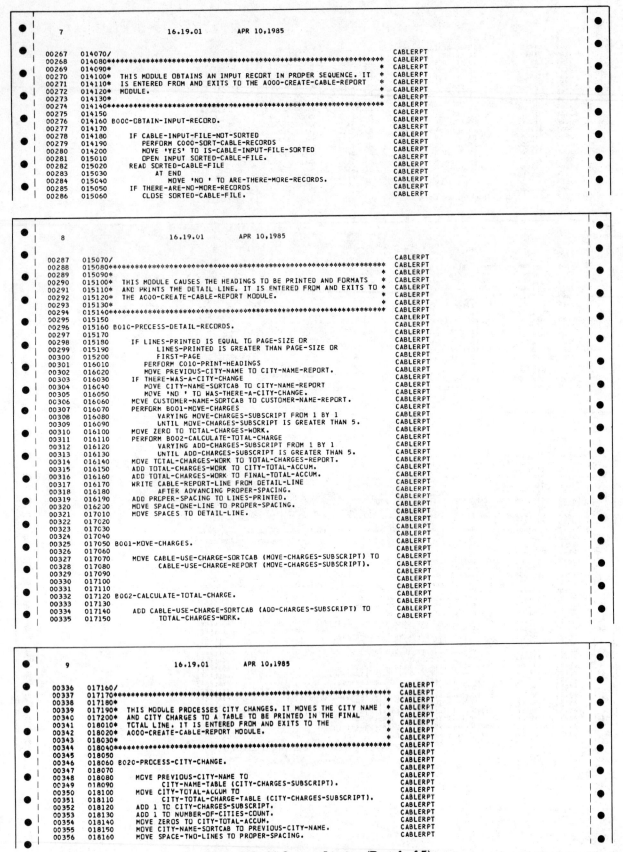

```
       7                       16.19.01       APR 10,1985

    00267   014070/                                                                CABLERPT
    00268   014080********************************************************         CABLERPT
    00269   014090*                                                      *         CABLERPT
    00270   014100*   THIS MODULE OBTAINS AN INPUT RECORT IN PROPER SEQUENCE. IT  * CABLERPT
    00271   014110*   IS ENTERED FROM AND EXITS TO THE A000-CREATE-CABLE-REPORT   * CABLERPT
    00272   014120*   MODULE.                                              *        CABLERPT
    00273   014130*                                                      *         CABLERPT
    00274   014140********************************************************         CABLERPT
    00275   014150                                                                 CABLERPT
    00276   014160 B00C-OBTAIN-INPUT-RECORD.                                       CABLERPT
    00277   014170                                                                 CABLERPT
    00278   014180       IF CABLE-INPUT-FILE-NOT-SORTED                            CABLERPT
    00279   014190          PERFORM C000-SORT-CABLE-RECORDS                        CABLERPT
    00280   014200          MOVE 'YES' TO IS-CABLE-INPUT-FILE-SORTED               CABLERPT
    00281   015010          OPEN INPUT SORTED-CABLE-FILE.                          CABLERPT
    00282   015020       READ SORTED-CABLE-FILE                                    CABLERPT
    00283   015030          AT END                                                 CABLERPT
    00284   015040             MOVE 'NO ' TO ARE-THERE-MORE-RECORDS.               CABLERPT
    00285   015050       IF THERE-ARE-NO-MORE-RECORDS                             CABLERPT
    00286   015060          CLOSE SORTED-CABLE-FILE.                               CABLERPT
```

```
       8                       16.19.01       APR 10,1985

    00287   015070/                                                                CABLERPT
    00288   015080********************************************************         CABLERPT
    00289   015090*                                                      *         CABLERPT
    00290   015100*   THIS MODULE CAUSES THE HEADINGS TO BE PRINTED AND FORMATS  * CABLERPT
    00291   015110*   AND PRINTS THE DETAIL LINE. IT IS ENTERED FROM AND EXITS TO* CABLERPT
    00292   015120*   THE A000-CREATE-CABLE-REPORT MODULE.                 *        CABLERPT
    00293   015130*                                                      *         CABLERPT
    00294   015140********************************************************         CABLERPT
    00295   015150                                                                 CABLERPT
    00296   015160 B01C-PROCESS-DETAIL-RECORDS.                                    CABLERPT
    00297   015170                                                                 CABLERPT
    00298   015180       IF LINES-PRINTED IS EQUAL TO PAGE-SIZE OR                 CABLERPT
    00299   015190          LINES-PRINTED IS GREATER THAN PAGE-SIZE OR             CABLERPT
    00300   015200          FIRST-PAGE                                             CABLERPT
    00301   016010          PERFORM C010-PRINT-HEADINGS                            CABLERPT
    00302   016020          MOVE PREVIOUS-CITY-NAME TO CITY-NAME-REPORT.           CABLERPT
    00303   016030       IF THERE-WAS-A-CITY-CHANGE                                CABLERPT
    00304   016040          MOVE CITY-NAME-SORTCAB TO CITY-NAME-REPORT             CABLERPT
    00305   016050          MOVE 'NO ' TO WAS-THERE-A-CITY-CHANGE.                 CABLERPT
    00306   016060       MOVE CUSTOMER-NAME-SORTCAB TO CUSTOMER-NAME-REPORT.       CABLERPT
    00307   016070       PERFORM B001-MOVE-CHARGES                                 CABLERPT
    00308   016080          VARYING MOVE-CHARGES-SUBSCRIPT FROM 1 BY 1             CABLERPT
    00309   016090          UNTIL MOVE-CHARGES-SUBSCRIPT IS GREATER THAN 5.        CABLERPT
    00310   016100       MOVE ZERO TO TCTAL-CHARGES-WORK.                          CABLERPT
    00311   016110       PERFORM B002-CALCULATE-TOTAL-CHARGE                       CABLERPT
    00312   016120          VARYING ADD-CHARGES-SUBSCRIPT FROM 1 BY 1              CABLERPT
    00313   016130          UNTIL ADD-CHARGES-SUBSCRIPT IS GREATER THAN 5.         CABLERPT
    00314   016140       MOVE TCTAL-CHARGES-WORK TO TOTAL-CHARGES-REPORT.          CABLERPT
    00315   016150       ADD TOTAL-CHARGES-WORK TO CITY-TOTAL-ACCUM.               CABLERPT
    00316   016160       ADD TOTAL-CHARGES-WORK TO FINAL-TOTAL-ACCUM.              CABLERPT
    00317   016170       WRITE CABLE-REPORT-LINE FROM DETAIL-LINE                  CABLERPT
    00318   016180          AFTER ADVANCING PROPER-SPACING.                        CABLERPT
    00319   016190       ADD PROPER-SPACING TO LINES-PRINTED.                      CABLERPT
    00320   016200       MOVE SPACE-ONE-LINE TO PROPER-SPACING.                    CABLERPT
    00321   017010       MOVE SPACES TO DETAIL-LINE.                               CABLERPT
    00322   017020                                                                 CABLERPT
    00323   017030                                                                 CABLERPT
    00324   017040                                                                 CABLERPT
    00325   017050 B001-MOVE-CHARGES.                                              CABLERPT
    00326   017060                                                                 CABLERPT
    00327   017070       MOVE CABLE-USE-CHARGE-SORTCAB (MOVE-CHARGES-SUBSCRIPT) TO CABLERPT
    00328   017080          CABLE-USE-CHARGE-REPORT (MOVE-CHARGES-SUBSCRIPT).      CABLERPT
    00329   017090                                                                 CABLERPT
    00330   017100                                                                 CABLERPT
    00331   017110                                                                 CABLERPT
    00332   017120 B002-CALCULATE-TOTAL-CHARGE.                                    CABLERPT
    00333   017130                                                                 CABLERPT
    00334   017140       ADD CABLE-USE-CHARGE-SORTCAB (ADD-CHARGES-SUBSCRIPT) TO   CABLERPT
    00335   017150          TOTAL-CHARGES-WORK.                                    CABLERPT
```

```
       9                       16.19.01       APR 10,1985

    00336   017160/                                                                CABLERPT
    00337   017170********************************************************         CABLERPT
    00338   017180*                                                      *         CABLERPT
    00339   017190*   THIS MODULE PROCESSES CITY CHANGES. IT MOVES THE CITY NAME * CABLERPT
    00340   017200*   AND CITY CHARGES TO A TABLE TO BE PRINTED IN THE FINAL     * CABLERPT
    00341   018010*   TCTAL LINE. IT IS ENTERED FROM AND EXITS TO THE            * CABLERPT
    00342   018020*   A000-CREATE-CABLE-REPORT MODULE.                     *        CABLERPT
    00343   018030*                                                      *         CABLERPT
    00344   018040********************************************************         CABLERPT
    00345   018050                                                                 CABLERPT
    00346   018060 B020-PROCESS-CITY-CHANGE.                                       CABLERPT
    00347   018070                                                                 CABLERPT
    00348   018080       MOVE PREVIOUS-CITY-NAME TO                                CABLERPT
    00349   018090          CITY-NAME-TABLE (CITY-CHARGES-SUBSCRIPT).              CABLERPT
    00350   018100       MOVE CITY-TOTAL-ACCUM TO                                  CABLERPT
    00351   018110          CITY-TOTAL-CHARGE-TABLE (CITY-CHARGES-SUBSCRIPT).      CABLERPT
    00352   018120       ADD 1 TO CITY-CHARGES-SUBSCRIPT.                          CABLERPT
    00353   018130       ADD 1 TO NUMBER-OF-CITIES-COUNT.                          CABLERPT
    00354   018140       MOVE ZEROS TO CITY-TOTAL-ACCUM.                           CABLERPT
    00355   018150       MOVE CITY-NAME-SORTCAB TO PREVIOUS-CITY-NAME.             CABLERPT
    00356   018160       MOVE SPACE-TWO-LINES TO PROPER-SPACING.                   CABLERPT
```

Figure 10-41 Source Listing (Part 4 of 5)

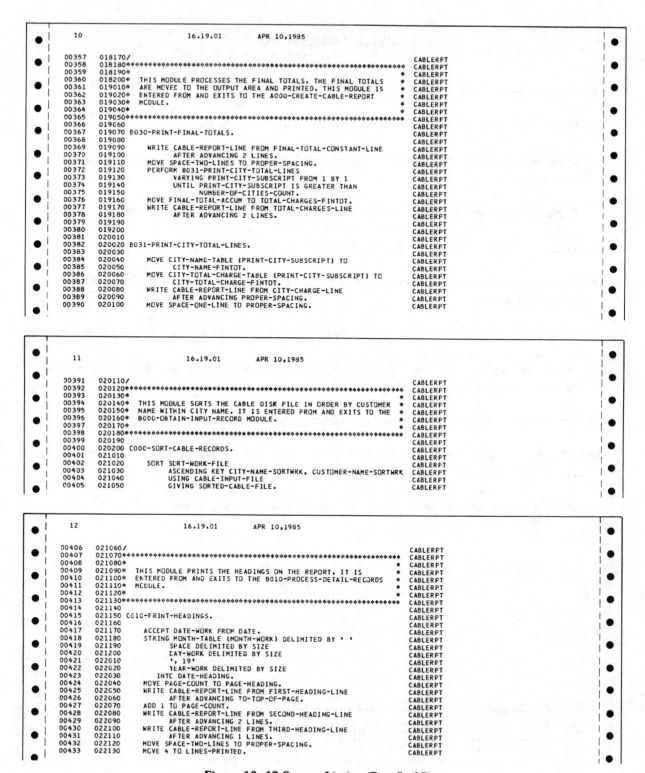

```
  10                    16.19.01        APR 10,1985

00357   018170/                                                                          CABLERPT
00358   018180*************************************************************************  CABLERPT
00359   018190*                                                                       *  CABLERPT
00360   018200*  THIS MODULE PROCESSES THE FINAL TOTALS. THE FINAL TOTALS             *  CABLERPT
00361   019010*  ARE MOVED TO THE OUTPUT AREA AND PRINTED. THIS MODULE IS             *  CABLERPT
00362   019020*  ENTERED FROM AND EXITS TO THE A000-CREATE-CABLE-REPORT               *  CABLERPT
00363   019030*  MODULE.                                                              *  CABLERPT
00364   019040*                                                                       *  CABLERPT
00365   019050*************************************************************************  CABLERPT
00366   019060                                                                           CABLERPT
00367   019070 B030-PRINT-FINAL-TOTALS.                                                  CABLERPT
00368   019080                                                                           CABLERPT
00369   019090     WRITE CABLE-REPORT-LINE FROM FINAL-TOTAL-CONSTANT-LINE                CABLERPT
00370   019100         AFTER ADVANCING 2 LINES.                                          CABLERPT
00371   019110     MOVE SPACE-TWO-LINES TO PROPER-SPACING.                               CABLERPT
00372   019120     PERFORM B031-PRINT-CITY-TOTAL-LINES                                   CABLERPT
00373   019130         VARYING PRINT-CITY-SUBSCRIPT FROM 1 BY 1                          CABLERPT
00374   019140         UNTIL PRINT-CITY-SUBSCRIPT IS GREATER THAN                        CABLERPT
00375   019150             NUMBER-OF-CITIES-COUNT.                                       CABLERPT
00376   019160     MOVE FINAL-TOTAL-ACCUM TO TOTAL-CHARGES-FINTOT.                       CABLERPT
00377   019170     WRITE CABLE-REPORT-LINE FROM TOTAL-CHARGES-LINE                       CABLERPT
00378   019180         AFTER ADVANCING 2 LINES.                                          CABLERPT
00379   019190                                                                           CABLERPT
00380   019200                                                                           CABLERPT
00381   020010                                                                           CABLERPT
00382   020020 B031-PRINT-CITY-TOTAL-LINES.                                              CABLERPT
00383   020030                                                                           CABLERPT
00384   020040     MOVE CITY-NAME-TABLE (PRINT-CITY-SUBSCRIPT) TO                        CABLERPT
00385   020050         CITY-NAME-FINTOT.                                                 CABLERPT
00386   020060     MOVE CITY-TOTAL-CHARGE-TABLE (PRINT-CITY-SUBSCRIPT) TO                CABLERPT
00387   020070         CITY-TOTAL-CHARGE-FINTOT.                                         CABLERPT
00388   020080     WRITE CABLE-REPORT-LINE FROM CITY-CHARGE-LINE                         CABLERPT
00389   020090         AFTER ADVANCING PROPER-SPACING.                                   CABLERPT
00390   020100     MOVE SPACE-ONE-LINE TO PROPER-SPACING.                                CABLERPT
```

```
  11                    16.19.01        APR 10,1985

00391   020110/                                                                          CABLERPT
00392   020120*************************************************************************  CABLERPT
00393   020130*                                                                       *  CABLERPT
00394   020140*  THIS MODULE SORTS THE CABLE DISK FILE IN ORDER BY CUSTOMER           *  CABLERPT
00395   020150*  NAME WITHIN CITY NAME. IT IS ENTERED FROM AND EXITS TO THE           *  CABLERPT
00396   020160*  B000-OBTAIN-INPUT-RECORD MODULE.                                     *  CABLERPT
00397   020170*                                                                       *  CABLERPT
00398   020180*************************************************************************  CABLERPT
00399   020190                                                                           CABLERPT
00400   020200 C000-SORT-CABLE-RECORDS.                                                  CABLERPT
00401   021010                                                                           CABLERPT
00402   021020     SORT SORT-WORK-FILE                                                    CABLERPT
00403   021030         ASCENDING KEY CITY-NAME-SORTWRK, CUSTOMER-NAME-SORTWRK           CABLERPT
00404   021040         USING CABLE-INPUT-FILE                                           CABLERPT
00405   021050         GIVING SORTED-CABLE-FILE.                                        CABLERPT
```

```
  12                    16.19.01        APR 10,1985

00406   021060/                                                                          CABLERPT
00407   021070*************************************************************************  CABLERPT
00408   021080*                                                                       *  CABLERPT
00409   021090*  THIS MODULE PRINTS THE HEADINGS ON THE REPORT. IT IS                 *  CABLERPT
00410   021100*  ENTERED FROM AND EXITS TO THE B010-PROCESS-DETAIL-RECORDS            *  CABLERPT
00411   021110*  MODULE.                                                              *  CABLERPT
00412   021120*                                                                       *  CABLERPT
00413   021130*************************************************************************  CABLERPT
00414   021140                                                                           CABLERPT
00415   021150 C010-PRINT-HEADINGS.                                                      CABLERPT
00416   021160                                                                           CABLERPT
00417   021170     ACCEPT DATE-WORK FROM DATE.                                           CABLERPT
00418   021180     STRING MONTH-TABLE (MONTH-WORK) DELIMITED BY ' '                      CABLERPT
00419   021190         SPACE DELIMITED BY SIZE                                           CABLERPT
00420   021200         DAY-WORK DELIMITED BY SIZE                                        CABLERPT
00421   022010         ', 19'                                                            CABLERPT
00422   022020         YEAR-WORK DELIMITED BY SIZE                                       CABLERPT
00423   022030         INTO DATE-HEADING.                                               CABLERPT
00424   022040     MOVE PAGE-COUNT TO PAGE-HEADING.                                      CABLERPT
00425   022050     WRITE CABLE-REPORT-LINE FROM FIRST-HEADING-LINE                       CABLERPT
00426   022060         AFTER ADVANCING TO-TOP-OF-PAGE.                                   CABLERPT
00427   022070     ADD 1 TO PAGE-COUNT.                                                  CABLERPT
00428   022080     WRITE CABLE-REPORT-LINE FROM SECOND-HEADING-LINE                      CABLERPT
00429   022090         AFTER ADVANCING 2 LINES.                                          CABLERPT
00430   022100     WRITE CABLE-REPORT-LINE FROM THIRD-HEADING-LINE                       CABLERPT
00431   022110         AFTER ADVANCING 1 LINES.                                          CABLERPT
00432   022120     MOVE SPACE-TWO-LINES TO PROPER-SPACING.                               CABLERPT
00433   022130     MOVE 4 TO LINES-PRINTED.                                              CABLERPT
```

Figure 10-42 Source Listing (Part 5 of 5)

REVIEW QUESTIONS

1. Define the term sorting.

2. Briefly explain the processing which occurs when using the Sort statement.

3. What files must be defined in the Environment Division and Data Division when using the Sort statement?

4. Explain the purpose of each of the files used in the sorting process in the sample program.

5. When is the entry SD used in the File Section of the Data Division?

6. What is the purpose of the Ascending Key clause, Using clause, and Giving clause as used in the Sort statement?

7. Explain the use of the From clause and By clause as used in the Perform Varying statement.

8. What criteria should be used to decide how many elements are to be contained within a table in which the exact number of elements is not known?

9. Briefly explain the difference between the String statement and the Unstring statement.

10. What is the purpose of the DELIMITED BY ' ' clause and the SPACE DELIMITED BY SIZE clause as used in the String statement?

11. What is the purpose of the INTO clause as used in the Unstring statement?

COBOL CODING EXERCISES

1. Write the COBOL coding to define the Input-Output Section of the Environment Division assuming a file named ACCOUNTING-INPUT-FILE is to be sorted and the report named ACCOUNTING-REPORT is to be produced. In addition to these two files, assign names to and define those files which are required for the sorting process.

2. Write the COBOL coding required in the Data Division to define all files required for the sort explained in problem #1 above. The ACCOUNTING-INPUT-FILE contains the ACCOUNT-NAME-INPUT (PIC X(15)), ACCOUNT-NUMBER-INPUT (PIC 9(4)), and ACCOUNT-TRANSACTION-INPUT (PIC 9(5)V99)) fields. The ACCOUNT-TRANSACTION-INPUT field contains a maximum of seven individual account transactions per input record. The ACCOUNTING-INPUT-FILE is to be sorted in ascending order by Account Number. The format of the report should be determined by the programmer.

3. Write the COBOL Sort statement to sort the ACCOUNTING-INPUT-FILE mentioned in problems #1 and #2 above.

4. Write the COBOL coding necessary to add the contents of the seven individual account transactions found in the ACCOUNTING-INPUT-FILE described in problem #2 above. The seven transactions should be added together using the Perform Varying statement and stored in the TOTAL-TRANSACTION-WORK field. For the purpose of adding the fields together, use the field named ADD-TRANSACTIONS-SUBSCRIPT as a subscript.

5. Write the COBOL coding necessary to define the ADD-TRANSACTIONS-SUBSCRIPT required in problem #4 above.

STRUCTURED WALKTHROUGH EXERCISES

The following portions of COBOL code contain one or more errors in program logic, in the use of the COBOL language itself, or in the programming standards which should be followed. Review the code in each exercise in the same manner used for structured walkthroughs. Identify the errors and make the appropriate corrections.

1.

```
003010  FILE CONTROL.
003020      SELECT PHONE-INPUT-FILE
003030          ASSIGN TO UT-S-PHONEIN.
003040      SELECT SORTED-PHONE-FILE
003050          ASSIGN TO UT-S-PHONESRT.
003060      SELECT SORT-WORK-FILE
003070          ASSIGN TO UT-X-SORTWORK.
003080      SELECT PHONE-REPORT-FILE
            ASSIGN TO PHONEOUT.
```

2.

```
004070  FD  PHONE-INPUT-FILE
004080      RECORD CONTAINS 62 CHARACTERS
004090      LABEL RECORDS ARE OMITTED
004100      DATA RECORD IS PHONE-INPUT-RECORD
004110  01  PHONE-INPUT-RECORD.
004120      05  FILLER                      PIC X(62).
004130
004140  FD  PHONE-REPORT-FILE
004150      RECORD CONTAINS 132 CHARACTERS
004160      LABEL RECORDS ARE OMITTED
004170      DATA RECORD IS PHONE-REPORT-LINE.
004180  01  PHONE-REPORT-LINE               PIC X(132).
004190
004200  SD  SORTED-PHONE-FILE
005010      RECORD CONTAINS 63 CHARACTERS
005020      DATA RECORD IS SORTED-PHONE-RECORD.
005030  01  SORTED-PHONE-RECORD.
005040      05  PHONE-NUMBER-SORTCAB        PIC X(7)
005050      05  CUSTOMER-NAME-SORTCAB       PIC X(20)
005060      05  PHONE-CHARGE-SORTCAB        PIC 99V99 OCCURS 9 TIMES
005070
005080  FD  SORT-WORK-FILE
005090      RECORD CONTAINS 63 CHARACTERS
005100      LABEL RECORDS ARE STANDARD
005110      DATA RECORD IS SORT-WORK-RECORD.
005120  01  SORT-WORK-RECORD.
005130      05  PHONE-NUMBER-SORTWRK        PIC X(7).
005150      05  FILLER                      PIC X(56).
005160
```

3.

```
007010 01   SUBSCRIPTS.
007020      05   ADD-CHARGES-SUBSCRIPT PIC X.
007030      05   PRINT-CITY-SUBSCRIPT PIC XX.
```

4.

```
014120 B000-SORT-PHONE-RECORDS.
014130
014140      SORT WORK-FILE
014150          ASCENDING KEY PHONE-NUMBER-SORTWORK
014160          USING PHONE-INPUT-FILE GIVING SORTED-PHONE-FILE.
```

5.

```
017010      MOVE ZERO TO TOTAL-CHARGES-WORK.
017020      PERFORM B003-CALCULATE-TOTAL-CHARGES
017030          VARYING ADD-CHARGES-SUBSCRIPT FROM 1
017040          UNTIL ADD-CHARGES-SUBSCRIPT IS GREATER THAN 10.
```

```
018050 B002-CALCULATE-TOTAL-CHARGE.
018060
018070      ADD CITY-CHARGE-SORTCAB ( ADD-CHARGES-SUBSCRIPT ) TO
018080          TOTAL-CHARGES-WORK.
```

PROGRAMMING ASSIGNMENT 1

INSTRUCTIONS

A Weekly TV Viewing Report is to be prepared. Design and write the COBOL program to produce the required report. An IPO Chart and Pseudocode Specifications should be used when designing the program. Use Test Data Set 6 in Appendix A.

INPUT

Input consists of TV Viewer Disk Records that contain the Station Name, the Show Title, and the number of Monday Viewers, Tuesday Viewers, Wednesday Viewers, Thursday Viewers, and Friday Viewers. The number of viewers field should be processed using a table in the input record definition. The input records must be sorted by Show Title within Station Name prior to processing. There are presently seven stations being viewed. It is estimated that there will never be more than ten stations. The format of the input record is illustrated below.

TV Viewer Disk Record				
FIELD DESCRIPTION	POSITION	LENGTH	DEC	ATTRIBUTE
Station Name	1 – 4	4		Alphanumeric
Show Title	5 – 24	20		Alphanumeric
UNUSED	25 – 48	24		Alphanumeric
Monday Viewers	49 – 52	4	0	Numeric
Tuesday Viewers	53 – 56	4	0	Numeric
Wednesday Viewers	57 – 60	4	0	Numeric
Thursday Viewers	61 – 64	4	0	Numeric
Friday Viewers	65 – 68	4	0	Numeric
UNUSED	69 – 79	11		Alphanumeric
Record Length		79		

OUTPUT

Output consists of a Weekly TV Viewing Report containing the Station Name, the Show Title, the number of viewers for each of the five weekdays, and the Total Viewers for each show. The headings should contain the date written out in long form (example: The date 01/13/86 would be printed in the headings as JANUARY 13, 1986).

When there is a change in Station Name, the Station Name and the total number of viewers for that station should be printed. Station Name should be group indicated on the report.

After all records have been processed, each station and the total number of viewers for each station should again be printed in the Station Summary. There are presently seven stations being viewed. It is estimated that there will never be more than ten stations in the future. The printer spacing chart for the report is illustrated on the following page.

PRINTER SPACING CHART

```
 2 XXXXXXXXXXXXXXXXXX          WEEKLY TV VIEWING REPORT                    PAGE ZZ9

 4 STATION           SHOW           MON.    TUES.    WED.    THUR.    FRI.      TOTAL
 5   NAME            TITLE         VIEWERS  VIEWERS  VIEWERS  VIEWERS  VIEWERS  VIEWERS

 7   XXXX    XXXXXXXXXXXXXXXXXXXX   Z,ZZ9    Z,ZZ9    Z,ZZ9    Z,ZZ9    Z,ZZ9   ZZ,ZZ9
 8           XXXXXXXXXXXXXXXXXXXX   Z,ZZ9    Z,ZZ9    Z,ZZ9    Z,ZZ9    Z,ZZ9   ZZ,ZZ9

10                                 STATION  XXXX  -  TOTAL  VIEWERS  ZZZ,ZZ9

12   XXXX    XXXXXXXXXXXXXXXXXXXX   Z,ZZ9    Z,ZZ9    Z,ZZ9    Z,ZZ9    Z,ZZ9   ZZ,ZZ9
13           XXXXXXXXXXXXXXXXXXXX   Z,ZZ9    Z,ZZ9    Z,ZZ9    Z,ZZ9    Z,ZZ9   ZZ,ZZ9

15                                 STATION  XXXX  -  TOTAL  VIEWERS  ZZZ,ZZ9

18 STATION SUMMARY   -
20 XXXX      -    ZZZ,ZZ9
21 XXXX      -    ZZZ,ZZ9
22 XXXX      -    ZZZ,ZZ9
24 TOTAL VIEWERS     -    Z,ZZZ,ZZ9
```

PROGRAMMING ASSIGNMENT 2

INSTRUCTIONS

A Nightly Basketball Report is to be prepared. Design and write the COBOL program to produce the required report. An IPO Chart and Pseudocode Specifications should be used when designing the program. Use Test Data Set 6 in Appendix A.

INPUT

Input consists of Scoring Records that contain the Team Number, Player Name, First Quarter Points, Second Quarter Points, Third Quarter Points, and Fourth Quarter Points. The four quarterly points should be processed using a table in the input record definition. The input records must be sorted by Player Name within Team Number prior to processing. The format of the input record is illustrated below.

Scoring Disk Record				
FIELD DESCRIPTION	POSITION	LENGTH	DEC	ATTRIBUTE
UNUSED	1 – 24	24		Alphanumeric
Team Number	25 – 26	2	0	Numeric
UNUSED	27 – 28	2		Alphanumeric
Player Name	29 – 48	20		Alphanumeric
1st Quarter Points	49 – 50	2	0	Numeric
2nd Quarter Points	51 – 52	2	0	Numeric
3rd Quarter Points	53 – 54	2	0	Numeric
4th Quarter Points	55 – 56	2	0	Numeric
UNUSED	57 – 79	23		Alphanumeric
Record Length		79		

OUTPUT

Output consists of a Nightly Basketball Report containing the Team Name, the Player Name, the number of points scored by a player in the four quarters of the basketball game, and the Total Points scored. The headings should contain the date written out in long form (example: The date 01/13/86 would be printed in the headings as JANUARY 13, 1986).

The Team Name should be group indicated on the report and should be extracted from the following table based upon the Team Number in the input record.

TEAM NUMBER	TEAM NAME
01	COUGARS
03	BULLDOGS
04	WARRIORS
06	LEOPARDS
07	MINERS
09	BOMBERS
11	CHEETAHS

When there is a change in Team Number in the input record, the name of the Highest Scoring Player for that team should be printed.

After all records have been processed, each team, the highest scoring player for that team, and the player's score should be printed. Presently there are seven teams, and it is estimated that the number of teams will never exceed ten in the future. The printer spacing chart for the report is illustrated below.

PRINTER SPACING CHART

```
 2 XXXXXXXXXXXXXXXX        NIGHTLY BASKETBALL REPORT                    PAGE ZZ9
 4    TEAM              PLAYER        FIRST     SECOND   THIRD    FOURTH   TOTAL
 5    NAME              NAME          QUARTER   QUARTER  QUARTER  QUARTER  POINTS
 7 XXXXXXXX    XXXXXXXXXXXXXXXXXXXXX     Z9        Z9       Z9       Z9     ZZ9
 8             XXXXXXXXXXXXXXXXXXXXX     Z9        Z9       Z9       Z9     ZZ9
10                          HIGHEST SCORING PLAYER  -  XXXXXXXXXXXXXXXXXXXXX
12 XXXXXXXX    XXXXXXXXXXXXXXXXXXXXX     Z9        Z9       Z9       Z9     ZZ9
13             XXXXXXXXXXXXXXXXXXXXX     Z9        Z9       Z9       Z9     ZZ9
15                          HIGHEST SCORING PLAYER  -  XXXXXXXXXXXXXXXXXXXXX
17 HIGHEST SCORING PLAYERS  -
19    TEAM              PLAYER        SCORE
21 XXXXXXXX    XXXXXXXXXXXXXXXXXXXXX    ZZ9
22 XXXXXXXX    XXXXXXXXXXXXXXXXXXXXX    ZZ9
24 NIGHT'S HIGHEST SCORING PLAYER  -  XXXXXXXXXXXXXXXXXXXXX
```

PROGRAMMING ASSIGNMENT 3

INSTRUCTIONS

A Telemarketing Sales Report is to be prepared. Write the COBOL program to prepare this report. An IPO Chart and Pseudocode Specifications should be used when designing the program. Use Test Data Set 6 in Appendix A.

INPUT

Input consists of Sales Records that contain the City Number, the Marketing Representative, the number of telephone calls made for Monday, Thursday, and Saturday, and the number of sales made for Monday, Thursday, and Saturday. The number of telephone calls and the number of telephone sales for the Monday, Thursday, and Saturday fields should be processed using a table in the input record definition. The input records must be sorted by Marketing Representative within City Number prior to processing. The format of the input record is illustrated below.

Sales Disk Record				
FIELD DESCRIPTION	POSITION	LENGTH	DEC	ATTRIBUTE
UNUSED	1 – 24	24		Alphanumeric
City Number	25 – 26	2	0	Numeric
UNUSED	27 – 28	2		Alphanumeric
Marketing Representative	29 – 48	20		Alphanumeric
UNUSED	49 – 56	8		Alphanumeric
Monday Calls	57 – 58	2	0	Numeric
Thursday Calls	59 – 60	2	0	Numeric
Saturday Calls	61 – 62	2	0	Numeric
Monday Sales	63 – 64	2	0	Numeric
Thursday Sales	65 – 66	2	0	Numeric
Saturday Sales	67 – 68	2	0	Numeric
UNUSED	69 – 79	11		Alphanumeric
Record Length		79		

OUTPUT

Output consists of a Telemarketing Sales Report containing the City Name, the Marketing Representative, and the number of telephone calls, number of telephone sales, and percentage of sales made on three days of the week: Monday, Thursday, and Saturday. The percentage of sales is calculated by dividing daily telephone sales by daily telephone calls. Headings should contain the date written out in long form (example: The date 01/13/86 should be written in the headings as JANUARY 13, 1986).

City Name should be group indicated on the report and should be extracted from the following table based upon the City Number in the input record.

CITY NUMBER	CITY NAME
01	PORTLAND
03	SAN DIEGO
04	HOUSTON
06	CHARLOTTE
07	DETROIT
09	ATLANTA
11	KNOXVILLE

When there is a change in City Number in the input record, the total number of telephone calls, the total number of telephone sales, and the percentage of sales made for that city are to be printed. In addition, the name of the day of the week (i.e. MONDAY, THURSDAY, or SATURDAY) with the highest percentage of sales for that city is to be printed, together with the total telephone calls for that day, total telephone sales for that day, and percentage of sales for that day.

After all records have been processed, a summary of the survey should be printed on a separate page containing headings and all city names, the day with the highest percentage of sales for that city, and the percentage of sales for that city.

The printer spacing chart is illustrated below.

PRINTER SPACING CHART

PROGRAMMING ASSIGNMENT 4

INSTRUCTIONS

A Golf Tournament Report and Golf Tournament Results Report are to be prepared. Write the COBOL program to prepare these reports. The IPO Chart and Pseudocode Specifications should be used when designing the program. Use Test Data Set 6 in Appendix A.

INPUT

Input consists of Tournament Records that contain the Team Number, Golfer Name, Round 1 Score, Round 2 Score, Round 3 Score, Round 4 Score, and Tournament Score. Note that Golfer Names are stored in last name, first name sequence. The scores for rounds 1, 2, 3, and 4 should be processed using a table in the input record definition. The format of the input record is illustrated below.

Tournament Record				
FIELD DESCRIPTION	**POSITION**	**LENGTH**	**DEC**	**ATTRIBUTE**
UNUSED	1 – 26	26		Alphanumeric
Team Number	27 – 28	2	0	Numeric
Golfer Name (Last Name, First Name sequence)	29 – 48	20		Alphanumeric
UNUSED	49 – 68	20		Alphanumeric
Round 1 Score	69 – 70	2	0	Numeric
Round 2 Score	71 – 72	2	0	Numeric
Round 3 Score	73 – 74	2	0	Numeric
Round 4 Score	75 – 76	2	0	Numeric
Tournament Score	77 – 79	3	0	Numeric
Record Length		79		

OUTPUT

Output consists of a Golf Tournament Report and Golf Tournament Results Report. The Golf Tournament Report contains the Team Number, Golfer Name, Round 1 Score, Round 2 Score, Round 3 Score, Round 4 Score, Tournament Score, and a message area. The message area should contain either the amount under par (PAR = 288) and the message UNDER PAR, the amount over par and the message OVER PAR, or the message EVEN PAR. For example:

TOURNAMENT PAR = 288

If Tournament Score = 296, the message area contains: 8 OVER PAR
If Tournament Score = 288, the message area contains: EVEN PAR
If Tournament Score = 271, the message area contains: 17 UNDER PAR

This report requires that the input records be sorted by Golfer Name within Team Number prior to processing.

When there is a change in Team Number in the input record, the Best Golf Score for that team, the amount over or under par and one of the following messages — OVER PAR, UNDER PAR, or EVEN PAR — and the name of the golfer with the best score for that team should be printed.

The printer spacing chart for the two reports is illustrated below.

PRINTER SPACING CHART

```
 2 XXXXXXXXXXXXXXXXX         GOLF TOURNAMENT REPORT                        PAGE ZZ9
 3                              (PAR = 288)
 5                           *** GOLF  SCORES ***  TOURNAMENT
 6  TEAM            GOLFER    ROUND    ROUND    ROUND    ROUND    SCORE
 7 NUMBER           NAME      1        2        3        4
 9   Z9    XXXXXXXXXXXXXXXXXXX  Z9       Z9       Z9       Z9       ZZ9    Z9 UNDER PAR
10         XXXXXXXXXXXXXXXXXXX  Z9       Z9       Z9       Z9       ZZ9    Z9 OVER PAR
11         XXXXXXXXXXXXXXXXXXX  Z9       Z9       Z9       Z9       ZZ9    EVEN PAR
13                           BEST GOLF SCORE:   ZZ9
14                           OVER/UNDER PAR:    Z9 UNDER PAR
15                           BEST GOLFER:       XXXXXXXXXXXXXXXXXXX
17   Z9    XXXXXXXXXXXXXXXXXXX  Z9       Z9       Z9       Z9       ZZ9
19                           BEST GOLF SCORE:   ZZ9
20                           OVER/UNDER PAR:    Z9 OVER PAR
21                           BEST GOLFER:       XXXXXXXXXXXXXXXXXXX
23                              (SEPARATE PAGE)
25 XXXXXXXXXXXXXXXXX         GOLF TOURNAMENT RESULTS        PAGE ZZ9
26                              (PAR = 288)
28 TOURNAMENT         GOLFER       TOURNAMENT   OVER/UNDER    PRIZE
29    RANK            NAME         SCORE        PAR           MONEY
31    1ST    XXXXXXXXXXXXXXXXXXX     ZZ9         -Z9        $65,000
32    2ND    XXXXXXXXXXXXXXXXXXX     ZZ9         -Z9        $32,000
33    3RD    XXXXXXXXXXXXXXXXXXX     ZZ9         -Z9        $23,000
34    4TH    XXXXXXXXXXXXXXXXXXX     ZZ9         +Z9        $14,000
35    5TH    XXXXXXXXXXXXXXXXXXX     ZZ9         +Z9        $ 8,000
36    6TH    XXXXXXXXXXXXXXXXXXX     ZZ9         +Z9        $ 2,000
39  TEAM           BEST          TOURNAMENT    OVER/UNDER
40 NUMBER          GOLFER        SCORE         PAR
42   Z9    XXXXXXXXXXXXXXXXXXX     ZZ9          -Z9
43   Z9    XXXXXXXXXXXXXXXXXXX     ZZ9          -Z9
44   Z9    XXXXXXXXXXXXXXXXXXX     ZZ9          +Z9
```

After the Golf Tournament Report has been printed, the Golf Tournament Results Report should be printed on a separate page with headings. The Golf Tournament Results Report contains the top six ranking golfers for the tournament, their ranks in the tournament, their Tournament Scores, the amount over or under par, and the prize money awarded. The input records must be sorted by Tournament Score to produce this report.

Following the top six ranking golfers is a list of all twelve teams in the tournament together with the Best Golfer for that team, the golfer's Tournament Score, and the amount over or under par.

Note that on both reports the golfer names are to be printed in first name, last name sequence while the golfer names are in last name, first name sequence in the input records. The format of the golfer names in the input record is last name followed by a comma, then one blank space, followed by the first name. Thus, the first golfer in the input file — JONES, MALCOLM — should be printed on the reports as MALCOLM JONES.

CHAPTER ELEVEN

ADDITIONAL COBOL STATEMENTS

ADDITIONAL COBOL STATEMENTS

INTRODUCTION

The previous chapters have covered the major elements of the COBOL language. There are, however, some elements of the language which have not been discussed and which, in some applications, can prove useful. This chapter will summarize these additional capabilities of the COBOL language.

DATA DIVISION

The following segments of the language are used in the Data Division.

Level 77 Data Items

In previous chapters, the level numbers 01, 05, 10, etc. have been used to define group and elementary items in the Data Division. Another method which may be used to define data in the Data Division is the level 77 data item. The use of level 77 data items is illustrated in Figure 11-1.

```
004020 77  SALES-TOTAL-ACCUM            PIC S9(5)V99 VALUE ZERO.
004030 77  ARE-THERE-MORE-RECORDS       PIC XXX     VALUE 'YES'.
004040     88  THERE-ARE-NO-MORE-RECORDS            VALUE 'NO '.
```

Figure 11-1 Level 77 Data Items

In Figure 11-1, the level number 77 appears in columns 8-9 of the coding form. A level 77 data item allows a single data item to be defined without it's being a member of a group. Although a level 77 data item can be used, it is a better programming technique to use a 01 group level item to identify the use of elementary items within the Data Division. The use of the 01 group level item leads to a more easily read Data Division. Therefore, it is suggested that the use of group and elementary items as illustrated in previous programs be used instead of level 77 data items.

Level 66 Renames Clause

Figure 11-2 illustrates the use of a level 66 data item to rename other data items within the Data Division.

003100		05	NAME-INPUT		PIC X(20).
003110		05	ADDRESS-INPUT.		
003120			10	STREET-INPUT	PIC X(15).
003130			10	CITY-INPUT	PIC X(15).
003140			10	STATE-INPUT	PIC XX.
003150			10	ZIP-CODE-INPUT	PIC 9(5).
003160		66	NAME-STREET-CITY RENAMES NAME-INPUT THRU CITY-INPUT.		

```
66  data-name-1; RENAMES data-name-2  [ { THROUGH / THRU }  data-name-3 ]  .
```

Figure 11-2 Level 66 Renames Clause

In Figure 11–2, a level 66 item is included on line 003160. This item renames the fields NAME-INPUT through CITY-INPUT to the name NAME-STREET-CITY. The data-name-1 in the Renames statement (NAME-STREET-CITY) is treated as a group item which includes all of the data items from data-name-2 through data-name-3. Thus, when NAME-STREET-CITY is referenced in the Procedure Division of the program, it refers to the fields NAME-INPUT, STREET-INPUT, and CITY-INPUT. In some applications, this can be a useful tool, but the programmer must be careful when using it to ensure that the correct data items are renamed. In addition, meaningful names should be chosen when renaming data items.

Condition Names with Group Level Items

The use of condition names for elementary data items has been extensively illustrated in previous chapters. Condition names can also be used for group items. This is illustrated in Figure 11–3.

004120		05	ADDRESS-INPUT.		
004130			88	ADDRESS-IS-NOT-IN-RECORD	VALUE SPACES.
004140			10	STREET-INPUT	PIC X(15).
004150			10	CITY-INPUT	PIC X(15).
004160			10	STATE-INPUT	PIC XX.
004170			10	ZIP-CODE-INPUT	PIC 9(5).

Figure 11-3 Condition Name with Group Item

In Figure 11–3, the 88 level condition name is specified immediately following the group name ADDRESS-INPUT. Therefore, the condition name ADDRESS-IS-NOT-IN-RECORD applies to the entire group as defined by ADDRESS-INPUT. If the entire ADDRESS-INPUT field contains spaces, then the condition will be true; if any of the elementary items within the group contains non-spaces, then the condition will be false.

Name Qualification

In previous examples of defining data within either the File Section of the Data Division or the Working-Storage Section, all data-names and identifiers which have been referenced have been unique; that is, each has been different. It is allowable, however, to have the same data-names reference different areas of main computer memory. The requirement is that there be some higher level name which is unique and which will qualify the data-name, and therefore, make it unique.

The ability to qualify names is illustrated in Figure 11-4.

```
003020    01   TRANSACTION-RECORD.
003030         05   NAME-EMPLOYEE.
003040              10   FIRST-NAME              PIC X(10).
003050              10   LAST-NAME               PIC X(15).
003060         05   ADDRESS-EMPLOYEE.
003070              10   STREET-NUMBER           PIC X(5).
003080              10   STREET-NAME             PIC X(10).
003090         05   CITY-EMPLOYEE                PIC X(20).
003100         05   STATE-EMPLOYEE               PIC X(15).
003110
003120    01   MASTER-RECORD.
003130         05   NAME-EMPLOYEE.
003140              10   FIRST-NAME              PIC X(10).
003150              10   LAST-NAME               PIC X(15).
003160         05   ADDRESS-EMPLOYEE             PIC X(15).
003170         05   CITY-EMPLOYEE                PIC X(20).
003180         05   STATE-EMPLOYEE               PIC X(15).
```

Figure 11-4 Example of Name Qualification

In Figure 11-4, there are two 01 level data-names — TRANSACTION-RECORD and MASTER-RECORD. Within these record descriptions there are both group and elementary items with identical names. For example, both records have a NAME-EMPLOYEE group field and a FIRST-NAME elementary item. In order to reference these different fields with the same names, each of the identical names must be "qualified" up to a point where they become unique. Thus, if one were to reference the name NAME-EMPLOYEE as belonging to the group TRANSACTION-RECORD or belonging to the group MASTER-RECORD, then these data-names would become unique. This process is known as qualification.

Figure 11-5 illustrates a Move statement which could be used to move the NAME-EMPLOYEE field in the TRANSACTION-RECORD to the NAME-EMPLOYEE field in the MASTER-RECORD.

```
014020         MOVE NAME-EMPLOYEE IN TRANSACTION-RECORD TO
014030              NAME-EMPLOYEE IN MASTER-RECORD.
```

Figure 11-5 Example of Move Statement with Name Qualification

In Figure 11-5, the field to be moved is identified as NAME-EMPLOYEE IN TRANSACTION-RECORD. This is known as name qualification because the name NAME-EMPLOYEE is used for more than one field in the program. The term IN TRANSACTION-RECORD uniquely identifies which NAME-EMPLOYEE field is being referenced. Thus, the compiler will be able to determine that the NAME-EMPLOYEE field within the group item TRANSACTION-RECORD is the sending field in the Move statement.

Similarly, the term NAME-EMPLOYEE IN MASTER-RECORD identifies the receiving field in the Move statement. The word OF is logically the same as the word IN when identifying qualified names. Thus, the data-name NAME-EMPLOYEE OF TRANSACTION-RECORD would also identify the NAME-EMPLOYEE field in the group item TRANSACTION-RECORD as the sending field in the Move statement.

Whenever the same data-names are used to define different areas in main computer memory, they must never be used as identifiers within an imperative statement without some qualification which will make them unique. More than one level of qualification may be used. Figure 11-6 illustrates this.

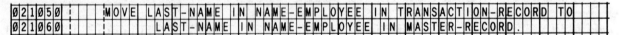

Figure 11-6 Example of Multi-Level Name Qualification

In Figure 11-6, there are two names, NAME-EMPLOYEE and TRANSACTION-RECORD, qualifying the data-name LAST-NAME for the sending field. The only requirement when specifying qualified names is that the name be qualified to a point where it is unique and can be identified by the COBOL compiler.

Justified Right Clause

In some applications, it may be desirable to right justify alphabetic data. Normally an alphabetic move results in left justified data. For example, in the segment of the printer spacing chart illustrated in Figure 11-7, the words DISCOUNT and TOTAL are right justified. This may be accomplished by use of the Justified Right clause in the Data Division. Figure 11-7 illustrates the use of the Justified Right clause.

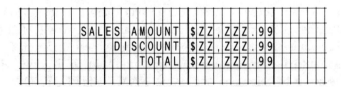

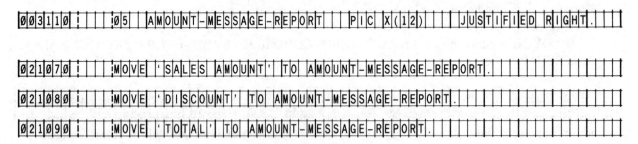

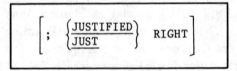

Figure 11-7 Justified Right Clause

The Justified Right clause may be written only for an elementary alphabetic or alphanumeric item. When non-numeric data is moved to a field for which JUSTIFIED RIGHT has been specified, the rightmost character of the source field is placed in the rightmost position of the receiving field. The moving of characters continues from right to left until the receiving field is filled. If the length of the source field is greater than that of the receiving field, truncation terminates the move after the leftmost position of the receiving field is filled. If the source field is shorter, the remaining leftmost positions of the receiving field are filled with spaces.

Blank When Zero Clause

The Blank When Zero clause can be used to blank a field when its value is zero. This is illustrated in Figure 11–8.

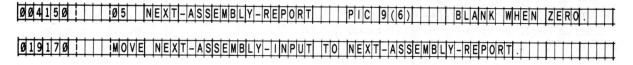

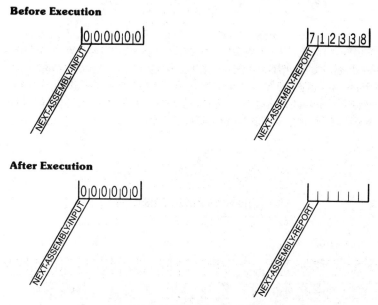

Figure 11-8 Blank When Zero Clause

In Figure 11–8 the NEXT-ASSEMBLY-REPORT field is defined as a numeric field with the BLANK WHEN ZERO clause. When the value in the NEXT-ASSEMBLY-INPUT field, which is zero, is moved to the report field, blanks will be placed in the field instead of zeros. The Blank When Zero clause can be used only for an elementary item whose Picture is specified as numeric or numeric edited.

Low-Values and High-Values

The figurative constants LOW-VALUES and HIGH-VALUES can be used to place the lowest character and highest character, respectively, of the collating sequence of a computer into an alphanumeric field. These values may be placed in a field through the use of either the Value clause when defining the field in the Data Division or through the use of the Move statement in the Procedure Division. These two methods are illustrated in Figure 11–9.

```
ØØ4Ø2Ø      Ø5   HIGH-FIELD-WORK            PIC  XXX        VALUE  HIGH-VALUES.
ØØ4Ø3Ø      Ø5   LOW-FIELD-WORK             PIC  XXX.
```

```
Ø23Ø6Ø      MOVE  LOW-VALUES  TO  LOW-FIELD-WORK.
```

After Execution

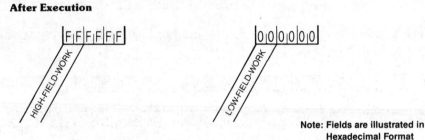

Note: Fields are illustrated in
Hexadecimal Format

Figure 11-9 High Values and Low Values

In Figure 11-9, the figurative constant HIGH-VALUES is specified in the Value clause of the HIGH-FIELD-WORK field. The figurative constant LOW-VALUES is moved to LOW-FIELD-WORK through the use of the Move statement. The values stored in the fields are represented in hexadecimal format. The lowest value is 000000, while the highest value is FFFFFF. Although these values are used on the IBM 4381, as well as other computers, some computers may have other values which represent the high and low values in the collating sequence.

ALL Figurative Constant

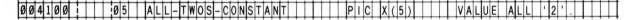

In order to give an alphanumeric field a repetitive sequence of one or more values, the ALL figurative constant can be used. This is illustrated in Figure 11-10.

```
ØØ41ØØ      Ø5   ALL-TWOS-CONSTANT          PIC  X(5)       VALUE  ALL  '2'.
```

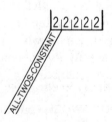

Figure 11-10 ALL Figurative Constant

In Figure 11-10, the field ALL-TWOS-CONSTANT contains the value 2 in each position even though only one 2 is specified in the Value clause. This is because the figurative constant ALL is specified. When the figurative constant ALL is specified, the one or more constant values within the apostrophes are repeated as many times as necessary to fill the field defined with the Picture clause.

Usage Clause

The Usage clause can be used to describe the form in which data is to be stored in the Data Division. In Figure 11–11, the clause USAGE IS COMP-3 is used. This clause will cause the areas referenced by INTEREST-AMOUNT-WORK and TOTAL-AMOUNT-WORK to be stored in the Computational-3 format on those computers which allow the Computational-3 format.

Ø Ø 5 Ø 7 Ø	Ø 1	WORK-AREAS.				
Ø Ø 5 Ø 8 Ø		Ø 5	INTEREST-AMOUNT-WORK	PIC S9(5)V99	USAGE IS COMP-3.
Ø Ø 5 Ø 9 Ø		Ø 5	TOTAL-AMOUNT-WORK	PIC S9(5)V99	USAGE IS COMP-3.

Figure 11-11 Example of USAGE IS COMP-3 Clause

If an area is reserved in the Data Division without specifying COMPUTATIONAL-3 or COMP-3, data is stored in the area in the Display format. Figure 11–12 illustrates how the amount 0023600 would be stored in the INTEREST-AMOUNT-WORK field if Usage is Comp-3 is not specified in the Picture clause.

F0 F0 F2 F3 F6 F0 F0
INTEREST-AMOUNT-WORK

Note: The format is that used by computers using the
Extended Binary Coded Decimal Interchange Code [EBCDIC].

Figure 11-12 INTEREST-AMOUNT-WORK Field in Display Format

Seven bytes of storage are reserved for the field and one byte or position in memory is used for each digit in the field. In Figure 11–12, each digit is preceded by an "F." The "F" is a hexadecimal representation of the high order bits of the byte containing the digit. Thus, the number 0 is represented internally as F0, the number 2 as F2, etc. The entire number 0023600 is stored internally as F0F0F2F3F6F0F0.

When the field is converted to a Computational-3 format, however, all of the sign positions (F) of the bytes are dropped except for the low-order sign which is the sign of the field. The hexadecimal F is a valid plus sign. This is illustrated in Figure 11–13.

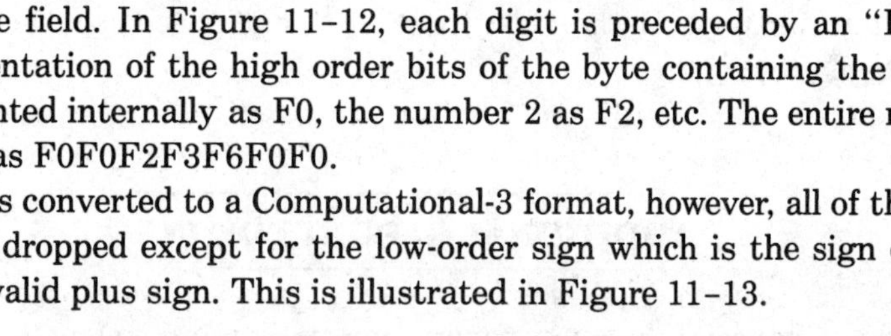

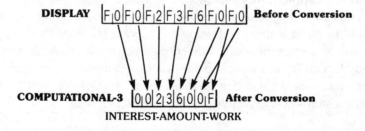

Figure 11-13 INTEREST-AMOUNT-WORK Field in Computational-3 Format

When numeric data is converted from the Display format to the Computational-3 format, the sign in the low-order position of the Display Field is placed in the rightmost four bits of the Computational-3 field, and then only the numeric portion of the bytes is placed in the Computational-3 field. Thus, numeric data which requires seven bytes in the Display format requires only four bytes in the Computational-3 format. The Computational-3 format is not found on all computers. It is found, however, on many computers used for business applications.

Format Notation

The general format of the Usage clause is illustrated in Figure 11–14.

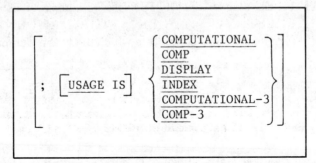

Figure 11 - 14 General Format of Usage Clause

In Figure 11–14, the word USAGE is required in the Usage clause. The word IS is optional. The Computational or Comp option specifies that the numeric data is to be stored in a binary format. The Display option indicates that the data is to be stored in the Display format.

The Index option specifies that the field is a special field used in table look-up operations. As noted previously, the Computational-3 or Comp-3 option specifies that the data will be stored in the Computational-3 format, which is also called the internal decimal format.

The Usage clause may be written either at the group level or the elementary level. At the group level, it applies to each elementary item within the group. If it is used at the group level, the usage of an elementary item must not contradict the usage specified for the group to which the elementary item belongs. If the Usage clause is not specified, the usage of an item is assumed to be Display.

ADDITIONAL REPORT EDITING

As explained in Chapter 4, business reports normally require some form of report editing. Report editing consists of suppressing leading zeros in numeric fields and inserting punctuation within a field to make it more legible on the report. Included in the discussion of report editing was the use of zero suppression, zero suppression with blank fill, zero suppression with asterisk fill, and the editing of numeric fields with special characters such as the dollar sign, comma, and decimal point. In addition to these report editing techniques, there exist several additional insertion characters available in the COBOL language.

Minus Sign

A minus sign (–) can be used at either end of the Picture clause for a numeric edited field. When the minus sign appears at either end of the Picture clause, the minus sign will be printed in the position in which it is placed when the data is negative. When the data is positive, a space is inserted in the position in which the minus sign appears. This is illustrated in Figure 11–15.

DATA IN MEMORY	PICTURE	PRINTED OUTPUT
4500	PICTURE -9999	4500
-4500	PICTURE -9999	-4500
4500	PICTURE 9999-	4500
-4500	PICTURE 9999-	4500-

Figure 11-15 Minus Sign

In addition to occupying a fixed position in a Picture clause, the minus sign can also be floated from the left side of the Picture by placing the minus symbol in each leading numeric position to be suppressed. Each leading zero is replaced with a space, and either a space or a minus sign is placed in the position of the last suppressed zero. The use of the floating minus sign is illustrated in Figure 11-16.

DATA IN MEMORY	PICTURE	PRINTED OUTPUT
12345	PICTURE ----99	12345
00034	PICTURE ----99	34
00000	PICTURE ----99	00
-12345	PICTURE ----99	-12345
-00045	PICTURE ----99	-45
-00006	PICTURE ----99	-06

Figure 11-16 Floating Minus Sign

In Figure 11-16, as with all editing, there must be enough room in the Picture clause to store the data which is being moved to the Picture. The data in memory contains five digits in Figure 11-16. Therefore, the Picture clause contains space for these five digits plus the minus sign. Whenever data is to be edited, there must always be room in the Picture for all of the digits in order for editing to take place properly.

Plus Sign

When the plus sign (+) appears at either end of a Picture clause, the sign of the data will be indicated in the position where the plus sign appears. If the data is positive, a + is inserted; if the data is negative, a - is inserted. The plus sign can also be floated in the same way as the minus sign. The use of the plus sign is shown in Figure 11-17.

DATA IN MEMORY	PICTURE	PRINTED OUTPUT
12	PICTURE +99	+12
-12	PICTURE +99	-12
-12	PICTURE 99+	12-
12	PICTURE 99+	12+

Figure 11-17 Plus Sign

Credit Symbol and Debit Symbol

When the CR symbol appears at the right side of a Picture clause, the sign of the data being edited will be indicated in the character positions occupied by the symbol. If the data is positive, two blanks are inserted; if the data is negative, the letters CR are inserted.

DATA IN MEMORY	PICTURE	PRINTED OUTPUT
12345	PICTURE $***.99CR	$123.45
-12345	PICTURE $***.99CR	$123.45CR
-012345	PICTURE $$,$$$.99 CR	$123.45 CR
-004560	PICTURE $$,$$$.99CR	$45.60CR

Figure 11-18 CR Symbol

When the letters DB appear at the right side of the Picture clause and the data to be edited is negative, the letters DB will appear in the positions in which they are placed; if the data is positive, two blanks are inserted.

DATA IN MEMORY	PICTURE	PRINTED OUTPUT
001256	PICTURE $Z,ZZZ.99DB	$ 12.56
001256	PICTURE $*,***.99DB	$***12.56
-001256	PICTURE $*,***.99DB	$***12.56DB
-001256	PICTURE $*,***.99 DB	$***12.56 DB
-001256	PICTURE $$,$$$.99 DB	$12.56 DB

Figure 11-19 DB Symbol

When using the CR and DB symbols, a space can be included in the Picture clause following the specifications for the data to be edited and before either the CR or DB symbols. This allows the symbols to be separated from the actual data which is edited and is many times used for a more readable report. The CR and DB symbols can only be used on the right side of the Picture clause.

"P" Symbol

If the assumed decimal point location is not within the field, the symbol P is used to indicate each scaling position beyond either end of the data in memory. In effect, each P represents an implied position.

DATA IN MEMORY	PICTURE	PRINTED OUTPUT
123	PICTURE 999PPP	123000.
123	PICTURE PP999	.00123

Figure 11-20 "P" Symbol

Blank, Zero (0), and Stroke (/)

In all the previous examples of editing, the data to be edited must be numeric; that is, it must be defined with a Picture 9 clause and it must contain actual numeric data. The Blank, Zero (0), and Stroke (/) insertion characters can be used with either numeric fields (Picture 9) or alphanumeric fields (Picture X). When used, these characters are inserted in the field in the positions in which they appear within the Picture clause. Although not widely used, in some applications their use is quite important. A competent COBOL programmer should understand these editing characters. Figure 11-21 illustrates the use of these editing characters.

BLANK

DATA IN MEMORY	PICTURE	PRINTED OUTPUT
00000	PICTURE 99B999	00 000
060978	PICTURE 99B99B99	06 09 78
249524667	PICTURE 999B99B9999	249 52 4667
FLJONES	PICTURE XBXBXXXXX	F L JONES
ABCDEF	PICTURE XXBXXXBX	AB CDE F

Figure 11-21 Blank Editing Character (Part 1 of 2)

ZERO SYMBOL

DATA IN MEMORY	PICTURE	PRINTED OUTPUT
125	PICTURE 99900	12500
125	PICTURE 00999	00125
125	PICTURE XXX0	1250
125	PICTURE 000XXX	000125

STROKE

DATA IN MEMORY	PICTURE	PRINTED OUTPUT
082987	PICTURE 99/99/99	08/29/87
ABCDEF	PICTURE X/XXX/X/X	A/BCD/E/F
007563	PICTURE Z/ZZZ/ZZ	75/63

Figure 11-21 Zero and Stroke Editing Characters (Part 2 of 2)

PROCEDURE DIVISION

As with the Data Division, there are statements not explained in previous chapters that can be used within the Procedure Division which are useful in some applications. These statements are explained in the remainder of this chapter.

Go To Statement

The Go To statement is used to pass control from one paragraph to another. This is illustrated in Figure 11-22.

```
015050      IF SALES-INPUT IS GREATER THAN SALES-QUOTA-CONSTANT
015060         GO TO C050-FIGURE-BONUS.
```

```
017090  C050-FIGURE-BONUS.
017100
017110      MULTIPLY SALES-INPUT BY BONUS-PCT GIVING SALES-BONUS-REPORT.
```

Figure 11-22 Go To Statement

In Figure 11-22, the Go To statement is used to transfer control to the first statement in the C050-FIGURE-BONUS paragraph. Thus, as a result of the Go To statement on line 015060, the next statement to be executed in the program is the Multiply statement on line 017110.

The Go To statement as illustrated in Figure 11-22 is not a useful statement in COBOL for two major reasons: First, if the program and logic of the program are designed properly, there is normally no reason to use the Go To statement; and second, with the use of the Go To statement there is the distinct possibility that the program will violate the rules of the three control structures which are used to arrive at a proper program. Therefore, the Go To statement is a dangerous statement in that it will likely lead to a program which is not easily read and maintained. As a consequence, it is suggested that the Go To statement not be used in a program unless there is an overwhelming and thoroughly thought-out reason for doing so.

Go To Depending Statement

A variation of the Go To statement which finds a more useful and practical application in a well-designed structured COBOL program is the Go To Depending statement. An example of the Go To Depending statement is illustrated in Figure 11-23.

```
018130        GO TO C001-ADD-A-RECORD
018140           C002-DELETE-A-RECORD
018150           C003-CHANGE-SALES-AMOUNT
018160           C004-CHANGE-CUSTOMER-ADDRESS
018170           C005-CHANGE-CREDIT-LIMIT
018180        DEPENDING ON TRANSACTION-CODE-INPUT.
```

```
GO TO procedure-name-1 [, procedure-name-2] ...    , procedure-name-n

DEPENDING ON identifier
```

Figure 11-23 Go To Depending Statement

In Figure 11-23, the Go To Depending statement will cause control to be passed to one of the five paragraphs specified, depending upon the value found in the TRANSACTION-CODE-INPUT field. If the value in the field is equal to 1, then the C001-ADD-A-RECORD paragraph would be entered. If the value is equal to 2, then the C002-DELETE-A-RECORD paragraph would be entered. If the value is equal to 3, the C003-CHANGE-SALES-AMOUNT paragraph would receive control, etc. Thus, if the value in the field is equal to 1, 2, 3, 4, or 5, the appropriate paragraph would receive control. If the value in the field was not equal to 1, 2, 3, 4, or 5, then the statement following line 018180 would be executed.

The identifier in the Go To Depending statement must be an elementary numeric field which contains positive integers. If the field contains a negative number, zero, or a number greater than the number of paragraph names specified, then control passes to the statement following the Go To Depending statement.

Case Structure

The Go To Depending statement finds application in the Case Structure, which is a control structure which has been introduced to Structured Programming in addition to the three major structures illustrated previously (Sequence, If-Then-Else, and Perform Until). The Case

Structure is used when there are a number of "cases" which must be processed, depending upon the value in a given field.

In order to illustrate the Case Structure, assume that a transaction record is to be read which contains a numeric code to specify the type of processing which is to take place. The codes are summarized below.

Code 1 — Add a Record
Code 2 — Delete a Record
Code 3 — Change the Sales Amount
Code 4 — Change the Customer Address
Code 5 — Change the Credit Limit

The coding to process the Case Structure through the use of the Go To Depending statement is illustrated in Figure 11-24.

```
015020        PERFORM B000-PROCESS-TRANSACTIONS THRU B000-EXIT.

016060  B000-PROCESS-TRANSACTIONS.
016070
016080        GO TO B001-ADD-A-RECORD
016090               B002-DELETE-A-RECORD
016100               B003-CHANGE-SALES-AMOUNT
016110               B004-CHANGE-CUSTOMER-ADDRESS
016120               B005-CHANGE-CREDIT-LIMIT
016130           DEPENDING ON TRANSACTION-CODE-INPUT.
016140        GO TO B006-PRINT-ERROR-MESSAGE.

017160  B001-ADD-A-RECORD.

018180        GO TO B000-EXIT.

019020  B002-DELETE-A-RECORD.

019140        GO TO B000-EXIT.

020070  B003-CHANGE-SALES-AMOUNT.

021090        GO TO B000-EXIT.

021110  B004-CHANGE-CUSTOMER-ADDRESS.

021130        GO TO B000-EXIT.

022150  B005-CHANGE-CREDIT-LIMIT.

023170        GO TO B000-EXIT.

023190  B006-PRINT-ERROR-MESSAGE.

025010        GO TO B000-EXIT.

025030  B000-EXIT.
025040
025050        EXIT.
```

Figure 11-24 Case Structure with Go To Depending Statement

In Figure 11–24, the processing of the Case Structure is initiated with the Perform statement on line 015020. This Perform statement includes the THRU clause. When the THRU clause is used, control does not return to the statement following the Perform statement when a single paragraph has been performed; rather, control is returned only after the paragraph whose name is specified following the word THRU is executed. In Figure 11–24, control would be returned to the statement following the Perform statement on line 015020 only after the B000-EXIT paragraph is executed.

The B000-PROCESS-TRANSACTIONS paragraph, which is the first one performed, contains the Go To Depending statement. This statement will direct control to one of the named paragraphs, depending upon the value found in the field TRANSACTION-CODE-INPUT. If the value 1–5 is not found, then the B006-PRINT-ERROR-MESSAGE paragraph will be entered. Regardless of which paragraph is entered as a result of the Go To Depending statement, the appropriate processing will take place and then a Go To statement at the end of each of the paragraphs will direct control to the B000-EXIT paragraph. This is the named paragraph in the Thru clause of the Perform statement (see line 015020). The only statement in the B000-EXIT paragraph is the EXIT statement. The Exit statement accomplishes no processing; it merely specifies that control is to be returned to the statement following the Perform statement.

Therefore, as a result of the coding illustrated in Figure 11–24, the Go To Depending statement will be executed to direct control to the proper processing paragraph. After the proper paragraph has been executed, control is passed to the B000-EXIT paragraph which in turn returns control to the statement following the Perform statement which initiated the processing.

Alternate Method for Case Structure

The previous example illustrated one method which can be used to process the Case Structure. It will be noted, however, that the use of the Go To Depending statement depends upon the code field containing a numeric value. If the field does not contain a numeric value, then the Go To Depending statement cannot be used.

If the code field does not contain a numeric field, or even when the code field does contain numeric data, the technique shown in Figure 11–25 can be used to process the case structure.

Data Division

```
004020        05  TRANSACTION-CODE-INPUT    PIC 9.
004030            88  CODE-IS-ADD-A-RECORD              VALUE 1.
004040            88  CODE-IS-DELETE-A-RECORD           VALUE 2.
004050            88  CODE-IS-CHANGE-SALES-AMOUNT       VALUE 3.
004060            88  CODE-IS-CHANGE-CUST-ADDRESS       VALUE 4.
004070            88  CODE-IS-CHANGE-CREDIT-LIMIT       VALUE 5.
```

Procedure Division

```
019020        IF  CODE-IS-ADD-A-RECORD
019030            PERFORM B001-ADD-A-RECORD
019040        ELSE IF  CODE-IS-DELETE-A-RECORD
019050            PERFORM B002-DELETE-A-RECORD
019060        ELSE IF  CODE-IS-CHANGE-SALES-AMOUNT
019070            PERFORM B003-CHANGE-SALES-AMOUNT
019080        ELSE IF  CODE-IS-CHANGE-CUST-ADDRESS
019090            PERFORM B004-CHANGE-CUSTOMER-ADDRESS
019100        ELSE IF  CODE-IS-CHANGE-CREDIT-LIMIT
019110            PERFORM B005-CHANGE-CREDIT-LIMIT
019120        ELSE PERFORM B006-PRINT-ERROR-MESSAGE.
```

Figure 11-25 Example of the IF-THEN-ELSE for Case Structure

In Figure 11-25, a Nested If statement is used to check for the appropriate code in the record. This Nested If statement is different from those seen in previous chapters in several respects. First, once one of the conditions is true, there will never have to be a check for a further condition. For example, once the code for Delete A Record is found, there will never have to be a further check of any of the other codes. Thus, instead of checking further conditions when one condition is true, as has been done in previous Nested If statements, the proper paragraph is performed and control will pass to the statement following the Nested If statement.

Second, this Nested If statement is written on the coding form in a different manner from previous Nested If statements. Note that the phrase ELSE IF is written on the same coding line, and there is no indentation of each Else statement as was done previously. The reason for this is that if the condition is true, there are no further If statements which must be executed. If the condition is not true, then the next If statement must be executed. Thus, there is no danger that the person reading the program will be misled by applying an ELSE clause to the wrong If statement. Whenever the case structure is to be implemented using the Nested If technique, the statement should be written as illustrated in Figure 11-25.

Although both the Go To Depending technique and the Nested If technique can be used for the case structure, the Nested If technique offers more flexibility since it can be used with alphanumeric as well as numeric fields. In addition, when used in conjunction with condition names, the Nested If technique will normally be more easily understood by the reader than the Go To Depending technique.

Alter Statement

Although some persons will argue that the Go To statement should be used in certain circumstances within a program, there is universal agreement that the Alter statement should NEVER be used in a program. In the past, however, programs have been written with this statement in them, so the Alter statement is presented here merely for general information. Again, the Alter statement should NEVER be used in a COBOL program.

The ALTER statement is used to modify an unconditional GO TO statement elsewhere in the Procedure Division, thus changing the sequence in which programs steps are to be executed. Figure 11-26 illustrates the Alter statement.

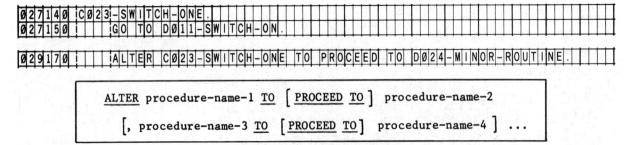

Figure 11-26 Alter statement

Procedure-name-1 designates a paragraph containing a single sentence consisting only of a Go To statement. The effect of the Alter statement is to replace the procedure-name specified in the Go To statement with Procedure-name-2 of the Alter statement. Thus, in Figure 11-26, before the Alter statement is executed, the Go To statement on line 027150 will cause control to be passed to the D011-SWITCH-ON paragraph. After the execution of the Alter statement, control will be passed to the D024-MINOR-ROUTINE paragraph.

Again, the Alter statement will appear in some programs which were written in the past, but should never be used in a program because it violates all rules pertaining to structured programming and the development of easily read and understood programs.

Display Statement

The function of the Display statement in a COBOL program is to display fields upon a CRT terminal screen or on the computer console. The format of the Display statement is illustrated in Figure 11-27.

$$\underline{\text{DISPLAY}} \quad \left\{ \begin{array}{l} \text{identifier-1} \\ \text{literal-1} \end{array} \right\} \quad \left[\begin{array}{l} , \ \text{identifier-2} \\ , \ \text{literal-2} \end{array} \right] \quad \cdots \quad \left[\underline{\text{UPON}} \ \text{mnemonic-name} \right]$$

Figure 11-27 Format Notation of Display Statement

The Display statement format in Figure 11-27 begins with the word DISPLAY. It is followed by the identifier or literal to be displayed. The UPON clause is optional, but if used, causes the identifier or literal to be displayed on the output device associated with the mnemonic-name. The mnemonic-name is a programmer chosen name that associates the use of the Display statement with displaying fields upon the CRT screen or computer console. Figure 11-28 illustrates the usage of the Display statement.

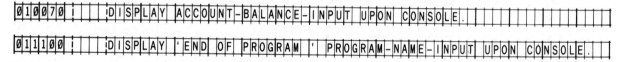

Figure 11-28 Display Statement Examples

The Display statement on line 010070 will display the contents of the ACCOUNT-BALANCE-INPUT field on the CRT screen associated with the device known as CONSOLE beginning in the leftmost position of the screen. On line 011100, the literal END OF PROGRAM would be displayed on the console screen beginning in the leftmost position, followed by the contents of the field PROGRAM-NAME-INPUT.

Move Corresponding Statement

In a previous example of name qualification, the same data-name could be used for an elementary data item as long as it belonged to a group item with a unique name. It should be noted that each Move statement which used name-qualification referenced only one data item within the group.

The Corresponding option may be used to reference all fields with common data names within two different groups. Figure 11-29 on page 11.18 illustrates the use of the Corresponding option when used with the Move statement.

In Figure 11-29, the word MOVE must appear in the Move statement as illustrated previously. The word CORRESPONDING or the abbreviation CORR must immediately follow the word Move, separated by one or more blanks.

```
003020  01  TRANSACTION-RECORD.
003030      05  NAME                    PIC X(25).
003040      05  ADDRESS                 PIC X(25).
003050      05  CITY                    PIC X(25).
003060      05  FILLER                  PIC X(4).
003070      05  CODE                    PIC X.
003080
003090  01  MASTER-RECORD.
003100      05  COUNT                   PIC XXX.
003110      05  NAME                    PIC X(25).
003120      05  ADDRESS                 PIC X(25).
003130      05  CITY                    PIC X(25).
003140      05  FILLER                  PIC XX.
```

```
019170      MOVE CORRESPONDING TRANSACTION-RECORD TO MASTER-RECORD.
```

```
                  ⎧ CORRESPONDING ⎫
         MOVE     ⎨               ⎬   identifier-1  TO  identifier-2
                  ⎩ CORR          ⎭
```

BEFORE MOVE

TRANSACTION-RECORD

NAME	ALFRED R. JOHONSKI
ADDRESS	7245 DRUMMOND AVE
CITY	NORTH LAKE, NEW YORK
CODE	3

MASTER-RECORD

COUNT	275
NAME	JAMES JILLIAN
ADDRESS	1927 HIWAY 37
CITY	BRUSHVILLE, TEXAS

AFTER MOVE

TRANSACTION-RECORD

NAME	ALFRED R. JOHONSKI
ADDRESS	7245 DRUMMOND AVE
CITY	NORTH LAKE, NEW YORK
CODE	3

MASTER-RECORD

COUNT	275
NAME	ALFRED R. JOHONSKI
ADDRESS	7245 DRUMMOND AVE
CITY	NORTH LAKE, NEW YORK

Figure 11-29 Move Corresponding

Identifier-1 is used to specify a group-item name which contains the sending fields to be moved by the Move statement. Identifier-2 specifies the group-item data name which contains the receiving fields. When the Move Corresponding instruction is executed, as illustrated in Figure 11-29, all data stored in fields within the group item specified by identifier-1 with the same data names as data stored in the fields within the group item specified by identifier-2 are moved. Thus, since the name NAME appears both in the group specified by identifier-1 and in the group specified by identifier-2, the data in the field NAME is moved from the sending group item (TRANSACTION-RECORD) to the receiving group item (MASTER-RECORD). The same is true for the fields ADDRESS and CITY, which are specified in both the TRANSACTION-RECORD group and the MASTER-RECORD group. The individual names of the fields need not be specified in order to move the data from one field to another. The use of the Corresponding entry causes these moves to take place by merely specifying the group-item data names.

Names within either group which do not have a corresponding name in the other group are not affected by the Move Corresponding statement. Thus, in Figure 11-29 the field CODE, for which there is not a corresponding name in the MASTER-RECORD group, is not moved; and the contents of the field COUNT in the MASTER-RECORD group remains unchanged because there is no correspondingly named field in the TRANSACTION-RECORD group. Any Fillers which are defined in either of the group items are not moved even though the names are the same.

The Corresponding option may be used with other instructions as well as the Move statement. For example, it may be used with the Add statement in order to add the values in fields with corresponding names within a group item. It must be remembered, however, that when the Add Corresponding statement is utilized, all of the fields which are to be added within the group item must be validly signed numeric fields. The same is true when the simple Add statement is used. Any invalidly signed numeric field may cause a cancellation of the program or other unpredictable results. The use of the corresponding option may be convenient in a few applications, but its use is discouraged in many installations because each field is not uniquely defined in the Move, Add, or other statements.

On Size Error Processing

It will be recalled from previous chapters that the On Size Error option can be used with various arithmetic statements. When used, it tests if the answer developed from the arithmetic operation is too large to fit into the field which was defined for it. If so, an "on size error" is said to have occurred. In addition, when it is used with the Divide statement, it can also mean that the divisor is zero.

The On Size Error option does present some problems, however, because it is a conditional statement which does not have an "else" possibility. This is illustrated in Figure 11-30 which is an INCORRECT EXAMPLE of the way in which to write the On Size Error.

```
015070        IF PERCENTAGE-INPUT IS GREATER THAN 10
015080           DIVIDE SALES-INPUT BY SALES-RETURN-INPUT GIVING
015090              RATIO-WORK
015100              ON SIZE ERROR
015110                 MOVE 'DIVISOR ZERO' TO MESSAGE-OUTPUT
015120           MOVE SALESPERSON-NAME-INPUT TO SALESPERSON-OVER-10-OUTPUT
015130           MOVE RATIO-WORK TO RATIO-OUTPUT.
```

Figure 11-30 Example of Incorrect Use of On Size Error Option

In Figure 11-30, if the Percentage is greater than 10, then the Divide statement is to be executed. It also appears that after the Divide statement is executed, the programmer intends that the Move statements on line 015120 and line 015130 should be executed. These statements, however, will be executed ONLY if an "on size error" occurs. This is because they follow the On Size Error statement within the Divide statement. Any statement following the On Size Error option in an arithmetic statement will be executed only if the size error occurs. The only way to end the effect of the On Size Error option is to place a period following the last statement in the On Size Error option or to use the End statement which is available with some compilers.

The programmer must be careful when using the On Size Error option so that the program will do what was intended. In order to have the above statement work properly if the End statement is not available, an indicator should be set. This is illustrated in Figure 11-31.

015020		IF	PERCENTAGE-INPUT	IS	GREATER	THAN	10			
015030			DIVIDE SALES-INPUT BY SALES-RETURNS-INPUT GIVING							
015040			RATIO-WORK							
015050			ON SIZE ERROR							
015060			MOVE 'YES' TO WAS-THERE-A-SIZE-ERROR.							
015070		IF	THERE-WAS-A-SIZE-ERROR							
015080			MOVE 'DIVISOR ZERO' TO MESSAGE-OUTPUT							
015090			MOVE 'NO ' TO WAS-THERE-A-SIZE-ERROR							
015100		ELSE								
015110			MOVE SALESPERSON-NAME-INPUT TO SALESPERSON-OVER-10-OUTPUT							
015120			MOVE RATIO-WORK TO RATIO-OUTPUT.							

Figure 11-31 Example of Correct Use of On Size Error Option

In Figure 11-31 when an On Size Error occurs, the indicator WAS-THERE-A-SIZE-ERROR is set to the value YES. The IF statement on line 015070 then checks to determine if there was an error — if so, the error message is moved to the output area, and then the indicator is reset to the value NO . Whenever an indicator is set to indicate a condition, it must be reset after that condition has been processed. If there is no size error, then the Salesperson Name and Ratio are moved to the output area. Thus, the required processing is accomplished despite the limitations of the On Size Error option.

Inspect Statement

The Inspect statement is used to examine fields and to either count the number of occurrences of certain characters within the field or to replace certain characters within a field with other characters, or both.

The general formats of the Inspect statement are illustrated in Figure 11-32.

FORMAT 1

```
INSPECT identifier-1 TALLYING

  { , identifier-2 FOR { ,  { ALL      } { identifier-3 } [ { BEFORE } INITIAL { identifier-4 } ] } ... } ...
                         { LEADING  } { literal-1    }   { AFTER  }         { literal-2    }
                         { CHARACTERS }
```

FORMAT 2

```
INSPECT identifier-1 REPLACING

  { CHARACTERS BY { identifier-6 } [ { BEFORE } INITIAL { identifier-7 } ]                              }
  {               { literal-4    }   { AFTER  }         { literal-5    }                                }
  { { ALL    } { , { identifier-5 } BY { identifier-6 } [ { BEFORE } INITIAL { identifier-7 } ] } ... } ...
  { { LEADING }     { literal-3    }    { literal-4    }   { AFTER  }         { literal-5    }
  { { FIRST  }
```

Figure 11-32 General Formats of Inspect Statement (Part 1 of 2)

FORMAT 3

```
INSPECT identifier-1 TALLYING

   ⎧                    ⎧ ⎧⎧ALL     ⎫ ⎧identifier-3⎫⎫ ⎡⎧BEFORE⎫         ⎧identifier-4⎫⎤⎫   ⎫
   ⎨ , identifier-2 FOR ⎨ ⎨⎨LEADING ⎬ ⎨literal-1   ⎬⎬ ⎢⎨AFTER ⎬ INITIAL ⎨literal-2   ⎬⎥⎬...⎬ ...
   ⎩                    ⎩ ⎩⎩CHARACTERS⎭            ⎭⎭ ⎣⎩      ⎭         ⎩            ⎭⎦⎭   ⎭

REPLACING

   ⎧                                                                                     ⎫
   ⎨  CHARACTERS BY ⎧identifier-6⎫ ⎡⎧BEFORE⎫ INITIAL ⎧identifier-7⎫⎤                      ⎬
   ⎪                ⎨literal-4   ⎬ ⎢⎨AFTER ⎬         ⎨literal-5   ⎬⎥                      ⎪
   ⎪                ⎩            ⎭ ⎣⎩      ⎭         ⎩            ⎭⎦                      ⎪
   ⎨  ⎧ ⎧ALL    ⎫ ⎧ ⎧identifier-5⎫    ⎧identifier-6⎫ ⎡⎧BEFORE⎫         ⎧identifier-7⎫⎤⎫    ⎬
   ⎪  ⎨ ⎨LEADING⎬ ⎨ ⎨literal-3   ⎬ BY ⎨literal-4   ⎬ ⎢⎨AFTER ⎬ INITIAL ⎨literal-5   ⎬⎥⎬... ⎪
   ⎩  ⎩ ⎩FIRST  ⎭ ⎩ ⎩            ⎭    ⎩            ⎭ ⎣⎩      ⎭         ⎩            ⎭⎦⎭    ⎭ ...
```

Figure 11-32 General Formats of Inspect Statement (Part 2 of 2)

In each of the three formats, identifier-1 must be a data item whose Usage is Display. It may also be a group item. Identifier-3 through identifier-n must reference either an elementary alphabetic, alphanumeric, or numeric item described as Usage is Display. Each literal must be nonnumeric and may be any figurative constant except ALL. In formats 1 and 3, identifier-2 must be an elementary numeric data item.

Figure 11-33 illustrates the use of the Inspect statement.

ADDRESS-INPUT |1|2|7| |S|M|I|T|H| |A|V|E| | |

BLANK-COUNT
[After Execution] |0|0|4|

Figure 11-33 Example of Inspect Statement

In Figure 11-33, the ADDRESS-INPUT field is to be inspected. The word TALLYING indicates that all of a certain character within the field are to be counted. The identifier-2 field, BLANK-COUNT, is where the count will be stored. The For All phrase says that a count is to be taken for all of the ' ' characters which are found; that is, all of the blanks which are found in the field. As can be seen, after the statement is executed, the field BLANK-COUNT contains the value 004, which is the number of blanks in the field.

In Figure 11-34, the Inspect statement is used to examine the NAME-INPUT field. A count is to be taken for each character A which is found in the field before the initial (first) blank (' ') is found. As can be seen, there are two A's in the field before the first blank is found. Therefore, the value in the field A-COUNT after the execution of the Inspect statement is 002.

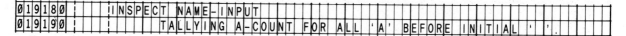

NAME-INPUT |A|R|M|O|N|A| |K|.| |J|O|A|N|

A-COUNT
[After Execution] |0|0|2|

Figure 11-34 Example of Inspect Statement

In Figure 11-35, the AMOUNT-INPUT field is to be inspected and all leading blanks (' ') are to be replaced by zeros (0). The word REPLACING must be specified when one character is to be replaced by another. The word LEADING indicates that the blanks in the field are to be replaced by zeros until a nonblank character is found in the field. At that point, the replacement process is to terminate. As can be seen from the field before the Inspect statement is executed, the AMOUNT-INPUT field contains four blanks in the leading positions of the field. After the execution of the Inspect statement, these leading blanks have been replaced by zeros.

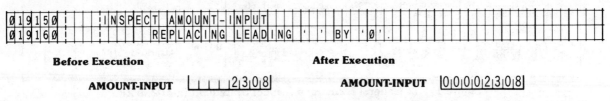

Figure 11 - 35 Example of Inspect Statement

In Figure 11-36, instead of the leading blanks being replaced, ALL blanks will be replaced by a slash ('/'). As can be seen from the field after the execution of the Inspect statement, the blanks have been replaced by slashes.

```
Ø29140    INSPECT DATE-FIELD
Ø29150       REPLACING ALL ' ' BY '/'.
```

DATE-FIELD |0|9| |2|7| |8|9| DATE-FIELD |0|9|/|2|7|/|8|9|

Figure 11 - 36 Example of Inspect Statement

The previous examples have illustrated Format 1 and Format 2 of the Inspect statement. Format 3 works just as if a Format 1 statement were written followed immediately by a Format 2 statement. The Inspect statement can be useful in some applications, particularly where checking and editing of data is required.

Calling and Called Programs

When a module which performs a commonly required function within an installation is required by many programs in the installation, often the module is made into a called program, which is a program that can be called by other programs in order to perform its function. Generally, this program will be placed in an operating system library located on disk so that whenever it is called, it will be available for use.

COBOL Called Programs

When writing in COBOL, the calling program (the program which requires a function to be performed) and the called program (the program which performs the function) will be compiled separately. They will then be linked together to form a single program by the Linkage Editor. This is illustrated in Figure 11-37.

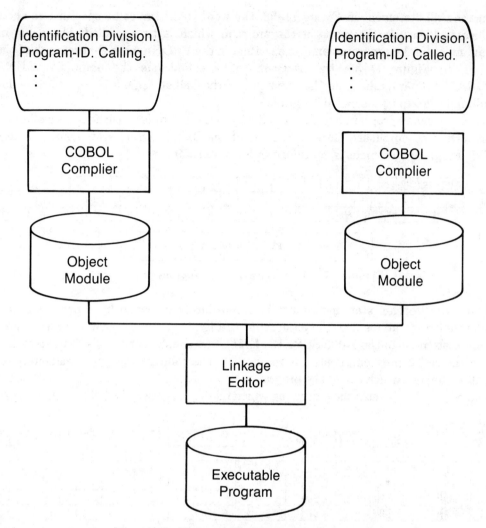

Figure 11-37 Example of Called Programs

In Figure 11-37, the calling program (CALLING) and the called program (CALLED) are compiled as separate programs. Separate object modules are produced as a result of the separate compilations, and then these separate object modules are linked together by the Linkage Editor to form a single program which can then be executed. The compilations do not have to take place at the same time; in fact, as mentioned, the called program will normally be compiled one time and stored in a library for use by other programs. It will be extracted from the library and inserted in the calling program by the Linkage Editor when the program is link-edited.

To call a COBOL program, the Call statement is used in the calling program. An example of a Call statement and the general format of the statement are illustrated in Figure 11-38.

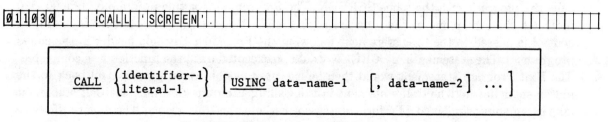

Figure 11-38 Example of Call Statement

In the Call statement in Figure 11–38, the word CALL must be specified as shown. The literal entry identifies the name of the program which is to be called. The value used for "literal" must be the program-name as specified in the PROGRAM-ID paragraph of the called program. In Figure 11–38, the program to be called has the name SCREEN in the PROGRAM-ID paragraph. The Using portion of the Call statement is used to pass data from the calling program to the called program.

After the called program has performed its function, it must return to the calling program. This return is accomplished through the use of the Exit Program statement. An example of the Exit Program statement is contained in Figure 11–39.

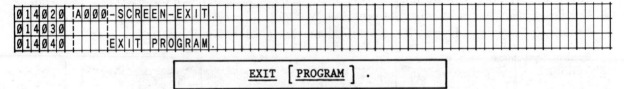

Figure 11-39 Example of Exit Program Statement

The Exit Program statement must be immediately preceded by a paragraph-name and must be the only statement in the paragraph. In Figure 11–39 the Exit Program statement is the only statement in the A000-SCREEN-EXIT paragraph. When this statement is encountered in the called program, control is returned to the calling program immediately following the Call statement which called the program.

Figure 11–40 illustrates the processing which takes place when the Call statement is executed.

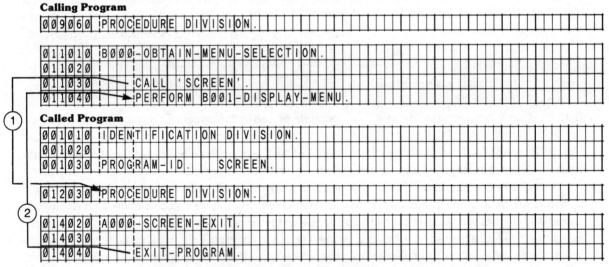

Figure 11-40 Example of Call Statement Execution

The Call statement on line 011030 in the B000-OBTAIN-MENU-SELECTION module calls the program with the name SCREEN. The Program-ID for this program on line 001030 indicates that the name of the program is SCREEN. When the Call statement is executed, control is passed to the first statement following the Procedure Division header in the called program (1). The statements in SCREEN would be executed until the function was completed. The Exit Program statement would then be executed, which would pass control back to the statement following the Call statement in the Calling Program (2). Thus, the Call statement acts in a manner similar to a Perform statement without the Until clause. The major difference is that the called program is compiled separately from the calling program.

Using Clause

Another difference between the Call statement and the Perform statement is that since the called program is compiled separately, it has no access to the data which is stored in the calling program, whereas a paragraph which is Performed would. In most cases, however, the called program must reference some data or storage areas within the calling program in order to receive data on which to operate or to pass back data to the calling program. In order to pass information back and forth between the calling program and the called program, the Using clause is used both in the Call statement which calls the program and the Procedure Division Header in the called program. An example of the Call statement used to call SCREEN and the Procedure Division header in the called program are illustrated in Figure 11-41.

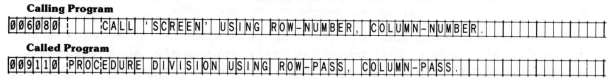

Calling Program

| 0 0 6 0 8 0 | | | | | CALL | 'SCREEN' | USING | ROW-NUMBER, | COLUMN-NUMBER. |

Called Program

| 0 0 9 1 1 0 | PROCEDURE | DIVISION | USING | ROW-PASS, | COLUMN-PASS. |

Figure 11-41 Using Clauses from the Called and Calling Programs

In the Call statement in Figure 11-41, the words CALL 'SCREEN' USING are followed by the data-names ROW-NUMBER and COLUMN-NUMBER.

The called program will be entered at the first statement following the Procedure Division header. The linkage to the called program is established by the Call statement in the calling program. The Using clause in the Call statement indicates that the addresses of the fields ROW-NUMBER and COLUMN-NUMBER are to be passed to the called program so that it may reference the data in the calling program. The Using clause in the called program, as specified with the Procedure Division Header statement, identifies the fields in the called program which will be used to reference the data in the calling program.

The order of the fields to be passed and the number of fields must be identical in the Call statement and the Procedure Division Using Header. Thus, the data-name ROW-NUMBER is first in the Using clause in the Call statement followed by the data-name COLUMN-NUMBER; and the ROW-PASS field is first in the Procedure Division Header followed by the COLUMN-PASS field. The data-names used in the Using clauses need not be the same but must be defined in their respective programs.

In the called program, SCREEN, the names used in the Procedure Division Using Header are defined in the Linkage Section of the Data Division. A Linkage Section is used to reference data fields which are passed from the calling program. The data-names defined in the Linkage Section DO NOT reserve any computer memory. Instead, they are used merely to reference fields which have already been defined in the calling program. The Linkage Section must follow all other Data Division sections in the called program. The Linkage Section from the called program, SCREEN, is illustrated in Figure 11-42.

Called Program

| 0 0 3 0 1 0 | DATA | DIVISION. |

0 0 5 0 5 0	LINKAGE	SECTION.
0 0 5 0 6 0		
0 0 5 0 7 0	0 1	ROW-PASS	PIC 99.
0 0 5 0 8 0	0 1	COLUMN-PASS	PIC 99.

Figure 11-42 Linkage Section of Called Program

There are two fields defined in the Linkage Section in Figure 11-42 — ROW-PASS and COLUMN-PASS.

There is no need for the references in the Linkage Section to be defined in the same order as the Procedure Division Using Header, although they have been in Figure 11-42. However, whenever a linkage section is used, the fields which are passed with the Using statement must be defined as level 01 fields in the called program. Thus, ROW-PASS and COLUMN-PASS are defined as level 01 fields.

Once the fields are defined as 01 level fields, they may be manipulated in whatever manner desired within the called program.

Copy Statement

When writing programs which require the same source statements, it is possible to store the source statements on disk and copy them into any programs requiring them. The most practical method to include source statements into a program is through the use of libraries and the Copy statement.

The Copy statement can be used in the Environment Division, Data Division, and Procedure Division to include source statements, which are stored in an Operating System library, in the program in which the Copy statement appears. This operation is illustrated in Figure 11-43.

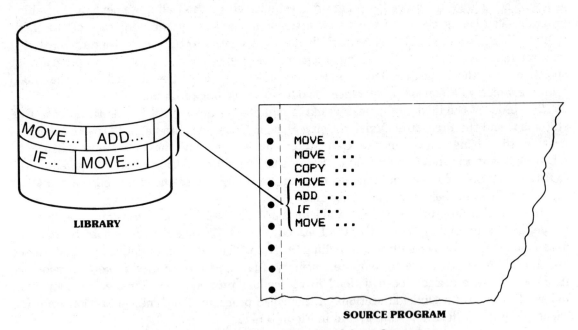

Figure 11-43 Example of Results of Copy Statement

In Figure 11-43, the source statements are stored on the disk in a library. The programmer would write the word Copy together with a library-name in the source program. When the program is compiled, the COBOL compiler will extract the source statements contained in the library and place them in the source program in the same manner as if the source statements in the library had been written in the source program.

Figure 11-44 illustrates the Copy statement to copy a set of printer control entries from the library into a source program and the results of using the Copy statement.

Results of the Copy Statement

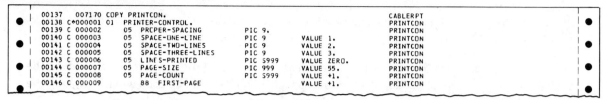

Figure 11-44 Example of Copy Statement in Working-Storage Section

In the coding in Figure 11–44, the Copy statement (line 007170) will copy the file PRINTCON from the library into the source program. As can be seen from the source listing, PRINTCON consists of the printer control entries which are used for proper line counting, page numbering, and line spacing in many of the sample programs explained previously.

The first statement in PRINTCON is a level 01 data-name (PRINTER-CONTROL). The remaining fields within the source coding which are copied into the source program can be referenced by their names in the same manner as if the coding were included in the source program as normal coding.

The source statements in PRINTCON must be catalogued in a library under the name PRINTCON prior to compiling the program with the Copy statement.

When the program is compiled, the statements in PRINTCON are placed in the program in the same manner as if the programmer had written them directly in the program without using the Copy statement. In addition, the letter C is included on the source listing to indicate that the statements were included as a result of the Copy statement. The asterisk appearing on the first line of the copied statements (line 000001) denotes a sequence number out of order. This is a normal occurrence because of the change in sequence numbers from the source program to the copied statements.

In addition to being used in the Working-Storage Section of the program, the Copy statement can also be used in the Environment Division and Procedure Division.

CASE STUDY 1
APPLIANCE REPAIR REPORT

INSTRUCTIONS

An Appliance Repair Report is to be prepared. Write the COBOL program to produce the required report. An IPO Chart and Pseudocode Specifications should be used when designing the program. Use the Test Data at the end of this assignment.

INPUT

The input consists of Appliance Disk Records containing the Truck Number of the repair-person, an Appliance Code describing the type of appliance repaired, the Total Amount of the repair, and the Warranty Code (W = on warranty, N = not on warranty). If the sort capability is available on the computer being used, the input records should be sorted by Appliance Code within Truck Number prior to processing. The format of the input record is illustrated below.

Appliance Disk Record				
FIELD DESCRIPTION	**POSITION**	**LENGTH**	**DEC**	**ATTRIBUTE**
Truck Number	1 – 3	3	0	Numeric
Appliance Code	4 – 5	2	0	Numeric
Total Amount	6 – 10	5	2	Numeric
Warranty Code	11	1		Alphanumeric
Record Length		11		

OUTPUT

Output consists of an Appliance Repair Report. The printer spacing chart is illustrated below.

PRINTER SPACING CHART

The report contains the Truck Number (group indicated), Appliance Code, Appliance Name, and Total Amount of all repairs. The Appliance Name is obtained from a table based upon the Appliance Code in the input record. For appliances on warranty, the report lists the number of appliances on warranty that were repaired, the amount of the total bill charged for Parts, the amount of the total bill charged for Labor, and the Total Amount of the repair bill. The same information is listed for appliances not on warranty.

Note that each line on the printer spacing chart represents one or more input disk records, but there is only one input record for each appliance repaired. Therefore, the values on each line of the report represent totals which have been accumulated and group printed. When there is a change in Truck Number, totals are to be printed; and after all records have been processed, final totals are to be printed.

The percent of the total amount charged for Parts is dependent upon the Application Code in the input record. These percentages are listed in the following table.

APPLIANCE CODE	APPLIANCE NAME	PERCENTAGE (PARTS)
07	REFRIGERATOR	30.0
19	ELECTRIC STOVE	23.0
22	GAS STOVE	22.0
27	WASHER	24.0
34	ELECTRIC DRYER	25.5
47	GAS DRYER	26.0
52	WATER HEATER	33.0
65	MICROWAVE	47.5
77	DISHWASHER	32.7

For example, if the Appliance Code is 27 (WASHER), the Percentage from the table is 24%. If the Total Amount of the repair bill is $35.00, the amount of billed charges for parts is 8.40 (35.00 x .24 = 8.40), and the amount of the billed charges for labor is 26.60 (35.00 - 8.40 = 26.60).

If an Appliance Code in an input record does not appear in the table above, the message UNKNOWN should appear on the report in the Appliance Name field, and 20% should be used for the percentage for parts.

If the sort capability is available on the computer being used, all input records should be sorted by Appliance Code within Truck Number prior to processing.

TEST DATA

The test data to be used for Case Study 1 is illustrated below. The test data is listed in sorted order. If the sort capability is available on the computer being used, the test data below should be scrambled to test the use of the Sort statement in the COBOL program being written.

```
1510703750W
1510705400W
1510706757N
1510702370W
1510704527W
1510701579N
1512202200W
1512204583W
1512203567N
1512207689N
1512202365N
1513403456W
1513401389N
1513402500W
1513403690W
1513403457N
1513400198N
1513400345N
1513408644W
1513407854N
1513403467W
1513404576W
2012704500N
2012704378N
2012702769N
2012703089N
2012703570W
2014702460W
2014702000N
2014702300N
2014701750N
2014702750N
2014703345W
2015205000W
2015201356W
2015201733W
2015203467W
2015201100W
3500707500N
3500710167N
3500705600N
3500704500N
3500703500W
3501005000W
3503407649W
3503409834W
3503405577W
3503406789W
3503405579N
3506506678N
3506505567W
3506509977N
3506510000W

TOTAL RECORDS = 53
```

CASE STUDY 2
BANKING REPORT

INSTRUCTIONS

A Credit Card Report is to be prepared. Write the COBOL program to produce the required report. An IPO Chart and Pseudocode Specifications should be used when designing the program. Use the Test Data at the end of this assignment.

INPUT

The input consists of Credit Card Disk Records containing the Branch Code, Account Number, Credit Limit, Previous Balance, Transaction Date (in MM/DD/YY form), Transaction Code (1 = Payment, 2 = Credit, 3 = Charge), and Transaction Amount. If the sorting capability is available on the computer being used, the input records should be sorted by Transaction Date within Account Number within Branch Code prior to processing. The format of the input record is illustrated below.

Credit Card Disk Record				
FIELD DESCRIPTION	POSITION	LENGTH	DEC	ATTRIBUTE
Branch Code	1 – 2	2	0	Numeric
Account Number	3 – 10	8		Alphanumeric
Credit Limit	11 – 16	6	2	Numeric
Previous Balance	17 – 22	6	2	Numeric
Transaction Date	23 – 30	8		Alphanumeric
Transaction Code	31	1	0	Numeric
Transaction Amount	32 – 37	6	2	Numeric
Record Length		37		

OUTPUT

Output consists of a Credit Card Report listing all credit card holders for the bank. The printer spacing chart is illustrated on the following page. The report contains the Branch Name, Account Number, Previous Balance, Transaction Date, Transaction Type, Transaction Amount, and New Balance.

The Branch Name should be extracted from a table based upon the Branch Code in the input record. The Branch Name table appears below.

BRANCH CODE	BRANCH NAME
01	STATE COLLEGE
17	CULVER STREET
39	DENVER AVENUE

If the Branch Code from the input record is not found in the Branch Name table, then the message UNKNOWN should be printed on the output report in the Branch Name field. The Transaction Type on the report should be extracted from a table based upon the Transaction Code in the input record. The Transaction Type table appears below.

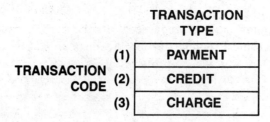

		TRANSACTION TYPE
TRANSACTION CODE	(1)	PAYMENT
	(2)	CREDIT
	(3)	CHARGE

The printer spacing chart is illustrated below.

PRINTER SPACING CHART

```
 2 MM/DD/YY                              CREDIT CARD REPORT                              PAGE ZZ9
 4     BRANCH          ACCOUNT     PREVIOUS      TRANS.         TRANSACTION       TRANSACTION        NEW
 5      NAME           NUMBER      BALANCE       DATE              TYPE             AMOUNT         BALANCE
 7 XXXXXXXXXXXXX     XXXX-XXX    Z,ZZZ.99     MM/DD/YY   XXXXXXXXXXXXXX        Z,ZZZ.99       Z,ZZZ.99
 8                                            MM/DD/YY   XXXXXXXXXXXXXX        Z,ZZZ.99       Z,ZZZ.99
 9                                                       FINANCE CHARGE        Z,ZZZ.99       Z,ZZZ.99
11 ACCOUNT SUMMARY -
13          PREVIOUS BALANCE  ----    Z,ZZZ.99
15 LESS     PAYMENTS                -  Z,ZZZ.99
16          CREDITS                 -  Z,ZZZ.99
18 PLUS     CHARGES                 -  Z,ZZZ.99
19          FINANCE CHARGE          -  Z,ZZZ.99
21               NEW BALANCE  ----    Z,ZZZ.99
23 CREDIT LIMIT        -  Z,ZZZ.99
24 AVAILABLE CREDIT    -  Z,ZZZ.99
25 MINIMUM PAYMENT     -  Z,ZZZ.99

28                               (SEPARATE PAGE)

30 BANK SUMMARY -
32     TOTAL PREVIOUS BALANCE  ----   ZZ,ZZZ.99
34     TOTAL PAYMENTS               -  ZZ,ZZZ.99
35     TOTAL CREDIT                 -  ZZ,ZZZ.99
36     TOTAL CHARGES                -  ZZ,ZZZ.99
37     TOTAL FINANCE CHARGES        -  ZZ,ZZZ.99
39     TOTAL NEW BALANCE        ----   ZZ,ZZZ.99
```

In addition to the three Transaction Types that appear on the report, every account is charged a Finance Charge. The Finance Charge should appear on the Credit Card Report as the last transaction for the Account Number being processed and should appear with the Transaction Date left blank, the words FINANCE CHARGE printed in the Transaction Type field, and the Finance Charge printed in the Transaction Amount field. To calculate the Finance Charge, the Amount Owed must be determined. The Amount Owed is calculated by subtracting Total Payments and Total Credits from the Previous Balance. The Finance Charge is then calculated by multiplying the Amount Owed by the appropriate interest rate from the table on the following page.

AMOUNT OWED	INTEREST RATE
UNDER $1000	1.65%
$1000 – $2500	1.55%
OVER $2500	1.40%

The New Balance of the first transaction within an account is calculated by subtracting the Transaction Amount from the Previous Balance if the transaction is a Payment or a Credit and adding the Transaction Amount to the Previous Balance if the transaction is a Charge. All other New Balances are calculated by subtracting the Transaction Amount from the Previous New Balance if the transaction is a Payment or a Credit and adding the Transaction Amount to the Previous New Balance if the transaction is a Charge.

Upon a change in the Account Number in the input record, an Account Summary is to be printed. The summary for that account contains the Previous Balance, Total Payments, Total Credits, Total Charges, Finance Charge, and New Balance. In addition, the Credit Limit (which appears in each input record associated with an account number), Available Credit, and Minimum Payment are to be printed. The Available Credit is calculated by subtracting the New Balance from the Credit Limit.

The Minimum Payment is calculated according to the instructions in the following table.

If New Balance is	Minimum Payment is
Under $10	Amount of New Balance
$10 to $250	$10 plus 5% of the New Balance
Over $250	$25 plus 7% of the New Balance

Thus, if the New Balance is $7.00, the Minimum Payment is $7.00. If the New Balance is $200, then the Minimum Payment is $20 ($10 + (5% × $200)).

If the New Balance is $400, the Minimum Payment is $53 ($25 + (7% × $400)).

All the transactions for one account and the corresponding Account Summary should appear on a page by themselves.

After the processing of all accounts, a Bank Summary should be printed on a separate page. The summary should contain the Total Previous Balances for all accounts, Total Payments, Total Credits, Total Charges, and Total New Balances of all accounts.

TEST DATA

The test data to be used for Case Study 2 is illustrated below. The test data is listed in sorted order. If the sort capability is available on the computer being used, the test data below should be scrambled to test the use of the Sort Statement in the COBOL program being written.

```
011198-44625000008756010/15/861010000
011198-44625000008756010/17/862002067
011198-44625000008756010/19/862014557
011198-44625000008756010/21/862003509
012098-56212000002036110/05/862010000
012098-56212000002036110/07/862006598
012098-56212000002036110/09/861010000
012098-56212000002036110/11/862007598
012098-56212000002036110/12/863001200
171037-63215000004507410/10/861035000
171037-63215000004507410/15/862004500
171037-63215000004507410/19/861010074
171037-63215000004507410/21/862009056
173347-56028000022837410/03/862008734
173347-56028000022837410/03/862014569
173347-56028000022837410/05/862003485
173347-56028000022837410/07/861020000
173347-56028000022837410/09/862005567
173347-56028000022837410/10/862010765
390983-87312000003458910/30/861034589
392256-90324000015469310/05/862003000
392256-90324000015469310/07/862004583
392256-90324000015469310/08/862003345
392256-90324000015469310/11/861050000
392256-90324000015469310/11/862007568
392256-90324000015469310/12/862010134
392256-90324000015469310/22/863003345
392256-90324000015469310/24/862003987
392256-90324000015469310/30/862004500

TOTAL RECORDS = 29
```

CASE STUDY 3
COLLEGE BUDGET REPORT

INSTRUCTIONS

A College Budget Report is to be prepared. Write the COBOL program to produce the required report. An IPO Chart and Pseudocode Specifications should be used when designing the program. Use the Test Data at the end of this assignment.

INPUT

The input consists of Budget Disk Records containing the Division Code, Department Code, Account Code, Last Year's Budget, Last Year's Expenses, This Year's Budget, and This Year's Expenses. If the sort capability exists on the computer being used, the input records should be sorted by Account Code within Department Code within Division Code prior to processing. The format of the input record is illustrated below.

Budget Disk Record				
FIELD DESCRIPTION	POSITION	LENGTH	DEC	ATTRIBUTE
Division Code	1 – 2	2	0	Numeric
Department Code	3 – 4	2	0	Numeric
Account Code	5 – 6	2	0	Numeric
Last Year's Budget	7 – 11	5	0	Numeric
Last Year's Expenses	12 – 16	5	0	Numeric
This Year's Budget	17 – 21	5	0	Numeric
This Year's Expenses	22 – 26	5	0	Numeric
Record Length		26		

OUTPUT

Output consists of the College Budget Report. A printer spacing chart is illustrated on the following page. The report contains the Division Name, Department Name, Account Name, Last Year's Budget, Last Year's Expenses, Last Year's Surplus (if any), This Year's Budget, This Year's Expenses, This Year's Surplus (if any), and the Percentage Change between last year's and this year's Budget and Expenses. In addition, on a separate page, the report contains the Department Summary and Division Summary. Contained in each summary are Last Year's and This Year's Budget, Expenses, and Surplus, plus the Percentage Change in budget and expenses.

The Surplus is calculated by subtracting Expenses from Budget. Percent Change in Budget is calculated by subtracting Last Year's Budget from This Year's Budget and dividing by Last Year's Budget. Percent Change in Expenses is calculated by subtracting Last Year's Expenses from This Year's Expenses and dividing by Last Year's Expenses.

```
                                    PRINTER SPACING CHART

 1
 2 MM/DD/YY                        COLLEGE BUDGET REPORT                              PAGE ZZ9
 3
 4 DIVISION   DEPARTMENT    ACCOUNT        --------LAST YEAR--------  --------THIS YEAR--------  - PERCENT CHANGE -
 5   NAME        NAME        NAME        BUDGET  EXPENSES  SURPLUS   BUDGET  EXPENSES  SURPLUS    BUDGET   EXPENSES
 6
 7 XXXXXXXXXX  XXXXXXXXXX  XXXXXXXXXXXXXXX  ZZ,ZZ9   ZZ,ZZ9  -ZZ,ZZ9  ZZ,ZZ9   ZZ,ZZ9  -ZZ,ZZ9  -ZZZ.99%  -ZZZ.99%
 8                         XXXXXXXXXXXXXXX  ZZ,ZZ9   ZZ,ZZ9  -ZZ,ZZ9  ZZ,ZZ9   ZZ,ZZ9  -ZZ,ZZ9  -ZZZ.99%  -ZZZ.99%
 9
10             XXXXXXXXXX  XXXXXXXXXXXXXXX  ZZ,ZZ9   ZZ,ZZ9  -ZZ,ZZ9  ZZ,ZZ9   ZZ,ZZ9  -ZZ,ZZ9  -ZZZ.99%  -ZZZ.99%
11                         XXXXXXXXXXXXXXX  ZZ,ZZ9   ZZ,ZZ9  -ZZ,ZZ9  ZZ,ZZ9   ZZ,ZZ9  -ZZ,ZZ9  -ZZZ.99%  -ZZZ.99%
12
13 XXXXXXXXXX  XXXXXXXXXX  XXXXXXXXXXXXXXX  ZZ,ZZ9   ZZ,ZZ9  -ZZ,ZZ9  ZZ,ZZ9   ZZ,ZZ9  -ZZ,ZZ9  -ZZZ.99%  -ZZZ.99%
14                         XXXXXXXXXXXXXXX  ZZ,ZZ9   ZZ,ZZ9  -ZZ,ZZ9  ZZ,ZZ9   ZZ,ZZ9  -ZZ,ZZ9  -ZZZ.99%  -ZZZ.99%
15
16             XXXXXXXXXX  XXXXXXXXXXXXXXX  ZZ,ZZ9   ZZ,ZZ9  -ZZ,ZZ9  ZZ,ZZ9   ZZ,ZZ9  -ZZ,ZZ9  -ZZZ.99%  -ZZZ.99%
17                         XXXXXXXXXXXXXXX  ZZ,ZZ9   ZZ,ZZ9  -ZZ,ZZ9  ZZ,ZZ9   ZZ,ZZ9  -ZZ,ZZ9  -ZZZ.99%  -ZZZ.99%
18
19
20                                      (SEPARATE PAGE)
21
22 MM/DD/YY                        COLLEGE BUDGET REPORT                              PAGE ZZ9
23
24 DEPARTMENT SUMMARY -    --------LAST YEAR--------  --------THIS YEAR--------  - PERCENT CHANGE -
25                     BUDGET   EXPENSES  SURPLUS    BUDGET   EXPENSES  SURPLUS    BUDGET   EXPENSES
26
27    XXXXXXXXXX    ZZZ,ZZ9  ZZZ,ZZ9  -ZZZ,ZZ9   ZZZ,ZZ9  ZZZ,ZZ9  -ZZZ,ZZZ9  -ZZZ.99%  -ZZZ.99%
28    XXXXXXXXXX    ZZZ,ZZ9  ZZZ,ZZ9  -ZZZ,ZZ9   ZZZ,ZZ9  ZZZ,ZZ9  -ZZZ,ZZZ9  -ZZZ.99%  -ZZZ.99%
29    XXXXXXXXXX    ZZZ,ZZ9  ZZZ,ZZ9  -ZZZ,ZZ9   ZZZ,ZZ9  ZZZ,ZZ9  -ZZZ,ZZZ9  -ZZZ.99%  -ZZZ.99%
30
31 DIVISION SUMMARY -      --------LAST YEAR--------  --------THIS YEAR--------  - PERCENT CHANGE -
32                     BUDGET   EXPENSES  SURPLUS    BUDGET   EXPENSES  SURPLUS    BUDGET   EXPENSES
33
34    XXXXXXXXXX   Z,ZZZ,ZZ9  Z,ZZZ,ZZ9  -Z,ZZZ,ZZ9  Z,ZZZ,ZZ9  Z,ZZZ,ZZ9  -Z,ZZZ,ZZ9  -ZZZ.99%  -ZZZ.99%
35    XXXXXXXXXX   Z,ZZZ,ZZ9  Z,ZZZ,ZZ9  -Z,ZZZ,ZZ9  Z,ZZZ,ZZ9  Z,ZZZ,ZZ9  -Z,ZZZ,ZZ9  -ZZZ.99%  -ZZZ.99%
36    XXXXXXXXXX   Z,ZZZ,ZZ9  Z,ZZZ,ZZ9  -Z,ZZZ,ZZ9  Z,ZZZ,ZZ9  Z,ZZZ,ZZ9  -Z,ZZZ,ZZ9  -ZZZ.99%  -ZZZ.99%
```

The Division Code, Department Code, and Account Code in the input record should be used to retrieve the Division Name, Department Name, and Account Name from the following tables.

DIVISION NAME TABLE

DIVISION CODE	DIVISION NAME
01	BUSINESS
02	ENGLISH
03	FINE ARTS
04	HUMANITIES
05	SCIENCE

ACCOUNT NAME TABLE

ACCOUNT CODE	ACCOUNT NAME
10	FULL TIME WAGES
15	PART TIME WAGES
20	TRAVEL EXPENSES
25	OFFICE SUPPLIES
30	TEACH. SUPPLIES
35	LAB ASSISTANTS

DEPARTMENT NAME TABLE

DEPARTMENT CODE	DEPARTMENT NAME
14	ACCOUNTING
28	ART
35	ANATOMY
43	BIOLOGY
49	CHEMISTRY
54	JOURNALISM
67	LITERATURE
76	HISTORY
79	MARKETING
83	MATH
85	MUSIC
89	PHILOSOPHY
91	PHYSICS
97	MANAGEMENT

If the Division Code, Department Code, or Account Code in the input record does not appear in its respective table, the message "UNKNOWN" should be printed in the corresponding field on the report. When there is a change in Department Code in the input record, the appropriate amounts should be stored for later printing in the Department Summary. When there is a change in Division Code in the input record, the appropriate amounts should be stored for later printing in the Division Summary. Both Division Name and Department Name on the report are group indicated.

TEST DATA

The test data to be used for Case Study 3 is illustrated below and on the next page. The test data is listed in sorted order. If the sort capability is available on the computer being used, the test data listed below should be scrambled to test the use of the Sort Statement in the COBOL program being written.

```
011410560005413559400581B9
011415135001201312500013054
01142000600005510060000410
011425005000038300500000413
011430002000015000200000200
011435016000154701700001656
017910870008650093200094500
017915235002785626000027336
017920009000088300900000900
017925004000013400300000211
```

```
01793000500004870050000567
01793500000000000000000000
01971028000280002960029500
01971511600089481100010433
01972000300003000030000275
01972500200001130015000167
01973000100000500010000060
01973500000000000000000000
02541026900270002700027200
02541509800086771000009213
02542000300003000030000300
02542500350003180035000436
02543000200001500020000200
02543500200001500020000159
02671026900269002760027600
02671509000082720900010620
02672000300002530030000300
02672500400003250040000389
02673000250002200025000200
02673500000000000000000000
03281032400324003370033400
03281515000146441900017838
03282000300002050030000300
03282500350002380035000298
03283000500004500050000550
03283501600013560160001549
03851026500270002700027400
03851516000141141600015579
03852000300000000030000178
03852500110001000011000097
03853000000000000020000150
03853501000009300100001245
04761029800287002980029700
04761513500135331460014307
04762000300003000030000300
04762500200001890020000200
04763000500003500050000389
04763500000000000000000000
04891031600310003290033000
04891508000074550900008410
04892000300003000030000275
04892500400003130040000398
04893000350003330035000278
04893500500000000000000000
05491087900870008900088800
05491527800240992900031731
05492000900006530090000900
05492500400002870040000392
05493000100001000020000200
05493502300021130230002476
05831059000588006300061000
05831517800155331800015599
05832000300002840030000233
05832500350003070035000321
05833000250002250025000289
05833500200003760040000475
05911027600289002900029500
05911501500016170170001878
05912000300003000030000300
05912500150001400015000180
05913000100001000020000150
05913500000000000000000000

TOTAL RECORDS = 72
```

APPENDICES

PROGRAMMING ASSIGNMENT TEST DATA

TEST DATA SET 1

Note: All data is presorted and need not be sorted to be used. Test Data Set 1 is used with Programming Assignment #1 in Chapter 2 and Chapter 3, Chapter 4, Chapter 5, Chapter 7, Chapter 8, and Chapter 9.

```
0000000000111111111122222222223333333333444444444455555555556
1234567890123456789012345678901234567890123456789012345678901

100101410ALBERS, STEVEN        FRONT DISC BRAKES    422034031045
100101561CANATERRA, CANDY      HEAD LIGHTS          163045075105
100101765CHENEY, MAXINE        NYLON GAS PEDALS     114034007016
100101813CRAIG, MARY LOU       BUCKET SEAT          243457010005
100301887DUFFY, MARCUS         1" TRAILER HITCH     122356002010
100301914EPPLY, DERVIS         TORQUE WRENCHES      413056110213
100301957FIEDLER, FERN         4 PLY RADIAL TIRES   150345056075
100502045GARCIA, FRANCIS       6' JUMPER CABLES     221233004011
100502076KOON, BARNEY L.       SETS OF 4 HEX NUTS   310340005017
100502189KOWALSKI, PATRICK     5" WINDSHIELD BLADES330567023020
100502201LICHFIELD, SANDRA     PLASTIC FLOOR MATS   660450047192
100502250LUBNER, SALLY R.      WOOD STEERING WHEELS545459102365
100602275MARQUARDT, MICHAEL    POINTS AND PLUGS     613455002078
100602323MARTIN, JUSTIN B.     LOCK DE-ICER         230983010045
100602357MCGILL, MARTIN J.     MOTORALL 10W30 OIL   345676023056
100602789MEEGAN, JULIE R.      GENERATORS           365678090900
100603578MUFFINS, ROBERT L.    1/2" VACUUM LINES    116787004098
100603971NAPOLITAN, SHEILA R.  METRIC SOCKET SETS   450123103134
100703989NOWICKI, OZZIE L.     FLOOR CLEANER        623456004021
100704456PEACOCK, GERALD M.    2 TON CAR RAMPS      610045010024
100704692PEREZ, MARTINIQUE A.  TRANSMISSION KITS    250173080076
100704789POSTEN, THOMAS E.     OIL PANS             541234011078
100704987REESES, LAURA W.      OPERATORS MANUALS    522894001099
100705139RENO, STEVEN B.       HI/LO DIMMER SWITCH  610639010020
100705983ROTHCHILD, RUTH C.    RACING STRIPE KITS   133404045089
100805999SAMMS, CARLA P.       OIL CHANGE KIT       669234090100
100806134SCHMIDT, CHUCK H.     INTERIOR LIGHT BULBS312302004050
100806297SHARP, CRAIG I.       SET OF 2 FOG LIGHTS  237809001008
100806356SHORT, BRENDA B.      DISTRIBUTOR CAPS     429834010023
100806489SKINNER, CARL S.      TIMING GEARS         250789110023
100806598SPRINGSTEIN, ALBERT   SECURITY SYSTEM      460929010067
100806701STROH, ALEXIS M.      CRUISE CONTROLS      342856055067
200107980SWEENEY, ROGER W.     SET OF 4 HUB CAPS    350345067078
200108379TEEPLE, THOMAS T.     AXLE GREASE (GALLON)512347001023
200108567TOMCHUCK, FREDERICK   NO-WIPE CAR POLISH   130375004056
200108673TOMLIN, PETER S.      CAR WAXERS           269845090020
200108674TOWNLEY, ASTIN R.     GREASE-B-GONE WASHER455628034056
200108732TOWNS, BEVERLY        SUNNY SUNROOF KIT    422345011045
200308845TRAKSO, ALLEN R.      ROAD MAPS            610304001005
200308913TRUSKOWSKI, MIKE      2-WAY OIL FILTER     123040010052
200308957TURNER, CHARLES A.    ENGINE BLOCKS        540378402098
200308975TYLER, MARY M.        TRANSMISSION FLUID   530923045045
200509003ULMER, FRED F.        NO-SLIP BRAKE FLUID  240450050067
200509156URMY, AMY A.          NO-LEAK RADIATORS    419340120344
200509245VARTY, VERNON S.      SPARKLES PAINT       620098009009
200509347VINCENT, BOBBY L.     CHROME POLISH        362984019090
200709467WADHAM, LARRY L.      VINYL TOP KITS       140086087078
200709610WALKER, JERRY F.      6" ROUND HEADLIGHTS  655870087090
200709763WENDT, WENDY Y.       NO-FUZZ FUZZ BUSTER  424598030030
200709990ZELLER, ARTHUR        GLASS WINDOWS        118890200230

TOTAL RECORDS = 50
```

TEST DATA SET 2

Note: All data is presorted and need not be sorted to be used. Test Data Set 2 is used with Programming Assignment #2 in Chapter 2 and Chapter 3, Chapter 4, Chapter 5, Chapter 7, Chapter 8, and Chapter 9.

```
00000000011111111112222222222333333333344444444445555555555566666666
12345678901234567890123456789012345678901234567890123456789012345678

072786100101ALBERT, PETER A.    CRT WORKSTATION      101202100308901
072786100103ALLENSON, SHEILA M. CONTEMPORARY DESK    202386800873403
072786100105ANDERSON, ARLENE T. EXECUTIVE DESK CHAIR3012593010050005
072786100107BILLINGS, BARBARA   ARMLESS SWIVEL CHAIR401378301105606
072786100109CANNON, CAROLE C.    PLASTICMAID FLOORMAT200673900300004
072786100310CHAPMAN, RONA L.     HAT & COAT RACK      301569400356702
072786100312CLAFFLIN, WALTER E.  5 DRAWER CABINET     401250100367803
072786100313COMPANA, ESTER      CRT STAND & PAD      101890100789576
072786100315COOPER, BART B.     CORRUGATED ORGANIZER100456700200034
072786100316CRAIGS, ELAINE      5" MESSAGE PADS      100127300506785
072786100318DOGGINS, CARL       LABEL & BADGE MAKER  301345700240582
072886100529DOWNING, EARLE S.   SELF-ADHESIVE LABELS304873101258991
072886100530DRIFT, CHRISTOPHER  #14 RUBBER BANDS     200053700348446
072886100531ERIKSON, BRIT E.    TRANSPARENT TAPE     402345601103406
072886100532FREEMAN, ROBERT F.   PHONE/ADDRESS BOOK   200579300600034
072886100535FRONT, CHARLES L.    ELMO'S SUPER GLUE    401457300293483
072886100537GARCIA, JOSE        FLOWCHART TEMPLATE   201453630101344 2
072886100738HATFIELD, FRED R.   EXPAND-O FILE FOLDER403568500806795
072886100739HELLER, KAREN S.    DESK TOP CARD FILE   300456700304591
072886100740HENDRIX, SHIRLEY D. GENERAL LEDGER CARDS300348200169523
072886100742ISLANDER, JENNE     WOOD ATTACHE CASE    203547801209865
072886100743LADA, LAWRENCE S.   STANDARD STAPLES     104500802475332
072886100745LADD, DAVID L.      MULTIPLE HOLE PUNCH  400346800204082
072886100947LAMB, EDWARD R.     PRESENTATION EASELS  203984402879906
072886100948LEELAND, WESLEY R.  MAGNIFYING GLASS     300738300607023
072986100949LOFTIS, DOUGLAS L.  DESK PAD & CALENDAR  100783700500092
072986100950MILLER, SUSAN S.    DESK TOP ORGANIZER   203759802184392
072986200151MUDGLEY, BRENDA     3' DESK LAMP         203568401568224
072986200152NICKELS, KATHY      WALL CLOCK & CORD    210308804108071
072986200154NOWAKOWSKI, ALLEN T.WASTE RECEPTACLES    403459300809545
072986200355PATTERSON, PATTI    SMOKING STANDS       108906701293424
072986200356PETERSON, JACK E.   CORRESPONDENCE FORM 403450900809693
072986200357PETERSON, TONY L.   WORK ORDER FORM PADS212009900459875
072986200358PLANTARA, CARLA P.  PRESSBOARD COVERS    406550900879336
073086200359RASKIN, RUTH E.     METAL HINGE BINDERS  309833104658262
073086200560SANDERSON, PAULETTE STENOGRAPHER'S PAD   412569300308551
073086200562SAUNDERS, GEORGE P. BINDER INDEXES       204050603459843
073086200564SINGER, ALEXIS E.   EXPENSE BOOKLET      300348500203484
073086200565SUMMERS, APRIL L.   COLUMNAR BOOKS       407890104593056
073086200567SWEET, SUSAN R.     CALCULATOR ROLLS     109345405056091
073086200769IANDY, TRICIA S.    HAND HELD CALCULATOR208394505010003
073086200770TERRY, RON          CATCH-A-CALL PHONE   305309204832296
073186200773TONEY, IRA L.       PENCIL SHARPENER     408398904007082
073186200775UPLAND, JILL I.     PEN & PENCIL SET     208987803567754
073186200779VANBUREN, ERIN F.   MECHANICAL PENCIL    304354403234735
073186200980WALLACE, STEVEN     COLORED PENCIL SET   208979903478541
073186200985WALTON, WOODROW R.  DUPLICATING FLUID    400783900638363
073186200987YULANE, ARTHUR M.   FILING ENVELOPES     301234500900045
073186200990ZIPPO, WANDA        EXECUTIVE PAD HOLDER400847500739156
073186200995ZOONEY, MARVIN B.   5" DISKETTE HOLDER   109385505033253

TOTAL RECORDS = 50
```

TEST DATA SET 3

> **Note:** All data is presorted and need not be sorted to be used. Test Data Set 3 is used with Programming Assignment #3 in Chapter 2 and Chapter 3, Chapter 4, Chapter 5, Chapter 7, Chapter 8, and Chapter 9.

```
00000000001111111111222222222233333333334444444444555555555566666
12345678901234567890123456789012345678901234567890123456789012345

100010002110101586GROUND BEEF LEAN     EPSTEIN'S CLOTHING   00345603
100010003210101586BEEF BAG-O-BONES     SUPERB TOBACCO       00346445
100010011310101586PORK CHOP CENTER CUTMAX'S 5 & 10           03250956
100010015410101586CHICKEN BREAST       HATTI'S HATTERY      00147560
100010045510101586SMOKED TURKEY BREASTTASTI-FREEZ CONES     00139334
100020005730101586MOZZARELLA CHESSE    15TH ST. DELI        00149859
100020079410101586CHEESE 'N' CRACKERS ART'S ART SUPPLIES    00284650
100020093710101586CHOC. CHIP COOKIES   VARTIES CABINETS     00154672
100020104210101586BLUE CHEESE DRESSINGERIE PIPE SUPPLY      00205341
100020158510101586JUMBO SIZE EGGS      BARTOFF BOOK DIST.   01080434
100020179610101586APPLE FLAVOR YOGURT RASKIN-BOBBINS        03365711
100030204210101586DRIED APRICOTS       JEANS FOR MORE       07256303
100030273310101686BELL PEPPER GREENS   SUITS A LA DUDE      07153009
100030340410101686PINEAPPLE SHERBERT   JOX ACCESSORIES      03093670
100030379510101686PEPPERONI PIZZA      DOGGY DOO HAIR-CUTS  06073608
100030400110101686CREAMED CHIP BEEF    BRITE-ON PAINTERS    01387854
100040425710101686DUTCH APPLE PIE      SHOCKING ELECTRONICS00490903
100040459110101686BROCOLLI CUTS        DOWN-TO-EARTH PLANTS00110906
100040479310101686LEMONADE FROZEN      PATTY'S PATIO SHOP   00229846
100040498410101686YELLOW CLING PEACHESKANNON DUPLICATORS    01333462
100040520610101786OREGON APPLE CIDER   WOODY & WALLPAPER    09143033
100050570410101786BAKED BEANS & FRANKSLIQUID WATER DIST.    00146723
100050620510101786FANCY TOMATO SAUCE   TREE-TOP TRIMMERS    00209245
100050624210101786SMOKED HERRING       DEEP-DOWN PLUMBERS   03198452
100050636710101786WORCESTERSHIRE SAUCESOFTWARE SALES        01076954
100050642610101786DICED GREEN CHILIES BOTTOM-LINE ACCTING.00083037
200060689210101886KOSHER DILL PICKLES GENERAL INSURANCE CO01139023
200060690510101886RED HOT MUSTARD      PRINT SUPPLIES       00389022
200060693110101886VIENNA SAUSAGE       WALT'S WINDOW WASH   09120934
200060720310101886DISPOSABLE DIAPERS   AIR-TO-YOU MESSAGES 02068752
200060744710101886LENTIL DRIED BEANS   ZIPPY CAR WASH       06127463
200060770610101886LONG GRAIN RICE      FIRST UNIVERSAL BANK01116740
200070794310101986SUPERMOIST CAKE MIX COLONEL MOTORS INC.  07101011
200070830410101986CAPTAIN CLASH CEREALCOZY ISLAND DOGS      02098990
200070855110101986MAPLE BLEND SYRUP    EAT-IT DONUT SHOP    10204030
200070873210101986STRAWBERRY JELLY     LEGALEZE LAW FIRM    07154933
200070890610101986WHOLE BASIL LEAVES   COZY & KOOKY CARDS   02056804
200070893710101986DISH DETERGENT- MILDLOOK-SEE PRIVATE EYE00139067
200080907110101986EARTHTONE NAPKINES   SHORTS & SHIRTS      00375863
200080914310101986PEPPERMINT CANDIES   TIES AND TACKS       05043951
200080938210101986SALTED SODA CRACKERSSCRUBS AND GRUB       06174322
200080945510101986FAMILY FUDGE BARS    PAMELA & HER PLANTS  08353345
200080952710101986CORN BREAD MUFFINS   PRICELESS JEWELRY CO01118733
200080964410101986SPAGHETTI SAUCE      ESCROW COMPANY       20089452
200090968510101986GENERIC DOG FOOD     ELAINE'S CURIOS      00111907
200090975410101986DINNER ROLLS 8 PACK J. C. NICKLES CO.     06154733
200090980210101986SHINE TOOTHPASTE     KIDDY LAND BICYCLES  06174922
200090987310101986GREEN CREME RINSE    CARP LOVERS FISH CO.00079231
200090989110101986624 EXPOSURE FILM    CLOTHES FOR KIDS     00057760
200090993610101986PARAKEET SEED        BIKES FOR TIKES      00153456

TOTAL RECORDS = 50
```

TEST DATA SET 4

Note: All data is presorted and need not be sorted to be used. Test Data Set 4 is used with Programming Assignment #4 in Chapter 2 and Chapter 3, Chapter 4, Chapter 5, Chapter 7, Chapter 8, and Chapter 9.

```
00000000001111111111222222222233333333334444444444555555555566666666667777
1234567890123456789012345678901234567890123456789012345678901234567890123

0105010010110ALBERT, CARL G.      010386ABCD COMPUTER CORP. 65378970367321
0205010030130BEZZEMEK, JENNEFER   010486ABACUS COMPUTERS    76474380345721
0305010040975BLAKE, DONALD        010986FIRST NATIONAL BANK 79346596453721
0405010051032BONADIO, JAMES S.    011286CANNONBALL EXPRESS  64658260654611
0505010061567CLAFLIN, WAYNE R.    012586EXPRESSO COFFEE CO. 88567789546621
0605020011673COLEMAN, THOMAS      020886AMERICAN CANNING INC97764599469621
0705020032133COLWELL, RICHARD L.  021586PRESTO METAL CORP.  85483490345222
0805020042252COOPER, JOHNATHAN    022586ERIE PIPE & TOOL CO.66567495453822
0905020052461COREY, SARAH D.      022886BRETT'S EXCAVATING  79983680456422
1005020062772CRACKLE, CYNTHIA     031086PETER PIZZA COMPANY 86653784546222
1105030012803CRAWFORD, TIMOTHY    031586COUNTRY GENTLEMAN   83487886635421
1205030032998CURRIE, RICHARD      040586NEWMAN PAPER CO.    81182090546321
1305030043110EPPLEY, DAVID        042086MIDLAND MACHINERY   93578399836412
1405030063375FIX, RALPH N.        042886LAKESIDE SAND CO.   90345099035422
1505040023461FRENCH, TERRY L.     050386PORT ELECTRONICS    80665394546322
1605040033705GALLAGHER, CLARENCE  051086BINARY BOOK BINDERS 79847887465322
1705040043931GENNERRO, TONY       051586SAINT PLASTIC WORKS 44567748748411
1805040054106GOEBEL, NANCY K.     052786WHAMO FIREWORKS     80465790034521
1905040064192HAINES, MARSHA L.    061386FREDERICKO FASHIONS 66483585463822
2005050014327HANCOCK, ELIZABETH   062086BOND AND RUN AGENCY 88735697463712
2105050034363HARTNETT, ROBERT L.  062886CRYSTAL GLASSES     90348590087622
2205050044434HORNBECK, NEIL       070286VACATION INN INC.   83546487563422
2305050054513HYATT, BRUSTER       070586BEAUTIFUL MUGS ETC. 70045686453621
2405050065001KURTZ, CHRISTOPHER   070986KELLY'S TOOL WORKS  64564086483912
2505060015123LEVANDOWSKI, JILL I. 072086BUGS BE GONE        90657495463721
2605060025246LUKASEK, LINDA L.    073186SUPERIOR THEATRE CO.89846790546222
2705060035257METZ, ARNOLD E.      081586EARLY BIRD ALARMS   70653590445322
2805060045309NORRIS, RICHARD P.   083086THE SOUP KITCHEN    93476493546312
2905060065323NOWAKOWSKI, ALLEN    090786TRAFFIC JAM DINER   74674884563822
3010010025415O'BOYLE, PATRICK     091886JACQUE'S TAVERN     90487599948521
3110010045493PATTERSON, LENNI R.  092386PEPE'S PIZZA PARLOR 54675060343622
3210010065854PERRY, ALLAN E.      093086EMERALD TREE FARM   90346790623411
3310010025947POPA, GEORGE         100486SWARTZ, SWARTZ & LEE71278670344422
3410020036128REED, ROBERT S.      101086BEST BUY HOMES CORP.70879171192322
3510020046287SANCHEZ, HANK        101386KERR OFFICE SUPPLIES66475082435622
3610020056491SANDELL, ROBERT A.   101586HOWARD'S FURNITURE  76467077629921
3710030026873SOULE, MICHAEL R.    102186SAMM'S MOVING CO.   84783087823421
3810030047203SWARTZ, RICHARD      103086CRISLER COMPANY     67483087342211
3910030057315TANSKY, ROBERT       110386CURIO'S JEWELRY     99999990263221
4010030067481TERRY, JONI          111086BLANKETS GALORE     82877090273522
4110040017731TESKY, ALLEN         112086VIDEO EXPERTS       72873490347811
4210040038315THIBODEAU, RALPH     113186BOWLERS WORLD       89393090067622
4310040048477THRUSHMAN, VICKY     120386TELLTALE SAILERS CO.80230386473221
4410040068064TOWNS, GAIL E.       120586BOOK ENDS           80838388864711
4510050018951TUTTLE, MICHAEL      121086SIMPLY PUT CURTAINS 90334497475521
4610050039372WARNER, ELINOR L.    121386GENERAL PORPOISE CO.74475888740322
4710050069417WESTON, BARBARA B.   121786LAZY CONSTRUCTION   66732870347822
4810060029539WIGGLE, BARBARA J.   122086DILLY'S BAR & GRILL 74646080672421
4910060039819WILEY, RICHARD A.    122586LYNWOOD TACO SHACK  99392090374822
5010060049903YAKES, KATHLEEN K.   123086FERRY FASHIONS      50664675646612

TOTAL RECORDS = 50
```

TEST DATA SET 5

Note: All data is presorted and need not be sorted to be used. Test Data Set 5 is used with all Programming Assignments in Chapter 6.

```
0000000000111111111122222222223333333334
1234567890123456789012345678901234567890

ARMSTEAD, WALTER      A103MDBM11ALA2500015
BADGER, KENNETH       B204N PM12NCA0750010
                      MABP21FAX300001X
BAILEY, HOWARD        B310MDBX1X  A2750014
BOSTICK, RAY          B350    32MGR1000007
BROWN, DONALD         C401M PCX1MGR1500019
CHIPMAN, DARRELL      C453N BC21FMA      13
DEERING, EARL         C489N BM21NEA0800011
FAIRMAN, MALVINA      D005X X 21APA0950007
FRIZZLE, ALLEN        D010MAPP12ALR3000013
GUTIERREZ, JOSE       D152N PP2XNXA4750009
HEIMBACK, DAVID       D161N B 11MC 1000017
                      E011MDPM23FXA3100014
HERNANDEZ, DAVE       E110N BPX1FAA045001X
JENSEN, KENNETH       E332    12AXA0800013
KIRBY, STANLEY        E357MAPM12NEA3000015
LANDSCHOOT, CYHTHIA   F409MDPC21  A3M40012
LLOYD, ELLEN          F519N BC4AMXR06500
LOSINSKI, GEORGE      G403MABM1XMGA3000007
MARION, LAWRENCE      G997    2XAPA0700005
                      MDPPX1NCA3750009
MARTIN, PHILLIP       H191MABX21FMR3000011
MCGINNIS, LEANNE      H231N PP24FAA5500016
MICALSKI, CHARLES     H304N P 21FMA1000014
MOSHER, SUSIE         H357MDBP12APA3500014
MUELLER, DAVID        H493N PM11APR0500010
O'CONNOR, PETER       H501MABC21NCR3000011
                      I610N PP3XNEA0750013
O'CONNELL, STEVEN     I630M PM12MCA1000017
PEACOCK, HARRIETT     I650MDBMXXX 2C00012
PEREZ, BRUCE          I719N PM23MGA035001X
PORRETT, JULIE        I800    11ALA2900014
RAYMO, ARNOLD         J100N B 21N R5000013
ROGERS, ANNE          J135N PC21FAA1200014
SASS, JOHNATHAN       K109MABP21MCX3000010
SHAMALY, GREG         K121N PP12NEA      09
                      MDPP11FMR3750016
SMITH, ALLEN          K130M BC12MGA2300013
STOCKWELL, BARBARA    L001N BM21A 0350016
STONE, BRENDA         L103MAPM24X A3000014
THOMPSON, EDWARD      L527N BPX M A0700012
THOMAS, CHARLES       L693X X 11F R0800013
TIBEDEAU, RALPH       M006MDPP21NEA6000012
TRACTOR, JAMES        M010N BC12ALA0600011
ULLENBRUCH, MICHAEL   M239MAPM2XAPA1X00007
WAGNER, BRENDA        M459N BM11APX0900012
WALKER, TONY          N019MDPP21NCR3750008
WESTBROOK, CAROLYN    N101MABP51FMR3000016
YAGER, CHUCK          N201N PM21NCA0600013
ZVANOVEC, ALVIN       N333N PP14ALA0550014

TOTAL RECORDS = 50
```

TEST DATA SET 6

Note: Data is **NOT** presorted and needs to be sorted per Programming Assignment instructions. Test Data Set 6 is used with all Programming Assignments in Chapter 10.

```
0000000000111111111122222222223333333333444444444455555555556666666666777777777
1234567890123456789012345678901234567890123456789012345678901234567890123456789

WUBCA DAY IN THE LIFE    0101JONES, MALCOLM       0910080444454222311972707068280
WKLQNEWS SPECIAL         0407WILTON, TOM          0511070332302824211968666872274
WKTZSPORTS ROUND UP      0703FREDERICK, AL        0404040223252914182274747472294
WBBBDOWN HOME BOYS       0311SANCHEZ, JOSE        0807080084640343128236768687 0273
WAIVBOSTON POPS ON TOUR  0902VALENTI, MARIO       0200020044453423241974767474298
WUBC6:00 PM NEWS SHOW    0109TREETER, JIM         0606080433442219301972687174285
WKLQLATE NIGHT TONIGHT   0608SAMUELS, ROGER       0006040239482921202572687474288
WKTZEMBASSY              0406HOLSTEIN, FRANK      0202020223232717151567687071276
WJKLPHILADELPHIA         1104PETERS, BOBBY        0002050832334021181776777980312
WPTVWEEKNIGHT FOOTBALL   0710MELTON, GARY         0200020422292314180476767779308
WATVL.A. TOWN            0305SHORTS, FRED         0806100842443417232068747667285
WUBCAEROBISIZE YOUR BODY1101ALBERT, ANDY         0410000239202222320176971706 9279
WKLQTHAT'S DANCING       0612PETERSON, LENNY      0202020429345020162765676771270
WKTZCOUNTRY HOEDOWN      0709TERRY, JO            0407080432283513271772727468286
WJKLPUPPETS ON PARADE    0108DUNNER, STEVEN       0606080823453915211483777979318
WPTVMR. DODGER'S         1112WESTON, GORDIE       0304060824373711141380788183322
WBBBWEATHER OR NOT       0902SCHULLER, CRAIG      0004040043352921171274767772299
WATVTHIS OLD BUILDING    0310GUSSIE, LARRY        0402020437384812091476757776304
WKIZNUTRITION AND YOU    1107STAIGER, HANK        0606081048364920142078808284324
WBBBTHREE ON THE TOWN    0411BLACKEN, MARK        0306040629374813162367707377287
WUBCTHE SUPER-HEROS SHOW0705SLOTE, DON           0200000637454812232166806874288
WJKLLIFE AT THE TOP      0603BRODSKY, MEL         1012060846354823162166676970272
WKLQWILD WEST ADVENTURES0109CRIMMINS, TONY       0504070933434712192170757981305
WKTZDAYTIME DRAMATIME    1101DELUTH, SANDY        0204081029455310123774808279315
WAIVJAZZIN WITH MUSIC    0304POPKINS, JERRY       0406071037372013262070736970282
WKLQFRENCH COOKING - OUI0702LANKERSHAM, KILE     0504040424352021321974767884312
WAIVKIDS AND COMPUTERS   0906SASSER, STEVEN       0002000636474432393779818387330
WPTVBLOOPERS AND JOKES   0412STREK, GARY          0404060627364521313676847983322
WJKLFAMILY CONNECTIONS   0610KLEINSCHMITT, BILL   0200020433445130234370707072282
WBBBBATTING FOR DOLLARS  0105GONZALEZ, RICK       0405081026375213234570697171281
WUBCTV COMMERCIAL AWARDS0308FOSSEE, KEVIN        0604040837452819231766697474283
WATVALL NIGHT VIDEO SHOW0711HASSIG, BILL         0314000384829334129657271692 77
WPTVADDING WITH GRANDPA  1104DAHL, JOHN           0506111025374321303270707477291
WKLQCOSMOTOLOGY AT HOME  0403MCCARTHY, BOB        0404080748362842312572727478296
WKIZNIGHTTIME CALLER     0606CUMMINS, CARLYLE     0810070727384025343874737175293
WBBBAMATEUR GOLF TIPS    0301NORTON, BOB          0402030733574131473779777983318
WJKLSPINNERS 'N' WINNERS0110SCHAFFER, ED         0202020442263632162070687571284
WPTVLATE NIGHT HORRORS   0711GIGER, ALLEN         0403020534375616133674736971297
WAIVEQUESTRIAN TREATS    0302WATTS, SAMUEL        0608070550423138231280827981322
WBBBTHE MONEY MAKERS     0407ALHAMBRA, PEPI       0200000227372713251572727074288
WUBCCREATIVE EXPRESSIONS0608WILSON, TED          0406070836414218211274787974305
WJKLSTARTING AT THE TOP  0909BROWNING, PETER      0204060448372924131978777775307
WPTVIN PURSUIT OF TRIVIA1104MCQUIRE, JULIO       0404040437362633192082848276324
WATVBREAKIN' IN THE PARK0107PETRIE, STAN         0200000027365723303873757771296
WKIZAUTUMN COLORS        0712POLLARD, RICHIE      0200020052423747363075717873297
WBBBMY OLD NEIGHBORHOOD  0905POHL, MARK           0504070823363318231972707272286
WKLQSELECTING A WINNER   1106HUGHES, GREG         0808060829354815223171717166279
WUBCHOLLYWOOD COUPLES    0403TAYLOR, JEFF         1011100240302232241766647269271

TOTAL RECORDS = 48
```

APPENDIX
RESERVED WORDS

B

The following is a list of the reserved words used in the COBOL language.

ACCEPT	COMPUTE	ENABLE	INITIAL
ACCESS	CONTAINS	EMI	INITIATE
ADD	CONTROL	END	INPUT
ADVANCING	CONTROLS	END-OF-PAGE	INPUT-OUTPUT
AFTER	COPY	ENTER	INSPECT
ALL	CORR	ENVIRONMENT	INSTALLATION
ALPHABETIC	CORRESPONDING	EOP	INTO
ALSO	COUNT	EQUAL	INVALID
ALTER	CURRENCY	ERROR	IS
ALTERNATE		ESI	
AND	DATA	EVERY	JUST
ARE	DATE	EXCEPTION	JUSTIFIED
AREA	DATE-COMPILED	EXIT	
AREAS	DATE-WRITTEN	EXTEND	KEY
ASCENDING	DAY		
ASSIGN	DE	FD	LABEL
AT	DEBUG-CONTENTS	FILE	LAST
AUTHOR	DEBUG-ITEM	FILE-CONTROL	LEADING
	DEBUG-LINE	FILLER	LEFT
BEFORE	DEBUG-NAME	FINAL	LENGTH
BLANK	DEBUG-SUB-1	FIRST	LESS
BLOCK	DEBUG-SUB-2	FOOTING	LIMIT
BOTTOM	DEBUG-SUB-3	FOR	LIMITS
BY	DEBUGGING	FROM	LINAGE
	DECIMAL-POINT		LINAGE-COUNTER
CALL	DECLARATIVES	GENERATE	LINE
CANCEL	DELETE	GIVING	LINE-COUNTER
CD	DELIMITED	GO	LINES
CF	DELIMITER	GREATER	LINKAGE
CH	DEPENDING	GROUP	LOCK
CHARACTER	DESCENDING		LOW-VALUE
CHARACTERS	DESTINATION	HEADING	LOW-VALUES
CLOCK-UNITS	DETAIL	HIGH-VALUE	
CLOSE	DISABLE	HIGH-VALUES	MEMORY
COBOL	DISPLAY		MERGE
CODE	DIVIDE	I-O	MESSAGE
CODE-SET	DIVISION	I-O-CONTROL	MODE
COLLATING	DOWN	IDENTIFICATION	MODULES
COLUMN	DUPLICATES	IF	MOVE
COMMA	DYNAMIC	IN	MULTIPLE
COMMUNICATION		INDEX	MULTIPLY
COMP	EGI	INDEXED	
COMPUTATIONAL	ELSE	INDICATE	NATIVE

NEGATIVE	QUOTES	SENTENCE	TIME
NEXT	RANDOM	SEPARATE	TIMES
NO	RD	SEQUENCE	TO
NOT	READ	SEQUENTIAL	TOP
NUMBER	RECEIVE	SET	TRAILING
NUMERIC	RECORD	SIGN	TYPE
	RECORDS	SIZE	
OBJECT-COMPUTER	REDEFINES	SORT	UNIT
OCCURS	REEL	SORT-MERGE	UNSTRING
OF	REFERENCES	SOURCE	UNTIL
OFF	RELATIVE	SOURCE-COMPUTER	UP
OMITTED	RELEASE REMAINDER	SPACE	UPON
ON	REMOVAL	SPACES	USAGE
OPEN	RENAMES	SPECIAL-NAMES	USE
OPTIONAL	REPLACING	STANDARD	USING
OR	REPORT	STANDARD-1	
ORGANIZATION	REPORTING	START	VALUE
OUTPUT	REPORTS	STATUS	VALUES
OVERFLOW	RERUN	STOP	VARYING
	RESERVE	STRING	
PAGE	RESET	SUB-QUEUE-1	WHEN
PAGE-COUNTER	RETURN	SUB-QUEUE-2	WITH
PERFORM	REVERSED	SUB-QUEUE-3	WORDS
PF	REWIND	SUBTRACT	WORKING-
PH	REWRITE	SUM	STORAGE
PIC	RF	SUPPRESS	WRITE
PICTURE	RH	SYMBOLIC	
PLUS	RIGHT	SYNC	ZERO
POINTER	ROUNDED	SYNCHRONIZED	ZEROES
POSITION	RUN		ZEROS
POSITIVE		TABLE	
PRINTING	SAME	TALLYING	+
PROCEDURE	SD	TAPE	-
PROCEDURES	SEARCH	TERMINAL	*
PROCEED	SECTION	TERMINATE	/
PROGRAM	SECURITY	TEXT	**
PROGRAM-ID	SEGMENT	THAN	>
	SEGMENT-LIMIT	THROUGH	<
QUEUE	SELECT	THRU	=
QUOTE	SEND		

APPENDIX
CODING STANDARDS

C

Documentation of a program is material prepared by the programmer which is intended to show what a program does, how a program works, how to operate the program, how to interact with the program, and in short, everything one must know concerning the program. The most important piece of documentation for a program when it must be maintained is the source listing of the program.

When a program is to be changed, the maintenance programmer will usually read the program documentation to determine what the program does and how it does it. Even though a variety of forms of documentation may be developed, the reason the most valuable piece of documentation is the source listing is because it is always up-to-date (whereas other forms of documentation may not be kept up-to-date) and because it specifies exactly what is going to take place within the program and how it is going to be accomplished.

It is extremely important, therefore, that the source listing be an easy to read document. Indeed, a source listing should be as easily read as any book which one would read. It is of little value to design a good program and then write it so poorly that no one can understand what the program does and how it does it.

In order to ensure that good source programs are written, it is necessary to establish and follow well-defined programming standards within an installation. The following guidelines are the standards used for all the programs within this textbook, and they should be followed when writing the program assignments at the end of each chapter; and indeed, whenever COBOL programs are written.

Identification Division

The Identification Division in the COBOL program is used to identify the program; therefore, as much information as possible should be specified in the Identification Division. All paragraphs in this division should be completed by the programmer; and in addition, comments should be included to indicate what the program does. This is illustrated in Figure C-1.

```
001010 IDENTIFICATION DIVISION.
001020
001030 PROGRAM-ID.    PAYRPT.
001040 AUTHOR.        FORSYTHE.
001050 INSTALLATION.  BREA.
001060 DATE-WRITTEN.  FEB 26,1985.
001070 DATE-COMPILED. FEB 27,1985.
001080 SECURITY.      UNCLASSIFIED.
001090
001100 ******************************************************************
001110 *                                                                *
001120 *    THIS PROGRAM READS THE PAYROLL DISK RECORDS AND CREATES THE  *
001130 *    PAYROLL REPORT CONTAINING EMPLOYEE NAME, EMPLOYEE NUMBER,    *
001140 *    HOURS WORKED, HOURLY PAY RATE, AND TOTAL WAGES.              *
001150 *                                                                *
001160 ******************************************************************
```

Figure C-1 Example of Identification Division

Note from Figure C-1 that the PROGRAM-ID, AUTHOR, INSTALLATION, DATE-

WRITTEN, DATE-COMPILED, and SECURITY paragraphs are all included in the Identification Division. These entries should be included for *every* COBOL program which is written. The comment entries to the right of the paragraph names should all begin in column 23 of the coding form so that they will be vertically aligned for ease of reading.

In addition, comments should be included which tell what the program does. The comments in the Identification Division should define the purpose of the program and basically what it does. These comments should be enclosed in asterisks with spacing as illustrated in Figure C-1. Blank lines should be included as illustrated to improve readability.

Environment Division

The Environment Division also has standards which must be followed. These standards are specified below.

1. The ENVIRONMENT DIVISION Header will begin after three blank lines have been inserted following the last line of the comments in the Identification Division.
2. All Section Names (Configuration Section, Input-Output Section, etc.) shall have one blank line both before and after they are written.
3. Section Names and Paragraph Names will begin in column 8 of the coding form.
4. The Source-Computer and Object-Computer paragraphs will always be included in the Configuration Section. The programmer-supplied entries for these fields will begin in column 25, as will any other programmer-supplied entries in the Configuration Section.
5. The Select statement will begin in column 12. The first line shall contain the name of the file only. The second line of the Select statement (Assign clause) shall begin in column 18.
6. All filenames used will fully indicate the purpose of the file. Each filename will include the suffix FILE. The following are examples of acceptable and unacceptable file names.

Acceptable	Unacceptable
CONSUMPTION-INPUT-FILE	CON-IN-FILE
SHIPPING-REPORT-FILE	SHIP-FILE
PROPERTY-INPUT-FILE	PRO-INPUT-FILE
BILLING-REPORT-FILE	BILL-FILE

A sample Environment Division is illustrated in Figure C-2.

```
002040 ENVIRONMENT DIVISION.
002050
002060 CONFIGURATION SECTION.
002070
002080 SOURCE-COMPUTER.    IBM-4381.
002090 OBJECT-COMPUTER.    IBM-4381.
002100 SPECIAL-NAMES.      C01 IS TO-TOP-OF-PAGE.
002110
002120 INPUT-OUTPUT SECTION.
002130
002140 FILE CONTROL.
002150     SELECT PAYROLL-INPUT-FILE
002160        ASSIGN TO UT-S-PAYDATA.
002170     SELECT PAYROLL-REPORT-FILE
002180        ASSIGN TO UT-S-PAYPRINT.
```

Figure C-2 Example of Properly Coded Environment Division

Data Division

As with other divisions in a COBOL program, there are coding standards for the Data Division of the COBOL program. These standards are specified below.

1. The DATA DIVISION Header will always begin on a new page. This can be accomplished through the use of the Eject statement or through the use of a slash in column 7 of the line before the line on which the Data Division Header appears. The choice will depend upon the COBOL compiler being used.

2. All Section Names (File Section, Working-Storage Section, etc.) shall have one blank line before and after they are written.

3. Section Names, Paragraph Names, FD Statements, and 01 level data-names will begin in column 8 of the coding form.

4. In the FD statement, each clause shall appear on a separate line and except for the first line containing the FD statement, shall begin in column 14.

5. Each successive level of data-names (i.e. 01, 05, 10) shall be indented four spaces from the next higher data-name. This is illustrated in Figure C-3.

```
007090  01  WORK-AREAS.
007100      05  DATE-WORK.
007110          10  YEAR-WORK           PIC  99.
007120          10  MONTH-WORK          PIC  99.
007130          10  DAY-WORK            PIC  99.
```

Figure C-3 Example of Level Indentation

6. The data-name will be separated from the level number by two spaces.

7. Each data-name used in the program will fully indicate the purpose of the field or record being defined. The following are examples of acceptable and unacceptable data-names:

Acceptable	Unacceptable
CUSTOMER-NAME-INPUT	CUST-NAME-IN
THE-RECORD-IS-IN-ERROR	RECORD-ERROR
TO-TOP-OF-PAGE	TOP
SHIPPING-ADDRESS-REPORT	SHIP-ADD-REPORT

8. No level 77 data items will be used within the program.

9. No level 01 data-name, with the exception of record names in the File Section of the Data Division, shall be an elementary data item. All data fields shall be identified by a group name. Figure C-4 illustrates this rule.

Acceptable

```
006010  01  TOTAL-ACCUMULATORS-COUNTERS.
006020      05  TOTAL-PAYROLL-ACCUM         PIC  S9(5)V99.
006030      05  TOTAL-RECORDS-COUNT         PIC  S999.
```

Unacceptable

```
006080  01  TOTAL-PAYROLL-ACCUM             PIC  S9(5)V99.
006090  01  TOTAL-RECORDS-COUNT             PIC  S999.
```

Figure C-4 Example of Level 01 Data

10. All Elementary Items within a Group Item will have their Picture clauses begin in the same column and will use the abbreviation "PIC." If possible, the Picture clauses will begin in column 40, but it is more important that all Picture clauses begin in the same column within group items. This is illustrated in Figure C-5.

Acceptable

```
008010 01  TOTAL-ACCUMULATORS-COUNTERS.
008020     05   HOURS-WORKED-COUNT          PIC  S999.
008030     05   OVERTIME-ACCUM              PIC  S9(5)V99.
```

Unacceptable

```
008010 01  TOTAL-ACCUMULATORS-COUNTERS.
008020     05   HOURS-WORKED-COUNT  PIC  S999.
008030     05   OVERTIME-ACCUM  PIC  S9(5)V99.
```

Figure C-5 Examples of Picture Clauses

11. If more than three digits are to be contained in a field, then parentheses should be used in the Picture clause rather than a series of X's or 9's. This is illustrated in Figure C-6.

Acceptable	Unacceptable
PIC 9(5)	**PIC 99999**

12. The Value clauses will be aligned within group items. If possible, they should begin in column 53.

13. If the value to be specified in the Value clause is short enough, it will be specified on the same line as the Value clause. If not, it will be contained on the next coding line, with the apostrophe one space to the left of the letter "V" in the word Value. This is illustrated in Figure C-6.

```
010040 01  HEADING-LINE.
010050     05   CARRIAGE-CONTROL           PIC  X.
010060     05   TOTAL-RECORDS-FINAL        PIC  ZZ9.
010070     05   FILLER                     PIC  XX        VALUE SPACES.
010080     05   FILLER                     PIC  X(13)     VALUE
010090                                                   'TOTAL RECORDS'.
```

Figure C-6 Example of Value Clause

14. There will be no continued values in the Value clause.

15. If a value which is specified in the Value clause contains more than two imbedded blanks, then a separate value clause must be used. This is illustrated in Figure C-7.

Acceptable

```
011020     05   FILLER                     PIC  X(3)      VALUE 'YES'.
011030     05   FILLER                     PIC  X(3)      VALUE SPACES.
011040     05   FILLER                     PIC  X(2)      VALUE 'NO'.
```

Unacceptable

```
011020     05   FILLER                     PIC  X(8)      VALUE 'YES    NO'.
```

Figure C-7 Example of Value Clause

16. The Occurs clause, Ascending Key Is clause, Usage clause, or any other clause used to define data within a field other than the Picture clause shall begin in column 53 of the coding form or in a column which makes the clause easy to read. This is illustrated in Figure C-8.

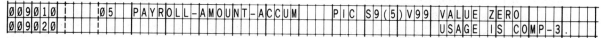

| 0 0 9 0 1 0 | | 0 5 | P A Y R O L L - A M O U N T - A C C U M | | P I C | S 9 (5) V 9 9 | V A L U E | Z E R O |
| 0 0 9 0 2 0 | | | | | | | U S A G E | I S | C O M P - 3 . |

Figure C-8 Example of Usage Clause

17. Condition names (Level 88) shall be assigned to a value within a field whenever that value will be used in a condition test.
18. Indicator names shall have as their names the question which is answered by the indicator. The following are examples.

Acceptable	**Unacceptable**
ARE-THERE-MORE-RECORDS	EOF
WAS-THERE-A-CONTROL-BREAK	CONTROL-BREAK-IND
THE-RECORD-IS-NOT-VALID	INVALID-REC

19. The only acceptable values in an indicator are YES or NO. Thus, all indicators have a picture PIC XXX.
20. All Level 01 data-names will be preceded by one blank line. In addition, blank lines can be inserted between other levels if needed for ease of reading.

In addition to these standards which must be followed, any additional techniques which make the Data Division more readable should also be implemented.

Procedure Division

The following standards should be followed when coding the Procedure Division.

1. The PROCEDURE DIVISION Header line should begin on a new page. This can be accomplished through the use of the Eject statement or through the use of a slash in column 7 of the line before the line on which the Procedure Division Header appears, depending upon the COBOL compiler being used.
2. All modules will begin on a new page. The first module can appear on the same page as the Procedure Division Header.
3. All modules will be preceded by comments (* in column 7) explaining the function of the module and the module(s) which call the module. In addition, the comments shall be enclosed within asterisks, and blank lines should be included as illustrated in Figure C-9.

0 2 1 1 8 0	*	* *
0 2 1 1 9 0	*	*
0 2 1 2 0 0	*	T H I S M O D U L E P R I N T S H E A D I N G S O N T H E R E P O R T . I T I S E N T E R E D	*
0 2 2 0 1 0	*	F R O M A N D E X I T S T O T H E B 0 0 0 - P R O C E S S - D E T A I L - R E C O R D M O D U L E .	*
0 2 2 0 2 0	*		*
0 2 2 0 3 0	*	* *

Figure C-9 Example of Comments in Procedure Division

4. All comments will be preceded by and followed by a blank line unless the comments

begin a page. If this is the case, they need not be preceded by a blank line.

5. The name of each module will be the same as the function performed by the module. These names should be spelled out in full for ease of reading. In addition, each module name will be preceded by a four-digit field representing the placement of the module within the structural hierarchy of the program. The following are examples of acceptable and unacceptable module names.

Acceptable	Unacceptable
A000-CREATE-INVOICE-REPORT	CREATE-INVOICE-REPORT
B010-PROCESS-DETAIL-RECORDS	B010-PROC-DET-REC
C020-EDIT-CUSTOMER-NAME	020-EDIT
C000-PRINT-HEADINGS	C000-HEADINGS

6. If a separate paragraph is required WITHIN a module because of the use of the Perform statement, the paragraph name shall be preceded by three blank lines. The paragraph will have a sequence number which contains the digits 1, 2, etc. in the low-order position, plus the sequence number of the module in which it appears. For example, paragraphs in the module B010 would have prefixes B011, B012, etc. The paragraph name must be meaningful and describe the purpose of the paragraph.

7. All module and paragraph names within the program will be followed by a blank line prior to the first program statement.

8. Program statements which are not executed as a result of prior conditional statements or which are not continuation statements will begin in column 12 of the coding form.

9. All conditional statements of clauses within a statement which indicate a condition under which certain processing is to take place will be placed on a line by themselves. In addition, statements to be executed as a result of a condition's being true or not true will be indented three spaces from the position where the statement stating the condition begins. This is illustrated in Figure C-10.

Acceptable

```
005020    READ PAYROLL-INPUT-FILE
005030         AT END
005040             MOVE 'NO ' TO ARE-THERE-MORE-RECORDS.
005050     IF CUSTOMER-NAME-INPUT = SPACES
005060         ADD 1 TO BLANK-NAME-COUNT.
```

Unacceptable

```
005020    READ PAYROLL-INPUT-FILE
005030         AT END MOVE 'NO ' TO ARE-THERE-MORE-RECORDS.
005040     IF CUSTOMER-NAME-INPUT = SPACES ADD 1 TO BLANK-NAME-COUNT.
```

Figure C-10 Example of Conditional Statements

Note particularly in the Read statement in Figure C-10 that the AT END clause is a conditional clause; therefore, it must be on a line by itself.

10. Any single statement must be on a line by itself; that is, only one statement can appear on one line. This is illustrated in Figure C-11.

Acceptable

003010		ACCEPT DATE-WORK FROM DATE.	
003020		MOVE MONTH-WORK TO MONTH-HEADING.	

Unacceptable

003010		ACCEPT DATE-WORK FROM DATE. MOVE MONTH-WORK TO MONTH-HEADING.

Figure C-11 Example of Single Statements

11. Any statement which must be continued to a second line will have the second line and all subsequent continued lines indented six spaces from the position where the statement being continued begins. This is illustrated in Figure C-12.

008040		IF NUMBER-OF-HOURS-WORKED-INPUT IS GREATER THAN
008050		MAXIMUM-HOURS-WORKED-CONSTANT
008060		PERFORM C000-CALCULATE-OVERTIME-PAY.
008070		WRITE PAYROLL-REPORT-LINE
008080		AFTER ADVANCING PROPER-SPACING.

Figure C-12 Example of Continued Statements

12. If Nested If statements are required to solve a problem, each IF and its corresponding ELSE will be vertically aligned; in addition, statements which are to be executed as a result of a condition's being true or not true will be indented three spaces in the same manner as any other conditional statement. This is illustrated in Figure C-13.

Acceptable

013050		IF EMPLOYEE-IS-SALARIED
013060		IF EMPLOYEE-RECEIVES-BONUS
013070		IF EMPLOYEE-EMPLOYED-TEN-YEARS
013080		PERFORM C010-AWARD-LONGEVITY-BONUS
013090		ELSE
013100		PERFORM C020-AWARD-REGULAR-BONUS
013110		ELSE
013120		PERFORM C030-AWARD-NO-BONUS
013130		ELSE
013140		PERFORM C040-AWARD-CERTIFICATE.

Unacceptable

013050		IF EMPLOYEE-IS-SALARIED IF EMPLOYEE-RECEIVES-BONUS
013060		IF EMPLOYEE-EMPLOYED-TEN-YEARS PERFORM
013070		C010-AWARD-LONGEVITY-BONUS ELSE PERFORM
013080		C020-AWARD-REGULAR-BONUS ELSE PERFORM
013090		C030-AWARD-NO-BONUS ELSE PERFORM C040-AWARD-CERTIFICATE.

Figure C-13 Example of Nested If Statements

13. If multiple conditions are to be checked by one IF statement, they must be continued on a second or third line. Each continued statement will be indented six spaces from the start of the IF statement, and each line will end with the "AND" or "OR," indicating to the reader that the line is to be continued. This is illustrated in Figure C-14.

Acceptable

```
021050    I F  HOURS-WORKED-INPUT IS LESS THAN MAXIMUM-HOURS-CONSTANT OR
021060         HOURS-WORKED-INPUT = MAXIMUM-HOURS-CONSTANT
021070       PERFORM C000-CALCULATE-REGULAR-PAY.
```

Unacceptable

```
021050    I F  HOURS-WORKED-INPUT IS LESS THAN MAXIMUM-HOURS-CONSTANT
021060         OR HOURS-WORKED-INPUT = MAXIMUM-HOURS-CONSTANT
021070       PERFORM C000-CALCULATE-REGULAR-PAY.
```

Figure C-14 Example of Multiple Conditions

14. The PERFORM THRU statement and the EXIT statement will only be used when the GO TO DEPENDING statement is used to implement a Case Structure. The Level-W diagnostic "EXIT FROM PERFORMED PROCEDURE ASSUMED BEFORE PROCEDURE-NAME" is an acceptable diagnostic.

15. The GO TO statement will not be used in a program except under unique circumstances and must be justified to others in a walkthrough prior to implementation.

16. Page/line numbers (columns 1-6) will always be included for each source statement.

17. Program identification (columns 73-80) will always be included for each source statement. The program identification should be the same as the PROGRAM-ID specified in the Identification Division.

Summary

The coding standards presented in this Appendix are not just good ideas; they are standards which absolutely should be adhered to. There is no doubt that some programmers will disagree with some of the standards specified here, but unless they propose a better way to code, that is, a way which is equally as clear to understand and read, then these standards should be followed to the letter.

APPENDIX
SAMPLE PROGRAM FLOWCHARTS

D

The logic used in this textbook is illustrated through the use of pseudocode. Although pseudocode is widely used, some installations prefer to illustrate logic through the use of flowcharts. Therefore, this appendix contains the flowcharts for the sample programs in this textbook. These flowcharts, shown on flowchart worksheets, can be used for a program-by-program, module-by-module comparison to the pseudocode contained in each chapter. A more in-depth explanation of the Flowchart Worksheets and the flowcharting symbols that appear in this appendix can be found in the textbook, *Structured COBOL: Flowchart Edition*, by Shelly/Cashman/Forsythe and published by Anaheim Publishing Company.

CHAPTERS 2 AND 3

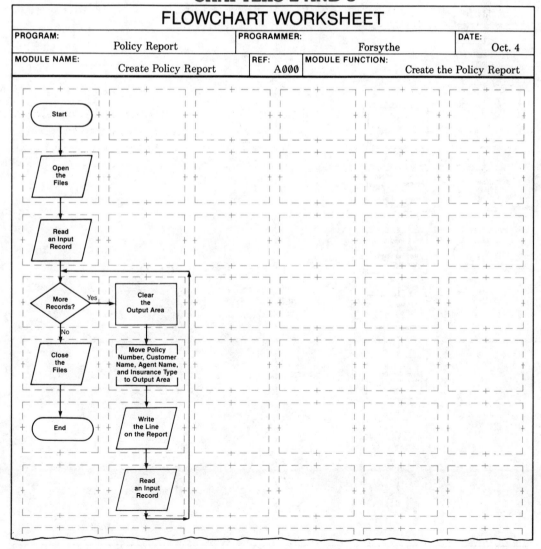

CHAPTER 4

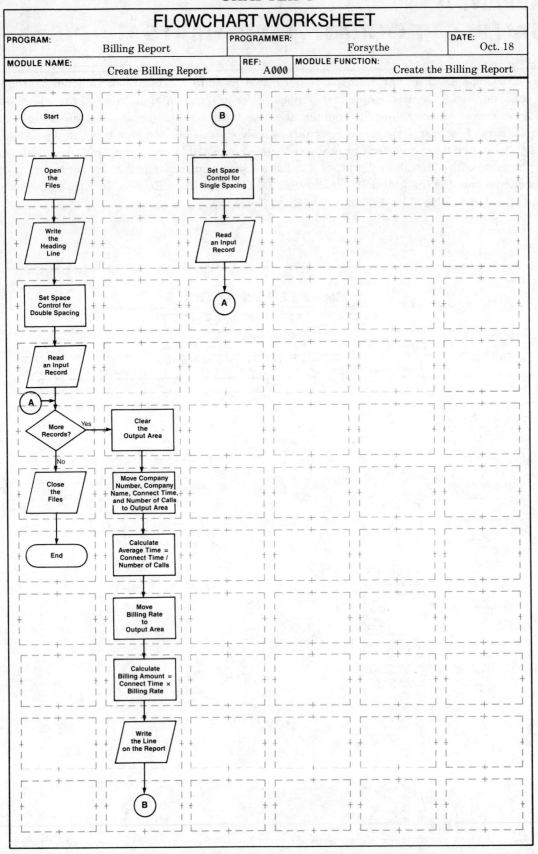

FLOWCHART WORKSHEET

PROGRAM: Billing Report	PROGRAMMER: Forsythe	DATE: Oct. 18
MODULE NAME: Create Billing Report	REF: A000	MODULE FUNCTION: Create the Billing Report

CHAPTER 5 (Part 1 of 3)

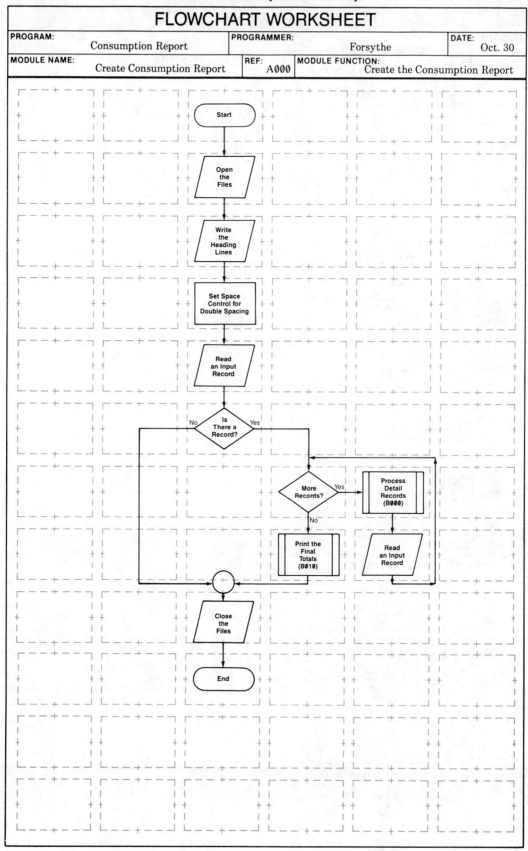

FLOWCHART WORKSHEET

| PROGRAM: Consumption Report | PROGRAMMER: Forsythe | DATE: Oct. 30 |
| MODULE NAME: Create Consumption Report | REF: A000 | MODULE FUNCTION: Create the Consumption Report |

Start

Open the Files

Write the Heading Lines

Set Space Control for Double Spacing

Read an Input Record

Is There a Record? — No / Yes

More Records? — Yes → Process Detail Records (B000)

No → Print the Final Totals (B010)

Read an Input Record

Close the Files

End

CHAPTER 5 (Part 2 of 3)

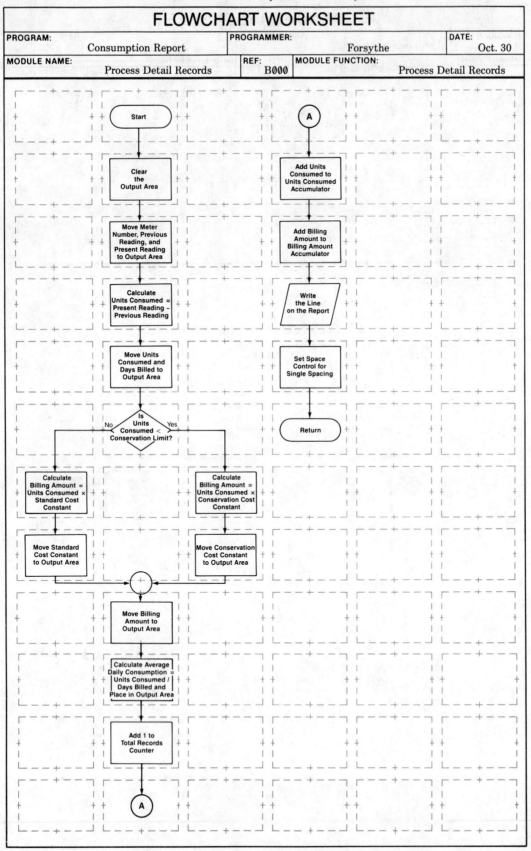

FLOWCHART WORKSHEET

PROGRAM:		PROGRAMMER:		DATE:
	Consumption Report		Forsythe	Oct. 30

MODULE NAME:		REF:	MODULE FUNCTION:	
	Process Detail Records	B000		Process Detail Records

CHAPTER 5 (Part 3 of 3)

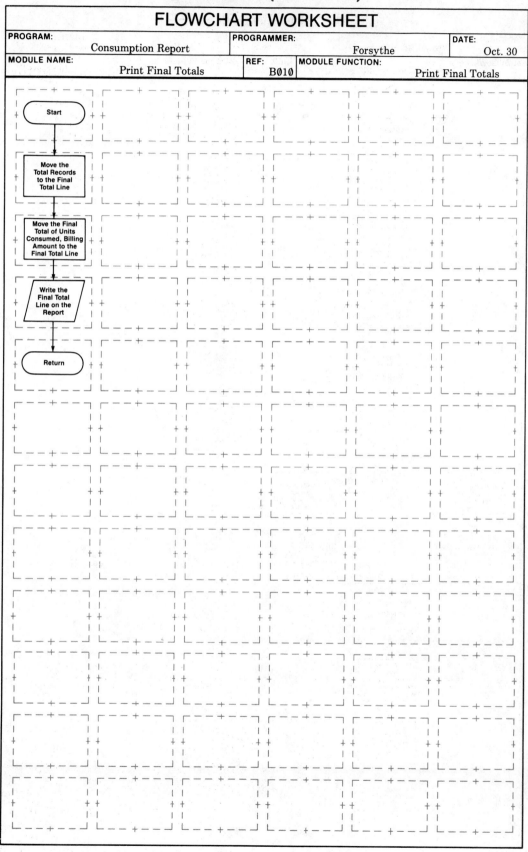

FLOWCHART WORKSHEET

PROGRAM: Consumption Report	PROGRAMMER: Forsythe	DATE: Oct. 30
MODULE NAME: Print Final Totals	REF: B010	MODULE FUNCTION: Print Final Totals

Start

Move the Total Records to the Final Total Line

Move the Final Total of Units Consumed, Billing Amount to the Final Total Line

Write the Final Total Line on the Report

Return

CHAPTER 6 (Part 1 of 6)

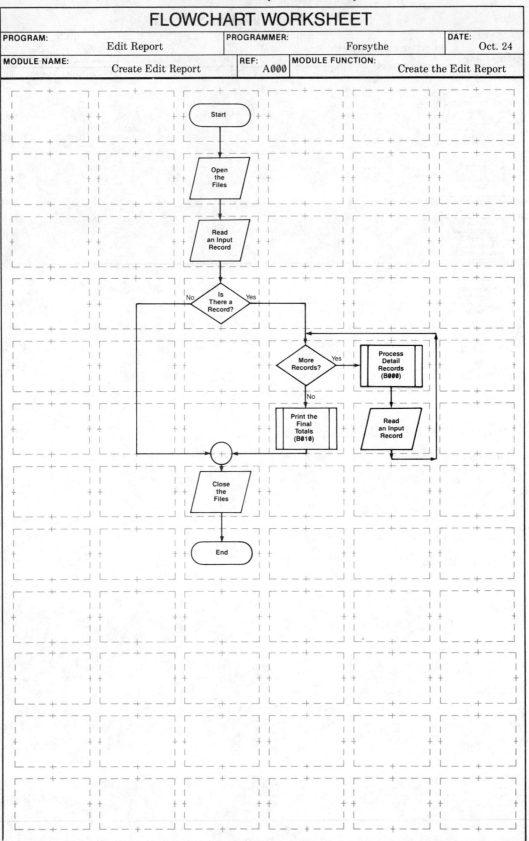

CHAPTER 6 (Part 2 of 6)

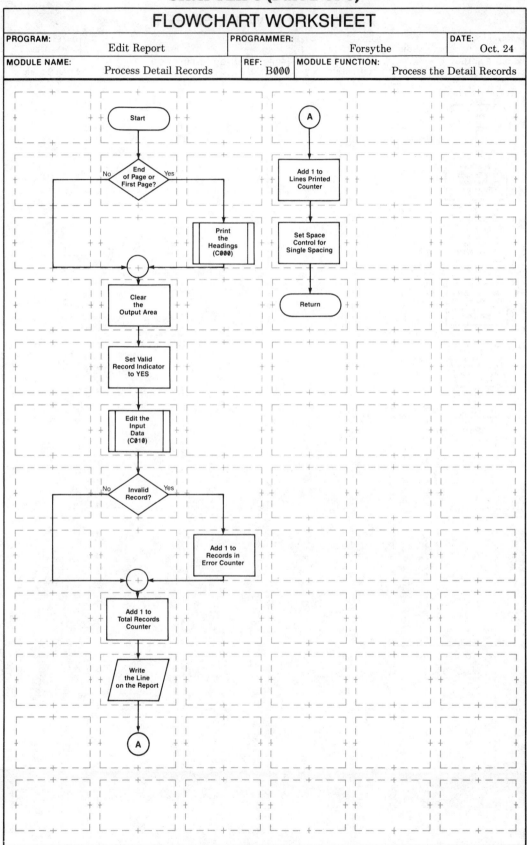

FLOWCHART WORKSHEET

PROGRAM: Edit Report	PROGRAMMER: Forsythe	DATE: Oct. 24

MODULE NAME: Process Detail Records	REF: B000	MODULE FUNCTION: Process the Detail Records

Start

End of Page or First Page? No — Yes

Print the Headings (C000)

Clear the Output Area

Set Valid Record Indicator to YES

Edit the Input Data (C010)

Invalid Record? No — Yes

Add 1 to Records in Error Counter

Add 1 to Total Records Counter

Write the Line on the Report

A

A

Add 1 to Lines Printed Counter

Set Space Control for Single Spacing

Return

CHAPTER 6 (Part 3 of 6)

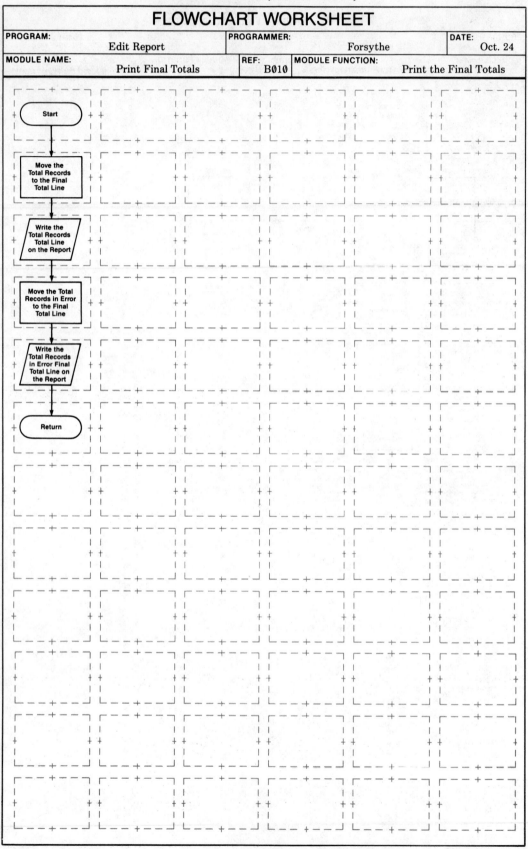

FLOWCHART WORKSHEET

PROGRAM: Edit Report	PROGRAMMER: Forsythe	DATE: Oct. 24

MODULE NAME: Print Final Totals	REF: B010	MODULE FUNCTION: Print the Final Totals

Start

Move the Total Records to the Final Total Line

Write the Total Records Total Line on the Report

Move the Total Records in Error to the Final Total Line

Write the Total Records in Error Final Total Line on the Report

Return

CHAPTER 6 (Part 4 of 6)

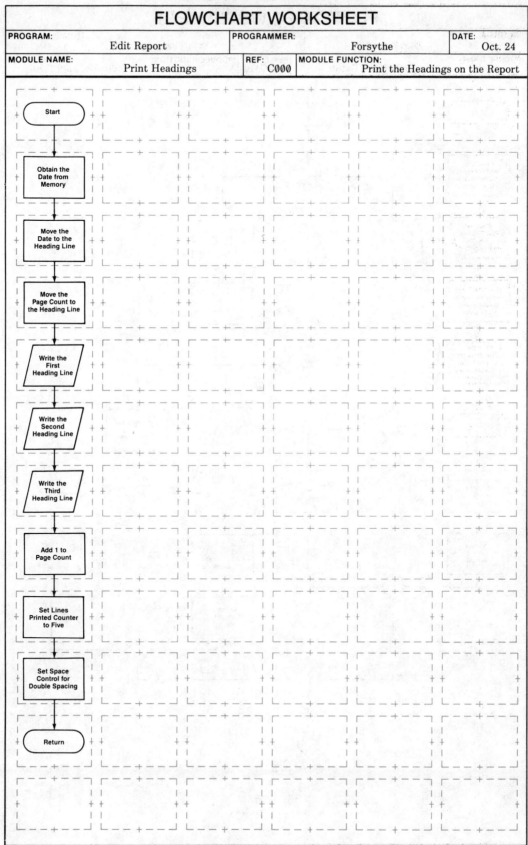

FLOWCHART WORKSHEET

PROGRAM: Edit Report	PROGRAMMER: Forsythe	DATE: Oct. 24

MODULE NAME: Print Headings	REF: C000	MODULE FUNCTION: Print the Headings on the Report

Start

Obtain the Date from Memory

Move the Date to the Heading Line

Move the Page Count to the Heading Line

Write the First Heading Line

Write the Second Heading Line

Write the Third Heading Line

Add 1 to Page Count

Set Lines Printed Counter to Five

Set Space Control for Double Spacing

Return

CHAPTER 6 (Part 5 of 6)

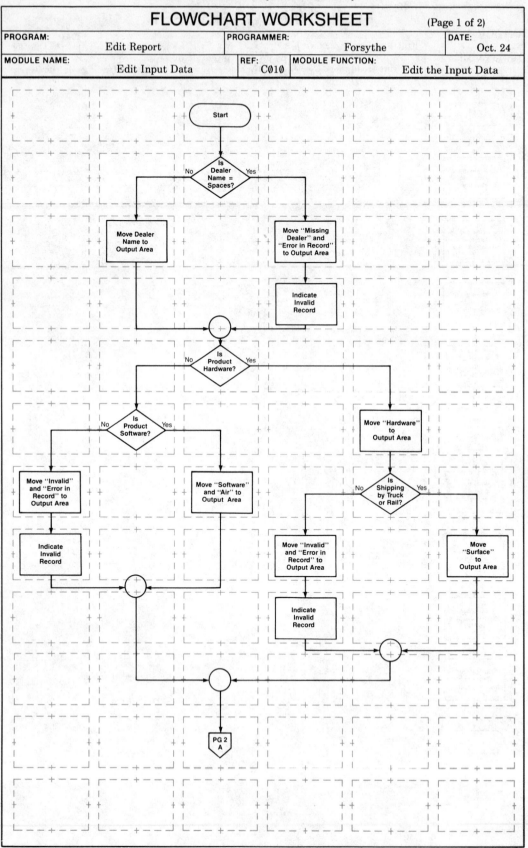

FLOWCHART WORKSHEET   (Page 1 of 2)

PROGRAM: Edit Report	PROGRAMMER: Forsythe	DATE: Oct. 24
MODULE NAME: Edit Input Data	REF: C010	MODULE FUNCTION: Edit the Input Data

CHAPTER 6 (Part 6 of 6)

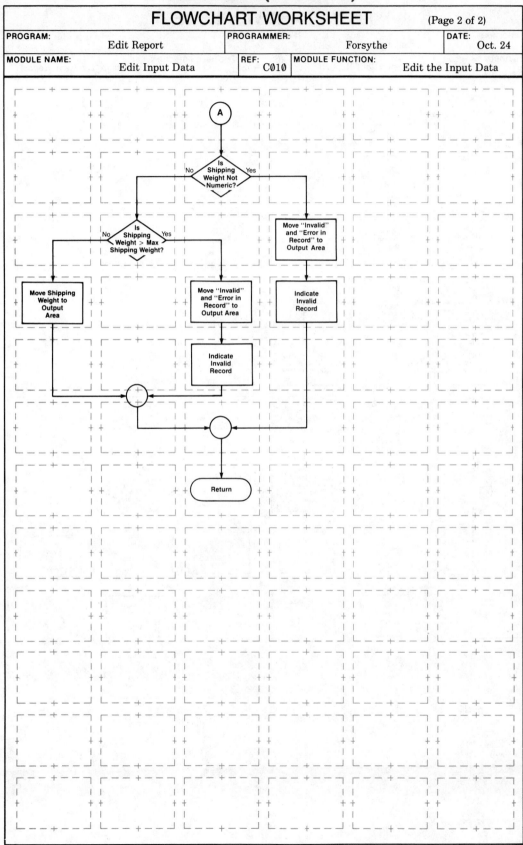

FLOWCHART WORKSHEET (Page 2 of 2)

PROGRAM: Edit Report

PROGRAMMER: Forsythe

DATE: Oct. 24

MODULE NAME: Edit Input Data

REF: C010

MODULE FUNCTION: Edit the Input Data

CHAPTER 7 (Part 1 of 5)

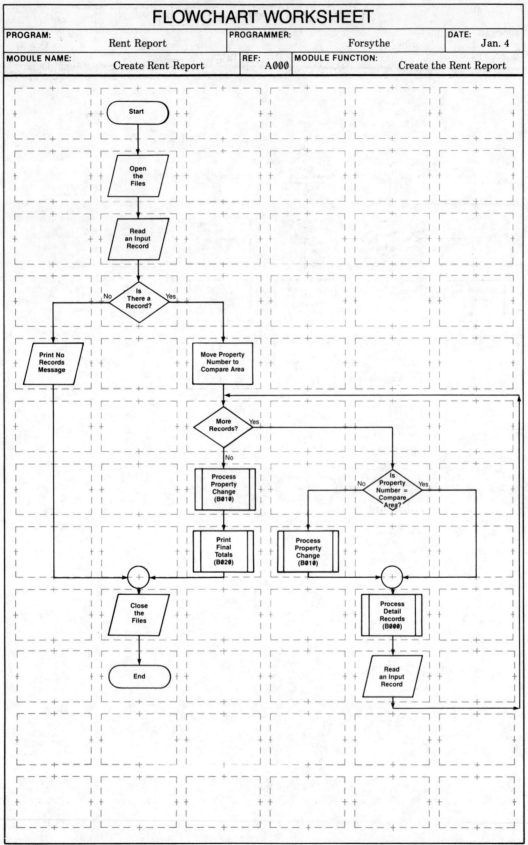

CHAPTER 7 (Part 2 of 5)

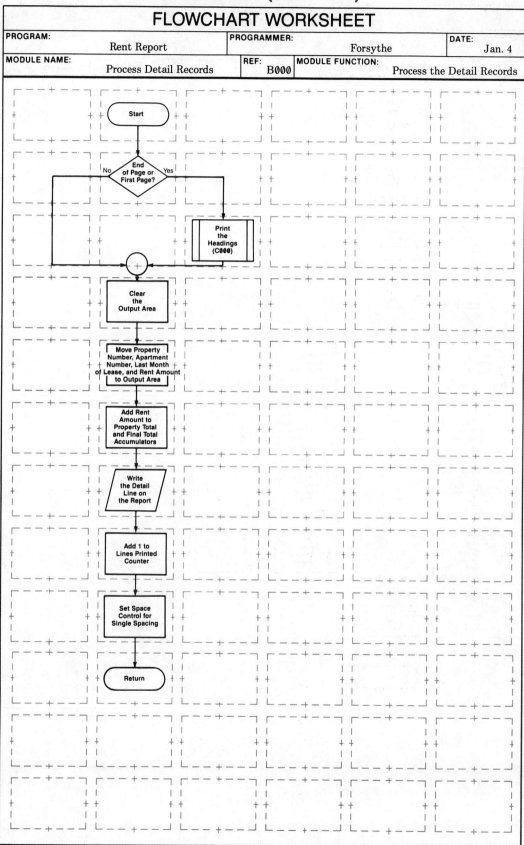

FLOWCHART WORKSHEET

PROGRAM: Rent Report	PROGRAMMER: Forsythe	DATE: Jan. 4
MODULE NAME: Process Detail Records	REF: B000	MODULE FUNCTION: Process the Detail Records

CHAPTER 7 (Part 3 of 5)

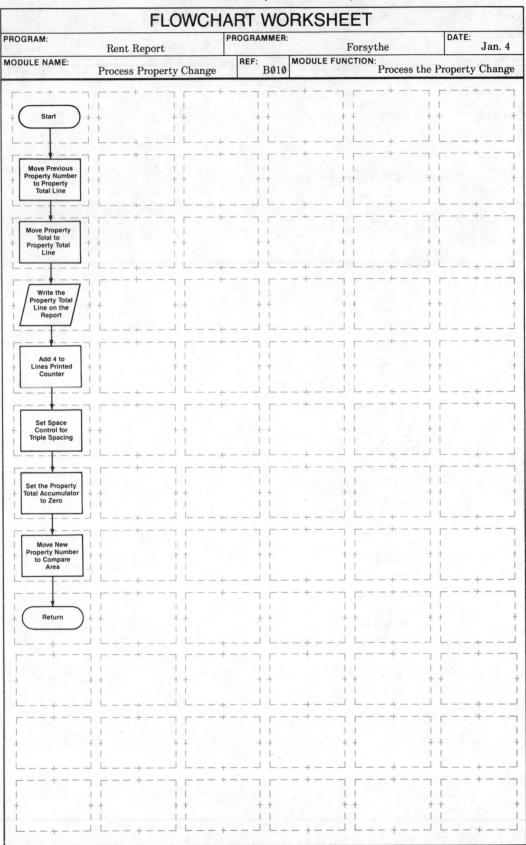

FLOWCHART WORKSHEET

PROGRAM: Rent Report

PROGRAMMER: Forsythe

DATE: Jan. 4

MODULE NAME: Process Property Change

REF: B010

MODULE FUNCTION: Process the Property Change

Start

Move Previous Property Number to Property Total Line

Move Property Total to Property Total Line

Write the Property Total Line on the Report

Add 4 to Lines Printed Counter

Set Space Control for Triple Spacing

Set the Property Total Accumulator to Zero

Move New Property Number to Compare Area

Return

CHAPTER 7 (Part 4 of 5)

CHAPTER 7 (Part 5 of 5)

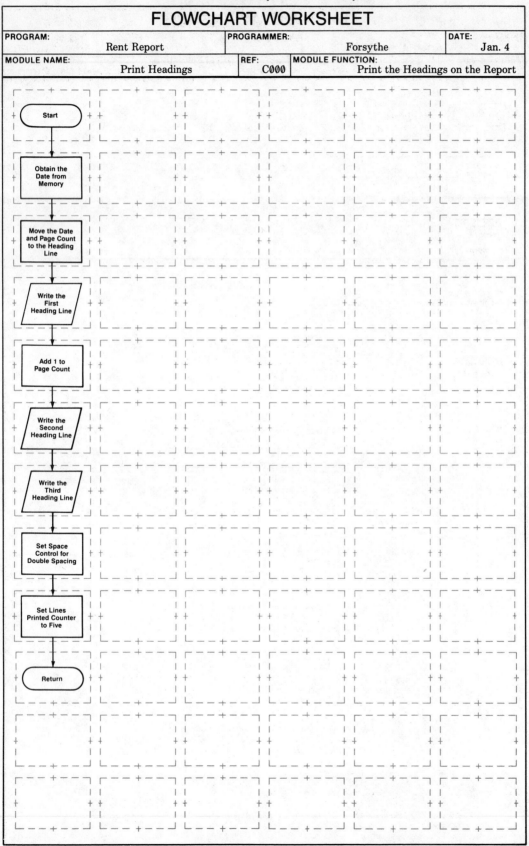

FLOWCHART WORKSHEET

PROGRAM: Rent Report

PROGRAMMER: Forsythe

DATE: Jan. 4

MODULE NAME: Print Headings

REF: C000

MODULE FUNCTION: Print the Headings on the Report

Start

Obtain the Date from Memory

Move the Date and Page Count to the Heading Line

Write the First Heading Line

Add 1 to Page Count

Write the Second Heading Line

Write the Third Heading Line

Set Space Control for Double Spacing

Set Lines Printed Counter to Five

Return

CHAPTER 8 (Part 1 of 8)

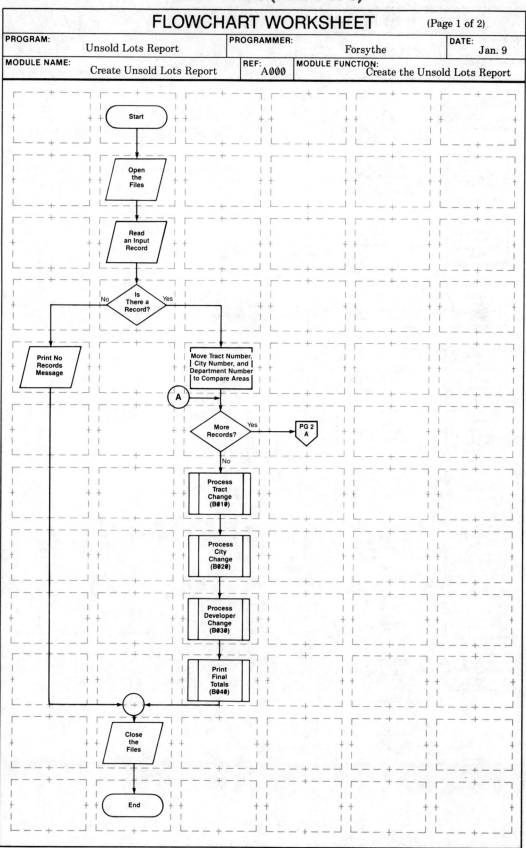

FLOWCHART WORKSHEET (Page 1 of 2)

| PROGRAM: Unsold Lots Report | PROGRAMMER: Forsythe | DATE: Jan. 9 |

| MODULE NAME: Create Unsold Lots Report | REF: A000 | MODULE FUNCTION: Create the Unsold Lots Report |

Start

Open the Files

Read an Input Record

Is There a Record?   No / Yes

Print No Records Message

Move Tract Number, City Number, and Department Number to Compare Areas

A

More Records?   Yes → PG 2 A   No

Process Tract Change (B010)

Process City Change (B020)

Process Developer Change (B030)

Print Final Totals (B040)

Close the Files

End

CHAPTER 8 (Part 2 of 8)

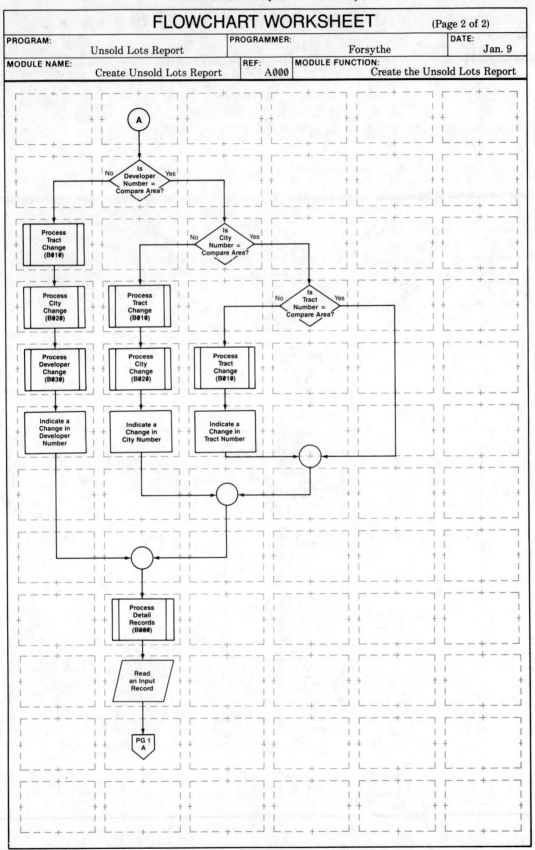

FLOWCHART WORKSHEET   (Page 2 of 2)

PROGRAM: Unsold Lots Report   PROGRAMMER: Forsythe   DATE: Jan. 9

MODULE NAME: Create Unsold Lots Report   REF: A000   MODULE FUNCTION: Create the Unsold Lots Report

CHAPTER 8 (Part 3 of 8)

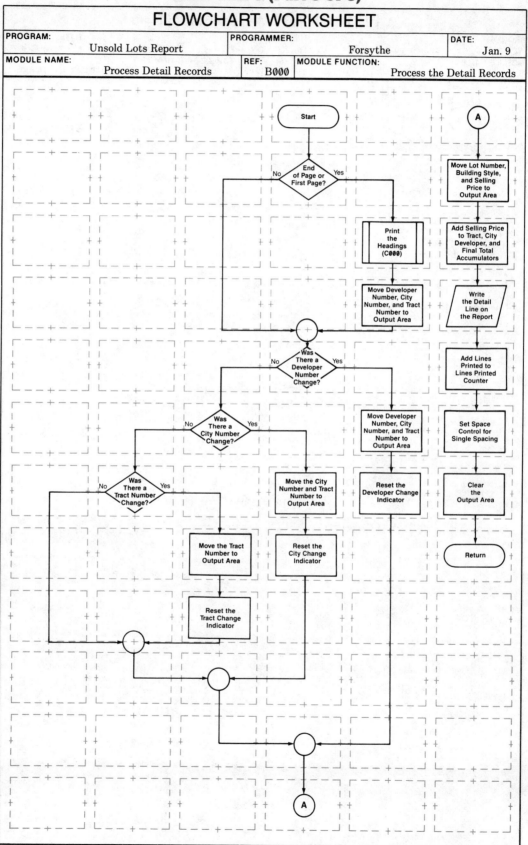

FLOWCHART WORKSHEET

PROGRAM: Unsold Lots Report	PROGRAMMER: Forsythe	DATE: Jan. 9
MODULE NAME: Process Detail Records	REF: B000	MODULE FUNCTION: Process the Detail Records

Start

End of Page or First Page? No / Yes

Print the Headings (C000)

Move Developer Number, City Number, and Tract Number to Output Area

Was There a Developer Number Change? No / Yes

Was There a City Number Change? No / Yes

Was There a Tract Number Change? No / Yes

Move Developer Number, City Number, and Tract Number to Output Area

Move the City Number and Tract Number to Output Area

Move the Tract Number to Output Area

Reset the Developer Change Indicator

Reset the City Change Indicator

Reset the Tract Change Indicator

A

Move Lot Number, Building Style, and Selling Price to Output Area

Add Selling Price to Tract, City Developer, and Final Total Accumulators

Write the Detail Line on the Report

Add Lines Printed to Lines Printed Counter

Set Space Control for Single Spacing

Clear the Output Area

Return

A

CHAPTER 8 (Part 4 of 8)

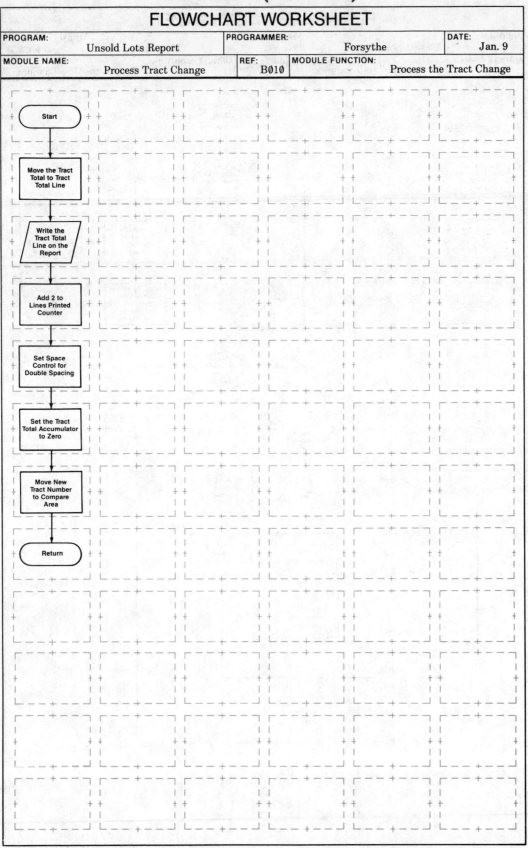

FLOWCHART WORKSHEET

PROGRAM: Unsold Lots Report	PROGRAMMER: Forsythe	DATE: Jan. 9

MODULE NAME: Process Tract Change	REF: B010	MODULE FUNCTION: Process the Tract Change

Start

Move the Tract Total to Tract Total Line

Write the Tract Total Line on the Report

Add 2 to Lines Printed Counter

Set Space Control for Double Spacing

Set the Tract Total Accumulator to Zero

Move New Tract Number to Compare Area

Return

CHAPTER 8 (Part 5 of 8)

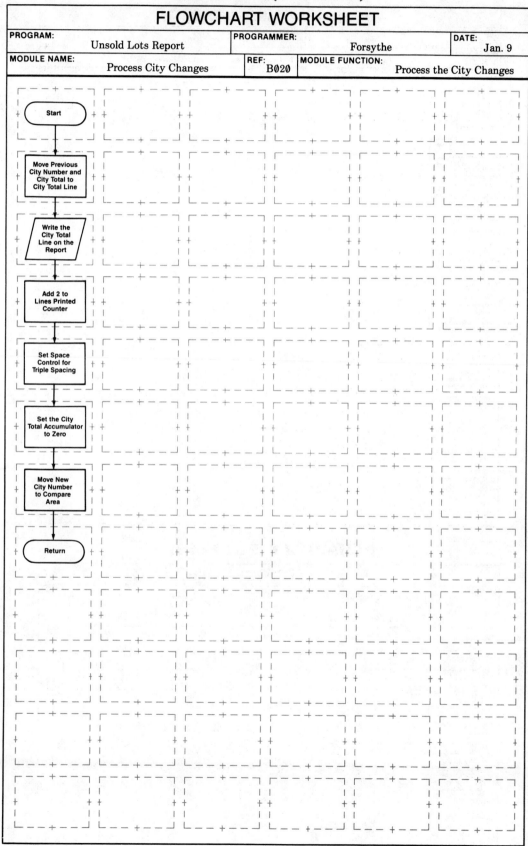

FLOWCHART WORKSHEET

PROGRAM: Unsold Lots Report	PROGRAMMER: Forsythe	DATE: Jan. 9
MODULE NAME: Process City Changes	REF: B020	MODULE FUNCTION: Process the City Changes

Start

Move Previous City Number and City Total to City Total Line

Write the City Total Line on the Report

Add 2 to Lines Printed Counter

Set Space Control for Triple Spacing

Set the City Total Accumulator to Zero

Move New City Number to Compare Area

Return

CHAPTER 8 (Part 6 of 8)

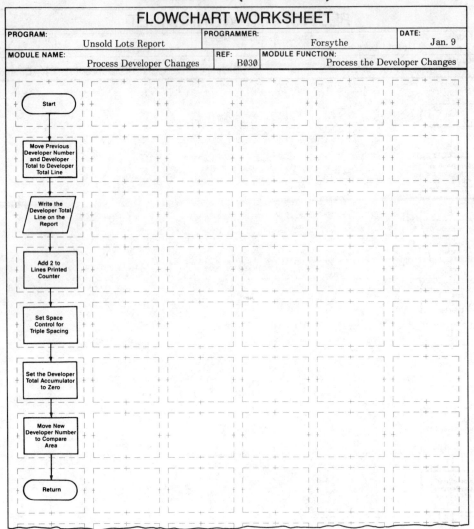

CHAPTER 8 (Part 7 of 8)

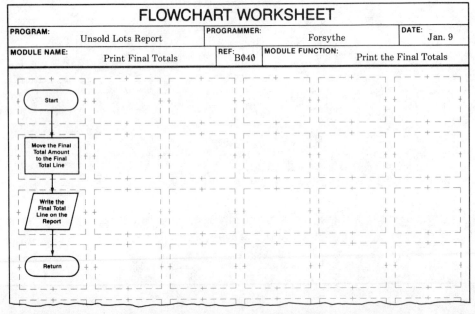

CHAPTER 8 (Part 8 of 8)

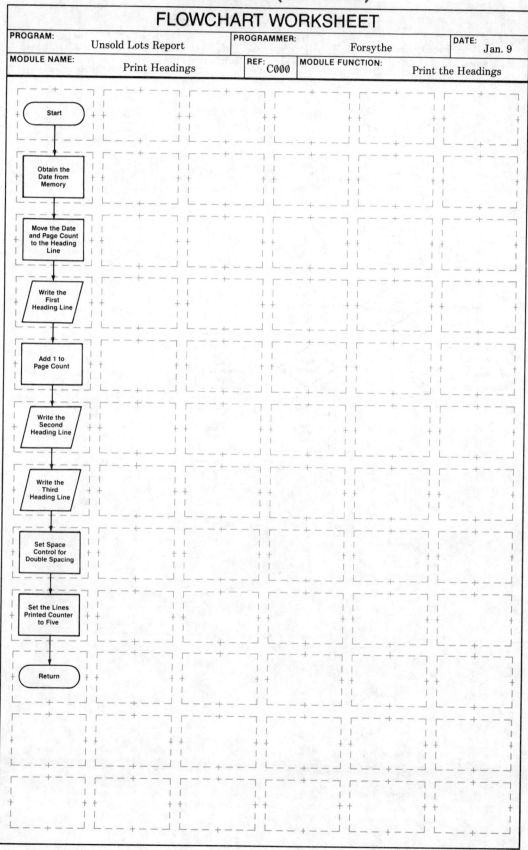

FLOWCHART WORKSHEET

PROGRAM: Unsold Lots Report	PROGRAMMER: Forsythe	DATE: Jan. 9
MODULE NAME: Print Headings	REF: C000	MODULE FUNCTION: Print the Headings

Start

Obtain the Date from Memory

Move the Date and Page Count to the Heading Line

Write the First Heading Line

Add 1 to Page Count

Write the Second Heading Line

Write the Third Heading Line

Set Space Control for Double Spacing

Set the Lines Printed Counter to Five

Return

CHAPTER 9 (Part 1 of 4)

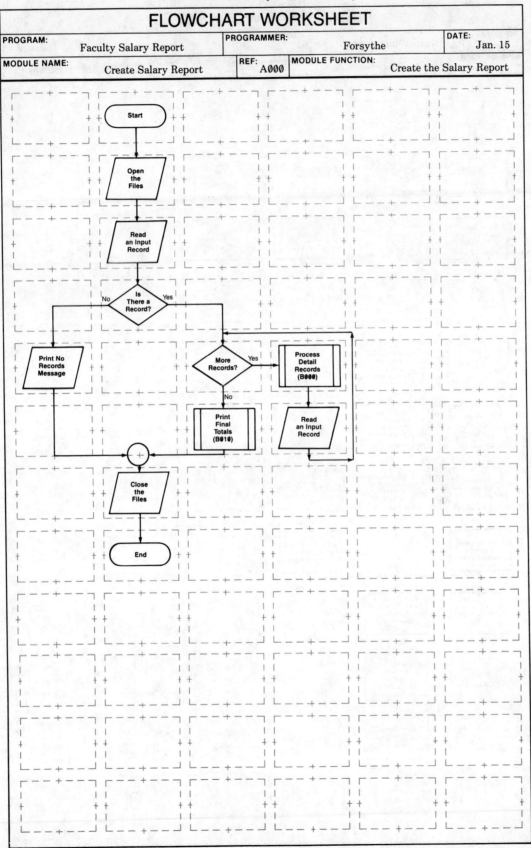

FLOWCHART WORKSHEET

PROGRAM: Faculty Salary Report	PROGRAMMER: Forsythe	DATE: Jan. 15

MODULE NAME: Create Salary Report	REF: A000	MODULE FUNCTION: Create the Salary Report

CHAPTER 9 (Part 2 of 4)

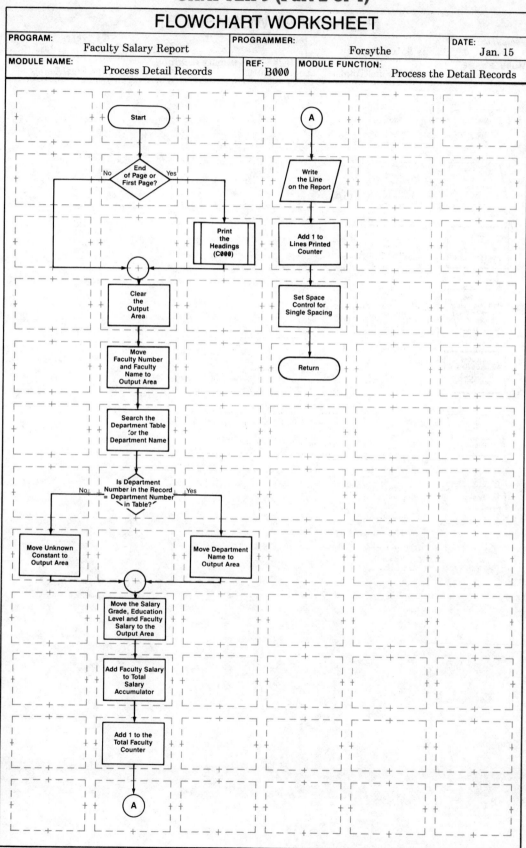

FLOWCHART WORKSHEET

PROGRAM: Faculty Salary Report	PROGRAMMER: Forsythe	DATE: Jan. 15
MODULE NAME: Process Detail Records	REF: B000	MODULE FUNCTION: Process the Detail Records

Start

End of Page or First Page? No / Yes

Print the Headings (C000)

Clear the Output Area

Move Faculty Number and Faculty Name to Output Area

Search the Department Table for the Department Name

Is Department Number in the Record = Department Number in Table? No / Yes

Move Unknown Constant to Output Area

Move Department Name to Output Area

Move the Salary Grade, Education Level and Faculty Salary to the Output Area

Add Faculty Salary to Total Salary Accumulator

Add 1 to the Total Faculty Counter

A

A

Write the Line on the Report

Add 1 to Lines Printed Counter

Set Space Control for Single Spacing

Return

CHAPTER 9 (Part 3 of 4)

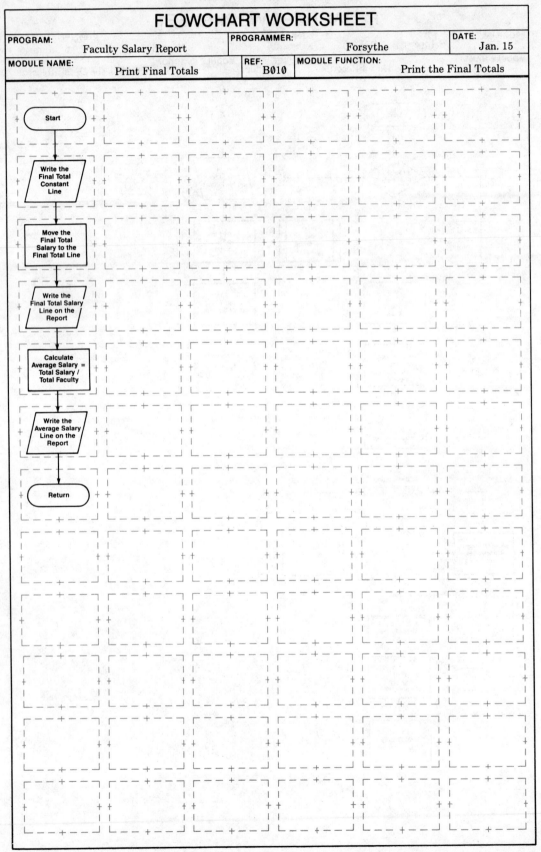

FLOWCHART WORKSHEET

PROGRAM: Faculty Salary Report

PROGRAMMER: Forsythe

DATE: Jan. 15

MODULE NAME: Print Final Totals

REF: B010

MODULE FUNCTION: Print the Final Totals

Start

Write the Final Total Constant Line

Move the Final Total Salary to the Final Total Line

Write the Final Total Salary Line on the Report

Calculate Average Salary = Total Salary / Total Faculty

Write the Average Salary Line on the Report

Return

CHAPTER 9 (Part 4 of 4)

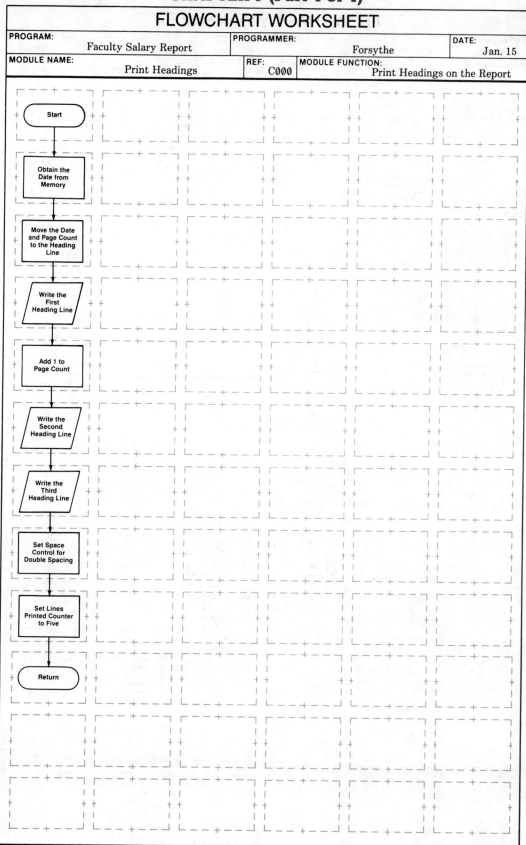

FLOWCHART WORKSHEET

PROGRAM:	PROGRAMMER:	DATE:
Faculty Salary Report	Forsythe	Jan. 15

MODULE NAME:		REF:	MODULE FUNCTION:
Print Headings		C000	Print Headings on the Report

Start

Obtain the
Date from
Memory

Move the Date
and Page Count
to the Heading
Line

Write the
First
Heading Line

Add 1 to
Page Count

Write the
Second
Heading Line

Write the
Third
Heading Line

Set Space
Control for
Double Spacing

Set Lines
Printed Counter
to Five

Return

CHAPTER 10 (Part 1 of 7)

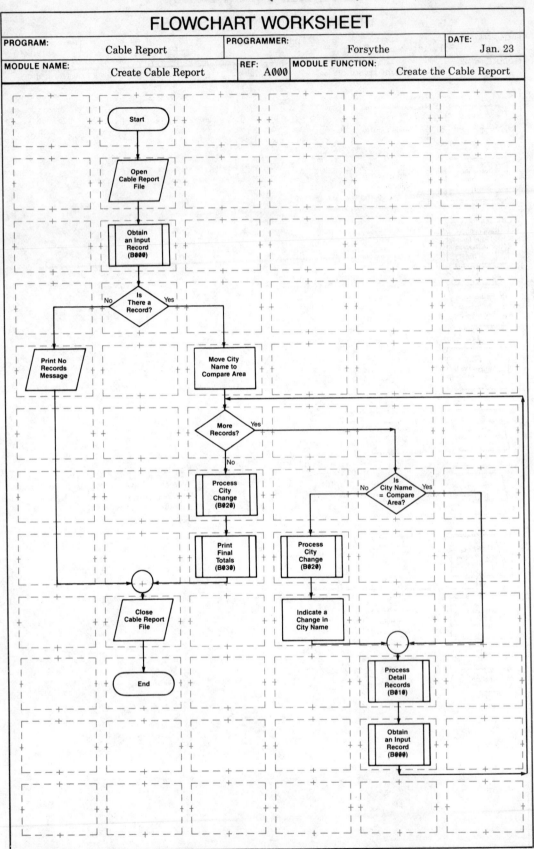

FLOWCHART WORKSHEET

| PROGRAM: Cable Report | PROGRAMMER: Forsythe | DATE: Jan. 23 |
| MODULE NAME: Create Cable Report | REF: A000 | MODULE FUNCTION: Create the Cable Report |

CHAPTER 10 (Part 2 of 7)

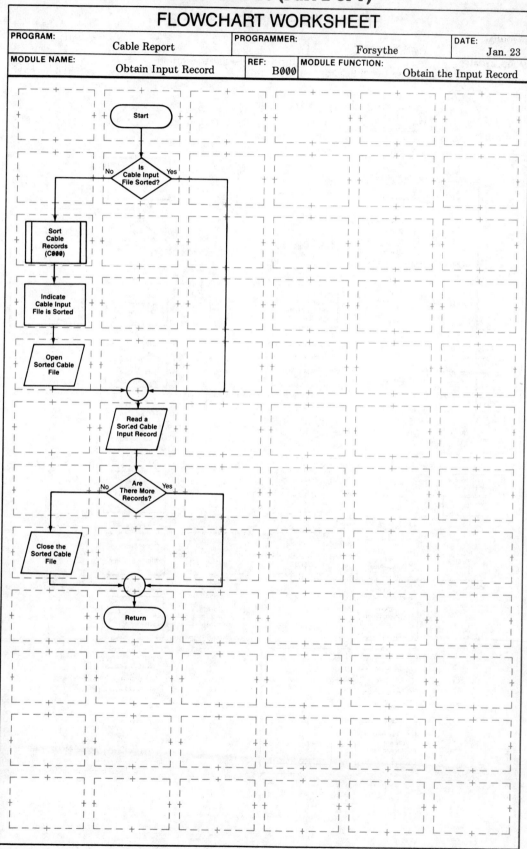

FLOWCHART WORKSHEET

PROGRAM:	PROGRAMMER:	DATE:
Cable Report	Forsythe	Jan. 23

MODULE NAME:	REF:	MODULE FUNCTION:
Obtain Input Record	B000	Obtain the Input Record

CHAPTER 10 (Part 3 of 7)

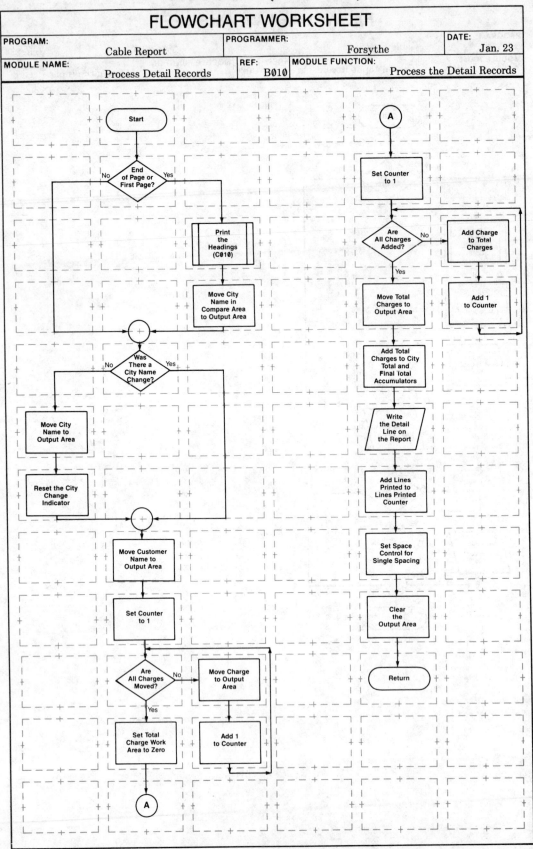

FLOWCHART WORKSHEET

PROGRAM: Cable Report	PROGRAMMER: Forsythe	DATE: Jan. 23
MODULE NAME: Process Detail Records	REF: B010	MODULE FUNCTION: Process the Detail Records

CHAPTER 10 (Part 4 of 7)

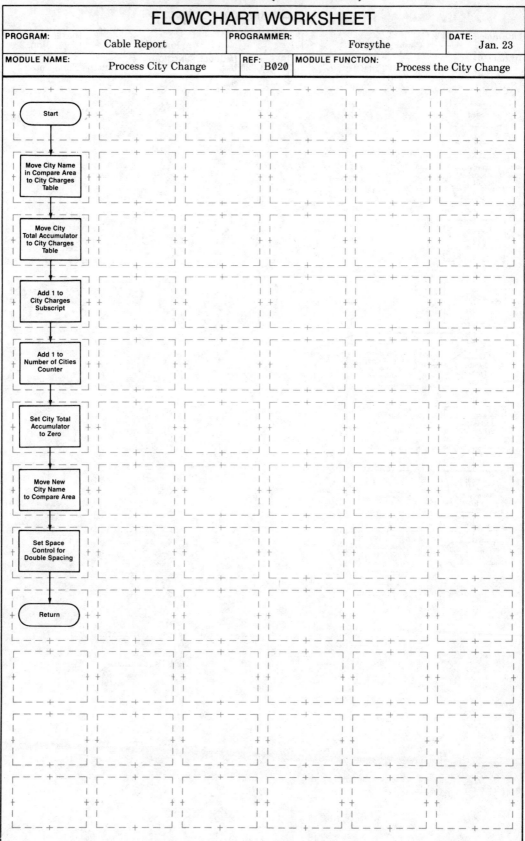

FLOWCHART WORKSHEET

| PROGRAM: Cable Report | PROGRAMMER: Forsythe | DATE: Jan. 23 |
| MODULE NAME: Process City Change | REF: B020 | MODULE FUNCTION: Process the City Change |

Start

Move City Name in Compare Area to City Charges Table

Move City Total Accumulator to City Charges Table

Add 1 to City Charges Subscript

Add 1 to Number of Cities Counter

Set City Total Accumulator to Zero

Move New City Name to Compare Area

Set Space Control for Double Spacing

Return

CHAPTER 10 (Part 5 of 7)

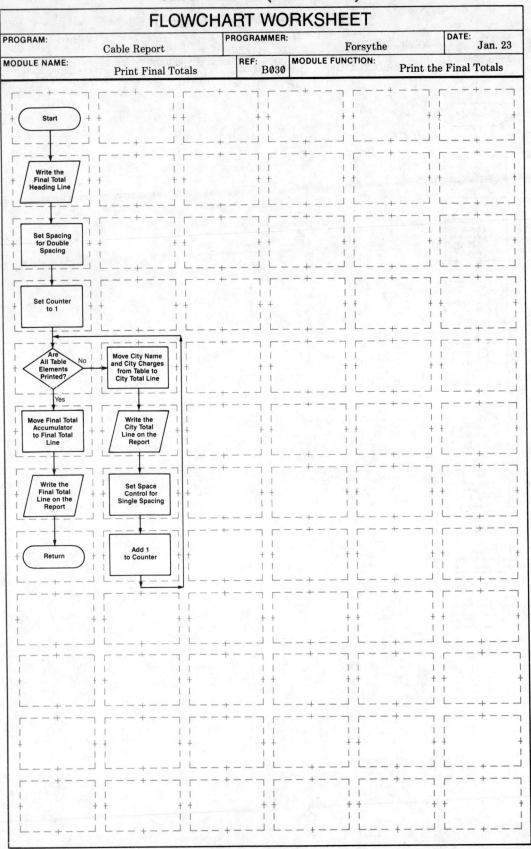

FLOWCHART WORKSHEET

PROGRAM: Cable Report

PROGRAMMER: Forsythe

DATE: Jan. 23

MODULE NAME: Print Final Totals

REF: B030

MODULE FUNCTION: Print the Final Totals

Start

Write the Final Total Heading Line

Set Spacing for Double Spacing

Set Counter to 1

Are All Table Elements Printed?

No → Move City Name and City Charges from Table to City Total Line

Yes

Move Final Total Accumulator to Final Total Line

Write the City Total Line on the Report

Write the Final Total Line on the Report

Set Space Control for Single Spacing

Return

Add 1 to Counter

CHAPTER 10 (Part 6 of 7)

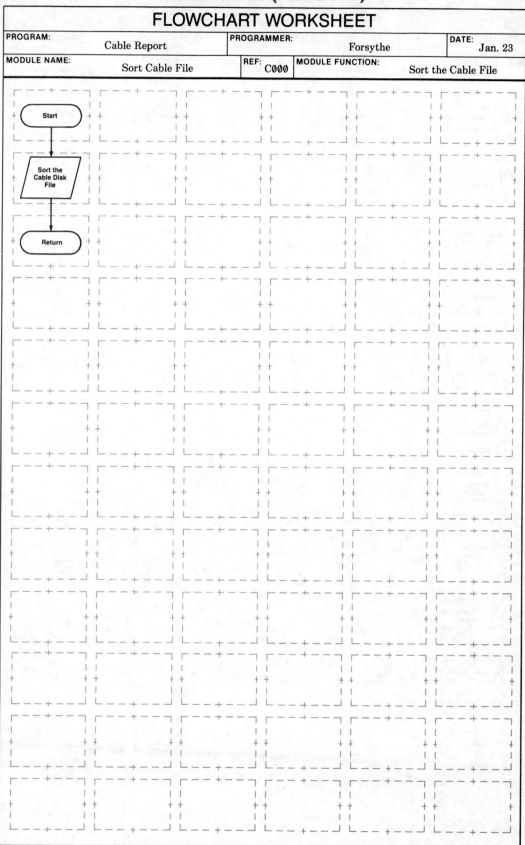

FLOWCHART WORKSHEET

PROGRAM:	Cable Report	PROGRAMMER:	Forsythe	DATE: Jan. 23
MODULE NAME:	Sort Cable File	REF: C000	MODULE FUNCTION:	Sort the Cable File

Start

Sort the
Cable Disk
File

Return

CHAPTER 10 (Part 7 of 7)

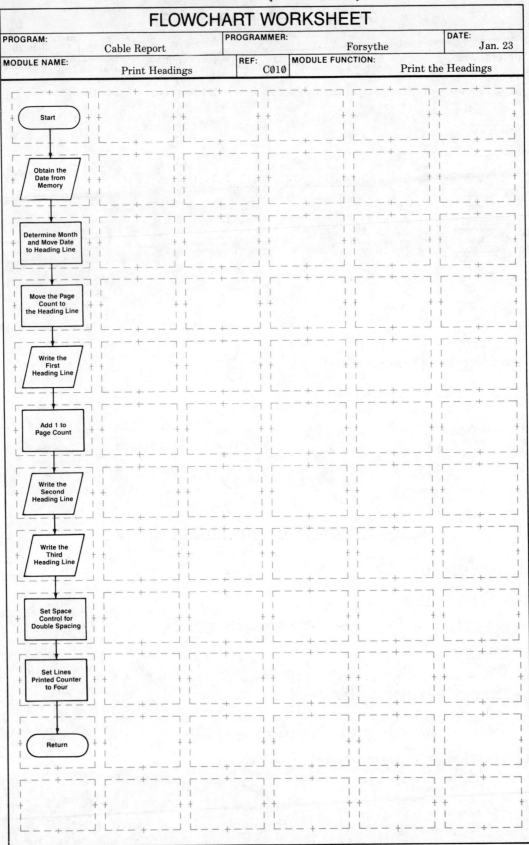

FLOWCHART WORKSHEET

PROGRAM: Cable Report	PROGRAMMER: Forsythe	DATE: Jan. 23
MODULE NAME: Print Headings	REF: C010	MODULE FUNCTION: Print the Headings

Start

Obtain the Date from Memory

Determine Month and Move Date to Heading Line

Move the Page Count to the Heading Line

Write the First Heading Line

Add 1 to Page Count

Write the Second Heading Line

Write the Third Heading Line

Set Space Control for Double Spacing

Set Lines Printed Counter to Four

Return

The following are the general formats for all COBOL statements used in this text.

Identification Division

GENERAL FORMAT FOR IDENTIFICATION DIVISION

IDENTIFICATION DIVISION.

PROGRAM-ID. program-name.

[AUTHOR. [comment-entry] ...]

[INSTALLATION. [comment-entry] ...]

[DATE-WRITTEN. [comment-entry] ...]

[DATE-COMPILED. [comment-entry] ...]

[SECURITY. [comment-entry] ...]

Environment Division

GENERAL FORMAT FOR ENVIRONMENT DIVISION

ENVIRONMENT DIVISION.

CONFIGURATION SECTION.

SOURCE-COMPUTER. computer-name [WITH DEBUGGING MODE] .

OBJECT-COMPUTER. computer-name

$$\left[, \text{MEMORY SIZE integer} \left\{ \begin{matrix} \text{WORDS} \\ \text{CHARACTERS} \\ \text{MODULES} \end{matrix} \right\} \right]$$

[, PROGRAM COLLATING SEQUENCE IS alphabet-name]

[, SEGMENT-LIMIT IS segment-number] .

$\left[\underline{\text{SPECIAL-NAMES}}. \left[, \text{implementor-name} \right. \right.$

$\left\{ \begin{array}{l} \underline{\text{IS}} \text{ mnemonic-name } \left[, \underline{\text{ON}} \text{ STATUS } \underline{\text{IS}} \text{ condition-name-1 } \left[, \underline{\text{OFF}} \text{ STATUS } \underline{\text{IS}} \text{ condition-name-2}\right]\right] \\ \underline{\text{IS}} \text{ mnemonic-name } \left[, \underline{\text{OFF}} \text{ STATUS } \underline{\text{IS}} \text{ condition-name-2 } \left[, \underline{\text{ON}} \text{ STATUS } \underline{\text{IS}} \text{ condition-name-1}\right]\right] \\ \underline{\text{ON}} \text{ STATUS } \underline{\text{IS}} \text{ condition-name-1 } \left[, \underline{\text{OFF}} \text{ STATUS } \underline{\text{IS}} \text{ condition-name-2}\right] \\ \underline{\text{OFF}} \text{ STATUS } \underline{\text{IS}} \text{ condition-name-2 } \left[, \underline{\text{ON}} \text{ STATUS } \underline{\text{IS}} \text{ condition-name-1}\right] \end{array} \right] \right]$ ...

$\left[, \text{alphabet-name } \underline{\text{IS}} \left\{ \begin{array}{l} \underline{\text{STANDARD-1}} \\ \underline{\text{NATIVE}} \\ \text{implementor-name} \\ \text{literal-1} \left[\left\{ \begin{array}{l} \underline{\text{THROUGH}} \\ \underline{\text{THRU}} \end{array} \right\} \text{literal-2} \\ \underline{\text{ALSO}} \text{ literal-3} \left[, \underline{\text{ALSO}} \text{ literal-4}\right]... \right] \\ \left[\text{literal-5} \left[\left\{ \begin{array}{l} \underline{\text{THROUGH}} \\ \underline{\text{THRU}} \end{array} \right\} \text{literal-6} \\ \underline{\text{ALSO}} \text{ literal-7} \left[, \underline{\text{ALSO}} \text{ literal-8}\right]... \right] \right]... \end{array} \right\} \right]$ ...

$\left[, \underline{\text{CURRENCY}} \text{ SIGN } \underline{\text{IS}} \text{ literal-9} \right]$

$\left[, \underline{\text{DECIMAL-POINT}} \text{ IS } \underline{\text{COMMA}} \right] .$ $\left. \right]$

$\left[\underline{\text{INPUT-OUTPUT}} \underline{\text{SECTION}}. \right.$

$\underline{\text{FILE-CONTROL}}.$

   $\{ \text{file-control-entry} \}$ ...

$\left[\underline{\text{I-O-CONTROL}}. \right.$

   $\left[; \underline{\text{RERUN}} \left[\underline{\text{ON}} \left\{ \begin{array}{l} \text{file-name-1} \\ \text{implementor-name} \end{array} \right\} \right] \right.$

   $\underline{\text{EVERY}} \left\{ \begin{array}{l} \left\{ \begin{array}{l} [\underline{\text{END}} \text{ OF}] \left\{ \begin{array}{l} \underline{\text{REEL}} \\ \underline{\text{UNIT}} \end{array} \right\} \\ \text{integer-1} \underline{\text{RECORDS}} \end{array} \right\} \text{OF file-name-2} \\ \text{integer-2} \underline{\text{CLOCK-UNITS}} \\ \text{condition-name} \end{array} \right\} \left. \right]$ ...

   $\left[; \underline{\text{SAME}} \left[\begin{array}{l} \underline{\text{RECORD}} \\ \underline{\text{SORT}} \\ \underline{\text{SORT-MERGE}} \end{array} \right] \text{AREA FOR file-name-3} \{ , \text{file-name-4} \} ... \right]$ ...

   $\left[; \underline{\text{MULTIPLE}} \underline{\text{FILE}} \text{ TAPE CONTAINS file-name-5} \left[\underline{\text{POSITION}} \text{ integer-3} \right] \right.$

   $\left[, \text{file-name-6} \left[\underline{\text{POSITION}} \text{ integer-4} \right] \right] ... \left. \right]$ ... $\left. . \right] \right]$

Environment Division

GENERAL FORMAT FOR FILE CONTROL ENTRY

FORMAT 1:

SELECT [OPTIONAL] file-name

    ASSIGN TO implementor-name-1 [, implementor-name-2] ...

    [; RESERVE integer-1 $\begin{bmatrix} \text{AREA} \\ \text{AREAS} \end{bmatrix}$]

    [; ORGANIZATION IS SEQUENTIAL]

    [; ACCESS MODE IS SEQUENTIAL]

    [; FILE STATUS IS data-name-1] .

FORMAT 2:

SELECT file-name

    ASSIGN TO implementor-name-1 [, implementor-name-2] ...

    [; RESERVE integer-1 $\begin{bmatrix} \text{AREA} \\ \text{AREAS} \end{bmatrix}$]

    ; ORGANIZATION IS RELATIVE

    $\left[\text{; ACCESS MODE IS} \left\{ \begin{array}{l} \text{SEQUENTIAL} \quad [, \text{RELATIVE KEY IS data-name-1}] \\ \left\{ \begin{array}{l} \text{RANDOM} \\ \text{DYNAMIC} \end{array} \right\} , \text{RELATIVE KEY IS data-name-1} \end{array} \right\} \right]$

    [; FILE STATUS IS data-name-2] .

Environment Division

GENERAL FORMAT FOR FILE CONTROL ENTRY

FORMAT 3:

SELECT file-name

    ASSIGN TO implementor-name-1 [, implementor-name-2] ...

    [; RESERVE integer-1 $\begin{bmatrix} \text{AREA} \\ \text{AREAS} \end{bmatrix}$]

    ; ORGANIZATION IS INDEXED

$$\left[\; ; \; \underline{\text{ACCESS}} \text{ MODE IS } \left\{ \begin{array}{l} \underline{\text{SEQUENTIAL}} \\ \underline{\text{RANDOM}} \\ \underline{\text{DYNAMIC}} \end{array} \right\} \right]$$

$$; \; \underline{\text{RECORD}} \text{ KEY IS data-name-1}$$

$$\left[\; ; \; \underline{\text{ALTERNATE}} \; \underline{\text{RECORD}} \text{ KEY IS data-name-2 } \left[\text{WITH } \underline{\text{DUPLICATES}} \right] \right] \; \ldots$$

$$\left[\; ; \; \text{FILE } \underline{\text{STATUS}} \text{ IS data-name-3} \right] \; .$$

<u>FORMAT 4</u>:

<u>SELECT</u> file-name <u>ASSIGN</u> TO implementor-name-1 [, implementor-name-2] ...

Data Division

<u>GENERAL FORMAT FOR DATA DIVISION</u>

<u>DATA</u> <u>DIVISION</u>.

[<u>FILE</u> <u>SECTION</u>.

[<u>FD</u> file-name

$$\left[\; ; \; \underline{\text{BLOCK}} \text{ CONTAINS } \left[\text{integer-1 } \underline{\text{TO}} \right] \text{ integer-2 } \left\{ \begin{array}{l} \underline{\text{RECORDS}} \\ \underline{\text{CHARACTERS}} \end{array} \right\} \right]$$

$$\left[\; ; \; \underline{\text{RECORD}} \text{ CONTAINS } \left[\text{integer-3 } \underline{\text{TO}} \right] \text{ integer-4 CHARACTERS} \right]$$

$$; \; \underline{\text{LABEL}} \left\{ \begin{array}{l} \underline{\text{RECORD}} \text{ IS} \\ \underline{\text{RECORDS}} \text{ ARE} \end{array} \right\} \left\{ \begin{array}{l} \underline{\text{STANDARD}} \\ \underline{\text{OMITTED}} \end{array} \right\}$$

$$\left[\; ; \; \underline{\text{VALUE}} \; \underline{\text{OF}} \text{ implementor-name-1 IS } \left\{ \begin{array}{l} \text{data-name-1} \\ \text{literal-1} \end{array} \right\} \right.$$

$$\left. \left[\text{, implementor-name-2 IS } \left\{ \begin{array}{l} \text{data-name-2} \\ \text{literal-2} \end{array} \right\} \right] \; \ldots \right]$$

$$\left[\; ; \; \underline{\text{DATA}} \left\{ \begin{array}{l} \underline{\text{RECORD}} \text{ IS} \\ \underline{\text{RECORDS}} \text{ ARE} \end{array} \right\} \text{ data-name-3 } \left[\text{, data-name-4} \right] \; \ldots \right]$$

$$\left[\; ; \; \underline{\text{LINAGE}} \text{ IS } \left\{ \begin{array}{l} \text{data-name-5} \\ \text{integer-5} \end{array} \right\} \text{ LINES } \left[\text{, WITH } \underline{\text{FOOTING}} \text{ AT } \left\{ \begin{array}{l} \text{data-name-6} \\ \text{integer-6} \end{array} \right\} \right] \right.$$

$$\left. \left[\text{, LINES AT } \underline{\text{TOP}} \left\{ \begin{array}{l} \text{data-name-7} \\ \text{integer-7} \end{array} \right\} \right] \left[\text{, LINES AT } \underline{\text{BOTTOM}} \left\{ \begin{array}{l} \text{data-name-8} \\ \text{integer-8} \end{array} \right\} \right] \right]$$

$$\left[\; ; \; \underline{\text{CODE-SET}} \text{ IS alphabet-name} \right]$$

$$\left[\; ; \; \left\{ \begin{array}{l} \underline{\text{REPORT}} \text{ IS} \\ \underline{\text{REPORTS}} \text{ ARE} \end{array} \right\} \text{ report-name-1 } \left[\text{, report-name-2} \right] \; \ldots \; \right] .$$

[record-description-entry] ...] ...

[SD file-name

    [; RECORD CONTAINS [integer-1 TO] integer-2 CHARACTERS]

    [; DATA $\left\{\begin{array}{l}\text{RECORD IS}\\\text{RECORDS ARE}\end{array}\right\}$ data-name-1 [, data-name-2] ...] .

{record-description-entry} ...] ...]

[WORKING-STORAGE SECTION.

$\left[\begin{array}{l}\text{77-level-description-entry}\\\text{record-description-entry}\end{array}\right]$ ...]

[LINKAGE SECTION.

$\left[\begin{array}{l}\text{77-level-description-entry}\\\text{record-description-entry}\end{array}\right]$ ...]

Data Division

GENERAL FORMAT FOR DATA DESCRIPTION ENTRY

FORMAT 1:

level-number $\left\{\begin{array}{l}\text{data-name-1}\\\text{FILLER}\end{array}\right\}$

  [; REDEFINES data-name-2]

  [; $\left\{\begin{array}{l}\text{PICTURE}\\\text{PIC}\end{array}\right\}$ IS character-string]

  [; [USAGE IS] $\left\{\begin{array}{l}\text{COMPUTATIONAL}\\\text{COMP}\\\text{DISPLAY}\\\text{INDEX}\end{array}\right\}$]

  [; [SIGN IS] $\left\{\begin{array}{l}\text{LEADING}\\\text{TRAILING}\end{array}\right\}$ [SEPARATE CHARACTER]]

  [; OCCURS $\left\{\begin{array}{l}\text{integer-1 TO integer-2 TIMES DEPENDING ON data-name-3}\\\text{integer-2 TIMES}\end{array}\right\}$

      [$\left\{\begin{array}{l}\text{ASCENDING}\\\text{DESCENDING}\end{array}\right\}$ KEY IS data-name-4 [, data-name-5] ...] ...

      [INDEXED BY index-name-1 [, index-name-2] ...]]

$$\left[; \left\{ \begin{array}{l} \underline{\text{SYNCHRONIZED}} \\ \underline{\text{SYNC}} \end{array} \right\} \left[\begin{array}{l} \underline{\text{LEFT}} \\ \underline{\text{RIGHT}} \end{array} \right] \right]$$

$$\left[; \left\{ \begin{array}{l} \underline{\text{JUSTIFIED}} \\ \underline{\text{JUST}} \end{array} \right\} \text{RIGHT} \right]$$

$$\left[; \underline{\text{BLANK}} \text{ WHEN } \underline{\text{ZERO}} \right]$$

$$\left[; \underline{\text{VALUE}} \text{ IS literal} \right] .$$

FORMAT 2:

66 data-name-1; $\underline{\text{RENAMES}}$ data-name-2 $\left[\left\{ \begin{array}{l} \underline{\text{THROUGH}} \\ \underline{\text{THRU}} \end{array} \right\} \text{data-name-3} \right] .$

FORMAT 3:

88 condition-name; $\left\{ \begin{array}{l} \underline{\text{VALUE}} \text{ IS} \\ \underline{\text{VALUES}} \text{ ARE} \end{array} \right\}$ literal-1 $\left[\left\{ \begin{array}{l} \underline{\text{THROUGH}} \\ \underline{\text{THRU}} \end{array} \right\} \text{literal-2} \right]$

$\left[, \text{literal-3} \left[\left\{ \begin{array}{l} \underline{\text{THROUGH}} \\ \underline{\text{THRU}} \end{array} \right\} \text{literal-4} \right] \right] \ldots \quad .$

Procedure Division

GENERAL FORMAT FOR PROCEDURE DIVISION

FORMAT 1:

$\underline{\text{PROCEDURE}}$ $\underline{\text{DIVISION}}$ $\left[\underline{\text{USING}} \text{ data-name-1} \left[, \text{data-name-2} \right] \ldots \right] .$

$\left[\underline{\text{DECLARATIVES}} . \right.$

$\left\{ \text{section-name} \underline{\text{SECTION}} \left[\text{segment-number} \right] . \quad \text{declarative-sentence} \right.$

$\left[\text{paragraph-name.} \left[\text{sentence} \right] \ldots \right] \ldots \right\} \ldots$

$\underline{\text{END}} \underline{\text{DECLARATIVES}} . \left.\rule{0pt}{2.5ex}\right]$

$\left\{ \text{section-name} \underline{\text{SECTION}} \left[\text{segment-number} \right] . \right.$

$\left[\text{paragraph-name.} \left[\text{sentence} \right] \ldots \right] \ldots \right\} \ldots$

FORMAT 2:

$\underline{\text{PROCEDURE}}$ $\underline{\text{DIVISION}}$ $\left[\underline{\text{USING}} \text{ data-name-1} \left[, \text{data-name-2} \right] \ldots \right] .$

$\left\{ \text{paragraph-name.} \left[\text{sentence} \right] \ldots \right\} \ldots$

COBOL Verb Formats

GENERAL FORMAT FOR VERBS

ACCEPT identifier [FROM mnemonic-name]

ACCEPT identifier FROM $\left\{ \begin{array}{l} \text{DATE} \\ \text{DAY} \\ \text{TIME} \end{array} \right\}$

ACCEPT cd-name MESSAGE COUNT

ADD $\left\{ \begin{array}{l} \text{identifier-1} \\ \text{literal-1} \end{array} \right\}$ $\left[\begin{array}{l} \text{, identifier-2} \\ \text{, literal-2} \end{array} \right]$ ...   TO identifier-m [ROUNDED]

  [, identifier-n [ROUNDED]] ...   [; ON SIZE ERROR imperative-statement]

ADD $\left\{ \begin{array}{l} \text{identifier-1} \\ \text{literal-1} \end{array} \right\}$, $\left\{ \begin{array}{l} \text{identifier-2} \\ \text{literal-2} \end{array} \right\}$ $\left[\begin{array}{l} \text{, identifier-3} \\ \text{, literal-3} \end{array} \right]$ ...

    GIVING identifier-m [ROUNDED] [, identifier-n [ROUNDED]] ...

    [; ON SIZE ERROR imperative-statement]

ADD $\left\{ \begin{array}{l} \underline{\text{CORRESPONDING}} \\ \underline{\text{CORR}} \end{array} \right\}$ identifier-1 TO identifier-2 [ROUNDED]

  [; ON SIZE ERROR imperative-statement]

ALTER procedure-name-1 TO [PROCEED TO] procedure-name-2

  [, procedure-name-3 TO [PROCEED TO] procedure-name-4] ...

CALL $\left\{ \begin{array}{l} \text{identifier-1} \\ \text{literal-1} \end{array} \right\}$ [USING data-name-1 [, data-name-2] ...]

  [; ON OVERFLOW imperative-statement]

CANCEL $\left\{ \begin{array}{l} \text{identifier-1} \\ \text{literal-1} \end{array} \right\}$ $\left[\begin{array}{l} \text{, identifier-2} \\ \text{, literal-2} \end{array} \right]$ ...

CLOSE file-name-1 $\left[\begin{array}{l} \left\{ \begin{array}{l} \underline{\text{REEL}} \\ \underline{\text{UNIT}} \end{array} \right\} \left[\begin{array}{l} \text{WITH NO REWIND} \\ \text{FOR REMOVAL} \end{array} \right] \\ \text{WITH} \left\{ \begin{array}{l} \text{NO REWIND} \\ \text{LOCK} \end{array} \right\} \end{array} \right]$

$\left[, \text{file-name-2} \left[\begin{array}{l} \left\{ \begin{array}{l} \underline{\text{REEL}} \\ \underline{\text{UNIT}} \end{array} \right\} \left[\begin{array}{l} \text{WITH NO REWIND} \\ \text{FOR REMOVAL} \end{array} \right] \\ \text{WITH} \left\{ \begin{array}{l} \text{NO REWIND} \\ \text{LOCK} \end{array} \right\} \end{array} \right] \right]$ ...

CLOSE file-name-1 [WITH LOCK] [, file-name-2 [WITH LOCK]] ...

COMPUTE identifier-1 [ROUNDED] [, identifier-2 [ROUNDED]] ...

  = arithmetic-expression [; ON SIZE ERROR imperative-statement]

DELETE file-name RECORD [; INVALID KEY imperative-statement]

DISABLE $\left\{ \begin{array}{l} \underline{INPUT} \\ \underline{OUTPUT} \end{array} [\underline{TERMINAL}] \right\}$ cd-name WITH $\underline{KEY}$ $\left\{ \begin{array}{l} identifier-1 \\ literal-1 \end{array} \right\}$

DISPLAY $\left\{ \begin{array}{l} identifier-1 \\ literal-1 \end{array} \right\}$ $\left[\begin{array}{l} , identifier-2 \\ , literal-2 \end{array} \right]$ ... [$\underline{UPON}$ mnemonic-name]

DIVIDE $\left\{ \begin{array}{l} identifier-1 \\ literal-1 \end{array} \right\}$ $\underline{INTO}$ identifier-2 [$\underline{ROUNDED}$]

[, identifier-3 [$\underline{ROUNDED}$]] ... [; ON $\underline{SIZE}$ $\underline{ERROR}$ imperative-statement]

DIVIDE $\left\{ \begin{array}{l} identifier-1 \\ literal-1 \end{array} \right\}$ $\underline{INTO}$ $\left\{ \begin{array}{l} identifier-2 \\ literal-2 \end{array} \right\}$ $\underline{GIVING}$ identifier-3 [$\underline{ROUNDED}$]

[, identifier-4 [$\underline{ROUNDED}$]] ... [; ON $\underline{SIZE}$ $\underline{ERROR}$ imperative-statement]

DIVIDE $\left\{ \begin{array}{l} identifier-1 \\ literal-1 \end{array} \right\}$ $\underline{BY}$ $\left\{ \begin{array}{l} identifier-2 \\ literal-2 \end{array} \right\}$ $\underline{GIVING}$ identifier-3 [$\underline{ROUNDED}$]

[, identifier-4 [$\underline{ROUNDED}$]] ... [; ON $\underline{SIZE}$ $\underline{ERROR}$ imperative-statement]

DIVIDE $\left\{ \begin{array}{l} identifier-1 \\ literal-1 \end{array} \right\}$ $\underline{INTO}$ $\left\{ \begin{array}{l} identifier-2 \\ literal-2 \end{array} \right\}$ $\underline{GIVING}$ identifier-3 [$\underline{ROUNDED}$]

REMAINDER identifier-4 [; ON $\underline{SIZE}$ $\underline{ERROR}$ imperative-statement]

DIVIDE $\left\{ \begin{array}{l} identifier-1 \\ literal-1 \end{array} \right\}$ $\underline{BY}$ $\left\{ \begin{array}{l} identifier-2 \\ literal-2 \end{array} \right\}$ $\underline{GIVING}$ identifier-3 [$\underline{ROUNDED}$]

REMAINDER identifier-4 [; ON $\underline{SIZE}$ $\underline{ERROR}$ imperative-statement]

ENABLE $\left\{ \begin{array}{l} \underline{INPUT} \\ \underline{OUTPUT} \end{array} [\underline{TERMINAL}] \right\}$ cd-name WITH $\underline{KEY}$ $\left\{ \begin{array}{l} identifier-1 \\ literal-1 \end{array} \right\}$

ENTER language-name [routine-name] .

EXIT [PROGRAM] .

GENERATE $\left\{ \begin{array}{l} data-name \\ report-name \end{array} \right\}$

$\underline{GO}$ TO [procedure-name-1]

$\underline{GO}$ TO procedure-name-1 [, procedure-name-2] ... , procedure-name-n

$\underline{DEPENDING}$ ON identifier

$\underline{IF}$ condition; $\left\{ \begin{array}{l} statement-1 \\ \underline{NEXT} \ \underline{SENTENCE} \end{array} \right\}$ $\left\{ \begin{array}{l} ; \ \underline{ELSE} \ statement-2 \\ ; \ \underline{ELSE} \ \underline{NEXT} \ \underline{SENTENCE} \end{array} \right\}$

$\underline{INITIATE}$ report-name-1 [, report-name-2] ...

$\underline{INSPECT}$ identifier-1 TALLYING

$\left\{ , identifier-2 \ \underline{FOR} \ \left\{ , \left\{ \begin{array}{l} \underline{ALL} \\ \underline{LEADING} \\ \underline{CHARACTERS} \end{array} \right\} \left\{ \begin{array}{l} identifier-3 \\ literal-1 \end{array} \right\} \left[\left\{ \begin{array}{l} \underline{BEFORE} \\ \underline{AFTER} \end{array} \right\} \ INITIAL \ \left\{ \begin{array}{l} identifier-4 \\ literal-2 \end{array} \right\} \right] \right\} ... \right\} ...$

INSPECT identifier-1 REPLACING

$$
\left\{
\begin{array}{l}
\underline{\text{CHARACTERS}}\ \underline{\text{BY}}\ \left\{\begin{array}{l}\text{identifier-6}\\\text{literal-4}\end{array}\right\}\left[\left\{\begin{array}{l}\underline{\text{BEFORE}}\\\underline{\text{AFTER}}\end{array}\right\}\ \text{INITIAL}\ \left\{\begin{array}{l}\text{identifier-7}\\\text{literal-5}\end{array}\right\}\right]\\[3mm]
\left\{,\ \left\{\begin{array}{l}\underline{\text{ALL}}\\\underline{\text{LEADING}}\\\underline{\text{FIRST}}\end{array}\right\}\ \left\{,\ \left\{\begin{array}{l}\text{identifier-5}\\\text{literal-3}\end{array}\right\}\ \underline{\text{BY}}\ \left\{\begin{array}{l}\text{identifier-6}\\\text{literal-4}\end{array}\right\}\left[\left\{\begin{array}{l}\underline{\text{BEFORE}}\\\underline{\text{AFTER}}\end{array}\right\}\ \text{INITIAL}\ \left\{\begin{array}{l}\text{identifier-7}\\\text{literal-5}\end{array}\right\}\right]\right\}\cdots\right\}\cdots
\end{array}
\right\}
$$

INSPECT identifier-1 TALLYING

$$
\left\{,\ \text{identifier-2}\ \underline{\text{FOR}}\ \left\{,\ \left\{\begin{array}{l}\underline{\text{ALL}}\\\underline{\text{LEADING}}\\\underline{\text{CHARACTERS}}\end{array}\right\}\left\{\begin{array}{l}\text{identifier-3}\\\text{literal-1}\end{array}\right\}\right\}\left[\left\{\begin{array}{l}\underline{\text{BEFORE}}\\\underline{\text{AFTER}}\end{array}\right\}\ \text{INITIAL}\ \left\{\begin{array}{l}\text{identifier-4}\\\text{literal-2}\end{array}\right\}\right]\ \cdots\ \right\}\cdots
$$

REPLACING

$$
\left\{
\begin{array}{l}
\underline{\text{CHARACTERS}}\ \underline{\text{BY}}\ \left\{\begin{array}{l}\text{identifier-6}\\\text{literal-4}\end{array}\right\}\left[\left\{\begin{array}{l}\underline{\text{BEFORE}}\\\underline{\text{AFTER}}\end{array}\right\}\ \text{INITIAL}\ \left\{\begin{array}{l}\text{identifier-7}\\\text{literal-5}\end{array}\right\}\right]\\[3mm]
\left\{,\ \left\{\begin{array}{l}\underline{\text{ALL}}\\\underline{\text{LEADING}}\\\underline{\text{FIRST}}\end{array}\right\}\ \left\{,\ \left\{\begin{array}{l}\text{identifier-5}\\\text{literal-3}\end{array}\right\}\ \underline{\text{BY}}\ \left\{\begin{array}{l}\text{identifier-6}\\\text{literal-4}\end{array}\right\}\left[\left\{\begin{array}{l}\underline{\text{BEFORE}}\\\underline{\text{AFTER}}\end{array}\right\}\ \text{INITIAL}\ \left\{\begin{array}{l}\text{identifier-7}\\\text{literal-5}\end{array}\right\}\right]\right\}\cdots\right\}\cdots
\end{array}
\right\}
$$

$$
\underline{\text{MERGE}}\ \text{file-name-1}\ \text{ON}\ \left\{\begin{array}{l}\underline{\text{ASCENDING}}\\\underline{\text{DESCENDING}}\end{array}\right\}\ \text{KEY data-name-1}\ [,\ \text{data-name-2}]\ \cdots
$$

$$
\left[\ \text{ON}\ \left\{\begin{array}{l}\underline{\text{ASCENDING}}\\\underline{\text{DESCENDING}}\end{array}\right\}\ \text{KEY data-name-3}\ [,\ \text{data-name-4}]\ \cdots\ \right]\cdots
$$

$$
[\ \text{COLLATING}\ \underline{\text{SEQUENCE}}\ \text{IS alphabet-name}\ ]
$$

$$
\underline{\text{USING}}\ \text{file-name-2, file-name-3}\ [,\ \text{file-name-4}\ ]\ \cdots
$$

$$
\left\{
\begin{array}{l}
\underline{\text{OUTPUT}}\ \underline{\text{PROCEDURE}}\ \text{IS section-name-1}\ \left[\left\{\begin{array}{l}\underline{\text{THROUGH}}\\\underline{\text{THRU}}\end{array}\right\}\ \text{section-name-2}\right]\\[3mm]
\underline{\text{GIVING}}\ \text{file-name-5}
\end{array}
\right\}
$$

$$
\underline{\text{MOVE}}\ \left\{\begin{array}{l}\text{identifier-1}\\\text{literal}\end{array}\right\}\ \underline{\text{TO}}\ \text{identifier-2}\ [,\ \text{identifier-3}]\ \cdots
$$

$$
\underline{\text{MOVE}}\ \left\{\begin{array}{l}\underline{\text{CORRESPONDING}}\\\underline{\text{CORR}}\end{array}\right\}\ \text{identifier-1}\ \underline{\text{TO}}\ \text{identifier-2}
$$

$$
\underline{\text{MULTIPLY}}\ \left\{\begin{array}{l}\text{identifier-1}\\\text{literal-1}\end{array}\right\}\ \underline{\text{BY}}\ \text{identifier-2}\ [\ \underline{\text{ROUNDED}}\ ]
$$

$$
[\ ,\ \text{identifier-3}\ [\ \underline{\text{ROUNDED}}\ ]\ ]\ \cdots\ [\ ;\ \text{ON}\ \underline{\text{SIZE}}\ \underline{\text{ERROR}}\ \text{imperative-statement}\ ]
$$

$$
\underline{\text{MULTIPLY}}\ \left\{\begin{array}{l}\text{identifier-1}\\\text{literal-1}\end{array}\right\}\ \underline{\text{BY}}\ \left\{\begin{array}{l}\text{identifier-2}\\\text{literal-2}\end{array}\right\}\ \underline{\text{GIVING}}\ \text{identifier-3}\ [\ \underline{\text{ROUNDED}}\ ]
$$

$$
[\ ,\ \text{identifier-4}\ [\ \underline{\text{ROUNDED}}\ ]\ ]\ \cdots\ [\ ;\ \text{ON}\ \underline{\text{SIZE}}\ \underline{\text{ERROR}}\ \text{imperative-statement}\ ]
$$

$$
\underline{OPEN} \left\{ \begin{array}{l} \underline{INPUT}\ \text{file-name-1} \left[\begin{array}{l} \underline{REVERSED} \\ \underline{WITH}\ \underline{NO}\ \underline{REWIND} \end{array} \right] \left[,\ \text{file-name-2} \left[\begin{array}{l} \underline{REVERSED} \\ \underline{WITH}\ \underline{NO}\ \underline{REWIND} \end{array} \right] \right] \ \dots \\ \underline{OUTPUT}\ \text{file-name-3} \left[\underline{WITH}\ \underline{NO}\ \underline{REWIND} \right] \left[,\ \text{file-name-4} \left[\underline{WITH}\ \underline{NO}\ \underline{REWIND} \right] \right] \ \dots \\ \underline{I\text{-}O}\ \text{file-name-5} \ \left[,\ \text{file-name-6} \right] \ \dots \\ \underline{EXTEND}\ \text{file-name-7} \ \left[,\ \text{file-name-8} \right] \ \dots \end{array} \right\} \ \dots
$$

$$
\underline{OPEN} \left\{ \begin{array}{l} \underline{INPUT}\ \text{file-name-1} \ [,\ \text{file-name-2}] \ \dots \\ \underline{OUTPUT}\ \text{file-name-3} \ [,\ \text{file-name-4}] \ \dots \\ \underline{I\text{-}O}\ \text{file-name-5} \ [,\ \text{file-name-6}] \ \dots \end{array} \right\} \ \dots
$$

$$
\underline{PERFORM}\ \text{procedure-name-1} \left[\left\{ \begin{array}{l} \underline{THROUGH} \\ \underline{THRU} \end{array} \right\} \text{procedure-name-2} \right]
$$

$$
\underline{PERFORM}\ \text{procedure-name-1} \left[\left\{ \begin{array}{l} \underline{THROUGH} \\ \underline{THRU} \end{array} \right\} \text{procedure-name-2} \right] \left\{ \begin{array}{l} \text{identifier-1} \\ \text{integer-1} \end{array} \right\} \underline{TIMES}
$$

$$
\underline{PERFORM}\ \text{procedure-name-1} \left[\left\{ \begin{array}{l} \underline{THROUGH} \\ \underline{THRU} \end{array} \right\} \text{procedure-name-2} \right] \underline{UNTIL}\ \text{condition-1}
$$

$$
\underline{PERFORM}\ \text{procedure-name-1} \left[\left\{ \begin{array}{l} \underline{THROUGH} \\ \underline{THRU} \end{array} \right\} \text{procedure-name-2} \right]
$$

$$
\underline{VARYING}\ \left\{ \begin{array}{l} \text{identifier-2} \\ \text{index-name-1} \end{array} \right\} \underline{FROM}\ \left\{ \begin{array}{l} \text{identifier-3} \\ \text{index-name-2} \\ \text{literal-1} \end{array} \right\}
$$

$$
\underline{BY}\ \left\{ \begin{array}{l} \text{identifier-4} \\ \text{literal-3} \end{array} \right\} \underline{UNTIL}\ \text{condition-1}
$$

$$
\left[\underline{AFTER}\ \left\{ \begin{array}{l} \text{identifier-5} \\ \text{index-name-3} \end{array} \right\} \underline{FROM}\ \left\{ \begin{array}{l} \text{identifier-6} \\ \text{index-name-4} \\ \text{literal-3} \end{array} \right\} \right.
$$

$$
\underline{BY}\ \left\{ \begin{array}{l} \text{identifier-7} \\ \text{literal-4} \end{array} \right\} \underline{UNTIL}\ \text{condition-2}
$$

$$
\left[\underline{AFTER}\ \left\{ \begin{array}{l} \text{identifier-8} \\ \text{index-name-5} \end{array} \right\} \underline{FROM}\ \left\{ \begin{array}{l} \text{identifier-9} \\ \text{index-name-6} \\ \text{literal-5} \end{array} \right\} \right.
$$

$$
\underline{BY}\ \left\{ \begin{array}{l} \text{identifier-10} \\ \text{literal-6} \end{array} \right\} \underline{UNTIL}\ \text{condition-3} \Bigg] \Bigg]
$$

$$
\underline{READ}\ \text{file-name}\ \text{RECORD}\ \left[\underline{INTO}\ \text{identifier} \right] \ \left[;\ \underline{AT}\ \underline{END}\ \text{imperative-statement} \right]
$$

$$
\underline{READ}\ \text{file-name}\ \left[\underline{NEXT} \right]\ \text{RECORD}\ \left[\underline{INTO}\ \text{identifier} \right]
$$

$$
\left[;\ \underline{AT}\ \underline{END}\ \text{imperative-statement} \right]
$$

$$
\underline{READ}\ \text{file-name}\ \text{RECORD}\ \left[\underline{INTO}\ \text{identifier} \right] \ \left[;\ \underline{INVALID}\ \text{KEY}\ \text{imperative-statement} \right]
$$

$$
\underline{READ}\ \text{file-name}\ \text{RECORD}\ \left[\underline{INTO}\ \text{identifier} \right]
$$

$$
\left[;\ \underline{KEY}\ \text{IS}\ \text{data-name} \right]
$$

$$
\left[;\ \underline{INVALID}\ \text{KEY}\ \text{imperative-statement} \right]
$$

$$
\underline{RECEIVE}\ \text{cd-name}\ \left\{ \begin{array}{l} \underline{MESSAGE} \\ \underline{SEGMENT} \end{array} \right\} \underline{INTO}\ \text{identifier-1}\ \left[;\ \underline{NO}\ \underline{DATA}\ \text{imperative-statement} \right]
$$

RELEASE record-name [FROM identifier]

RETURN file-name RECORD [INTO identifier] ; AT END imperative-statement

REWRITE record-name [FROM identifier]

REWRITE record-name [FROM identifier] [; INVALID KEY imperative-statement]

SEARCH identifier-1 [VARYING {identifier-2 / index-name-1}] [; AT END imperative-statement-1]

   ; WHEN condition-1 {imperative-statement-2 / NEXT SENTENCE}

   [; WHEN condition-2 {imperative-statement-3 / NEXT SENTENCE}] ...

SEARCH ALL identifier-1 [; AT END imperative-statement-1]

   ; WHEN {data-name-1 {IS EQUAL TO / IS =} {identifier-3 / literal-1 / arithmetic-expression-1} / condition-name-1}

     [AND {data-name-2 {IS EQUAL TO / IS =} {identifier-4 / literal-2 / arithmetic-expression-2} / condition-name-2}] ...

   {imperative-statement-2 / NEXT SENTENCE}

SEND cd-name FROM identifier-1

SEND cd-name [FROM identifier-1] {WITH identifier-2 / WITH ESI / WITH EMI / WITH EGI}

   [{BEFORE / AFTER} ADVANCING {{{identifier-3 / integer} [LINE / LINES]} / {mnemonic-name / PAGE}}]

SET {identifier-1 [, identifier-2] ... / index-name-1 [, index-name-2] ...} TO {identifier-3 / index-name-3 / integer-1}

SET index-name-4 [, index-name-5] ... {UP BY / DOWN BY} {identifier-4 / integer-2}

$$\underline{\text{SORT}} \text{ file-name-1 ON } \left\{ \begin{matrix} \underline{\text{ASCENDING}} \\ \underline{\text{DESCENDING}} \end{matrix} \right\} \text{ KEY data-name-1 } \left[\text{, data-name-2} \right] \text{ ...}$$

$$\left[\text{ON } \left\{ \begin{matrix} \underline{\text{ASCENDING}} \\ \underline{\text{DESCENDING}} \end{matrix} \right\} \text{ KEY data-name-3 } \left[\text{, data-name-4} \right] \text{ ...} \right] \text{ ...}$$

$$\left[\text{COLLATING } \underline{\text{SEQUENCE}} \text{ IS alphabet-name} \right]$$

$$\left\{ \begin{matrix} \underline{\text{INPUT}} \underline{\text{ PROCEDURE}} \text{ IS section-name-1 } \left[\left\{ \begin{matrix} \underline{\text{THROUGH}} \\ \underline{\text{THRU}} \end{matrix} \right\} \text{ section-name-2} \right] \\ \underline{\text{USING}} \text{ file-name-2 } \left[\text{, file-name-3} \right] \text{ ...} \end{matrix} \right\}$$

$$\left\{ \begin{matrix} \underline{\text{OUTPUT}} \underline{\text{ PROCEDURE}} \text{ IS section-name-3} \left[\left\{ \begin{matrix} \underline{\text{THROUGH}} \\ \underline{\text{THRU}} \end{matrix} \right\} \text{ section-name-4} \right] \\ \underline{\text{GIVING}} \text{ file-name-4} \end{matrix} \right\}$$

$$\underline{\text{START}} \text{ file-name } \left[\underline{\text{KEY}} \left\{ \begin{matrix} \text{IS } \underline{\text{EQUAL}} \text{ TO} \\ \text{IS } = \\ \text{IS } \underline{\text{GREATER}} \text{ THAN} \\ \text{IS } > \\ \text{IS } \underline{\text{NOT LESS}} \text{ THAN} \\ \text{IS } \underline{\text{NOT}} < \end{matrix} \right\} \text{ data-name} \right]$$

$$\left[\text{; } \underline{\text{INVALID}} \text{ KEY imperative-statement} \right]$$

$$\underline{\text{STOP}} \left\{ \begin{matrix} \underline{\text{RUN}} \\ \text{literal} \end{matrix} \right\}$$

$$\underline{\text{STRING}} \left\{ \begin{matrix} \text{identifier-1} \\ \text{literal-1} \end{matrix} \right\} \left[\begin{matrix} \text{, identifier-2} \\ \text{, literal-2} \end{matrix} \right] \text{ ... } \underline{\text{DELIMITED}} \text{ BY } \left\{ \begin{matrix} \text{identifier-3} \\ \text{literal-3} \\ \underline{\text{SIZE}} \end{matrix} \right\}$$

$$\left[\text{, } \left\{ \begin{matrix} \text{identifier-4} \\ \text{literal-4} \end{matrix} \right\} \left[\begin{matrix} \text{, identifier-5} \\ \text{, literal-5} \end{matrix} \right] \text{ ... } \underline{\text{DELIMITED}} \text{ BY } \left\{ \begin{matrix} \text{identifier-6} \\ \text{literal-6} \\ \underline{\text{SIZE}} \end{matrix} \right\} \right] \text{ ...}$$

$$\underline{\text{INTO}} \text{ identifier-7 } \left[\text{WITH } \underline{\text{POINTER}} \text{ identifier-8} \right]$$

$$\left[\text{; ON } \underline{\text{OVERFLOW}} \text{ imperative-statement} \right]$$

$$\underline{\text{SUBTRACT}} \left\{ \begin{matrix} \text{identifier-1} \\ \text{literal-1} \end{matrix} \right\} \left[\begin{matrix} \text{, identifier-2} \\ \text{, literal-2} \end{matrix} \right] \text{ ... } \underline{\text{FROM}} \text{ identifier-m } \left[\underline{\text{ROUNDED}} \right]$$

$$\left[\text{, identifier-n } \left[\underline{\text{ROUNDED}} \right] \right] \text{ ... } \left[\text{; ON } \underline{\text{SIZE}} \underline{\text{ ERROR}} \text{ imperative-statement} \right]$$

COBOL Verb Formats

GENERAL FORMAT FOR VERBS

$$\underline{\text{SUBTRACT}} \left\{ \begin{matrix} \text{identifier-1} \\ \text{literal-1} \end{matrix} \right\} \left[\begin{matrix} \text{, identifier-2} \\ \text{, literal-2} \end{matrix} \right] \text{ ... } \underline{\text{FROM}} \left\{ \begin{matrix} \text{identifier-m} \\ \text{literal-m} \end{matrix} \right\}$$

$$\underline{\text{GIVING}} \text{ identifier-n } \left[\underline{\text{ROUNDED}} \right] \left[\text{, identifier-o } \left[\underline{\text{ROUNDED}} \right] \right] \text{ ...}$$

$$\left[\text{; ON } \underline{\text{SIZE}} \underline{\text{ ERROR}} \text{ imperative-statement} \right]$$

$$\text{\underline{SUBTRACT}} \begin{Bmatrix} \text{\underline{CORRESPONDING}} \\ \text{\underline{CORR}} \end{Bmatrix} \text{identifier-1} \ \text{\underline{FROM}} \ \text{identifier-2} \ \left[\text{\underline{ROUNDED}} \right]$$

$$\left[\ ; \ \text{ON} \ \text{\underline{SIZE}} \ \text{\underline{ERROR}} \ \text{imperative-statement} \right]$$

<u>SUPPRESS</u> PRINTING

<u>TERMINATE</u> report-name-1 [, report-name-2] ...

<u>UNSTRING</u> identifier-1

$$\left[\text{\underline{DELIMITED}} \ \text{BY} \ \left[\text{\underline{ALL}} \right] \begin{Bmatrix} \text{identifier-2} \\ \text{literal-1} \end{Bmatrix} \left[\ , \ \text{\underline{OR}} \ \left[\text{\underline{ALL}} \right] \begin{Bmatrix} \text{identifier-3} \\ \text{literal-2} \end{Bmatrix} \right] \ ... \right]$$

$$\text{\underline{INTO}} \ \text{identifier-4} \ \left[\ , \ \text{\underline{DELIMITER}} \ \text{IN} \ \text{identifier-5} \right] \left[\ , \ \text{\underline{COUNT}} \ \text{IN} \ \text{identifier-6} \right]$$

$$\left[\ , \ \text{identifier-7} \ \left[\ , \ \text{\underline{DELIMITER}} \ \text{IN} \ \text{identifier-8} \right] \left[\ , \ \text{\underline{COUNT}} \ \text{IN} \ \text{identifier-9} \right] \right] ...$$

$$\left[\text{WITH} \ \text{\underline{POINTER}} \ \text{identifier-10} \right] \left[\text{\underline{TALLYING}} \ \text{IN} \ \text{identifier-11} \right]$$

$$\left[\ ; \ \text{ON} \ \text{\underline{OVERFLOW}} \ \text{imperative-statement} \right]$$

$$\text{\underline{USE}} \ \text{\underline{AFTER}} \ \text{STANDARD} \ \begin{Bmatrix} \text{\underline{EXCEPTION}} \\ \text{\underline{ERROR}} \end{Bmatrix} \ \text{\underline{PROCEDURE}} \ \text{ON} \ \begin{Bmatrix} \text{file-name-1} \ [\ , \ \text{file-name-2}] \ ... \\ \text{INPUT} \\ \text{\underline{OUTPUT}} \\ \text{I-O} \\ \text{\underline{EXTEND}} \end{Bmatrix} \ .$$

$$\text{\underline{USE}} \ \text{\underline{AFTER}} \ \text{STANDARD} \ \begin{Bmatrix} \text{\underline{EXCEPTION}} \\ \text{\underline{ERROR}} \end{Bmatrix} \ \text{\underline{PROCEDURE}} \ \text{ON} \ \begin{Bmatrix} \text{file-name-1} \ [\ , \ \text{file-name-2}] \ ... \\ \text{INPUT} \\ \text{OUTPUT} \\ \text{I-O} \end{Bmatrix} \ .$$

<u>USE</u> <u>BEFORE</u> <u>REPORTING</u> identifier.

$$\text{\underline{USE}} \ \text{FOR} \ \text{\underline{DEBUGGING}} \ \text{ON} \ \begin{Bmatrix} \text{cd-name-1} \\ [\text{\underline{ALL}} \ \text{REFERENCES OF}] \ \text{identifier-1} \\ \text{file-name-1} \\ \text{procedure-name-1} \\ \text{\underline{ALL}} \ \text{\underline{PROCEDURES}} \end{Bmatrix}$$

$$\left[\ , \ \begin{Bmatrix} \text{cd-name-2} \\ [\text{\underline{ALL}} \ \text{REFERENCES OF}] \ \text{identifier-2} \\ \text{file-name-2} \\ \text{procedure-name-2} \\ \text{\underline{ALL}} \ \text{\underline{PROCEDURES}} \end{Bmatrix} \right] ... \ \ .$$

<u>WRITE</u> record-name [<u>FROM</u> identifier-1]

$$\left[\begin{Bmatrix} \text{\underline{BEFORE}} \\ \text{\underline{AFTER}} \end{Bmatrix} \ \text{ADVANCING} \ \begin{Bmatrix} \begin{Bmatrix} \text{identifier-2} \\ \text{integer} \end{Bmatrix} \begin{bmatrix} \text{LINE} \\ \text{LINES} \end{bmatrix} \\ \begin{Bmatrix} \text{mnemonic-name} \\ \text{\underline{PAGE}} \end{Bmatrix} \end{Bmatrix} \right]$$

$$\left[\ ; \ \text{AT} \ \begin{Bmatrix} \text{\underline{END-OF-PAGE}} \\ \text{\underline{EOP}} \end{Bmatrix} \ \text{imperative-statement} \right]$$

<u>WRITE</u> record-name [<u>FROM</u> identifier] [; <u>INVALID</u> KEY imperative-statement]

Condition Formats

GENERAL FORMAT FOR CONDITIONS

RELATION CONDITION:

$$
\left\{
\begin{array}{l}
\text{identifier-1} \\
\text{literal-1} \\
\text{arithmetic-expression-1} \\
\text{index-name-1}
\end{array}
\right\}
\left\{
\begin{array}{l}
\text{IS [NOT] } \underline{\text{GREATER}} \text{ THAN} \\
\text{IS [NOT] } \underline{\text{LESS}} \text{ THAN} \\
\text{IS [NOT] } \underline{\text{EQUAL}} \text{ TO} \\
\text{IS [NOT] } > \\
\text{IS [NOT] } < \\
\text{IS [NOT] } =
\end{array}
\right\}
\left\{
\begin{array}{l}
\text{identifier-2} \\
\text{literal-2} \\
\text{arithmetic-expression-2} \\
\text{index-name-2}
\end{array}
\right\}
$$

CLASS CONDITION:

identifier IS [NOT] $\left\{ \begin{array}{l} \underline{\text{NUMERIC}} \\ \underline{\text{ALPHABETIC}} \end{array} \right\}$

SIGN CONDITION:

arithmetic-expression is [NOT] $\left\{ \begin{array}{l} \underline{\text{POSITIVE}} \\ \underline{\text{NEGATIVE}} \\ \underline{\text{ZERO}} \end{array} \right\}$

CONDITION-NAME CONDITION:

condition-name

SWITCH-STATUS CONDITION:

condition-name

NEGATED SIMPLE CONDITION:

NOT simple-condition

COMBINED CONDITION:

condition $\left\{ \left\{ \begin{array}{l} \underline{\text{AND}} \\ \underline{\text{OR}} \end{array} \right\} \text{ condition} \right\}$ ...

ABBREVIATED COMBINED RELATION CONDITION:

relation-condition $\left\{ \left\{ \begin{array}{l} \underline{\text{AND}} \\ \underline{\text{OR}} \end{array} \right\} \text{ [NOT] [relational-operator] object} \right\}$ ...

Miscellaneous Formats

MISCELLANEOUS FORMATS

QUALIFICATION:

$\left\{ \begin{array}{l} \text{data-name-1} \\ \text{condition-name} \end{array} \right\}$ $\left[\left\{ \begin{array}{l} \underline{OF} \\ \underline{IN} \end{array} \right\} \text{data-name-2} \right]$ ...

paragraph-name $\left[\left\{ \begin{array}{l} \underline{OF} \\ \underline{IN} \end{array} \right\} \text{section-name} \right]$

text-name $\left[\left\{ \begin{array}{l} \underline{OF} \\ \underline{IN} \end{array} \right\} \text{library-name} \right]$

SUBSCRIPTING:

$\left\{ \begin{array}{l} \text{data-name} \\ \text{condition-name} \end{array} \right\}$ (subscript-1 [, subscript-2 [, subscript-3]])

INDEXING:

$\left\{ \begin{array}{l} \text{data-name} \\ \text{condition-name} \end{array} \right\}$ ($\left\{ \begin{array}{l} \text{index-name-1} \left[\{\pm\} \text{ literal-2} \right] \\ \text{literal-1} \end{array} \right\}$

$\left[, \left\{ \begin{array}{l} \text{index-name-2} \left[\{\pm\} \text{ literal-4} \right] \\ \text{literal-3} \end{array} \right\} \left[, \left\{ \begin{array}{l} \text{index-name-3} \left[\{\pm\} \text{ literal-6} \right] \\ \text{literal-5} \end{array} \right\} \right] \right]$)

IDENTIFIER: FORMAT 1

data-name-1 $\left[\left\{ \begin{array}{l} \underline{OF} \\ \underline{IN} \end{array} \right\} \text{data-name-2} \right]$ ... [(subscript-1 [, subscript-2

[, subscript-3]])]

IDENTIFIER: FORMAT 2

data-name-1 $\left[\left\{ \begin{array}{l} \underline{OF} \\ \underline{IN} \end{array} \right\} \text{data-name-2} \right]$ ... [($\left\{ \begin{array}{l} \text{index-name-1} \left[\{\pm\} \text{ literal-2} \right] \\ \text{literal-1} \end{array} \right\}$

$\left[, \left\{ \begin{array}{l} \text{index-name-2} \left[\{\pm\} \text{ literal-4} \right] \\ \text{literal-3} \end{array} \right\} \left[, \left\{ \begin{array}{l} \text{index-name-3} \left[\{\pm\} \text{ literal-6} \right] \\ \text{literal-5} \end{array} \right\} \right] \right]$)]

COPY Statement

<u>GENERAL FORMAT FOR COPY STATEMENT</u>

$$
\underline{\text{COPY}}\ \text{text-name}\ \left[\left\{\begin{array}{l}\underline{\text{OF}}\\ \underline{\text{IN}}\end{array}\right\}\ \text{library-name}\right]
$$

$$
\left[\underline{\text{REPLACING}}\ \left\{,\ \left\{\begin{array}{l}\text{==pseudo-text-1==}\\ \text{identifier-1}\\ \text{literal-1}\\ \text{word-1}\end{array}\right\}\ \underline{\text{BY}}\ \left\{\begin{array}{l}\text{==pseudo-text-2==}\\ \text{identifier-2}\\ \text{literal-2}\\ \text{word-2}\end{array}\right\}\right\}\ \ldots\right]
$$

INDEX